WINNING AND
LOSING THE
NUCLEAR PEACE

WINNING AND LOSING THE NUCLEAR PEACE

the RISE, DEMISE, *and* REVIVAL *of* ARMS CONTROL

Michael Krepon

STANFORD UNIVERSITY PRESS
Stanford, California
A Henry L. Stimson Center book

STANFORD UNIVERSITY PRESS
Stanford, California

Printed in the United States of America on acid-free, archival-quality paper

ISBN 9781503638143
First paperback printing, 2024

The Library of Congress has cataloged the hardcover edition as follows:

Names: Krepon, Michael, 1946– author.
Title: Winning and losing the nuclear peace : the rise, demise, and revival of arms control / Michael Krepon.
Description: Stanford, California : Stanford Security Studies, an imprint of Stanford University Press, 2021. | "A Henry L. Stimson Center book."
  Identifiers: LCCN 2021014056 (print) | LCCN 2021014057 (ebook) |
  ISBN 9781503629097 (cloth) | ISBN 9781503629615 (ebook)
Subjects: LCSH: Nuclear arms control—History. | Nuclear arms control—United States—History. | United States—Foreign relations—1945–1989. | United States—Foreign relations—1989–
Classification: LCC JZ5665 .K72 2021 (print) | LCC JZ5665 (ebook) |
  DDC 327.1/747—dc23
LC record available at https://lccn.loc.gov/2021014056
LC ebook record available at https://lccn.loc.gov/2021014057

Cover design: Kevin Barrett Kane
Cover art: Adobe Stock
Typeset by Newgen North America in 9.5/14 Sabon LT

This book is dedicated to all those who pushed the boulder uphill, and to those who will do so again.

The more we know of our nuclear history, the harder it will be to lose our way.

The Beginning and the End are in your hands, O Creator of the Universe. And in our hands, you have placed the fate of this planet. We, who are tested by having both creative and destructive power in our free will, turn to you in sober fear and in intoxicating hope. We ask for your guidance and to share in your imagination in our deliberations about the use of nuclear force. Help us to lift the fog of atomic darkness that hovers so pervasively over our Earth, Your Earth, so that soon all eyes may see life magnified by your pure light. Bless all of us who wait today for your Presence and who dedicate ourselves to achieve your intended peace and rightful equilibrium on Earth. In the Name of all that is holy and all that is hoped. Amen.

—George Shultz's "Nuclear Prayer," conceived
and written by Bishop William Swing

CONTENTS

ACRONYMS

ABM	anti-ballistic missile
ACDA	Arms Control and Disarmament Agency
AEC	Atomic Energy Commission
AFL-CIO	American Federation of Labor and Congress of Industrial Organizations
ALCM	air-launched cruise missile
CFE	Conventional Armed Forces in Europe
CIA	Central Intelligence Agency
CTBT	Comprehensive Test Ban Treaty
CWC	Chemical Weapons Convention
IAEA	International Atomic Energy Agency
ICBM	intercontinental ballistic missile
INF	Intermediate-Range Nuclear Forces
JSTPS	Joint Strategic Target Planning Staff
MAD	mutual assured destruction
MAP	Multiple Aim Point
MIRV	Multiple Independently Targetable Reentry Vehicle
MIT	Massachusetts Institute of Technology
MLF	Multilateral Nuclear Force
MRV	Multiple Reentry Vehicle
NATO	North Atlantic Treaty Organization
NPT	Nonproliferation Treaty
NSC-68	National Security Council Paper no. 68
NSDD-75	National Security Decision Directive no. 75

PNI   Presidential Nuclear Initiatives
ROTC   Reserve Officers' Training Corps
SALT   Strategic Arms Limitation Talks
SDI   Strategic Defense Initiative
SIOP   Single Integrated Operational Plan
SIPRI   Stockholm International Peace Research Institute
SLBM   submarine-launched ballistic missile
START   Strategic Arms Reduction Treaty
UN   United Nations
UNESCO   United Nations Education, Scientific and Cultural
             Organization
USSR   Union of Soviet Socialist Republics
WHO   World Health Organization

WINNING AND
LOSING THE
NUCLEAR PEACE

INTRODUCTION

This book is a history of the rise and demise of nuclear arms control. The story begins with dashed hopes for abolition, moves on to halting first steps, followed by agreements that broke new ground but could not stop the momentum of the nuclear arms competition. The apogee of success is reached at the end of the Cold War, followed by a willful unraveling of agreements in order to pursue freedom from constraints. In between there are high-wire acts and periods of extreme nuclear danger. Throughout these ups and downs, there is one surprising constant: nuclear weapons have not been used in warfare since 1945. This isn't due to happenstance; it has taken concerted effort. This great accomplishment seemed impossible to our grandparents and parents; we now take this accomplishment for granted. If we continue to do so, we invite a world of cataclysmic hurt. My book ends with a call for the revival of arms control.

How has it come to pass that nuclear weapons—"war-winning" weapons as they were initially called—haven't been used in warfare for three-quarters of a century? How have they been stigmatized to such an extent that states do not even test them the way they regularly test other instruments of warfare? Why are there not more states that possess nuclear weapons? We are inundated with warnings of nuclear proliferation, and yet its pace is very slow. The last state to acquire nuclear weapons, North Korea, demonstrated this capability in 2006. Only one country—Iran—is positioning itself to acquire nuclear weapons within this decade but faces stiff penalties in trying to do so. How has the norm of nuclear nonproliferation taken root?

The comforting answer to these questions, as some would have it, gives credit to nuclear deterrence. The threat of terrible destruction has kept the peace, we are often told. This is a half-truth, because relying on deterrence alone is too dangerous. Deterrence is by its very nature threatening; otherwise, nuclear weapons would cease to deter. When states take steps to strengthen deterrence, they typically make threats to use nuclear weapons more credible. Sharper threats then prompt threatening responses. The ethos of escalation is baked into deterrence because if the threat of inflicting greater violence is absent, a nuclear-armed rival might be emboldened. Rivals therefore sharpen threats to use nuclear weapons. These strengthening measures do not make rivals safer. Still, rivals are obliged to compete, either in search of advantage or to avoid disadvantage.

These intellectual constructs work well enough on the printed page or in war-fighting plans, but they can collapse like a house of cards after first use. Nuclear deterrence works until it fails, after which restraint rests on truly heroic assumptions. One assumption is that nuclear-armed rivals can signal each other effectively because they have sufficient information and because they are on the same page—even after resorting to nuclear warfare. Another assumption is that decision makers would retain control over the use of nuclear weapons once the first mushroom cloud appears; otherwise, rational choice gives way to panic and unauthorized use. A third assumption, most heroic of all, is that the disadvantaged side will accept loss without resorting to spasm attacks aimed at killing that which its adversary holds most dear.

After first use, nuclear-armed rivals may not be on the same page. Escalation control and escalation dominance become blurry constructs; even escalation control—assuming both rivals seek it in nuclear warfare—is predicated on the threat of further escalation. And then what? After first use, war plans are spring-loaded to seek advantage or to avoid disadvantage. This is how nuclear deterrence strategists think and this is how they plan. Their underlying constructs are likely to fail catastrophically once the nuclear threshold is crossed and retaliation begins. After first use, nuclear deterrence dies, and once deterrence dies, escalation takes over.

The belief system and dynamics of nuclear deterrence are far too unstable to explain the absence of mushroom clouds in warfare since 1945. To the contrary, deterrence beliefs and dynamics are necessarily skewed toward use; otherwise, they cease to deter. The dictates of nuclear deterrence do not reduce nuclear danger; they increase it. They do not reduce nuclear weapons; they add to weapon stockpiles and targeting lists. All this is by rational choice; deterrence constructs have no utility against the accidental or unauthorized use of nuclear weapons.

To give nuclear deterrence its due, it has so far helped to prevent nuclear exchanges and full-scale conventional war. These are major accomplishments—so far—but nuclear deterrence has a poor track record in lesser cases. There have already been two limited wars between nuclear-armed states—China and the Soviet Union in 1969 and Pakistan and India in 1999. Nor does nuclear deterrence preclude clashes over contested borders, as is the case between China and India and between Pakistan and India.

Nuclear deterrence needs diplomacy to prevent mushroom clouds. Diplomacy has to provide what deterrence cannot offer—reassurance that national leaders are not inclined to use their most threatening weapons. There have been no mushroom clouds in warfare since 1945 because in one harrowing crisis after the next, national leaders have chosen not to rely on the intellectual constructs devised by deterrence strategists. They have followed a higher calling, seeking to avoid Armageddon. There have been no mushroom clouds in warfare for three-quarters of a century because leaders have recognized that national security and public safety require cooperation as well as competition with a nuclear-armed rival. National leaders have understood—especially after severe crises—that deterrence alone is too unwieldy and dangerous to keep the nuclear peace. Nuclear deterrence requires guardrails and stabilization measures. Deterrence requires effective lines of communication, codes of conduct, tacit understandings, political compacts, and formal treaties to help prevent the battlefield use of nuclear weapons. We call these diplomatic methods of reassurance arms control. The fundamental purposes of arms control are to stabilize nuclear rivalries and reduce nuclear danger.

The practice of arms control did not come naturally. It was a learned behavior that went against the grain of domestic politics and global rivalry. Deterrence was always easier and more straightforward to pursue than reassurance. Arms control rejected the very premise of winning in nuclear warfare. This corpus of diplomatic activity obliged leaders to distinguish between acceptable and unacceptable behavior, even in warfare. The practice of arms control helped to establish a fundamental norm against the battlefield use of nuclear weapons even though the dictates of deterrence rested on being willing to cross this threshold.

The tension between the dictates of arms control and the dictates of nuclear deterrence have always been at odds even as they needed to be lashed together. Only by softening the sharpest edges of deterrence through arms control has the norm of not using nuclear weapons in warfare held for three-quarters of a century. The practice of arms control has limited and then reduced the most powerful weapons ever devised. It has stopped the testing of nuclear weapons and foreclosed widespread nuclear proliferation. This surprisingly successful body of work constitutes the greatest unacknowledged diplomatic successes of the Cold War.

This book provides a condensed diplomatic history of halting first steps, followed by extraordinary achievements, followed by the demise of treaties after the Cold War ended. The story of arms control isn't told in books about deterrence, of which there is no shortage. This book repays a debt: The remarkable individuals who conceptualized and then practiced the diplomacy of nuclear arms control deserve to have their stories told. We owe them for their trials, and we can learn much from them.

These pages describe pitched battles between those who believed in strengthening deterrence and those who believed in arms control. One camp habitually sought to sharpen swords while the other sought to sheath them. Tensions between these camps were endemic and occasionally disabling for U.S. presidents who sought treaties. And yet these tensions could also enable remarkable achievements. Ironies abound in these pages, not the least of which is that the apogee of arms control occurred when deterrence strategists practiced what arms controllers preached.

The nuclear peace was won as a result of the combined efforts of arms controllers and deterrence strategists. My definition of nuclear peace does not rest solely on the norm of nonbattlefield use. The nuclear peace was codified by treaties and backstopped by less formal agreements seeking to prevent dangerous military practices. The nuclear peace required the norm of nonproliferation. It was built on the acceptance of vulnerability to nuclear attacks and on the acceptance of international borders and national sovereignty.

My definition of nuclear peace is clearly contestable, especially to those who equate peace with the absence of war or with nuclear abolition. These equations reflect aspirational standards that have been beyond reach for every generation that has lived uneasily with nuclear danger. Friction, crises, and war remain with us. In some instances, possessing the Bomb has abetted risk taking. The human costs of continued warfare have been great, but not anywhere near as great as in wars fought before the Bomb was invented.

The great successes of arms control lie in the rearview mirror. We have lost sight of the contributions of arms control to our national security and public safety. Treaties that helped codify the nuclear peace during the Cold War have been jettisoned in favor of freedom of action. There are now four nuclear-armed rivalries; each rival seeks security by strengthening nuclear deterrence and not by diplomatic engagement. Nuclear danger is rising on all four fronts—the United States and Russia, the United States and China, China and India, and India and Pakistan.

The geometry is even more complicated than this. The four rivalries are embedded in two interlocking triangular competitions, where the United States, Russia, and China jockey for position in one, while China, India, and Pakistan compete in the second. Guardrails and stabilization measures are lacking for all four pairings and both triangular competitions. Their absence invites crises. Triangular competitions do not lend themselves to numerical limitations and are inherently hard to stabilize when two states act in concert against the third.

Making matters worse, nuclear-armed rivals have not respected the national sovereignty of others, have badly overreached, and have engaged in serious risk taking. Every nuclear-armed rival is taking steps to strengthen deterrence in ways that appear threatening and that prompt countermeasures by a competitor. Diplomatic initiatives to allay concerns about the possible use of nuclear weapons are out of favor. Relations between Washington and Moscow and between Washington and Beijing have been poor. Border clashes between China and India and between India and Pakistan have become more severe. Cyber intrusions have become increasingly bold. Space warfare capabilities have grown. The status quo is no longer sacrosanct.

The founding fathers and practitioners of arms control never dealt with such complex geometry; their challenges were mostly binary in nature. Current circumstances do not lend themselves to traditional and dearly held arms control remedies. The pursuit of abolition defies trend lines that are all too evident. Nuclear competitions are too unwieldy and domestic politics too fractious in the United States to negotiate ambitious new treaties that harken back to those described in these pages. Only one pairing of nuclear-armed rivals—the United States and Russia—lends itself to numerical constraints. Negotiations on a multilateral treaty ending the production of bomb-making material have never gotten started; a treaty ending nuclear testing has been negotiated but remains in limbo. A cascade of stabilizing ratifications by the United States, China, India, and Pakistan begins in the Senate, where Republican support is lacking. Confidence-building and nuclear risk reduction measures are needed for every pairing; they can help at the margins but beg larger questions. The time has come to consider new conceptual frameworks.

The revival and reimagination of arms control are needed because old remedies have lost traction and because deterrence without arms control is a story that does not end well. The work ahead of us cannot be accomplished by cynics. Cynics don't succeed in reducing nuclear danger; pragmatic realists and idealists do. Every important and successful human endeavor requires vision. The two biggest visionaries in these pages are Ronald Reagan and Mikhail Gorbachev. Others have succeeded by tempering their vision and accepting more modest remedies.

Because nuclear weapons were different, and because the health hazards posed by these weapons were so great, President John F. Kennedy and Premier Nikita Khrushchev agreed to a treaty ending atmospheric tests in 1963. Because nuclear weapons were different, President Richard Nixon and General Secretary Leonid Brezhnev agreed in 1972 to a treaty that acknowledged national vulnerability. Nothing of this kind had ever been negotiated before.

Their Anti-Ballistic Missile Treaty banning nationwide missile defenses was supposed to help place limits and then reductions on nuclear weapons. But the companion agreement limiting offenses signed by Nixon and Brezhnev was purposefully porous, as neither superpower was prepared to forego plans to strengthen deterrence. The arms competition amped up, and attempts by Presidents Gerald Ford and Jimmy Carter to cap the competition could not withstand domestic opposition at a time when the Soviet Union seemed to be on the advance.

Ronald Reagan's first term was marked by heightened nuclear danger. His measures to strengthen deterrence were met by intense opposition at home and abroad. Arms control negotiations collapsed. Then, deus ex machina, the apogee of the nuclear peace became possible when aging Politburo members handed Mikhail Gorbachev the reins of a failing Soviet Union. Gorbachev was ready to trash deterrence orthodoxy and found a kindred spirit in Reagan, whose virulent anticommunism coexisted with a fervent abolitionism. Together, they said that a nuclear war could not be won and must not be fought, and they sincerely meant it.

The apogee of the nuclear peace followed, a ten-year period encompassing Reagan's second term, the remarkable presidency of George H.W. Bush, and President Bill Clinton's first term. During this period treaties eliminated entire classes of ground-launched missiles and mandated deep cuts in longer-range strategic forces as well as conventional forces in Europe. In addition, Clinton secured a treaty negotiated by Bush prohibiting chemical weapons and completed a decades-long pursuit of a treaty prohibiting nuclear testing. During this decade, the Nonproliferation Treaty was indefinitely extended and an Open Skies Treaty—first conceived by President Dwight Eisenhower as a mechanism to prevent surprise attack—was belatedly realized.

After the Cold War ended, arms control seemed superfluous. Treaties were victimized by their own successes, by shifting national priorities, by new fears of vulnerability, and by renewed U.S.-Russian friction. Strategic arms reduction negotiations stalled out during the second term of the Clinton administration. The process of treaty unraveling began with George W. Bush and Vladimir Putin, both of whom wanted freedom to maneuver and so they dispensed with treaty constraints. Putin disregarded treaties that he believed reflected the weakness and concessions of his predecessors. The demise of arms control was greatly accelerated with the pairing of Putin and Donald Trump and by the drift toward "America First" that, after a century's hiatus, seized parts of the Republican Party.

We didn't recognize winning the nuclear peace, but we will surely notice its loss. I use the terms winning and losing metaphorically rather than literally. Few wins in the demanding practice of nuclear arms control are permanent; losses can be temporary, as well. Losing the nuclear peace does not necessarily equate to the battlefield use of nuclear weapons and the resumption of nuclear testing. Deterrence remains in place, as does the central norm of not detonating mushroom clouds in warfare. Any leader who authorizes use of a nuclear weapon for the first time since 1945 will live in infamy for the remainder of recorded history.

This isn't sufficient protection against battlefield use, but it is meaningful, nonetheless. And while all states that possess nuclear weapons carry out nuclear experiments, nuclear testing has been strictly and verifiably constrained. The norm of not testing nuclear devices is now a quarter of a century old despite the siren call of conducting such tests to improve military utility and demonstrate resolve. Only one outlier remains, North Korea, and no responsible state wishes to be in this company. We have come a long way since testing in the atmosphere or at significant yields underground was deemed essential. Moratoria on nuclear testing, like the absence of battlefield use, can be broken tomorrow, or the day after. But every day without a nuclear test attaches greater stigma to the national leader who breaks this norm.

While losing the nuclear peace does not mean a reversion to worst practices, it does mean greater nuclear danger. We haven't come full circle to the time when the dangers posed by the Bomb had yet to be fenced in by the practices of arms control. There is time to regain our equilibrium. At the dawn of the nuclear age, when newspaper readers were introduced to the atomic bomb, when they saw the first images of mushroom clouds and read about the devastating consequences to Hiroshima and Nagasaki, few expected that the world could be spared atomic warfare. Previous generations lived with the presumption of when, and not whether, mushroom clouds would reappear. Josef Stalin ruled the victorious Soviet Union with an iron fist, his Iron Curtain descended on a divided Europe, and he was hellbent to obtain the Bomb. Stalin's successors worked hard not to fall behind in the nuclear competition; at times, many U.S. deterrence strategists thought the Kremlin was ahead.

A massive nuclear arms race ensued. Its extent surprised everyone. Existential angst was so great as to justify and prompt the production of more than 125,000 nuclear weapons. Each of these weapons had a defensive purpose—to deter use. To deter use, however, doctrine required the demonstration of malignant potential. Approximately 70,000 weapons were manufactured in the United States; another 55,000 in the Soviet Union. Other states—Great Britain, France, China, India, Pakistan, Israel, and North Korea—added to these numbers. The actual use of any one of these weapons on a battlefield invited uncontrolled escalation since no one offered a convincing explanation as to how leaders could exercise control once finding themselves at an impasse so great as to require mushroom clouds.

These weapons needed to be tested, in the atmosphere, over sacrificial islands, and beneath fragile atolls in the Pacific, underground or in colonial possessions. Almost two thousand of these tests were carried out; over half by the United States and over seven hundred by the Soviet Union. Every test was a demonstration of resolve and deterrence.

Deterrence generated these numbers; arms control was needed to survive them. So far, we have not suffered worst cases. We have survived close calls, accidents, and near catastrophes. Strategic bombers carrying nuclear weapons with rudimentary safety devices crashed, but no mushroom clouds resulted.

False warnings were recognized as such, rather than prompting doomsday procedures. Three officers on board a Soviet submarine being depth-charged to the surface during the Cuban missile crisis voted on whether to fire a nuclear-armed torpedo—one that the U.S. Navy was unaware of—having previously agreed to do so only by unanimous choice. One officer voted "nyet." These stories, too, are in the pages that follow. Amazingly, we have survived our overzealous, risk-laden nuclear past. The keys to our success can still serve us, if we are wise enough to remember them.

This book appears at a time of severe, dysfunctional partisanship in the United States and the advent of "strongman" leaders in states that possess nuclear weapons. Many have written obituaries for nuclear arms control in the past. Treaty withdrawals by George W. Bush, Vladimir Putin, and Donald Trump have prompted additions to this literature. And yet nuclear arms control will be resurrected because national leaders will continue to recognize the need for diplomacy to take the sharpest edges off deterrence.

How can I be so sure? Because Archimedean principles and Sir Isaac Newton's Third Law of Motion have always applied to the practice of nuclear arms control. Every action generates reaction. Seeds of success are typically planted in prior failures, just as success yields to backsliding. Granted, it will be very hard to forge a working consensus in the United States on how best to reduce nuclear danger and nuclear weapons. A nuclear peace won with great difficulty and persistence has been lost, but we can regain it if we recognize the dangers that lie ahead and take remedial steps.

Those who believe in classical arms control and in abolition are inclined to view treaties as the way to accomplish their vision. I suggest an alternative approach to revive arms control and to reduce nuclear danger in these pages, one based on the life extension of three essential norms—no use of nuclear weapons in warfare, no further testing of nuclear weapons, and nonproliferation.

Numbers and treaties still matter greatly, but norms matter more. Norms are easier to defend than numbers are to reduce. If we focus our efforts on re-affirming these three crucial norms, we can establish conditions for far fewer numbers. Everything we hold dear depends on the absence of mushroom clouds. No matter how hard deterrence strategists try to limit and fine-tune nuclear weapon effects, in the absence of escalation control, the use of these weapons is fundamentally reckless and contrary to the humanitarian laws of warfare. Every negotiation to reduce nuclear danger conveyed this implicit underlying message, even when no treaty explicitly prohibited first use. We have succeeded in the past because national leaders recognized that controlling nuclear escalation was a near-impossible task. The norm of no battlefield use can be extended upon this bedrock assumption.

The norm of no use is buttressed by the norms of no testing and nonproliferation. The task before us, as with those who succeeded in the past, is to set nuclear weapons apart from other instruments of warfare. We will proceed the same way that previous generations succeeded in keeping the nuclear peace—one day at a time and one crisis at a time. We can succeed by pairing deterrence with arms control. Success is possible because breaking these norms is very hard for national leaders to do.

I propose that we aim to extend these three norms to the hundredth anniversary of Hiroshima and Nagasaki. Imagine, if you can, a world in which nuclear weapons have not been used on battlefields for a hundred years, and a world in which nuclear weapons have not been tested for fifty years. Imagine, too, that North Korea remains the last nuclear-armed state. Now imagine the perceived utility of nuclear weapons in 2045. How many of them would be required for deterrence? How high would the barriers against use and testing be?

Aiming for a century of nonbattlefield use, a half-century of not testing nuclear weapons, and forty years of successful nonproliferation might seem too ambitious and even otherworldly. Perhaps, but the accomplishments of arms control recounted in these pages also seemed too ambitious and otherworldly. In 1945, it was absurdly ambitious to envision a world in which nuclear weapons were not used in warfare for three-quarters of a century. When conversations began about nuclear testing in the Eisenhower administration, it was absurd to envision a world in which states possessing the Bomb didn't conduct tests for a quarter-century. Those who conceived of global nonproliferation expected twenty or more states to rely on nuclear weapons.

The hardest part of establishing these three norms is behind us. The nuclear taboo against use in warfare now extends to further testing. These two norms have been extended because they are the most difficult to break. Every day that passes without use and testing strengthens them. Success happens one day at a time. When crises happen, we rise in defense of these norms. When a state seems intent to acquire nuclear weapons, other states take diplomatic steps and consider military strikes to protect this norm.

The history of nuclear arms control recounted in these pages is necessarily abbreviated. A deeply annotated, multivolume history of nuclear arms control is sorely needed, but I don't have the time, patience, and skills to write it.

And besides, we can't wait for historians to sift through declassified material to regain our footing and to resume the essential work of reducing nuclear danger and nuclear weapons. I recognize that contraction requires selectivity, and selectivity can lack balance. I have tried to avoid this pitfall; whether I have done so is your call.

I have benefited greatly from first-person accounts, interviews, oral histories, and official records. My sources are mostly U.S. nationals. New accounts by Russian academicians and practitioners could provide a fuller picture of the decision making described here. Perhaps these accounts will correct errors of analysis on my part but, again, it will take time for these accounts to appear.

My focus is on nuclear diplomacy, not grand strategy. Diplomacy is one element of a coherent strategy of national security and public safety. I end this book on a positive note. The revival of nuclear arms control is possible because its absence is too unsettling and dangerous. I have written this book in a way that I hope is accessible to lay readers, useful for students and teachers, and insightful for practitioners. I have kept jargon and acronyms to a minimum. Public safety requires public engagement. The field of arms control needs public insistence and energy, a new generation of practitioners, interested students, and willing teachers. I invite you to lend a hand to help repair and revive the practice of arms control.

PROLOGUE

Chapter 1

A PREHISTORY OF NUCLEAR ARMS CONTROL

We have learned to live with the Bomb without domesticating it. We belong to a species with a hunger for symbols, and no symbol is more
powerful than the mushroom cloud. It is buried in the subconscious even
when nuclear anxiety has ostensibly subsided. No symbol compels more rapt
attention, fear, and dread.[1] By comparison, the chemistry set imagery of the
novel coronavirus does not mesmerize, even though it has produced a pandemic. The compelling image of a massive hurricane might come closest to
the mushroom cloud but is far from comparable. Hurricanes are local phe-
nomena. We can see them coming a week in advance and follow their tracks.
There is time to gather family and precious belongings, to take adequate
precautions, and to move out of their path. The wreckage they leave behind
reminds us of what might be in store in the event of something worse.

The worst case is a nuclear war. Chroniclers of nuclear anxiety refer to
the mushroom cloud as a permanent neural trace that is carried down, one
generation to the next, evoking mental clusters of massive death. The Bomb
is the universal Frankenstein monster, transmogrified by the silver screen into
Godzilla, Them (giant ants), *The 50-Foot Woman,* and other mutated threats
to our global village. Missile defenses are like pitiable pitchforks against this
man-made Golem.

Prior to the appearance of mushroom clouds, warheads released from
long-range missiles would arc overhead, creating vapor trails in the sky. As
is often the case, the terminology for this warhead-release mechanism atop

a missile desensitizes us from its genocidal potential; it is called a "bus," releasing warheads en route to their targets akin to the way a yellow school bus carries and drops off children. Arcing downward toward their intended targets, pictures of these vapor trails also mesmerize but are not well known. Staring at them during flight tests is to imagine the beginning of the end of human mental evasion to deny nuclear peril.

Ever since the sudden and shocking appearance of the atomic bomb, we have lived in a permanent Age of Anxiety. W.H. Auden's epic poem with this title, published in 1947, is about four disconnected souls, living in numbness, their lives dissociated from affirmative meaning. Auden offered an extremely small sample size. Feelings of nuclear fear, dread, and numbness have affected humanity writ large. They are now manifested in bloodless computer games about Armageddon and public fascination with superheroes that prevent the end of days on variably sized screens.

Atomic physicists in the crucible of World War II used their intellectual gifts to disturb the universe, forever disturbing we, the people, by their creation. The chronicler of nuclear anxiety Spencer Weart writes, "During the first few years, people did not fear anything specific or immediate. The public simply felt that the ground had fallen away from under them."[2] The noted essayist E.B. White, writing in the August 18, 1945 issue of the *New Yorker*, sensed this with typical acuity: "For the first time in our lives we can feel the disturbing vibrations of complete human readjustment."

White asked, "What does one do when appalling dangers became a normal part of daily life?" The very same question has emerged with the novel coronavirus that spread globally in 2019. Another masterful account of the public's handling of nuclear anxiety asked the right framing question: "How does a people react when the entire basis of its existence is fundamentally altered?"[3] One of the scenes from *Star Wars* reminds us of this feeling—when Obi-Wan, played by Alec Guinness, feels the shudder of a powerful menacing force "in the field." But the *Star Wars* trilogy offered the expected feel-good ending. After the Bomb's appearance, there was little prospect of a happy ending.[4]

Henry L. Stimson, the secretary of war who oversaw the making of the atomic bomb and who authorized its use to end a global conflagration as soon as possible, warned that to view nuclear weapons in military terms would be a grave mistake. Instead, the Bomb represented no less than "a new relationship of man to the universe."[5] Stimson, like many others, worked afterward to control the evil he helped create. His quest remains with us and with future generations.

During intense crises, when vulnerabilities are exposed like open wounds, a deep sense of anxiety and dread rises from our collective consciousness. We respond in very different ways. Some demand caution, others demand proactive steps. Overwrought decisions to prevent worst cases from coming true have generated an intense nuclear competition. Key junctures during this Age of Anxiety included 1949, when the Soviet Union tested its first atomic bomb and allied with a victorious Communist China; in 1962 when the Cuban missile crisis brought us the closest we have yet come to nuclear disaster; in 1983 when Reagan administration hardliners pushed buttons to evoke the Kremlin's deepest anxieties without realizing it; and in 2001 after 9/11—the domestic equivalent of Pearl Harbor—when the George W. Bush administration launched wars in Afghanistan and Iraq for the publicly stated purposes of fighting evil, preventing the worst actors from acquiring the worst weapons, and spreading democracy.

Some of the Bomb's deadly effects came as a surprise even to most of its creators, who were focused on its blast and shockwave, but not the firestorms atomic bombs generated nor their widespread radiation.[6] The Bomb's unnerving weapon effects were magnified by the recognition that attacks could come out of the blue. A new fear—the "fear of irrational death," as the writer and editor Norman Cousins described it—took hold. It was hopelessly irrational for death to be so sudden, on such a large scale, and so purposeless.[7]

The Bomb was quickly recognized as an ideal instrument of surprise attack. Its means of conveyance—bombers to begin with, but the prospect of ocean-spanning missiles that took less than thirty minutes to reach their targets could soon be envisioned—compounded anxieties. Relief from anxiety after Hiroshima could only be temporary, measured by the period of time it would take before the Soviet Union joined the United States in possessing this city-killing weapon. Most expert opinion held that it might take four or five years for Josef Stalin's physicists, working under great duress, to match the feats of America's atomic scientists. Two prominent outliers—Vannevar Bush, a senior overseer of wartime research, and General Leslie R. Groves, the head of the Manhattan Project—offered more comforting estimates of around twenty years for the Soviets to match U.S. feats.[8] When Stalin proved Groves and Bush wrong in 1949, another strong wave of fear washed over American society.

The Kremlin could now pay America back using the Manhattan Project's own currency—or strike America first. More waves of anxiety were breaking unseen on the horizon. U.S. atomic scientists demonstrated the feasibility of making "hydrogen" or thermonuclear bombs a thousand times or greater in destructive force than the atomic bomb. Popular accounts called this weapon the "Hell Bomb." Then came the merger of the Sino-Soviet bloc, quickly followed by the outbreak of war on the Korean Peninsula. More waves of anxiety followed: Soviet mastery of how to make hydrogen bombs; atmospheric testing and fallout; a presumed bomber gap; the launch of Sputnik atop a missile that could carry nuclear weapons; a presumed missile gap; heightened fear of surprise attack; multiple warhead-bearing missiles and a new window of vulnerability they foreshadowed. These waves kept crashing ashore, disturbing national equilibrium and prompting remedies that only reinforced a national sense of peril.

The Bomb was extraordinarily divisive as well as destructive, evoking responses to peril that were poles apart. One expert on ethics and public policy wrote, "The fear of the bomb is not the beginning of wisdom," adding, "Fearful men have a kind of foresight, but in their partial view of the future all signs point to a foregone conclusion. How else could the frightening consequences of nuclear fission justify both McCarthyism and pacifism?"[9] Both advocates and opponents of nuclear weapons resorted to fear to make their arguments. One side needed to rouse Americans to be properly armed at the ramparts; the other side, calling for a world without the Bomb, also spread fear, as Weart noted, not only because this emotion represented their own feelings but also because "fear could move a listener."[10]

DUELING ANXIETIES

The result was a national echo chamber of dueling anxieties. Some feared the Bomb, others feared being disadvantaged by the Bomb. For three decades, American nuclear superiority provided an insurance policy against anxiety, but the premiums of maintaining superiority kept growing, as did the Soviet nuclear arsenal. The Kremlin resolved to compete no less hard than the United States. Superpower nuclear stockpiles rose to unanticipated heights. No one at the outset of this competition came close to accurately predicting that stockpiles would grow to five-digit-sized arsenals. The wells of nuclear anxiety were plumbed and found to be bottomless.

Those propelling the arms race and those trapped by it knew that it didn't take more than a small fraction of the arsenals being readied for use to ensure destruction beyond historical experience, but the competition was impervious to such calculations. To compete was admittedly dangerous; not to compete was deemed more dangerous still. Diplomacy offered an exit strategy, but it took decades—and the impending collapse of the Soviet Union—for diplomacy to gain greater traction than the arms race. Nuclear weapons reflected impasses and widened them. Disarmament was impossible, so a brilliant group of conceptualizers at the end of the Eisenhower administration began to formulate the principles of what they called arms control. Their new and risky concepts were unable to stop arms racing. A different set of brilliant minds had already begun to conceptualize deterrence. It was far easier to make nuclear weapons and missiles than to negotiate treaties.

One great source of anxiety was that effective defenses against the Soviet Bomb and its means of delivery were inconceivable. None of the original conceptualizers of nuclear deterrence offered this hope; it was instead viewed as a fool's errand. Only later, when defensive technologies advanced, did the pursuit of national defenses arise, fueled on moral and strategic grounds. But offensive technologies also advanced, nullifying defensive technologies. The nuclear-armed state and its citizens seemed hopelessly vulnerable. By extension, civilization itself could end with uncontrolled atomic warfare.

Protective countermeasures to atomic bombing, such as creating satellite cities instead of building out from city centers to suburbs and exurbs, as humans have been wont to do, was initially considered and quickly dropped as being impractical. Civil defenses were also contemplated early on. In due course, many basement fallout shelters were constructed and major facilities to protect leadership were built underground with reams of bank notes, safely wrapped in plastic, stored in protective custody to rebuild civilization.[11]

There was, however, no safety from being targeted or from being downwind. Herman Kahn, who was easily caricatured because of his attempt to rationalize nuclear war-fighting scenarios, asked a central question: "Would the living envy the dead?"[12] With improved accuracies for bomb delivery and greater destructive yields, command bunkers and hardened missile silos could not survive attacks. To be at or near a designated ground zero meant death, either quickly or over time. Hospital beds would be far too limited—assuming that hospitals were not destroyed. Medical supplies would run out quickly. Air traffic would be shut down in the immediate aftermath of nuclear strikes even if some runways were usable. First responders would have to steer clear of radiation zones or be so encumbered by protective gear as to have limited effectiveness. Survivors would face radiation exposure if they escaped the immediate blast effects and firestorms. Food supplies would be radiated if not wiped out.

Escape from this new, ominous reality could be found in black humor, in popular culture, and even in a new swimsuit design, called the bikini after an atoll in the South Pacific sacrificed by nuclear testing. Escapism through denial was one route to being held captive to the Bomb's destructive effects. Others sought extraordinary steps to prevent the production of atomic weapons. A third approach was to seek safety by outcompeting the Soviet Union.

Atomic scientists working on the Manhattan Project that created atomic weapons were at the forefront of those having second thoughts about their advances. They had "known sin," in the words of J. Robert Oppenheimer, the orchestra leader of the geniuses assembled at Los Alamos.[13] These scientists were divided about their handiwork; some, led by Oppenheimer, accepted the responsibility to help explain the incomprehensible and to devise mechanisms of relief from nuclear danger. Some veterans of the Manhattan Project lobbied against using the atomic bomb against Japan. Oppenheimer was a central figure in drafting the Acheson-Lilienthal Plan, a blueprint of international control to ban the Bomb and to promote the peaceful uses of the atom. Veterans of the Manhattan Project were also central in starting up a bulletin to circulate their views, which evolved into the *Bulletin of the Atomic Scientists*.[14]

ONE LAST CHANCE FOR NONUSE

Scientists based at the Metallurgy Laboratory in Chicago established proof of concept for a nuclear chain reaction and then handed their calculations and designs to Los Alamos, Hanford, and Oak Ridge. They had more time and distance than their colleagues who remained on deadline, leading some to question their prospective achievements. The man who chaired their secret deliberations was James Franck, a Nobel Prize–winning physicist who served as director of the Chemistry Division. Franck, like Hans Bethe, John von Neumann, Leo Szilard, Edward Teller, Rudolf Peierls, Enrico Fermi, Stanislaw Ulam, Eugene Wigner, George Gamow, and Victor Weisskopf, found refuge in the United States and purpose in defeating Fascism by working on the Bomb. Two months before Hiroshima, Franck, with drafting help from Eugene Rabinowitch, Glenn Seaborg, and especially Szilard, wrote a memorandum urging the Truman administration to carry out a demonstration shot of the atomic bomb rather than to use it without advance warning against a Japanese city.[15]

Franck and his colleagues warned, "If no efficient international agreement is achieved, the race of nuclear armaments will be on in earnest not later than the morning after our first demonstration of the existence of nuclear weapons." They were right, of course, but this would be true whether Truman authorized a demonstration shot or used the weapon against a city. One reason for a demonstration shot was on moral grounds; another was the need for trust between the United States and the Soviet Union: "Only lack of mutual trust, and not lack of desire for agreement, can stand in the path of an efficient agreement for the prevention of nuclear warfare." The signers of the Franck Report argued that "the way in which nuclear weapons . . . will first be revealed to the world appears of great, perhaps fateful importance." They wrote that using the Bomb against a Japanese city "may easily destroy all our chances of success" to control nuclear weapons. It would be very difficult, they argued, to persuade the world that the nation capable of "secretly preparing and suddenly releasing" a weapon as indiscriminate as the atom bomb could be trusted "in its proclaimed desire to having such weapons abolished by international agreement." Trust could be engendered, they argued, with a demonstration test "made before the eyes of all United Nations, on the desert or a barren island."[16]

Secretary of War Stimson sought counsel to consider the Franck Report's recommendations and reasoning in late May and June of 1945. These advisers, who included Oppenheimer, identified problems with the idea of a demonstration shot, such as wondering whether it would diminish or whet Josef Stalin's appetite for the Bomb. Stimson and his advisers found the Franck Report's recommendations to be unpersuasive. The task at hand, as they saw it, was to end the war as quickly as possible. Stimson could not explain to the parents of those to whom he signed letters of condolence why he did not end the U.S. invasion of the Japanese home islands when he had the opportunity to do so.

STIMSON, THE ADVISER

Stimson was the ultimate insider, serving every president but one from William Howard Taft to Truman. As secretary of war for Presidents Franklin Delano Roosevelt and Truman, Stimson oversaw and approved of the bomb's use as "the least abhorrent choice." His justification: "The destruction of Hiroshima and Nagasaki put an end to the Japanese war. It stopped the fire raids, and the strangling blockade; it ended the ghastly specter of a clash of great land armies." In a memorandum to Truman that they discussed on

April 25, 1945, more than three months before the destruction of Hiroshima, Stimson advised, "The world in its present state of moral advancement compared with its technical development would eventually be at the mercy of such a weapon. In other words, modern civilization might be completely destroyed." He added, "No system of control heretofore considered would be adequate to control this menace."

Stimson challenged Truman to consider that "our leadership in the war and in the development of this weapon has placed a certain moral responsibility upon us which we cannot shirk." Then Stimson pivoted: to avoid disaster, "we would have the opportunity to bring the world into a pattern in which the peace of the world and our civilization can be saved." Here he differed with Truman's confidante and Secretary of State James F. Byrnes, who viewed the Bomb as helpful in dealing with the Kremlin on a variety of postwar issues. Stimson once thought likewise, but his focus on how to control the Bomb led him to an opposite view: "that having the weapon rather ostentatiously on our hip" would only harm prospects for international control. Truman was on the fence; initially he was inclined to follow Stimson's advice, but then swung to Byrnes's position.[17]

Stimson didn't shirk from his duty. He chose the targets to be struck, repeatedly deleting Kyoto from General Groves's suggested list. He had visited Kyoto before the war and was well aware of its importance as a religious and cultural center as well as the absence of consequential military production facilities within its confines. Hiroshima had no such protections. It was home to significant army and naval facilities. Moreover, it was relatively unscathed from aerial bombardment, making it a better target to assess the new weapon's effects.

Nuclear historian Alex Wellerstein has dug deeply into the circumstances of Stimson's exchanges with Truman about Hiroshima and their aftermath. Truman may well have misunderstood—or wanted to misunderstand—that he was approving the destruction of an entire city. Instead, he might have believed, as he publicly stated, that he was authorizing the destruction of a military target. The pictures of Hiroshima's destruction taken by an aircraft trailing the *Enola Gay* and placed in front of Truman within forty-eight hours demolished this conceit.

Try to imagine how jarring the briefings Groves prepared for Truman, Stimson, and other top officials of the A-bomb's effects must have been. Back then, briefings of this kind consisted of images pasted on two-by-three-foot cardboard slabs that were placed on easels. McGeorge Bundy gifted the

Stimson Center with the same folio of images Truman saw, replicated in the briefing Groves gave to his father, Harvey Bundy, who was Stimson's close confidante at the War Department. To see this folio of images is to reimagine the shock and awe that Truman and his top advisers most probably felt—reactions so profound that they sought to partner with Josef Stalin, proposing a bold scheme to prevent further military uses of atomic energy, despite the odds.[18]

Nagasaki's death by atomic bombing was already well in train when Truman saw the images of Hiroshima. He then decreed a stop to the further use of atomic bombs. Truman publicly professed to be unbothered by the decision to drop atomic bombs on Japanese cities, but his private thoughts and subsequent decisions suggest otherwise. At a cabinet meeting two short days after Nagasaki, Truman acknowledged that the thought of wiping out another 100,000 people was too horrible to contemplate. His private references to the use of atomic bombs repeatedly dwelled on the deaths of innocents, a connection that he didn't make with city-killing aerial bombardment by other means. Truman was especially bothered after meeting Oppenheimer, who spoke of having blood on his hands. With good reason: if Oppenheimer had blood on his hands, Truman would have been bathed in it.[19]

The briefing of aerial images that Groves, the son of an army chaplain, circulated might have been one contributing factor in Truman's decision not to use this "war winning" weapon in Korea, even when the war dragged on, even after Chinese troops crossed the Yalu, sending American GIs reeling. Truman's restraint during this crucible was the beginning of the norm of nonbattlefield use. The public reason he gave for this uncommon but crucial restraint was direct: "It should not be used on innocent men, women and children who have nothing whatsoever to do with this military aggression. That happens when it is used."[20]

THE BIGGEST BOMBSHELL OF A STORY

It was immediately clear in August 1945 on the day after the atomic bombing of Hiroshima that nuclear weapons were of world historic consequence. This initial impression didn't change over time. Journalists and historians surveyed in February 1999 ranked the first use of a nuclear weapon in warfare as the "Story of the Century." The Associated Press's ranking of the most important headline stories of the twentieth century concurred.

These were the lead paragraphs of the 2,500-word report in the *New York Times* on the atomic bombing of Japan:

The White House and War Department announced today that an atomic bomb, possessing more power than 20,000 tons of TNT, a destructive force equal to the load of 2,000 B-29's and more than 2,000 times the blast power of what previously was the world's most devastating bomb, had been dropped on Japan.

The announcement, first given to the world in utmost solemnity by President Truman, made it plain that one of the scientific landmarks of the century had been passed, and that the "age of atomic energy," which can be a tremendous force for the advancement of civilization as well as for destruction, was at hand.[21]

One historian who studied public opinion after the shock of atomic bombing characterized emotional reactions as awe, fear, satisfaction, hope, uncertainty, and bewilderment.[22] To which we might add pride and moral revulsion. A distinctly minority view strongly held that the Bomb's use was unnecessary and immoral. The majority view in 1945 expressed a strong sense of relief and approval that the use of atomic bombs ended the carnage of a world war as soon as possible. In a Gallup poll taken days after Hiroshima and Nagasaki were razed, 85 percent of Americans expressed approval of the use of the atomic weapons.[23]

The relief most Americans felt was mixed with a sense of foreboding and anxiety about what might follow. There was also hope that this new destructive force could somehow be corralled by heroic efforts to transform international relations and place effective international controls over the most dangerous weapons ever devised.

THE SMYTH REPORT

Just three days after the bombing of Nagasaki, on August 12, 1945, General Groves released an "administrative history of the Atomic Bomb project and the basic scientific knowledge on which the several developments were based." It was known as the Smyth Report, after its author, Professor Henry DeWolf Smyth, who taught physics at Princeton before and after his stint at Los Alamos. The report's official title was *A General Account of the Scientific Research and Technical Development That Went into the Making of Atomic Bombs.* It could be purchased at a cost of thirty-five cents from the superintendent of documents.

The Smyth Report was part history, part elementary physics text, and must reading for all those—foreign nationals included—keenly interested in the Bomb and the extent of U.S. efforts to produce it. One possible reason for its public release was to justify the extraordinary cost of the Manhattan Project. Beyond the particulars, Smyth offered an unnerving but obvious conclusion: "A weapon has been developed that is potentially destructive beyond the wildest nightmares of the imagination; a weapon so ideally suited to sudden unannounced attack that a country's major cities might be destroyed overnight." He continued, "This weapon has been created not by the devilish inspiration of some warped genius, but by the arduous labor of thousands of normal men and women working for the safety of their country."[24]

Democratic societies grappled with how best to proceed. Vocal opposition occasionally interfered with planning behind closed doors, especially on the question of nuclear testing and on constructing national missile defenses. But the votes that weighed most heavily on nuclear decision-making were few in number. These voters were members of an exclusive club. They were senior government officials and advisers, leaders of the scientific elite who created this "gadget," and a few members of Congress. The renowned Yale University political scientist Robert Dahl worked on this dilemma early in his career. In November 1953, Dahl edited a slim book, *The Impact of Atomic Energy*, a collection of essays that previously appeared in *The Annals*, the journal of the American Academy of Political and Social Science. In his introductory essay, Dahl wrote, "As a plain statement of fact . . . the political processes of democracy do not operate effectively with respect to atomic energy policy." He wrote that the "institutionalization of secrecy has concentrated, in the hands of a few people," power equivalent to "any old-fashioned authoritarian leader." As a result, "atomic energy seems to present choices that defy wide popular understanding and control." The result was "a kind of indigestible element in the operation of American politics."[25]

MORAL INDIGNATION

A distinct minority of the American public expressed moral indignation against the Bomb and its use against Japan. Among these prominent voices were essayist Dwight MacDonald, noted educator Robert M. Hutchins, polymath and humanist Lewis Mumford, perennial socialist presidential candidate Norman Thomas, and Norman Cousins, a young, dynamic magazine editor. Writing in the fall of 1945, MacDonald, a caustic social critic, characterized the atomic bomb as "the natural product of the kind of society we have created. It is as easy, normal and unforced expression of the American Way of Life as electric iceboxes, banana splits, and hydromatic-drive automobiles." MacDonald's heroes were the scientists who refused to work on the Bomb: "This," he wrote, "is 'resistance,' this is 'negativism' and in it lies our best hope."[26]

Other critiques were no less pointed but more restrained. Hutchins, the son of a Presbyterian minister and a foot soldier amidst the slaughter of World War I, rose quickly to become the dean of Yale Law School and chancellor of the University of Chicago, from which he penned *The Atomic Bomb vs. Civilization* in 1945. Hutchins opened with the assertion, "There is only one subject of really fundamental importance"—the atomic bomb—for "if we do not survive, there is no use discussing what we are going to do with our lives." Secrecy didn't matter, because others could figure out how to make atom bombs. "We might make better bombs than other countries," he readily conceded, then added, "But in the event of nuclear weapons' use . . . whether we won or lost the war, our cities would be destroyed."

The Bomb, Hutchins wrote, "produces a world which must live in perpetual fear." He didn't place much stock in the prospect of world government, but he heartily endorsed steps along the way. The situation was not hopeless, however. The remedy was "to increase our rate of moral progress tremendously . . . We must see to it, if we can, that our social and cultural advances for once exceed the advances in the technology of destruction."

Hutchins joined with others who sought to allay Soviet mistrust after the Bomb's dramatic unveiling by disclosing atomic secrets, as doing so "would show we have no intention of using it." He was among the first to propose that Washington "seek to enter into international agreements renouncing the bomb as an instrument of warfare." He acknowledged, "The task is overwhelming, and the chance of success is slight." Even so, "We must take the chance or die."[27]

Mumford was a utopian who wrote gracefully on many topics. In *Values for Survival*, published in 1946, he wrote, "We must give as much weight to the arousal of emotions and to the expression of moral and esthetic values as we now give to science, to invention, to practical organization. One without the other is impotent." Thomas, the Socialist Party's quadrennial candidate for president, reacted to the Bomb with deep sorrow. Rather than rejoicing over the ending of a victorious war, he felt "a sense of shame for the horror which the atomic bomb released on earth . . . I shall always believe that the war might have been ended before the first atomic bomb was dropped on Hiroshima bringing death to at least a hundred thousand men, women and children."[28]

Well before revisionist historians entered the fray to argue that the use of atomic weapons was directed more against the Kremlin than against a prostrate Japan, religious leaders and editorialists struck this very theme. The Catholic Church was the most vocal on these matters. *Commonweal*, an influential American Catholic journal, editorialized that Hiroshima and Nagasaki "are names for American guilt and shame."[29]

Protestant denominations and leaders held mixed views about the Bomb. Leading theologian Reinhold Niebuhr endorsed its use against two Japanese cities, but later had second thoughts.[30] Other voices were fiercely opposed. *Christian Century*, a leading voice of American Protestantism, published an editorial in its August 29, 1945 issue under the headline "America's Atomic Atrocity": "Our leaders seem not to have weighed the moral considerations involved . . . The atomic bomb can fairly be said to have struck Christianity itself . . . The churches of America must dissociate themselves and their faith from this inhuman and reckless act of the American Government."[31]

Jewish leaders naturally felt mixed emotions about the Bomb: gratitude that it ended war in the Pacific, regret that it hadn't been ready sooner for use against Nazi Germany, and uneasiness about the moral peril that lay ahead. One account in the Boston-based *Jewish Advocate* expressed pride that Jewish scientists played prominent roles in the Manhattan Project.[32]

ACHESON-LILIENTHAL

Atomic scientists and others with influence were like electrons orbiting at varying distances to the nucleus of power. Those at the outer rings, like the contributors to the Franck Report, readily offered dissenting views. The closer scientific expertise and influencers orbited near the nucleus of power, such as those who deliberated on the Bomb's use along with Stimson, the more consensual decision making became. Those who held strong reservations about using the Bomb dropped out of insider deliberations. One of the last to drop out was Oppenheimer, rightly called an "American Prometheus" by his foremost biographers, Kai Bird and Martin J. Sherwin.

Oppenheimer needed a laser-like focus to prove worthy of the challenge General Groves entrusted to him and the challenge he set for himself—to help win the war effort. In doing so, he demonstrated leadership and management skills that were barely visible in his prior intellectual pursuits. His past flirtations, political and personal, didn't matter; building a workable bomb did. Oppenheimer stood out and stood apart even among the extraordinary cast of characters he assembled at Los Alamos, including many Nobel Prize winners. He harnessed this assemblage of talent and ego with seeming ease. They included Edward Teller, who played sonatas on the piano in the wee hours, John von Neumann, who recited Thucydides in Greek and Voltaire in French, and a stellar international cast of characters and homegrown genius.[33]

After accomplishing his mission, Oppenheimer permitted himself a wider aperture. Circumstances dictated a more active policy role. Edward Teller, Ernest Lawrence at Berkeley, Lewis Strauss of the Atomic Energy Commission, and others were pushing privately for bombs that could dwarf Los Alamos's first bomb designs in terms of their destructive power. Oppenheimer could not accept this development mutely. Having succeeded at overseeing the creation of a war-winning weapon, he set his sights on new missions, just as urgent as the last: to conceptualize international control of nuclear weapons and, failing that, to place limits on the Bomb's destructive capacity. In this, he had widespread support, not just among atomic scientists but also in the highest echelon of the Truman administration. Stimson was very much on this wavelength, but he was a tired and unwell man who was about to retire. David Lilienthal, a rising star as head of the Tennessee Valley Authority, was similarly inclined. The immediate challenge was to prevent a race to manufacture atom bombs. Otherwise, the world would be under the perpetual threat of mushroom clouds.

Truman asked Byrnes, his new secretary of state, to set up a Committee on Atomic Energy to draft a plan that could be presented to the fledgling United Nations. The task was given to Byrnes's deputy, Dean Acheson, who was joined by an All-Star cast consisting of General Groves, James Conant of Harvard University, Vannevar Bush, and John J. McCloy, one of Stimson's advisers. A board of consultants, led by Oppenheimer, helped with conceptualization and drafting. Three members of the board were captains of industry (Chester Barnard of Bell Telephone, Charles Allen Thomas of Monsanto, and Harry Winne of General Electric) who naturally turned to Oppenheimer for guidance. Lilienthal was the final member of the board of consultants and its chairman.

Victor Weisskopf, yet another refugee who contributed to the work at Los Alamos, helped Niels Bohr draft a memorandum to Oppenheimer in April 1944 predicting this moment: "Unless some agreement about the control [of fissionable material] . . . can be obtained in due time, any temporary advantage, however great, may be outweighed by a perpetual menace to human security."[34] Oppenheimer was then at the peak of his prowess and authority. The fifty-nine-page Acheson-Lilienthal Report—more of a blue-print—was largely his handiwork, with an assist from I.I. Rabi and other unattributed colleagues.

After the war ended, Oppenheimer was in a position to try to do something heroic about the dilemma he helped create. No insider deliberations ever produced a more radical set of blueprints than the plan Oppenheimer designed and Lilienthal conveyed to Deputy Secretary of State Dean Acheson. The Acheson-Lilienthal Plan was a systematic and comprehensive first draft for international control of atomic energy. Completed after only two short months of intensive effort, it was a plan worthy of the moment.

The Acheson-Lilienthal Plan's underlying assumptions were that there was no effective defense against the Bomb's destructive power, and that no nation could maintain a monopoly on its production. Its central underlying concept was "to prevent the use of atomic energy for destructive purposes and to promote the use of it for the benefit of sovereignty." The authors emphasized that their plan wasn't the final word; instead, it "was a place to begin, a foundation on which to build." It was, they stressed, a "hopeful" and "affirmative" approach, not one built around "police powers," although inspections were an essential element of its implementation. Inspections could only succeed if undertaken within a cooperative ethos. Otherwise, "suspicion by one nation of the good faith of another and the fear engendered thereby are themselves strong incentives for the first to embark on secret illicit operations."

The Acheson-Lilienthal Plan laid out conditions necessary for success, labeled as "safeguards," and stressed that the problem had "definable boundaries," making it conceptually feasible. The plan essentially sought to remove the production of bomb-making material from other aspects of international rivalry by placing every stage of mining, manufacturing, and production within the ambit of an Atomic Development Authority that would be entrusted with international observation and control. It would have "exclusive jurisdiction to conduct all intrinsically dangerous operations in the field."[35]

The Acheson-Lilienthal Plan could be no more than a conceptual outline. It lacked crucial specifics, such as the modalities of inspection, the composition and workings of the international atomic energy agency, and the transitional arrangements whereby the United States would relinquish its atomic monopoly as effective safeguards came online. Truman and Byrnes gave Bernard Baruch the task of transmitting the recommendations embedded in the plan to the United Nations. Baruch's father was a field surgeon for the Confederate army during the Civil War. Baruch moved the family to

New York City, where his son attended City College, then worked his way up from office boy in the linen business to wealthy Wall Street financier. He was a wartime adviser to Presidents Woodrow Wilson and Franklin Delano Roosevelt as well as a public figure with a flair for the dramatic.

Baruch felt the plan he inherited lacked adequate safeguards for American security. By this time, Stimson's influence had waned in retirement and Acheson's views had hardened. Acheson was obliged to transfer the plan devised by Oppenheimer and Lilienthal to Truman and Byrnes, but he had no vested interest in it. He heard out Oppenheimer and then asked a colleague, "How can you persuade a paranoid adversary to disarm 'by example'?"[36]

Baruch amended the Acheson-Lilienthal Plan by mandating that its implementation and operation not be subject to the Soviet Union's veto power at the UN Security Council. On June 14, 1946, he introduced what was now called the Baruch Plan before the UN's Atomic Energy Committee with the quip, "We are here to make a choice between the quick and the dead." His insistence on doing away with the Soviet veto on matters pertaining to atomic energy insured that the Acheson-Lilienthal Plan was quickly dead.[37]

A public relations contest ensued thereafter between Washington and Moscow over who wanted disarmament more and who was mostly responsible for failure. Even had Baruch employed greater finesse at the United Nations, failure seemed inevitable. Trust between Washington and Moscow was in very short supply, especially on a matter of such supreme national interest. Moscow's foreign minister, Andrei Gromyko, wanted U.S. disarmament first, to be followed by international control; Washington wanted veto-proof international control before relinquishing the Bomb. As the historian Barton Bernstein concluded, "Divided by deep mistrust, both nations were unprepared to make the concessions necessary for agreement and to risk bestowing advantages on the other great power."[38]

Acheson-Lilienthal was the right, bold plan for the threat posed by the Bomb, but that threat coincided with the outset of the Cold War and the division of Europe. The failure of the plan—the first and best hope for international control to prevent atomic bomb making—prompted a profound wave of despair. Oppenheimer turned to mordant irony. The pages of the *Bulletin of the Atomic Scientists* offered prophetic warnings rather than hope. The U.S. government went to great lengths to keep secrets about the Bomb and to neuter the influence of those—including Oppenheimer himself—who were deemed suspect. Anxieties were boundless. Some sought relief by tuning out. Others sought relief by keeping ahead of the competition. The third option—abolition—now seemed beyond reach. A fourth option, arms control, awaited conceptualization.

ESCAPING FROM PERIL

In 1946, Winston Churchill spoke of an "Iron Curtain" descending upon Europe. Stalin announced that the Soviet Union would remain on a wartime footing. It was depressingly clear that U.S. and Soviet leaders were at loggerheads in the newly created United Nations. The plan devised by Oppenheimer and David Lilienthal to place the means of producing nuclear weapons under international control fell by the wayside. World Federalism—another escape route—was a hopeless dream. Those in authority sought protection from the Soviet Union's eventual possession of the Bomb by competing and competing hard. A national security state was required to deal with anxieties prompted by a nuclear competition, undergirded by secrets that needed to be protected, ample funds for nuclear laboratories and production lines, and nuclear weapons ready for prompt use, if need be.

Some placed their hopes in the pursuit of war-winning capabilities, but this presumed the ability to execute "splendid" first strikes and Moscow's inability to compete effectively or retaliate with devastating effect. Those who proposed constructs and plans to win a nuclear war were, in their own way, every bit as audacious and ambitious as those who championed world government or international control over the means of bomb making. Both were forms of escapism. The only way to hope to win a nuclear war was to strike first, but President Harry Truman deemed this unacceptable. Truman equated preventive war with the infamy of the Japanese attack on Pearl Harbor; to engage in such an infamous act was, in his view, downright un-American. In an address during the Korean War, he said, "We do not believe in aggressive or preventive war. Such is the weapon of dictators, not of free democratic countries like the United States."[39]

There were other impediments to military escapism. To begin with, nuclear war-winning capabilities couldn't be measured because there were no fact-based estimates of the Soviet threat. Precise targeting was problematic, even when ocean-spanning, "intercontinental" ballistic missiles, or ICBMs, became available, because the Soviet Union was a closed society. By the time targeting information became known, thanks to risky U-2 overflights and reconnaissance satellites, the Soviet Union had begun to accumulate its own missiles in sufficient number to dissuade presidents from striking first. Programs of ballistic missile defenses of U.S. cities began to be pursued in the mid-1950s, but the radars needed to send interceptor missiles toward incoming warheads could be blacked out by nuclear detonations. Still another constraint against launching a surprise attack was the widespread assumption that the Kremlin would respond with another ground war in Europe along with retaliatory strikes against U.S. cities.

The diminishment of hope cut both ways. Those who sought escape by means of abolition and World Federalism found themselves defeated, just as the keys to a successful preventive war were beyond the reach of military strategists. Although the pursuits of abolition and nuclear war-winning capabilities were tamped down, they were never extinguished. Neither camp lost hope. These contradictory, instinctive responses to nuclear peril resurfaced whenever the competition became dangerously intense.

What remained, as a matter of practicality and eventually policy, was the acceptance of mutual vulnerability to nuclear attack, an acceptance that could, many hoped, provide the basis for successful negotiations. Mutual vulnerability was, however, no guarantee against mushroom clouds. Even after the advent of arms control, the primary restraint against using nuclear weapons in war was characterized as "mutual assured destruction," or MAD. MAD was a deeply imperfect answer because reliance on mass slaughter to preserve the peace was immoral and because deterrence could break down. Doves sought diplomatic means of reassurance and controls along with sufficient deterrence to prevent use. Hawks placed their faith in nuclear weapons. They doubted that the Kremlin accepted mutual assured destruction and presumed that Moscow harbored war-winning aims. Deterrence strengtheners in the United States and the Soviet Union took steps that suggested war-winning objectives. National security establishments are supposed to find more comfort in victory than in ties, or failing that, in comparative advantage.

The goal of outright victory in a nuclear war was rarely vocalized or written about. It was less unnerving to talk in code. Comparative advantage had two rationales. One was the leverage advantage presumably provided in an intense crisis, another was an advantageous outcome, albeit at horrific cost, if deterrence failed. The first could be palatably sold to an attentive domestic audience; the second was usually beyond the pale and mostly left unsaid. But the plain fact of the matter was that Washington and Moscow both pursued comparative advantage and the avoidance of disadvantage. Arms control accords were initially unable to dent these twin pursuits. Until the Soviet Union was on the brink of dissolution, each treaty was accompanied by an intensified competition. Anxiety never took an extended holiday. A collective sense of peril grew with the size of nuclear stockpiles, and then, when stockpiles finally began to decline in the late 1960s, anxieties were propelled by qualitative improvements in nuclear capabilities.

In his last address to the House of Commons in 1955, as hope ebbed and the Bomb became even more ubiquitous, Winston Churchill prophesized a "sublime irony" that "safety will become the sturdy child of terror, and survival the twin brother of annihilation."[40] For once, Churchill's way with words failed him. There was nothing sublime about this irony. Bomb building was resolute work; the mysteries of the atom were being exploited for destructive purposes. There would be no slacking, as national security required ceaseless vigilance. For those toiling in what Eisenhower called the military-industrial complex, safety meant leading a nuclear competition that seemed both inevitable and irreversible.

ATOMIC SCIENTISTS AS POLITICAL ACTORS

Atomic scientists felt relief and a sense of pride in helping to end a global conflict. Some comfort could be found in the knowledge that even greater destruction was wreaked on cities like Tokyo and Dresden by aerial bombardment. Then John Hersey personalized the damage by telling the stories of six victims in Hiroshima. His reporting first appeared in the August 31, 1946 issue of the *New Yorker* and was subsequently available as a Book-of-the-Month Club selection. Hersey obliterated the distance between the actors and the act itself, between the bomb makers and the consequences of their accomplishment.[41]

Some introspective atomic scientists were particularly susceptible to feelings of remorse. Oppenheimer advised it would not help to "try to rub the edges off this new terror that we have helped bring to the world."[42] The powerful, authoritative voices of atomic scientists were central to the push for international control to prevent another military use of atomic energy. Arguably, the voices of scientists in public policy never carried more weight than in the period immediately after the atomic bomb's unveiling.

Personal responsibility was a key driver in the activation of atomic scientists. Robert Wilson, a pacifist who nonetheless joined the Manhattan Project because "neutrality would have been a selfish luxury" in light of the Nazi menace, framed the challenge this way: "We physicists cast our lot with building it. We therefore bear the responsibility for our choice."[43] Oppenheimer, the most prominent atomic scientist of them all, joined a blue-ribbon panel of advisers to devise instruments of international control so that the "cosmic" bomb—a moniker used by the War Department that soon fell into disuse—would not threaten civilization. But how could this be done when the potential for change in international relations and perceived national interests lagged so stubbornly behind advances in the killing power of modern weaponry? As Albert Einstein warned, "The unleashed power of the atom has changed everything save our modes of thinking and we thus drift toward unparalleled catastrophe."[44]

The hopeful, insistent voices of scientists involved in the Manhattan Project were collected in a thin volume published by the newly formed Federation of American (Atomic) Scientists in 1946, *One World or None*, which became a national best seller. In it, Frederick Seitz, who worked on plutonium production at the Manhattan Project, and Hans Bethe, a theoretical physicist who worked on the A-bomb's design at Los Alamos, asked the question, "How Close Is the Danger?" Their correct answer was between four and five years—the time it would probably take for Russian scientists to figure out how to duplicate this accomplishment. And what then? "We may find ourselves alienated in a hostile world, a world in which the proximity of sudden death on a larger scale is greater than it ever was in the primordial jungle that cradled the human tribes."[45]

Arthur H. Compton was the head of the Metallurgical Laboratory in Chicago where the first self-sustaining chain reaction of atom splitting—and thus a key proof of principle for the A-bomb's destructive force—occurred under the stands of an athletic facility. The "Met Lab" then handed off this work to others in the Manhattan Project. Compton wrote in the Introduction to *One World or None*: "The terrific blast at Hiroshima shocked the world into a realization that catastrophe lies ahead if war is not eliminated . . . We now have before us the clear choice between adjusting the pattern of our society on a world basis so that wars cannot come again, or of following the outworn tradition of national self-defense, which if carried through to its logical conclusion must result in catastrophic conflict."[46]

A nonscientist was enlisted to contribute to *One World or None*—General H.H. "Hap" Arnold, the army's chief of air staff during World War II (an independent air force did not yet exist). Arnold wrote, "The greatest need facing the world today is for international control of the human forces that make for war." Failing this, he warned that these bombs would be necessary for national protection.[47]

Among the multiple anxieties unleashed by the Bomb was the first expression of fear that a nuclear war could result by accident or poor judgment.

Louis M. Ridenour, a physicist working on radar rather than the Bomb during World War II, penned a playlet, *Pilot Lights of the Apocalypse*, that appeared in the January 1946 issue of *Forbes*. Ridenour's doomsday scenario begins with an earthquake destroying San Francisco that prompts an excitable, patriotic colonel to go haywire. *Dr. Strangelove* and *Fail Safe* can trace their lineage to Ridenour.

For others, international control of atomic energy to prevent A-bombs from being built was necessary but insufficient. Norman Cousins, writing in his *Saturday Review of Literature*, emphatically argued, "The only real protection for a democracy in an atomic age is an organized peace under world law."[48] Cousins had illustrious company. Einstein's contribution to *One World or None* concluded, "It is necessary for that the individual state be prevented from making war by a supranational organization supported by a military power that is exclusively under its control."[49]

Oppenheimer's contribution to *One World or None* was optimistic: "These weapons call for and by their existence will help to create radical and profound changes in the politics of the world." Oppenheimer succinctly clarified "the truly radical character" of atomic weapons as "their vastly greater powers of destruction [and] in the vastly reduced effort needed for such destruction." He hoped that "the common interest of all in the prevention of atomic warfare would seem immensely to overshadow any purely national interest." On this, the world community of scientists would need to take the lead.[50]

Oppenheimer's naivete was short-lived, overtaken by mordant cynicism. The world wasn't capable of such "radical and profound" changes. Still, Oppenheimer soldiered on until his security clearance was revoked in 1954 for suspect views and early associations, but primarily for his cautionary influence among his cohort of atomic scientists. Oppenheimer's ambivalence about bomb making and his intent to remain an influential insider would become his undoing.

INSTITUTIONALIZING ANXIETY THROUGH DETERRENCE

With the failure of the Acheson-Lilienthal Plan, it was painfully clear that preventing atomic warfare required preparations to wage it. Hap Arnold's essay in *One World or None* suggested as much. Failing to place effective controls over atomic energy would mean that "our first defense is the ability to retaliate even after receiving the hardest blow the enemy can deliver."[51] Diplomacy needed to take a backseat to deterrence, and the requirements for deterrence would need to be exacting: "Our counteroffensive must be made by a force in being—not a force which has to be mobilized in weeks and even days." Another advocate of radical solutions, Walter Lippmann, the renowned author and columnist for the New York *Herald Tribune*, also acknowledged in his contribution to *One World or None* that "peaceable nations have to be willing to wage total war in order to prevent total war."[52]

The first drafters of deterrence theory were located at Yale University's Institute of International Studies. The most trenchant among them was Bernard Brodie, a historian of naval strategy and warfare who turned his attentions to the new field of nuclear strategy. Brodie gathered his colleagues, Frederick S. Dunn, Arnold Wolfers, Percy Corbett, and William T.R. Fox, to apply their powers of analysis to the coming revolution of military affairs. The result was a slim volume, *The Absolute Weapon*, published in 1946, that included the most prescient, earliest forecasts of the implications of "atomic power and world order" (the book's subtitle), as well as the origins of the strategy of deterrence.

Brodie's essays were the best of the lot. His analysis was grounded in what he believed was "unalterable reality." He wrote, "Everything about the atomic bomb is overshadowed by the twin fact that it exists and that its destructive power is fantastically great." There was no choice but to accept the uncomfortable fact that "no adequate defense against the bomb exists, and the possibility of its existence in the future are exceedingly remote." Brodie rejected escapism: "the absolute weapon" was ideally suited for aggressors, "and the elements of surprise and terror are as intrinsic to it as are the fissionable nuclei."

Brodie introduced readers to the concept of deterrence. Without the "fear of substantial retaliation," the atomic bomb would "clearly encourage aggression." It therefore followed that "the first and most vital step in any American security program for the age of atomic bombs is to take measures to guarantee to ourselves in case of attack the possibility of retaliation in kind." Deterrence could provide safe passage during the Nuclear Age. "Thus far," he wrote, "the chief purpose of our military establishment has been to win wars. From now on its chief purpose must be to avert them."[53]

Deterrence became the watchword. Building nuclear weapons was more reassuring than putting faith in international agreements with closed societies that couldn't be pried open—at least not until satellite technology produced astonishing pictures of military installations in closed societies. It took almost three decades more for the Kremlin to grudgingly permit circum-scribed inspections of military exercises. This led quickly to intrusive on-site inspections at nuclear missile and production sites in the 1987 Intermediate Nuclear Forces Treaty signed by Mikhail Gorbachev and Ronald Reagan. This level of transparency and cooperation was inconceivable when Brodie and others penned the outlines of deterrence theory.

The great minds who wrote about deterrence quarreled with each other about the requirements necessary to succeed and over definitions of success. Deterrence strategists were captives to their brainpower. They didn't dwell on accidents, screw-ups, and irrational acts because to acknowledge the central-ity of these factors could turn their sturdy theorems into sandcastles. Instead, they focused on definitions and requirements for success. Was success about reinforcing strategic stalemate or was success about winning—or at least, not losing? Deterrence strengtheners worried that the Kremlin was playing by a different set of rules—that they weren't seeking deterrence but rather war-winning capabilities. The Kremlin's interest in blockbuster missiles and mis-sile defenses seemed to confirm this thesis. What Moscow seemed to seek was something that U.S. deterrence strategists also wanted. The best deterrent was a strong offense, complemented by missile defenses. Both could provide leverage in crises and, if deterrence failed, a winning advantage in the event of a nuclear war. The Kremlin, of course, viewed U.S. programs that placed a premium on qualitative improvements rather than size in a similar light.[54]

The "absolute" weapon lent itself to the twin pursuits of relative advan-tage and avoiding disadvantage. There were other accelerators of the arms race, to be sure. Constituencies that supported strategic modernization pro-grams were usually more powerful than those advocating restraint. Techno-logical imperatives also played a significant role. As Herbert York wrote, the United States, as the richer and more technically advanced competitor, could innovate its way forward, especially after being caught napping. "The root of the problem," he wrote, "has not been maliciousness, but rather a sort of technological exuberance that has overwhelmed the other factors that go into the making of overall national policy."[55]

The arms race required the testing of new bomb designs. Initially, testing occurred mostly in the atmosphere. National populations facing the threat of nuclear attacks became unwilling hostages to the Bomb's destructive powers. Childhood leukemia rates downwind from testing in Nevada were 400 per-cent above the national average.[56] Absent effective means of national defense against nuclear attacks—another unending but seemingly unachievable pursuit—the guardians of nuclear arsenals knowingly and with deadly earnestness risked public health to keep the Cold War from becoming hot.

THE H-BOMB DECISION

The key juncture in nuclear peril following the proof of concepts for atomic bombs was the decision in the Truman administration to engage in a crash effort to develop and test far more powerful thermonuclear or hydrogen bombs. To oversimplify, in a first-generation atomic bomb, fissile material (plutonium or highly enriched uranium) is compressed with high explosives until it achieves the very high densities required for a runaway fission chain reaction. In a hydrogen or H-bomb, atomic scientists believed and subsequently proved that the energy released from an A-bomb could compress and heat a much larger mass of material more efficiently. In H-bombs, a two-stage process of fission-powered fusion could have previously unimaginable destructive effects.

In 1949, the Soviet Union demonstrated its ability to build A-bombs. Moscow seemed to be working hand-in-glove with Beijing, and a war was brewing on the Korean Peninsula. It was a time when U.S. national security seemed to be slipping away. Only a few individuals were privy to the push to proceed with H-bombs. One was Oppenheimer, who had grave misgivings. The H-bomb decision was Oppenheimer's last stand, and he lost everything but his security clearance. That would come later.

Oppenheimer still held considerable sway in 1949. Don DeLillo characterized the A-bomb as "the sun's own heat that swallows cities" in his novel, *Underworld*. Oppenheimer, the overseer of two weapon designs that swallowed two cities, sought to avoid building weapons with far more destructive capacity. His redoubt was the Atomic Energy Commission's General Advisory Committee. He saw no need for a crash program to build the H-bomb and found no design then under discussion to be militarily feasible. The design that H-bomb advocates like Edward Teller was then working on could only be delivered by oxcart, if it could be made to work at all.[57] Oppenheimer argued that diversifying the U.S. arsenal of atomic weapons would suffice to hedge against the Soviet threat.

Other members of the General Advisory Committee shared Oppenheimer's views. The committee concluded, "We are all reluctant to see the United States take the initiative in precipitating this development. We are all agreed that it would be wrong at the present moment to commit ourselves to an all-out effort toward its development." A six-member majority of the committee, including Oppenheimer, James Conant (president of Harvard University and former head of the wartime National Defense Research Committee) and Lee DuBridge (presidential science advisor for Truman, Eisenhower, and Nixon) based their recommendation "on our belief that the extreme dangers to mankind inherent in the proposal wholly outweigh any military advantage that could come from this development." They went on to write, "Its use would involve a decision to slaughter a vast number of civilians . . . If super bombs will work at all, there is no inherent limit in the destructive power that may be attained with them. Therefore, a super bomb might become a weapon of genocide."

No one using the word "genocide" when referencing nuclear weapons would subsequently be welcome in the highest councils of government. Committee members Enrico Fermi and I.I. Rabi went further. In their minority annex to the General Advisory Committee Report, they wrote, "It is clear that the use of such a weapon cannot be justified on any ethical ground which gives a human being a certain individuality and dignity even if he happens to be a resident of an enemy country."[58]

Teller, a refugee from Hungary, was an avid anticommunist. His colleagues at Los Alamos did not share his passion for the "Super"—the hydrogen bomb. Teller was not a member of the Atomic Energy Commission's General Advisory Committee, but he had friends in Washington who were Oppenheimer's enemies, especially Lewis Strauss, who headed the commission. Teller's reaction to the launch of Sputnik was typical of him: "If the Russians pass us in technology, there is very little doubt who will determine the future of the world."[59] Teller felt the same way about advances in nuclear weapons. Staying ahead in this race was essential; falling behind was not an option. When their relations were still collegial, Teller and York would sit on York's back porch debating these matters in La Jolla, California, overlooking the ocean. When York's young daughter would join them as darkness fell over the swells, Teller would tell her that if she didn't go to bed the Russians would get her. He was joking, of course, but not entirely.[60]

In York's account of the H-bomb decision, Teller won by a nontechnical knockout. Oppenheimer's arguments were stronger on the merits, but nuclear anxiety won out. "The side with the weaker formal position won the debate."[61] Truman took Teller's side because he could not be sure that Stalin would exercise similar restraint. Indeed, he had good reason to believe otherwise. Nobel Prize winner Harold Urey vocalized the clinching argument this way: "I am very unhappy to conclude that the hydrogen bomb should be developed and built. I do not think we should intentionally lose the armaments race; to do this will be to lose our liberties."[62]

Strauss, the chairman of the Atomic Energy Commission, agreed with Teller that it was necessary to cripple Oppenheimer's influence. The opportunity came when Strauss, who thought Oppenheimer to be "dangerous" and his proposals "fatal," suspended Oppenheimer's security clearance shortly before it was due to expire on the grounds that he was a security risk, thereby prompting the accused to fight to clear his name. When Oppenheimer appealed this ruling, a star chamber proceeding was arranged to consider the matter, at which Teller testified.

During this proceeding, Teller testified that Oppenheimer's judgment and actions were "exceedingly hard to understand," and "I feel that I would like to see the vital interests of this country in hands which I understand better, and therefore trust more." When pressed, Teller concluded that it "would be wiser not to grant clearance." Two years earlier, a new lab was launched at Livermore to compete with Oppenheimer's creation at Los Alamos in designing the H-bomb. Teller served on its Scientific Steering Committee.[63]

Stanislaw Ulam, a Polish refugee, helped Teller figure out how to design a militarily usable H-bomb. Oppenheimer, who proposed a wider variety of atomic bombs to meet military contingencies instead of pursuing the H-bomb, acknowledged this technical achievement. Subsequently, the yields of H-bombs were downsized to serve the purposes proposed by Oppenheimer. Hans Bethe, a Nobel Prize–winning theoretical physicist, was torn between hating the Bomb and hating the thought of a Hitler or a Stalin having it before the United States. After helping on the A-bomb and H-bomb, Bethe ruefully observed, "What history will remember is not the ideals we were fighting for, but the methods we used to accomplish them."[64]

Another step-jump in the strategic competition was taken, bringing with it more waves of nuclear anxiety. York, who was on the ground floor of bomb making as the founding director of the Lawrence Livermore Lab, counted the ways in which the failure to control the military uses of the atom grew in the decade after 1945: "Over the next ten years, the power of individual bombs grew a thousandfold, the stock of bombs increased more than a thousandfold, and so the potential atomic fury was multiplied more than one million times."[65]

Within the counsels of government, the standings of Oppenheimer and Teller were reversed as a result of the behind-closed-doors controversy over the H-bomb. The die was cast against Oppenheimer after the General Advisory Committee's deliberations on the H-bomb. His influence as a government consultant was shredded and his employment of the word "genocide" was fatal, since this critique could apply, by extension, to the entire enterprise of nuclear deterrence.

NSC-68

In 1949, the last vestiges of U.S. insulation from nuclear dangers vanished. In August, Stalin presided over the first test of an atomic bomb, ending the U.S. monopoly and signaling an accelerated nuclear arms race. To make matters worse, in October Mao Zedong's forces defeated Chang Kai-Shek's army. America's ally retreated to Taiwan and a new Communist state ruled the mainland. Worse still, U.S. officials harbored fears that Mao would link up with Josef Stalin, forming a Communist behemoth challenging U.S. allies in both Europe and the Pacific. The Communist master plan for disruption and victory seemed to be playing out when war on the Korean Peninsula broke out in 1950. A few months before the war erupted, the head of the State Department's Policy Planning Staff, Paul Nitze, had proposed what was needed to hold back the Communist tide. That plan was NSC-68.

NSC-68 was a comprehensive, sixty-five-page, single-spaced assessment of the nature of the Soviet threat and what to do about it—a manifesto of how best to respond to an existential Soviet challenge. It characterized the Soviet leadership as "animated by a new fanatic faith," driven "to impose its absolute authority over the rest of the world." Conflict with the USSR in varied forms was inevitable; indeed, it was "endemic." The U.S. response must be no less than "the rapid building up of the political, economic, and military strength of the free world" to deter Soviet aggression "as rapidly as possible." The elements of this buildup in conventional and nuclear capabilities were not spelled out. NSC-68 interred the Acheson-Lilienthal Plan, concluding that "no system of international control could prevent the production and use of atomic weapons in the event of a prolonged war." Negotiations with the Kremlin were necessary, but until Soviet objectives were fundamentally muted, the primary purpose of engagement would be "gaining support for a program of building strength . . . while helping to minimize the risks of war."[66]

NSC-68 was bedrock Nitze, forecasting a period of maximum danger, perhaps only a few years away. His prescriptions included an across-the-board militarization of George Kennan's policy of containment. Kennan, who preceded Nitze as head of the State Department's Policy Planning Staff, opposed NSC-68 on these grounds, as did Truman's secretary of defense, Louis Johnson, on budgetary grounds. But after the shocks of 1949 and the onset of the Korean War, the U.S. nuclear posture would be locked and loaded. A nuclear arms race was on in earnest. With it came the unavoidable irony that the quest to alleviate nuclear anxieties accentuated them.

EYEWITNESSES TO PERIL

Very few have now personally witnessed the dark, bellowing, mutating image of the mushroom cloud. There are the remaining Hibakusha—witnesses of the Bomb's use on Hiroshima and Nagasaki, and there are the dwindling eyewitnesses of nuclear weapon testing in the atmosphere. The experience of observing early tests in the Pacific protected men like Herbert York, Herbert Scoville, and Gerard Smith from the slings and arrows of those who questioned their judgment while advocating arms control. York, a physicist who was the Lawrence Livermore Laboratory's first director, became a strong advocate of stopping nuclear tests while advising Eisenhower. Smith, who later became the Nixon administration's nuclear negotiator in the Strategic Arms Limitation Talks, tried and failed to convince John Foster Dulles and Dwight Eisenhower to witness a test, as he was convinced that it would bring them around to support a moratorium on testing. Smith and his boss, Atomic Energy Commissioner Thomas Murray, thought they were gazing into the Gates of Hell after witnessing the 1952 test at Eniwotek, the sacrificial atoll in the Marshall Islands where the new hydrogen bomb was tested.

Witnesses reacted in different ways. Scoville, who worked on technical issues at the Central Intelligence Agency before becoming an advocate of arms control, wrote home that the tests were "unbelievably beautiful to watch."[67] Senator Henry "Scoop" Jackson, who was also present in 1952 at a massive test at Eniwotek, reacted by turning to Smith and asking, "Where is the nearest bar?" Nothing about the Bomb generated unanimity, except agreement on its destructive power.[68]

The United States and the Soviet Union finally stopped atmospheric testing in 1962. By then, a groundswell of public revulsion against mushroom clouds and the health hazards they posed left advocates of continued testing with but one option—to continue testing refinements to weapon designs underground. Great Britain, dependent on U.S. test sites, had no choice in the matter. Paris and Beijing reluctantly followed suit. The last atmospheric test was carried out by China in 1980.[69] And yet the image of the mushroom cloud has lost none of its power to induce dread; it mesmerizes us still. Once seen on film or online, it is unforgettable, quickly and indelibly imprinted on the brain. The power of this image is so compelling that it can generate action to prevent its reappearance or it can foster somnambulant resignation. Our nuclear future depends on this choice.

EISENHOWER'S BURDEN

Public and official anxieties fell upon the shoulders of President Dwight Eisenhower. Eastern Europe was under Soviet control. The Kremlin seemed implacably hostile, even after Stalin's death in 1953. On Capitol Hill, a Wisconsin Republican senator named Joseph McCarthy would hold hearings blaming Communists embedded in the State Department and elsewhere for America's slackness in dealing with the Soviet threat. Eisenhower and his secretary of state, John Foster Dulles, were inclined to use nuclear weapons to end a wasting war on the Korean Peninsula. Eisenhower was also advised to use nuclear weapons to bail out the French from losing a colonial war in Indochina. Eisenhower's interest in nuclear weapons was driven, in part, by an aversion to government spending and deficits that explained his reluctance to endorse the recommendations in NSC-68.

And then came the launch of Sputnik in 1957, the satellite that the whole world could track in a clear night sky. The rocket that launched Sputnik could also carry the atomic bomb. Eisenhower's popularity plummeted; the image of him playing golf began to grate. A demeanor that once felt comforting subsequently conveyed tiredness and age. His presidency ended as it began, with a sense of increased nuclear danger. Every atmospheric nuclear test punctuated public anxiety while posing health hazards. Eisenhower needed to do something besides building bombs and testing them. And so, he authorized the first discussions with Soviet representatives on preventing surprise attacks and stopping nuclear tests. The history of nuclear arms control was about to begin, haltingly at first, and then in earnest.

RISE

Chapter 2

EISENHOWER'S HALTING STEPS

P resident Dwight Eisenhower inherited a ground war on the Korean Peninsula, a policy of containment toward the Soviet Union, and stale proposals for general and complete disarmament after Moscow vetoed the Acheson-
Lilienthal and Baruch plans at the United Nations. The nascent practice of
Kremlinology was mostly literal and pictorial. Since U.S. experts knew so
little about the machinations and thinking of Russian leaders, they relied
heavily on their public statements and the lineup that occasionally appeared
on the balcony of the Kremlin above Lenin's mausoleum. Public statements
were brutish and estimates of Soviet missile and bomber production were
uncertain until a new secret reconnaissance plane, the U-2, began its high-
altitude flights over Soviet territory.

Before the diplomacy of arms control began in the Kennedy administration, Washington and Moscow exchanged rhetorical volleys over who was
to blame for the failure of disarmament, supplemented with parrying over
manpower reductions, challenges to stop the production of bomb-making
materials, and the cessation of nuclear testing. Nuclear dangers were rising
precipitously with stockpile sizes. The U.S. nuclear arsenal grew, on average,
by over 1,300 weapons per year in the 1950s. During this decade, the United
States and Soviet Union carried out, on average, one nuclear test every two
weeks.[1] No less than 243 of these tests were in the atmosphere. Children in
the worst-affected areas downwind from test sites were as severely exposed
as children affected by the 1986 Chernobyl nuclear plant accident.[2]

At the outset, Washington and Moscow had no basis for trust, no common language for negotiation, and no familiarity with each other's thinking about nuclear weapons—key elements of successful diplomacy. Public anxieties were boundless. New, more powerful nuclear weapons were in the offing, as well as new, faster means to deliver them. The launch in 1957 of the first human object in space, Sputnik, further intensified public anxieties. The same Soviet rocket that placed a satellite in orbit could also carry a nuclear weapon.

There was no basis for Eisenhower to succeed at nuclear arms control—but he could and did lay the groundwork for subsequent success. The principal accomplishment during Harold Stassen's rocky tenure as Eisenhower's special adviser on disarmament was to shift the focus of U.S. attention from grand objectives to first steps.[3] Eisenhower had to try something; he couldn't simply be on the receiving end of Soviet propaganda.

The Eisenhower administration responded to public fears and to the perceived need to lead by proposing meetings of experts to consider measures to reassure against surprise attack and for ways to monitor a ban on nuclear testing. These meetings occurred in the summer and fall of 1958. The problem of surprise attack was pressing because the United States knew so little about the disposition of Soviet conventional forces and even less about its growing nuclear forces. Discussing the prevention of surprise attack also made sense because Washington wasn't going to authorize one. After the Japanese attack on Pearl Harbor, a U.S. preventive war was deemed downright un-American.

THE SURPRISE ATTACK CONFERENCE

The Surprise Attack Conference convened in Geneva for five weeks in November and December 1958. Leading the U.S. delegation was William C. Foster, one of the dark-suited, white-shirted, thin dark tie–wearing businessmen who answered the call of government service during World War II. Foster's counterpart was a Soviet Foreign Ministry official, Vasily Kuznetsov. Two members of Foster's delegation—George Kistiakowsky and Jerome Wiesner, who served as the U.S. delegation's staff director—gained subsequent renown as presidential science advisors. Both came from the Harvard–Massachusetts Institute of Technology corridor in Cambridge, Massachusetts.

The subject matter for discussion was compelling: U.S. and Soviet stockpiles were presumed to be rising significantly, as were the means to deliver these weapons from long distances. Neither superpower had the ability to monitor the extent to which these threats were growing, nor the ability to observe force buildups at points of likely engagement. Alleviating these concerns required technical means of intelligence collection that were on the horizon but not in hand, leaving on-site inspections as the primary means of alleviating strategic concerns. These inspections were anathema to military leaders on both sides. A quarter-century would pass before agreement was reached on the first on-site inspections. Besides, the same means required to discern preparations for surprise attack in 1958 could actually facilitate plans for surprise attack.

Negotiations to provide reassurance were bound to fail. Foster was Eisenhower's third choice to lead the talks, after the president had been turned down by two generals. By the time Foster came on board, there was little time to arrive at a U.S. government position for the talks. When that position was hammered out, it was defined more by what could not be discussed than by what might be considered.

Interagency differences over the scope of the negotiations precluded the tabling of a specific U.S. negotiating proposal, and Foster's negotiating instructions, at the Defense Department's insistence, fenced off broader talks on possible political settlements. U.S. negotiators doggedly pursued technical measures that would provide assurance against force buildups and other troubling military preparations. In the absence of overhead reconnaissance, U.S. ideas invariably dwelled on the conduct of on-site inspections. Soviet negotiators viewed these proposals in the same light as Eisenhower's previous proposal for cooperative aerial overflights as a mechanism to reassure against surprise attack. The Kremlin's reaction to "Open Skies," as with on-site inspections, was to view these proposals as clever devices to simplify targeting and reacted accordingly.[4] Moscow viewed secrecy as a necessary safeguard of national security. Nonintrusive technical measures might be considered, but only in tandem with political settlements.

Kistiakowsky characterized the discussions at the Surprise Attack Conference as "two railroad trains going on separate tracks."[5] With the shock of Pearl Harbor still very much in mind, Washington wanted to focus on the means and techniques of observation and inspection, while Moscow wanted to focus on practical political steps and on partial disarmament measures. The conference was all shadow boxing and no real engagement. Kistiakowsky, who described himself as "a fresh conscript into the diplomatic army," felt like a character in Lewis Carroll's *Alice in Wonderland*: "The same words used by the two sides had opposite meanings and neither side was willing to state its clear intentions."[6]

Positive outcomes at the Surprise Attack Conference required mutual transparency to measure force buildups. Other preconditions for success included a U.S. willingness to explore Soviet proposals, a softening of superpower relations in general, and a mutual willingness to entertain on-site inspections. None of this was in the cards. During this period, U.S.-Soviet relations darkened considerably. Khrushchev threatened to tighten Western access to Berlin and the Eisenhower administration considered speeding up the rearmament of West Germany, possibly to include stockpiling nuclear weapons there.

Even so, discussions on means for reassurance against surprise attack were not a complete washout. Those involved learned valuable lessons. The takeaway of James Killian, Eisenhower's science advisor, was "the deficiencies of ad hoc and hurried preparations for such negotiations."[7] The subject of discussion—especially points of difference—was necessary and useful, planting the first seeds of diplomatic breakthroughs that would come decades later.

The Surprise Attack Conference talks were a "useful educational device," according to James Goodby, who was present as the Atomic Energy Commission's representative to the talks.[8] The large U.S. contingent of experts included individuals who later became mainstays of strategic assessment, including Henry Rowen and Albert Wohlstetter. Wohlstetter's major impact centered around the problem of surprise attack, initially highlighting the vulnerability of the Strategic Air Command's bomber basing. He believed deeply in a "delicate" balance of terror, premised on a willingness of the Kremlin to strike first.[9]

The two biggest beneficiaries of the experience gained at the Surprise Attack Conference were William C. Foster and Jerome Wiesner. Both went on to play key roles in the Kennedy administration, Wiesner as the president's science advisor and Foster as the first director of the U.S. Arms Control and Disarmament Agency. One of Foster's takeaways from this failed effort was that technical issues could not be divorced from political ones.[10] It was abundantly clear to Foster that the Surprise Attack Conference failed because of the absence of a confluence of interests and deteriorating superpower relations. Learning about failure helped Foster to succeed once he became the director of ACDA.

FIRST STEPS TO STOP NUCLEAR TESTING

Anxieties prompted by the failure of the Surprise Attack Conference were amplified by the drumbeat of nuclear testing during 1958, when the United States and the Soviet Union combined to average more than two tests per week—seventy-five by the United States and thirty-four by the Soviet Union. Nuclear fallout was a pressing public concern because ninety-five of these tests were detonated in the atmosphere. The Kremlin, sensitive to international opinion against testing and fearing U.S. technological advances, began to call for the cessation of tests as early as 1954. There was no cost to taking the diplomatic initiative since Moscow could rely on the standard U.S. rejoinder that stopping tests needed to be accompanied by stopping the production of bomb-making materials.

Fallout negated these arguments. Serious public health concerns were reinforced by the discovery of radioactive traces in mother's milk and children's bones and teeth. No scientist was able to identify the extent of these consequences; it was too soon to assess damage, given the periods of latency before various types of cancer would appear, but linkages could not be credibly disputed. It was hard to accept predictions that the consequences would be minimal, as proffered by the pro-testing lobby, led by the Atomic Energy Commission.

Those who wanted more tests did their most successful work behind closed doors. Opposition took to the streets. A new activist organization, the National Committee for a SANE Nuclear Policy, was created in 1957 to channel and amplify public revulsion against testing.[11] SANE had 150 chapters nationwide, including one in Hollywood led by actors Steve Allen and Robert Ryan. In May 1960, SANE staged a rally to end testing before a capacity crowd at Madison Square Garden. The American Friends Service Committee lent its support and moral authority to the cause. As was the case during subsequent public debates, renowned scientists played central roles. Linus Pauling won his second Nobel Prize for helping to lead this campaign. In doing so, he became a subject of FBI scrutiny for having communist sympathies, leading to the revocation of his passport.[12]

Soviet premier Nikita Khrushchev left Eisenhower and his key advisers flat-footed on March 31, 1958, by announcing a unilateral moratorium on nuclear testing and by issuing a direct challenge to Eisenhower and British prime minister Harold Macmillan to join him. The timing was ideal for Khrushchev, as the Soviets had just completed a long test series, and awkward for Eisenhower, as the Kremlin's challenge was timed just before another round of U.S. tests were about to begin. Eisenhower's advisers held mixed views. Secretary of State John Foster Dulles was sensitive to the shellacking the United States would receive by turning down Khrushchev's challenge. Eisenhower's Science Advisory Committee, including such luminaries as Killian, Kistiakowsky, Wiesner, Bethe, I.I. Rabi, and Herbert Scoville, were in favor of immediately taking Khrushchev up on his offer. The creation of this advisory body was one of the Eisenhower administration's initiatives undertaken after the launch of Sputnik. During this period, the scientific advisory committee was the strongest locus of support within the executive branch for slowing down the nuclear competition.

The scientific advisors were outvoted. In strong opposition were Atomic Energy Commission chairman Strauss and the Joint Chiefs of Staff. The Los Alamos and Livermore laboratories were also opposed. Both were pursuing new design concepts that they wished to confirm by means of atmospheric and underground tests. Herman Kahn wrote, with characteristic enthusiasm, that "for the first time in history, we are having a complete technological revolution in the art of war approximately every five years." With the advent of new types of nuclear weapons and their means of delivery, he wasn't exaggerating.[13]

The Foreign Policy Research Institute at the University of Pennsylvania was a strong locus of opposition against a testing moratorium. This group, led by Robert Strausz-Hupé and Robert Kintner, published *Protracted Conflict* in 1959, a description of Soviet strategy. They published *A Forward Strategy for America* in 1961 with prescriptions. In their view, "the United States and the Free World have steadily lost ground in the international struggle with communism," a process that, if continued "within the foreseeable future," would become irreversible. Eisenhower's "defeats and embarrassments at the conference table" were due to a "fundamental failure to see the totality" of the U.S.-Soviet conflict." Negotiations were a zero-sum game: "For the communist revolutionaries, diplomacy is a continuation of war by other means." The objectives of the United States and the Soviet Union in negotiations were too profound to expect arms control to serve a useful purpose. "Low-level" arms control was too "risky" and disarmament was folly. They argued that "the greatest hope for progress toward mutual arms security lies in the technological-military competition itself."[14]

The key figure of influence at Livermore at this time was Edward Teller, a brilliant Hungarian refugee who thought seriously about becoming a concert pianist before being drawn to physics. Teller studied with renowned mentors in Europe before leaving in 1935 for the safety of the United States. He was blessed with a photographic memory but not collegial skills. After his testimony against Oppenheimer, he was both admired and scorned. Teller's view, as heard often by Herbert York, Livermore's first director, was that "if we were behind, we had to catch up . . . and if we were ahead, we had to test to stay there. There was no circumstance under which a test ban could be in our interest."[15]

In addition to being a strong advocate of new H-bomb designs, Teller was also keenly interested in the pursuit of what he called "clean" nuclear weapons that would not cause worrisome fallout. In public forums he asserted that "we are making great strides toward nonradioactive weapons." Teller also argued that a moratorium would impede progress toward the "clean" bomb's development. This device was later called the "neutron bomb," which wasn't "clean," as its impact would be derived primarily from radiation rather than physical destruction. During the Jimmy Carter administration, the political backlash to its production was fierce. Opponents readily caricatured the "neutron" bomb as a capitalist tool that killed people while leaving buildings intact. Carter canceled deployment plans for West Germany.[16]

During the Eisenhower administration, Teller was embroiled in debates with Linus Pauling over the effects of fallout. Writing with Albert Latter in *Life* magazine and in *Our Nuclear Future*, Teller argued, "Radiation in small doses need not necessarily be harmful—indeed may conceivably be helpful." He and Latter asserted that a wristwatch with a luminous dial subjected the wearer to far more radiation than fallout, and that "the worldwide fallout is as dangerous to human health as being one ounce overweight."[17] Willard F. Libby, a University of California physical chemistry professor turned Atomic Energy commissioner, went further, claiming that fallout could be increased 15,000 times without hazard.[18] Libby later won the Nobel Prize for discovering and advancing radiocarbon dating techniques.

Pauling, the son of a small-town drugstore owner in Oregon, received his first Nobel Prize for researching the nature of chemical bonds. His rebuttal to Teller and Libby, *No More War*, reads like a science class for concerned citizens, politely demolishing their claims. His response to Teller's arguments in *Life* magazine was far more pointed, claiming parts of Teller's article to be false, misleading, inaccurate, and "pure propaganda," then adding, "The whole article is an apology for evil, a plea for the continued use of force, an attack on the effort to introduce reason into world affairs."[19]

Pauling and Teller appeared in a debate on public television over nuclear testing, fallout, and disarmament shortly before Khrushchev announced his March 1958 moratorium and his public challenge to Eisenhower. In their debate, Teller argued that dangers from radioactive fallout had not been proven, but mostly he rested his case on strategic imperatives: Whatever damage might be caused by nuclear testing paled in comparison to the damage caused by war, and continued testing was essential to deter war. As for genetic damage caused by fallout—a key element of Pauling's bill of particulars—Teller acknowledged, "The great many of these changes will be damaging. Yet without some change evolution would be impossible." Teller also cited research suggesting that genetic mutation might be caused by tight clothing and other factors unrelated to nuclear testing.[20]

At this juncture, it was too soon to prove Pauling's arguments. Monitoring the public health consequences of atmospheric testing would take time, the study of medical records, and statistical measuring devices that had yet to be developed. Most Americans were inclined to side with Pauling over Teller, and subsequent data backed up their reservations.[21] Joining Teller in arguing against a moratorium was Sidney Hook, a professor of philosophy at New York University and a champion of Liberty in the battle against Communism. "Whatever the facts of past testing," Hook asserted, "these effects must be regarded as part of the tragic costs of freedom."[22]

Herbert York was a select member of a rare breed familiar with the cultures of both bomb making and negotiating arms control. He observed that presidents could expect stiff opposition to stopping nuclear testing from the usual quarters. In such cases, "Higher authorities have to be ready and able to overrule such opposition; they cannot simply repress it or hope to convert it."[23] Eisenhower was inclined to seek ways to slow down the nuclear arms race, but he wasn't ready to overrule Pentagon civilians, the Joint Chiefs, the Atomic Energy Commission, and the nuclear weapon labs. He dismissed Khrushchev's call for a moratorium and green-lighted what became a total of seventy-five tests that advocates insisted were necessary—one series involving high-yield atmospheric tests in the South Pacific and South Atlantic to measure weapon effects, and a second series of low-yield tests underground.

At the same time, Eisenhower proposed to Khrushchev that a group of experts meet to consider technical matters associated with a test ban. After some back-and-forth, Khrushchev agreed to this proposal, perhaps because Eisenhower appeared to relax his position that constraints on testing needed to be linked to a cutoff on production of bomb-making material. Or perhaps

Khrushchev had growing concerns about a Chinese bomb and onward pro-liferation, which experts labeled as the "Nth country" problem.[24]

Khrushchev and Eisenhower sent teams of technical experts to Geneva for seven weeks of talks beginning in July 1958. The results were surprisingly promising and prescient. The U.S. team was led by James B. Fisk of Bell Laboratories, the Soviet team by Yevgeni Fedorov of the Academy of Sciences. Technical experts backstopped the delegations, led on the U.S. side by Hans Bethe, who reluctantly contributed to the original designs of atomic and hydrogen bombs. The Soviet team included N.N. Semenov, who won his country's first Nobel Prize two years earlier.

The "Conference of Experts to Study the Possibility of Detecting Violation of a Possible Agreement on the Suspension of Nuclear Tests" reached positive conclusions about the ability to detect nuclear testing, even at low yields. U.S., Soviet, British, and other delegations identified the types of monitoring techniques required for a test ban. They enumerated the monitoring stations needed—160–170 on land and another ten posts on ships—as well as their geographical distribution. They agreed in principle that on-site inspections could supplement this network of sensors but disagreed over specifics.

These concepts and the monitoring stations that were envisioned became known as the "Geneva system." They bore a striking resemblance to the monitoring system adopted almost four decades later for the Comprehensive Test Ban Treaty, which settled on fifty primary and 120 auxiliary seismic stations. There were, however, areas of disagreement, presaging sticking points in negotiations to come. The Conference of Experts notably disagreed over the number of inspections, the composition of inspection teams (with the Soviet team expressing the need for veto powers), and the procedures governing their visits.[25]

The day after the end of this round of talks, Eisenhower enthusiastically announced his readiness to proceed with negotiations on a test ban and its control system. The Pentagon, the Joint Chiefs, the Atomic Energy Commission, and the nuclear laboratories remained skeptical. Perhaps as a consequence, U.S. testing continued until October 31, 1958, the day before the United States was set to begin a moratorium on testing, coinciding with the start of a second round of expert talks. This test series, consisting of over thirty detonations, was nicknamed "Operation Deadline." Moscow also resumed testing for most of the month of October, carrying out fourteen shots, half of which were in the megaton range.

Thus fortified, both superpowers were ready to move from technical talks to negotiations in Geneva. James Wadsworth, a highly pedigreed New York state assemblyman, led the U.S. team. Wadsworth was previously tapped by Eisenhower to be the second-ranking U.S. diplomat at the United Nations. His counterpart was Semyon Tsarapkin, an accomplished career diplomat who participated at the founding conference of the United Nations and served at the Soviet embassy in Washington. Wadsworth claimed no technical expertise. For this, he turned to Robert F. Bacher, a veteran of the Manhattan Project, an adviser to many high-level advisory bodies, and a charter commissioner of the Atomic Energy Commission.

The second round of talks was rockier than the first, reflecting a pattern of approach/avoidance that would become all too apparent in subsequent negotiations. The nearer both sides came to a possible agreement, the sharper the disagreements over particulars became. The negotiations got off to a difficult start when the Kremlin conducted two or three low-yield devices and then mysteriously stopped, amidst speculation that they were planned earlier and were delayed. Henry Kissinger also threw sand in the gears in his lead article in the October 1958 issue of *Foreign Affairs*, raising concerns about the advisability of a test ban.[26]

Matters were complicated further when the *New York Times* revealed details of the secret atmospheric tests Eisenhower authorized before agreeing to join Khrushchev's proposal for a moratorium. The purpose of the high-altitude tests, according to the *New York Times*, was to aid weapon and ballistic missile defense research. The *Baltimore Sun* ran a banner, scare-inducing headline, "U.S. Puts 'Electron Sheet' over Earth in Search for an Anti-Missile Shield," prompting the Eisenhower administration to qualm fears.[27] The greatest impediment to an early agreement ending nuclear testing proved to be the underground test series that Eisenhower authorized. Data from low-yield tests suggested that monitoring difficulties would be harder than previously thought.

The two sides couldn't agree on a common agenda. Since the United States was unable to offer a draft treaty, the focus of discussion was a Soviet draft that proposed a complete moratorium on testing without provisions to monitor compliance. Only the United States, the Soviet Union, and Great Britain were to be signatories. Predictably, the key points of disagreement were over the scope of a test ban, the numbers of control posts needed to monitor compliance, the composition and nationalities of the control commission, and the nationalities of the technicians that would be present at the control posts. The United States wanted to discuss the particulars of the control regime; Soviet negotiators parried by insisting that they needed to know what the treaty was about before they could reach conclusions about monitoring arrangements.

Drawing from U.S. practice negotiating the 1922 and 1930 treaties governing naval limitations, the Eisenhower administration included selected members of Congress to observe these negotiations. The leading congressional figure was Senator Albert Gore, an energetic Democrat from Tennessee serving on both the Joint Atomic Energy Committee and the Foreign Relations Committee. (Gore's son also served in the Senate, almost becoming president of the United States.) Gore voiced concerns over verification of underground tests—concerns greatly amplified after U.S. technical experts sifted through test data to conclude that the proposed "Geneva System" of perhaps 170 seismic stations employing 1950s technologies and methods would be woefully inadequate to detect low-yield tests, perhaps increasing requirements for these posts tenfold.

As U.S. negotiator James Wadsworth later recounted, the tabling of these preliminary technical findings in early 1959 "spread a pall over the negotiations from which they never completely recovered."[28] Hans Bethe revised his initial calculations and conceded that more stations would be needed, while noting that their number could be greatly reduced if the capabilities of each station were enhanced. Additional bad news arrived with the calculations of Albert Latter of the RAND Corporation—Teller's co-author of the *Life* essay and *Our Nuclear Future*—that seismic signals from underground tests could be "decoupled" if tests were carried out in large cavities, making their detection difficult. This concern discounted detectable signs associated with large-scale excavations and was later addressed by advances in seismology, but at the time, Latter's argument greatly weakened prospects for a comprehensive test ban.

The situation in Geneva wasn't completely bleak, however. The Soviet delegation accepted the need for an annex to their draft treaty dealing with verification and the U.S. delegation accepted the treaty's indefinite duration rather than linking this to progress on other fronts. On central aspects of a test ban, however, much distance between Washington and Moscow remained.

The Kremlin and the White House each suspected bad faith. Eisenhower announced that the United States would no longer commit to a moratorium but would provide prior notice of a resumption of testing. The moratorium breaker turned out to be France—an absentee from the negotiations—which tested its first device in February 1960 in the Algerian desert. Negotiations limped along with Washington and Moscow swapping proposals. Eisenhower offered an end to atmospheric and large-yield underground testing, while Khrushchev countered with a complete test cessation but without intrusive monitoring. The talks were on life support when Francis Gary Powers was shot down flying a U-2 reconnaissance mission over Russia, after which plans for a summit meeting in Paris collapsed.

The moratorium on testing wasn't sustainable; the superpower competition was too intense and there were far too many advances in warhead designs in the offing, including designs for missiles to be based on nuclear-powered submarines. The Soviet Union ended the sixteen-month-long superpower moratorium in October 1961 with a fifty-seven-megaton behemoth that was subsequently nicknamed "Tsar Bomba"—the highest-yield nuclear test ever conducted. This test had a significant psychological impact. Some in the United States, led by General Curtis LeMay, Teller, and Senator Henry Jackson, called for higher-yield warhead designs to close a "megatonnage gap." This would later become one of the issues raised against ratifying the 1963 Limited Test Ban Treaty ending U.S., Soviet, and British atmospheric tests.[29]

Outrage over the Tsar Bomba test, magnified by the U-2 shootdown and the collapse of the summit meeting between Eisenhower and Khrushchev, put hopes for a test ban temporarily on hold. Eisenhower's foray into nuclear negotiations nonetheless served as an important icebreaker. The moratorium and the initial test ban talks provided a taste of negotiating dynamics to come, highlighted traps to avoid (such as not offering a proposal, thereby yielding a starting point for negotiations to Moscow), and whetted appetites for success. The groundwork laid in the Eisenhower administration helped to quicken the pace of negotiations for the Limited Test Ban Treaty banning atmospheric testing—the first major success of nuclear arms control.

Chapter 3

KENNEDY, JOHNSON, AND EARLY SUCCESSES

John F. Kennedy's election was a breath of fresh air for voters ready for a Democratic administration and generational change. Kennedy was joined by men of significant achievement on Wall Street and the corporate world. His choice for secretary of defense, Robert McNamara, was president of the Ford Motor Company. He chose Dean Rusk of the Rockefeller Foundation to be his secretary of state. Many others with glowing and gilded resumés joined the administration from prominent law firms and academic posts, including members of "the Charles River Gang"—academics from Harvard and MIT who put into practice new ideas about arms control.

THE BIG RETHINK

When the Bomb first appeared, men like Stimson, Lilienthal, and Oppenheimer sought to abolish it. Domestic and international political conditions made general and complete disarmament impractical and impossible. Talks on surprise attack and nuclear testing were useful, but they needed to be placed in a broader framework. What was the best way for the United States to go about reducing nuclear danger? And what would this practice be called?

The Charles River Gang had begun to formulate answers to these and other questions before Kennedy was elected. Many of the key conceptualizers were neighbors. Key figures in the Charles River Gang included Donald G. Brennan, Robert R. Bowie, Henry Kissinger, Jerome Wiesner, Paul Doty, Bernard Feld, Thomas C. Schelling, and a young PhD candidate in search of a mentor, Morton H. Halperin. Halperin found his man in Schelling. Herman Kahn, Edward Teller, and William Frye brought additional intellectual firepower to these deliberations.

Several study groups were convened, one by the American Academy of Arts and Sciences, which sponsored a summer study in 1960 on its premises. There was also a Harvard-MIT study group on arms control. "Everybody wanted in," Halperin recalled.[1] The field was new, intellectually challenging, and hugely consequential. The central challenge was to find a framework to prevent rampant, destabilizing arms racing. A new central organizing principle was needed to replace general and complete disarmament. The new concept needed to provide coherence to disparate initiatives and to help generate expert and public support for long-term undertakings. The degree of difficulty involved was immense. Another challenge was to forge a domestic consensus. A third was to convince the Kremlin to accept a work program based on a common framework.

Three very important volumes emerged from these deliberations. The first was a collection of essays that appeared in the Fall 1960 issue of *Daedalus*, the American Academy's journal. A larger collection of essays, edited by Brennan, appeared as *Arms Control, Disarmament, and National Security*. Several of these essays were identified as being especially appropriate for classroom use. The third volume was the most influential of all. *Strategy and Arms Control*, by Schelling and Halperin, synthesized this new thinking, becoming a primer for students and practitioners.[2] This was an overwhelmingly male enterprise. Of the fifty participants and visitors in the Summer Study, exactly two were women: Nancy Hoepli, who became a central figure in the Foreign Policy Association, and Miriam Salpeter from the Physics Department at Cornell. Only one female participant, Betty Goetz, is noted in Brennan's long list of acknowledgments. She worked for Senator Hubert Humphrey, promoting this agenda on Capitol Hill.

The central organizing principle that emerged from these deliberations was identified as arms control. The terminology had been used before, but its centrality was new. Brennan addressed this shift without apology in the Preface of *Arms Control, Disarmament, and National Security*, pushing back against those who championed disarmament and who argued that this narrower construct was "wicked" and even immoral since it countenanced the Bomb. The rejoinder was obvious: disarmament wasn't happening, and arms control had a possibility of success.[3] Jerome Wiesner, a participant in the ill-prepared Surprise Attack Conference, modestly hoped that this collection of essays would "stimulate public discussion . . . and, if possible, . . . make a contribution to the serious literature in the field."[4]

The conceptualizers of arms control achieved far more than that. Arms control succeeded in placing controls on the most powerful weapons ever devised, and then reducing them. They succeeded in setting nuclear weapons apart and, in doing so, helped to prevent their use in crises and in wars. Brennan's definition of arms control was more modest—"to reduce the hazards of present armament policies by a factor greater than the amount of risk introduced by the control measures themselves."[5] Bowie defined arms control as "any agreement among several powers to regulate some aspect of their military capability or potential." Even profound adversaries could have "possible common or parallel interests in preventing an unintended all-out war and in minimizing the burden of the deterrent."[6] Here, Bowie argued, arms control could have the greatest practical effect. Schelling reasoned that arms control was necessary because "we and the Russians are trapped by our military technology . . . [Weapon developments] have enhanced the advantage, in the event war should come, of being the one to start it. They have inhumanely compressed the time available to make the most terrible decisions."[7]

Schelling's writing stood apart. He was later awarded the Nobel Prize in Economics for applying game theory to problems of conflict and cooperation. His razor-sharp mind and succinct powers of analysis were hallmarks of a career that began with the Bureau of the Budget and the Marshall Plan, ending at the University of Maryland, with stops at Yale, RAND, and Harvard along the way. After Schelling's death in 2016, his family auctioned off his Nobel Prize to raise money for the Southern Poverty Law Center.

Schelling's father was a Naval Academy graduate; his mother earned undergraduate and graduate degrees. Teaching was one of the few professions available to accomplished women back then, so she taught, stopping to become a homemaker, raising three children. According to Schelling's sister, the future Nobel Laureate was a quiet, unremarkable student until his mother said, "Tommy, it grieves me that you don't get better grades. I would like you to get A's." Thereafter he did.[8]

In high school Schelling read *How to Win Friends & Influence People* by Dale Carnegie and other books of that ilk. The family didn't stay put for very long, moving around with his father's postings. He started college at San Diego State and transferred to Berkeley, where he majored in economics to learn tools to prevent another Great Depression. He couldn't get into the navy because of a stomach ulcer, so went to Harvard instead to pursue a doctorate.[9]

Schelling's junior partner, Morton Halperin, was born in Bensonhurst, Brooklyn, to first-generation Jewish immigrants from Ukraine and Hungary. His father was a trained lawyer who chose to be a title examiner—an occupation that appeared to be Depression-proof. His mother was a homemaker. Faraway places and politics captured his imagination early on from reading the *New York Times*. He excelled at school and entered Columbia at sixteen. The Upper West Side of Manhattan seemed like a distant land from Bensonhurst. At Columbia, he had the good fortune to take courses from two extraordinary, young professors, Warner Schilling and Kenneth Waltz. As a senior, he took a course from a graduate student, Glenn Snyder, filling in for Waltz. The course was on the theory of nuclear deterrence, and Halperin was hooked.

From Columbia he went to study and write about nuclear strategy at Yale, which boasted not only a great political science faculty but also an institute of international affairs. To his dismay, the international relations stalwarts he hoped to study with left in a dispute with the university president, leaving him marooned. Schelling visited Yale to give a talk, easily persuading Halperin to pursue his doctorate remotely at Cambridge, where he met Henry Kissinger and other members of the Charles River Gang. One plum assignment after another fell into his lap.[10]

Halperin badgered Schelling about the need for a holistic picture rather than detailed essays about parts of the problem. "You have to write this book," he argued, and Schelling eventually consented to a collaborative work.[11] The result, *Strategy and Arms Control*, situated arms control as an element of U.S. foreign and military policy, and "to demonstrate how naturally it fits rather than how novel it is . . . We believe that arms control is a promising, but still only dimly perceived enlargement of the scope of our military strategy."

The pursuit of arms control was possible, Schelling and Halperin argued, because "our military relation with potential enemies is not one of pure conflict and opposition." There could still be common approaches to achieve three core objectives: "the avoidance of war that neither side wants, in minimizing the costs and risks of the arms competition, and in curtailing the scope and violence of war in the event it occurs." Collaborative efforts were possible and advisable "to avoid false alarms and misunderstandings." Arms control could also help "in avoiding the kinds of crises in which withdrawal is intolerable" and in providing "reassurance that restraint on the part of potential enemies will be matched by restraint of our own." Arms control, if properly pursued, could codify or implicitly reaffirm "a mutual interest in inducing and reciprocating arms restraint."[12]

Arms control could entail more or less of certain types of weapons, unilateral initiatives, tacit or negotiated arrangements. Schelling and Halperin deliberately avoided suggesting an end state or "ultimate goal." The challenge at hand was to avoid catastrophe: "Man's capability for self-destruction cannot be eradicated—he knows too much! Keeping that capability under control—providing incentives to minimize recourse to violence—is the eternal challenge." In their concluding remarks, Schelling and Halperin wrote that "arms control, if properly conceived, is not necessarily hostile to, or incompatible with, or an alternative to, a military policy properly conceived . . . The aims of arms control and the aims of a national military strategy should be substantially the same." They recognized how difficult the practice of arms control would be: "Military collaboration with potential enemies is not a concept that comes naturally." It would be simple to view arms control "as an alternative, even antithetical field" from military strategy. Avoiding this trap would require a sophisticated process of blending. Failing this, concepts of arms control and nuclear deterrence would be at loggerheads.[13]

CREATING ACDA

Conceptualizing arms control was one predicate for success. Another was creating a place in the executive branch that could be staffed with experts, carry out research, conceive of proposals, champion these proposals in bureaucratic deliberations, and engage in as well as backstop negotiations. Edmund A. Gullion, a holdover from the Eisenhower administration's State Department, wrote a memo to the new president advising him to embed the new agency within the State Department. Gullion later became dean of the Fletcher School at Tufts.[14]

John J. McCloy persuaded President Kennedy otherwise. McCloy believed that a semi-autonomous agency devoted to the pursuit of arms control was needed; otherwise, creative initiatives could be smothered by the State Department, which was primarily focused on other matters of diplomacy. The State Department did not distinguish itself on the first halting arms control initiatives in the Eisenhower administration. Instead, its approach to Khrushchev's maneuverings was ad hoc and reactive. Eisenhower's appointee as disarmament adviser, a three-term governor of Minnesota, Harold Stassen, had little clout nor much of a staff.[15] In retirement, Eisenhower was sympathetic to bulking up efforts within the executive branch to work on arms control and disarmament. President Kennedy gave this task to McCloy.

McCloy had impeccable credentials, but not because he was a blue blood. Far from it: His mother was a hairdresser and then a nurse. His father, an insurance salesman, died young. McCloy's parents produced a smart and ambitious young man with an unerring ability to gravitate to power. The Establishment was open to such ambitious young men, depending on their skin color and religious affiliation. McCloy went to college at Amherst, served as an artillery officer on the western front in World War I, and then went to Harvard Law School. Another artillery officer in World War I was Henry L. Stimson. Stimson enlisted after serving as secretary of war for William Howard Taft. McCloy then found a home on Wall Street lawyering for wealthy clients. Franklin Delano Roosevelt, in need of Republican support for a looming conflict in Europe and Asia, recruited Stimson to serve a second tour of duty as secretary of war. Stimson, in turn, recruited McCloy to serve as one of his assistant secretaries.

Both men were stanchions of Republican internationalism, fighting the tide of isolationism. They were key links in a long chain of the Grand Old Party's engagement with the world that has now mostly atrophied. Stimson served every president but one from Taft to Truman; McCloy advised presidents from FDR to Ronald Reagan, serving along the way as World Bank president, high commissioner to Germany, and chairman of the Chase Manhattan Bank, among other posts.

McCloy was politically bulletproof, even though his record on Wall Street was tarred by having German chemical manufacturers as clients and later, as assistant secretary of war, by advising in favor of interning Japanese Americans and against bombing the rail lines into Auschwitz. (Stimson was on board with both decisions.) Before email contact lists, there were little cards in alphabetical order with names and mailing addresses in a twirling desktop file called a rolodex. Nobody's rolodex was more impressive than McCloy's. He lined up support for the new agency even among skeptics who were deferential to him. Assisting McCloy in this effort was William C. Foster, another Republican with impeccable credentials, having previously served as deputy secretary of defense and the lead U.S. negotiator to the Surprise Attack Conference. Kennedy assiduously recruited Foster to become the agency's first director.

With international control to prevent the production of nuclear weapons a lost cause, Kennedy set his sights on creating an agency of government to come up with implementable ideas. McCloy assembled a small team, including Adrian "Butch" Fisher, Betty Goertz, and George Bunn, to help draft the enabling legislation of what was to become the Arms Control and Disarmament Agency. Foster helped out. One measure of the persuasiveness of McCloy and Foster was that former secretary of defense Robert Lovett testified in favor of the agency's creation. Previously, he worried that it could become "a Mecca for a wide variety of screwballs" and that "it would be a great pity to have this Agency launched and shortly become known as a sort of bureau for beatniks."[16] Others who testified in favor of the bill were Secretary of State Dean Rusk, the deputy secretary of defense, the chairman of the Joint Chiefs of Staff, the head of the Atomic Energy Commission, key officials from the Eisenhower administration, including his former secretary of defense and secretary of state, two ambassadors to the United Nations, and the former supreme allied commander in Europe.

The youngest supporting witness was Herbert York. York was instrumental in the development of hydrogen bombs as the first director of the new nuclear laboratory in Livermore, California. He then served as the Pentagon's director of research and engineering during the Eisenhower administration. York came to see nuclear weapons in a different light after leaving Livermore and rubbing elbows with big-picture scientists like James Killian, George Kistiakowsky, and Jerome Wiesner. York also hints that the strong views of his colleague at Livermore, Edward Teller, contributed to his intellectual evolution.[17]

While his former colleagues at the nuclear laboratories at Livermore and Los Alamos were pressing for continued testing, York supported a moratorium and believed that the creation of a disarmament agency was overdue. As he testified before the Foreign Relations Committee, "Uncontrolled arms races have a habit of leading to war, and if the global war that this modern arms race is leading to happens, the words 'victory and defeat' will not be applicable afterwards. The only words that would make sense are 'complete and utter disaster, catastrophe.'"[18]

The initial name proposed for this agency in the draft legislation McCloy conveyed to congressional leaders was "The Disarmament Agency for World Peace and Security." No one testifying in the Senate hearings to review the legislation blanched at this name, which was par for the course in the battle of public diplomacy back then. The agency's name was subsequently toned down at the suggestion of Eisenhower and others, with a view toward aligning it with the Charles River Gang's new central organizing principle. The Arms Control and Disarmament Agency and a new acronym, ACDA, were born in the fall of 1961.

The senator most consequential in this bill's passage was Hubert Horatio Humphrey, Jr., the chairman of the Senate Foreign Relations Subcommittee on Disarmament. Humphrey, "the Happy Warrior," was the face of liberalism in the Senate who would subsequently champion the 1963 Limited Test Ban Treaty banning atmospheric testing and the 1964 Civil Rights Act. Humphrey worked as tirelessly as McCloy to make ACDA a reality despite skepticism about its aims. Skeptics were most concerned that its director could get crosswise with the secretary of state and that the agency could impair the requirements of national defense. Humphrey's rejoinders reflected his core optimism and innate sense of decency: "There are those who feel that the real test of patriotism is whether you can rattle the saber a little louder than somebody else or wave the flag a little higher. Actually, I suppose the greatest patriot of them all would be one who discovers the path to peace."[19]

As for the new agency's critical function of helping the executive branch to prepare for and conduct diplomacy, Humphrey argued that it was as important to be ready for disarmament discussions as it was to be prepared for the nation's defense. Humphrey's cause was advanced by the fumbling and reactive way the Eisenhower administration handled a nuclear test moratorium in 1958. Those who wished to create ACDA received a boost when the stolid, graying lineup of Soviet leaders on display above Lenin's tomb during military parades seemed more agile than Eisenhower and his key advisers, Secretary of State John Foster Dulles and Chairman of the Atomic Energy Commission Lewis Strauss.

Humphrey and McCloy lined up overwhelming support for the new agency, but its powers were contested at the outset. The Senate wanted it to be integrated into the State Department, while the House wanted an independent agency. The Conference Committee arbitrated these differences by splitting them down the middle. The White House's executive order implementing the statute creating ACDA gave the director responsibility for "the preparation for and management of United States participation in international negotiations" for arms control and disarmament but constrained the director's independence by having him report to the secretary of state. Both were expected to work in harness. The director was empowered to meet directly with the president, with the foreknowledge of the secretary of state. President

Kennedy signed the bill creating ACDA in his hotel suite at the Carlyle in New York. Attending the signing ceremony was William C. "Bill" Foster, who set aside his business plans to accept Kennedy's offer to become its first director. He was paid the princely sum of $22,000. ACDA's influence and its accomplishments were never greater than during Foster's tenure.

The executive order creating ACDA empowered its director to "exercise leadership in assuring that differences of opinion concerning arms control and disarmament policy are resolved expeditiously and shall take such steps as may be appropriate in order to produce common or harmonious action among the agencies concerned." This was more easily accomplished in multilateral negotiations in which the State Department and Pentagon had only limited interest or modest complaint than in bilateral nuclear arms control negotiations. The Senate Armed Services Preparedness Investigating Committee took an early interest in ACDA's remit. In its hearings, Foster expressed the view that "essentially . . . this is an independent agency." Committee chairman John C. Stennis, Henry "Scoop" Jackson, Stuart Symington, and others pushed back vigorously against Foster's assertion. An appearance by Secretary of State Dean Rusk was needed to smooth these ruffled feathers.[20] The tensions between ACDA and the State Department and the Pentagon were, however, baked into its founding legislation. The more ACDA pursued its mandate, the more feathers would be ruffled, leading eventually to its demise and merger into the State Department during the Clinton administration.

AN AUSPICIOUS START

Washington and Moscow continued to trade affirmations of their pursuit of general and complete disarmament even after ACDA's creation.[21] The new agency drew up yet another proposal in 1962 and presented it to the United Nations, but ACDA's main focus was elsewhere. Arms control, not disarmament—what might be doable rather than an ambitious end state—would be the central pursuit of its dedicated public servants and technical expertise. Many of ACDA's critics believed otherwise. They assumed that every proposed arms control step would lead inexorably to disarmament, and that each step with a sworn geopolitical and ideological foe would be a snare and a delusion.

The odds were stacked against ACDA from the start, as the fledgling agency was seriously overmatched by the Pentagon and the Atomic Energy Commission. Its workforce was also dwarfed by the State Department, which was typically hesitant to proceed with arms control initiatives that complicated ties with friends and allies. ACDA could only succeed with the support of the secretary of state and the president. And succeed it did—never more so than under its first director, Foster, and his able deputy director, Adrian "Butch" Fisher.

Foster was the son of a mechanical engineer who worked on the Hoover Dam and the Panama Canal. He grew up driven to succeed in Westfield, New Jersey. Foster interrupted his schooling at MIT to serve as an army pilot during World War I. He then pursued a career in business, but business always took second fiddle to public service. He married well and lived comfortably, establishing a salon for the well connected in Georgetown.[22]

Foster was reserved, formal, low-key, and confident in his capabilities. He was a public relations–savvy, transatlantic businessman, having served as director and vice president for public affairs of the Olin Mathieson Chemical Corporation. He looked like one of the martini-drinking "Mad Men" in the fictional Sterling Cooper Draper Pryce Advertising Agency. But Foster was no mere PR flack. He had solid government credentials, having previously served as director of the Purchases Division at the War Department during World War II, as a leading figure and then administrator of the Marshall Plan, as under secretary of commerce and then as deputy secretary of defense, working with Robert Lovett during the Korean War.

Foster's credentials as a defender of national security were indisputable. Besides leading the U.S. delegation to the 1958 Surprise Attack Conference, he was a key figure in the Security Resources Panel, more commonly known as the Gaither Commission, named after and briefly led by Ford Foundation chairman H. Rowan Gaither. The Gaither panel recommended major increases across the board in defense spending, particularly on strategic forces and nuclear weapons. Foster's role in the Gaither Committee not only reaffirmed his bone fides as a supporter of defense preparedness but also strengthened his ties with fellow committee member John J. McCloy.[23]

During Kennedy's run for the presidency, he asked Foster to join his campaign brain trust on national security, but Foster politely declined as he had agreed to serve in the same capacity for Richard Nixon the previous day. He told Kennedy that his choice was on political party lines, since he was a Republican and it didn't seem "quite proper to sit formally on both advisory groups." Tellingly, however, he added that he "would always be available to help."[24] Kennedy continued to pursue Foster after his election. Initially Foster begged off, as he was in the process of setting up new business opportunities.

The delayed timing of ACDA's creation in September 1961 proved to be a good fit. Foster severed his business ties and corporate board memberships and signed up for the job. He was well aware that one reason for his selection was to help round up Republican support, which he did willingly. Foster was transformed by his eight years as the head of ACDA from the man who led the Gaither Committee to a committed believer in arms control. Before he died, Foster arranged that donations in his name be sent to the Arms Control Association, a nongovernmental organization he helped establish in 1971 after retiring from ACDA.

Adrian Fisher was Foster's highly effective partner. Fisher was a gregarious personality with well-honed political skills and a bulging rolodex file. The son of a Tennessee congressman, Fisher led a charmed life, attending St. Albans and the Chaote School, then off to Princeton where he played football, followed by Harvard Law and the *Law Review*. Fisher then clerked for Supreme Court justices Louis Brandeis and Felix Frankfurter. He also worked short stints at the War and State Departments. In World War II, Fisher navigated bombing missions over Europe, after which he served as a legal adviser during the Nuremburg trials. He worked more short stints at the Commerce Department and the Atomic Energy Commission before a tour as Dean Acheson's legal advisor at the State Department.

Resumés like this were rare, even in those heady days for Establishmentarians. Fisher tried lawyering at a prestigious firm but his heart wasn't in it. He then became a vice president and counsel for the *Washington Post*, but this, too, didn't satisfy. He wanted to be in on the action, where his lawyering and political skills could be applied to matters of high policy. In Fisher's retelling, on New Year's Day in 1961, "My wife and I were having milk punch with Felix and Marian Frankfurter and Dean and Alice Acheson over at the Frankfurters' house. And I sort of said, 'You know, I think I'd like to get back into government. Maybe the thing for me to do is to call McCloy and see if he'd like an assistant.'"[25] Needless to say, his high-ranking position at ACDA was a done deal.

Kennedy and McCloy chose well, given the sensitivity of ACDA's mandate and its potential to clash with the State Department, the Pentagon, and skeptics of arms control on Capitol Hill. ACDA never had a more powerful and effective team. During these early years, Foster was the button-down, accomplished company man with strong credentials and ties to Republican heavyweights, with an innate ability to deal with complexity and an interest in organizational charts. Fisher was a driving force with a flair for politics and a sharp mind for treaty law. McCloy, the chairman of ACDA's General Advisory Committee, was the agency's shield against skeptics. McCloy assembled the strongest group of advisers ACDA ever had, including former secretary of defense Robert Lovett, atomic scientists Herbert York and I.I. Rabi, former Pentagon officials Trevor Gardner and Dean McGee, AFL-CIO president George Meany, and former air force chief of staff Thomas White. This Republican-tinged cast was choreographed by McCloy to reassure doubters that the agency would be operating within the mainstream while advocating agreements that other government agencies were, at best, ambivalent about.

ACDA IN HARNESS

During Foster and Fisher's tenure, ACDA officials helped to engineer the 1963 Limited Test Ban Treaty, the 1963 "Hotline" agreement, the 1967 Outer Space Treaty, and the 1968 Nuclear Nonproliferation Treaty. In addition, ACDA lent support to the 1967 Treaty of Tlatelolco, making the Southern Hemisphere a nuclear weapon–free zone. The latter three achievements were negotiated on Lyndon Baines Johnson's watch, a president not remembered for his interest in arms control. This was a period of significant norm building for arms control and for nuclear weapon–free zones, as well as for international law governing the peaceful uses of outer space and nuclear nonproliferation. A core group of activists within ACDA looked for these opportunities against general indifference or modest resistance elsewhere in the executive branch. They included Laurence Weiler, George Bunn, and Betty Goetz. Members of this group met on Saturday mornings, usually at Adrian Fisher's house, to plot strategy and plan for the coming week's challenges.

It takes a surprisingly small, dedicated cadre of government officials and Capitol Hill staffers to create something remarkable or to dismantle prior accomplishments. This was the case with ACDA's rise and, later on, its demise. Larry Weiler was born in Salt Lake City. He attended the University of Utah before moving on to Stanford, where he received a master's degree and a doctorate. After serving in the army during World War II, he joined the State Department, first working on the United Nations, where debates over disarmament occurred in the 1950s. Weiler then moved to the White House to work with Harold Stassen, and eventually settled in at ACDA. He was Fischer's special assistant during ACDA's halcyon years.[26]

George Bunn grew up in St. Paul, Minnesota, the son of a writer of children's books and a lawyer who was more inclined toward teaching. He moved often but was eventually drawn to Madison, Wisconsin, where he and his dad taught and where he later became dean of the Law School. Bunn served in the navy at the end of World War II. Intent on becoming a physicist, he had a life-changing experience reading the Acheson-Lilienthal Plan. Treaties needed lawyers, so off he went to Columbia Law School. His introduction to arms control, like many others back then, was at the Atomic Energy Commission, where he helped write regulations desegregating its facilities. The work wasn't satisfying, so he joined a well-connected law firm where he did pro bono work desegregating Washington's restaurants. He returned to the executive branch because McCloy needed help writing ACDA's statute. McCloy hired Fisher, and Fisher recruited Bunn. There was connective tissue between Bunn and Fisher—both worked earlier as legal counsels for the Atomic Energy Commission and they had a common link to Felix Frankfurter. Fisher clerked for him and Bunn's father co-taught the "hot dog" course (Frankfurter and Bunn) one year at Harvard Law.[27]

Betty Goetz, later Betty Goetz Lall, was born in Chicago, the daughter of a businessman. She received her bachelor's and master's degrees from the University of Minnesota, where she was politically active with the League of Women Voters. There she came to the attention of Senator Humphrey, who hired her as the staff director of his Senate Foreign Relations Committee's Subcommittee on Disarmament, where she helped her boss create ACDA. She worked at ACDA from 1961 to 1963 as Fisher's special assistant, a rare female professional amidst a raft of males. She left ACDA to accompany her husband, a retired Indian diplomat, at Cornell, where she taught industrial and labor relations. After leaving ACDA, she was able to complete work on her doctorate from the University of Minnesota.[28]

Herbert "Pete" Scoville, Jr., added heft to ACDA's ranks, arriving in 1963 after rising through the ranks of technical expertise at the Central Intelligence Agency to become its deputy director for research. As ACDA's assistant director for science and technology, he helped backstop negotiations on the Limited Test Ban Treaty, a fitting coda to a professional life that began with monitoring weapon effects, including those he witnessed during Operation Crossroads at Eniwetok in the Marshall Islands.

Scoville worked closely with Herbert York, a fellow eyewitness at Eniwetok. Their lives intersected more than they knew, starting from different sides of the tracks on the Buffalo to Rochester railroad line, where York's dad worked as a messenger on the trains and Scoville's ancestors made a fortune building railroad car wheels in Buffalo during and after the Civil

War. Scoville and York both received PhDs from the University of Rochester and then applied themselves to defense issues during World War II. They both took several years to disentangle themselves from workplace affiliations to become active and effective skeptics of the utility of nuclear weapons. They worked side by side on the front lines to end nuclear testing and the arms race.[29]

Foster and Fisher harnessed ACDA's modest number of employees to push the envelope for treaty making. They needed powerful allies and found them in the White House on the Limited Test Ban Treaty and in the Pentagon on the Nonproliferation Treaty, overcoming the State Department's lukewarm interest. State's primary mission was improving relations with foreign capitals, not promoting initiatives to prevent armament that friendly leaders might have an interest in acquiring. Dean Rusk and his Foreign Service officers were particularly ambivalent, if not somewhat opposed to the Nonproliferation Treaty, because it could harm key bilateral ties with countries like West Germany that might be better positioned to fend off challenges from the Soviet Union if they possessed nuclear weapons.

NEGOTIATING THE BAN ON ATMOSPHERIC TESTING

The outlook for test ban negotiations was not promising after the Cuban missile crisis. The United States was engaged in a significant strategic arms buildup, doubling its warhead totals and increasing its land-based, ocean-spanning missiles tenfold in the period between 1961 and 1963. After breaking the testing moratorium in August 1961, the Soviet Union tested, on average, one device every two days for the next three months. After the Soviet test series, the resumption of U.S. tests was a given; whether they would include atmospheric tests was not. A public and private debate ensued on this issue. Edward Teller again weighed in with a book, *The Legacy of Hiroshima*, serialized in the *Saturday Evening Post*, arguing that radioactive fallout "was not worth worrying about."[30] The Pentagon, the Atomic Energy Commission, and the nuclear laboratories prevailed in this debate with an assist from ACDA director Foster, who argued that a full rejoinder to Soviet testing was warranted.[31] Kennedy reluctantly signed off on a resumption of atmospheric testing, at least for a short time.

The test ban negotiations at the end of the Eisenhower administration ended on a sour note with both sides reverting to stale proposals for general and complete disarmament. In reality, Washington and Moscow were closer to an agreement than outward appearances suggested. In 1961, test ban negotiations resumed in Geneva, led on the U.S. side by Arthur Dean, a lawyer and diplomat who previously helped negotiate the Korean Armistice Agreement. Washington tabled two draft treaties, one for a comprehensive test ban and another for a partial ban that permitted testing underground but nowhere else.

This two-track approach was James Goodby's idea, then a young ACDA official. Goodby sold the idea to his superiors and joined with George Bunn, Alan Neidle of ACDA, Thomas Pickering from the State Department, and Pentagon general counsel John McNaughton to do the drafting.[32] The comprehensive proposal would be backed up by on-site inspections and black boxes for monitoring seismic events; on-site inspections were less critical for a partial treaty. Dean tabled the two drafts in August 1962.

The Kremlin promptly rejected both. There was some hesitation among Kennedy's advisers around making another run at a test ban. Foster, for one, had second thoughts, thinking it was "a little undignified" after the Tsar Bomba test and those that followed. Kennedy held a different view. In Foster's recollection, JFK's thinking was, "Let us take another crack at this thing, because this is too important to let nature take its course. He, of course, was so right."[33]

The Cuban missile crisis clarified the urgency of steps to reduce nuclear danger and lent impetus to a search for common ground. The obvious place to start was nuclear testing. By the end of 1962, there was reason to hope that both superpowers could live without additional testing in the atmosphere. Kennedy and Khrushchev both felt chastened by their brush with Armageddon. Kennedy decided to make a major address and a direct appeal to Khrushchev. Speech preparation was rushed, the final draft readied by Theodore Sorenson just before delivery of Kennedy's commencement address at The American University in June 1963. The time seemed ripe for a diplomatic breakthrough.

"I speak of peace," Kennedy said, "because of the new face of war. Total war makes no sense in an age when great powers can maintain large and relatively invulnerable nuclear forces and refuse to surrender without resort to those forces." Then Kennedy turned to the environmental degradation and health hazards from testing in the atmosphere: "It makes no sense in an age when the deadly poisons produced by a nuclear exchange would be carried by wind and water and soil and seed to the far corners of the globe and to generations yet unborn."

Leaders can sometimes accomplish great things by matching the right words to the right moment. Kennedy had two audiences in mind—one domestic, the other within the walls of the Kremlin:

> Let us examine our attitude toward peace itself. Too many of us think it is impossible. Too many think it unreal. But that is a dangerous, defeatist belief. It leads to the conclusion that war is inevitable—that mankind is doomed—that we are gripped by forces we cannot control. We need not accept that view. Our problems are manmade—therefore, they can be solved by man.

Speaking with perfect pitch, Kennedy continued, "Let us reexamine our attitude toward the Soviet Union," adding, "No government or social system is so evil that its people must be considered as lacking in virtue." Powerful words at the right moment are important but insufficient. A symbolic gesture can be crucial in clarifying intent. As a predicate to his gesture, Kennedy offered an aphorism: "We can seek a relaxation of tension without relaxing our guard." And then the gesture: "The United States does not propose to conduct nuclear tests in the atmosphere so long as other states do not do so. We will not be the first to resume. Such a declaration is no substitute for a formal binding treaty, but I hope it will help us achieve one." Kennedy announced that Khrushchev, British prime minister Harold Macmillan, and he had agreed to high-level discussions in Moscow to conclude an agreement.[34]

The stage was set for a successful outcome. The question at hand was which of the two treaties—comprehensive or partial—would be chosen. Correspondence from Khrushchev indicated some softening on the issue of on-site inspections, but given the Kremlin's qualms, the odds strongly favored a partial rather than a comprehensive ban. With Dean's departure in 1962, Foster and Fisher alternated as heads of the U.S. delegation in Geneva where test ban negotiations were ongoing. To signify a change from negotiating business as usual and to place his personal imprint on the team headed for Moscow, Kennedy chose the under secretary of state for political affairs, W. Averill Harriman, as his emissary.

The bloodstream of the Kennedy administration ran blue. Harriman's credentials were impeccable. The son of a railroad magnate who joined the board of directors of the Union Pacific Railroad Company while a senior at Yale, Harriman became chairman of the board at the tender age of 41. He pursued investment banking at Brown Brothers Harriman on the side. Harriman served as Franklin Delano Roosevelt's emissary to Great Britain during and after the Blitz to implement the Lend-Lease program, then served as the

U.S. ambassador to both the Soviet Union and Great Britain before becoming President Truman's commerce secretary. Harriman helped administer the Marshall Plan before being elected governor of New York. He was someone the Kremlin could do business with.[35]

Harriman brought with him a small but powerful team, including Carl Kaysen from the National Security Council staff, John McNaughton, the general counsel at the Department of Defense, William Tyler from the State Department, Franklin Long from ACDA and one outsider, Frank Press from the California Institute of Technology, to have a seismologist available. Adrian Fisher was Harriman's second in command. Lord Hailsham led the small British delegation while Foreign Minister Andrei Gromyko led the Soviet delegation. Khrushchev himself appeared at the opening session. According to Harriman, he was in a jovial mood and declared his readiness to sign a partial treaty.

The Moscow talks coincided with the public breakup of the Sino-Soviet bloc. Khrushchev was disinterested in bringing China into the treaty's obligations, which undermined the Soviet position to include France. Khrushchev tabled a simple draft treaty banning testing in three environments—the atmosphere, underwater, and space—without verification, a withdrawal clause, and a provision allowing peaceful nuclear explosions. Harriman's team tabled the partial test ban treaty offered the previous year in Geneva and tested the waters for a comprehensive ban. Finding no takers, Harriman and his team focused on nailing down a partial test ban and, with no need for a seismologist, Press left for home.

The drafters of the agreed treaty text were Fisher, Semyon Tsarapkin, and Charles Darwin, a British civil servant and a lineal descendant of his namesake. Peripheral Soviet interest in a nonaggression pact dropped away. After wrangling over language regarding peaceful nuclear explosions and the withdrawal clause, the treaty text was ready for initialing by Harriman, Hailsham, and Gromyko ten days after the start of their deliberations.[36]

The Limited Test Ban Treaty banned testing in the atmosphere, underwater, and in outer space. It was of indefinite duration, but states could give three months' notice of withdrawal in the event of extraordinary circumstances. The treaty was silent on the issue of nuclear testing for nonmilitary purposes—to the distress of the Atomic Energy Commission, which wanted an endorsement—but explicit insofar as tests of whatever kind could only be carried out underground, with the proviso that they did not produce fallout beyond national borders. A signing ceremony with Rusk, Gromyko, and

British foreign secretary Alec Douglas-Home followed in Moscow on August 5. The treaty's entry into force was conditioned on the deposit of instruments of ratification by the three signatories, which was done on October 19, 1963, after the Senate and the Soviet Praesidium provided their consent.

The biggest "if only" in the reminiscences and historical accounts of these negotiations is if only Kennedy and Khrushchev had been able to split the difference between the U.S. demand for an annual quota of seven on-site inspections to investigate the possibility of cheating and the Soviet insistence that no more than three inspections was permissible. As Glenn Seaborg wrote in his account of the negotiations, "I regard the failure to achieve a comprehensive test ban as a world tragedy of the first magnitude."[37] In reality, splitting the difference was informally tried but to no avail. ACDA director Foster exceeded his instructions once by asking his counterpart, Semyon Tsarapkin, "What about this?" while raising five fingers. He got a scowl in return.[38] Earlier, U.S. ambassador Arthur Dean misspoke and suggested that two or three inspections might be acceptable, but this was quickly walked back amidst much consternation and embarrassment.

The failure to negotiate a comprehensive test ban treaty in 1963 set the template for agreements that followed, with both superpowers accelerating technical advances to guard against diplomatic risk taking. The pace of underground testing picked up after the Limited Test Ban Treaty, abetting the next phase of the arms race. The ensuing competition clarified that a comprehensive ban was beyond reach. The gulf was far wider than splitting the difference over the number of inspections. Kennedy was hammered for dropping down to seven from earlier estimates of twenty or more inspections that many presumed to be essential. After his unofficial attempt to split the difference was rejected, Foster, for one, advised against going lower than seven.[39] Khrushchev was also under heavy pressure as powerful figures around him wanted no inspections whatsoever. A reading of declassified, Secret, Eyes Only memoranda of conversations with Khrushchev clarifies how wide the gap between Kennedy and Khrushchev actually was. Khrushchev only agreed to "symbolic," not substantive inspections. This gulf, as gaping as that over the number of inspections, was too wide to bridge.

Before Harriman's arrival, on April 24, 1963, U.S. ambassador Foy Kohler had met with Khrushchev to deliver a letter from President Kennedy trying to cross this bridge. Kennedy and Macmillan closely coordinated their messaging to Khrushchev. The UK's ambassador to Moscow conveyed the same letter, signed by Macmillan, at the same time. The translation of

Khrushchev's reaction, transmitted to Secretary of State Dean Ruck the next day, was of a "not unfriendly, but relatively subdued" Soviet leader who had reached the conclusion that Washington was "playing" with the Kremlin. When he agreed to two or three inspections, "he was sure that the matter was solved." But then came demands for more inspections, and he was given a "cold shower." The diplomatic cable continued, "He demanded to know what sort of fool he should be if he were to permit espionage organizations" to roam around his country. The Soviet side had offered three inspections "as symbolic inspections and not ones of substance. Then West would want to fly around country, and go wherever it please." Khrushchev, Kohler reported, was not about to allow CIA director John McCone to do this.

The memorandum of the meeting summarized Khrushchev's response as wanting an agreement "very much," but he was now "cursing himself, because it had been his initiative to make [the] offer of three inspections." Here the summary quoted Khrushchev directly as saying that by opening this door he "had ruined everything" and that "I made a fool of myself." Underground testing was very expensive; the Americans could do this as much as they wanted. The Soviet Union had conducted one underground test to show the Americans that they could detect it. Upping the number of inspections and raising the ante in this way indicated "a lack of seriousness." There would be no agreement on nuclear testing on these terms.[40]

Granted, this is but one encounter of many in the run-up to the Limited Test Ban Treaty, but it is an evocative one. Khrushchev comes across as the genuinely aggrieved, morose party, not as the cunning figure scheming to deceive the West by concealing underground tests—the narrative favored by treaty skeptics. Both leaders wanted more than a partial test ban but were satisfied with settling for less than a comprehensive one. Mutual distrust was too great and the demands of the testers and their backers too insistent to stop this aspect of the nuclear arms competition completely. During the negotiating endgame, it was clear that every member of the Joint Chiefs would testify against a comprehensive ban. Key Republicans on Capitol Hill were also geared up to oppose a comprehensive ban; indeed, they had serious reservations about a limited one.

Representative Craig Hosmer, the Republican leader of the Joint Committee on Atomic Energy, was among the skeptics. He was a believer in the military utility of nuclear weapons, having served as an army officer with the first U.S. occupation forces in Hiroshima. Hosmer chaired a newly created Republican Conference Committee in the House that issued assessments, including one by Edward Teller, against treaty making. Senator Henry "Scoop" Jackson was also deeply skeptical of a comprehensive treaty, along with a majority of his fellow members of the Senate Armed Services Preparedness Investigating Subcommittee. Senator Joseph Clark, a strong treaty supporter, counted heads and found no more than fifty-seven votes in favor of a comprehensive ban. Senator William Proxmire, another strong supporter, spoke on the Senate floor to advise against trying.[41]

Harriman and his team brought back a Limited Test Ban Treaty. A comprehensive ban wasn't in the cards given the Soviet position regarding on-site inspections, problems with detecting low-yield tests, the opposition by the Joint Chiefs, and the prospect of not having enough votes for consent to ratification in the Senate. Harriman, Fisher, and Kaysen met with Kennedy immediately on the way back from Moscow for a debriefing. Rusk and Foster joined them from Washington. They sat around Kennedy's living room in Hyannis Port enjoying drinks and the balmy weather. There were "well dones" all around. The three-environment ban on testing was a major accomplishment. Kennedy was elated and forward-looking. Fisher recalled his parting message as, "Let's not rest now. This is a first step. Let's get cracking on something else."[42]

Arguments against the Limited Test Ban Treaty were easily rebutted. Edward Teller and others expressed concerns that the United States would be unable to learn more about weapon effects that could be useful for ballistic missile defenses by foregoing further tests in the atmosphere and in space. He also dwelled on the constraining effects the treaty would have on possible applications for peaceful nuclear explosions. Senator Jackson, a dogged skeptic of arms control, shared General Curtis LeMay's concerns that the Soviets were advantaged by their high-yield tests, and that the ban on atmospheric tests would prevent the United States from catching up. Dr. John S. Foster, the director of the Livermore Laboratory, joined Teller in opposing the treaty, but their views were not as important as Harold Brown's, another distinguished veteran of Livermore who had moved on to become the Pentagon's director of defense research and engineering. Brown joined Herbert York, Eisenhower's science advisor George Kistiakowsky, and the director of the Los Alamos Laboratory, Norris Bradbury, in rebutting Teller and Foster. Several former chiefs weighed in against the treaty, but the views of the sitting chiefs offset their opposition. The concerns of Teller, Jackson, and LeMay were not persuasive, since addressing them would have required more atmospheric testing.

The required two-thirds majority vote in the Senate was assured after President Kennedy persuaded Republican minority leader Everett McKinley Dirksen to offer his support. Dirksen explained his vote in the Senate debate this way: "I should not like written on my tombstone: 'He knew what happened at Hiroshima but did not take the first step.'" Jackson's redoubt on the Armed Services Preparedness Investigating Subcommittee offered a harsh critique, finding that the treaty would "result in serious, and perhaps formidable, military and technical disadvantages," but Jackson also voted "aye" because the administration endorsed a package of "safeguards" presented by the chairman of the Joint Chiefs of Staff, General Maxwell Taylor.

The administration's four safeguards were to pursue a strong underground test program, healthy funding for nuclear weapon research, a readiness to resume atmospheric testing if need be, and improvements to monitor clandestine test programs. The two overriding concerns of reluctant but persuadable senators were whether the treaty would have a lulling effect, and whether it meant that the United States was foregoing superiority for equality with respect to the nuclear competition with the Soviet Union. The safeguards package was designed to assure senators that the Kennedy administration would not be lulled into a false sense of security and that it intended to field superior nuclear capabilities. With these assurances, the Senate consented to its first nuclear arms control treaty on September 24, 1963, by a vote of 80 in favor and 19 against.[43]

The strong wariness to even a Limited Test Ban Treaty attested to its value, symbolic and otherwise. The treaty was a significant breakthrough, albeit at the cost of far more underground tests. It signified that Washington and Moscow could accomplish a meaningful agreement limiting one aspect of their nuclear competition—the one posing the most serious, demonstrable public health hazards. The treaty also signified that a nuclear war was not inevitable, and that Kennedy and Khrushchev were seized with a mutual responsibility to reduce nuclear danger. By way of compensation, U.S. and Soviet nuclear laboratories proceeded to conduct aggressive underground testing to remain on the cutting edge. The only significant operational constraint imposed on nuclear weapons by the Limited Test Ban Treaty was the devaluation of very high-yield bomb designs that maximized nuclear overkill—designs that had limited military value in any event.

The nuclear competition didn't miss a beat after the Limited Test Ban Treaty was signed—a pattern that would be repeated after the first Strategic Arms Limitation accords negotiated almost a decade later by Richard

Nixon and Leonid Brezhnev. In the thirty-three years between the signing of the Limited and Comprehensive Test Ban treaties, Washington and Moscow carried out a total of 1,197 tests underground—703 by the United States and 494 by the Soviet Union. The Limited Test Ban Treaty was an important breakthrough, but several more breakthroughs were needed before bringing the nuclear arms competition to heel.

THE OUTER SPACE TREATY

The easiest arms races to stop are the ones that haven't begun. The launch of Sputnik was worrisome enough; the notion of nuclear weapons orbiting overhead was a nightmare that Kennedy and later Lyndon Johnson sought to avoid. After the Cuban missile crisis, Kennedy pressed his bureaucracy not only to seek limits on nuclear testing but also to prevent placing nuclear weapons in outer space. This was the only instance in the history of arms control agreements where a president overrode the unanimous opposition of the Joint Chiefs of Staff. The Joint Chiefs wanted to keep open the option of deploying nuclear weapons in space but had no support elsewhere in the executive branch. With prodding from the White House, opposition to a diplomatic initiative banning the placement of weapons of mass destruction in outer space melted. The State Department and ACDA worked in concert to close this potential arena of nuclear competition and Kennedy chose a low-key way to gain its international blessing by means of a UN General Assembly resolution. President Johnson subsequently lent his support to turn this resolution into a treaty, by which time the reservations of the Joint Chiefs had evaporated.

The Soviet Union championed a draft treaty for general and complete disarmament, of which bans on space weapons were a part. The long-standing U.S. talking point against ambitious Soviet declaratory proposals was that they had to be verifiable, and that verification demanded on-site inspections. In 1963, ACDA proposed to switch gears and to carve out and pursue a ban on nuclear weapons in space from proposals on general and complete disarmament.

Initially, the Office of the Secretary of Defense, the Joint Chiefs of Staff, the National Reconnaissance Office (responsible for newly launched U.S. satellites), and the Central Intelligence Agency all opposed a separate ban on nuclear weapons in space. The Joint Chiefs took an all-or-nothing position: either general and complete disarmament under strict controls and inspection, or no constraints on space capabilities whatsoever. The State Department initially joined others in opposition to a separate ban because established policy was to oppose hollow Soviet "declamatory" measures. Kennedy didn't reject this counsel outright. Instead, his deputy national security advisor, Carl Kaysen, conveyed Kennedy's message asking for a deeper investigation of U.S. options. Might a nuclear weapons' ban in space serve U.S. national security interests if nothing better were available? And was the standard insistence on inspections feasible in space or acceptable on the ground before space launches?

At this point, ACDA director Foster received help from the State Department, whose position was being coordinated by Raymond Garthoff, a young Kremlinologist drawn to policy and negotiation. The civilian leadership of the Pentagon also came around. Deputy Secretary of Defense Roswell Gilpatric delivered a carefully crafted speech announcing that the United States had "no program to place any weapons of mass destruction in orbit," inferentially inviting the Kremlin to make a parallel statement along these lines. In September 1963, Foster circulated a draft "U.S. Approach to a Separate Arms Control Measure for Outer Space," which generated a strong dissent by the Joint Chiefs, but they no longer had support elsewhere.

This near-consensual approach was relayed to Kennedy in October 1963. Kennedy then authorized Foster to propose a ban on stationing weapons of mass destruction in outer space to Soviet foreign minister Gromyko, which he did later that month. The Kremlin needed two clarifications—whether the ban applied to missiles flying through space, and whether inspections were required. Hearing the right answers—no in both cases—the groundwork was laid for an agreement. The Kennedy administration did not pursue a treaty, perhaps in deference to the opposition of the Joint Chiefs. It focused instead on a UN General Assembly resolution (also opposed by the chiefs), co-sponsored with the Soviet Union and other countries, led by Mexico and Canada.

Beginning in 1963, annual UN General Assembly resolutions co-sponsored by Washington and Moscow preventing the placement of nuclear weapons in outer space became the placeholder for a moratorium until both superpowers were ready to upgrade the UN resolution into a treaty. President Johnson, whose strong interest in outer space dated back to his Senate days as an ardent critic of the Eisenhower administration after the launch of Sputnik, announced his interest in completing the Outer Space Treaty in May 1966. Both Washington and Moscow introduced draft treaty texts the following month. Differences were ironed out quietly in the Legal Subcommittee of the UN Committee on the Peaceful Uses of Outer Space.

Kennedy's gambit of defusing domestic opposition by means of a UN resolution proved prescient. By the time Johnson was ready to proceed to treaty making, the Joint Chiefs were satisfied that a ban on weapons of mass destruction in space was consistent with U.S. national security interests. The Senate consented to the Outer Space Treaty's ratification without a single dissenting vote in 1967.[44]

THE NONPROLIFERATION TREATY

The Nonproliferation Treaty deserves pride of place as ACDA's highest achievement, accomplished despite considerable hesitation from the State Department. The NPT proved the value of having a semi-autonomous agency of government prioritizing arms control with a direct line to the White House. In this instance, the State Department's overriding priority was maintaining strong ties with NATO—a worthy priority, to be sure—but not by means of its preferred instrument—a Multilateral Force.

The concept behind the MLF gained standing from a State Department study in 1960 led by Robert Bowie, who previously served as director of policy planning for Eisenhower. Bowie and other strong Atlanticists developed a concept for surface ships carrying U.S. missiles and warheads, manned by mixed European crews, with the U.S. supreme allied commander in Europe retaining control over nuclear use. The Rube Goldberg nature of this idea, which initially began as submarines with NATO crews, was driven by the presumed need to present an alternative to having nuclear weapons in West German hands. This plan survived critical scrutiny in the Eisenhower administration and continued on autopilot at the outset of the Kennedy administration where Rusk, seized with the responsibility for alliance cohesion, was the MLF's principal, albeit unenthusiastic supporter. He received help from Gerard Smith, who later succeeded Foster as the director of ACDA.

A nonproliferation treaty became an obvious alternative to the MLF since it would disallow transferring nuclear weapons to other states. Washington could circumvent this obligation by not relinquishing actual control or authority over nuclear weapons' use to its NATO allies, but definitions of the nontransfer obligation would require hard negotiations with Moscow, strongly opposed to nuclear weapons in German hands. Rusk didn't want to invite Moscow into NATO's nuclear knickers, and could avoid doing so by placing a higher priority on creating an MLF than on the negotiation of a nonproliferation treaty.

Rusk was swimming against the tide. The concept of a Nonproliferation Treaty was gaining adherents. Ireland's foreign minister, Frank Aiken, broke new ground at the United Nations by drafting resolutions around "nondissemination." Aiken, a former commandant of the Irish Republican Army, gained renown (and notoriety) for derailing a train carrying King George V's cavalry regiment. He settled into a life of politics in the Republic of Ireland, becoming a fixture as minister for external affairs. In defending his initiative, which evolved into a core Nonproliferation Treaty obligation for nuclear weapon states not to transfer their wares or knowledge to non-nuclear-weapon states, Aiken argued that "while we all wish for complete nuclear disarmament . . . it is quite vain to expect it in the immediate future."[45]

Aiken's departure from UN resolutions calling for general and complete disarmament was the first tentative incursion by non-nuclear-weapon states on the freedom of action by nuclear-armed states. In 1961, after four years of redrafting, Aiken came up with a formula for nonproliferation that assuaged Washington's concerns about NATO solidarity and Moscow's demand for the absence of inspections on its soil.

But before the Nonproliferation Treaty could see the light of day, the idea of an MLF had to sink like a stone. Torpedoes came from many directions. The Atomic Energy Commission was deeply skeptical, as were key senators on Capitol Hill who would be against amending the Atomic Energy Act to allow for the MLF. At the private urging of Adrian Fisher, Senator John Pastore held hearings on nonproliferation, a goal that had significant support in the Senate. The newly elected British prime minister, Harold Wilson, held a negative view of the MLF, unlike his predecessor. France was strongly opposed. The idea of mixed manning made more sense on paper than in practice. And there were better ways to engage NATO in nuclear planning than to do so on board ships. By the end of 1965, the MLF was a ghost fleet.

President Johnson still needed to be convinced that a nonproliferation treaty merited his strong endorsement. Those in ACDA pushing and prodding for a treaty—Bunn, Alan Neidle, Charles Van Doren, and Robert Rochlin—had convinced Foster. They also had fellow believers at working levels in the State Department. A cabal of Nonproliferation Treaty supporters, led by Fisher, John McNaughton at the Pentagon, and Spurgeon M. Keeny on the National Security Council staff, conceived of a plan to convert President Johnson into a treaty backer. They employed Bill Moyers to make the case. Moyers was Johnson's press secretary and confidant. He was also a more sympathetic listener than McGeorge Bundy's successor as national security advisor, Walt Rostow. Toward the end of 1966, Johnson was on board and Rusk knew it.[46]

The coup de grâce came from a blue-ribbon committee chaired by Roswell Gilpatric. Blue-ribbon committees can dim prospects for arms control, like the 1957 Gaither panel, or they can open doors. The Gilpatric Committee's secret report opened doors. Gilpatric was one of the best and the brightest. He went to school at Hotchkiss, Yale, and Yale Law. His resumé included the chairmanship of the Federal Reserve Bank of New York and a "presiding" partnership at the prestigious New York law firm of Cravath, Swain & Moore. He learned the ropes of bureaucratic maneuver as McNamara's deputy secretary of defense, a post he held until 1964.

The Gilpatric Committee's charter was to help Johnson deal with the fallout from China's first nuclear test in 1964. How might China's growing influence be contained? The State Department was already toying with the idea of combatting Chinese influence by arming U.S. allies and friends in Asia, including Japan and India, with nuclear weapons. The Pentagon as well as ACDA thought this unwise; they wanted Johnson to make nuclear nonproliferation a high national priority. Before stepping down as national security advisor, McGeorge Bundy rounded up the usual graybeards—including Arthur Dean, Allen Dulles, Alfred Gruenther, George Kistiakowsky, John McCloy, and Herbert York, then conspicuously without a single gray hair— to rethink strategy. Gilpatric, fresh from his Pentagon assignment, was given the delicate task of forging a consensus.

Nothing matters more than the composition and timing of a commission of heavy hitters. The timing and composition of Gilpatric's panel were well suited to achieve significant results. The Johnson administration was at a policy crossroads, and significant decisions could not be postponed further. While some at the State Department still believed that having European crews join U.S. Navy crews in manning nuclear-armed surface combatants was a sound idea, concerns over a proliferated world were beginning to swell. It was also evident that prospects for improved U.S.-Soviet relations and ending the deep freeze with Beijing would be stillborn if U.S. nuclear weapons were shared with Bonn and Tokyo.

No blue-ribbon commission advanced the prospects of arms control more than the Gilpatric Committee report, which warned, "The world is fast approaching a point of no return in the prospects of controlling the spread of nuclear weapons." Its unanimous bottom line: "Preventing the further spread of nuclear weapons is clearly in the national interest. . . . The United States must, as a matter of great urgency, substantially increase the scope and intensity of our efforts if we are to have any hope of success." Gilpatric called for the negotiation of formal multilateral agreements, applying influence on states contemplating nuclear weapons, and by exemplary "policies and actions."

Gilpatric and his fellow panelists stressed the importance of collaborating with the Soviet Union on nonproliferation, and that bilateral steps to slow down the arms race were an essential component of a successful nonproliferation strategy. In addition to calling for the nuclear Nonproliferation Treaty and the initiation of strategic arms reduction talks with the Kremlin, they supported the establishment of nuclear weapon–free zones, a comprehensive nuclear test ban treaty, a fissile material "cutoff" agreement, a verifiable freeze of new deployments of strategic delivery vehicles along with 30 percent reductions in deployed force levels, and a halt in ballistic missile defense construction. These proposals were far outside the box of establishment thinking in 1965. In making their case the Gilpatric Committee argued, "The rewards of long-term success would be enormous; and even partial success would be worth the costs we can expect to incur."[47]

The Gilpatric Committee's report was like manna from heaven to ACDA's activists. The best way to deal with the Chinese test was to push nonproliferation, and the way to push nonproliferation was to ditch plans for mixed manning of ships carrying U.S. nuclear weapons and their means of delivery. Once plans for the MLF completely collapsed, the State Department joined ACDA in championing the Nonproliferation Treaty. The Kremlin, which did not want West Germany to have the Bomb, readily co-sponsored this initiative.

Johnson had soundly defeated the Republican presidential candidate, Barry Goldwater, who was sympathetic to selective U.S. proliferation to allied states. The Senate was overwhelmingly supportive of a nonproliferation accord. Robert F. Kennedy's maiden floor speech as a newly elected senator from New York wasn't on Vietnam—it was on the threat of proliferation. Senator Pastore's resolution to this effect in 1966 passed without a single dissenting vote. The Gilpatric Committee sank the MLF fleet. The stars were aligned for a treaty designed to prevent the spread of nuclear weapons.

President Johnson initially broached the concept of a nonproliferation treaty to Khrushchev in 1964, along with other sweeping initiatives that soon fell by the wayside. By the fall of 1966, Foster, Fisher, Bunn, and Samuel

DePalma at ACDA had collaborated on a draft text of the Nonproliferation Treaty's central provisions. After extensive consultations with allies and fortified by conversations between Johnson and Soviet premier Alexei Kosygin at their 1967 summit in Glassboro, New Jersey, the United States tabled its proposal for a nonproliferation treaty in Geneva that summer. The biggest points of contention in deliberations with Moscow were over safeguards, whether facilities of nuclear-armed states would be included, and how to deal with multilateral approaches for the peaceful uses of the atom.

The issue of peaceful nuclear explosions for major excavations had earlier complicated negotiations on the Limited Test Ban Treaty. Adrian Fisher's answer remained constant: The only place where peaceful nuclear explosions were technologically feasible was "the delegates' lounge of the UN."[48] The Kremlin wasn't about to allow its nuclear facilities to be inspected but was happy to push for safeguards for states that abstained from weapons building.

After a gestation period of six years, the time had come for the Nonproliferation Treaty. ACDA director Foster, the strongest advocate for the NPT at the highest level, knew that success was at hand. The treaty's date of conception could be traced back to the Cuban missile crisis, when Khrushchev conveyed to Kennedy a Soviet interest in some form of nonproliferation compact. Washington and Moscow began to exchange language about a nontransfer pledge as early as 1963. Negotiations took place in Geneva within a forum then consisting of five Western states, five Eastern bloc states, and eight neutral and nonaligned states. The United States and the Soviet Union were co-chairs of this Eighteen Nation Committee on Disarmament, an unusual arrangement, but one that fostered private cooperation and a sense of common purpose. ACDA's William Foster and Alexi Roshchin from the Soviet Foreign Ministry worked in concert. With the help of their deputies, George Bunn and Roland Timerbaev, they found language acceptable to their capitals. As early as July 1964, Foster's Soviet interlocutors told him "that if we will give up the MLF, they will sign a non-proliferation agreement with us tomorrow morning."[49] With the Gilpatric Committee Report and with Johnson as a backer, it was time to seal the deal.

In 1967, the United States and the Soviet Union tabled identical drafts of what would become the treaty's first three articles. Article I was an obligation by nuclear-weapon states not to transfer weapons or control over them, or to help non-nuclear-weapon states to manufacture or otherwise acquire them. Article II was an obligation by non-nuclear-weapon states of continued abstinence. Article III was an obligation by non-nuclear-weapon states to accept safeguard arrangements with the International Atomic Energy Agency to prevent diversions from peaceful to military uses of the atom.

That was as far as Washington and Moscow got in their private deliberations. It wasn't far enough for the neutral and nonaligned members around the table in Geneva. In early 1968, the United States and the Soviet Union tabled another draft treaty. Foster was hospitalized with a heart problem, so Fisher took over. Foster continued to send missives from his hospital bed over the hard bargaining that ensued. The group of eight neutral and nonaligned states wanted provisions supportive of peaceful uses on a nondiscriminatory bases (the eventual basis for Articles IV and V of the treaty), as well as pledges by nuclear-armed states to abolish their weapons. The language everyone settled on in Article VI was that weapon possessors were obliged "to pursue negotiations in good faith on effective measures relating to cessation of the nuclear arms race at an early date and to nuclear disarmament, and on a treaty on general and complete disarmament under strict and effective international control." The duration of the treaty was set for twenty-five years, instead of indefinitely as Moscow and Washington wanted. The treaty provided for a conference at the twenty-five-year mark to decide on its fate.

One of the devices employed by the neutral and nonaligned states to leverage weapon possessors was UN General Assembly resolutions. The resolution adopted without dissent on November 23, 1965, stated that "the treaty should embody an acceptable balance of mutual responsibilities and obligations of the nuclear and non-nuclear powers." Sweden, Mexico, Brazil, India, and Egypt played active roles among the bloc of neutral and nonaligned states. Alva Myrdal from Sweden and Alphonso Garcia Robles from Mexico were later recognized with the Nobel Peace Prize for their nonproliferation and disarmament efforts.

Washington and Moscow continued to collaborate on treaty drafting. On March 14, 1968, they steered draft treaty text from Geneva to New York where the UN General Assembly could commend or reject their handiwork. They sidestepped a vote at the Eighteen Nation Committee on Disarmament, where the two superpowers would have been outvoted. The bargains struck between weapon possessors and abstainers were insufficient for Brazil and India, the most vocal skeptics in Geneva. West Germany, Italy, Japan, France, and Romania were balky, but unwilling to torpedo the negotiations or the transfer of treaty text to New York.

The biggest challenge the NPT faced in 1968 was delaying tactics. When Secretary of State Rusk, ever mindful of West German sensibilities, expressed readiness to delay a vote at the United Nations, ACDA director Foster threatened to resign. Rusk relented and the vote proceeded on June 12, 1968. Israel voted "aye," but later withheld its instrument of ratification. The only negative votes came from Albania, Cuba, Tanzania, and Zambia. There were significant abstentions, however. China and France abstained, as did Pakistan, India, Argentina, Brazil, Saudi Arabia, Portugal, and several African nations.

China and France subsequently joined the treaty in 1992. Argentina and Brazil kept the nuclear option open until joining in 1995 and 1998, respectively. During the Geneva negotiations, New Delhi did not receive satisfactory assurances from Washington, London, and Moscow to come to its aid in the event of another war initiated by a nuclear-armed China. New Delhi therefore decided not to sign, leaving the door to the Bomb ajar with a stated interest in "peaceful" nuclear explosions. Pakistan would not commit unless India was on board. North Korea joined the treaty and then in 2003 announced its withdrawal as a prelude to testing a nuclear device three years later. [50]

Since perfection eludes diplomats, the strength of treaties and norms can be measured by how long they are respected and how rarely they are broken. A half century after its entry into force, the Nonproliferation Treaty has gained 191 adherents. It has established strong norms for responsible states that have chosen not to possess nuclear weapons and has lent authority to sanctions against states unwilling to abide fully to its terms. Four states have violated their obligations under the NPT—North Korea, Iraq, Syria, and Iran. South Africa joined the NPT after disassembling its small, covert nuclear arsenal, after which it turned over power to Nelson Mandela's African National Congress. Iraq's covert nuclear program was discovered and dismantled after the 1991 Gulf War prompted by Saddam Hussein's invasion of Kuwait during the George H.W. Bush administration. The George W. Bush administration also waged war on Saddam, justified on the presumed reconstitution of Iraq's nuclear capabilities, a presumption that could have been disproven by international inspectors if given enough time on the ground.

India, Pakistan, Israel, North Korea, and Iran stand out as outliers in the Nonproliferation Treaty regime. The treaty has succeeded in braking but not completely stopping proliferation. The value of this treaty and its accompanying international safeguards system can best be appreciated by a simple thought exercise: imagine a world of nuclear danger and weapons in which this treaty didn't exist.[51]

SPREADING THE NUCLEAR SAFETY NET

The norms established in the Nonproliferation Treaty reinforced and extended those of a precursor agreement—the 1967 Treaty of Tlatelolco. Initially promoted by Brazilian diplomats and then championed by an extraordinary Mexican diplomat, Alphonso Garcia Robles, the treaty established a Latin American nuclear-free zone. Signatories pledged to keep their territories free of nuclear weapons and to work with the International Atomic Energy Agency on safeguards agreements for nuclear power plants. The United States did not have a seat at this negotiating table. Mexico took the lead and dealt with complex negotiating dynamics, marked by balkiness by Argentina and Brazil.

ACDA had few qualms about a Latin American nuclear free zone; other parts of the U.S. government did. The Joint Chiefs were wary of infringements on freedom of navigation, and State Department officials were initially wary of any enterprise in which Garcia Robles had a significant role, as he prided himself in ruffling feathers in Foggy Bottom. Another concern was that a nuclear weapon–free zone without Cuba's ratification might be too qualified. The U.S. Atomic Energy Commission was once again wary of placing any constraints on peaceful nuclear explosions.

As the pendulum swung within the Johnson administration away from sharing nuclear weapons with allies and toward the Nonproliferation Treaty, the State Department's reservations about a nuclear-free zone in Latin America waned. Progress toward the Latin American nuclear-free zone reinforced progress in negotiating the Nonproliferation Treaty. The concerns of the Joint Chiefs about freedom of navigation could be ameliorated with the anodyne language of a U.S. reservation, while the peaceful nuclear explosion issue would fall of its own dead weight.

ACDA and the State Department shepherded the treaty's two protocols through the Senate process of advice and consent. Protocol I entailed the obligation of states with territorial interests in Latin America to keep their possessions free of nuclear weapons. Protocol II—an explicit formulation, unlike the side assurances provided by nuclear-armed states in the Nonproliferation Treaty—obliged nuclear-weapon states neither to use nor threaten the use of nuclear weapons against parties to the treaty. As is often the case,

Senate consent to both protocols was a lengthy process but was completed in 1981.

The concept of a populated region free of nuclear weapons, born in Latin America, was subsequently extended to the South Pacific, Southeast Asia, Africa, and Central Asia. Additional treaties extended nuclear-weapon-free zones to Antarctica, outer space, and the globe's seabeds. The Global South is a nuclear-weapon-free zone in its entirety. Regions free of nuclear weapons lend credence to abolition movements and reinforce the Nonproliferation Treaty.[52]

The Nonproliferation Treaty is the thickest strand of the nuclear safety net, woven by both nuclear- and non-nuclear-weapon states. The International Atomic Energy Agency oversees implementation. Its technical experts oversee safeguards on civil nuclear power programs and provide early warning if they contribute to covert plans to build nuclear weapons. Over time, inspections became routinized—too much so. The fine print of safeguards agreements and the International Atomic Energy Agency's inspections became newsworthy only when they were circumvented or ignored, such as with the belated discovery of Saddam Hussein's covert nuclear arms program in 1990. A push to strengthen safeguards and the ambit of international inspectors followed. The Nonproliferation Treaty, nuclear-weapon-free zones, and the International Atomic Energy Agency's safeguard system remain bulwarks of the global nuclear order.

LEDGER SHEET

The rise of nuclear arms control was propelled by evident need, including the need to brake proliferation. ACDA deserves pride of place in these foundational efforts. The need for a semi-autonomous agency was never more evident than in the creation of the Nonproliferation Treaty. The State Department was more inclined to tend to bilateral relations and to nuclear weapon sharing, especially with West Germany. The design of the nonproliferation system was the greatest, but far from the only contribution of the Johnson administration to weaving a global nuclear safety net. States that seek the Bomb face significant risks and consequences, thanks in part to the Nonproliferation Treaty. A lasting nuclear peace is inconceivable without the Nonproliferation Treaty.

The foundation laid by the Kennedy and Johnson administrations was built to accommodate new construction. The big challenge ahead was to control and then reduce strategic arms. With the Nonproliferation Treaty in hand, President Johnson immediately turned to this task, but he ran out of time. His successors worked this problem intensively. Once again, ACDA played a critical role with its advocacy and expertise. Progress was halting, but success in the form of deep reductions in nuclear forces came two decades after the Nonproliferation Treaty was negotiated. The promise given by Washington and Moscow to non-nuclear-weapon states was kept, only to be broken later.

Chapter 4

JOHNSON AND THE QUEST FOR STRATEGIC ARMS CONTROL

B eing relentless by nature, Lyndon Johnson wasn't satisfied after securing the Nonproliferation Treaty. Strategic arms control was next on his agenda. One reason to do so was to help convince fence-sitters to join the NPT. By beginning strategic arms limitation talks, Johnson could demonstrate that Washington took seriously the NPT's obligation that nuclear-armed states take steps toward disarmament. There was a more important reason, however. Secretary of Defense Robert McNamara convinced Johnson of the need to move quickly to avoid a quantitative and qualitative strategic arms race.

Washington and Moscow were working hard to build new land-based missiles, nuclear-powered submarines to carry missiles, and new warheads. Both were working on missile defenses to blunt attacks. Conceptualizers of deterrence and arms control were worried about this intensified strategic competition. McNamara, the most nuclear arms race–averse secretary of defense ever to hold this position, could see no end to this competition except through an arms control breakthrough, and time was running out.

As early as 1964, the Arms Control and Disarmament Agency's representatives at the Eighteen Nation Disarmament Conference in Geneva had tabled a proposal for a freeze on offensive and defensive strategic arms—a concept that would later be incorporated in U.S. negotiating proposals. What was to be frozen? "Strategic nuclear delivery vehicles" were defined by U.S. experts as consisting of ocean-spanning or "intercontinental" land-based ballistic missiles, submarine-launched ballistic missiles, and long-range bombers. In addition, the earliest U.S. proposals for strategic arms control included missiles of less-than-intercontinental range as well as strategic defenses. The presumed unit of account for strategic defenses was the number of interceptors based on national soil that were designed to shoot down incoming warheads. Technologies to "hit to kill" incoming warheads by conventional means didn't exist. The only conceivable way to carry out these intercepts during this period was by means of nuclear detonations in the atmosphere or above it.

The Pentagon's force structure for strategic offensive arms was largely set during the Eisenhower administration. After jockeying between McNamara and his bright civilian "whiz kids" and the service chiefs, these numbers were reaffirmed during the Kennedy and Johnson administrations. The United States would deter the Soviet Union with approximately 1,000 ocean-spanning, land-based missiles, 656 ballistic missiles to be carried on 41 nuclear-powered submarines, and another 600 or so B-52 bombers. This force was built out quickly during McNamara's tenure and was essentially completed in 1967. With quantitative limits mostly in place due to budgetary constraints, the Pentagon's attention turned to qualitative improvements in order to compete effectively with the Soviet Union. The most important qualitative advance on the horizon was placing more than one warhead atop ocean-spanning missiles. Added compulsion to do so was provided by Moscow's interest in missile defense deployments and by Soviet missile programs. What Soviet designers lacked in sophistication, they made up for in brute force.

Insight into the Kremlin's thinking was provided decades later, thanks to Mikhail Gorbachev's endorsement of *glasnost*, or openness. According to two Soviet insiders who took advantage of the opportunity provided by Gorbachev to write about the Soviet style of competition, the Kremlin's negotiating objectives were to compete effectively with the Pentagon and to secure advantages whenever possible. The two defining events for the members of the Soviet leadership—events that "burned imprints" on the Russian soul—were the Great Patriotic War (World War II) and the Cuban missile crisis. These experiences convinced Soviet leaders that allowing U.S. strategic superiority would invite aggression and result in unwelcome outcomes. Strategic superiority would therefore be sought and disadvantage would be avoided at all costs. At a minimum, "equal security" was required, in both offensive and defensive systems.[1]

McNamara clearly wanted to keep a lid on further increases in defense spending for nuclear forces and to avoid missile defense deployments that would lend even greater impetus to a strategic arms competition. But McNamara left for the World Bank before the negotiations started. No one in the Johnson administration was as committed as McNamara in placing restraints on the arms race, and no one could be sure what might be achievable in talks with the Soviet Union. This was terra incognita as negotiations of this kind had never been attempted before. Skeptics of arms control assumed that the Kremlin would seek strategic superiority. The Kremlin was similarly convinced about Washington's intentions. If these suppositions were correct, deal making would be impossible.

The United States began full-scale development funding for a nationwide defense against missile attacks in 1963. The system was then known as Nike Zeus, but the more engineers struggled to succeed at intercepts, the more it became apparent that radars were the system's weakest link. Proposed solutions begat new problems. Radars were required to direct where intercepts needed to be aimed, but killing incoming warheads required arming interceptor missiles with nuclear warheads, which would result in blacking out radars. Two types of interceptors were planned for use in the anti-ballistic missile system that was readied during the Johnson administration. One type carried a five-megaton warhead for use above the earth's atmosphere; another used a five-kiloton warhead to serve as a last-ditch defense.

Using nuclear detonations to defend against incoming warheads heading toward cities prompted another problem that was political rather than technical in nature. Those to be protected around Boston, Chicago, Seattle and other metropolitan areas didn't want to be defended with nuclear detonations.[2] There was yet another problem, as well: If either superpower sought to intercept incoming warheads, the other would seek ways to improve the means by which warheads could reach their targets. McNamara called this the "action-reaction syndrome."[3]

One way to defeat defenses would be to build more missiles and to dig more missile silos. Early on, McNamara fended off preliminary air force interest in building 10,000 silos. A "cost-effective" alternative was to enhance the ability of a far smaller force of missiles to reach their targets by means of "penetration aids"—devices to confuse radars so that they couldn't send interceptors to the right aim points. The Pentagon began funding for penetration aids in 1965. One kind of penetration aid was "chaff," or thin metallic strips released en route to confuse radars. Another was to load up dummy warheads along with real ones atop missiles. It didn't take too much mental calculation to arrive at the conclusion that real warheads would be more effective than dummy warheads, especially when the Soviet Union began preparations to deploy missile defenses. Thus, the concept of unguided, multiple reentry vehicles atop missile launchers, or MRVs, was born. Even better, each warhead atop a ballistic missile could be guided to separate targets. The acronym for these independently targetable reentry vehicles—MIRVs—became the nemesis for successful strategic arms control.

McNamara could see this coming. His tenure at the Pentagon was a series of severe trials, especially dealing with the Vietnam War and preparing for nuclear negotiations. It was his lot to tell his fellow citizens about the Pentagon's plans for missile defenses and for MIRVs just before leaving the Pentagon. That's why he insisted that Johnson hurry up and start negotiations with the Kremlin.

While ACDA was busy negotiating the Nonproliferation Treaty, Robert McNamara and two of his whiz kids, Morton Halperin and Ivan Selin, were seized with the problem of how to contain the prospect of MIRVs and antiballistic missile defenses, two mutually reinforcing technologies that could wreck prospects of strategic arms control and, in the bargain, shred McNamara's efforts to constrain growth in the Pentagon's budget for strategic forces. MIRVs were "technically sweet," to use Oppenheimer's phrase. Just as the deployment of H-bombs became inevitable once it became clear that they were technically feasible, so, too, were multiple warheads atop a single ballistic missile. After that, improved targeting capabilities for each warhead also became technically sweet. Deploying three, six, ten, or even more MIRVs atop a single missile would be far more cost-effective—a term favored by McNamara and his whiz kids—than deploying an equivalent number of missiles carrying individual warheads. Each warhead would pack the punch of an H-bomb.

The allure of MIRVs inevitably became stronger as evidence mounted that the Soviet Union was pursuing defenses against nuclear attack. The Kremlin began deploying defenses near the Baltic Sea in 1964. This "Tallinn" system seemed to be oriented against bombers, but in an oft-repeated dynamic of "worst casing," U.S. strategic analysts worried that the system might be upgraded to intercept ballistic missiles. Then, in 1967, satellites provided incontrovertible evidence that the Kremlin had begun to construct an anti-ballistic missile system to protect Moscow.

Johnson, who led the charge on Capitol Hill criticizing Eisenhower over Soviet gains in space after the launch of Sputnik, wasn't about to have the tables turned on him by being a laggard in any aspect of the strategic competition. His opponent in 1964, Barry Goldwater, wrote a book titled *Why Not Victory?*, and victory in nuclear warfare against the Soviet Union wasn't remotely possible in the absence of effective missile defenses. Johnson refused to be politically vulnerable on this issue, but he understood McNamara's pleadings. He was willing to give his secretary of defense a chance to avoid costly anti-ballistic missile defense deployments if he could persuade the Kremlin.

Johnson convened his key advisers in Austin, Texas, in June 1966 to consider whether to proceed at full speed on a nationwide anti-ballistic missile (ABM) system. The Joint Chiefs were ready to do so, as was National Security Advisor Walt Rostow. McNamara was in opposition. Johnson agreed to a down payment on missile defenses while giving McNamara one budget cycle to seek the basis for a diplomatic settlement. In 1966, the Soviet ambassador to the United States, Anatoly Dobrynin, indicated to Llewellyn Thompson, then between stints as U.S. ambassador to Moscow, that the Kremlin would be willing to consider discussions on offensive and defensive arms. Time was of the essence, as MIRVs and ABMs were gaining momentum.

ABM SKEPTICS

Several strategic thinkers concluded early on that a nationwide anti-ballistic missile system might do far more harm than good. One early heretic was Jack Ruina. Ruina came to America in 1927 as a young child with his parents and eight other siblings, traveling from a Polish shtetl to Brooklyn. Ruina was the only member of his family to attend college. With the help of the GI Bill after serving in the army, he went to graduate school and then received a PhD in electrical engineering. Ruina's aptitude in defense applications of advanced technology was evident early on, and a mentor recruited him in 1959 to work with the chief scientist of the air force on a range of pressing issues. There he met Herbert York, then the director of defense research and engineering. York was another first-generation college student. He made his way to the Pentagon from upstate New York by way of Berkeley, Oak Ridge, and the Livermore labs. York and Ruina plunged into the technical challenges associated with missile defenses. Thanks to York, Ruina became the head of the Pentagon's Advanced Research Projects Agency, where he started work the same day as John F. Kennedy's inauguration.

Ruina recalled that the first person to raise the idea that a mutual U.S.-Soviet agreement not to deploy national missile defenses might be worthwhile—half in jest, in 1961 or 1962—was Jerome Wiesner, Kennedy's science advisor.[4] In the Pentagon, Ruina worked on a short concept paper about banning nationwide ballistic missile defenses that he shared with his boss, Harold Brown. Brown did not then endorse it but suggested that Ruina run it up the flagpole with Roswell Gilpatric, McNamara's deputy. Gilpatric grasped the concept and urged Ruina to work on it further, which he did after leaving the Pentagon in 1963 to lead the Institute for Defense Analyses. The small group that Ruina worked with initially included Wiesner, York, George Rathgens, and Paul Doty. Rathgens and Doty—one a professor at MIT, the other at Harvard—were key participants along with Wiesner in the Charles River Gang that helped conceptualize the practice of arms control.

At a 1964 Pugwash meeting in India, Ruina, Carl Kaysen (who had recently left the National Security Council staff as McGeorge Bundy's deputy), and Murray Gell-Mann, a professor at the California Institute of Technology and soon to be awarded the Nobel Prize for his work on subatomic particles, first introduced the idea of refraining from national missile defense deployments to their Russian counterparts. The reaction was both quizzical and skeptical. More conversations followed, along with greater receptivity.

The most important ABM skeptic was McNamara, who was softened up on this subject by Gilpatric and later tutored by Paul Warnke and Morton Halperin. Warnke was recruited by Cyrus Vance to join the Pentagon in 1966 as general counsel, which McNamara used as a springboard for promotion to important policy slots. Once Warnke had proven himself, he was elevated in 1967 to become the assistant secretary of defense for international security affairs. Halperin, Warnke's go-to staffer and the youngest of the Charles River Gang, found himself presented with the opportunity to turn the concepts he and Thomas Schelling wrote about in *Strategy and Arms Control* into practice.

Warnke credited McNamara as being the person who "basically invented strategic nuclear arms control."[5] McNamara was convinced by the Pentagon's former research directors that deploying nationwide ballistic missile defenses would not work effectively. In turn, he planted the seeds of doubt about the utility of strategic defenses in Moscow—no mean feat. He warned about the "mad momentum" of the nuclear competition, where one superpower felt obliged to respond to the other's strategic modernization program.[6]

McNamara oversaw the first draft of the U.S. negotiating position in strategic arms limitation talks, managing to keep the Joint Chiefs on the reservation. He understood how much fuel nationwide defenses would add to the fire building around him to increase the U.S. nuclear arsenal. MIRVs and accuracy increases would reorient deterrence strategy away from assured destruction toward war-fighting strategies against military, economic, and leadership targets. McNamara was not completely unsympathetic to MIRVs, since they would help him fend off the air force's demands for additional thousands of globe-spanning missiles. But he was all-too-aware of the lose-lose trade-offs involved as MIRVs would also result in additional thousands of warheads.

McNamara arranged for Johnson to meet in January 1967 with a blue-ribbon collection of presidential science advisors and former directors of defense research and engineering to discuss nationwide ballistic missile defenses. The attendees—Harold Brown, John S. Foster, Donald Hornig, James Killian, George Kistiakowsky, Jerome Wiesner, and Herbert York—had the best grasp of the technical challenges involved. Johnson asked the participants whether an anti-ballistic missile system should be deployed. York's summary of the meeting was that the answer with respect to the Soviet Union was an unequivocal, unanimous "no." With respect to China, York recounts that there was "some divergence of views," but the majority view was again a "no."[7]

Johnson gave McNamara his chance to persuade Soviet premier Alexei Kosygin that the more missile defenses were pursued, the stronger the case became for offensive upgrades to defeat them. The summit took place at Glassboro, New Jersey, in June 1967. The agenda was already full, headlined by a recent Middle East crisis where the Hotline had been used for the first time. Also on the agenda were the Chinese nuclear program and the Vietnam War. McNamara's pitch against ballistic missile defenses would have to be squeezed in over lunch. Time was short, it was difficult to hear over the clamor, and Johnson framed the issue too narrowly—over why defenses were a bad idea, rather than how this might fit within a broader freeze of offenses and defenses that the Kremlin indicated a readiness to discuss. Johnson wasn't going to buck hawkish sentiments on Capitol Hill and among the Pentagon brass, but there was no harm in allowing McNamara to try.

Much later, McNamara recounted his version of the Glassboro meeting, imploring Kosygin to think differently about strategic defenses, warning that Soviet deployment of ballistic missile defenses would result in expanded offenses.[8] Kosygin normally wore a poker face, but in McNamara's retelling, "He absolutely erupted. He became red in the face." McGeorge Bundy, who stepped down as LBJ's national security advisor before Glassboro, offers a different account—that Kosygin "had himself a good time" arguing the standard Soviet line, that defense was a moral imperative and that a nuclear arms race was immoral.[9] Archival research also rebuts McNamara's version. The note taker at the luncheon found Kosygin to be composed, as did Walt Rostow, who replaced Bundy as Johnson's national security advisor.[10]

The luncheon discussion was rushed and not worthy of the topic. Kosygin, part of a collective leadership, wasn't empowered to make a decision, in any event. Llewellyn Thompson was dispatched once more to Moscow to deliver the message that the United States was willing to send a high-level delegation to Moscow to begin preliminary discussions. He was to lead the U.S. delegation, but was left cooling his heels. Thompson conveyed three subsequent messages from Washington, but there was still no reply.

The decision to begin strategic arms control talks tied the Kremlin into knots. Soviet ambassador Anatoly Dobrynin raised one important concern in a discussion with Secretary of State Dean Rusk: What, exactly, did the United States want to achieve? Superiority? Or would Washington accept parity? Rusk was evasive. Kosygin expressed the concern to Thompson that the U.S. nationwide defense could be 100 times better than anything the Soviet Union could build. The Soviet Union lagged behind in MIRV technology, as well. Another reason for delay was that the Soviet Union was far behind the United States in missile deployments. Raymond Garthoff, the State Department Kremlinologist who would later join the U.S. negotiating team, thought Moscow's delay was due to correctly anticipating that Washington would propose to freeze deployments, which would place the Kremlin in an inferior position unless they stalled in order to catch up.[11]

The Soviet reply expressing readiness to talk finally came in late June 1968—one long year after the Glassboro Summit. The delay was costly as MIRV and ABM programs continued to advance. The Joint Chiefs shot down efforts by Pentagon civilians to slow down MIRV flight testing. Halperin and Selin proposed an eight-month delay that would not affect the first projected MIRVed missile deployment, but the chiefs would have none of this. In interagency deliberations, ACDA officials tried to place MIRVs on the negotiating table, but they were also rebuffed.

The most the Johnson administration was prepared to accept was a discussion of MIRV limitations only if Moscow raised the issue. This was unlikely, since the Kremlin lagged behind U.S. MIRV capabilities, and Moscow was unlikely to seek controls on MIRVs from a position of weakness. The first U.S. flight test of a MIRV capability occurred in August 1968—the same month as the first Soviet test of a less technically advanced MRV.

Johnson didn't want a nuclear arms race, but he was going to negotiate from a position of strength. McNamara literally and figuratively ran out of time. Funding for the first two ballistic missile defense sites would be included in the defense budget to be transmitted to the Congress in January 1968. Johnson was willing to make one concession, however: McNamara could frame the rationale for going forward with missile defenses any way he wanted.

Halperin was the principal drafter of the speech McNamara would give—surely one of the strangest ever made by a secretary of defense. The speech would dwell on reasons why anti-ballistic missiles were a bad idea before its last paragraph endorsing a "thin" defense against China. Much back-and-forth ensued on drafting McNamara's speech, with Paul Warnke repeatedly seeking to excise the China rationale. McNamara's plaintive response was, "What else can I blame it on?" To blame the Soviet Union would add even more fuel to the "mad momentum of the arms race" that he was about to decry in his speech. By blaming China, perhaps limits on missile defenses might be easier to negotiate while fending off extravagant Pentagon plans. No one around McNamara could come up with a better rationale for a move that Johnson decided he had to make.[12]

McNamara was a tragic figure—and not only because of Vietnam. He was the prophet who warned about a serious ratcheting up of the nuclear competition but was unable to affect the political and technological forces driving it. Instead, he found himself endorsing military programs he thought were unwise, programs that fueled the strategic competition that he publicly warned against. There wasn't enough time to convince the Kremlin to move quickly on stopping anti-ballistic missile defenses. And so, before the strategic arms talks were set to begin in 1968, McNamara announced Johnson's decision to deploy a "thin" nationwide defense, after clarifying in great detail the reasons why this was an unwise decision.

On September 18, 1967, McNamara delivered his address on "The Dynamics of Nuclear Strategy" to a meeting of United Press International editors and publishers in San Francisco. Here he introduced themes that would become staples in subsequent critiques of missile defenses. An ABM system, McNamara cautioned, would not provide an "impenetrable shield," even in the foreseeable future. With currently available technologies, "such a system can rather obviously be defeated by an enemy sending more offensive warheads, or dummy warheads than there are defensive missiles."

McNamara explicitly acknowledged the danger of arms racing and warned against starting with a "light" missile defense system against China and turning it into a "heavy, Soviet-oriented ABM system." A "heavy" ABM defense would "be no adequate shield at all against a Soviet attack, but rather a strong inducement for the Soviets to vastly increase their own offensive forces." After all these cautionary notes, McNamara went on to announce the deployment of a "light" national missile defense.[13] Never has a U.S. official ever made a more powerful public case against the course of action he was directed to advocate.

The speech and the missile defense plan it endorsed made no sense. Johnson's "Sentinel" missile defense system against China seemed well designed to prompt the very outcome that McNamara warned about. On paper, this "light" defense, if fully deployed, would include 672 interceptor missiles at seventeen locations in the continental United States. Another 28 interceptors were planned for Hawaii, making the total 700 in all. At the time of the Sentinel system's unveiling, the Soviet Union possessed almost 900 land- and sea-based launchers capable of reaching the United States. China, the ostensible reason for deployment, would not flight-test a ballistic missile capable of reaching the United States for another thirteen years.

Despite McNamara's careful parsing, Moscow's concerns could not possibly be assuaged. Instead, they were reinforced after President Richard Nixon subsequently reoriented the system's rationale to defend the U.S. deterrent against Soviet attack and changed the system's name to "Safeguard." Secondary missions were to defend against a small Chinese attack and against accidental or unauthorized launches. Much of the system architecture remained the same, however. From Moscow's perspective, whether the system was called Sentinel or Safeguard, it seemed best suited to nullify what might remain of the Soviet deterrent after a U.S. first strike. Safeguard wasn't about to be built because of domestic political opposition, economic cost, and technical reasons. But the prospect of its being built was sufficient for the Kremlin to arrive at the conclusion that nationwide ABM systems were a bad idea. McNamara got the outcome he wanted. The progression from Sentinel to Safeguard eventually led to the Anti-Ballistic Missile Treaty. Many more ironies would follow.

MIRVS

Meanwhile, the technologies to place several warheads atop a single missile and guide them independently to separate targets were advancing. MIRVs, unlike ballistic missile defenses, could perform quite effectively. And with advances in accuracy, as was entirely foreseeable (despite the Nixon administration's fleeting attempt to downplay this prospect), MIRVs could be deeply unsettling to calculations of strategic stability, even if nationwide ballistic missile defenses never saw the light of day.

McNamara had one more unwanted duty before leaving the Pentagon for the World Bank. Just eleven days after his "mad momentum" speech decrying the "action-reaction syndrome," his interview for *Life* magazine revealed the Pentagon's MIRV program.[14] One reason for going public was that the lid of secrecy over MIRVs would soon be lifted with the beginning of flight tests in the summer of 1968. A second reason was that McNamara wanted to get ahead of a deployment he couldn't stop but might somehow empower others to control.

McNamara and others hoped that MIRVs could be controlled in the upcoming negotiations. There was a strong interest in doing so at the Arms Control and Disarmament Agency, where William Foster and Adrian Fisher led the charge, as expected. McNamara agreed completely with the arguments advanced by Warnke, Halperin, and Selin, but the Pentagon's top brass, backed by their allies on Capitol Hill, insisted on having no constraints on MIRVs. The Soviet Union was racing to catch up to U.S. launcher numbers, including a new "heavy" missile—the SS-9—that could carry three warheads, with each warhead packing a five-megaton wallop. A "window of vulnerability" was opening for U.S. land-based missiles—vulnerability that plagued nuclear negotiations for the next two decades. MIRVs were the U.S. counter to the Soviet missile buildup with its silo-busting capabilities. The instructions written for the U.S. negotiating team in 1967 were explicit in rejecting constraints on qualitative improvements for U.S. missiles.[15]

The United States would be loaded for bear in the forthcoming talks on limiting strategic offensive and defenses forces. McNamara had provided public notice for both nationwide ballistic missile defenses and MIRVs. The Kremlin would likewise do whatever was necessary to avoid being placed at a disadvantage in these strategic arms limitation talks. A new acronym, SALT, was born. Both superpowers were primed for an intense strategic arms competition, one that SALT couldn't tamp down.

The principal drafters of the U.S. negotiating position in 1967 were Halperin and Selin from the Office of the Secretary of Defense, General Royal Allison (a bomber pilot during World War II) from the Joint Chiefs, Raymond Garthoff and Philip Farley from the State Department, and Adrian Fisher from ACDA. With McNamara at the World Bank, Dean Rusk took the reins to prepare for the onset of SALT. The U.S. proposal called for 1,200 intercontinental ballistic missiles with no external upgrades permitted other than to harden their silos; limitations on missiles with ranges in excess of 1,000 kilometers; a building freeze on missile-carrying submarines and ICBMs as of September 1, 1968; a five-year naval building holiday for ballistic missile-carrying submarines, after which replacements were permissible, and mutually agreed but unspecified limitations on ballistic missile defenses. Pentagon drafters initially proposed setting a limit on missile defense interceptors at 1,000 each—sufficient to cover the proposed Sentinel deployment and the Soviet "Tallinn line" plus the Moscow system. Before leaving the Pentagon, McNamara balked at this high number, proposing instead that missile interceptor limits be equal but unspecified. The Joint Chiefs were opposed to a freeze on anti-ballistic missile defenses, so this was stripped from the draft U.S. proposal that would be conveyed to Moscow.

The key to banning MIRVs was a flight test ban since neither side could be confident in the effectiveness of MIRVs without them, and since remotely based intelligence capabilities could monitor flight tests. But McNamara and Rusk were unwilling to fall on their swords to ban the flight-testing of MIRVs. Besides, monitoring MIRV flight tests wasn't a simple matter at that time. Distinguishing between the flight tests of unguided and independently targetable warheads posed challenges. The arms control solution would be to ban all flight tests of multiple warheads or their simulation. Failing this, the only way to have confidence in a ban on MIRVed missile deployments would be through on-site inspections, which both the Kremlin and the Pentagon strongly resisted.

The Joint Chiefs and their allies strongly opposed an arms control solution banning MIRVs. A ban on flight testing and deploying MIRVs would foreclose a primary U.S. comparative advantage and a counter to the Soviet missile buildup. A ban on MIRVs would also be a very hard sell on Capitol Hill. Johnson would have none of this.[16]

At long last, talks were set for early September. Johnson wanted to be present at the opening ceremony. Rusk was also ready to attend. Ambassador Llewellyn Thompson was tapped to lead the U.S. delegation, to be joined by Paul Nitze representing the Office of the Secretary of Defense, General Allison representing the Joint Chiefs, and Fisher from ACDA. Harold Brown—then at the California Institute of Technology—would provide outside technical expertise, Garthoff was slated to be the delegation's executive secretary, and ACDA would "backstop" the negotiations in Washington, coordinating the executive branch's support for the negotiating team.

One day before the proposed joint announcement of the beginning of talks, Soviet tanks and troops invaded Czechoslovakia to put an end to the Prague Spring. Negotiations would have to await the incoming Nixon administration. More time would be lost while MIRVs proceeded apace.[17]

Chapter 5

NIXON, KISSINGER, AND THE SALT I ACCORDS

R ichard Nixon had ideal credentials to oversee the challenge of negotiating
SALT. The new president prided himself on his grasp of world affairs and
he had impeccable anticommunist credentials dating back to his congressional career. Nixon's choice as national security advisor, Henry Kissinger,
showcased his grasp of international politics and grand strategy in weighty
books, along with trenchant commentary in *Foreign Affairs*. During the
Eisenhower administration, Kissinger honed his grasp of nuclear issues by
staffing a Council on Foreign Relations study group on pressing strategic
matters, from which emerged his critique of John Foster Dulles's doctrine
of massive retaliation, *Nuclear Weapons and Foreign Policy*. Kissinger had a
knack for affixing himself to ambitious politicians and making an intellectual
impact in the salons of power.

Both Nixon and Kissinger prided themselves on being supreme realists.
They were skeptical of arms control and committed to negotiating from
strength. They were a fitting team. They shared similar instincts and conspiratorial tendencies, which raised hackles during the SALT negotiations that
later came back to haunt Presidents Gerald Ford and Jimmy Carter. Nixon
and Kissinger were inclined toward the big picture; neither was all that interested in detail, which led to missteps. They would put the bureaucracy to
work while minimizing its input and excluding cabinet members from their
maneuvering. At key junctures, even their negotiating team, led by a true-blue
Republican, Gerard Smith, was in the dark.

Nixon chose William Rogers to be secretary of state, a competent man with prior cabinet-level experience in the Eisenhower administration, where he served as attorney general. As secretary of defense, he chose Melvin Laird, a veteran from Capitol Hill with a deep understanding of military issues from his years on the Defense Appropriations Subcommittee. Laird could affect decision making on SALT by clarifying the penalties for not protecting strategic modernization programs. Rogers had little means of leverage.

FIRST UP: BIOLOGICAL WEAPONS

SALT wasn't the only arms control issue facing Nixon. Laird urged Nixon to make decisions about biological weapons as well as inert toxins like botulinum that could be produced from living organisms. Chemical and biological weapons were then closely intertwined in the public mind. They were also in the news. Open-air testing of nerve agents created political firestorms in Utah, as did the revelation that these stocks were stored in Okinawa, Japan. The use of Agent Orange to defoliate dense vegetation during the Vietnam War created political difficulties for the administration and grievous health consequences for villagers and U.S. troops. Laird wanted a policy to deal with biological weapons that he believed to have little or no military utility or deterrent effect.

The Pentagon was divided on these matters but eventually the Joint Staff was again isolated, as ACDA and the State Department sided with Laird. Kissinger and his National Security Council staffer, Michael Guhin, at first sought to split the difference—destroying biological weapon stocks while carving out the possibility for subsequent production of toxins—but then had second thoughts. The public relations aspects of defending this nuanced position seemed far more than the traffic could bear. Nixon agreed, and in February 1970, announced his decision: The United States would unilaterally renounce biological and toxin warfare while continuing to maintain defensive preparation against their use by others.

This was the first and only time that a president unilaterally renounced the possession and use of stockpiles categorized as weapons of mass destruction. Nixon's rationale was straightforward: "Biological weapons have massive, unpredictable, and potentially uncontrollable consequences." For good measure, he declared, "They may produce global epidemics and impair the health of future generations." Laird felt it was important to distinguish between biological and chemical weapons. The former would be subject to renunciation by Nixon; the latter would be addressed later in negotiations that were successfully concluded at the end of the George H.W. Bush administration.

The diplomat charged with negotiating the Biological Weapons Convention was James Leonard, an ACDA official serving as ambassador to the Conference on Disarmament in Geneva. The United Kingdom had already tabled a draft convention stigmatizing and renouncing biological weapons, but the Soviet Union initially wanted a convention covering chemical weapons, as well. When Moscow changed its mind, its negotiators joined with U.S. and British diplomats to present others in Geneva with a draft text reflecting Washington's view that renunciation be unaccompanied by verification. Monitoring procedures would have to be intrusive and neither Washington nor Moscow welcomed on-site inspections. Negotiations over monitoring procedures could result in endless haggling, which Nixon wished to avoid.

Laird got what he wanted. Nixon hosted the signing ceremony for the Biological Weapons Convention in Washington, accompanied by the Soviet and British ambassadors to the United States in April 1972. The Kremlin readily signed up to the convention while blithely ignoring its obligations.[1]

THE SALT I NEGOTIATIONS

Gerard Smith, William Foster's successor at ACDA, didn't have his predecessor's pro-defense credentials. Instead, Smith rose through the ranks as an exemplary civil servant. In 1954, he left the Atomic Energy Commission to join the State Department as John Foster Dulles's special assistant for atomic energy affairs. In 1957, he was elevated to become assistant secretary of state for policy planning, a post he held until the incoming Kennedy administration. Before leaving the State Department in 1960, he pressed Dulles's successor as secretary of state, Christian Herter, to pursue a "Hotline" agreement with the Kremlin, a novel idea urged by a colleague, Henry Owen, that became a reality after the Cuban missile crisis.

Foster, Adrian Fisher, and their colleagues at ACDA could boast a remarkable track record, but it largely consisted of placing constraints on others (the NPT) and on foreclosing options that had not yet been pursued (Tlatelolco and the Outer Space Treaty). They also helped to end atmospheric testing that was politically and literally toxic. As hard as these accomplishments were for Foster and Fisher, Smith's job was harder. His task was to seek parallel constraints on U.S. and Soviet strategic offensive and defensive capabilities—technologies that were advancing headlong toward deployment. This challenge would place him in the direct line of fire of the uniformed services, conservative-minded national security strategists, and elected officials on Capitol Hill supportive of the Pentagon's preferences. Smith provided them with plenty of ammunition; everyone knew what he was advocating behind closed doors. He opposed missiles bearing multiple warheads and nation-wide ballistic missile defenses, much to the annoyance of the president and his national security advisor.

Gerard Smith's grandparents immigrated to the United States from Ire-land during the potato famine. His mother taught school. His father was a first-generation college-goer, a dynamo who graduated at the top of his class at Creighton University and then with high honors from Yale Law School. Smith's father joined General Motors where he became general counsel, a post he held for thirty years. Gerard Smith was born to privilege in New York City and enjoined by his type A father to be useful in life. After attend-ing Yale and Yale Law School, Smith was commissioned in the U.S. Navy during World War II and posted in Washington, where he caught Potomac fever. A law practice interested him far less than international affairs, so he jumped at the offer to become a special assistant to Thomas E. Murray, a rare breed of atomic energy commissioner who recoiled at the power of hydrogen weapons.

Policy planning and nuclear issues obviously suited Smith. He was a highly regarded veteran presence by the time Nixon and Kissinger were looking for someone to lead the strategic arms limitation talks that the Johnson adminis-tration had hoped, but failed, to initiate. Smith's Republican credentials were beyond question and he was also in good standing with Democrats, having been enlisted during the Kennedy administration to help advance the Multi-lateral Force concept, an uphill and eventually futile task.

"Gerry" Smith was a square-jawed straight shooter. He knew nuclear is-sues and NATO. He was widely recognized as a man of talent and integrity. And he had the blessing of the chairman of the Joint Chiefs of Staff, General Earl Wheeler. In January 1969, Secretary of State William Rogers told Smith he was going to be tapped as ACDA's second director. Like Foster, Smith wasn't an "arms controller" at the start. A case in point was his opposition to a moratorium on nuclear testing during the Eisenhower administration. Like Foster, his views evolved. The more he worked at the problems of controlling nuclear weapons, the more of an advocate he became.

After fending off the Nixon White House's first choice as his deputy—William Casey, later to become Ronald Reagan's pick as an adventurous

Central Intelligence Agency director—Smith secured his favored choice, Philip Farley.[2] Arms controllers have arrived at this calling from varied backgrounds and by serendipity. In Farley's case, he received his doctorate in philosophy from Berkeley in 1941 on the pattern, structure, and form of Thomas Hardy's novels. After graduating, he taught English at a junior college in East Texas before joining the army, where, by chance, Paul Nitze found and recruited him to join the Strategic Bombing Survey investigating the effects of air power during World War II. Farley then found himself sifting through the rubble and writing the Strategic Bombing Survey's report on Hiroshima and Nagasaki.

Afterward, Farley and Smith rose through the ranks together at the Atomic Energy Commission. As a staffer there, Farley helped to prepare Henry De-Wolf Smyth's lone dissent to the revocation of Robert Oppenheimer's security clearance in 1954. He and Smith then moved over to the State Department, where Farley was Smith's deputy and successor as the secretary's special assistant for disarmament affairs. Farley wasn't unique in being a profoundly gentle man who devoted his career to the control of genocidal weapons. He eased his life's contradictions by listening to Berlioz operas and playing the piano. Farley and Smith were a well-functioning team: Smith was bred for leading roles, while Farley was comfortable behind the scenes.

Smith was ready to tackle the SALT negotiations and to pursue what Raymond Garthoff characterized as "the single most ambitious undertaking of the détente experiment." Smith was not prepared, however, for dealings with Nixon and Kissinger. He was, in Farley's apt characterization, "a gentleman from the old school." They both were. Smith was a firm believer in bureaucratic process and respectful policy engagement, where the national security advisor fairly presented alternative views for arbitration to the president.[3]

Nixon and Kissinger weren't gentlemen from the old school. They were brass-knuckle masters in the arts of exercising and manipulating power. Although Smith had extraordinary "face time" with Nixon—forty-six meetings—he quickly became suspect as too eager to strike ambitious deals that would have curtailed the Pentagon's programs. When Smith pitched a negotiating proposal for a complete ban on anti-ballistic missile systems, he was taken aback when Nixon cut him off, saying it was "bullshit." He was helpless, as were the other members of his negotiating team, when Kissinger engaged in backchannel negotiations with Soviet ambassador Anatoly Dobrynin. In his memoirs, Smith wrote, "I must say that he had us all buffaloed." The

problem wasn't just that Kissinger offered different proposals than those being advanced by the U.S. negotiating team but also that he seemed to have
carte blanche from Nixon to proceed. To Smith, "it seemed quite clear that
Kissinger was often acting as a principal, not an agent."[4]

This wasn't what Smith signed up for, nor what he was led to expect.
Initially, the Nixon White House reaffirmed ACDA's leading role. Smith was
chosen to be dual-hatted as ACDA director and head of the delegation, dis-
placing the Johnson administration's choice of a highly esteemed Kremlinologist, Ambassador Llewellyn Thompson. Thompson would be the State Department's representative on the team, but his health was failing. Nixon and
Kissinger also signaled confidence in ACDA by selecting a sterling group to
serve on its General Advisory Committee, extending John J. McCloy's tenure
as its chairman and inviting four veterans of the Kennedy-Johnson years—
Foster, Rusk, Douglas Dillon, and Cyrus Vance—to join. Also included were
I.W. Abel of the United Steelworkers Union, William Casey, Peter G. Peter-
son, General Lauris Norstad, and four stalwarts with backgrounds in science—James Killian, Harold Brown, Jack Ruina, and John Wheeler.

The future looked bright for ACDA. Smith mastered his briefs and undertook to learn Russian. No SALT negotiator was ever surrounded by a
stronger team. Nitze, the Pentagon's civilian representative, prided himself
in his mastery of nuclear strategy as well as detail. He used the phrase "the
devil is in the details" so often he could have copyrighted it. Ambassador
"Tommy" Thompson was a superb Kremlinologist and served twice as U.S.
ambassador to Moscow.[5] Lt. General Royal Allison had the confidence of the
Joint Chiefs. A B-25 pilot who flew ninety combat missions during World
War II, he subsequently held key positions overseeing plans and operations
in Europe and in the Pacific. Harold Brown, moonlighting from the California Institute of Technology, was there to help on technical matters. Another
participant, Howard Stoertz, who did his graduate work at Yale University,
where Bernard Brodie and others wrote about *The Absolute Weapon*, was
the Central Intelligence Agency's top expert on Soviet strategic programs.[6]

How serious the Kremlin would be in the upcoming negotiations and
whether the two sides could reach agreement were unknowns. This was the
superpowers' first attempt to stabilize the strategic balance, and there was little reason to expect success and many reasons to expect failure. Concepts of
"strategic stability" were completely abstract and alien to the Kremlin. It was
by no means clear how the Soviet military's goal of winning a nuclear war
could mesh with the Foreign Ministry's diplomatic goal "to end uncertainty

in the accelerating arms race."[7] The two sides did not share a common vocabulary. Methods of developing and reacting to negotiating positions needed to be choreographed. The United States intended to discuss information that was previously withheld by the Soviet military from its diplomats, which sent shivers up the spine of the chief Soviet negotiator, Vladimir Semyonov.

The Kremlin chose Semyonov as lead negotiator in part because of his unfamiliarity with the weapon systems to be discussed. Semyonov and his delegation, before leaving for the negotiations, were instructed by Brezhnev not to divulge state secrets. With the Soviet delegation present, Brezhnev pointedly asked Semyonov his preference: Lubyanka (the KGB prison) or "a place of execution" if he or his colleagues revealed classified information. According to Georgii Korniyenko, a Foreign Ministry delegation member who was present, Brezhnev's reference to prison had a "paralytic effect" on those present. Earlier in his career, Semyonov narrowly avoided being one of Stalin's victims, so he took this warning to heart. In a final parting message, Brezhnev told the delegation not to be in a hurry and to keep him apprised. The Defense Ministry would be the final arbiter of negotiating positions and requirements.[8]

The U.S. negotiating team would carry the load when it came to providing data and initiating proposals, which caused discomfort within the Soviet delegation. After Allison made a presentation on forces in the field, the Soviet military representative, Nicolai Ogarkov, reproached him, saying, "General, I would appreciate it if you wouldn't talk about those things in front of our civilians because they're not cleared for that information."[9] The problem of Soviet secrecy could be circumvented at the outset in this way; over time, the Kremlin accommodated itself to data exchanges and, later, transparency measures and on-site inspections.

Before tackling matters of nuclear offense and defense, the Nixon administration undertook a strategic assessment, led by Deputy Secretary of Defense David Packard. This assessment's top-line conclusions were highlighted in President Nixon's first foreign policy report to the Congress. Nixon announced that vulnerability to Soviet nuclear capabilities was an "unescapable reality." The pursuit of strategic superiority would be both unobtainable and dangerous. Therefore, the strategic goal of the United States could best be described as "sufficiency." If Moscow wished to arrive at strategic arms control reflecting a rough strategic balance, it would have a partner in the Washington.[10]

Nixon was breaking new ground and wasn't being entirely candid. While "sufficiency" would be the watchword for public and Soviet consumption, the Pentagon continued to seek war-winning capabilities in the event deterrence failed. So, too, did the Soviet General Staff. James Cameron has characterized this as a "double game."[11] In actuality, Cameron was undercounting, since other games accompanied the first SALT negotiations. Nonetheless, this was the first time that an American president told his fellow citizens that seeking strategic superiority would be unobtainable and dangerous. The Eisenhower and Kennedy administrations unapologetically sought superiority, and the Limited Test Ban Treaty was sold to the Senate partially on the basis that it would lock in U.S. superiority in advanced warhead designs.

Those who deeply distrusted Soviet ambitions found it hard to swallow the new watchword of sufficiency. Given the quite different nuclear force structures of the United States and the Soviet Union, it would also be hard to judge—and easy to dispute—the sufficiency of agreements reached. The Kremlin had its own questions about whether the United States was ready to settle for sufficiency or would continue to seek superiority under this guise. The feeling was entirely mutual. But at least there was now a public basis for negotiations to proceed.

NEGOTIATIONS BEGIN

The Soviet negotiating team was as accomplished as its U.S. counterpart. Semyonov was a senior deputy foreign minister with a strong background in dealing with Central Europe, especially Germany. Semyonov remained as the principal SALT negotiator through the Carter administration, after which he was replaced by his deputy, Viktor Karpov. Ogarkov represented the Soviet General Staff and Defense Ministry. He was later promoted from colonel general to marshal. Other key figures were Aleksandr Shchukin, a distinguished academician and an urbane man, who helped with technical issues, and Ambassador Georgii Korniyenko, a veteran of the U.S.A. Division of the Soviet Foreign Ministry.

Much preparatory work had already been done for the U.S. team at the tail end of the Johnson administration, but Nixon and Kissinger understandably opted for a fresh look. ACDA was initially given the lead in this process, but Kissinger moved early on to exercise control. In mid-1969 he created a parallel (and quite obviously overriding) process of interagency assessment, which became known as the Verification Panel. The agreements that were eventually reached had no intrusive verification arrangements. They were to be monitored by "national technical means"—satellites and other intelligence-gathering devices—reinforced by provisos not to interfere with intelligence collection from afar.

The easiest place to start a new negotiation was to call for a freeze in new deployments. ACDA continued to favor a "Stop Where We Are" proposal to lock in numerical advantages that it advanced in the Johnson administration. The longer the negotiations took, however, the less advantageous a "freeze" would become, as the Kremlin was building new missile silos and submarines, while the Pentagon was not. Smith received the backing of Secretary of State Rogers for the "Stop Where We Are" concept, but Nixon dismissed it as a propaganda gimmick before accepting it.[12] The most practical place to start negotiations was with the facts on the ground.

Smith also proposed to stop MIRVs, armed with force projections and technical arguments from Benjamin Huberman and Sidney Graybeal at ACDA. U.S. flight testing had already begun in 1968, but Soviet flight tests had not. As on-site inspections were out of the question, a ban on flight testing was the only practical way of stopping MIRV deployments, since they were necessary to confirm proof of concept. Smith again had an ally in Rogers but encountered powerful opposition from the Pentagon against stopping flight tests, just as Warnke and Halperin had in the Johnson administration.

Since a ban on flight tests had support on Capitol Hill, those who wanted MIRVs to be deployed on U.S. missiles adopted an indirect approach, linking a ban to controls that were beyond reach, including strict Soviet radar limits and extensive radar dismantlement, strategic arms reductions, and on-site inspections. Demanding inspections that would reveal sensitive information was sure to be anathema to the Kremlin. It would also be anathema to the Pentagon, but a Soviet veto would relieve the Pentagon of the requirement for inspections.

ACDA was also strongly inclined to limit ballistic missile defenses to the extent possible, drawing strength from rising opposition to nationwide defenses on Capitol Hill. The White House had no fixed position on the question of how many missile defense sites were required. At different times during the negotiations, Kissinger directed the delegation to offer the numbers zero, one, three, and four deployment sites, only to withdraw them later. The number four was an obvious nonstarter; while the United States would be permitted this number, the Kremlin would be limited to one site to defend Moscow.

That there was no clear bottom-line U.S. requirement for strategic defense attested to the weakness of technologies then under consideration and to the strength of domestic opposition. The most comprehensive, coherent, and effective arms control agreement would have banned MIRVs, all but the most modest missile defense deployments, and major upgrades of land-based missiles. There was a clear logic for doing so, since the case for MIRVs rested on the need to penetrate missile defenses and to counter upgrades in Soviet land-based missiles with heavy carrying capacity or throw-weight. Bigger Soviet missiles meant more throw-weight, and more throw-weight would eventually translate into larger warhead numbers. An ambitious proposal to ban MIRVs, limit ABMs, and curtail qualitative missile upgrades would have choked off and stabilized the strategic arms competition.

This package deal was conceptually sound but impossible to negotiate. Washington and Moscow were at square one. They barely trusted each other enough to begin negotiations, let alone pursue far-reaching outcomes. Powerful constituencies in both countries opposed ambitious trade-offs. No agency of government—not even ACDA—made the case for a radical offer dealing with MIRVs, ABMs, and qualitative missile upgrades. Melvin Laird's Pentagon and its supporters on Capitol Hill were dead set against a MIRV ban, since MIRVs were the counter to the Soviet missile launcher buildup and the possibility of a nationwide Soviet ABM system. With controls on MIRVs off the table, and with MIRVs being the only leverage Washington possessed to limit the Soviet missile buildup, significant constraints on offensive forces in SALT were beyond reach.

Missile modernization programs were given a free rein in the Nixon administration. Melvin Laird, not Robert McNamara, ran the Pentagon. As Smith wrote in his memoirs, "A serious effort to ban both MIRVs and ABMs might well make serious trouble for SALT." In Smith's retelling, strict limits on ABMs was all the traffic would bear—"the traffic in this case being the Secretary of Defense, the Joint Chiefs, their supporters in Congress and their constituencies."[13]

Nixon and Kissinger tasked the negotiators and their backstopping team to work up proposals for varied options. Garthoff, the delegation's executive secretary, did much of the drafting. His paper proposed equal aggregate ceilings of 1,710 land- and sea-based missile launchers—reflecting the U.S. force structure. Harking back to the Johnson administration, Garthoff also proposed 1,000 missile defense interceptors per side. This could accommodate the full Safeguard deployment at twelve locations, even though no one believed the full system would be built. The Kremlin had 64 interceptors around Moscow and hundreds more air defense interceptors along the

"Talinn line" that, in the view of the intelligence community with the exception of the U.S. Air Force, were incapable of being upgraded for use against long-range ballistic missiles.

During the first round of negotiations, the U.S. delegation offered "illustrative elements" of an agreement rather than proposals, reflecting the numbers worked up at the end of the Johnson administration. Land- and sea-based missile launchers would be limited to those presently operational, with each side having the freedom to mix. Medium-range ballistic and cruise missiles would be limited to those presently operational, and there would be agreed, unspecified limits on anti-ballistic missile interceptors. The U.S. proposal made no mention of MIRVs.

THE GREAT SENATE ABM AND MIRV DEBATES

The Nixon administration had to deal with three powerful constituencies during the SALT negotiations. One, of course, was the Kremlin. The second constituency was the hawks on Capitol Hill who were foursquare behind the Pentagon's preferences, distrustful of Soviet intentions, and worried that Nixon and Kissinger would not be tough enough in the negotiations. Senator Henry "Scoop" Jackson, tenacious and well informed, led this camp, whose center of gravity was the Armed Services Committee. The third constituency that mattered was strongly opposed to the Nixon administration's plans for ABMs and MIRVs. This camp was clustered in the Senate Foreign Relations Committee and led by Senators J. William Fulbright and Albert Gore, Sr., whose son would also go on to distinguish himself in the Senate on nuclear issues. The lead Republican in this camp was Edward Brooke, an internationalist-minded freshman senator from Massachusetts.

The first great debate between hawks and doves was over ballistic missile defenses in 1969. The second, the following year, was over MIRVs. These debates came at a chaotic and pivotal time. Everyone understood the stakes involved. The Vietnam War intruded regularly in hearings on missile defenses and MIRVs. The Senate was a land of giants in 1969. Fulbright, the chairman of the Foreign Relations Committee, was a larger-than-life figure. He and President Johnson butted against each other over Vietnam like two elephant seals competing for mating rights over U.S. public opinion. Powerful Republican senators like Clifford Case, John Sherman Cooper, and Jacob Javits gravitated toward the Foreign Relations Committee, representing the GOP's commitment to constructive internationalism forged during World War II and the onset of the Cold War.

Southern legislators with long tenures controlled defense matters. Richard Russell had just passed the chairmanship of the Armed Services Committee to John Stennis after his elevation to become chairman of the Appropriations Committee. But the man who set the terms of debate on these matters was Scoop Jackson, a nickname given to him by his sister because of his resemblance to a comic book character. Jackson was the son of Norwegian immigrants. His tenacity and work ethic were evident early on, as he earned every rung on the ladder of career advancement. Defense-minded Democrats as well as conservative Republicans were inclined to follow Jackson's lead. Stuart Symington, the first secretary of the air force before entering politics, was a unique figure, serving on both the Armed Services and Foreign Relations Committees. He was a bellwether of sorts, starting his career as a pro-defense Democrat. Symington was now inclined toward questioning official rationales. The deck for and against the ABM deployments seemed evenly stacked.

Critics of ABMs and MIRVs on Capitol Hill, as with those in ACDA and the State Department, felt the need to prioritize. Tackling everything at once might overload the circuits. Gore, the chairman of the Foreign Relations Subcommittee handling these matters, initially viewed MIRVs as a digression. In his view, one target rather than two improved the chances of a successful blocking action. Gore chose to focus first on the ABM for several reasons. The Johnson administration's rationale—a thin defense against China—made no sense because Beijing was a long way from building missiles with the range to threaten the U.S. homeland. The Nixon administration's change of rationale to defend the land-based missile leg of the U.S. deterrent seemed to invite arms racing. Pentagon funding for the first two sites ABM sites had already been committed; a request for more funding to expand the system was before Congress. The Pentagon's support seemed soft, suggesting the possibility for a successful blocking action.

There was sound logic behind Gore's thinking, and he had the full support of other Foreign Relations Committee heavyweights to fend off the request of Senator Brooke to seek a simultaneous blocking action against MIRVs. ABMs could be challenged as being unworkable in a nuclear environment, whereas there was no doubt about the technical feasibility of MIRVs. There was already a strong public education campaign focused against ABMs. In comparison, public attention on MIRVs was relatively muted.[14]

The crucial debate over nationwide defenses was the first time that congressional hearings and arguments over a strategic weapon system occurred in public and not behind closed doors. Gore invited former presidential science advisors and Pentagon officials to explain their opposition on technical grounds. James Killian, George Kistiakowsky, Hans Bethe, Wolfgang Panovsky, George Rathgens, Jack Ruina, and Herbert York testified. The hearings were a senior seminar for veteran senators that knew their own minds but struggled to grasp technical detail. The witnesses had a rapt audience, eager to learn about penetration aids and blackout effects on radars.[15]

Chairman Fulbright flummoxed the Pentagon's chief technical expert, John S. Foster, by asking him whether "any reputable or well-known scientists . . . not in the employ of or paid by the Government" could support his hopeful assessment of the viability of ballistic missile defense in a nuclear environment. Foster was unable to offer names.[16] Secretary of Defense Laird and his deputy, David Packard, did not offer technical rebuttals. Instead, they rested their case on other grounds. Funding for an ABM system would, in Laird's view, offer the Kremlin "added incentive for productive arms control talks," and besides, the Kremlin had already put in place a defense of its capital area.

Laird was a veteran of Capitol Hill—"the Richelieu of the cheese belt"–and an expert on how to leverage members of Congress to get what he wanted.[17] Packard was a titan of Silicon Valley before there was a Silicon Valley, the co-founder of Hewlett-Packard and, like many others of his generation, inclined toward taking time off from business pursuits or lawyering to pursue public service. Packard reinforced Laird's arguments, also highlighting the need for Safeguard as a "hedge against the failure of arms control."[18] For good measure, Packard argued that he did "not see that it would make any significant difference" between a MIRVed and an un-MIRVed world.[19]

Gerard Smith was in a tight spot. As the lead witness, he had yet to receive his first paycheck as ACDA director. The Nixon administration had not settled on its negotiating position when he was called to testify. A staunch opponent of ABM deployments in internal deliberations, Smith walked this tightrope by offering his personal view that a limited system would not spoil negotiations, whereas proceeding with a thick nationwide system would.[20]

Two technical difficulties seemed insuperable and not subject to effective rebuttal. One was discerning real warheads from dummies and other confusion generated by penetration aids. The other was radar blackout, either due to the detonations by incoming warheads or by nuclear-armed interceptor missiles. Without radars able to track incoming warheads and guide interceptors, the system would quickly fail catastrophically.

On top of this, there was a public backlash against proposed missile defense sites near ten cities, including Seattle, Boston, and Chicago. City dwellers, in particular, were not keen on being protected by nuclear-armed interceptor missiles. New data on cancer incidence rates from atmospheric testing in the 1950s and early 1960s were becoming available, projecting increased mortality rates. Notable first-person accounts reinforced public apprehension. One telling example was the case of Patrick Stout, the military driver of the Manhattan Project's leader, General Leslie Groves. On a trip for the press to the Alamogordo test site in New Mexico where the proof of principle for the bomb design that destroyed Nagasaki occurred, Groves asked Stout to stand where the fireball turned the desert sand into an eerie greenish glass in order to demonstrate how safe the site was. Stout did so for thirty minutes, smiling and waving for the reporters and photographers. Twenty-two years later, on the eve of the ABM debate, he was diagnosed with leukemia. Stout died in 1969.[21]

The debate on Capitol Hill was reflected in the public square. Former deputy secretary of defense Roswell Gilpatric and former UN ambassador Arthur Goldberg created Citizens Concerned About the ABM, an advocacy group to stop deployments. Paul Nitze, Dean Acheson, and Albert Wohlstetter countered with the Committee to Maintain a Prudent Defense Policy, staffed by two of Wohlstetter's talented students, Paul Wolfowitz and Richard Perle. Perle remembered with fondness Wohlstetter's willingness to take on multiple opponents at once and to do so almost with "a good-natured glee."[22] William Casey bankrolled another advocacy group supporting ABM deployments, the Citizens Committee for Peace and Security. Hastily compiled compendiums of arguments for and against the ABM appeared in print.[23] Technical and policy-oriented journals weighed in. Dennis Flanagan, the editor of *Scientific American*, published no less than five technical and analytical assessments to help inform the congressional debate.[24] *Foreign Affairs* published pro and con essays by Donald Brennan and McGeorge Bundy.[25]

Paul Warnke argued that defense in the nuclear age was a futile endeavor. "We cannot now, with any amount of money, buy physical safety from a Soviet attack of indescribable devastation," he warned. "But the real pressures for a ballistic-missile defense—and perhaps even its lulling designation as the 'Safeguard' system—derive from our unwillingness to accept emotionally what we have every factual reason to comprehend."[26] Edward Teller countered: "In not more than five years the [Kremlin] may have the ability to wipe out our retaliatory forces with a sudden 'first strike.' Missile defense would at least cast a doubt into the minds of Communist planners. If they cannot be certain of success they probably will not attack."[27] To offset the Foreign Relations Committee's parade of witnesses, the Senate Armed Services Committee enlisted testimony from proponents of ABM deployments, including Paul Nitze and Wohlstetter.[28]

On August 6, 1969, the roll was called. Everyone knew that the vote on ABM funding for additional deployments would be close, so Vice President Spiro Agnew was on hand if the need arose to break a tie. Most Democrats were opposed to ABM funding, but twenty-one joined Senator Jackson in breaking ranks to support it. Most Republicans voted in favor of ABM funding, but fourteen defected, including the amendment's lead sponsor, Senator Margaret Chase Smith. Agnew's vote was indeed needed to break the fifty–fifty tie. The ABM program survived, but it was a Pyrrhic victory. After this vote, there was no way that a nationwide defense, let alone a four-site defense of land-based missiles that Nixon and Jackson wanted, was going to happen, regardless of its rationale.

AN EMPTY CONSENSUS ON MIRVS

The decisive MIRV debate took place early in 1970. The first public inkling that multiple warheads were in the offing came three years earlier in a *New York Times* report.[29] Another *New York Times* story in early 1967 introduced the acronym MIRV.[30] Even with these press accounts, MIRVs weren't center stage, as public and congressional attention was focused on ABMs. This changed when Secretary of the Air Force Robert Seamans let slip that MIRV deployments could begin as soon as the summer of 1970.

The Foreign Relations Committee, again under the lead of Senator Albert Gore, Sr., then hurriedly scheduled hearings in March 1970, with Senator Edward Brooke as the lead witness. Gore's preferred sequential approach to dealing first with ABMs and then MIRVs was foiled by the speed with which the Pentagon was proceeding. Meanwhile, Brooke and his key legislative assistant, Alton Frye, had signed up forty-three senators to a resolution calling for a mutual suspension of MIRV flight tests and deployments, "subject to national verification." Brooke and his allies knew that after adequate flight-testing, the prohibition of MIRV deployments could only be monitored with close-up inspections that neither side would agree to. The only chance of stopping MIRVs lay in prohibiting further flight-testing, a prohibition that could be monitored by remote means.

The campaign to stop MIRVs was a steep uphill battle in 1970, as the U.S. flight-testing program was already well advanced when Seaman's announcement lent urgency to the proceedings. The Soviet Union had also begun to flight-test multiple warheads atop a single missile, but these early tests, beginning in 1968, were of unguided warheads, or MRVs. The Pentagon, which enjoyed a projected five-year lead, was speeding ahead with warheads that could be independently targeted. Pentagon officials, led by Secretary Laird, conflated MRVs and MIRVs. Laird professed disinterest in "semantics," testifying that "the Soviets are going forward with multiple warheads, and so are we." This was a shrewd argument, undercutting the efforts of advocates to pause MIRV flight testing.[31]

The Nixon administration's response to the Brooke resolution was conveyed by John S. Foster, director of defense research and engineering. Foster testified that the Pentagon had "no intrinsic objection" to a MIRV flight-test moratorium, "provided that appropriate collateral provisions" were in place. Since MIRVs were designed to counter missile defenses and the possibility that Soviet air defenses might be upgraded, he argued that both kinds of defenses would need to be constrained and that those constraints must be verified by on-site inspections.

Foster also testified that the Pentagon "was unable to determine any reliable method, using national means only, for verifying with certainty Soviet adherence to a ban" on MIRV tests. This assertion was questionable but required technical expertise to deconstruct that was well beyond the reach of skeptical senators. Foster also made the valid point that the multimegaton yields of Soviet warheads compensated for inaccuracy. Additionally, Foster distinguished between the lethality of Soviet and U.S. MIRVs. He warned that Soviet high-yield warheads would be silo killers, while U.S. MIRVed warheads did not then have yields and accuracies sufficient to kill Soviet missiles in silos. The Soviet program would therefore be ideal for nuclear war fighting, in Foster's view, while the U.S. program would be defensive in nature and not first-strike weapons.[32]

Foster's contention that Soviet MIRVs would be silo killers while U.S. MIRVs would not have this lethality was soon overtaken by events, with easily predictable increases in U.S. missile accuracy. All this was unpacked with a parade of technical experts. Herbert York (soon to be added to President Nixon's enemies list) and Wolfgang Panovsky again provided seminars, and were joined by Sidney Drell, Marvin Goldberger, Donald Hornig, George Kistiakowsky, Herbert Scoville, and Jerome Wiesner. Also weighing in were

McGeorge Bundy and Adrian Fisher. Bundy asked senators to recall arguments used to oppose the Limited Test Ban Treaty that now resided in "the dustbin of dead fantasy"—for example, that the Soviets could test secretly behind the moon—and to reject short-sighted arguments against a MIRV fight-test ban.[33] The strongest rejoinder was offered by Secretary of Defense Laird, who provided sobering testimony about the pace of the Soviet missile buildup, its throw-weight advantages, the impending vulnerability of U.S. land-based missiles, and the dangers invited by unreciprocated restraint. Laird also made the case for providing U.S. negotiators with leverage.

Brooke and Gore could clearly generate a high number in support of their initiative. They weren't asking the Senate to deny the Pentagon funding for MIRV research and development; their intention was more modest—to refrain from actions that were injurious to negotiating a restraint regime. As amended by Republican senators Jacob Javits and John Sherman Cooper, the language of the Brooke resolution was broadened to encompass ABMs as well as MIRVs in the proposed moratorium. Finally, in April 1970, with two ABM sites under construction and two months before the deployment of MIRVs, the Senate embraced a more comprehensive approach.

It was too late. Senators were attuned to the argument by Laird and Senator Jackson that they ought not to tie the hands of U.S. negotiators. Jackson opposed any action on Capitol Hill "whose effect would seriously disrupt both our efforts to negotiate a SALT agreement and important programs to maintain the credibility of our deterrent."[34] The Brooke resolution didn't do this, however, because it was nonbinding. Even Jackson could vote for it. The resolution passed on March 20, 1970, by a vote of 72 to 6. It was a "free" vote that expressed concerns and aspirations without blocking deployments then in train.

Brooke hoped that strength in numbers would induce caution by the administration. He was greatly disappointed. The day after the Senate voted, Nixon was asked for his reaction at a news conference. He responded with unusual frankness: "I think the Resolution is irrelevant to what we are going to do."[35] Senator Brooke's persistence did, however, elicit a pledge from the Nixon White House that "there is no current U.S. program to develop a so-called 'hard-target' MIRV capability," and that "we have not developed, and are not seeking to develop a weapon system having, or which could reasonably be construed as having, a first strike potential."[36] These promissory notes were recalled in early 1974 when Secretary of Defense James Schlesinger announced such plans.

The Senate voted again on ABMs in 1970, but this time opponents lost ground, gaining fewer than fifty votes, in part because SALT negotiator Gerard Smith transmitted a letter asking members of Congress not to weaken his hand in the negotiations. The Senate Foreign Relations Committee continued to hold hearings on MIRVs with presidential frontrunner Edmund Muskie now leading the charge. Muskie questioned whether "arming to parlay" was a sound approach, as this "might threaten the progress of the SALT talks." Warnke, the most fearless witness, argued that "we can afford to exercise greater restraint and . . . in fact, we cannot afford not to."[37] By then, however, MIRV deployments had already begun.

The toothless consensus behind the 1970 Brooke resolution hid the reality that prospects on Capitol Hill for blocking MIRV flight tests and deployments were slim before vanishing completely with emerging Soviet ballistic missile capabilities. Nixon and Kissinger were determined to let MIRVs run free and Brooke didn't have the votes to stop funding. Once MIRVs were deployed, it was but a short distance to providing them with accuracies required for "prompt hard-target-kill" capabilities. Superior U.S. missile accuracy was the counter to superior Soviet missile throw-weight. Schlesinger, Laird's successor in the Pentagon, was primed to lead this charge.

The great Senate debates over ABMs and MIRVs proceeded in full view of the Kremlin. As for ABMs, proselytizing by McNamara, U.S. participants at Pugwash meetings, and arms controllers had their intended effect. The Kremlin supported strict limits, not wanting to compete on missile defense technologies. The Soviet SALT delegation proposed three alternatives—a complete ban, very limited deployments, or a defense of a single area within national territories. The Soviet leadership was eager to proceed with an ABM treaty first and willing to deal with restraints on offenses later. Nixon and Kissinger refused. There was sound logic to agree to both, but at the same time.

Beside differences over ABMs, the initial Soviet negotiating position also proposed including bombers—an area of distinct U.S. advantage—while resisting limits on medium and intermediate-range missiles between 1,000 and 5,500 kilometers in range. The Kremlin also wanted limits on "forward-based systems"—perhaps 850 aircraft on carriers or based in Europe and Asia capable of reaching targets in the Soviet Union, plus British and French ballistic missile-carrying submarines. The Kremlin succeeded only in excluding missiles of less-than-ocean-spanning range.

The Nixon administration got what it wanted on MIRVs, a decision that came back to haunt Ford and Carter when they tried to cap the strategic competition. The passage of time wasn't working in favor of a U.S. negotiating stance predicated on a freeze on missile deployments. The United States had stopped constructing new land- and sea-based missile launchers in 1967, when the notion of a freeze was first conceived. The Kremlin rushed to catch up to and to exceed U.S. numbers. Between 1967 and 1970, the Soviet Union adding between 250 and 300 missile launchers per year. Even after pressing ahead of U.S. missile launcher totals, the Kremlin kept building during the Strategic Arms Limitation Talks, but at a slower pace, adding a total of eighty more. Most of these missiles would eventually be MIRVed. MIRVs started out by being linked to prospective Soviet missile defense deployments. As Herbert York argued, "ABM and MIRV are . . . inseparable; each one requires and inspires the other."[38] Moscow changed its mind on ABMs but gave Washington another rationale for MIRVs.

There were many "what ifs" associated with the decision to let MIRVs run free. The world would have been a safer place had MIRVs not been flight-tested and deployed, but it is hard to see how Nixon and Kissinger could have chosen differently. A grand bargain on MIRVs, missile defenses, and missile upgrades wasn't politically feasible. No agency, not even ACDA, was willing to advocate putting all these chips on the table. At the very outset of negotiations, in the midst of technological advances in strategic offenses, radical solutions were out of bounds to the Pentagon, on Capitol Hill, and in Moscow. Senator Gore didn't help matters by resisting a comprehensive approach with time running out in 1969, thinking it was best to stop ABMs first, a prospect that he believed "might be adversely affected by the injection of the MIRV issue."[39] Even if Gore had tackled ABMs and MIRVs at the same time, he would have faced fierce resistance. The technologies behind MIRVs were in hand, and the Kremlin was modernizing its land-based missiles in ways that suggested a commitment to war-fighting strategies. Even had Johnson managed to start negotiations in 1968, he would have been no less averse than Nixon to a package deal halting ABM, MIRV, and missile modernization programs. Nixon and Kissinger played the hand they were dealt cautiously and reluctantly. The result was both historic and deeply flawed.[40]

NEGOTIATING OUTCOMES

The SALT I negotiations produced in 1972 the Anti-Ballistic Missile Treaty and an "Interim Agreement" on strategic offenses. The ABM Treaty codified equal numbers and effective constraints on national missile defenses. Both superpowers accepted strict limits on missile defense interceptors at two sites each, one for the national capital area and another to defend missile silos in a circumscribed area. Given the large numbers of offensive missiles and warheads permitted by the Interim Agreement, the ABM Treaty confirmed mutual vulnerability. Washington and Moscow arrived at this outcome circuitously, after the U.S. delegation previously suggested four other choices for missile defense deployments and then withdrew all of them.[41]

The Interim Agreement affirmed realities on the ground. Those realities resulted in unequal numbers and ineffective limitations. The United States could have no more than 656 launchers on nuclear-powered submarines, whereas the Soviet Union could have 740 launchers on nuclear-powered submarines. The numbers were similarly lopsided with respect to land-based missiles, reflecting continuing Soviet missile launcher construction before and during the negotiations. At the date of signing, the United States possessed 1,054 operational land-based ICBMs, with none under construction. The Soviet numbers weren't completely clear; the U.S. State Department's official release on the Interim Agreement tellingly offered an "estimated" number of 1,618 ICBMs operational and under construction—a lack of precision that was duly noted by critics of the agreement.

Washington and Moscow reached agreement by not constraining their areas of advantage. For the United States, this meant letting MIRVs run free and not counting bombers and forward-based systems. For the Soviet Union, this meant excluding missiles of less-than-ocean-spanning range and resisting tight constraints on the dimensions of their missile upgrades. No one argued strenuously for constraints on cruise missiles, about which the Kremlin would soon have second thoughts.

Neither Washington nor Moscow thought the limits reached on offensive forces treaty-worthy. Instead, the five-year Interim Agreement was to be supplanted by more ambitious constraints in the not-too-distant future. The Kremlin viewed the Interim Agreement's lopsided numbers as "major concessions" by the United States.[42] Washington could, however, take comfort in what the Interim Agreement didn't limit, including the U.S. lead in missile guidance technology, a five-year head start in MIRVs, superior U.S. antisubmarine warfare capabilities, and bombers that were also excluded.

Reaching these numbers was complicated by Kissinger's penchant for negotiating in the backchannel with Soviet ambassador Dobrynin. The U.S. SALT delegation learned to its consternation that Kissinger expressed his indifference to Dobrynin in the backchannel as to whether submarines and their launchers would be covered under the limitations. Eventually, the U.S. side clawed back their inclusion, but at the cost of accepting unequal numerical constraints, reflecting the rush of new Soviet submarine construction.

The U.S. SALT delegation was unable to nail down strict constraints on permissible upgrades for replacement Soviet missiles. The best formulation they could elicit from their Soviet counterparts was a pledge not to "increase substantially" silo dimensions, with an agreed interpretation that "substantial" meant increases of 10 to 15 percent. Left unclear was whether this applied to one dimension—depth or diameter—or both, in which case upgrades correlated to an increase in throw-weight of over 30 percent. The Soviet delegation refused to be tied down because machine tooling for new missiles was already underway. The Kremlin's negotiators were not permitted to override the blueprints from which missile design bureaus were operating.

Failing to secure tight limitations, the Nixon administration resorted to a unilateral statement offering its restrictive view of permissible upgrades, adding, "The United States proceeds on the premise that the Soviet side will give due account to this consideration." The Soviet Union proceeded to build new missiles then in its pipeline, all of which disregarded the U.S. "premise" that could not be won at the negotiating table. This fine print later turned into a heated controversy over Soviet "cheating."

MIRVs ran free, bedeviling the next rounds of SALT negotiations. Washington wasn't going to negotiate away an advantage, while Moscow wasn't going to negotiate from weakness. William G. Hyland, Kissinger's closest associate in the negotiations, readily acknowledged that this ensured an intensified arms competition—"a truly fateful decision that changed strategic relations, and changed them to the detriment of American security." Nonetheless, he believed that trying to ban MIRVs at the outset of negotiations would have been a "weak move," as well as provoking a bloody fight with the Pentagon and in Congress.[43]

Gerard Smith thought a MIRV ban was worth the effort, and that letting MIRVs run free would weaken U.S. national security. But he acknowledged that it was by no means clear that the Soviet Union would accept a ban on MIRV flight testing and deployment even had the U.S. delegation been authorized to offer this without disabling conditions. After all, U.S. flight tests had already provided proof of feasibility and effectiveness. By not offering up MIRVs, Smith had no leverage to stop Soviet missile modernization programs in their tracks. As he later reflected, a MIRV-less world would have been a safer world, but while this "may have been an opportunity missed, it was not a clear one."[44]

When President Ford, with Kissinger's help, later negotiated a framework for capping the arms competition at Vladivostok in 1974, the consequences of letting MIRVs run free became painfully evident. The Vladivostok Accord permitted no less that 1,320 launchers carrying MIRVs, reflecting U.S. plans. Kissinger fleetingly offered that, "in retrospect, I wish I had thought through the implications of a MIRVed world more thoughtfully in 1969 and 1970 than I did."[45] Kissinger subsequently retracted this disingenuous remark. Both he and Nixon foresaw the pernicious effects of MIRVs and increased missile accuracy on the arms competition, weighed the domestic and international consequences of foregoing MIRVs, and chose to rely on U.S. technological prowess rather than on sharply curtailing strategic arms against the Pentagon's wishes. Nixon's memoir offered this thin veneer: "I believed that the only effective way to achieve nuclear arms reduction was to confront the Soviets with an unacceptable alternative in the form of increased American armaments and the determination to use them."[46]

In a *Time* magazine essay published on March 21, 1983, Kissinger claimed that "the Soviets ignored our hints to open the subject of a MIRV ban in the SALT talks."[47] This, too, was disingenuous. Why hint about a topic so central to strategic stability? The memoirs of Ambassador Dobrynin, Kissinger's counterpart in the backchannel, offered a more straightforward account: "The Americans did not exert themselves to discuss MIRVs during the SALT talks and definitely were not eager to ban them." Thus, allowing MIRVs to run free was "rather skillfully hidden under the cover of a condition which the Nixon administration (and Kissinger especially) knew Moscow could not accept: a link between a ban on MIRVed missiles and on-site inspections to verify the ban."[48] Actually, the conditions the Nixon administration required for a MIRV ban were far more onerous. They included on-site inspections of surface-to-air missile deployments, constraints on their upgrade, and the dismantling of early warning radars. Another reason for the Soviet rejection of the Nixon administration's nonserious offer was that Washington's proposed ban was on flight testing but not production.

Moscow's counterproposal was equally disingenuous, proposing a ban on MIRV production and deployment—without on-site inspections necessary to verify these controls—while permitting flight testing, so as to catch up to the United States. Garthoff notes in the first volume of his magisterial history of détente that his Soviet negotiating counterpart confided in him that "we had been hoping you would make a serious MIRV proposal."[49] This was not to be. As Smith wrote in his memoirs, the U.S. and Soviet proposals were an ingenious and disingenuous mismatch. Nixon and Kissinger recognized the downside risks of letting MIRVs run free, but they weren't about to eliminate the main U.S. counter to the Soviet buildup. The U.S. proposal did succeed in one sense: it held arms controllers on Capitol Hill in abeyance. Kissinger could tell them that the Nixon administration had raised the subject of a MIRV ban at SALT, but that no solution could be found.[50]

NIXON AND KISSINGER'S BALANCE SHEET

Nixon and Kissinger were a compelling team whose considerable powers of intellect and will produced a deeply flawed result in the Interim Agreement, while removing one impetus for arms racing in the ABM Treaty. The flaws in the Interim Agreement were so great, however, that continued arms racing was unavoidable, even with the ABM Treaty. Moscow protected the modernization of its land-based missiles and Washington protected its counter—MIRVs. Nixon and Brezhnev were not about to alienate their military-industrial complexes or their most hard-nosed allies. The best arms control outcome would have been tight controls on ABMs and a trade-off between MIRVs and significant constraints on Soviet missile upgrades, but this wasn't in the cards.

Nixon and Kissinger viewed themselves as geopolitical strategists of the highest rank, not bean counters. Their initial interest in SALT lay less in the negotiating outcome than in the possibility of using the talks to leverage the Kremlin's help on Vietnam, the Middle East, and elsewhere. The name given to this diplomatic practice was "linkage." The Kremlin similarly believed that linkage might be possible during the SALT negotiations, but quickly realized otherwise.[51]

Nixon and Kissinger were tripped up by their concepts of détente and linkage, the initial linchpins of their negotiating strategy. Détente proved to be a weak foundation for strategic arms control because the concept was conceived as one-sided. Instead, gaining something of value required trade-offs. Moscow, like Washington, made decisions based on perceived national security interests. The Politburo could negotiate SALT while the Pentagon was mining Haiphong Harbor. It could also negotiate while challenging Washington's interests in the Middle East.

The notion that linkage was a one-way street was pure hubris; Moscow as well as Washington would seek preferred outcomes elsewhere while seeking limits on each other's strategic arms. It remains a mystery why Nixon and Kissinger, supreme realists, harbored the fantasy that linkage could affect changes in Moscow's calculations. When the shoe was on the other foot—when Moscow behaved in unwelcome fashion, whether during the 1973 Middle East war or in seeking footholds in states in postcolonial tumult—prospects for arms control suffered.

Nixon also entertained the possibility of deriving leverage from a "madman" theory of deterrence and bargaining, especially in a crisis. In *The Real War*, Nixon explained, "International relations are a lot like poker—stud poker with a hole card." He wrote that "our only covered card is the will, nerve, and unpredictability of the President—his ability to make the enemy think twice about raising the ante." Nixon's takeaway: "If the adversary feels you are unpredictable, even rash, he will be deterred from pressing you too far."[52]

In practice, the madman role is played better by weak leaders who depend on unpredictability backed up by weapons of mass destruction to hold off stronger foes. Countries that have much to lose have had less leeway to gain leverage from nuclear threats that leave something to chance.[53] Madman diplomacy was for crises, not SALT.[54] And even in crises, madman diplomacy didn't work for Nixon and Kissinger. They were, and were seen to be, hard-nosed realists rather than supreme risk takers. They were entirely capable of taking chances, but not foolhardy ones involving nuclear weapons.

Nixon and Kissinger did poorly in negotiating restraints on strategic offensive forces because the Kremlin held a better hand. The Soviet Union had more active production lines for missiles and submarines. In contrast, U.S. modernization programs were either on the drawing boards or just entering production—a time-phasing problem that bedeviled subsequent negotiations. Ballistic missile defenses were the Nixon/Kissinger hole card, because concern over advanced U.S. technologies resided deep in the Kremlin's DNA. But the White House was stymied on this front, as well, because of congressional and public opposition to national missile defense deployments. Besides, technical problems were insurmountable in the 1970s, even against rudimentary offenses. The Pentagon didn't have enough money for missile defenses as well as strategic modernization programs. When left to choose, sound military judgment opted for more offense rather than a deeply suspect defense.

Nixon and Kissinger generated criticism on both flanks. Arms controllers were deeply uneasy about MIRVs and new strategic modernization programs. Deterrence strategists were unhappy with how cavalier Nixon and

Kissinger were about fine print and about how they rushed to conclude the SALT accords in the run-up to the 1972 presidential election. Their inattention to detail left heavyweight strategic analysts like Paul Nitze seething. Nitze not only took pride in his grasp of big-picture issues, but he waded into detail with the avidness of a fly fisherman wetting a line in a pristine stretch of water. He was, after all, a member of the Strategic Bombing Survey that placed "calipers on the rubble."[55]

The last unresolved issues at the Moscow summit were technical in nature. Kissinger and Nixon tried to nail down details while their negotiators were cooling their heels in Helsinki. Kissinger sent messages back to Smith for his views, while asking him not to share information with the rest of his team. The "Moscow White House" didn't want last-minute complications or resistance; Nixon and Kissinger wanted a signing ceremony before leaving for home. They engaged in the cardinal sin of negotiating against a self-imposed deadline.

Within two years, the handiwork of Nixon and Kissinger generated a harsh backlash against SALT. The numerical advantages accorded to Moscow in the Interim Agreement rankled, and Soviet missile modernization programs made matters worse. Administrations face a clear choice when presenting arms control agreements to Capitol Hill. They can undersell or oversell. Making tall claims can come back to haunt—usually a succeeding administration—but they can help secure the two-thirds majority required for the Senate's consent to treaties under the Constitution. The ABM Treaty and the Interim Agreement were too important to undersell. The administration's oversell prompted a backlash against SALT when Ford and Carter sought to set ceilings on the resulting competition.

Nixon returned directly from Moscow to Capitol Hill to address a joint session of Congress, where he claimed, "It is clear that the agreements forestall a major spiraling of the arms race—one which would have worked to our disadvantage."[56] Kissinger generously overpromised, as well. In his briefing to members of Congress sixteen days after the Moscow Summit, he declared, "By setting a limit to ABM defenses the treaty not only eliminates one area of potentially dangerous competition, but it reduces the incentive for continuing deployment of offensive systems."[57] Secretary of State Rogers hailed the accords as a break in the action-reaction phenomenon, when in actuality the Interim Agreement ensured more of it. Secretary of Defense Laird went further, declaring that the Interim Agreement "stops the momentum of the Soviet Union in the strategic offensive weapon area."[58]

These claims had little connection to reality, given that MIRVs ran free and the constraints on Soviet missile modernization were loosely drawn. Even with the ABM Treaty, another cycle of arms racing was clearly in the offing, requiring generous funding from the Congress. Leonid Brezhnev told Nixon that he would do the same—a not-so-veiled reference that the constraints U.S. negotiators wished to impose on new Soviet ICBMs were not going to happen. Nixon conveyed Brezhnev's message to Congress, along with the proviso that to succeed at stabilization, his arms control accords required serious down payments on new missiles, submarines, and bombers.

Kissinger judged the outcome of the 1972 SALT accords a success, partly because "as long as [the ABM Treaty] lasts, offensive missile forces have, in effect, a free ride to their targets. Beyond a certain level of sufficiency, differences in numbers are therefore not conclusive."[59] The Soviet missile buildup steadily undercut his case and called into question the Nixon administration's premises that SALT and sufficiency would be stabilizing, and that the Kremlin was on the same page.

One intense critic of the Interim Agreement, William Van Cleave, argued that attempts at "joint strategic planning" were "chimerical" and bound to fail. In his view, nothing less than deep cuts in Soviet land-based missiles and throw-weight were needed.[60] Edward Teller, who opposed Kennedy's Limited Test Ban Treaty, was kinder to Nixon, expressing lukewarm support for the Interim Agreement, "even though . . . [it] puts us at a disadvantage." His reasoning was that it was "the best bargain we can strike under these circumstances."[61]

Senator Jackson's primary complaint was over permissible allowances for Soviet missile upgrades. The bigger the missiles, the more throw-weight they could carry, and throw-weight conveyed more warheads packing more powerful destructive capacity. The U.S. delegation was not in a good position to constrain Soviet upgrades partly because, early on, Kissinger blithely assured Dobrynin in backchannel talks that no limitations on modernization were necessary.[62] This, too, needed to be clawed back as much as possible, but the art of the possible depended on the blueprints of Soviet design bureaus. The Soviet General Staff was seeking advantage and avoiding disadvantage no less than the Pentagon.

In his initial negotiating instructions to the SALT delegation, Nixon wrote, "I am determined to avoid, within the Government and in the country at large, divisive disputes regarding Soviet compliance or non-compliance with an understanding or agreement. Nor will I bequeath to a future President the seeds of such disputes."[63] The Nixon White House did exactly this by misrepresenting missile upgrade provisions while seeking to leverage Soviet behavior by means of a feckless unilateral statement, conveyed to the Congress.[64] The Nixon administration's representations to Congress to finesse this issue were "a complete fraud" in the view of Thomas Graham, Jr., one of ACDA's lawyers during the SALT I negotiations.[65]

The resentments of SALT skeptics were compounded by the hurried negotiation in Moscow to secure agreements in time for Nixon's reelection bid. Nixon and Kissinger not only negotiated against a self-imposed deadline at a summit meeting, but also were without technical expertise at their side and without American translators. There was ample, earlier evidence of the Nixon White House's wariness of leaks and suspicions of the bureaucracy, beginning with creation of the Verification Panel and Kissinger's backchannel. Nixon also proposed that Nitze, the secretary of defense's representative at SALT, report through a backchannel via a special mechanism that the Joint Chiefs of Staff could provide. The reason for doing so, Nixon explained, was that Gerard Smith needed careful oversight that Secretary Rogers was not capable of providing. Nitze declined, but Smith remained wary of end runs from his own delegation, once issuing a warning to Nitze in this regard.[66] Nixon and Kissinger subjected selected administration officials with worse indignities and illegalities, including phone taps in search of leakers to the press.[67]

These machinations perfectly suited Nixon's obsessions and Kissinger's penchant for control, but at a cost, since the backchannel to Dobrynin and the resulting dual-track negotiations fostered confusion among U.S. negotiators and strengthened the Kremlin's hand. Both Nixon and Kissinger excelled at high strategy; the backchannel immersed them in obscure details about construction, numbers, and dimensions of missiles to be limited. In Moscow, Nixon and Kissinger relied on a Russian interpreter—a practice that wasn't invented by Donald Trump—while keeping the U.S. negotiating team at arm's length. Kissinger had the self-assurance to try to pull this off. "It was," as Gerard Smith subsequently wrote in his account of the negotiations, "a one man stand, a presidential aide against the resources of the Soviet leadership."[68]

Secretary of Defense Laird told Smith that he had been "shafted" by Kissinger.[69] Smith wasn't alone: also unaware of Kissinger's maneuvering were Laird himself, Secretary of State Rogers, and Admiral Thomas Moorer, the chairman of the Joint Chiefs. Only later did the negotiators and cabinet members realize that Kissinger had agreed to loosen provisions they sought to tighten. "This rather contemptuous treatment of high administration officials was," as Glenn Seaborg, the chairman of the Atomic Energy Commission noted, "a hallmark of the Nixon-Kissinger way of doing business."[70]

After recording this litany of complaint, we are obliged to ask whether it would have made an appreciable difference if Nixon and Kissinger had not been so conspiratorial and if they had managed the bureaucracy and the U.S. SALT delegation properly. Probably not. An appreciably better outcome could only have come by means of trade-offs that neither man was in the least bit inclined to pursue. Even so, the irregular way in which the Interim Agreement and ABM Treaty were negotiated had punishing aftereffects. Nixon and Kissinger accentuated grievances about a process that was deeply suspect before it even began. SALT's severest critics thought it was unnatural to reach agreements with a geopolitical and ideological foe to control "war-winning" weapons. For some, any agreements reached had to be disadvantageous—otherwise, why would the Kremlin agree to them? Any agreement would, in this view, be provisional, until it no longer suited the Kremlin and was violated. Nikita Khrushchev once bragged that the Soviet Union would "bury" the United States. From the perspective of SALT's most trenchant critics, U.S. negotiators were handing the Kremlin the shovels to do so. In this view, the fine print that Nixon and Kissinger treated cavalierly mattered greatly.

Arms controllers were also deeply unhappy with the Interim Agreement. Warnke offered lukewarm support, while testifying that the missile numbers game was "a mindless exercise." Secretary Laird's "triple play for peace"— linking strategic modernization programs to congressional acceptance of the ABM Treaty and Interim Agreement—especially rankled. Laird dispensed with the sugarcoating before the hawkish Senate Armed Services Committee, testifying that "peace cannot be bought cheaply."[71] Fulbright warned about the "danger of having our actions belie our words."[72] The Interim Agreement's allowances for MIRVs and its lax provisions for missile upgrades provided perverse incentives, as William Perry later observed, to build up in order to avoid being left behind.[73]

The two most powerfully aggrieved figures by the behavior of Nixon and Kissinger—Paul Nitze and Senator Jackson—became SALT's severest critics. Nitze had issues with Kissinger's grasp of the subject matter dating back to a Council on Foreign Relations study group in which they both participated, prompting Nitze to write a cutting review of the book Kissinger wrote from this effort, *Nuclear Weapons and Foreign Policy*.[74] Nitze's preferred negotiating proposal to reduce land-based missiles on both sides, especially Soviet missiles carrying the most throw-weight, was only briefly considered before Nixon and Kissinger moved on to more negotiable formulas. Nitze and everyone else helping with the negotiations suspected what would become clear later with the release of a thousand pages of memoranda, meeting notes, and transcripts of conversations about SALT. These documents revealed Nixon as someone with only glancing familiarity with the hardware involved and a weak grasp of detail. They also confirmed that Nixon delegated great authority to Kissinger, who also focused more on the big picture than on details.[75]

Kissinger was a stern gatekeeper who repeatedly fed Nixon's vanity, grievances, and paranoia. Nixon didn't question Kissinger's narrative of events. A glaring example of Nixon's insularity and Kissinger's stroking methods occurred on April 23, 1971, when the national security advisor met with the president and his chief of staff H.R. Haldeman to get them up to speed on the SALT negotiations. Kissinger buoyed Nixon with his assessment that the Soviets, "to all practical purposes, [have] given in on this SALT thing . . . they have yielded 98 percent. They've practically accepted our position on the SALT." Sharp critics believed that the opposite to be true.[76]

The Kremlin didn't feel the victory that domestic critics of SALT in the United States were ready to confer. The Soviet Union did confirm advantages, especially with regard to missile numbers and throw-weight, but rightly worried that the Pentagon was seeking war-fighting advantages, as well. SALT supporters tried to rebut worst-case thinking, arguing that the assured destruction codified in the ABM Treaty made relative differentials in missile size and throw-weight irrelevant, but the high ground in this domestic debate was won by those sounding the tocsin, not muffling its sound.

Despite the ABM Treaty, the terms of the Interim Agreement ensured an intensified competition. The Pentagon was intent on modernizing all three legs of the Triad—land-based missiles, bombers, and missile-carrying submarines—while pursuing MIRVs and belatedly grasping the utility of cruise missiles. The Soviet General Staff was also off to the races. Dobrynin, the most seasoned and attuned go-between during the negotiations, concluded that Nixon and Kissinger were not "thinking in terms of bringing about a major breakthrough in Soviet-American relations, and of ending the Cold War and the arms race." Instead, U.S. national security policy continued to be "essentially based on military strength, and on the accommodation of national interests only when they found it desirable to do so. Their arms control efforts thus disguised this policy of strength, but only slightly."[77]

Because of its temporary provisions, the Interim Agreement was presented to Congress as an executive agreement. Both chambers would therefore need to approve its provisions by majority vote rather than the requirement for two-thirds of the Senate to consent to treaties. Kissinger initially suggested that the Interim Agreement be 18–24 months in duration before agreeing to extend it to five years. Despite all of the warnings by deterrence strategists of the Soviet throw-weight advantage, only two senators and two congressmen voted against the Interim Agreement. The ABM Treaty was of indefinite duration. It received a surprisingly easy ride on Capitol Hill. Opposition on strategic and moral grounds had little traction at first. The Senate debate was cursory, lasting only eight hours. Only two senators voted against the ABM Treaty.

BLOWBACK

It didn't take long for opposition to the Interim Agreement to build. Concerns were muffled at first during Nixon's reelection campaign but would gain enough strength during Gerald Ford's run for the presidency in 1976 that he struck the word "détente" from his vocabulary. Ford's challenger in the Republican primaries, Ronald Reagan, issued stark warnings of the advent of Soviet strategic superiority, aided and abetted by the Interim Agreement. All this came to pass within four years of Nixon's triumphant return from the Moscow summit.

Nitze held his fire until resigning from the SALT negotiating team in 1974 when he "could no longer function under the steadily darkening cloud of Watergate," wary that Nixon might seek to save himself by striking unfavorable deals with the Kremlin.[78] He soon became the most authoritative spokesperson warning against the trend lines facilitated by the Interim Agreement. Thomas Moorer, the former chairman of the Joint Chiefs who felt burned by the Nixon White House's end-arounds, joined Nitze in strenuous opposition. Moorer pointedly did not offer prepared remarks in the Senate Foreign Relations Committee hearings on the SALT accords. When asked whether the Joint Chiefs strongly supported the agreements, he answered that they were "consulted prior to signature" and that they would be acceptable if strategic modernization programs were carried out.[79] Critical voices gained strength through mass. Nitze and Moorer joined other heavyweights on the Committee on the Present Danger, organized by Eugene Rostow, Dean Acheson, and others, which strenuously opposed the terms of the Carter administration's subsequent effort to negotiate a more comprehensive treaty.

Festering resentments to the way in which the Interim Agreement was negotiated and its unequal provisions found expression in a sense of the Senate resolution crafted by Senator Jackson and his articulate aide, Richard Perle. The side that frames an argument in a simple, rhetorical way that leaves opponents sputtering and requiring paragraphs of rebuttal usually carries the day on Capitol Hill. Jackson hammered away at the dangers posed by the Interim Agreement due to its permissive allowances for Soviet missile upgrades and throw-weight, but his arguments about being disadvantaged in nuclear war-fighting scenarios sounded too Strangelovian to gain popular traction. Jackson and Perle then found a winning formula by asking, "What could be wrong with parity?" If sufficiency no longer meant superiority, it certainly meant parity, or for some, parity in the guise of maintaining strategic advantage.

Jackson's resolution urged and requested "the President to seek a future treaty that, *inter alia*, would not limit the United States to levels of intercontinental strategic forces inferior to the limits provided for the Soviet Union." During Senate debate, Jackson explained the practical meaning of his formulation in different ways, leaving himself enough leeway to be the arbiter of whether or not the executive branch had fulfilled his guidelines.

Just as Nixon and Kissinger "buffaloed" the SALT negotiators (in Gerard Smith's characterization), so, too, did Jackson and Perle buffalo the architects of the 1972 SALT accords. The Nixon White House supported Jackson's resolution even though it indirectly repudiated its handiwork; Nixon and Kissinger didn't want to be even more embarrassed by losing a vote they opposed. The Jackson resolution garnered 56 votes in support. The 35 naysayers, led by Fulbright, understood the downside risks of handing Jackson arbitration rights over his resolution. When President Carter finally completed negotiations on comprehensive SALT limits seven years later—an agreement codifying equal limits for both sides—Senator Jackson judged the result as being not good enough to meet his standard of parity.

Jackson, the epitome of a species now virtually extinct—the "yellow dog" Democrat who was strong on national defense and progressive on domestic issues—exacted his pound of flesh. In return for his supporting votes for the ABM Treaty and the Interim Agreement, he pushed on Nixon's open door to build new missiles and bombers, to purge ACDA and reduce its budget, and to place his surrogate, General Edward Rowny, on the negotiating team to represent the Joint Chiefs, replacing Royal Allison, whom he felt did not defend the Pentagon's interests strongly enough. On these matters, Nixon, Kissinger, and Jackson were in complete accord.

The virtues of the SALT accords were dimmed by what followed—rising warhead totals, MIRV deployments, and growing nuclear war-fighting capabilities. SALT's severest critics warned of a "window of vulnerability" that would soon be wide open. The opening chapter of strategic arms control, which was supposed to calm jitters, had the opposite effect.

SUCCESS THAT WOULD LEAD TO FAILURE

The critiques of the Interim Agreement were overdrawn, but in essence accurate. The strategic arms competition ramped up as a result, even with the ABM Treaty in place. Even so, the Interim Agreement was an historic accomplishment. For the first time, Washington and Moscow began to codify and set limits to their nuclear competition. They began to discuss what were considered state secrets in the Soviet Union. Nixon and Kissinger initiated a process for the subsequent negotiation of comprehensive controls, a necessary precursor to achieve deep cuts. They proved the hypothesis that agreements were possible. The Kremlin could agree to SALT despite the Nixon administration's conduct in the Vietnam War and its opening to China. For their part, Nixon and Kissinger could agree to sign the SALT I accords even though they were unable to change the Soviet pursuit of geopolitical advantage in distant locales. Linkage proved to be a fiction; strategic arms control would eventually become real, to be followed by deep reductions.

Nixon, Kissinger, and the SALT negotiating team deserve credit for achieving the first-ever limitations on strategic offensive forces. They deserve more credit for the ABM Treaty that foreclosed expensive and ineffective defenses against ballistic missile attacks. The ABM Treaty was a necessary but insufficient condition for deep cuts in strategic offenses. This could occur only when political conditions permitted after Gorbachev was elevated to negotiate with Ronald Reagan and George H.W. Bush. Nixon, Kissinger, and their SALT negotiators also opened multiple lines of communication that could be employed in crises and to curtail dangerous military practices. Two of the lesser accords negotiated during this period—measures to reduce the risk of accidental nuclear war and upgrades to the 1963 Hotline Agreement—clearly demonstrated the utility of strategic dialogue. They were among the first drafts of reassurance, lagging far behind measures to strengthen deterrence, but they were a start.[80]

Laying the basis for strategic stability was, in William Hyland's view, a "profound accomplishment" that survived changes of leadership on both sides for the duration of the Cold War. The ABM Treaty was central in this regard, as "the two superpowers had agreed that they would remain vulnerable to a nuclear attack and would not attempt to build a significant defense against it."[81] Gerard Smith wrote that, "contrary to cynical expectations, SALT resulted in solid areas of agreement," proving that it was possible to negotiate "to reduce the risks of war and the costs of security."[82] Kissinger's view during this period was that "for the first time in history two major powers deliberately rested their security on each other's vulnerability."[83]

These claims were valid. They were also strongly contested, contributing to the demise of subsequent efforts by Presidents Ford and Carter to make the Interim Agreement's porous constraints more comprehensive. The Interim Agreement's constraints were far too permissive, but the Pentagon and the Soviet General Staff would have it no other way. The arms competition would significantly intensify before it could be capped and reduced. The 1972 SALT accords were path-breaking achievements, but they were extremely lax and badly oversold, fanning blowback when unreal expectations were dashed.

In contrast to the Interim Agreement, the Anti-Ballistic Missile Treaty was an immediate and longer-lasting accomplishment. Despite those who would subsequently rail at a treaty mandating national vulnerability, the technologies for successful intercepts against even rudimentary missile threats were clearly beyond reach in 1972. The odds were plainly stacked against nationwide defenses during Nixon's administration. The public living near proposed missile defense installations didn't want to be defended by nuclear detonations, the Pentagon was leery of spending considerable sums of money in this way, and the Congress was starkly divided about their utility. The ABM Treaty reflected the realities facing the Nixon administration.

In 1973, one chronicler of SALT deemed the results to be "inconclusive."[84] The passage of time confirms this judgment. By agreeing to a treaty strictly limiting missile defenses, Nixon and Kissinger established a framework that eventually resulted in comprehensive controls and deep cuts. The ABM Treaty provided a basis for eventual reductions while the Interim Agreement abetted arms racing. The 1972 SALT accords were deeply inconsistent, but they reflected ground realities.

Nixon and Kissinger were opportunists as well as realists. Nixon par-layed the SALT accords to a landslide victory at the polls. He, Kissinger, and their SALT negotiators ventured into the unknown and returned home with a limited and contestable proof of concept for strategic arms control. They left messes in their wake, with the strategic competition poised to accelerate, setting in motion fierce debates about how best to proceed.

CAPPING THE ARSENALS

Chapter 6

NIXON FALLS AND SALT II STALLS

Nixon's landslide reelection was ensured when Democratic activists, inflamed by the Vietnam War and the emerging Watergate scandal, nominated a gentle prairie populist and former B-24 bomber pilot, George McGovern, as their standard bearer. McGovern won Electoral College votes from Massachusetts and the District of Columbia, but nowhere else. Thus fortified, Nixon asked his entire cabinet to resign and began to reshuffle the deck.

The Arms Control and Disarmament Agency was particularly hard-hit, slated to lose one-third of its budget and fifty employees. Fourteen of the agency's top seventeen executives were asked to leave. As Gerard Smith wryly noted, somebody had to take the blame for complaints about the 1972 SALT accords, and it wasn't going to be the Nixon White House.[1] Richard Perle of Senator Jackson's staff was directly involved in ACDA staffing decisions. Raymond Garthoff, the State Department's arms control expert and the drafter of fine print, was exiled to the inspector general's office. Key figures in the Office of the Secretary of Defense left their posts. The Joint Chiefs of Staff representative, General Royal Allison, was reassigned, took the hint, and retired from the air force. Among the negotiators on Smith's original team, only Paul Nitze and Harold Brown remained on board.[2] Nitze's tenure would be limited; he resigned as the Watergate scandal grew.

EARLY STEPS

As a courtesy and for continuity's sake, Gerard Smith briefly led the U.S. negotiating team to consider a treaty to replace the five-year Interim Agreement, but his days were obviously numbered. Smith was replaced as ACDA's director by an accomplished defense intellectual, Fred Charles Iklé. Iklé was a reliable skeptic on nuclear arms control but not steeped in the arts of bureaucratic maneuver. John Lehman, a hawkish staffer on the National Security Council, subsequently joined Iklé as his deputy, providing sharp elbows. New analysts were brought on board, the beginning of a schism within the agency between strong enthusiasts and deep skeptics of strategic arms control.

Henry Kissinger succeeded William Rogers as Nixon's secretary of state in September 1973, while holding on to his position as national security advisor. He was at the pinnacle of his powers, but he left a stream of grievances in his wake. With ACDA greatly diminished and no longer serving as a foil, he was now in the direct line of fire for criticism, especially with a powerhouse like Nitze on the outside, able to speak freely, and with Senator Jackson directing withering criticism from Capitol Hill. Kissinger selected a career Foreign Service officer, U. Alexis Johnson, to replace Smith as the head of the U.S. SALT delegation, and a new acronym was born—SALT II. Johnson had no desire to be dual-hatted as ACDA director. The agency would be run for the duration of the Nixon-Ford years by Iklé who, in Johnson's view, "spun finely drawn analyses that quickly lost most people's attention, including the President's, and did not reveal where he stood." James Schlesinger and Donald Rumsfeld posed far greater impediments to progress on SALT II as secretaries of defense. After the 1972 accords, the Joint Chiefs also dug in their heels. "Defense and the JCS were strenuously regressing," Johnson wrote in his memoirs. Consequently, "nothing resembling a consensus emerged."[3]

Ural Alexis Johnson was a long way from Falun, Kansas, an isolated farming town on the Great Plains where he was born. A map-loving mother named him after the Ural mountain range. Johnson had a storied diplomatic career. He was stranded in Manchuria after the Japanese attack at Pearl Harbor and helped out with truce negotiations at the end of the Korean War. He rose through the ranks quickly, witnessing the Bay of Pigs fiasco and the Cuban missile crisis as a deputy to the third-ranking State Department official during the Kennedy years. He then went on to serve as ambassador to Japan, Thailand, and Czechoslovakia, before being appointed by William Rogers to be the State Department's top Foreign Service officer. From there, Kissinger tapped him to become the chief of the SALT delegation. It was Johnson's least favorite and most frustrating post, which speaks volumes from someone who worked on the truce negotiations for the Korean War.

Assisting Johnson were Boris Klosson of the State Department, Sidney Graybeal and then Ralph Earle II, representing ACDA, Nitze representing the Office of the Secretary of Defense, and General Edward Rowny representing the Joint Chiefs, Senator Jackson's hand-picked choice. Harold Brown continued to provide technical expertise. Sitting across from the U.S. negotiators were a familiar cast, led by Vladimir Semyonov, making the same case as before for including forward-based systems—aircraft based in Europe or on carriers, as well as British and French nuclear capabilities—and for maintaining numerical advantages won in the Interim Agreement. The Joint Chiefs continued to resist MIRV constraints but could accept a freeze now that U.S. deployments were well along, with the Soviet Union's deployments lagging behind with flight tests beginning in 1973.

The Jackson amendment loomed over preparations for the SALT II negotiations. Jackson was stung by the negotiating techniques of Nixon and Kissinger as well as their rejection of his favored negotiating positions. His corrective was deceptively simple—that the United States not be limited to "levels of strategic forces inferior to the limits provided for the Soviet Union," with Jackson being the arbiter of equality. Nitze attempted to revisit throw-weight limits, with Kissinger's initial consent. After these proposals were dropped from the U.S. negotiating stance, Nitze took his leave, replaced by Michael May of the Lawrence Livermore Laboratory.

Jackson greeted the initiation of SALT II negotiations with an amendment to a trade bill the Kremlin wanted, tying the grant of "most-favored nation" trading status to easing restrictions on Jewish emigration. Jackson's legislation, subsequently adopted in the House of Representatives in an effort led by Charles Vanik, was known thereafter as the Jackson-Vanik amendment. Jackson-Vanik was another variation of linkage—pocketing something of value in return for an outcome the Kremlin presumably wanted. Whereas Nixon and Kissinger sought changes in Soviet behavior abroad, Jackson conditioned economic and trade benefits to changes in the Kremlin's domestic policies. Jackson was successful when Nixon and Kissinger were not: Even after the advent of Mikhail Gorbachev and the exodus of Russian Jews to Israel, the Congress still didn't grant the Kremlin most-favored-nation trading status.

The Nixon White House's instructions to the U.S. delegation were to seek a "permanent agreement" based on "essential equivalence in central strategic systems." Subsequent instructions called for a ten-year timeframe and equal aggregates that included bombers as well as land- and submarine-based missiles. There would be freedom to mix within this aggregate figure. The initial U.S. proposal for SALT II also called for equal ceilings on ICBM launchers and ICBM throw-weight—a nod by Nixon and Kissinger to the views of Secretary of Defense Melvin Laird, Nitze, and Jackson. This proposal would have allowed the Pentagon to build an equivalent number of "heavy" missiles to match those of greatest concern in the Soviet force structure—something that wasn't in the Pentagon's plans. Alternatively, the Kremlin could eliminate their heavies. There was no initial mention of MIRVs. The Kremlin didn't deign to respond to this proposal.[4]

The Soviet SALT negotiators matched their counterparts with one-sided offers. They proposed to maintain numerical advantages and constrain U.S. strategic modernization programs. Flight testing and deployment of entirely new missiles, like that to be carried by the new Trident submarine, as well as the new B-1 bomber, would be banned for the duration of the agreement, while upgrades of existing systems (to include the next generation of existing Soviet missiles) would be allowed. The U.S. delegation didn't deign to discuss the Soviet proposal. The one positive outcome of this first round of SALT II negotiations was the creation of a Standing Consultative Commission to address questions of SALT implementation and compliance.

In the months after Nixon's reelection there was a marked lack of enthusiasm to negotiate a treaty to supersede the Interim Agreement. It was as if both Washington and Moscow needed a respite from the pressures associated from novel bilateral deal making. The primary focus in both capitals was to proceed with the strategic modernization programs permitted within the lax confines of the Interim Agreement.

The prospect of a summit in May 1973 prompted revisions in the U.S. negotiating position. Kissinger instructed the U.S. delegation to offer new proposals, including equal aggregates of 2,350 land-based missile launchers, submarine-launched missiles, and heavy bombers, essentially splitting the difference between the lower U.S. and higher Soviet aggregate force levels. To demonstrate seriousness of purpose, Kissinger also discarded U.S. proposals for equality in land-based missile launchers and throw-weight that were anathema to the Kremlin. Kissinger was also amenable to range restrictions for cruise missiles.[5] Jackson and Perle now had a direct line into the U.S. SALT delegation through Rowny, and they turned up the heat whenever Kissinger offered fallback positions.

Kissinger didn't entirely give up on seeking constraints on Soviet land-based missiles and their throw-weight. Instead of seeking equal limitations or unilateral, deep reductions in areas of Soviet advantage, which remained nonnegotiable, Kissinger decided to offer up MIRVs in trade. He proposed a freeze on their testing and deployment atop land-based missiles if the Kremlin would be prepared to accept a ceiling on ICBM throw-weight. Kissinger's proposal was unacceptable, since it would have foreclosed the testing Moscow needed for MIRVed missile deployments. Kissinger was also willing to discuss numbers for permissible MIRVed launchers.[6]

Soviet negotiators were also ready to discuss MIRVs for the first time, expressing a willingness to accept unequal numbers for MIRVed missiles, as long as suitable compensation was provided. As Garthoff, détente's most capable chronicler, wryly noted, this exchange came three years too late. Had the U.S. proposed a ban on MIRVed flight-testing and deployment early in the SALT negotiations, while demanding offsetting reductions in Soviet missile capabilities, the nuclear arms race could have been substantially downsized. Three years later, when this topic was finally discussed, the Pentagon possessed 350 MIRVed land-based missile launchers with 1,050 warheads, while the Soviet Union possessed none. The Kremlin wasn't interested in a freeze in this particular area of competition, as it was playing catch-up.[7]

The Joint Chiefs of Staff, still bruised from their previous dealings with Kissinger, offered far stronger resistance to his preferences and had a strong ally in Deputy Secretary of Defense William Clements. Clements rose from working as an oil-field roughneck to running the world's largest offshore drilling company, based in Texas. The Pentagon demanded equal rights to "heavy" land-based missiles and no constraints on MIRVs, which Kissinger characterized to Nixon as a "massive" negotiating problem. As Alexis Johnson noted in his memoirs, "The fact was the Chiefs did not want any SALT agreement that was negotiable."[8]

By the time Leonid Brezhnev arrived in Washington for a June 1973 summit, impeachment hearings were about to begin with White House counsel John Dean as the lead witness. Brezhnev was often dismissed as a slow-witted Soviet apparatchik, but this portrait, as Soviet defector Arkady Shevchenko later wrote, was faulty. In his view, Brezhnev "retained both the limitations of his origins and the cunning which had enabled him to rise above them." While by no means an "eminent leader," he was "a shrewd intriguer who was open minded enough to break significant new ground in East-West relations." Brezhnev "owed his longevity in office first of all to the stability he promised and delivered to the elite."[9] By now, Brezhnev was comfortable with summitry. Nixon and Kissinger reveled in the summit spotlight, but the ground was shifting from under their feet.

At the summit, Nixon and Brezhnev signed an agreement on "Basic Principles of Negotiations on Strategic Arms," which pledged "active negotiations" and "serious efforts" to reach a framework accord reflecting mutual recognition of "equal security interests" and to avoid "efforts to obtain unilateral advantage, directly or indirectly." The Basic Principles Agreement clarified that verification would be by national means and not by on-site inspections, and that modernization programs would be permitted under agreed terms.[10]

A SALT II framework agreement eluded Nixon and Brezhnev in 1973. Differences on numbers and what would be included or excluded in agreed totals were too great. They did, however, sign off on a Prevention of Nuclear War Agreement that affirmed a common stated desire "to remove the danger of nuclear war and the use of nuclear weapons." They also pledged to refrain from the threat or use of force, including against each other's allies, and to engage in urgent consultations to avoid nuclear dangers.[11]

Garthoff concluded that the Basic Principles and Prevention of Nuclear War agreements helped launch détente and contributed to its failure when these principles proved to be brittle.[12] The Prevention of Nuclear War Agreement was tested and found wanting less than four months after it was signed when Israel was attacked by Egyptian and Syrian forces, with backing from the Kremlin. The 1973 war in the Middle East provided additional proof that linkage (and détente) were not going the Nixon administration's way. Nixon deemed Moscow's actions aiding the Egyptian army in distress to be so troubling as to warrant increasing the nuclear alert rate of U.S. nuclear forces.

After Brezhnev left Washington, debates within the administration became, if anything, increasingly contentious. Kissinger found himself surrounded by hardliners in interagency deliberations. The Joint Chiefs, the Office of the Secretary of Defense, ACDA, and even some at State were championing positions that had no prospect of successful negotiation. The situation worsened when James Schlesinger transitioned from being the director of the Central Intelligence Agency to become secretary of defense in July 1973.

Verification Panel meetings became free-for-alls. As Kissinger's close associate, William Hyland, advised in a memo, "There is a wide gap between the bureaucracy and your own thinking on SALT. As I understand your views, you are convinced we must expect to pay a real price, in terms of ongoing U.S. programs, to stop ongoing Soviet programs. No agency will acknowledge this."[13] To complicate matters further, Senator Jackson again weighed in, this time with a letter to Nixon proposing deep reductions in strategic forces and equal throw-weight levels. This proposal, he argued, would "go quite far in diminishing the importance of MIRV as a destabilizing factor in the strategic balance."[14]

As in the Interim Agreement, neither side was willing to trade off its own modernization programs for reductions in the other's capabilities, so the framework they eventually approved during the Ford administration necessarily accommodated growth. In addition to new missiles, submarines, and bombers to replace existing types, the newest form of growth came in the form of cruise missiles—jet-powered vehicles that reached targets by flying in the atmosphere, unlike missiles that flew in ballistic trajectories through space.

The earliest cruise missiles were used by Germany in World War II—the "buzz bombs" that terrorized and killed British city dwellers. After the war, the superpowers shifted their focus to ballistic missiles, an unstoppable fast-flyer that Nazi Germany also previewed. The era of modern cruise missiles began when Nixon and Kissinger were looking for leverage in negotiations to follow the Interim Agreement. It seemed perfectly natural that, as negotiators were trying to squeeze air out of the ballistic missile competition, other compartments of the arms race would balloon up. With both military establishments seeking advantage and seeking to avoid disadvantage, trade-offs were not yet possible. If an agreement were to be reached, it would be additive, not subtractive.

Advanced cruise missiles weren't bargained away. Even though they moved far more slowly toward their targets than ballistic missiles, they had great maneuverability and their profiles could be masked by stealthy techniques so as to make them difficult to find once launched. Nuclear-armed cruise missiles could not only supplement the Triad of land-based missiles, ballistic missile-carrying submarines, and bombers, they could also be armed with conventional warheads, offering significant military applications for naval warfare and land attack.

Richard Nixon's days in office were numbered. He and Kissinger had no means to quell acts of insubordination, especially by Schlesinger, who saw eye to eye with Senator Jackson. As the Watergate revelations mounted, Nixon took to foreign travel to demonstrate his mastery of foreign policy and to add to his significant list of accomplishments. He traveled to Egypt in June 1974, where Washington was replacing Moscow as Cairo's chief ally. He then traveled to Moscow in June, one month before his resignation. The goal of a breakthrough on SALT II was not in the cards as the Kremlin leadership would wait for Watergate to play out before deciding on next moves. Nixon and Brezhnev did, however, agree to a protocol to the ABM Treaty that reduced each side's deployment to a single site. Not even Senator Jackson was interested in the second allowable site near Washington. They also agreed to a treaty limiting underground tests to 150 kiloton yields—approximately ten times more than the bomb dropped on Hiroshima.

THE THRESHOLD TEST BAN TREATY

Nixon's last summit meeting with Brezhnev in June 1974 was suffused with melancholy and disappointment. After a day of desultory talks, Kissinger huddled with his team around midnight to discuss the state of play. With a framework agreement on SALT II beyond reach, a signing ceremony was needed and the best on offer was a Threshold Test Ban Treaty. Kissinger directed Jan Lodal to put the finishing touches on the paperwork. Kissinger always had a "whiz kid" nearby, someone exceptionally smart who could help with technical details. Lodal was the fourth whiz kid in the succession of Kissinger aides.

Lodal grew up in San Antonio, Texas, the son of an engineer and a homemaker. The family's politics was progressive, with Democratic senator Ralph Yarborough serving as patron saint. (The political affiliation of talented staff didn't matter to Kissinger.) Lodal was a student leader. At age 14 his eyes were opened by attending a Scout Jamboree in England followed by travel around Europe. He attended a then-segregated Rice University where he stumped for civil rights and took up engineering. With a commission from the U.S. Army, he attended Princeton to receive one master's degree from the Woodrow Wilson School and another from the Engineering Department. At the tender age of 23, he then found himself at the Pentagon doing systems analysis of the consequences of nuclear exchanges.

In Moscow Lodal had in his possession the outline of a draft treaty setting a threshold limit for underground testing. The origin of this draft treaty lay in the need to parry Soviet calls for a comprehensive test ban. Business as usual at the Nevada test site was no longer possible since the higher the yields of underground tests, the more the casinos in Las Vegas would shake. In March 1974, Kissinger and Soviet foreign minister Gromyko agreed to "technical discussions" on a threshold treaty. The U.S. team was led by Walter Stoessel, a highly accomplished diplomat who was then serving as U.S. ambassador to the Soviet Union. Stoessel's deputy was Edward Ifft, a civil servant who had been working on SALT. The Soviet negotiator was Igor Morokhov, a deputy minister working in the Soviet nuclear complex. His deputy was Roland Timerbaev, one of the drafters of the Nonproliferation Treaty. Both delegations benefitted from strong technical expertise including, on the U.S. side, seismic experts outside of government.

These teams carried out technical discussions in Moscow that soon morphed into negotiations. Both delegations worked intensely and collaboratively, helped by the presence of Soviet technical experts who were unlikely to be able to travel abroad. The talks were strikingly informal, with U.S. and Soviet experts using blackboards to work on problem solving. In just five weeks, a draft treaty text was ready in time for the Moscow summit. The takeaway by Ifft, who had previously worked on delegations where progress could be measured at a snail's pace: "You can succeed if you give the delegations authority to succeed and if you send the right people."[15]

The agreement authorized the positioning of seismic stations at test sites and the exchange of geophysical data to help reduce uncertainties in monitoring yields. Even so, uncertainties regarding the upper boundary of Soviet tests would bedevil the treaty's prompt ratification. The negotiators also facilitated an agreement by setting aside how to deal with "peaceful" nuclear explosions for a separate treaty. They agreed to leave the threshold number blank, to be filled in at the summit. ACDA and State Department representatives preferred a 100-kiloton threshold; others on the U.S. delegation preferred a 200-kiloton number.

Lodal put the finishing touches on the paperwork for Nixon to finalize the Threshold Treaty Text around three in the morning. As for the treaty's yield, Lodal proposed 100 kilotons, agreeing with the State Department and ACDA positions. He carried his handiwork to Kissinger for approval, but Kissinger was indisposed, so he called Brent Scowcroft for guidance. Scowcroft, who was minding the store at the White House, told him to place the text in Nixon's folder for his meeting with Brezhnev the next morning.

Nixon handed Brezhnev the proposal for a 100-kiloton threshold test ban. After consulting briefly with his side of the table, Brezhnev agreed. There ensued much passing of notes on the U.S. side of the table amidst obvious discomfort by Kissinger, who interjected that the threshold should be raised to 150 kilotons. Nixon was puzzled and a brief conference ensued. At some point before the meeting, Scowcroft had reached Kissinger and Kissinger had talked to Schlesinger, who objected to the 100-kiloton threshold. Nixon then proposed the higher limit, Brezhnev again conferred with his side of the table, and a new deal was struck.[16]

The Threshold Test Ban Treaty faced rough sledding thereafter. Opponents of nuclear test constraints argued that the threshold would be difficult to monitor, and later on that the Soviets cheated by surpassing the 150-kiloton limit. Those in favor of test limitations argued that this threshold was far too high. The Senate's consent to ratification was deferred until a companion accord imposing similar constraints on "peaceful" nuclear explosions was negotiated in the Ford administration. Both treaties remained in limbo until joint verification experiments were conducted during the second term of the Reagan administration to address monitoring concerns. The Threshold and Peaceful Nuclear Explosions treaties finally entered into force in 1990.

UNFINISHED BUSINESS

The framework agreement on strategic offensive forces continued to elude Nixon. The more his administration delved into details, the more the Joint Chiefs and Schlesinger offered lopsided and nonnegotiable proposals. The overwhelming level of Republican support for the Interim Agreement dissolved quickly. The terms of debate shifted markedly to focus on the threat posed by the Soviet Union's new missiles—missiles that Nixon and Kissinger seemingly promised would be foreclosed by the Interim Agreement, and were thus considered violations by treaty opponents. The task of completing a framework agreement would fall to Nixon's successor and unelected vice president, Gerald Ford. Ford became vice president when Nixon's running mate, Spiro Agnew, was forced from office for bribe-taking and corrupt practices originating when he was governor of Maryland that extended into his tenure as vice president.

Throughout, Kissinger was dogged by Senator Jackson's critique of his handiwork that was informed by Rowny, who "reported privately and regularly to Jackson," according to the Arms Control and Disarmament Agency's lawyer for SALT II, Thomas Graham. Rowny would take extensive notes of meetings and convey them to his military assistant in Washington who would forward them to Richard Perle. "That channel of communication remained in place until the very end of SALT II and it was used as a device to try to destroy SALT II."[17]

As evidence mounted of no fewer than four new Soviet MIRVed missiles— three by land and one by sea—critics argued that the Kremlin was pursuing war-winning capabilities instead of operating on the Nixonian watchword of sufficiency. In a moment of exasperation after a meeting with the Kremlin leadership trying to advance a framework agreement in July 1974, Kissinger asked the assembled press, "What in the name of God is strategic superiority? What is the significance of it, politically, militarily, operationally, at these levels of numbers? What do you do with it?"[18] For once, Kissinger sounded like Paul Warnke. The numbers, details, and loopholes of the Interim Agreement, as well as the enemies he made negotiating it, had caught up with him. With his powers of control and manipulation greatly diminished, Kissinger found himself on the defensive. Any agreement within reach would be subject to withering fire.

Chapter 7

FORD, KISSINGER, AND THE DEATH OF DÉTENTE

erald Ford was the accidental president who told his fellow citizens that their "long national nightmare" was over, now that Nixon was heading west to his temporary exile in San Clemente, California. Ford was the perfect antidote to Nixon, an uncomplicated man who personified decency.[1] He downsized Kissinger's role, feeling more at ease with Brent Scowcroft as his national security advisor. James Schlesinger remained at the Pentagon until Ford forced his resignation in November 1975. Schlesinger's replacement was Donald Rumsfeld. Rumsfeld's deputy, Dick Cheney, became Ford's chief of staff at the age of 34.

The Kremlin had been observing the spectacle of Nixon's fall with puzzlement while slow-walking the negotiations for a SALT II framework agreement. With Ford in the White House, prospects for an agreement improved. Ford inherited proposals of equal aggregate levels of land- and sea-based missiles and heavy bombers, of which 1,320 could be missiles carrying multiple warheads. The Kremlin's proposed framework was "equal security," which meant including or compensating for U.S., British, and French forces within striking distance of the Soviet Union. The White House, abiding by the Jackson amendment, demanded equality and the exclusion of U.S. "forward-based" and allied nuclear forces. Kissinger surmised in a memo to Ford that it was highly unlikely the Kremlin would accept the exclusion of forward-based systems, equal limits, and "a fair accounting of the overwhelming US advantage in heavy bombers."[2] Kissinger predicted wrongly on all three counts.

THE VLADIVOSTOK ACCORD

Brezhnev wanted an agreement and lined up the support he needed. The Kremlin accepted equal aggregates, checking off an important box in terms of the Jackson amendment. Forward-based systems were excluded, while the inclusion of "heavy" bombers, of which the United States held an overwhelming advantage, could be viewed as an offset to the Soviet Union's "heavy" missiles. For their part, Ford and Kissinger conceded that the Backfire bomber did not have enough range to be included in these totals. The terms of a framework agreement that would outline comprehensive limits were at hand. The deal was sealed in November 1974 in the freezing cold of the Soviet Far East at Vladivostok.

The Vladivostok Accord's language included references to both equal security and equality, reflecting Brezhnev's talking point and Ford's need to acknowledge the Jackson amendment. The accord's most important provision was its limits on missiles carrying multiple warheads. This number—1,320—protected and reflected U.S. force structure, a defining aspect of deal making until the Cold War ended and nuclear excess could be readily pared. Since "essential equivalence" was the guiding principle for the Vladivostok Accord, 1,320 also became the ceiling for Soviet missiles carrying MIRVs. At the time of the accord, the United States possessed approximately 800 MIRVed missile launchers, and the Kremlin had exactly none. Its first MIRVed deployments began the following year, in 1975.

The Kremlin offered a one-third reduction in its "heavy missiles" at Vladivostok, but only if the United States would forego cruise missiles. This trade-off appealed to Kissinger, but Ford nixed it. The framework agreement prohibited construction of land-based missile silos at new locations and additional numbers of "heavy" missiles, confirming the Soviet Union's sole possession of these missiles. The Pentagon did not intend to build heavy missiles, in any event. Both sides were allowed "freedom to mix"—for example, to move from land to sea, where missiles would be harder to target. The two leaders agreed to a summit in Washington within a few months to celebrate this achievement. The negotiating record at Vladivostok was unclear about how cruise missiles would be counted, which subsequently became a major stumbling block.

Ford and Kissinger expressed strong satisfaction with the Vladivostok Accord. Ambassador Johnson was surprised by this result, considering it "a major accomplishment."[3] After returning from the summit, Ford addressed his cabinet, but his primary audience was Schlesinger. "The main accomplishment," Ford said, "was that we went from non-equivalence to equivalence" and that "we put a cap on the arms race." An added benefit was reductions in launcher numbers from the Interim Agreement.[4]

It didn't take long for the euphoria to wear off. The high level of allowable missiles carrying multiple warheads upset deterrence strategists and arms controllers alike. Discussions at Vladivostok were vague on how to count bombers, depending on whether they carried ballistic or cruise missiles. The Kremlin wanted to count heavy bomber launchers by the number of cruise missiles they carried—perhaps twenty or even more—which was unacceptable to Washington. As U. Alexis Johnson recounted, Deputy Secretary of Defense Clements "suddenly developed an enthusiasm" for cruise missiles "in which neither the Navy nor the Air Force had previously shown much interest."[5] There was also grumbling about the exclusion of the Backfire, a medium-range bomber, in the Soviet totals. Inclusion of the Backfire wasn't initially a serious negotiating pursuit. Rather it was, as Johnson wrote in his memoirs, "a bargaining chip [that] had been transmuted, by deft Pentagon political maneuvering, into a major obstacle to concluding and ratifying SALT II."[6]

The primary concern for deterrence strategists remained the Soviet advantage on missile throw-weight, which they believed conferred war-fighting advantages to the Kremlin and leverage in severe crises. Schlesinger pointedly framed the issue in the final National Security Council meeting before the Vladivostok summit as one between "arms balance" and "arms stability." The former would be numerically based; the latter would address imbalances in capabilities, particularly throw-weight.[7]

Schlesinger claimed he wasn't expressing a preference, but everyone present knew otherwise. His preferred approach, supported by Jackson, Nitze, and others disaffected by the Interim Agreement, lost out. Ford sided with Kissinger, and blowback would follow. Kissinger lent fuel to these attacks in his post-summit briefing in defense of the Vladivostok Accord, intoning, "I believe that the throw-weight issue has been vastly overstated." It could be meaningful only if translated "into numbers of warheads and accuracy." Here Kissinger was out of his element, as Soviet throw-weight would be converted into large warhead numbers, and these warheads would gain greater accuracy. With predictable increases in Soviet nuclear war-fighting capabilities, the terms of debate had shifted to favor Jackson and Nitze.[8]

Kissinger was hamstrung. Opposition by Schlesinger and the Joint Chiefs delayed the tabling of a U.S. draft treaty text based on the Vladivostok Accord. The Soviet draft treaty reflected its preferences on counting rules for bombers and cruise missiles. Progress was made on subsidiary issues, such as the permissible range of air-launched cruise missiles carried by bombers, counting rules for the numbers of warheads atop MIRVed missiles, and the definitions of "light" and "heavy" missiles. But progress was hard-won and, with the 1976 election season looming, the Pentagon's resistance to an agreement intensified. Ford's replacement of Schlesinger with Donald Rumsfeld didn't help matters.

Kissinger's memoir, *Years of Upheaval*, characterizes the Vladivostok Accord as a major achievement. Equal aggregates were negotiated by "counterbalancing asymmetries," but this result had "no bureaucratic or domestic support."[9] Opposition came from all directions. Senator Jackson found the numbers enshrined by the Vladivostok Accord to be "astonishingly high," a conclusion shared by Wolfgang Panofsky, who testified that "there is no justification for the large numbers." What remained of centrist thinking was reflected by Adrian Fisher's testimony that Vladivostok was, on balance, better than nothing, with "the clear understanding that this agreement was not a hunting license under which everyone did what they could up to the maximum of the agreement."[10]

Fisher's fears were subsequently realized. It was hunting season. Paul Nitze took direct aim at the accord for failing to address the throw-weight imbalance. He wrote in *Foreign Affairs,* "There is every prospect that . . . the Soviet Union will continue to pursue a nuclear superiority that is not merely quantitative, but designed to produce a theoretical war-winning capability." Nitze allowed that Vladivostok was a "considerable improvement" to prior U.S. negotiating positions, but that it would still "codify a potentially unstable situation caused by the large disparity in throw-weight."[11]

To be sure, the Vladivostok Accord's numbers were high, and they clarified the costs of letting MIRVs run free in the Interim Agreement. Vladivostok was, nonetheless, "a significant advance over SALT" in Garthoff's view.[12] SALT negotiator Gerard Smith agreed. "The ABM Treaty and the Vladivostok accord go a good way," he wrote, "toward making the limitation of Soviet and American strategic arms an irreversible process." Its limits were high, but they established boundaries for defense planning purposes, and could be subsequently lowered. Soviet acceptance of equal limits and the exclusion of forward-based systems in the totals were advances that could facilitate future progress. There were ambiguities in the Vladivostok framework that needed to be detailed, and the throw-weight issue could be problematic, but all in all, Smith was supportive.[13]

Taking the long view, Vladivostok was a step toward more meaningful controls and a precursor to eventual reductions. The framework for a SALT II treaty brought the bomber leg into numerical equations and placed a ceiling on MIRVs. But Vladivostok, like the Interim Agreement, had negligible effect on strategic offensive programs. It reflected comfortable trade-offs—a diet without sacrifice, resulting in weight gain rather than loss. With the advent of widespread MIRV deployments, deployed warhead totals would climb to five figures for the two heavyweight competitors.

The anticipated Washington summit to celebrate the Vladivostok Accord never happened. There was no finished product, nothing for the Senate to consider. Instead, Washington and Moscow wrangled over allowable cruise missile totals and the Backfire bomber that, in the view of the U.S. intelligence community, had an intercontinental range—on one-way missions. From the perspective of those most alarmed at Soviet nuclear war-fighting capabilities, it seemed reasonable enough to include the Backfire in SALT II, as bombers in a general nuclear war would be flying one-way missions. The Ford administration, increasingly mindful of its right flank, dug in its heels to include Backfire in the Vladivostok totals. Brezhnev would have none of this. Kissinger surmised that Brezhnev didn't include 400 Backfires when briefing the Politburo about the deal struck at Vladivostok and was thus facing a "massive" problem.[14]

The fallout from the Interim Agreement made the Vladivostok Accord radioactive. The implications of not constraining MIRVs in the Interim Agreement were now plainly apparent. Deterrence strategists felt deeply aggrieved and arms controllers were, at best, unenthusiastic. A moderate Republican administration tried its best to pull together the outlines of a treaty, but the party's right flank was having none of it. A Democratic administration would try next and would also come up short.

THE COUNTERFORCE COMPULSION INTRUDES

Whatever value strategic superiority might have, the Soviet Union could not be allowed to claim or derive benefit from it. It was only a matter of time before the Pentagon would be in a position to improve the accuracy of U.S. warheads atop missiles. That time came after the SALT accords were negotiated, when the breadth of new Soviet ICBM deployments and growth of throw-weight were painfully evident. Nitze, Jackson, and Albert Wohlstetter led a large chorus of complaint about the prospective vulnerability of U.S. land-based missiles. In the absence of mobile missile basing—many years off and very hard to do, given political constraints and financial costs—there was no way to remedy this condition.

There was, however, a way to even the score. Released from the constraints of being on the U.S. SALT delegation, Nitze sounded the tocsin in *Foreign Affairs*. The need of the hour was "high quality deterrence." The Kremlin worked hard to establish advantage and their leaders would "consider themselves duty-bound by Soviet doctrine to fully exploit that strategic advantage through political or limited military means." The best deterrent of Soviet designs was a war-winning capability, "if that is attainable." Failing that, denying the Soviet Union a war-winning capability was urgently needed.[15]

On this issue, Perle was in complete agreement with Nitze. "Improvement in the accuracy of American weapons," Perle testified, "will help to restore some balance in that particular capability. That is, we will have some limited capability as well to strike and destroy Soviet hardened targets."[16] This was a rare Perle understatement. U.S. deterrence was well distributed to sea-based missiles on quiet submarines and to bombers that were being enhanced by long-range cruise missiles. Given that the preponderance of Soviet strategic capabilities resided in land-based missiles, the window of vulnerability was about to open far wider for Moscow than Washington, since Soviet submarines were noisy and U.S. anti-submarine warfare capabilities tracked the Kremlin's missile-carrying submarines. The Kremlin didn't have much of a bomber force.

The Nixon administration assured the Congress during the crucial early debate over MIRVs that it did not then have plans to seek lethal accuracies on the thousands of warheads that MIRVing would permit. But conditions had changed, and Nixon's new secretary of defense, James Schlesinger, was the change agent for new targeting capabilities. Schlesinger was born to Jewish parents in New York City. His mother was an immigrant from Lithuania; his father's family came from Austria. He was schooled at Harvard where he received his bachelor's, master's, and doctorate degrees in economics. He converted to Lutheranism and taught briefly at the University of Virginia. A rapid rise then followed from the RAND Corporation to a series of cabinet posts. When called to testify on Capitol Hill, he responded to antagonistic questions in measured tones, sometimes accompanied by a pipe, unruffled and supremely confident in his analytical prowess.

Speaking at the Overseas Writers Club in January 1974, Schlesinger unveiled the U.S. rejoinder to the Soviet missile buildup. He propounded a new, more flexible nuclear-targeting doctrine that would provide a president with options between "massive response and doing nothing." These "prompt hard-target kill capabilities" could leverage outcomes and escalation.[17] Schlesinger acknowledged, "The Soviets would not necessarily draw reassurance from this. It is not our objective to give them reassurance. In order to have deterrence one must have a credible threat."[18]

Presidents always had the means to carry out limited strikes; henceforth, they would have far more of them. The purpose of these changes, Schlesinger testified, was "to shore up deterrence."[19] The United States was pursuing a significant range of strategic modernization programs to effectively counter the Soviet buildup. As George Brown, air force chief of staff, explained, "If the Soviets insist on an arms race, there will be an arms race."[20]

Schlesinger's changes provided a platform for rebuttal by presidential aspirant Edmund Muskie, who replaced Albert Gore, Sr., as chairman of the Senate Foreign Relations Arms Control Subcommittee. Muskie was deeply skeptical of Schlesinger's initiatives but he picked his battles carefully and this one wasn't in his wheelhouse. Not deeply versed on the particulars, he passed this baton to Senator Thomas McIntyre, who chaired the Subcommittee on Research and Development of the Armed Services Committee, and Edward Brooke, who had led the 1970 battle over MIRVs.[21]

Since the 1970 Senate debate, opposition to MIRVs on Capitol Hill had waned. New Soviet missiles nullified the argument that U.S. initiatives would fuel the arms race. As for the dangers posed by prompt hard-target kill capabilities, that barn door was opened with high-yield warheads atop Soviet ICBMs. Even if they lacked precision accuracy, they could still kill silos. In 1974, the Senate Armed Services Committee proposed a down payment of $77 million on accuracy improvements. McIntyre warned against placing a hair trigger on the nuclear arms competition and argued that there were better ways to counter Soviet moves. Senator Jackson responded by asking, "Does it make any sense for us to deny our Government unilaterally the opportunity to improve our ICBM systems? Should we throw away a source of leverage here?"[22] It was also hard to rebut the simple assertion of John Stennis, the chairman of the Armed Services Committee, that "accuracy is always desired in weaponry."[23] The amendment co-sponsored by McIntyre and Brooke to strike funding for accuracy improvements failed by a vote of 49 to 37.[24]

It was a crucial battle, but the war was lost years before, when Presidents Johnson and Nixon declined to trade off MIRVs for tight constraints on Soviet land-based missiles. A new generation of the Kremlin's land-based missiles threatened their U.S. counterparts. Soon the shoe would be on the other foot. Soviet leaders and military planners would have to contend with the prospective vulnerability of their own ICBM force. From Moscow's perspective, Schlesinger's doctrinal changes accentuated disadvantage, since the Kremlin couldn't count on the survivability of its missile-carrying submarines that were subject to tracking at sea and the bomber leg of its Triad, which was decidedly inferior to that of the United States. The next phase of the nuclear competition would be marked by mutual concerns over strategic stability—the central problem that the founding fathers of arms control warned against. The strategic arms race was accelerating while negotiations were losing steam.

THE DOLDRUMS AFTER VLADIVOSTOK

The post-Vladivostok negotiations were going nowhere. The Pentagon was making strong representations that the Backfire be included in Moscow's totals. Kissinger vented that "our position is impossible" and that "the Backfire issue is a fraud. If the Backfire is strategic, then our Forward Based Systems are strategic."[25] Another sticking point was cruise missiles that could be militarily useful for both nuclear and conventional attacks. The Pentagon held perhaps a five-year technological advantage on advanced cruise missiles, just as it did for MIRVs at the outset of the SALT negotiations. Their deployment would, however, pose monitoring problems and add great complexity to the Vladivostok framework.

A cabinet shakeup, with Schlesinger shown the door, replaced by Donald Rumsfeld, didn't ease these logjams. Brent Scowcroft took over as national security advisor, and George H.W. Bush replaced William Colby as head of the Central Intelligence Agency. Despite these changes, National Security Council meetings continued as before, with the Pentagon resisting deals. Kissinger wrote in his memoir that "procrastination became the critics' new strategy."[26] Having been burned earlier for his inattention to details, Kissinger had now mastered them, but he no longer could leave others in the dark or command the bureaucracy. The Pentagon was dug in. "As the debate went on and on," Kissinger wrote, "its cumulative impact transformed Vladivostok from a spur to improving Soviet-American relations into a further obstacle to them."[27]

Among those strongly critical of any treaty that might result from the Vladivostok Accord were those who felt most aggrieved by Kissinger's manipulation while negotiating the SALT accords. Admiral "Bud" Zumwalt, chief of naval operations during this time, later testified, "I consider him a man who is extremely skillful at making strategic defeat look like tactical victory."[28] U. Alexis Johnson offered a more measured but telling characterization of Kissinger in his memoirs: "Henry, like most geniuses, has spectacular talents but corresponding faults. He was amazingly successful juggling a profusion of balls while pirouetting atop a highwire. When some of these balls dropped, however, it was obvious that devotion to truth was not always his guiding principle."[29]

There were bigger targets than the Vladivostok Accord. The knives were out for détente, as attempts at linkage to engineer more accommodating Soviet behavior had failed. The reasons for its failure included an unwillingness to offer the Kremlin something of value in return for concessions, but these trade-offs were politically unacceptable at home. Ford went to Finland in August 1975 to sign the Helsinki Final Act, which recognized European borders, promoted trade, emphasized human rights, and prompted implementation measures that later helped to open the Soviet Union to emigration and on-site inspections. "Basket I" of the Final Act listed "Principles Guiding Relations," including respect for sovereignty, nonresort to the threat or use of force, and the inviolability of frontiers. Later, these provisions helped to free Warsaw Pact nations, and later still, a revanchist Russia under Vladimir Putin ignored them. All this lay in the future; when Ford signed the Helsinki Final Act, he was flayed by critics of détente for throwing Eastern Europe and the "captive" Baltic states under the bus.

Linkage, is this view, was a sham and détente a delusion. Former secretary of defense Melvin Laird wrote an essay for *Readers Digest* the month before Ford traveled to Helsinki, arguing that the United States made "major concessions" to induce good Soviet behavior and had been "sorely disappointed." Laird concluded that it was time to "shed any lingering illusions."[30] Presidential candidate Ronald Reagan campaigned against détente, and Ford stopped using the word, let alone trying to defend the concept.

Kissinger titled the second volume of his memoirs *Years of Upheaval*. His considerable powers of manipulation were by then depleted. Ford, the accidental president, was fighting a strong Republican challenger who railed against détente and the Soviet strategic buildup. The voters were ready for change. The Vladivostok Accord twisted in the wind. Rumsfeld was impossible to pin down. The Joint Chiefs wouldn't budge. The Kremlin was strongly opposed to making additional concessions, especially about the Backfire.

Brezhnev conveyed disappointment that Ford and Kissinger had allowed peripheral issues to become so freighted with meaning. Ford tried to defer contentious issues and move forward with the Vladivostok framework, but the Kremlin wasn't buying, deciding to wait for the outcome of the 1976 presidential election.

Chapter 8

CARTER, SALT II, AND THE RECKONING

Nixon and Kissinger, the architects of détente and linkage, were gone, working on books to rehabilitate their reputations maligned by resurgent conservatives within the Republican Party. Jimmy Carter brought new concepts to the task of improving the Vladivostok framework, but he was soon to be schooled by old school beliefs within the Kremlin. Carter was not steeped deeply in international affairs and national security. He chose his mentor at the Trilateral Commission, Zbigniew Brzezinski, to become his national security advisor. Underneath the "just folks" persona of the man from Plains, Georgia, was a burning ambition. The presidential candidate who carried his own clothing bag coming down the ramp of his campaign plane was now followed wherever he went by a military officer carrying a black satchel—the "football" that permitted his authorization to use nuclear weapons. Carter was determined not to use that football. In this, he was no different than his predecessors. Where he differed was in his disinclination to use a nuclear arms buildup to help convince the Kremlin to exercise similar restraint.[1]

Carter was scheduled to serve on the *USS Seawolf*, the navy's second nuclear-powered submarine, but left active duty after his father's death. His stint in the navy didn't change Carter's strongly held skeptical views about the utility of nuclear weapons and the uselessness of nuclear excess. In his inaugural address, he pledged to work for a world without nuclear weapons. Deterrence strengtheners shuddered. No previous president assumed office with a more explicit or broader arms control agenda than Jimmy Carter. He was intent on negotiating strategic arms reductions, a comprehensive nuclear test ban, a ban on the use of anti-satellite weapons, and controls on arms sales. Carter would be foiled on all these counts, as well as on his disinclination to seek an arms buildup in order to build down.

CARTER'S TEAM

Brzezinski didn't share Carter's passion for arms control. He was more inclined toward competitive superpower dynamics than collaborating with the Soviet Union. Brzezinski was resolved to counter even modest gains by pro-Soviet proxies in faraway places. He was born in eastern Poland, the son of a diplomat posted to Nazi Germany and Stalin's Russia. His father was in Montreal when Hitler and Stalin carved up Poland. Thus stranded, he studied at McGill and then at Harvard. He was two years behind Henry Kissinger at Harvard, where a competition between two men with such extraordinary intellectual powers and expansive egos was foreordained. There was room at Harvard for one of them, and Kissinger was awarded a tenured appointment. Brzezinski moved to Columbia where he published important books and looked for chances to follow in Kissinger's footsteps. Jimmy Carter provided that opportunity.[2]

Carter valued Brzezinski's brainpower but didn't share his instincts. Carter resolved to look at inherited strategic modernization programs—especially the B-1 bomber—on their merits, not as part of a grand negotiating strategy. He had the smartest person in the room to help him make hard choices. That would be Harold Brown, born in Brooklyn, the son of a lawyer and a diamond merchant's bookkeeper, who became president of Caltech, the Pentagon's director of defense research and engineering, secretary of the air force, director of the Lawrence Livermore Laboratory, and a SALT negotiator for Richard Nixon and Gerald Ford. Brown would go on to add other significant achievements, including success as a partner in the investment banking firm of Warburg Pincus. Walter Slocombe, who worked on SALT and other policy issues for Brown, believes the "smartest person in the room" moniker was an understatement. "He was," Slocombe recalled, "the smartest person I ever met."[3]

Brown, in turn, conferred with William Perry, his director of defense research and engineering, to help assess weapon systems and to introduce stealth technologies. Perry had a knack of being in the right place when advances in defense technologies beckoned. He was at the cutting edge of developing intelligence monitoring sensors and digital technology as the director of Sylvania's Electronic Defense Systems (later merged with TRW) when he was told to fly to Washington quickly to assess images of Soviet missile sites in Cuba. Pouring over the daily "rushes" of the U-2 missions during the Cuban missile crisis was the first of his several rendezvous at the nuclear brink, the title of his memoir. Reflecting on these close calls, Perry believed that luck—plain dumb luck—was to be credited for the absence of mushroom clouds; his keenly analytical mind ruled out the possibility of divine intervention.[4]

Walter Slocombe was often Harold Brown's "plus one"—the person accompanying the boss in restricted, high-level meetings. Raised by a single mother, a psychologist, Slocombe grew up in Erie, Pennsylvania, and Ann Arbor, Michigan. He excelled at Princeton, Oxford (on a Rhodes scholarship) and Harvard Law School, after which he clerked for Justice Abe Fortas on the Supreme Court. He was then selected by Henry Kissinger—one of several Democratic-leaning high achievers—to work on his National Security Council staff in 1969, where he got his first taste of SALT. Slocombe stayed barely a year before leaving to join Caplin & Drysdale, the law firm that would be his home base in between government posts. Slocombe was active in Carter's presidential campaign, working on defense and national security issues, and was rewarded with a position helping Brown.

The State Department's team was led by Cyrus Vance, who had been Robert McNamara's deputy at the Pentagon. Before that, Vance served as the Pentagon's general counsel, then becoming secretary of the army. He was born in the small town of Clarksburg, West Virginia, the son of an insurance broker who moved the family to Bronxville, New York, to commute to Manhattan for work. His father died of pneumonia when Vance was five years old. As a young man, Vance was drawn to the law, public policy, and politics, perhaps due to his uncle, John W. Davis, who lost his campaign to become president in 1924 to Calvin Coolidge. He excelled at three sports and in the classroom at the Kent School in Connecticut, an Episcopalian institution that inculcated the responsibility to do good works for those in need. Then it was on to Yale, where he spent his summers in Labrador working on a mission of "muscular Christianity" helping the poor. After receiving his degree from Yale Law School, he enlisted and served as a gunnery officer in the Pacific during World War II. He then went to Simpson, Thacher & Bartlett to practice law on Wall Street until McNamara called him to public service.[5]

Vance would butt heads with Brzezinski repeatedly. He chose Warren Christopher to be his deputy. Christopher, like Vance, was born in an out-of-the-way place (Scranton, North Dakota), excelled in school, and was drawn to the law and to Democratic politics. His father was a bank manager whose health was shattered during the Depression. His mother moved the family to Los Angeles, where he attended Hollywood High School. Christopher graduated from the University of Southern California and Stanford Law School, where he was editor of the *Law Review*. He, too, served in the navy and fought in the Pacific, after which he clerked for Supreme Court justice William O. Douglas. He joined the Los Angeles–based firm of O'Melveny & Myers, leaving for a stint as deputy attorney general in the Johnson administration.

Vance and Paul Warnke, Carter's choice to lead ACDA, were very close. They did most of the heavy lifting on SALT II, with the help of Assistant Secretary of State Leslie Gelb, whose last name was bestowed on his father by tax collectors in the Carpathian Mountains along the Hungarian-Czechoslovakian border. Jews living in villages there went by patronymics rather than last names, hardly suitable for record keeping. As a remedy, the tax collectors assigned colors to be last names. Max's new last name was Gelb—the color yellow. One of ten children, Max Gelb showed promise. He was designated to make a new life for himself in America, thereby improving prospects for the entire family. He settled in New Rochelle where he and his wife, an immigrant from the Czech-Hungarian border, ran a delicatessen.

His son, Leslie, went to college at Tufts and, with the help of one of his professors, got into Harvard where he got to know Henry Kissinger and his teaching assistant, Morton Halperin. He wrote his doctoral dissertation on theories of alliances and briefly tried his hand at college teaching, then went to work for Jacob Javits, an internationally minded Republican senator from New York. Hooked on public policy, Gelb was recruited by Halperin to join him at the Pentagon. There Gelb delved into the history of U.S. involvement in Vietnam, compiling what became known as the "Pentagon Papers," worked on policy planning, and got his feet wet working on nuclear arms control. He was eager to try his hand at the SALT negotiations when the opportunity arose.

Jimmy Carter was surrounded by extraordinary talent, but he was yoked to the Vladivostok Accord, "an ill-defined commitment and a well-defined stalemate," in the apt characterization of Strobe Talbott, *Time* magazine's chronicler of nuclear negotiations.[6] Carter was intent on negotiating strategic arms control differently. He observed Nixon, Kissinger, and the Pentagon embrace bargaining chips, purportedly for leverage, that were not bargained away. Instead, they added new dimensions to the arms competition, offending Carter's analytical mind. His choice to be the chief SALT negotiator, Paul Warnke, felt the same way—that bargaining chips were unnecessary for national security and fueled an arms race. Warnke's views offended deterrence strengtheners, already deeply concerned about the Soviet strategic buildup. Warnke believed the Kremlin was playing catch-up; his opponents believed the Politburo had more ambitious, deeply malevolent plans.

PAUL WARNKE, THE LIGHTNING ROD

Paul Warnke's lasting importance radiated from his belief system rather than his treaty making. Warnke came to epitomize what arms controllers were about. His sharp arguments set terms of debate that others would embrace and emulate. He eschewed the politesse of William Foster and Gerard Smith, two ACDA directors who preceded him. When challenged, he was pugnacious. He was a change agent, not a seat warmer, at a time when the winds of change were blowing against him.

Warnke's father had a sixth-grade education but found success in the shoe business that flourished in mostly blue-collar Massachusetts towns like Marlborough, where the Warnke family was raised. His son was a voracious reader and a good student in a weak public school system. Paul Warnke was first generation college-bound, headed for Holy Cross until one of his father's business acquaintances in New York suggested that this bright young man aim higher. He got into Yale and struggled in classes until he found his footing. With enlistment choices limited by a heart murmur, Warnke joined the U.S. Coast Guard during World War II, serving in combat in the Pacific. After the war, with help from the GI Bill, he headed to Columbia University and its Journalism School. The school's enrollment was full, but there was a vacancy in the Law School. There everything clicked and the *Law Review* followed.

Warnke landed at Covington & Burling, an elite law firm in Washington, DC, that provided a pipeline into public service. He was a natural litigator and became a partner in 1956. But the law was not nearly as interesting as national security, foreign policy, and the world of politics. He took leave from Covington & Burling to work for John F. Kennedy's presidential campaign, spending six weeks in Ohio. He then served on JFK's defense transition team but declined the two jobs he was offered at the Pentagon as lacking sufficient heft. His opening finally came when Robert McNamara offered him the general counsel's job in 1967, a position that McNamara used not only for the Department's legal matters but also to audition talent for policy slots.

When Cyrus Vance, then McNamara's deputy, recruited Warnke to be the Pentagon's general counsel, Warnke warned his friend that he was strongly antiwar. Don't worry, Vance responded, most of the civilians working on Vietnam were, too, and McNamara wouldn't hold it against him. Only later did it become clear that McNamara privately held a similar view. Warnke excelled at the Pentagon and soon moved up to become the assistant secretary of defense for international security affairs, where his primary preoccupation was the war he opposed. His most intriguing outlet was preparing for the strategic arms limitation talks that Johnson and McNamara were prodding the Kremlin to begin. He worked alongside Nitze, who had moved from being secretary of the navy to deputy secretary of defense. The two Pauls got along well in the Pentagon. They opposed the Vietnam War for different reasons: Warnke thought it was a tragic mistake, while Nitze thought it an unwise diversion of resources and military power.

Vietnam profoundly influenced Warnke's thinking about arms control. In Vietnam, early decisions trapped presidents and killed soldiers carrying out senseless orders. The politics of extrication were unforgiving, even when it was clear that the war wasn't winnable. The lessons Warnke learned from Vietnam were to make hard choices early, to take the political heat, to cut losses, and to avoid entrapment. The same tactics to prevent tens of thousands of dead American soldiers were also applicable to preventing a futile strategic arms race.

To Warnke, numbers mattered less than finding the right approach to stabilize the nuclear competition. There was no sense in arming to parlay when the parlays didn't result in trade-offs and reductions. Avoiding an arms race required making sound decisions even if the Kremlin made foolish ones. Otherwise, both superpowers would become "apes on the treadmill." Warnke used these words in an essay in *Foreign Policy* magazine, which he helped to launch. He was prone to sharp argument—it was the litigator in him. His combative nature got him into hot water, but when faced with reasoning he thought foolish, he reacted with unvarnished rebuttals.

Initially, his biggest foil was Albert Wohlstetter, a brilliant mind with eclectic intellectual interests who worked at RAND and then taught at the University of Chicago. Unlike Warnke, Wohlstetter drew strength and certainty from numbers—they were remorseless, offering no respite from the nuclear competition. Nitze felt the same way. Some who witnessed atmospheric tests and viewed the rubble after World War II came away with the view that a nuclear war would be senseless and differentials in nuclear firepower meaningless. Nitze calibrated the rubble and concluded otherwise. Nuclear numerology could be translated into leverage in crises. Numbers could also spell the difference between victory and defeat in fighting a nuclear war. Nitze's views were clearly stated during the Eisenhower administration, when he wrote that a nuclear war could be won or lost "decisively," depending on the postwar position of the adversaries.[7]

Later in his remarkably full life, after the Cold War ended, Nitze changed his views and lent his voice to those seeking abolition of nuclear weapons.[8] But in the 1970s, Nitze was a deeply worried man. To him, the numbers suggested a Soviet quest for strategic superiority. Wohlstetter's numbers pointed in the same direction, to a "delicate balance of terror," a theme he first raised during the Eisenhower administration. His focus then was on the vulnerability of strategic bombers to a surprise attack. Wohlstetter returned to this theme when the Soviet missile buildup in the 1970s threatened U.S. land-based missiles. Wohlstetter's numbers contested the relaxed view that the Kremlin merely wished to catch up to the United States in nuclear capabilities. Instead, his charts pointed to the conclusion that the Soviet Union sought nuclear war-winning capabilities. U.S. restraint would not be reciprocated; the Kremlin was embarked on an implacable quest for nuclear superiority, a quest that people like Warnke would likely abet.[9]

Wohlstetter and Warnke dueled on the pages of *Foreign Policy* magazine. It was Ali vs. Frazier, except with typewriters. Wohlstetter was a product of Washington Heights, DeWitt Clinton High School, and City College of New York. He never received a PhD nor wrote a book, but his influence was far-reaching, first with his studies at the RAND Corporation and later in life as a mentor for Paul Wolfowitz and Richard Perle. Both Wohlstetter and Warnke could be caustic. Their debate was ostensibly over the meaning of numbers, but it was really over worldviews. For Wohlstetter, numbers were sacrosanct. For Warnke, "the numbers game" was a losing proposition, leading to dangerous, excessive behaviors. Warnke's scarring experience in the Pentagon dealing with Vietnam showed. The arms race was a quagmire of a different sort, and one that could only be avoided by restraint and negotiation.[10]

Wohlstetter's jousting with Warnke was polite compared to Nitze's. Neither Warnke nor Nitze suffered fools gladly, and they thought each other's views on the Soviet Union and arms control to be foolish. Feeling manipulated by Nixon and Kissinger, appalled by Watergate, preoccupied by the Soviet strategic buildup, and unwanted by president-elect Jimmy Carter, Nitze took direct aim at Warnke. As Nicholas Thompson wrote, "Without a doubt, the explosion was sparked in part by his jealousy at Warnke's nomination and his pique at Carter for passing him over."[11] Nitze felt used; he was only a nominal adviser for optical purposes who had no chance on being offered a serious job.[12]

Nuclear arms and arms control were Nitze's bailiwicks; he had been thinking hard about nuclear issues since his work on the Strategic Bombing Survey. He was deeply troubled by his tour of duty negotiating SALT I when he believed that Nixon and Kissinger had made profoundly unwise, politically expedient decisions providing a pathway for the Soviet Union to achieve strategic superiority.[13] This outcome could only be avoided, in Nitze's view, by a tough negotiating stance backed by a major strategic buildup.

At a briefing session convened by presidential nominee Carter to familiarize himself with issues and to size up possible cabinet members, Nitze found himself the odd man out. He was a Democrat of the Dean Acheson–Scoop Jackson School, surrounded in Jimmy Carter's Pond House by men deeply chastened by Vietnam and appalled by nuclear overkill. Nitze had only one kindred spirit at this briefing session—James Woolsey. There was one woman in the room—Lynn Davis—besides Roslyn Carter. Nitze's personality had rough edges. He could lack situational awareness, being stiff, prickly, and utterly sure of himself. At the Pond House he launched into a briefing about the importance of throw-weight and the rising dangers it entailed. With rebuttals, including by Warnke, there was hardly time left in the two-hour meeting to discuss other topics. Nitze could be an exasperated listener, and his sense of urgency and authoritativeness didn't sit well with the presidential candidate. Warnke was no less self-confident than Nitze, but he was at ease. His instincts and approach to global issues were good matches to the Democratic presidential nominee. Warnke was in, and for the first time in his life, Nitze didn't belong in a Democratic administration.[14]

The only question for Warnke was whether he might realize his ambition to become secretary of state or secretary of defense. Neither position was on offer. When Vance, Carter's pick to become secretary of state, asked him to take the Arms Control and Disarmament Agency job, Warnke turned it down—and then had gnawing thoughts that he would again sit on the sidelines, the way he did during the first six years of the Kennedy and Johnson presidencies. When his wife, Jean, met Vance at a social function soon thereafter, Vance mentioned how much he regretted that her husband would not be joining the team as head of ACDA. Jean Warnke responded, "You haven't tried hard enough." Carter then called and made an offer that Warnke couldn't refuse.

Meanwhile, Nitze sat on the sidelines as Carter selected others for jobs for which he was superbly qualified. The upcoming SALT II negotiations were a particular sore point. Warnke had a long paper trail declaring that the numbers were not all that important. Nitze was acutely alert to the geopolitical threat posed by the Soviet Union. Warnke felt the Soviet threat was overdrawn.

Then Warnke made a decision that provided Nitze with an opening. Gerard Smith was confirmed for the ACDA job and subsequently assigned the lead in the SALT negotiations. Warnke wanted to be confirmed for both jobs to signal the president's confidence in him and to improve his standing with the Kremlin. Even after his grueling hearings, Warnke continued to believe that dual confirmations were a wise choice. But by opting to be confirmed for both, he provided his critics with the opportunity to wound him deeply, and they seized it.

Senator Jackson wasn't inclined to seriously contest Warnke's dual appointments. In his view, Carter would have chosen someone with similar views even if Warnke withdrew after an intense and closely fought battle. But Nitze felt otherwise: Contesting Warnke's nomination would send an important message to Carter, and denying Warnke a two-thirds majority vote for his ambassadorial appointment would influence Carter's negotiating and defense procurement decisions. Nitze called Jackson and persuaded him to contest Warnke's nomination. Just before the Senate hearings, Nitze was with Alton Frye at an event in Colorado Springs. Frye knew Capitol Hill well, having just written a book on congressional politics and national security and having served as an aide to Senator Edward Brooke, who led the campaign on Capitol Hill against MIRVs. Frye heard Nitze rehearse his intense views for the hearings and knew that Warnke would be severely attacked. Warnke was anathema to the negotiation-from-strength school, of which Nitze was the headmaster. Even so, the ugliness of the proceedings came as a surprise.[15]

Nitze's testimony was an eerie repeat of Oppenheimer's auto-da-fé, when his security clearance, about to expire, was formally revoked. In Oppenheimer's case, the most memorable testimony to strip Oppenheimer of his influence and access to decision makers came from Edward Teller. Nitze played

Teller's part in Warnke's ordeal, and unlike the Oppenheimer proceedings, Warnke's were in public view.

With Jackson leading the witness, Nitze testified that Warnke's judgment was "demonstrably unsound." He added that Warnke's positions were not "reasonably understandable." Nitze's testimony prompted the following exchange with Senator Thomas McIntyre, who was sympathetic to Warnke:

> McIntyre: "Are you saying that you impugn his character as an American citizen?"
> Nitze: "If you force me to, I do."
> McIntyre: "Do you think you are a better American than he is?"
> Nitze: "I really do."[16]

Nitze subsequently expressed regret about this exchange, but never offered Warnke an apology worthy of the defamation.[17]

Warnke later expressed surprise at the vehemence of Nitze's opposition. "I always thought it was a personal thing that Paul always thought he was going to be a more important figure in politics than he was, and I don't think he realized his personality was aggravating to a number of people." Warnke added, "Never to me, but a lot of people just thought he was very intolerant, that he looked down on them. I could never figure out why it became so personal. I mean he was just determined that I was not going to get that job."[18]

Warnke received seventy votes to become director of ACDA, but only fifty-eight to be ambassador for the SALT negotiations—less than the two-thirds vote necessary for the Senate to consent to ratify a treaty. Warnke survived this gauntlet with spirit intact. He was a fighter, and he would fight no less for SALT, but Nitze and Jackson got what they wanted—a warning shot across the bow. Warnke's nomination fight was, as Nitze later recounted, purposefully instructive—"a warning to the Carter administration to adopt a more realistic view of the Soviet Union and of our defense needs."[19]

When Oppenheimer was savaged in private, he already had diminished influence. His security clearance was not being renewed, making its revocation an entirely gratuitous affront. Warnke, in contrast, was at the crest of his influence, which was why he was targeted. With Jackson, unlike with Nitze, it wasn't personal. As Warnke later recalled, "The principal problem [for him] was that he was not a believer in arms control. He thought that I was, and he was right." Warnke reflected back on this painful episode with a characteristic quip—that if power corrupts, the absence of power corrupts absolutely.

The Warnke house had a long corridor for inscribed portraits of important colleagues, a hallowed Washington tradition. A picture of Nitze was among them, with a warm inscription to a comrade in arms. Jean Warnke took it down after the hearings.[20]

JIMMY CARTER'S TRAVAILS

Intent on doing far better than Nixon and Kissinger in SALT, Carter made missteps, attributed by Raymond Garthoff to "his lack of experience and knowledge of the ways of Washington, as well as world politics."[21] His biggest mistake, in the view of Leslie Gelb, was not to seek a quick agreement based on the Vladivostok numbers, but the details were complex and took time to resolve internally and with the Kremlin. Most accounts of the administration's initial deliberations place Vance and Warnke as proponents of moving quickly to complete the Vladivostok Accord.[22] Gelb remembered otherwise, having strenuous arguments with Vance and Warnke, who preferred a more ambitious approach. They even invited Soviet ambassador Anatoli Dobrynin to the State Department for counsel. Dobrynin argued for finishing up rather than reopening negotiations. Harold Brown and National Security Advisor Zbigniew Brzezinski were inclined otherwise, as was Carter, who authorized the pursuit of deeper reductions in the Vladivostok framework. Carter approved a modest fallback approach, as well.[23]

Brezhnev greeted Carter's election with an important policy speech declaring that the Kremlin did not seek military superiority. Carter received a different greeting with a diametrically opposite assessment from "Team B," a group opposed to détente. Ford's last director of the Central Intelligence Agency, George H.W. Bush, commissioned Team B to critique in-house estimates of the Soviet threat. Never have the results of an intelligence "counterassessment" been more foreordained. Team B was led by Richard Pipes, a Harvard University professor of Russian history who was an extremely literal reader of Soviet military doctrine. Pipes was joined by General Daniel O. Graham, who previously resigned as the director of air force intelligence, and William Van Cleave, an academic with profoundly pessimistic views of Soviet intentions who favored severe remedies. They received support from Nitze and Paul Wolfowitz, who agreed with his mentor, Wohlstetter, that the Central Intelligence Agency was guilty of chronically underestimating Soviet strategic modernization programs and intentions. Joining them were Foy Kohler, a former ambassador to the Soviet Union, and Seymour Weiss, a State Department official bitterly disaffected from Nixon and Kissinger.[24]

The essence of Team B's critique was distilled in an essay Pipes wrote for *Commentary* magazine, "Why the Soviet Union Thinks It Could Fight and Win a Nuclear War." Pipes stated categorically that U.S. and Soviet nuclear doctrines were "starkly at odds." U.S. doctrine discounted the possibility of winning; Soviet doctrine, in contrast, held that "the country better prepared for it and in possession of a superior strategy could win and emerge a viable society." This tenet was drawn, almost word for word, from Nitze's 1956 essay in *Foreign Affairs*, subsequently updated in another *Foreign Affairs* essay published in 1976.[25] Pipes disregarded Schlesinger's counterforce initiatives beginning in 1974 that placed U.S. nuclear employment policies on the same footing presumably embraced by the Soviet General Staff.

In reality, the Pentagon and the Soviet General Staff were in like-minded pursuit of advantage. The primary difference was that the Pentagon substituted greater missile accuracies for the Soviet Union's greater throw-weight, but to the same practical effect. Nitze called this "high quality deterrence." This evolution was well underway but had no bearing on Pipes or his Team B colleagues. Both U.S. and Soviet nuclear doctrines were in the process of becoming dangerously aligned; Pipes was railing against Robert McNamara long after McNamara was replaced by James Schlesinger.

Pipes's distinctive difference was to add an ethno-nationalist characterization to the strategic competition. He viewed Soviet doctrine as a reflection of *muzhik* thinking. Soviet peasants—*muzhiks*—"had been taught by long historical experience that cunning and coercion alone ensured survival." In stark contrast, "Middle-class American intellectuals simply cannot assimilate this mentality, so alien is it to their experience and view of human nature." His presumed competition between *muzhiks* and middle-class America was, in effect, no contest at all. Moscow, in Pipes's view, rejected the concept of mutual deterrence, while Washington was using it as a safety blanket.[26] This was a sweeping extrapolation, but it wasn't too far afield from what Nitze, Schlesinger and others had been arguing. In their view, deterrence could hold as long as U.S. strategic modernization programs and especially counterforce capabilities proceeded: the best defense was a sharper offense. Pipes reached his conclusions by drawing from doctrinal literature fifteen years old while discounting contemporaneous, authoritative statements by Soviet leaders. There was no need to take these statements seriously, in his view, because they were a ruse.

Jimmy Carter was deluged by contradictory advice and torn by conflicting instincts. He wanted to move quickly and decisively to translate the

Vladivostok Accord into a SALT II treaty, but he also wanted deep cuts. Team B's warnings were being amplified by the Committee on the Present Danger, a collective who's who of veteran Cold Warriors that served powerful notice during the Warnke nomination fight. Warnke's blood was already in the water. Senator Jackson offered Carter private counsel in the form of a twenty-page memorandum written by Perle. Jackson's advice was not to rush SALT, make a clean break from Kissinger's handiwork, include the Backfire bomber in SALT totals, and not "compromise the development of the cruise missile program."[27]

Brezhnev wrote to Carter that a deal could be struck if there was political will to do so, and if cruise missiles were included and the Backfire excluded. The complexity involved was mind numbing. Carter's instinct to immerse himself in detail was reinforced by his decision-making apparatus. The options memo he received from Brzezinski prior to the visit by Vance and Warnke to Moscow bearing proposals ran to seven pages of fine print.[28]

Carter's "preferred" option was reducing Vladivostok numbers from 2,400 to between 1,800 and 2,000 launchers, to be achieved as soon as possible. MIRVed missile launchers would be reduced by 10–15 percent from Vladivostok's 1,320 number. He proposed a freeze on new ICBM programs—to include the new ten-warhead-capable missile in development to replace smaller Minutemen missiles, provisionally named the M-X. The Kremlin would be expected to reduce their heaviest missiles in return. There would be a freeze on ICBM upgrades and equal limits of 550 land-based missiles per side. Carter further proposed a ban on all "transcontinental" cruise missiles, however armed, with ranges over 2,500 kilometers. If the Kremlin were favorably inclined to this proposal, Carter suggested that the Backfire bomber issue could be effectively set aside. To top this off, "the US side would be prepared to consider favorably, if the Soviet side raises the B–1 and Trident issues, a comprehensive freeze on all strategic systems, including the Backfire, banning their deployment and testing."[29]

This proposal reflected extraordinary ambition: If the Kremlin were willing to recast its strategic force structure to look much like that of the United States and dramatically reduce its throw-weight advantage, the United States would be willing to forego major strategic modernization programs. It amounted to, as Brzezinski's deputy David Aaron said, "giving up future draft choices in exchange for cuts in their starting lineup."[30]

Carter's preferred option was dead prior to Vance and Warnke's arrival in Moscow. As Thomas Graham, the ACDA's legal representative to the negotiations, recalled, "Brzezinski saw fit to leak it to the press before Vance got there." The Soviets first learned about it from reading the *New York Times*. With studied understatement, Graham noted, "This did not make a favorable impression on the Soviet leadership."[31]

Carter was willing to parlay to reduce arms, but U.S. modernization programs were in development while Soviet programs were being fielded. Carter lacked the leverage that Ronald Reagan enjoyed to secure deep cuts, leverage that was multiplied manyfold by Reagan's dream of the Strategic Defense Initiative. Carter wanted deep cuts, but Brezhnev wasn't interested, preferring a quick agreement. Vance and Warnke also broached Carter's fallback position in Moscow: If the Kremlin was disinclined to make ambitious trade-offs, Carter proposed to defer the cruise missile and Backfire issues and turn the Vladivostok Accord into a treaty as soon as possible with slight reductions to convey subsequent intent.[32]

Brezhnev summarily rejected the fallback proposal, as well, insisting that cruise missiles be limited in SALT II. Brezhnev took offense that both Carter's proposals were "deliberately unacceptable." Carter felt that his good intentions went unrecognized.[33] Vance surmised the main reason for the Kremlin's rejection was that they departed too greatly from the Vladivostok formula. This view was reinforced when Warnke was given a ride to the airport by Gromyko's deputy, Georgii Korniyenko. As Warnke later recounted, Korniyenko said, "I do not understand you Americans. Comrade Brezhnev spilled a lot of political blood at Vladivostok," reaching concurrence in the Politburo to accept equal aggregates and to exclude forward-based systems. He therefore could not consider departures from this framework.[34] As Vance and Warnke later commiserated to Carter, the problem wasn't with his ambition, but that "the Soviets proved unready to match this vision."[35]

In short order, Carter dropped his pursuit of an ambitious restructuring of the Soviet Union's land-based missiles, deferring serious reductions to a subsequent treaty. He also faced reality about the impossibility of including the Backfire bomber into SALT II's ceilings, seeking instead constraints on training exercises, production rates, and deployment. Nitze, Jackson, and the Committee on the Present Danger redoubled their opposition. Carter shifted his attention to cruise missile–related issues, with the goal of reaching a quick agreement of two years' duration by the fall of 1977. This, too, proved wildly ambitious.

Carter was intent to judge strategic modernization programs on their merits. He tasked Secretary of Defense Brown to assess whether the B-1, a new manned penetrating bomber program he inherited from Richard Nixon and Gerald Ford, made sense, given Soviet investments in air defenses. Brown and his director of research and engineering, William Perry, answered in the negative. Stealth technologies were on the way, and the B-1 didn't have them. In their view, the B-1 would be a poor investment compared to air-launched cruise missiles that could be fired in great number from safe distances and would be far more likely to reach their intended targets. Carter canceled the B-1 bomber. It was, as Vance later recalled, "the most courageous and politically costly decision of his presidency" and subsequently a "millstone" during the ratification debate.[36] Carter was right on the merits, but the road to securing the Senate's consent to SALT II's ratification became steeper. A cardinal principle of SALT negotiations, passed down from Nixon and Kissinger, was to negotiate from strength and to err on the plus side of strategic modernization programs.

Carter also decided after some vacillation to cancel the "enhanced radiation warhead" commonly known as the "neutron bomb." This low-yield tactical nuclear warhead was designed to have reduced blast effect. Samuel Cohen claimed parentage of the neutron bomb. Its principal backer was Edward Teller, who viewed it as one way to address public concerns about fallout.

The neutron bomb was a windfall for Kremlin propagandists, readily characterized by protesters as a "capitalist" nuclear weapon that would kill people but not buildings. As a practical matter, the prospective use of tactical nuclear weapons in tank or urban warfare had little operational appeal to the Pentagon. The West German government, torn between wanting the trappings of extended U.S. deterrence and not wanting the headaches of having neutron bombs on its soil, asked the Carter administration to find an additional basing country on the Continent. At this point, Carter decided to cut his losses.[37] As with the decision to cancel the B-1 bomber and rely on cruise missiles to strengthen the "air breathing" leg of the Triad, Carter was correct on the merits in deferring production of the neutron bomb, but subject to further criticism when defending SALT II. President Reagan would revisit the neutron bomb's deployment but fared no better. Its military utility was barely evident, and its political disutility was great.

Carter pressed ahead. In September 1977, Washington and Moscow moved closer to enumerating a series of limits and "sub-limits" to the SALT II framework. Carter and his team acknowledged that the Soviet Union would retain 308 "heavy" land-based missile launchers, regardless of Washington's preferences. Air-launched cruise missiles would have a range limit of 2,500 kilometers. The Backfire would not be included in the aggregate total, but constraints would be placed to reaffirm that it was not designed for nuclear warfare against the U.S. homeland.

Still there was no deal. Wrangling continued over the particulars of cruise missile limits, the collateral constraints over the Backfire bomber, and a host of other minor issues. Vote counters in the Senate presumed that some constraints on the Backfire were essential to counter expected criticisms during the ratification process, especially from General Edward Rowny, who had served as the Joint Chiefs' representative in the negotiations from 1973, leaving the U.S. delegation in 1979 to oppose SALT II. The Soviet General Staff insisted this was none of Washington's business. Marshal Ogarkov pointedly told Vance during one of his trips to Moscow that Rowny was welcome to fly a Backfire from the USSR to Cuba without refueling. Ogarkov promised to send flowers to Rowny's widow.[38]

As with the earlier negotiations over SALT and the Vladivostok Accord, every step forward seemed to make the remaining issues more contestable. Carter, Vance, and Warnke were under relentless attack for backing away from their initial, ambitious proposals; every step back was categorized as a dangerous concession and a reflection of weakness. Nothing Carter could hope to negotiate would change the vulnerability of U.S. silo-based missiles; that horse had left the barn when the Interim Agreement failed to stop upgrades in Soviet missiles, reduce throw-weight, and prevent MIRVs. Advances in missile accuracy merely confirmed the reality that fixed aimpoint targets like silo-based missiles would be vulnerable to attack.

Critics of SALT focused on the nightmare scenario of a massive Soviet surprise attack, one that laid to waste the concept of mutual assured destruction along with much of the U.S. strategic deterrent. In this worst-case scenario, the Kremlin would still have enough warheads remaining after a bolt-out-of-the-blue attack to dissuade whoever survived to command U.S. forces from retaliating. During a time of heightened anxiety, these scenarios held many in their sway. Nuclear arms control was still a new and untested practice. The first agreements produced by Nixon and Kissinger—agreements that received overwhelming support—now seemed woefully insufficient to arms controllers and downright dangerous to deterrence strengtheners.

Carter, Vance, and Warnke were caught in a vice. Deep cuts were not possible; neither were the remedies proposed by their severest critics. Technological advances favored the United States; the treaty they were negotiating would reflect U.S. advantages at sea, confirm improved U.S. accuracy and lethality on land-based missiles, and a clear superiority in the "air breathing" leg of the Triad, with bombers upgraded by new cruise missiles with stealthy characteristics. Only later did it become clear that the Soviet Union was anything but on the march; instead, it was dying from economic paralysis and suffocation. None of this mattered as Carter sought to bring the SALT II negotiations to a close. Treaty critics had seized the terms of debate.

In November 1977, Brzezinski advised Cater to slow down on SALT. A "premature" national debate over SALT II would conflict with ratification of the Panama Canal treaties, another high priority facing determined Republican opposition.[39] In January 1978, Secretary of Defense Brown reinforced this message, weighing in with a long memorandum detailing nine Pentagon concerns about making concessions that would constrain U.S. choices, particularly regarding air-launched cruise missiles.[40] Vance and Warnke jousted with Brzezinski and Brown in internal debates, with Carter instinctually inclined toward deal making but pulled in the opposite direction by political necessity.

Friction grew between Brzezinski and Vance, who didn't think that Brzezinski always characterized internal debates fairly to Carter.[41] For his part, Brzezinski took issue with the "soft" approaches favored by Vance and Warnke. Differences in view between the State Department, ACDA, and the Pentagon were modest compared to the Ford administration, where the Pentagon was opposed to any feasible agreement. Even so, delays were endemic. The minutiae mattered and internal negotiations took time, and then more time to iron out with the Kremlin.

The ratification debate over the Panama Canal treaties had priority. Brzezinski thought the long public education process would be a replicable model and that a successful outcome would strengthen Carter's hand on SALT. But Democratic presidents usually have only one bite of the apple when it comes to treaty ratification; the first time might end in success, while the second can be chastening. The support of the Republican Senate leader is crucial; without it, a Democratic president will be hard-pressed to muster the necessary two-thirds vote for treaty ratification. Republican minority leader Howard Baker had presidential ambitions. He could see the wisdom of supporting Carter on the Panama Canal treaties against his right flank but would later join the chorus of opposition to SALT II.[42] President Bill Clinton would later experience the same dynamic when Republican majority leader Trent Lott supported ratification of the Chemical Weapons Convention against a sizable minority of his colleagues, and subsequently opposed ratification of the Comprehensive Test Ban Treaty.

After canceling the B-1 bomber, Carter was in no position to fend off the Pentagon's pursuit of the M-X missile. Capable of carrying ten silo-killing warheads, the M-X would be the Pentagon's rejoinder to the new generation of Soviet land-based missiles. Its accuracy would help offset Soviet throw-weight advantages, and it would provide the "prompt hard-target kill" capabilities that deterrence strengtheners deemed essential. The problem with the M-X was how and where to base it. If deployed in silos, the M-X would be vulnerable to a Soviet first strike, and could provide a perverse incentive to strike first, given its silo-killing lethality. This was the classic case of using or losing one's deterrent. To avoid this dilemma, Brown, Perry, and their colleagues had to come up with a plan for mobile basing—a plan that U.S. SALT negotiators needed to protect.

The acronym for this plan was called MAP, for "multiple aim point" system. The M-X could be moved along 8,000 miles of roads laid out in a racetrack-like course on which there would be 4,600 shelters to hide the exact whereabouts of 200 missiles. Soviet military planners could not target all of these shelters, thereby neutralizing Soviet advantages in ICBMs and their throw-weight. MAP basing would be situated in mostly deserted public lands in Utah and Nevada equivalent to the combined size of New Jersey, Delaware, and Rhode Island. This plan was sound from a systems engineering perspective, as one would expect from Brown and Perry. It was also hopelessly impractical, beginning with the inconvenient truth that the scale of construction required would drain water supplies in barren lands. The citizens of Utah and Nevada were strongly opposed to using public lands as sponges for thousands of Soviet warheads. In what might have been the coup de grâce, the Mormon Church came out against M-X basing.[43]

The proposed "racetrack" basing mode for the M-X was a graphic case of how deterrence orthodoxy could lead smart, capable people to make tortured choices. Try as they might, Pentagon officials could find no better mobile basing schemes. A joke within the Pentagon after Carter ordered thermostats turned down to save taxpayer dollars was that the building could be heated with M-X basing studies.[44] The underlying premises behind the racetrack system—that a large new land-based missile was needed to strengthen deterrence and that it was unacceptable for the land-based leg of the Triad to be vulnerable—led to an infeasible solution. It was a classic case of Herbert

York's axiom that if the answer to a question makes no sense, then you are asking the wrong question. Once land-based missiles in fixed silos became vulnerable to attack, the way to fix this problem—if it indeed was a critical problem—was to move deterrent capability to sea in submarines that would be very difficult to find and therefore target. The presumed necessity for war-fighting capabilities on land-based missiles could also be replicated at sea. But the Triad was sacrosanct, and the vulnerability of its land-based leg was deemed to entail unacceptable risk during the Carter administration.

The result was the racetrack basing mode that Carter, Vance, and Warnke would have recoiled against in circumstances other than the need to secure the Senate's consent to ratify SALT II. Perry later wrote, "I have always regretted that I let myself be stampeded by the prophets of doom into that unnecessary exercise."[45] But these weren't normal circumstances. SALT critics were focused on the vulnerability of U.S. Minuteman missiles and the nuclear war-fighting potential of Soviet land-based missiles. As Brown told Carter, "The US response to this challenge is among the most fundamental defense policy decisions you will face."[46] The Joint Chiefs argued that perceptions of the strategic balance shifting in the Kremlin's favor needed to be addressed, and that missile capabilities needed to be upgraded. The racetrack was the answer.

Later in the Reagan administration, when alternative ways to address the vulnerability of land-based missiles were tried and found similarly wanting, Brent Scowcroft was enlisted to put to bed the "crisis" of land-based missile vulnerability. The Scowcroft Commission's answer was that if the bomber and submarine legs of the Triad were strong, the land-based leg of the Triad could still be valuable while being vulnerable. Thus, the M-X should be deployed in missile silos and work should begin on a much smaller, mobile ICBM. Joining Scowcroft were Alexander Haig, William Perry, Harold Brown, Henry Kissinger, Melvin Laird, Donald Rumsfeld, and James Schlesinger.[47] Reagan could accept land-based missile vulnerability; Carter did not have this luxury.

By the fall of 1978, hopes to employ arms control to reverse the permissive provisions of the Interim Agreement were extinguished. Instead, the focus became, as chairman of the Joint Chiefs General David Jones argued, "to get a cap on strategic forces. Maybe in SALT III we can get real reductions."[48] There was still important work to be done nailing down definitions and procedures that would enhance verification and facilitate subsequent reductions. The only way forward to a better deal for Carter, Vance, and Warnke was to ratify SALT II. Overselling the results, as the Nixon administration did, was out of the question; the Joint Chiefs would only say that SALT II constraints were "modest but useful."[49]

The biggest issue of political consequence was still the Backfire bomber. The Backfire wasn't just a symbolic issue for the Joint Chiefs. Their chairman, General Jones, said that they were "trying to be helpful" on SALT ratification but were "close to the edge of what is acceptable." While the Backfire might not be used on intercontinental missions, the Joint Chiefs were still concerned that it gave the Soviet Union a "breakout" capability, meaning that if the arms competition were to accelerate, the Backfire would give the Kremlin a head start. Warnke rebutted: "Backfire is an issue of tactics not substance. The issue is how to best use Backfire to get what we want on other things. There is no chance of counting Backfire." In this, he and Kissinger were of one view. It was illusionary to demand the inclusion of the Backfire and then trade this off for something of value in a negotiating endgame.[50]

With the final details still to be worked out but with the contours of a SALT II Treaty in hand, Warnke bid his leave in October 1978, much to Brzezinski's relief.[51] Negotiating arms control was no longer a creative challenge, having devolved into a bureaucratic slog over minutiae. Warnke had a large family to take care of, his relations with Brzezinski had deteriorated, Jimmy Carter's support waned, and it was time to go back to lawyering.[52] Plus, he wanted the focus to be on the SALT II Treaty rather than on its chief negotiator. Warnke's place as head of delegation was taken by his deputy, Ralph Earle II. With a contentious Senate debate ahead, Carter chose a retired general, George Seignious, to become director of ACDA. Seignious then left his post as president of the Citadel and resigned his membership in the Coalition for Peace Through Strength, an anti-SALT group.

The final negotiating issues were sorted out in the first few months of 1979, capped off by a summit meeting between Carter and Brezhnev in Vienna on June 18, 1979. By then, Brezhnev was a spent force, barely able to sign one copy of the treaty, let alone four.[53] Carter tried to mollify Jackson by not rushing to complete SALT II and by initially seeking deep cuts, but Jackson's opposition never softened. When SALT II was finally completed, the campaign season was close at hand and the Kremlin was about to give SALT critics more ammunition. An indicator of troubles that lay ahead came in 1978 in Yemen, Angola, and the Horn of Africa, where Soviet advisers and Cuban forces were active. Brzezinski's instinct was to raise the stakes, especially by improving U.S. ties to China.

A TREATY IN FULL AND IN LIMBO

U. Alexis Johnson estimated that 80 percent of the SALT II Treaty was completed when Gerald Ford left office.[54] Carter couldn't claim a bipartisan achievement, however, because SALT critics were bitterly opposed to the outlines of the agreement he inherited from Ford and Kissinger. Carter couldn't even count on Kissinger's support, since the former secretary of state and national security advisor was mending fences with hard-right figures in the Republican Party. Carter, Vance, and Warnke, like Nixon and Kissinger before them, reached the conclusion that the Kremlin and the Soviet General Staff would not radically alter their nuclear forces to suit Washington. The Carter administration turned to more achievable tasks, closing loopholes and nailing down particulars. This process took two years. The resulting limits were unavoidably high but could be reduced in subsequent negotiations. SALT critics could not be appeased. It was a time of reckoning: the permissive provisions of the Interim Agreement and the Vladivostok Accord had poisoned the well. A battle royal over ratification was inevitable, but the Carter administration still thought it could secure the required two-thirds vote in the Senate.

Treaty opponents and supporters formed coalitions to engage public opinion that went into high gear with the negotiating endgame and the ratification fight. The Committee on the Present Danger was led by Eugene Rostow. Its executive director was Charles Kupperman, who had been a student of Van Cleave. Nitze, the committee's chairman of policy studies, penned a pamphlet, "Is SALT II a Fair Deal for the United States?" that successfully framed the terms of debate. Nitze's sense of the Kremlin's global strategy reflected and refined his analysis in NSC-68, the report in 1950 that backstopped the U.S. response to the Soviet test of an atom bomb, the Communist capture of mainland China, and the outbreak of the Korean War. Nitze now presumed a Politburo's campaign to "outflank" Europe "by achieving dominance over the Middle East." And to dominate the Middle East, Moscow sought "controlling positions" in Afghanistan, Iran, Iraq, Yemen, Eritrea, Ethiopia, and Mozambique.

This seemed to be a rather indirect and difficult slog to dominate Europe. In contrast, there was nothing meandering about the Soviet military buildup: "It is a copybook principle of strategy," wrote Nitze, "that, in actual war, advantages tend to go to the side in a better position by expanding the scope, duration, and destructive intensity of the conflict. By the same token, at junctures of high contention short of war, the side better able to cope

with the potential consequences of raising the stakes has the advantage."
The Kremlin's land-based missiles and throw-weight were key pieces on this
chessboard. The Politburo wasn't competing for a tie, nor seeking strategic
stability. It was instead seeking to "take over and nail down the advantage
which the U.S. has appeared willing to relinquish."[55]

Nitze's critique was aimed no less at Henry Kissinger and Richard Nixon
than at the Carter administration. In March 1976, Kissinger defended the
transition from U.S. strategic superiority to "rough equilibrium" this way:
"No policy decision on our part brought this about. Nothing we could have
done would have prevented it. Nothing we can do will make it disappear."[56]
Carter, Vance, and Warnke essentially adopted the same stance, but they were
being flayed for it. Enduring U.S. strategic advantages were being greatly
discounted. And besides, nuclear warfare was different from conventional
combat; Nitze's "copybook" principles didn't apply to sane national leaders
who recognized the consequences of nuclear warfare.

These counterarguments were not persuasive. Republican and Democratic presidents seeking treaty ratification face different burdens of proof.
Republican presidents were presumed to be stronger guardians of national
security; they could reliably expect support from Democrats in the Senate
on treaty ratification. Democratic presidents after Kennedy, who believed in
nuclear superiority rather than sufficiency, faced rougher sledding in the Senate. Carter was on the defensive. He closed the barn door that Nixon and
Kissinger opened when they allowed MIRVs to run free. Carter tried and
failed to trade off strategic modernization programs for deep cuts in Soviet
missiles. The resulting numbers and war-fighting capabilities in SALT II were
high but could be reduced over time. The characterization of the Joint Chiefs
that the resulting agreement was modest but useful was completely accurate.
It was equally true that the strategic environment would be more troubling in
the absence of an agreement. These arguments provided no comfort to SALT
critics. The Coalition of Peace Through Strength, an affiliate of the American
Security Council, was more active than the Committee on the Present Danger.
Its broadside against SALT II consisted of numerous "technical flaws" and
the "fundamental" failings, such as disregarding the Soviet military's "first
strike" posture, the Carter administration's "unilateral disarmament," the
treaty's negative impact on NATO, and the failure of linkage.[57]

Treaty supporters banded together to form Americans for SALT. The
board of directors of the Arms Control Association, founded in 1971 by
former administration officials from the Kennedy, Johnson, and Nixon years,

issued a release strongly supporting SALT II, characterizing the treaty as "a significant, if long overdue, achievement in defining and maintaining the strategic nuclear balance." They highlighted four "major accomplishments"—the establishment of equal aggregates, a lower sub-ceiling on land-based missiles carrying MIRVs, restrictions on new types of ICBMs, and new measures to monitor compliance. They also noted the "historic" accomplishment of requiring the first reductions in strategic forces.[58] This endorsement helped convince reluctant Democrats to support ratification.

To shore up support among Republicans, Carter announced his decision to proceed with M-X deployments shortly before the Vienna summit with Brezhnev in June 1979 where SALT II was signed. Senator Jackson countered with a pre-summit announcement of opposition to Carter's policies of "appeasement," including the treaty. In one respect, Jackson was right: Carter sought to appease Jackson by allowing General Rowny to remain on the U.S. delegation until his resignation on the eve of the treaty-signing ceremony to campaign publicly against SALT II. Carter was not a popular president going into this fight, with approval ratings comparable to Nixon circa 1974. Gas prices, inflation, and interest rates were very high, and Senate Republicans, having agreed to support the Panama Canal treaties, were disinclined to give Carter another accomplishment.

TREATY TERMS AND CONTENTIOUS HEARINGS

The SALT II Treaty established a tiered system of constraints. Both superpowers would be obliged to reduce their Triads to 2,250 land- and sea-based long-range missile launchers as well as heavy bombers. Of this total, 1,320 launchers would be permitted for MIRVed missile launchers and heavy bombers carrying air-launched cruise missiles; 1,200 missile launchers for MIRVs would be permitted, of which 820 could be MIRVed land-based missiles with intercontinental range. SALT II banned new construction of ICBM launchers and limited new types of strategic offensive arms. It was to remain in effect through 1985, to be replaced, presumably, by a more ambitious undertaking. Two supplementary agreements were signed. One was a protocol lasting three years including cruise missile constraints, qualitative constraints on land-based missiles, and pledges not to deploy mobile land-based missiles for this limited duration. These issues would be taken up again in SALT III negotiations. A Joint Statement of Principles was also signed, reflecting aspirations for a follow-on treaty.

Contentious ratification hearings on Capitol Hill signaled trouble ahead to reach the 67 votes needed for the Senate's consent.[59] The administration's lead witness, Secretary of State Vance, argued that the treaty preserved a stable military balance, enhanced U.S. knowledge of the status of Soviet nuclear programs and capabilities, strengthened alliances, and reaffirmed U.S. leadership. Secretary of Defense Brown offered tempered reassurance about the strategic balance, saying it was "adequate" until 1985 and that it would improve thereafter. Chairman of the Joint Chiefs Jones offered very qualified support. His key concern was that SALT II not "be allowed to become a tranquilizer to the American people." Gerard Smith testified that SALT II compared "very favorably" with the Interim Agreement, urging the Senate to proceed step by step. Warnke defended the treaty by noting, "In any negotiation what you can get from the other side depends in very large part what you are willing to give up yourself . . . We have given up very little in SALT II." Warnke advised that "a better treaty can be negotiated, but only after this treaty."[60]

The Carter administration was unalterably on the defensive. It "cornered itself," in Leslie Gelb's view; the rules of the game were set by hawks.[61] Nitze testified to the treaty's "unequal and one-sided accommodation" but stopped short of calling for the treaty's outright rejection. Instead, he argued that the United States should never "concede" strategic superiority to the Soviet Union. Like General Jones, Nitze worried that it would "sap" U.S. willingness to compete.[62] Eugene Rostow, Nitze's partner in creating the Committee on the Present Danger, went further, arguing that ratification in the treaty's current form "would be an act of submission on our part." Edward Teller argued, "We cannot be saved except by mobilizing our scientists and our industry." Warnke returned to testify, this time expressly to address the concerns of liberal senators, calling for SALT II ratification to be used as a stepping-stone to deeper cuts and more stabilization measures.[63] Kissinger's testimony satisfied no one. He aligned himself with SALT critics by acknowledging a time of "grave danger" and "shifting strategic balance," but he didn't repudiate SALT II. Instead, he offered the nuanced view that its terms "do not improve our strategic situation, [nor] do they prevent our remedying it."[64]

The Senate Armed Services held concurrent hearings with Nitze and Rowny as the primary witnesses for the prosecution. Also testifying were Ford's secretary of defense, Donald Rumsfeld, who concluded that the treaty did not merit approval. Former ACDA director Fred Iklé suggested renegotiation to correct major flaws. Warnke argued that the defeat of SALT wouldn't change the strategic balance in the U.S. favor and, "as a matter of fact, its defeat would make it worse."[65]

The arguments of SALT supporters satisfied no one. Closing loopholes and capping arsenals after the permissive provisions of the Interim Agreement left both superpowers with bloated war-fighting capabilities. Arms controllers and deterrence strengtheners all had serious cause for complaint. After nearly four months of hearings and review, the Foreign Relations Committee voted its approval by a margin of nine to six. Liberals did not abandon the treaty, with Senator George McGovern, the Democratic Party's nominee in 1972, concluding that it "holds out more hope . . . than would rejection."[66] Both the chairman and the ranking Republican member of the Senate Foreign Relations Committee—Frank Church and Jacob Javits—supported SALT II and would soon lose their bids for reelection.

Over the objections of the Senate Armed Services Committee chairman John Stennis, Senator Jackson persuaded nine other senators on the committee to issue a report against ratification, including swing Republicans William Cohen and John Warner. The report, largely drafted by Richard Perle, concluded that SALT II was "not in the national security interest of the United States," and that "major changes" were necessary to make it acceptable.[67] The heart of the case against SALT II was that it permitted, and indeed facilitated, the vulnerability of U.S. land-based missiles that conveyed unacceptable advantages to the Kremlin. At a press conference following the committee vote, Senator Jackson underscored this point, describing the treaty as "a license for a massive buildup in strategic arms" that granted unilateral advantages to the Soviet Union.[68]

To beef up ratification prospects and to settle jitters in Europe, the Carter administration made preparations to deploy ballistic and cruise missiles on NATO soil. The Soviet Union had begun to deploy new MIRVed missiles in its western military districts that could reach Europe but not the United States—a move that NATO leaders felt compelled to answer. These counter-deployments would take center stage during the Reagan administration.

The Pentagon also announced a basing mode for the M-X. Brzezinski slowed down negotiations on a Comprehensive Test Ban Treaty so as not to provide more grist for the anti-SALT mill. In addition, the Carter administration proceeded with plans to place twenty cruise missiles on individual B-52 bombers and was entertaining the possibility of loading even more on specially designed, wide-bodied aircraft. Carter also announced defense budget increases, with Secretary Brown enumerating the particulars on Capitol Hill. Earlier, Carter's Pentagon had fully embraced Schlesinger's counterforce initiatives.

From the Kremlin's perspective, there wasn't much to lose when a rump minority of the Politburo decided to send troops into Afghanistan to protect its investment in a pro-Soviet government. This was the last nail in the coffin for SALT II ratification; others preceded it, including the fall of the Shah of Iran (and the loss of sensitive intelligence gathering posts), the extended Iranian hostage crisis, and the long-belated discovery of a Soviet "combat" brigade in Cuba. Ralph Earle, who was ACDA's SALT negotiator and subsequently its director, was convinced that the brouhaha over the Soviet brigade, which had been in Cuba since the 1960s, was crucial because "as long as they thought we were going to ratify SALT, they weren't going to invade Afghanistan." The Kremlin viewed the subsequent furor as "completely concocted and phony." Korniyenko, Gromyko's deputy, told Earle in Vienna that the "discovery" of Soviet troops in Cuba was proof positive that "Mr. Carter did not want SALT ratified." Earle was incredulous; he reacted by saying that this "was a stupid mistake. It was not intentional." Then Korniyenko looked Earle directly in the eye and said, "No government could be that stupid." Earle's reply: "Boy, you really don't know the United States." The lack of understanding was mutual.[69]

SALT II'S BALANCE SHEET

SALT II was significantly more effective and comprehensive than the Interim Agreement and the Vladivostok Accord. For the first time, it mandated reductions in aggregate force levels, albeit modest ones. It limited the numbers of Soviet weapon systems of greatest concern—ICBMs and land-based missiles carrying MIRVs. It established limits on the number of warheads that heavy missiles could carry. By including bombers into the aggregate totals—an area of distinct U.S. advantage—SALT II diminished throw-weight differentials. U.S. missile accuracy and counterforce capabilities were advancing, further offsetting the Soviet missile throw-weight advantage. SALT II corrected the numerical advantages in launchers accorded the Soviet Union in the Interim Agreement, while confirming the Vladivostok Accord's accomplishment of excluding forward-based systems, whether U.S., British, or French, in the totals.

There were additional benefits. SALT II belatedly clarified agreed limits on "new types" of ICBMs and upgrades of existing missile types. It established ceilings on missile throw-weight, banned "rapid reloads" of land-based missiles, and required advance notification of missile launches and other provisions to facilitate monitoring of flight tests. There were agreed statements and common understandings to avoid the compliance issues generated by the looseness of the Interim Agreement's provisions, as well as an agreed database of weapon systems covered under the treaty and "counting rules" for limitations on MIRVs. SALT II chronicler Strobe Talbott called the treaty "a masterpiece of modern diplomacy."[70] This seems overly generous, but compared to the Interim Agreement, it was. There was still one significant loose end—cruise missiles—and loose ends with perceived military utility would be dealt with in the usual way, by essentially being unconstrained.

SALT II was state of the art. It was as comprehensive as it could be for its time. Its level of detail and transparency were remarkable considering where the two parties were a decade earlier, when Brezhnev warned his SALT negotiators with prison if they spilled state secrets. SALT II was a promissory note. Reinforced by the ABM Treaty, it finally capped the strategic arms race, albeit at high levels—an outcome foreordained by earlier decisions. The treaty laid the groundwork for deeper cuts that became possible later, when political conditions permitted. But at the time of its completion, SALT II was either widely unloved or strenuously opposed.

The Joint Chiefs were essentially right in concluding that SALT II was modest but useful.[71] The Soviet General Staff might well have reached similar conclusions. Washington and Moscow had come a long way after almost a decade of negotiations, but their agreed limits did not fundamentally assuage the strategic concerns of either side, since neither was willing to forego an area of advantage in trade.[72]

SALT II, like the Interim Agreement fashioned by Nixon and Kissinger, reflected rather than altered the geopolitical competition between Washington and Moscow. Linkage did not fare well for either side in the SALT negotiations. This ambition was bound to fail since neither side was prepared to concede anything of value in order to gain something of equivalent value.

A far more relevant and realistic yardstick was whether SALT helped regulate and begin to dampen the nuclear competition in useful ways. One criterion of judging SALT II's worth in this regard is whether its provisions were respected even after Carter dropped his pursuit of ratification and Ronald Reagan, a harsh critic of SALT, was elected. By this measure, SALT II was clearly in the U.S. national security interest, as Reagan adhered to its limits until May 1986, beyond its expiration point in 1985 had the treaty been ratified. None of the criticisms levels by those opposed to SALT II could be remedied during this period, as U.S. strategic modernization programs were not ready for deployment.

The reckoning resulting from decisions made by Nixon and Kissinger in the Interim Agreement came due during the Carter administration. Carter closed the barn door and capped MIRVs. He laid the basis for deeper cuts that would be realized later. He could do no more. Just as the Interim Agreement was the most realistic outcome available to Nixon and Kissinger in 1972, SALT II was the most realistic outcome available in 1979.

SALT II bore the weight of the Interim Agreement's permissiveness. It was subject to withering fire, with Senator Jackson and Nitze leading the fusillades. They deemed missile throw-weight disparity exceedingly dangerous and not meeting the standards for equality under the Jackson amendment. The Backfire bomber wasn't counted in the totals. The tabling of an ambitious SALT II proposal in March 1977 was, in Garthoff's view, "fatefully unwise."[73] SALT opponents depicted every climb-down from Carter's ambitious offer as a measurement of retreat. Time was of the essence for Carter in 1977, just as it was for Ford in 1975; every delay decreased chances for the Senate's consent to ratification.

A series of disturbing Soviet actions, mostly in countries in Africa that most Americans couldn't identify on maps, helped to tip the scales against SALT II. Brzezinski set as one of his three top objectives upon becoming Carter's national security advisor "to improve America's strategic position"—not only with the Soviet Union and China but also to counter Soviet exploitation of "Third World turbulence."[74] The reverse seemed to be happening: the Kremlin was putting countries in the red column, while America's influence appeared to be shrinking.

Then came the coup de grâce for SALT II—the Soviet military expedition to keep Afghanistan in the "friendly" column. There were rumors that Brezhnev had previously promised Carter that he would not upset the applecart pending SALT II ratification, but by December 1979, this cart had no carrying capacity.[75] Bilateral relations were already at a low point. The invasion of Afghanistan seemed both an accentuation of negative dynamics and a harbinger of the future. Carter asked Senate majority leader Robert Byrd to suspend Senate consideration of the treaty, calling his failure to secure SALT II's ratification "the most profound disappointment" of his presidency.[76]

The RAND Corporation's leading SALT analyst, Thomas W. Wolfe, concluded that the "symbiotic" relationship between SALT and détente helped sink SALT II when détente turned sour.[77] With the benefit of hindsight, the Kremlin's move to secure a friendly government in Kabul can clearly be seen as a great strategic blunder, the beginning of a quagmire that contributed to the Soviet Union's demise. But in 1979, deep pessimism reigned. One year earlier, Carter delivered a televised "malaise" speech in which he talked about a crisis of confidence afflicting the country. In the fourth year of his presidency, Carter seemed to many to embody that malaise. He was the same extraordinary person revealed fully in his postpresidential years, but he was the wrong person to turn U.S. fortunes around. The man to do so was Ronald Reagan, riding horseback, promising a massive defense buildup and Morning in America.

THE PIVOT

Chapter 9

REAGAN'S ROLLER COASTER RIDE

Four decades after his presidency, Ronald Reagan continues to mystify. A gifted biographer, Edmund Morris, was granted extended access to Reagan and remained baffled. The public persona was easy enough for Morris to describe, but he had to resort to fiction in order to convey an inner life.[1] Reagan was remote and enigmatic even to his children, and a distant star to everyone else.

Reagan was a strident anticommunist and a fervent nuclear abolitionist. Prior to his arrival in the Oval Office, this was considered to be a null set; no president fully embraced both sets of belief. The anticommunist Reagan was on public display during his first term, the man who predicted that communism would collapse on the ash heap of history in an address before the British Parliament and railed against the Evil Empire before a gathering of evangelicals. This was the Reagan who authorized a significant defense buildup and tabled one-sided proposals to build down the Soviet nuclear arsenal as the United States built up. His abolitionism wasn't public knowledge until revealed from his encounters with Mikhail Gorbachev. George Shultz, his secretary of state, was unaware of it until a snowy evening on February 12, 1983, when the Reagans, unable to leave the White House for Camp David, invited the Shultzes to dine.[2]

The Left vilified Reagan during his first term. Arthur Schlesinger, Jr., forecast doom as a result of "the seizure of foreign policy by a boarding party of ideologues" who believed that "negotiation with evil is futile if not dangerous."[3] The Right forecast doom during Reagan's second term after his engagements with Gorbachev. Pat Buchanan, a veteran of the Nixon White House, wrote, "The Great Communicator who preached Peace through Strength today preaches peace through parchment."[4] Kenneth Adelman, Reagan's second director of the Arms Control and Disarmament Agency, wrote that "the Reagan administration most resembles March: in like a lion, out like a lamb."[5] Upon reflection, Adelman subsequently penned a generous tribute to Reagan.[6] Reagan left his critics sputtering and invited reassessment.

Reagan's embrace of the Strategic Defense Initiative and nuclear abolition was strange but was held together by the common thread of his abhorrence of nuclear weapons. Threading this needle so as to result in deep cuts in nuclear forces and the grounding of his beloved space shield required Shultz's deft maneuvering, Paul Nitze's formidable expertise, and, not least, the advent of a Soviet counterpart equally inclined to dispense with nuclear orthodoxy and force structure.

The Reagan administration's record of accomplishment in partnering with Gorbachev to break the back of the nuclear arms race should speak for itself, but what role the president himself played in this drama remains a matter of conjecture. The first assessments, written primarily by journalists, were not kind to Reagan, picturing him as woefully deficient on substance and easily manipulated by those around him. Strobe Talbott of *Time* magazine and the author of four books about the Reagan administration reflected this view, characterizing Reagan as "a President who confused nostrums with policies and dreams with strategy."[7] Raymond Garthoff, the chronicler of superpower competition and détente, held a similar view—that "Reagan was in many ways like a ceremonial monarch, entirely dependent on his viziers and courtiers."[8]

These accounts gave most of the credit for the breakthroughs reached during his presidency to others—especially to Gorbachev and secondarily to Shultz and his éminence grise, Nitze. A second wave of accounts by administration officials and Reagan's diary picture the president sufficiently in command to act opportunistically to seize the momentous developments occurring on his watch.[9]

One account by Jack Matlock, a diplomat with ringside seat, first on the National Security Council staff and then as U.S. ambassador to Moscow, finds coherence in Reagan's approach. In Matlock's view, Reagan always wanted peace and the reduction of nuclear dangers and weapons but needed to increase leverage first. Reagan challenged the Kremlin to change its operating assumptions and its behavior. Matlock objects to the conventional wisdom of a "turn" in U.S.-Soviet relations prior to and immediately after Reagan's reelection, arguing instead that conditions changed in the Soviet Union, allowing Reagan to execute his original game plan.[10]

Matlock's account is the outlier. Other than in hagiographical accounts, Reagan comes across as a president with strong instincts and gifts but with shallow depth. When advised poorly, he stumbled badly; with wise guidance, he recorded historic achievements. His presidential record on arms control proves that depth is optional and that strong political skills, wise counsel, and an enlightened Kremlin leader essential. Adelman sees Reagan as an actor who, when on set, was attentive and focused, but in between takes he could be disinterested and out of focus.[11]

John F. Kennedy was thoroughly immersed in detail, demanding daily updates in the Limited Test Ban Treaty negotiating endgame. Jimmy Carter was also detail oriented. Lyndon Baines Johnson was sound on the big picture of arms control and left the details of negotiating treaties to others—unlike his approach to the Vietnam War. Nixon wasn't familiar with technical detail and somewhat disinterested in nuclear numerology, but he superintended major agreements.

Reagan was sui generis. He was weak on details and held unshakable beliefs that didn't cohere. Jacques Attali, a French intellectual distant from the fray of American politics, described Reagan as a man of "formidable will, based on a mediocre understanding of the facts. As often in politics, ignorance sustains."[12] Far more important than mastery of detail is mastery of communicating with the public, and on this score, Reagan excelled. Reagan flummoxed opponents and confounded allies, but he accomplished much.

Presidents do not have to be grand strategists, nor do they have to hire grand strategists as national security advisors to gain public confidence in negotiating arms control with the Soviet Union. Reagan didn't pose as a grand strategist; it sufficed that he was a staunch anticommunist. Reagan's grasp of the particulars of deterrence and arms control was anecdotal and surface layered. He assembled a fractious crew under his big tent. Both dealers and squeezers who opposed deals with the Kremlin were welcome. Cabinet officers were at loggerheads and the captain of this ship disliked imposing discipline.

Some who observed Reagan at close hand were uncharitable toward him. Reagan's first secretary of state, Alexander Haig, characterized the president as an absentee captain: "The White House was as mysterious as a ghost ship; you heard the creak of the rigging and the groan of the timbers and sometimes even glimpsed the crew on deck. But which of the crew had the helm?" Adelman considered him "a man singularly endowed with an ability to hold contradictory views without discomfort." Reagan's first director of the Office of Management and Budget, David Stockton, asked, "What do you do when your president ignores all the relevant facts and wanders in circles?" Republican speechwriter Peggy Noonan had perhaps the unkindest cut of all: "The battle for the mind of Ronald Reagan was like the trench warfare of World War I: never have so many fought so hard for such barren terrain."[13]

There was ample evidence to support these views, but they failed to explain Reagan's role in breaking the back of the nuclear arms race. Placing all the credit on others, particularly Mikhail Gorbachev, is too simple an answer. How, then, can we properly decipher a leader with such instinctual powers and natural showmanship, but with a weak grasp of substance and loose grip on his subordinates? Lewis Dunn, who led the Reagan administration's efforts on nuclear nonproliferation, points us in the right direction: "Good instincts can produce opportunities and good results; bad instincts cannot be saved or overcome."[14]

Reagan accomplished what his predecessors could not, in part because he wasn't subject to normal political consequence for poor judgment, lax management, and being in thrall to fantasy. His instincts were overriding; their contradictions could be managed by wise counselors and skilled diplomats to produce extraordinary results. Reagan was preternaturally gifted and was readily absolved for his limitations and errors by all except the implacably unforgiving. He glided through life and his presidency without needing help from the astrological readings his wife compulsively consulted. Reagan created, by virtue of his obtuseness and unshakable beliefs, extraordinary opportunities that Shultz and the dealmakers around him exploited. To be sure, they would not have succeeded without Gorbachev's intense restlessness and neediness. Gorbachev realized that Shultz was "a serious man of sound political judgment."[15] Together, they would help engineer an extraordinary outcome, but this would not have been possible without Reagan.

REAGAN AND GORBACHEV

One key to deciphering Reagan's success in ending the Cold War nuclear competition was the human bond he forged with Gorbachev. That bond began at their first summit in Geneva in 1985 and became stronger when

they met at their unscripted summit at Reykjavik in 1986, where they contemplated the complete abolition of nuclear weapons. The Reykjavik summit started and ended badly, but their bond held. Despite their differences,
they both wanted historic accomplishments. They grasped at achievements
that were, by dint of their belief systems and extraordinary political circumstances, oddly within reach. Their human bond was essential to break the
back of the nuclear arms race.[16]

Shultz knew in his gut that if he could engage Reagan directly with a
Soviet leader like Gorbachev, he could win battles with Secretary of Defense
Caspar Weinberger and the Pentagon.[17] Gorbachev believed that personal
engagement was the key, as well.[18] He and Reagan had more in common than
met the eye; they were both big dreamers with a positive outlook on life, and
they were both lost without their wives. They could connect past their talking
points. Since bonding is an analytical concept in chemistry and not political
science, those scrutinizing the results of their interaction were baffled by it.

Gorbachev was, as many around Reagan understood, a transitional figure. He was the Soviet leader to end all Soviet leaders. He elevated Andrei
Gromyko to an honorific post from which Gromyko assumed he could still
control the Foreign Ministry. Then Gorbachev chose Eduard Shevardnadze
as his new foreign minister and together they threw out the Russian negotiating playbook.[19] Gorbachev was in a great hurry, recognizing that the Soviet
economic model, with its egregious deference to inflated defense requirements, and the Warsaw Pact model of control over Eastern Europe were both
unsustainable. As his interpreter wrote, Gorbachev embraced the "primacy
of universal values over class or ideological struggles."[20] Gorbachev was the
Great Disruptor, but he and Soviet society lacked the skills to reform a broken system. Gorbachev knew that reform required an end to the Cold War,
but he didn't know what to do after ending it. He did know, however, how
to end the nuclear arms race. Only he could do this, and only with Reagan
as his unlikely partner.

Reagan, too, was on a mission. He was convinced that nuclear deterrence
was immoral, and he was determined that Armageddon would not happen
on his watch. Reagan and Gorbachev were a spectacularly odd couple, and
yet a strangely appropriate match. They could take liberties with deterrence
orthodoxy and both could get away with it. Nixon and Kissinger carped
at Reagan and Gorbachev's greatest feat—the 1987 Intermediate Nuclear
Forces Treaty that eliminated entire categories of ground-based missiles—because this would weaken alliance bonds and remove rungs on the escalation

ladder reinforcing nuclear deterrence.[21] Reagan couldn't be bothered, and he was right. With Shultz at his side, stolid and Buddha-like, waiting for and reeling in Gorbachev's concessions, Reagan's radical abolitionist instincts were at least partially realized. Getting there was an adventure.

LAUNCHING THE SHIP OF FEUDS

Because he was so disengaged, Reagan could only be as effective as his closest advisers—and his advisers were, as his first chief of staff, James Baker, described, "a witches' brew of intrigue, elbows, egos, and separate agendas."[22] When surrounded by advisers that lacked common sense and tended toward ideological crusades, embarrassment followed, like the Iran-Contra affair— a hare-brained scheme to sell arms to Iran, using the proceeds to support Contra fighters in Nicaragua. When Reagan relied upon deft deal makers like Shultz and Baker, major accomplishments followed.

Strife was endemic during Reagan's first term, just as it was when President Ford and Kissinger sought to turn the Vladivostok Accord into a treaty over the objections of the Pentagon and hardliners on Capitol Hill. Republican politics had changed. Reagan was both the beneficiary and victim of this change; he rode hard-edged Conservatism to the White House, only to preside nominally over trench warfare between dealmakers and oppositionists during his first term.

Reagan's new team included over thirty members of the Committee on the Present Danger. Its co-founder, Eugene Victor Debs Rostow, took the helm of ACDA. His parents emigrated from Tsarist Russia with their socialist ideals intact. One brother, Walt Whitman Rostow, was Johnson's national security advisor when the Vietnam War was spiraling downward. A third brother was named after Ralph Waldo Emerson. "Gene" Rostow was superbly credentialed, having previously served as the dean of Yale Law School and as an under secretary of state in the Johnson administration. Rostow's major contribution during his short stint at ACDA was to help reframe the U.S. negotiating objective from strategic arms control and limitation to strategic arms reductions. SALT would henceforth become START.

Rostow's co-founder of the Committee on the Present Danger, Paul Nitze, joined the Reagan administration to focus on a "dual track" approach to hold the Atlantic Alliance together while deploying intermediate-range missiles below the 5,500-kilometer range threshold covered in SALT. The genesis of the dual-track approach came late in the Carter administration. One measure of the extent to which arms control constructs had taken hold was that negotiations had become a necessary complement to new missile deployments. If NATO countries wished to host counterdeployments to offset Soviet MIRVed missiles of less than ocean-spanning range, deployments and negotiations had to proceed on parallel tracks to assuage allied and public concerns.

Nitze was entirely focused on the challenge of keeping NATO together despite intense public opposition fanned by an all-out Soviet campaign to split the Atlantic Alliance and block their installation. No U.S. negotiator was made of sterner stuff. A self-described "assertive, hard-nosed pragmatist," the essential Nitze was a man who "sorted out matters of belief," then applied "clear and rigorous logic, based upon a cold and unemotional assessment of the objective evidence concerning the relevant facts, and a careful analysis of the probable outcomes and probable material and moral costs of alternative courses of action." Only then could one "get from where one is to where one wants, and should want, to be."[23] Employing this mindset, Nitze would utterly disregard his negotiating instructions to work out a deal limiting U.S. and Soviet Euro-missile deployments. He received no backup from the Reagan White House or from the Kremlin but was so essential to the dual-track strategy that he remained in place, with his sense of purpose undiminished. The only other person aware of Nitze's freelancing was a supportive Rostow.

Reagan chose Weinberger as his secretary of defense, a fellow Californian with deep roots in the Republican Party. Weinberger grew up in San Francisco, the child of a lawyer of Bohemian Jewish descent and a violinist-turned-homemaker. He was hooked on history and government at an early age, reading the *Congressional Record* and Winston Churchill, and avidly following the fortunes of Herbert Hoover. After a stint at Harvard, where he edited the *Harvard Crimson*, and at Harvard Law School, he enlisted as an infantryman during World War II and served in the Pacific. He returned to San Francisco, briefly clerked for a judge and worked in a law firm, and then focused on a life in politics. He represented the San Francisco Bay area in the State Assembly and served as the California state chairman of the Republican Party during the rise and defeat of presidential candidate Barry Goldwater.

With Nixon's election, Weinberger joined Shultz in Washington, serving first at the Federal Trade Commission and then followed in Shultz's footsteps as the director of the Office of Management and Budget. Weinberger was determined to succeed at whatever challenge he took on. When appointed by Reagan to lead the Defense Department, he tenaciously defended the Pentagon's support for more funding with as much single-minded focus as he cut budgets when he led the budget bureau. In between the Nixon and Reagan administrations, Weinberger, like Shultz, went into business at Bechtel. Shultz was Bechtel's president; Weinberger was the corporation's general counsel, who Shultz was sometimes obliged to rein in.

Reagan's initial choice to be secretary of state, Alexander Haig, proved to be a poor fit. Weinberger described him as being "constitutionally unable to present an argument without an enormous amount of passion and intensity, heavily overlaid with a deep suspicion of the competence and motives of anyone who did not share his opinion."[24] Blustery and not averse to the use of force, Haig readily tried to assume authority that was not relinquished by others, most notably after Reagan was shot and the secretary of state appeared on camera trying to calm his fellow citizens by announcing, "I, Al Haig, am in control here at the White House." This brought back memories of his role as White House chief of staff during Nixon's final days. Haig tried to resuscitate the concept of linkage between progress on strategic arms negotiations and improvements in problematic Soviet behavior elsewhere, starting with Cuba. His manner didn't suit Reagan who, after seventeen months of turmoil, picked up the phone to ask George Shultz to replace him.

Shultz dispensed with linkage while challenging the Kremlin on a range of issues, including human rights, while pursuing nuclear arms reductions. He made a practice of calling for freer emigration before every discussion about nuclear arms control. Deals were possible when national security interests were in alignment, while other issues would remain contested. Shultz needed all of his considerable powers of management and bureaucratic maneuver, gained from cabinet positions during the Nixon administration and then running Bechtel. When Shultz replaced Haig, he and Weinberger would be operating at the same level. Weinberger was resolutely opposed to the kinds of deals Shultz was contemplating. There always seemed to be unfinished business between them. Clashes were inevitable.

Shultz's demeanor disguised a man driven to accomplishment in academia, business, and government. Often described as unflappable, Shultz acknowledged that this was untrue; he had fits of anger, but said that it did no good, so he moved on.[25] His mother was the daughter of a Presbyterian missionary. His father, raised a Quaker on a farm in Indiana, was a self-made man who took a job at the New York Stock Exchange. An only child, Shultz never wanted for anything. He went to Princeton, then joined the marines and fought in the Pacific. After World War II, he went to MIT to earn his PhD in economics, followed by a brief stint in Washington in the office of President

Eisenhower's Council of Economic Advisers. He left Washington to make his mark in academia, rising to become a dean at the University of Chicago. Nixon brought him back to Washington to serve in two cabinet posts—as secretary of labor and as treasury secretary in addition to running the Office of Management and Budget. Then came his stint running Bechtel before being called back east by Reagan.

Shultz inherited Lawrence Eagleburger and Richard Burt from Haig. Both were avowed Atlanticists and believers in deterrence. Their most important responsibility was to keep the dual-track decision of deploying new Euromissiles while pursuing arms control moving forward in parallel. They overcame resistance from administration hardliners who wanted to ditch negotiations, and from skeptical arms controllers, who wanted to ditch the new missiles. These battles were won, at least temporarily, by whomever could succeed in inserting language into the president's prepared remarks. Eagleburger, deeply suspect for his association with Henry Kissinger, managed to insert language in Reagan's welcoming remarks for a visit by British prime minister Margaret Thatcher reaffirming the dual-track decision.

Burt was smart, ambitious, and new to the workings of government. He made a name for himself at the International Institute of Strategic Studies and as a diplomatic correspondent at the *New York Times*, following in Leslie Gelb's tracks to leave journalism to engage directly in nuclear negotiations. His opposite number in the Pentagon, Richard Perle, was well armed in the arts of legislative maneuver from eleven years on Senator Henry Jackson's staff. He proved equally adept at devising blocking maneuvers within the executive branch. Burt described him as a "talented and creative guy who could entice the birds out of the trees." He was also "fundamentally opposed to arms control," both process and outcome.[26] Perle's detractors labeled him the "Prince of Darkness." He was articulate and especially masterful in framing terms of debate. His rejoinder to critics was that he wasn't being unreasonable; he was instead setting higher standards. Reasonableness had led to bad deals, he argued; he would hold fast for better ones. The only deal that Reagan accomplished—the Intermediate Nuclear Forces Treaty—didn't meet his standards.

There were six national security advisors in the Reagan administration. The first was Richard Allen, a foreign policy adviser to Richard Nixon who was displaced by Kissinger. Candidate Ronald Reagan provided Allen with a second chance. Allen's area of expertise was Soviet Communism, and he lined up with hardliners deeply skeptical of Moscow's intentions, recruiting

Richard Pipes, lead author of the "Team B" report, to be his Soviet expert on the National Security Council staff. The president's views, expressed at his first news conference on January 29, 1981, were that "so far, détente's been a one-way street," adding for good measure that the Kremlin's goal "must be the promotion of world revolution and a one-world Socialist or Communist state."[27] If the Kremlin still harbored hopes that the Reagan administration would fit into the familiar Nixon mold, they were shaken by Reagan's early pronouncements. Allen lasted less than one year before resigning for receiving money from Japanese journalists to interview Mrs. Reagan.

Eugene Rostow had scant ties to Reagan, ruffled feathers easily, and was not indispensable. He was escorted out of the administration six months after Haig left, replaced by Kenneth Adelman, Jeane Kirkpatrick's deputy at the United Nations. Adelman grew up on the South Side of Chicago in a neighborhood where Michelle Obama was subsequently raised. Adelman was a go-getter. He worked his way through college and began his professional life as an Africanist. He was Muhammed Ali's translator in Zaire and sat ringside for Ali's championship fight with George Foreman. Then he found himself, thanks to an ex-campaign manager for Donald Rumsfeld, working in Nixon's newly created Office of Economic Opportunity with Rumsfeld and Dick Cheney. Adelman, a devotee of Shakespeare, was young, iconoclastic, and an outsider to the ranks of arms controllers, resulting in a rough confirmation fight and, later on, telling observations about Reagan.[28]

GETTING DOWN TO DEADLOCK

The first decision facing the Reagan administration was whether it would seek to retrieve SALT II from the Senate's calendar, a procedural move that would have the practical effect of repudiating the treaty. To do so required a majority vote. This decision was more consequential than it appeared because if SALT II remained with the Senate, the United States would be obliged by customary practice in international law to respect the treaty's object and purpose. In other words, even without the Senate's consent to ratification, SALT II would provide guardrails and netting under the high-wire act to follow.

Reagan asked for the advice of three civilians—Allen, Weinberger, and CIA director William Casey—and three men with military backgrounds—Haig, chairman of the Joint Chiefs David Jones, and National Security Agency director Bobby Inman. Allen and Weinberger wanted to withdraw from SALT II, while the military men all argued against doing so. Casey expressed no opinion at this meeting. SALT II stayed on the Senate's calendar.[29]

The Reagan administration's order of priority in dealing with negotiations was Euro-missiles first and ocean-spanning missiles second. The negotiation on intermediate-range, ground-based missiles was ahead in the queue because of the urgency attached to countering the deployment of new Soviet MIRVed missiles that could target Europe but not the United States. At a talk given in October 1977 before the International Institute of Strategic Studies in London, German chancellor Helmut Schmidt challenged the United States to rectify the resulting imbalance as well as to pursue arms control. The Carter administration responded by drawing up plans for deployments in five NATO countries, a painstakingly difficult process. Preliminary discussions on Euro-missiles with the Soviet Union began at the end of the Carter administration. At the State Department's urging, Reagan promised to begin negotiations by the end of his first year in office.

Carter and Reagan administration defense strategists presumed that the purpose of Soviet intermediate-range missiles was not only to provide additional war-fighting capabilities but also to divide and to apply political leverage on NATO countries. The Soviet ambassador to the United States, Anatoly Dobrynin, disputed this conventional wisdom as it ascribed more cohesion to Soviet decision making than was warranted. Instead, he described an uncoordinated approach where "military justifications were the only ones advanced" without input from the Foreign Ministry.[30]

Even though Reagan talked differently, the Kremlin expected more continuity than was outwardly apparent from one administration to the next. Jimmy Carter tried to improve markedly on the Vladivostok Accord, but Carter relented. Soviet foreign minister Andrei Gromyko assumed the same dynamics from the incoming Reagan administration.[31] Even though presidential candidate Reagan declared SALT II to be "fatally flawed," Gromyko believed Reagan would be obliged to negotiate within familiar parameters.

The Kremlin was in for a rude shock. To begin with, Reagan's team was in no hurry to table new proposals; Weinberger argued that a six-month wait was advisable.[32] It took longer—ten months—for Reagan to announce his administration's position and for Euro-missile negotiations to begin. Reagan called for the Kremlin to dismantle its missiles; in return, NATO would not deploy counters. Moscow promptly rejected the "Zero Option" and awaited a more realistic proposal. Reagan accepted the advice of the Pentagon and played hardball. The only answer to Soviet missiles that threatened NATO countries was the deployment of a comparable threat. Paul Nitze, the bane of SALT II's ratification, would lead the U.S. negotiating team.

For its strategic arms reduction negotiator, the Reagan team chose to reward retired general Edward Rowny for his steadfast opposition to SALT II. Rowny was also considered to become the director of ACDA, but this was an awkward fit, as Rowny didn't seem to believe in the agency's mission statement. When Adelman was tapped for this job, Rowny wrote him a memo suggesting individuals who ought to be culled from the agency's ranks because they believed too unreservedly in arms control. One of those who Rowny sought to blacklist, Jack Mendelsohn, recalled, "Rowny's problem was that he could not win an argument with anybody. He could 'boss' an argument, he could order an end, but he couldn't win it because he wasn't intellectually up to it."[33]

Rowny's choice as START negotiator had the intended effect of reassuring hardliners, but his influence inside the administration was slight. He was, in Nitze's view, "neither an impressive figure nor an effective bureaucratic infighter." He employed a "cumbersome, ham-fisted style of argument that often made those who agreed with him wince."[34] His theory of bargaining when representing the Joint Chiefs during the Ford and Carter administrations was, as U.S. delegation chief U. Alexis Johnson noted, "to state and restate our position without making any concession until the Soviets agreed to it. In relatively short order the Soviet [delegation] refused to talk to Rowny," requiring discussions in other channels.[35] More workarounds were in store.

NEGOTIATING FROM STRENGTH

Reagan took steps to strengthen his hand in the negotiations before announcing the Zero Option. Large hikes in the defense budget were announced. In October 1981, one month before the beginning of negotiations, the administration announced the resurrection of the B-1 bomber canceled by Carter and a more advanced missile for Trident submarines. The U.S. inventory of long-range cruise missiles would be enlarged. Reagan also scrapped Carter's costly and improbable plans for mobile, racetrack basing of the M-X, opting to place these missiles, now renamed the "Peacekeeper," in closely spaced silos in Wyoming. This basing concept was nicknamed "Dense Pack." These missiles would be vulnerable to attack, but the fratricide effects of the first Soviet detonations would have the effect of destroying later arrivals. The Dense Pack basing scheme died quickly.

If the Peacekeeper were to be deployed, the issue of ICBM vulnerability in silos—so central in the campaign against SALT II—would have to be defused. This was the purpose of the blue-ribbon commission led by Brent Scowcroft, which included five former secretaries of defense. The 1983 Scowcroft panel effectively closed the window of vulnerability by noting that the other two legs of the Triad were being strengthened. Mobility for land-based missiles would be pursued in the future. The Reagan team settled on 100 Peacekeepers, half the total proposed by the Carter administration. For good measure the Pentagon retired the largest throw-weight-bearing missiles in the U.S. inventory, the Titan II, citing their age and maintenance costs. Carter would have been flayed for these moves; Reagan glided above them.

Weinberger's new defense guidance, approved three months after the beginning of negotiations, dispensed with the bromides of "essential equivalence" and having nuclear capabilities "second to none." Instead, the Pentagon's new marching orders were that, if deterrence failed and mushroom clouds appeared, "United States nuclear capabilities must prevail even under the condition of prolonged war," forcing "the Soviet Union to seek earliest termination of hostilities on terms favorable to the United States." This new war-fighting strategy was promptly leaked to the press.[36] When challenged during congressional testimony, Weinberger returned fire with "You show me a Secretary of Defense who's planning not to prevail and I'll show you a Secretary of Defense who ought to be impeached."[37]

Weinberger entrusted Richard Perle, whom he recruited from Senator Jackson's staff, to help counter Shultz and Nitze. Perle argued that arms control as practiced by Nixon, Ford, and Carter was a soporific. Serious arms control, in Perle's view, required the Kremlin's acceptance of outcomes that previous presidents presumed were beyond reach. Perle, like his mentors Senator Jackson and Albert Wohlstetter, believed that better outcomes were possible as long as the Pentagon deployed new missiles, submarines, and bombers. If the Kremlin leadership was sufficiently worried about losing a strategic competition, Moscow would be more accommodating.

The first year of the Reagan administration was jarring, domestically and internationally. A senior strategic analyst at the Pentagon and advocate of civil defense measures, T. K. Jones, reassuringly told a journalist that three feet of dirt could make all the difference in saving lives in the event of nuclear war: "If there are enough shovels to go around, everybody's going to make it."[38] Equally stunning was the opinion of ACDA director Rostow, who previously surmised, "We are living in a pre-war and not a post-war world."[39]

The Reagan administration's rhetoric, personnel choices, and policies left Democrats dazed. U.S. allies were wary; the Kremlin was at first puzzled and then alarmed. The SALT process was disappointing, even to its supporters, but it had finally established guardrails on the nuclear competition—one that the Reagan team now seemed prepared to win. Anxieties about nuclear war were growing, and doubts about the administration's bone fides to negotiate agreements with the Kremlin were widespread. The unveiling of the Zero Option didn't help matters—until it succeeded, much to the surprise of its backers and opponents. Prospects for its success improved after Haig was shown the door and Reagan recruited Shultz to replace him. Reagan didn't mind conflicting advice from Shultz and Weinberger, but only up to a point. He ultimately sided with Shultz, who deftly outmaneuvered hardliners. The deal breakers then left, one by one.

THE ZERO OPTION

Perle disliked the dual-track decision and attempted to derail it, but the political imperatives to proceed were overriding. To make the best of what he feared would be a bad bargain in negotiating with Moscow, Perle sold Weinberger and the Joint Chiefs on the Zero Option. State Department officials from Secretary Haig on down were convinced that the United States wouldn't want zero even if it were achievable, which they doubted. In their view, zero would be detrimental to deterrence.

The interagency deliberations to craft a negotiating position were cochaired by Perle and Burt, who argued intensely. When Perle tabled a draft of the Zero Option for three types of medium- and intermediate-range nuclear missiles, Burt threw the paper aside, saying, "Come on, Richard." Perle drove back to the Pentagon after the meeting with John Woodworth, the director of Theater Nuclear Policy in the Office of the Secretary of Defense, who was soon to be the Pentagon's representative in the INF talks. Perle told Woodworth that he would circumvent the interagency process and take a direct route to Reagan to sell his idea. He assumed that the Kremlin would oppose whatever the Reagan administration proposed. If so, why not propose something simple, yet dramatic? "We're playing to the public," Woodworth recalled Perle saying, "and this will get the high ground." Perle succeeded, outmaneuvering the State Department, which was focused on an interim solution far short of zero. "He never thought anything would come of this," Woodworth recalled. With negotiations deadlocked, U.S. counterdeployments would then proceed, eventually placing the Kremlin at a great disadvantage.[40]

To make the Zero Option somewhat more palatable, Richard Burt and his State Department colleagues crafted a negotiating position calling for equal warheads on Euro-missiles at the lowest level possible, with the ultimate goal being zero. Haig offered this formula—"equal, effective and verifiable outcomes at the lowest levels of forces on the basis of the principle of equality and equal security"—in his September 1981 meeting in New York with Gromyko.[41] Gromyko unsurprisingly expressed opposition to any formula that smacked of reductions, especially one-sided reductions. The Pentagon also opposed reductions—unless they were one-sided.

Reagan announced the Zero Option at the National Press Club in November 1981. If the Kremlin would dismantle missiles carrying 1,100 warheads, his administration would not proceed with deployment of 108 Pershing II ballistic and 476 ground-launched cruise missiles in five NATO basing countries. The Pershing II missiles could arrive at their targets—which the Kremlin presumed to include Moscow itself—in a matter of minutes, likely detonating before detection. Stealthy cruise missiles would take longer to arrive at their targets but would be hard to detect before their detonation.

Public and editorial reaction to the Zero Option ranged from dismay to discomfort. Paul Warnke wrote that it could lead to "the worst of all possible results: no reduction in the Soviet intermediate-range nuclear-missile force, no deployment of the new American missiles in Western Europe and a perceived Soviet veto on NATO's weapons decisions."[42] Herbert Scoville wrote that it was "palpably nonnegotiable."[43] The *Wall Street Journal* editorialized, "The Soviets are no more likely to accept an interim solution than a zero option."[44] The *Los Angeles Times* opined, "It will take a miracle if prospective negotiations with Moscow . . . produce a satisfactory agreement."[45] Given the Pentagon's intentions, these prognostications were on the mark. Given Gorbachev's penchant for turning the tables, they were wrong.

Deterrence strategists were also uncomfortable with the Zero Option. It was clear to the U.S. negotiating team led by Nitze and his deputy, Maynard "Mike" Glitman, that the Kremlin sought to decouple the United States from its European allies by making it political untenable for basing countries to carry out their pledges of counterdeployments. Some NATO deployments were better than none, and West Germany was the key. There was an active and growing movement against new missile deployments within Western Europe; the more Moscow campaigned against counterdeployments, the more Washington needed to persuade NATO to stand fast. In Nitze's view, nothing less than the future of NATO was at stake. The Kremlin's Euro missiles posed a direct threat to NATO allies but not to the United States. NATO allies were "anxious for a prompt agreement" reducing this threat. They didn't expect to eliminate it.[46]

According to Woodworth, the Pentagon's representative to the negotiations, "never, in his wildest dreams," did Perle expect the Kremlin to accept the Zero Option; no one did.[47] A negotiating deadlock seemed very likely, so every Soviet proposal at the talks—and there were many variations—was designed to convey the impression of flexibility, placing the onus for stalemate on Reagan administration hardliners while fueling the burgeoning peace movement in European and American cities.

The INF negotiations in Geneva began shortly after the imposition of martial law in Poland in December 1981. The Reagan administration decided to proceed despite this crackdown. The Kremlin and the Pentagon were only nominally negotiating with each other. The Kremlin was playing to the galleries in Europe and the United States. Deadlocked negotiations served the purposes of Weinberger and Perle, as well. By calling and raising the Kremlin's hand, they could deploy new war-fighting capabilities placing the Soviet command and control system at far greater risk. As Glitman wrote, "The stakes were high—nothing less than the ultimate outcome of the Cold War."[48] Glitman wasn't exaggerating.

When the negotiations began in November 1981, the Kremlin tabled a "Statement of Intentions" calling for both sides to reduce their existing medium-range missiles and aircraft. U.K. and French forces were included in these proposals, which required reductions in "dual-capable" aircraft that could be used in conventional or nuclear warfare. The Kremlin proposed a moratorium on "new" and "medium-range" systems, leaving no room for new U.S. Euro-missile deployments. Modernization and replacement would be permitted on a one-for-one basis, in effect allowing Russian, British, and French missile replacements, but not those of the United States.

Both delegations tabled draft treaties in early 1982, but Moscow and Washington seemed hopelessly deadlocked over negotiating principles as well as outcomes. As Glitman wrote, "The underlying differences were fundamental."[49] The Soviet side refused to accept the legitimacy of any new NATO deployments of Euro-missiles that could reach Russian soil, while insisting on the right to be able to target NATO with missiles of comparable range. The two sides also disagreed fundamentally on whether the outcome of their negotiations should be based on equal reductions—the Soviet position—or equal outcomes. The Soviet side insisted on including British and French forces; their ballistic missile submarines would count, while Soviet submarines would not. The Kremlin wished to limit the scope of an agreement to systems deployed in Europe or "intended for use" in Europe. This was as unacceptable to the Reagan administration as the Zero Option was to the Kremlin. The U.S. treaty sought equal outcomes, the exclusion of British and French forces, and "dual-capable" aircraft. Washington also sought constraints to prevent the Kremlin from repositioning its missiles closer to Europe.

FROM SALT TO START TO FULL STOP

Stark differences in U.S. and Soviet negotiating positions in the INF talks were soon to be replicated in the new Strategic Arms Reduction talks. The infighting between the Pentagon and the State Department was over how to frame demands that the Kremlin would reject. Weinberger, Perle, and Fred Iklé, now at the Pentagon, called for missile throw-weight limits to slightly below the U.S. level. The State Department, with Richard Burt in the lead, proposed a two-phased system of reductions in launchers and warheads that would significantly reduce Soviet missile throw-weight.

Burt and James Goodby, the State Department's choice as Rowny's deputy, forged common cause with the Joint Chiefs at the Pentagon, proposing a two-phased approach: the first focusing on missiles and the warheads they carried, and the second focusing on even deeper, one-sided, throw-weight reductions. Those most concerned about Soviet missile throw-weight, led by the Pentagon, Rostow, and Rowny, assumed that the State Department would lose interest in the second phase of their proposal if they somehow succeeded in phase one.

It fell to Robert McFarlane on Reagan's National Security Council staff to reconcile these differences. He did do with a classified codicil to the National Security Decision Directive signed by Reagan. The codicil embraced hardline proposals. A first phase of reductions would reduce Soviet missile throw-weight by 50 percent; phase two would draw it down further, by a total of two-thirds. In May 1982, Reagan laid out the U.S. negotiating position for START in a commencement speech at his alma mater, Eureka College. Labeling his proposals as "a practical, phased reduction plan," Reagan called for deep cuts on land-based missiles to equal ceilings at least a third below existing levels, with no more than half of each side's warheads to be land-based.

In numerical terms, the U.S. going-in position for START would require Soviet land- and sea-based missile launchers to be reduced from 2,300 to

850; warheads atop land-based missiles were to be reduced from approximately 6,000 allowable in SALT II to 2,500. The Kremlin would be obliged to reduce by two-thirds its force of "heavy" missiles and their next largest land-based missile, while U.S. strategic modernization programs would proceed as planned. The practical effect of these proposals, as one Soviet negotiator relayed to Raymond Garthoff in 1983: "You want to solve your vulnerability problem by making our forces vulnerable."[50]

Like the administration's proposed Zero Option, Reagan was proposing equal outcomes. And like the Zero Option, these outcomes would be reached by Soviet reductions in forces of greatest concern to the United States. Reagan's initial offering was so one-sided as to suggest to the Kremlin and to domestic critics a disinterest in negotiations while the Pentagon could pursue new nuclear war-fighting capabilities on missiles, submarines, and bombers.

As opening negotiating gambits go, the Reagan administration's position on START was over-the-top but not unprecedented. The opening Soviet gambits on Euro-missiles were likewise one-sided and would presumably be altered over time. Every U.S. administration negotiates with itself before tabling proposals, and at the outset of the Reagan administration, opinions ranged between deep skepticism and outright opposition to negotiating steep arms reductions. The State Department sought useful outcomes while the Pentagon and ACDA felt that "useful" outcomes were useless. Coming on the heels of the Zero Option, Reagan's initial START proposal seemed disingenuous, at best, as the Pentagon seemed implacably opposed to fallback positions.

Dobrynin's assessment was that "the administration's arms control proposals seemed designed to subvert rather than advance the process."[51] The Kremlin countered in predictable ways. Brezhnev delivered a speech one week after Reagan's Eureka College commencement address calling for a freeze in strategic modernization programs. The most recent cycle of Soviet programs was almost completed, while the Reagan program, inherited from Carter, had yet to be fielded. The Kremlin's proposed freeze was therefore as one-sided in its effects as the Reagan administration's proposal. The Kremlin also proposed reductions from 2,250 to 1,800 launchers—an uncharacteristic move, as Moscow usually resisted reductions—but this was predicated on no additional forward-based systems, meaning that a START deal was linked to blocking NATO's new Euro-missiles. If the Reagan administration could backtrack from SALT, so, too, could the Kremlin. Brezhnev demanded that all cruise missiles would need to be banned—air-, ground- and sea-based.

START, like the INF negotiations, seemed to be going nowhere. Meanwhile, public opposition in the United States and Europe to the diplomatic impasse was growing.

THE FREEZE MOVEMENT

Archimedes postulated that magnitudes were relative, and that they changed in relationship to moves and countermoves. In every chapter of the nuclear competition, Archimedean properties have applied. If either superpower took a significant step in the nuclear competition, sooner or later the other would react accordingly. Sir Isaac Newton arrived at the same general conclusion in his Third Law of Motion—that actions prompted reactions. In nuclear arms control, the reactions are not necessarily equal, but they are definitely oppositional. McNamara called this the action-reaction phenomenon. The two superpowers rarely acted in parallel, as sequencing was out of phase. Sometimes Washington would gear up first, and at other times Moscow would. The superpower playing catch-up wasn't about to formalize an inferior position. In the case of INF deployments, the United States was playing catch-up.

Another variation on Archimedes and Newton was that every strong push a U.S. administration made to increase nuclear capabilities in ways that appeared to increase nuclear danger elicited a concerted domestic political reaction. In the United States, reactions to arms racing could be reliably measured by pushback on Capitol Hill and by the number of protesters taking to the streets. The proposed deployment of U.S. missiles in five NATO countries meant that pushback could also be measured by protests in European cities. The climactic inflection point in this dynamic—the fulcrum where action and reaction fused—was the vote in the German Bundestag over accepting Euro-missiles.

Moscow wasn't betting on winning arguments over Euro-missiles at the negotiating table; the Kremlin was betting on antinuclear legislators and demonstrators. The Reagan administration's hard talk about prevailing in a nuclear war, its one-sided negotiating proposals that seemed designed to fail, and its nuclear buildup generated powerful domestic opposition that crystalized in the Freeze Movement. The movement's principal conceptualizer was Randall Forsberg.

Forsberg followed her husband, a Swedish national, to Stockholm, where she found a job as a typist at the Stockholm International Peace Research Institute. She quickly rose through the ranks to become a researcher and published analyst. Returning to the United States as a single parent, she pursued a doctorate at MIT. This ambition was prolonged because more pressing matters intervened. She didn't fit into the world of work for women as it was then ordered. She wasn't credentialed enough to make a career in academia, and besides, she felt drawn to mobilize public opinion. There weren't many opportunities for women in the field at nongovernmental organizations and working on the inside didn't suit her. So, she created her own think tank, the Institute for Defense and Disarmament Studies, in 1980 to conduct research on military expenditures and the arms race—modeled on her experience in Sweden but on a smaller scale.

Purposeful leadership is necessary for a successful start-up lacking an endowment. The timing must also be right, and in 1980, Forsberg's timing was perfect. The notion of a moratorium was already circulating among peace groups in late 1979. Forsberg reframed this idea as a "freeze." She issued a "Call to Halt the Nuclear Arms Race" in December 1980. This call rejected the synchronicity problem, when actions and reactions are typically out of phase. It was instead premised on the assumptions that there already existed rough equivalence in strategic forces and that a NATO response to Soviet missiles along with the Reagan buildup would be dangerously destabilizing.

The "Call to Halt the Nuclear Arms Race" was addressed to Washington and Moscow. It called for a mutual freeze on nuclear weapon testing, production, and deployment, as well as on missiles and new aircraft designed to carry them. This would constitute an "essential, verifiable first step of lessening the risk of nuclear war and reducing the nuclear arsenals." Arsenals were growing, as were nuclear war-fighting capabilities. Negotiations seemed unlikely to reverse this course. The remedy was simple and persuasive to many on the outside looking in. It was, in effect, to "just say no" to the nuclear arms race. The freeze would "hold constant" existing nuclear parity and "eliminate excuses for further arming of both sides." Advocates of the freeze argued that later, after its adoption, its terms could be codified in a treaty. The remainder of the "call" explicated particulars—which systems would be covered, how the freeze would be verified, and how it would relate to existing agreements. It was signed by leading peace groups, prominent individuals, and liberal members of Congress.

Forsberg channeled generalized angst into political activism over a specific goal. She fought her way into conversations and rooms where she was previously excluded. In the politics of arms control, no woman before her had carved out such a large role. Forsberg attracted followers through her vision, her sense of strategy, and her public charisma.[52] Other women had begun to make their mark playing the inside game—Lynn Davis, Susan Koch, and Rose Gottemoeller, for example. Ruth Adams amplified the voices of rising talent and established figures at the *Bulletin of the Atomic Scientists*, later funding them from her perch at the MacArthur Foundation. Betty Goetz Lall was a pioneer, working for Hubert Humphrey to help create ACDA, but she wasn't a role model because, as Judith Reppy noted, there weren't that many women in the field back then.[53] Dorothy Fosdick, the daughter of Rev. Dr. Harry Emerson Fosdick, the pacifist pastor of Riverside Church, was a formidable figure working for Senator Jackson for nearly three decades. She, too, preferred to work behind the scenes. Forsberg was different; she ignited a movement.

The INF negotiations were accompanied by massive street demonstrations calling for a freeze and for blocking the Reagan administration's plans and policies. In Hamburg, Chancellor Helmut Schmidt's hometown, 100,000 took to the streets in June 1981. Four days of peace rallies in West Germany in April 1982 gathered almost half a million protesters. In Rome, 300,000 turned out. In New York's Central Park, 800,000 rallied in June 1982. The Federation of American Scientists sponsored a public conversation on the freeze with Forsberg, and Paul Warnke lent his endorsement. Ronald Reagan, speaking before a gathering of evangelical broadcasters where he denounced the "Evil Empire," dismissed the freeze this way: "The truth is that a freeze now would be a very dangerous fraud, for that is merely the illusion of peace. The reality is that we must find peace through strength. I would agree to a freeze if only we could freeze the Soviets' global desires." Reagan argued that "a freeze would reward the Soviet Union for its enormous and unparalleled military buildup."

The House and Senate held hearings in 1982, where Forsberg and Randy Kehler, the national director of the freeze, testified. The witness list at these hearings was long and diverse. Perle testified: "A freeze now would be dangerously irresponsible. It would perpetuate the current imbalance in nuclear forces, undercut the long-term deterrent value of our nuclear forces, and doom to failure our efforts to achieve deep and meaningful reductions in the START and INF negotiations."[54] Warnke testified that some aspects of the nuclear competition might be frozen quickly, while others would take time and negotiations.[55] Harold Brown testified as a private citizen that the freeze served "a useful political purpose in pushing for resumption for arms control and reduction negotiations . . . [but] having said that, I have to add that I do not think that putting those proposals into effect would be very helpful to U.S. security."[56] On August 5, 1982, the House of Representatives came within two votes of passing a resolution supporting an immediate freeze.[57]

NITZE UNBOUND

Everyone knew that 1983 would be the "Year of the Missile," when protests and deployment schedules would come to a head. Schmidt's government folded even before the year of the missile began and his Social Democratic Party turned against Euro-missile deployments. If West Germany followed through with the course of action Schmidt prompted, it would be up be up Helmut Kohl and his Christian Democratic Union Party.

Nitze was the master of withering criticism; now he was on the receiving end from antinuclear activists and hardliners within the Reagan administration. Nitze wanted to shore up deterrence and to keep NATO united. He believed, along with Glitman and Woodworth, that the Zero Option could not achieve either of these objectives. Nitze was convinced that an "interim" arms control deal was needed to hold NATO together and to strengthen deterrence. He was willing to take enormous risks to succeed, including rampant disregard for his negotiating instructions. To achieve both of his core objectives, he sought an agreement allowing some, but not all, U.S. deployments and some Soviet reductions. This outcome would establish meaningful rungs on the escalation ladder that he and other U.S. deterrence strategists deemed essential, while checking off the arms control box.[58]

Nitze's negotiating instructions provided no flexibility for deal making. Seeking changes to his instructions would face a wall of resistance from the Pentagon. So Nitze went off on his own. He proposed to his Soviet counterpart, Yuli Kvitzinsky, who also had a bit of a reckless streak, to explore whether a deal might be struck. On July 16, 1982, they drove off together and took a walk in the woods on a rain-soaked trail in the Jura Mountains, where Nitze offered his proposal for an interim agreement. No one else in Geneva or Washington was aware of Nitze's freelancing, except for Eugene Rostow, his soulmate at ACDA. Nitze was running roughshod over his instructions because "the potential payoffs seemed immense and I was prepared to run the risk."[59] He was someone that the Reagan administration couldn't fire because he was indispensable for NATO cohesion and for a negotiated outcome.

The high ground of the Zero Option was losing altitude with every Soviet variant of their basic position that there be no NATO Euro-missiles and that the Soviet Union retain new missiles threatening NATO capitals. By offering new proposals, Moscow suggested the appearance of flexibility, while

Washington's serial refusals increasingly suggested a my-way-or-the-highway approach.

Nitze's proposed deal, labeled a "joint exploratory package" would allow each side to deploy 75 missile launchers in the European theater. Moscow would be allowed 75 of its newest missiles, each missile carrying three warheads, for a total of 225 warheads. The United States would forego deployments of fast-flying Pershing II ballistic missiles and be permitted 75 launchers of ground-launched cruise missiles. With four missiles per launcher and with each missile carrying one warhead, this equated to 300 warheads. These numbers would be accompanied by a freeze of Soviet missile deployments in the Far East. Nitze also proposed equal levels of 150 medium-range nuclear-capable aircraft, with British and French aircraft excluded. Kvitzinsky made some alterations at the margins; the plan was mostly Nitze's.

The delegations were due to recess. Nitze advised Kvitzinsky where he could be reached and left for home. The Kremlin never got back to him or to anyone else in Washington. Moscow was undertaking a reevaluation of the negotiations that summer, and Nitze's plan didn't meet their twin objectives of blocking new NATO deployments and opening stress fractures within NATO. In that sense, as Glitman acknowledged, "the 'package' from the walk in the woods was always problematic."[60] Silence from Moscow signaled a negative reaction.

Nitze returned to brief Secretary of State Shultz, who was new to the job and not well versed in these particulars. Richard Burt joined them in the secretary's private dining room. Shultz, true to his nickname as "the Buddha," didn't react to Nitze's presentation over lunch. Neither did Burt, who was stunned by Nitze's freelancing but held his tongue. After lunch, Burt returned to Shultz's office and explained the difficulties in maintaining a united front in Europe as the ground hadn't been prepared for Nitze's gambit.[61]

Pentagon officials were outraged by Nitze's freelancing. Nitze was suspect in hawkish circles for his role in negotiating the 1972 SALT accords and in dovish circles for his role in torpedoing SALT II. Arms controllers did not expect him to make amends in the Reagan administration, while hardliners sensed the need to be ever vigilant against Nitze's pragmatic streak. He was, in Perle's characterization, "an inveterate problem-solver."[62] Nitze had helped launch Perle's career, but now Perle framed the principal argument against what Nitze was proposing—giving up "fast fliers" while the Kremlin would retain theirs. Weinberger declared this to be a "staggering concession."[63] Moreover, Nitze had weakened the Zero Option. These arguments resonated with Reagan. Nitze's gambit, in Perle's view, constituted nothing less than "an act of intellectual and political cowardice."[64] The Pershing II missiles were the strongest arrow in the U.S. negotiating team's quiver since the Kremlin feared its capacity, with extended range, to carry out decapitating strikes against Moscow. Moreover, Nitze's proposed deal allowed mobile SS-20 missiles in Asia, to the detriment of allies in the Pacific.

With strong opposition to Nitze's handiwork at the Pentagon and no high-level backing at the State Department, Shultz was prepared to move on. Concerned that the Kremlin would seek to pocket the desirable elements of Nitze's proposal, hardliners proposed a public disavowal of Nitze's free-lancing. Reagan authorized a softer approach. He directed Shultz to express negativity over the unequal aspects of the proposal and willingness to continue these exchanges—but only if Soviet foreign minister Andrei Gromyko raised the issue first when they were to meet at the United Nations. Gromyko kept silent. When the negotiations resumed, Kvitzinsky met with Nitze and conveyed the message that the proposed formula was received in a "wholly negative" way. The Kremlin aimed to stop all NATO missile deployments, not just some of them.[65]

Both sides would remain dug in until the German Bundestag voted in November 1983. The State Department succeeded in convincing Reagan to endorse a variation of its "equal outcomes" approach in May, proposing 300 warheads-on-missiles per side. Shultz gave Dobrynin a preview of the proposal and the Soviet ambassador didn't need to wait for the Kremlin's response. He told Shultz, "We will never agree to U.S. deployments in Europe, whatever the number." This confirmed Shultz's judgment "that the Soviets would not bargain seriously in Geneva until they were convinced we would deploy and that probably the only way of convincing them would be by actually deploying the weapons."[66]

Negotiations were at an impasse, and Kvitzinsky hinted that once the U.S. missiles were flown to their basing sites in Europe, the Soviet side would stage a walkout. In October 22, 1983, over a million protesters marched in West Germany, Italy, and Great Britain—three of the basing countries. (The other two were the Netherlands and Belgium.) The following day, Moscow announced the movement of missiles westward, a progression that would continue if NATO missiles were deployed. Two days after that, Soviet general secretary Yuri Andropov announced his country's willingness to reduce SS-20 warhead numbers to 420—the Soviet count of British and French warheads—but only if NATO deployed no new missiles. Washington couldn't stand pat. On November 14, 1983, the Reagan administration proposed another variation of its equal outcome principle—a 420 limit on warheads on INF missile deployments. On that day, the first ground-launched cruise missiles were delivered to the Greenham Common air base in the United Kingdom. The Soviet team remained in Geneva.

On November 22, 1983, the Bundestag voted. Nitze was as taut as a drawn bowstring, as if the meaning of his professional life depended on the outcome. The Bundestag voted to approve missile deployments by a vote of 286 to 226. The next day, the first Pershing II missile parts were flown to West Germany. The Soviet delegation then declared a recess in Geneva without setting a date for the resumption of talks. The heart of the matter for Moscow was no Pershing II missile deployments, and no deployments whatsoever in West Germany. The Kremlin threw all it had into this campaign and lost. NATO held up under unprecedented strain, while the Warsaw Pact was showing signs of restiveness. This was a pivotal moment. In retrospect, George Shultz felt that the deployment of Pershing II missiles in Germany was "the turning point of the Cold War."[67] He, Nitze and Glitman were completely sure that the Kremlin would come back to the negotiating table, holding a much weaker hand.

1983, ANNUS HORRIBILIS

Nineteen eighty-three was a terrible year for U.S.-Soviet relations. By its end, some in the Kremlin, including General Secretary Andropov, believed that the Reagan administration was preparing for war. Nuclear dangers were rising markedly while channels of communication and negotiation broke down. Hawkish U.S. defense strategists were convinced that the Soviet Union was on the march, cashing in on huge investments in strategic forces that provided room and leverage for risk taking. Under Secretary of Defense Iklé told a World Affairs Council meeting in Washington that the Kremlin was "outflanking the perimeters of containment."[68] The entirety of Western Europe was in play, seemingly hinging on the outcome of Euro-missile deployments.

Reagan, Weinberger, and others used the phrase "decade of neglect" to characterize the reversal of the strategic balance and superpower fortunes. In this view, U.S. strategic superiority was magnanimously given away; Nixon and Kissinger had consciously chosen to forego strategic superiority in order to negotiate nuclear arms limitation based on "essential equivalence," and failed to achieve even that. Kissinger seemingly made this a virtue out of necessity; when speaking at a Dallas World Affairs Council meeting in 1976, he intoned, "Nothing we could have done would have prevented it. Nothing we can do will make it disappear."[69] Four years later, at the outset of the Reagan administration, Kissinger joined those declaring imminent danger, warning, "Never in history has . . . a nation achieved superiority . . . without trying to translate it at some point into foreign policy benefit."[70] In this narrative, Jimmy Carter and the arms controllers around him made matters worse, hastening America's slide, which mandated opposition to SALT II. The vulnerability of U.S. land-based missiles to Soviet attack became symptomatic of a broader sense of vulnerability and national disadvantage.

While hawkish strategists were firmly convinced of negative trend lines, Soviet analysts and key figures in the Kremlin leadership were becoming convinced that the correlation of forces was working against the USSR.[71] During the "decade of neglect," the United States spent over one trillion dollars on defense. The total of U.S. warheads available for use on strategic forces more than doubled, from 4,250 to 9,200. Of this total, warheads based at sea, where the Soviet navy would be at a loss to find them, grew from 1,000 to 5,000. Sea-based missiles, like their land-based counterparts, were being upgraded with improved guidance for high accuracy, placing at risk the entire land- and bomber-based legs of the Soviet deterrent. In addition, Soviet submarines were noisy and subject to trailing by quieter U.S. attack submarines. On top of this, the Reagan administration was intent on deploying Euromissiles that had the potential of attacking and destroying Soviet command centers before incoming warheads could even be detected.

There was much more for the Kremlin to worry about. The Solidarity Movement in Poland had popular backing. Warsaw Pact countries were increasingly unreliable. Afghanistan was proving to be a quagmire. Defense spending had taken a toll on Russia's economy, which showed signs of internal rot. During the last half of the 1970s, when hawkish strategists were touting the inexorable and purposeful rise of Soviet strategic ambitions, the Central Intelligence Agency reduced its estimates of the Kremlin's annual spending increases from 4–5 percent down to 2 percent, an indicator of difficulties in meeting pressing domestic needs.[72] Dobrynin concluded that the Soviet defense buildup contributed "only marginally" to the Soviet Union's decline. What killed the USSR, in his view, were "internal contradictions" accentuated by Washington's occasional embrace of détente.[73]

None of the unnerving events in 1983 described below changed the perspective among hawkish defense strategists that the Kremlin was on the advance, while all of the events that year reinforced the view among Soviet strategists that they were in deep trouble. Washington and Moscow were like two ships fueled by suspicion headed on a collision course in a dense fog. The U.S. intelligence community was in the dark. As Robert Gates wrote in his memoirs, "We did not really grasp just how much the Soviet leadership felt increasingly threatened by the United States and by the course of events."[74] A few key members of the Politburo were particularly paranoid about the Reagan administration's intentions. One was the captain of the sinking ship, Yuri Andropov.

Andropov was incorruptible, implacable, and more capable than anyone else in his age bracket in the Politburo. His mentee, Mikhail Gorbachev, described him as a "brilliant and large personality" and a "true intellectual." He was also a "man of his time, and as one of those who were unable to break through the barrier of old ideas and values." He was capable of imparting much needed energy within the ranks, but his long years as head of the KGB "left an imprint on his attitudes and perceptions, making him a suspicious man condemned to serve the system."[75] As Oleg Gordievsky, a Soviet spy and double agent, explained to a Western counterpart, "A closed political system dominated by men of weak intellect, with little understanding of the world and ideological blinders, is prone to self-indoctrination."[76] Andropov was a true believer who wore out his body climbing to the top of the ladder. Soon after his ascension, he needed a dialysis machine to survive.

The run-up to this year of living dangerously was marked by highly provocative U.S. air and naval operations that were reaffirmed by National Security Decision Directive Number 75, issued in January 1983. It declared that the central focus of national security policy toward the Soviet Union would be "to contain and over time reverse Soviet expansionism by competing effectively on a sustained basis . . . in all international arenas—particularly in the overall military balance and in geographical regions of priority concern." This required a full-court press employing military, economic, and ideological elements. "There are," NSDD-75 noted, "a number of important weaknesses and vulnerabilities within the Soviet empire which the United States should exploit." The administration's game plan was to turn the tables on the Kremlin, since it couldn't take the offensive when it was playing defense.[77]

A succession of incidents prompted the Kremlin to believe that the Reagan administration was preparing for a war in 1983. Jack Chain, then the air force deputy chief of staff for plans and operations, reminisced, "Sometimes we would send bombers over the North Pole and their radars would click on. Other times fighter-bombers would probe their Asian or European periphery." This report adds, "During peak times, the operation would include several maneuvers in a week. They would come at irregular intervals to make the effect all the more unsettling. Then, as quickly as the unannounced flights began, they would stop, only to begin again a few weeks later." William Schneider, an under secretary of state in the Reagan administration, recalled, "It really got to them . . . They didn't know what it all meant. A squadron would fly straight at Soviet airspace, and other radars would light up and units would go on alert. Then at the last minute the squadron would peel off and return home."[78]

Naval operations were designed to sensitize the Kremlin of vulnerabilities to U.S. power projection. John Lehman moved from ACDA to become secretary of the navy, where he enthusiastically endorsed large fleet exercises to expose Soviet vulnerabilities. Between 1981 and 1983, no less than twenty-five fleet exercises were carried out in sensitive waters, including the Norwegian Sea, the Barents Sea, and in waters adjacent to the Aleutian Islands and the Kola Peninsula. Navy fighters practiced simulated attacks. FLEETEX 83–1, held in early 1983, was the largest U.S. naval exercise in forty years, involving over 40 ships and submarines, 300 aircraft, and three carriers. Its locus was 400 miles from the Kamchatka Peninsula, near the Sea of Okhotsk, one of the "bastions" where the Soviet Navy deployed and sought to protect its ballistic missile-carrying submarines.[79]

President Reagan knew how to push the Kremlin's buttons but didn't realize how effective he was in stoking paranoia. Speaking before the British Parliament in June 1982, Reagan enjoined freedom lovers to help deposit the Soviet Union on the "ash heap of history." Then in March 1983, before a gathering of evangelicals, he prefaced remarks directed at the Kremlin with a pronouncement: "There is sin and evil in the world, and we're enjoined by Scripture and the Lord Jesus to oppose it with all our might." Reagan called the Soviet Union an "evil empire" and "the focus of evil in the modern world." He summoned his audience to embrace a crusade opposing evil. "I believe," he said, "that communism is another sad, bizarre chapter in human history whose last pages even now are being written."[80]

A self-confident superpower would have brushed these rhetorical volleys aside, but Moscow was anything but confident. Andropov's dialysis treatments began in February 1983. Members of the Politburo were feeling a profound sense of vulnerability that the U.S. intelligence community, deeply set in its underlying assumptions about Soviet intentions, failed to recognize. William Casey, the Central Intelligence Agency director, viewed the Soviet

Union through an ideological lens. His deputy, Robert Gates, who rose through the ranks as a Soviet analyst, found it hard to diagnose change favorable to the United States. Residues of the Team B exercise and its worst-case assumptions lingered. The intelligence community's "National Estimate" of the Soviet Union's nuclear capabilities covering the period of 1982 to 1992— by which time the Soviet Union no longer existed—concluded, "They seek superior capabilities to fight and win a nuclear war . . . and have been working to improve their chances of prevailing in such a conflict."[81] A companion estimate on Soviet strategic intentions concluded, "The Soviets believe that they enjoy some strategic advantages over the United States and view their current overall position as supporting the conduct of an assertive foreign policy and the expansion of Soviet influence abroad."[82] Shultz, who was far more attuned to geo-economics than others in the administration, was frustrated. "Our knowledge of the Kremlin was thin," he wrote in his memoir, "and the CIA, I found, was usually wrong about it."[83]

Dobrynin's memoir dwells on a memorandum to the Politburo prompted by Reagan's Evil Empire speech, co-signed by Foreign Minister Gromyko, Defense Minister Dmitri Ustinov, and Andropov. They angrily accused Reagan of "a propaganda cover-up for the aggressive militarist policy of the United States" aimed at splitting off Moscow's Warsaw Pact allies and liquidating the Soviet system. Dobrynin wrote that Andropov "did not favor confrontation with the United States, but he believed Reagan to be a dangerous individual whose actions might trigger a military confrontation," adding, "The Soviet leadership had collectively arrived at the conclusion that any agreement with Reagan was impossible." The Soviet Union's top military officer, Marshal Nicolai Ogarkov, writing in *Red Star*, stressed "the sharply growing aggressiveness" of Washington's actions, adding, "The United States is intensively building up its strategic nuclear forces with a view of giving them the capability to inflict a disarming nuclear strike."[84]

THE STRATEGIC DEFENSE INITIATIVE

Two weeks after declaring the Soviet Union to be the focus of evil, Reagan announced his Strategic Defense Initiative, the pursuit of defenses so effective that they would help make nuclear weapons "impotent and obsolete." Since ground-based defenses continued to be hobbled by technological constraints, Reagan's vision was elevated to space. The State Department and the Pentagon didn't know about Reagan's fulsome embrace of strategic defenses until shortly before his announcement. Shultz, Weinberger, and

Perle all worked feverishly to stifle it. Eagleburger's reaction was that "the president seems to be proposing an updated version of the Maginot Line."[85] Shultz, Eagleburger, and Burt worried about its impact on U.S. allies that depended on extended deterrence. Perle believed that Reagan's vision of a world without nuclear weapons was "a disaster, a total delusion" and "the product of millions of American teenagers putting quarters into video machines."[86] In his memoir, Weinberger allowed that the initiative was hurt by the secrecy surrounding it, and that the Pentagon scrambled to provide a late heads-up so that "our colleagues had some notice and were not totally surprised by their major ally."[87]

Shultz understood that the driver behind the Strategic Defense Initiative was the president himself, but was annoyed with the president's national security advisor, William Clarke, who knew little about the decision's ramifications, and with Clarke's deputy, Robert McFarlane, who could foresee them. Shultz also blamed the Joint Chiefs for being too solicitous toward the president's dreamscape. The chiefs had no business, in Shultz's view, lending credence to the president's vision, since they weren't scientists. He told McFarlane that they "should have their necks wrung."[88] The chiefs were no less surprised by Reagan's decision and felt chastened that they didn't try to disabuse his musings. Their chairman, General John Vessey, recommended against giving the speech announcing the Strategic Defense Initiative and privately denounced the plan as lunacy.[89]

Reagan's attachment to the Strategic Defense Initiative was rooted in his belief in the Biblical prophesy of Armageddon. McFarlane's memoir sheds light on Reagan's motivation: "He was convinced that we were in fact heading toward Armageddon, the final battle between good and evil. 'I'm telling you, it's coming,' he would say. 'Go read your scripture.'"[90] The Soviet Union seemed to be on the march. U.S. land-based missiles were vulnerable, and the Pentagon was having trouble finding a survivable basing mode. Advanced technology was an area of U.S. advantage. There were the arguments for applying jiujitsu to the nuclear competition in the furtherance of Reagan's core beliefs. The counterarguments weren't offered until the cake was already baked.

On March 23, 1983, Reagan announced the Strategic Defense Initiative at the end of a public address on the defense budget and national security. He began: "Let me share with you a vision of the future which offers hope. It is that we embark on a program to counter the awesome Soviet missile threat with measures that are defensive." Reagan then asked, "What if free people could live secure in the knowledge that their security did not rest upon the threat of instant U.S. retaliation to deter a Soviet attack, that we could intercept and destroy strategic ballistic missiles before they reached our own soil or that of our allies?" One of the most memorable rhetorical questions in the history of the arms race followed: "Would it not be better to save lives than to avenge them?"

Reagan acknowledged that there would be technical challenges ahead and that allies needed help with deterrence. In a nod to deterrence orthodoxy, Reagan allowed that strong defenses could "raise certain problems and ambiguities. If paired with offensive systems, they can be viewed as fostering an aggressive policy, and no one wants that." Reagan, the Great Communicator, could not hope to make this sale to the Kremlin, especially when he summoned "the scientific community in our country, those who gave us nuclear weapons, to turn their great talents now to the cause of mankind and world peace, to give us the means of rendering these nuclear weapons impotent and obsolete."

The ensuing debate over strategic defenses played out in newspaper op-eds, journals, and quickly produced books.[91] Members of the arms control community were in a state of shock and disbelief. No one wanted to render nuclear weapons impotent and obsolete more than they did, but Reagan and the pursuit of strategic defenses in space seemed totally antithetical to the cause. Reagan was consistent in his beliefs, and those beliefs included an astrodome defense, significant arms reductions, and abolition. No one else appeared to share all three. For good measure, he added one more rhetorical question and flourish: "Isn't it worth every investment necessary to free the world from the threat of nuclear war? We know it is." To those around him, Reagan's instincts were at cross-purposes. Full-scale bureaucratic warfare ensued over his aspirations.

Andropov's response came three days later. Reagan's vision was "a bid to disarm the Soviet Union" that would launch a new phase of the arms competition in both offensive and defensive weapons.[92] A KGB message later provided to British intelligence from a defector, Oleg Gordievsky, mirrored Andropov's thinking—that "the Americans expect to be able to ensure that the United States territory is completely invulnerable to Soviet intercontinental ballistic missiles which would enable the United States to count on mounting a nuclear attack on the Soviet Union with impunity."[93] Paranoia feeds on worst-case assumptions, of which the Reagan administration offered the Kremlin a rich feast.

America's allies were shaken. First the Zero Option, then a deep cuts proposal for intercontinental ballistic missiles that also seemed unlikely to be negotiated, and now a plan for an astrodome defense that couldn't succeed in its stated purpose, but that could make strategic arms reductions even more remote and unhinge NATO's reliance on extended deterrence. Margaret Thatcher resolved to employ her formidable powers of persuasion on Reagan to corral the Strategic Defense Initiative. Her message was characteristically direct: "I'm a chemist. I know it won't work."[94]

Reagan was undeterred. After their initial stunned reaction to the pursuit of an astrodome defense, Weinberger and Perle became staunch supporters, as the president's vision could help with "spiking the wheels of the arms control process." For Shultz and Nitze, it was, as Shultz recounted in his memoir, "the ultimate bargaining chip. And we played it for all its worth."[95] The president held seemingly unshakable beliefs in astrodome defenses and deep cuts. Henceforth, deal breakers in the administration steered Reagan toward protecting his vision of effective strategic defenses; deal makers steered him toward deep cuts.

KAL-007

The speech unveiling the Strategic Defense Initiative was a new low for U.S.-Soviet relations in 1983. Worse was soon to come. On the night of August 31, KAL-007, a hopelessly off-course Korean airliner, was shot down by Soviet air defense forces. There were 269 fatalities, including Congress's only member of the John Birch Society and sixty other Americans. Secretary of State Shultz rejected harsher public formulations but still unloaded quickly on the Kremlin, declaring, "We can see no excuse for this appalling act."

Shultz believed there was no way that Soviet air defense forces could mistake a 747 airliner for a spy plane, even in the dead of night. But in trying to nail down facts, he found "the intelligence community was being very elusive," which was not a good sign. The reason was that a U.S. signals collection aircraft was in the area of the Kamchatka Peninsula, where Soviet missile testing often occurred, and had actually crossed paths with the doomed airliner. The shootdown was a case of bumbling and mistaken identity rather than a deliberate act of downing a civilian airliner. This particular intelligence-gathering flight was part of the Pentagon's campaign around the Soviet periphery, not only to gather intelligence on Soviet missile testing and air defenses but also to practice training runs in the event of a conflict. The Soviet air defense command had detected and lost track of the U.S.

intelligence-gathering plane and was at a heightened level of readiness, under orders not to allow the intrusion of a U.S. spy plane over Russian territory. The Soviet pilot sent to intercept the plane recognized an important anomaly, as the plane had blinking lights, whereas U.S. spy planes didn't. He fired warning shots, without affecting the airliner's course. As it continued over Soviet territory, the pilot was ordered to destroy the "intruder."

Public reaction in the United States was fierce. The day after the shootdown, Reagan employed rhetorical questions with devastating effect. "What can be the scope of legitimate and mutual discourse," he asked, "with a state whose values permits such atrocities?" *Time* magazine's cover for the September 12, 1983 issue was a graphic depiction of a civilian airliner exploding with a Soviet jet in the foreground. Patrick Buchanan wrote that it was an act of "the criminal regime that rules the Russian people—and the KGB assassin who heads it."[96]

The Kremlin reeled from news of the shootdown. Korniyenko at the Foreign Ministry took the risky step of trying to convince a hospitalized Andropov and Defense Minister Ustinov to acknowledge the error and express regret over the loss of life, but Ustinov would hear none of it. When the Politburo convened on September 2 for a damage assessment with Konstantin Chernyenko in the chair in place of Andropov, Raymond Garthoff's translation of the meeting's transcript has all Politburo members in harness, believing the KAL's deep incursion to be a deliberate provocation. Someone in the military chain of command had approved the shootdown, but the responsibility was placed on a local commander.[97] Dobrynin's memoir depicts Andropov as furious about the shootdown, calling it a "gross blunder" and the generals involved "blockheads." In Dobrynin's view, "Our leaders were convinced that [Reagan] deliberately and disproportionately used the incident against them, and that American secret services were involved."[98]

ABLE ARCHER

The depths of the Kremlin's paranoia were plumbed further during the ten-day Able Archer command post exercise in early November. U.S. and NATO officials participating in Able Archer 83 practiced communication and control procedures for "nuclear release." There was no movement of troops and military equipment, since the exercise was about decision making to authorize the use of the Bomb.

The Soviet Union had nominally adopted a doctrine of "No First Use" of nuclear weapons, but this was pure fiction. In reality, Soviet military plans embraced the detonation of tens and, if necessary, hundreds of tactical nuclear weapons in quick-hitting operations to pave the way for tank armies to cross Germany into France. Soviet marshal Ogarkov patiently explained these plans in 1983 to Oleg Grinevsky, the Kremlin's negotiator on confidence- and security-building measures for Europe, before sending him back to the talks in Stockholm. Ogarkov, who participated in the early SALT negotiations, stood before a large map of a war plan predicated on taking the initiative. There was no way, he explained to Grinevsky, that the Kremlin could accept obligatory notifications of military exercises, information exchanges, and transparency measures, as these would compromise military plans.[99]

Able Archer 83 was designed to counter presumed Soviet war-fighting plans. Deterrence and NATO doctrine required quick nuclear release authority to counter a Soviet armored advance. The 1983 iteration of Able Archer was particularly realistic in this regard. So realistic, as Soviet marshal Ustinov subsequently wrote in *Pravda* and in the General Staff journal *Military Thought*, that these exercises "are becoming increasingly difficult to distinguish from a real deployment of armed forces for aggression."[100]

Soviet intelligence services were already on heightened alert. Beginning early in the Reagan presidency, the heads of these services directed operatives to look for indicators that the Reagan administration was ready to use nuclear weapons to place the Soviet Union on the ash heap of history. This operation was code-named RYAN. Andropov and Ustinov were particularly wary of the threat of surprise attack. During Able Archer 83, operatives were assigned to observe blood banks and lights on at night at the Pentagon, State Department, Britain's Ministry of Defence and Foreign Office, looking for possible indicators of preparations to launch preemptive strikes.[101]

The Team B exercise still cast a pall over the U.S. intelligence community's strategic analysts. In the 1970s, they had underestimated the Soviet strategic buildup. During the Reagan administration the U.S. intelligence community overestimated Soviet defense spending and underestimated the Kremlin's paranoia, which was heightened during Able Archer. Corrective insight into the Kremlin's thinking came from Oleg Gordievsky, the double agent and Soviet spy based in London. When MI-6 transmitted Gordievsky's information to the Central Intelligence Agency's headquarters in Langley, it triggered reassessments of the CIA's Soviet estimates that projected the Kremlin to be on the march rather than deeply unnerved.

Two "Special National Intelligence Estimates" were commissioned in 1984 to review whether there was an intelligence failure, the latter with the benefit of Gordievsky's reporting. The intelligence estimators gave themselves passing grades. While there was evidence that some Soviet land-based missiles and nuclear-capable aircraft based in Europe were on heightened alert, the alert did not extend to hurriedly sending Soviet missile-carrying submarines to sea or other extreme measures. While some members of the Politburo—including its most powerful members—exhibited paranoid tendencies, others did not.

There would be no Team B in this instance. In reviewing their own work, the estimators found they were not very far off base. Even with the benefit of Gordievsky's reporting, their 1984 reassessment "indicated a very low probability that the top Soviet leadership is seriously worried about the imminent outbreak of nuclear war . . . The available evidence suggests that none of the military activities discussed in this Estimate have been generated by a real fear of imminent US attack."[102] After Reagan left office, a more rigorous assessment by President George H.W. Bush's Foreign Intelligence Advisory Board gave the agency's Kremlinologists lower marks.[103]

The final chapter of the annus horribilis of 1983 ended with the deployment of cruise and ballistic missiles in NATO countries—missiles that the Kremlin's early warning network was unlikely to detect en route to their targets. The Kremlin's decision to declare a recess in the Geneva negotiations on Euro-missiles and START followed. Its campaign to stop Euro-missile deployments was an abject failure. After the Kremlin's walkout, Moscow was unable to influence public opinion in Europe and the United States. The KAL-007 shootdown was a terrible blow to the Kremlin's image. The Reagan administration's hardliners seemed victorious. Negotiations were on hold and money continued to be poured into the Strategic Defense Initiative. It was the worst of times for arms control. It would soon become the best of times, as pragmatists and dealmakers around Reagan were about to stage a comeback.

Chapter 10

BREAKTHROUGH

The second term of the Reagan administration was quite different than the first. Out of the depths of U.S.-Soviet relations, the golden age of arms control was born. The story of nuclear arms control is suffused with irony, buttressed by Archimedean principles and consistent with Sir Isaac Newton's Third Law of Motion. There can be light at the end of dark tunnels, as darkness is followed by the dawn. For every action, expect a reaction. The more arms control seems to be in peril, the stronger its prospects of recovery. Expect the unexpected, and the unexpected isn't always bad.

After learning of the Soviet war scare prompted by exercise Able Archer 83, Reagan was a genuinely surprised and chastened man. His takeaway, conveyed to his national security advisor, Robert McFarlane, was that he had dodged a "sequence of events that could lead to the end of civilization as we know it."[1] Reagan was again preoccupied with thoughts of Armageddon. He resolved to be more careful in his use of language and more sensitive to the Kremlin's paranoia.

Reagan was given a private screening of *The Day After*, an ABC Television drama about average Americans around Lawrence, Kansas, trying to cope with the consequences of a nuclear war. This movie affected him deeply. He then traveled to Japan where he vowed to the Japanese Diet in November 1983 that a nuclear war could not be won and must not be fought. Nine days later, 100 million viewers watched *The Day After*. When Shultz met with Reagan in December 1983, he found the president receptive to giving a speech trying to reset the U.S.-Soviet relationship. Shultz does not believe that the reporting on Able Archer by the Soviet double agent, Oleg Gordievsky, was particularly critical in the orchestration of Reagan's shift, but it could only have reinforced Reagan's commitment to turn the page.[2]

There were tentative steps to build upon. Before the INF negotiations broke down in 1983, Washington and Moscow expressed a readiness to ease provisions in their respective lopsided START positions. Washington was amenable to raising allowable missile launcher levels, and Moscow was conditionally willing to entertain deeper cuts. The turn began in earnest early in 1984. On the eve of the resumption of the Stockholm talks on European security in January, Reagan delivered the speech Shultz sought, describing 1984 as "a year of opportunities for peace." With the Reagan defense buildup well underway, there was a sound foundation to "establish a constructive and realistic working relationship" with the Kremlin. Shultz gave Dobrynin an advance look at Reagan's conciliatory remarks, but the Kremlin remained dug in.[3]

In February 1984, Reagan sent a letter to an ailing Andropov conveying the message that the United States had "fresh ideas" on nuclear arms control if he was inclined to break the stalemate and return to negotiations.[4] The next month he sent a letter to Andropov's successor, Konstantin Chernenko, reinforcing the offer with this handwritten postscript: "I have reflected at some length on the tragedy and scale of Soviet losses in warfare . . . Surely those losses which are beyond description, must affect your thinking . . . I want you to know that neither I nor the American people hold any offensive intentions toward you or the Soviet people." Reagan knew from the pollsters helping with his reelection campaign that he needed to do better on peace and security issues, but these were heartfelt messages.[5]

There were other modestly positive developments, even in the horrific year of 1983. In June, Moscow allowed Shultz's deputy, Kenneth Dam, to make an uncensored speech on Soviet television. The Kremlin allowed Pentecostals who had taken refuge in the U.S. Embassy to emigrate. Diplomats working under the ambit of the 1975 Helsinki Final Act agreed to convene a European-wide conference on confidence- and security-building measures— the prompt for the cautionary briefing that Ambassador Grinevsky received from Marshal Ogarkov. In July a grain agreement was reached, upping U.S. exports to the Soviet Union, and consular ties, broken after the invasion of Afghanistan, were resumed. In September, with his reelection a sure bet, Reagan spoke before the UN General Assembly. He again emphasized that now, with U.S. strength renewed, he was ready for "constructive negotiations."

Momentum from these steps was halted by the KAL-007 shootdown and Able Archer 83. But Shultz had found the template for forward progress. He made it a habit to raise concerns over human rights while taking small, pragmatic steps to make relations less contentious. He would revert to this formula when conditions permitted. As long as there were no negotiations, however, there was no way to engage successfully.

NUCLEAR NEGOTIATIONS RESUME

In July 1984 there was another modest step forward—an agreement to upgrade the "Hotline" with facsimile capabilities. In November 1984, after an exchange of letters between Reagan and Chernenko, Washington and Moscow announced that Shultz and Gromyko would meet in January to work out the terms of reengagement to discuss nuclear and space weapons. These were to be called the Nuclear and Space Talks. There would be three forums of negotiations—Euro-missiles, strategic arms reductions, and strategic defense. The prospect of resuming negotiations generated another round of strenuous bureaucratic warfare between the State and Defense Departments, but once negotiations resumed, Shultz's position would be strengthened in debates with the Pentagon. He knew that Reagan wanted to prevent Armageddon and secure deep cuts as much as he wanted to make nuclear weapons impotent and obsolete by means of the Strategic Defense Initiative.[6] Reagan's vision of effective strategic defenses would give him and Paul Nitze even more leverage than the deployments of Euro-missiles, and they would make good use of it.

Chernenko's tenure as general secretary was destined to be short. He was 73 and in failing health when he succeeded Andropov in February 1983. Grinevsky described Chernenko as an old, crooked, coughing man who had no interest in substance. "He wanted only one thing—that everything would go well, as in Brezhnev's time."[7] Chernenko died thirteen months after reaching the top, a sclerotic figure in a failing country. His signal accomplishment was to accept a formula to resume nuclear negotiations, but the Kremlin didn't have much choice. The longer the Soviet walkout lasted, the longer Moscow was unable to negotiate reductions in nuclear danger, whether from new NATO Euro-missiles, Reagan's strategic buildup, and especially his plan for an astrodome defense. The most dynamic Politburo member among the graying elite—Mikhail Gorbachev—visited Great Britain in December 1984. Margaret Thatcher promptly sensed that he was person with whom Reagan could do business. This turned out to be a great understatement.

If 1983 was the year of the missile and the year of living dangerously, 1984 was the year of the pivot, to be followed by a year of opportunity. Negotiations would resume on intermediate-range missiles and ocean-spanning strategic forces, but with different torque provided by Reagan's Strategic Defense Initiative. This third topic of negotiation was essential for the Kremlin to justify reengagement and for Shultz to achieve deep cuts. After Chernenko's death, the talks would play out under new Kremlin management. To give himself more running room, the newly appointed general secretary, Mikhail Gorbachev, elevated Foreign Minister Andrei Gromyko—the man who had nominated him to succeed Chernenko—to the honorific position of chairman of the Praesidium. Gorbachev replaced Gromyko with a neophyte, Eduard Shevardnadze, the Communist Party boss of Georgia. Gorbachev also replaced Marshal Ogarkov with the more pliable, but still deeply resistant Marshal Sergey Akhromeyev.

The Reagan administration also needed to make key personnel choices. Nitze had become Shultz's indispensable man. His wife was dealing with health issues, so he would remain in Washington. Nitze's deputy in the INF talks, Mike Glitman, provided continuity as the top U.S. negotiator on Euromissiles. As for the Strategic Arms Reduction Treaty talks, Edward Rowny was replaced by John Tower, a Republican senator on the Armed Services Committee, newly retired. For coordinator of the U.S. team and lead negotiator in the defense and space talks, Shultz recruited Max Kampelman. Weinberger found no support for his preferred choice, Edward Teller, to become the lead negotiator for the defense and space talks.[8]

Kampelman was a unique amalgam of Senator "Scoop" Jackson and Hubert Humphrey—a progressive Democrat with antinuclear sentiments who nonetheless joined the Committee on the Present Danger. He was skilled as a mediator, conciliator, and arbitrator but not deeply versed in nuclear negotiations. When he parachuted in to address negotiating impasses, problems usually ensued.[9] The appointments of Kampelman and Tower left Rowny without a formal role in the negotiations. He lost his chief benefactor on Capitol Hill when Senator Jackson died in September 1983 and he alienated many he worked with.[10] Rowny was named a special adviser to the president and given responsibilities to keep Asian allies informed.

The Soviet negotiating team for the talks on nuclear and space issues consisted of familiar faces. Viktor Karpov, a veteran of the Strategic Arms Limitation Talks who was Rowny's opposite number at the outset of the START negotiations, returned as the head of the Soviet delegation. His deputy, Alexei Obukhov, was given the assignment of leading the delegation on Euro-missiles. Yuli Kvitzinsky—Nitze's companion in their walk in the woods—returned to lead the defense and space delegation.

NEW NEGOTIATING MANEUVERS

The opening round of the nuclear and space talks began in March 1985. With the onset of NATO's Euro-missile deployments, the Kremlin clearly needed to reassess its negotiating stance. It was obvious, as two of the Kremlin's leading arms control officials recounted, that "the Soviet side overestimated the potential of the anti-war/anti-missile movement in Europe." The walkout was a mistake. "The Soviet position was at its least flexible: it was all or nothing."[11] The U.S. negotiating position on Euro-missiles did not need tweaking. Just before the Soviet walkout, the administration had proposed an interim agreement allowing equal numbers of warheads on Euro-missiles as a fallback to the Zero Option. There was flexibility on what that number might be. The Pentagon insisted that any interim agreement be "militarily viable."[12] The Pentagon preferred over 400 warheads, Nitze proposed 275 in his walk in the woods, and Richard Burt at the State Department managed to have the Reagan administration explore the number 300 prior to the Soviet walkout.

With the resumption of negotiations after a sixteen-month hiatus, deal making was imperative for Moscow to halt continued NATO deployments, which meant jettisoning positions that were "absolutely unreal."[13] The Kremlin initially derided the Zero Option as absurd and as unilateral disarmament. Now zero could work in Moscow's favor to at least eliminate the Pershing II ballistic missiles—fast fliers that could quickly turn Moscow's command and control network into rubble, thereby changing "the strategic situation in Europe."[14] The Kremlin was prepared to pay a very high price to eliminate these missiles.

The logic of the Zero Option, originally conceived by Richard Perle as a means to facilitate NATO's Euro-missile deployments, was now turned on its head. Moscow could embrace zero to eliminate not only the Pershing II and ground-launched cruise missiles but also shorter-range missiles in West German hands that might be upgraded. The Kremlin moved toward this decision in stages. The Soviet General Staff still resisted the Zero Option in its entirety, preferring to keep 100–120 ground-launched cruise missiles. The Soviet military also wanted to retain missiles for Asian contingencies involving China.

An interim deal with far lower numbers than Nitze sought in his walk in the woods was now in play. The Kremlin grew more inclined toward extending its scope with reports that West Germany's shorter-range Pershing missiles might be extended. The Kremlin also wished to foreclose U.S. deployments of intermediate-range missiles in Alaska. Both were unlikely, but published reports contemplating these moves increased Moscow's willingness to deal.[15] The more appealing the Zero Option became to Moscow, the more necessary it became for Moscow to jettison its long-held position that nuclear capabilities of Great Britain and France be factored into the outcome. Moscow gave up on including these forces in the Vladivostok Accord; it was only a matter of time before it would do so again in the Euro-missile negotiations.

Gorbachev's visit to Paris in July 1985 presaged the possibility of a surprising outcome on Euro-missiles, one that would be unveiled later at the Reykjavik summit. In August 1986, Soviet experts hinted at their willingness to exclude British and French forces and to include shorter-range missiles at a high-level meeting in Moscow. There was one other major roadblock: If an INF Treaty were to be concluded, the Kremlin would need to change its traditional opposition to on-site inspections. This breakthrough occurred in the Stockholm negotiations on confidence and security-building measures, which continued despite the walkout in Geneva. One of the issues in dispute at the Stockholm talks was over permitting observers at military exercises.

DEATH AND BIRTH OF ON-SITE INSPECTIONS

In March 1985, Major Arthur D. Nicholson, Jr., was shot and killed by a jumpy Soviet sentry in East Germany. Nicholson was permitted to spy—within murky boundaries. He was a member of the U.S. Military Liaison Mission, established at the end of World War II to maintain a residual presence around Berlin to help with the collection of human remains, prisoner swaps, and detainees. The Soviet Union, the United States, Great Britain, and subsequently France all had liaison missions. They agreed to coordinate activities in their separate zones of occupation. The Western missions were quartered outside of Berlin in Potsdam. The initial rationales for liaison missions quickly faded. When the Cold War began and the iron curtain descended, the military liaison missions evolved into a means to assess the status of forces facing off against each other across the German divide.

Major Nicholson was poking around for information about new Soviet military hardware when he was killed. Liaison officers were empowered to carry out unarmed, unescorted travel in properly marked vehicles everywhere except in designated keep-out zones. The four powers could assign places of permanent and temporarily restricted access, which evolved on the basis of reciprocity. Soviet forces in East Germany didn't want Western officers prying into their business, but they also wanted to observe the U.S. military posture in West Germany. Trade-offs were necessary and possible.

Brigadier General Gregory Govan, who served a total of twelve years at the military liaison mission—including a two-year overlap with Nicholson—and as the defense attaché at the U.S. Embassy in Moscow, described working in East Germany this way: "You were tolerated but not welcome; the key was not being observed." "Touring" could be very dangerous. Another head of the U.S. Military Liaison Mission, Roland Lajoie, described serving in East Germany as a "wartime mission in peacetime." Serious incidents were part of doing business. As Govan recalled, the Western liaison officers "energetically pursued observations of military activity and the Soviets pushed back. Chases, blockading, and sometimes crashes occurred. There were deliberate rammings with probable intent to harm, and shots fired at vehicles and personnel." Nicholson poked hard in a nonrestricted area and paid for it with his life.[16]

Being assigned as a military liaison mission officer was, in Govan's description, "a real-world mission"—a way for young officers to make a significant contribution on the front lines of the Cold War. "The duty was dangerous and clandestine enough to be exciting, important enough to be fulfilling, obscure enough to be easily overlooked by big bureaucracies, enough like hunting to satisfy primal urges, and enough like actual combat to challenge their manhood."[17] Lajoie described being a military liaison mission officer as an experience in "congenital insecurity."[18]

Purposeful wandering about East Germany was excellent training for military personnel who would become on-site inspectors or who gravitated toward work on security issues at the intersection of diplomacy and military operations. Lajoie became the first director of the On-Site Inspection Agency to carry out the 1987 the Intermediate Nuclear Forces Treaty inspections. Govan became its third director. William Odom, an army officer who worked with Zbigniew Brzezinski in the Carter administration, was a military liaison mission officer, as was Lynn Hansen, an air force officer who helped negotiate procedures for military observers to conduct inspections in the 1986 Stockholm Agreement.

The liaison missions constituted the foundation for a much larger construction project. The U.S. Military Liaison Mission officers helped gain information and tamped down worst-case assessments by analysts confined to desk jobs. The Soviet Military Liaison Mission provided reassurance that West Germany was not rearming in dangerous ways. The liaison missions demonstrated the feasibility of well-trained military officers to carry out confidence- and security-building measures as well as on-site inspections.[19] These cooperative monitoring measures subsequently became embedded in agreements leading up to and codifying the end of the Cold War.

What started in a divided Germany evolved into compulsory on-site inspections to help monitor treaty compliance. At the time of Major Nicholson's death, it was beyond comprehension that compulsory, short-notice inspections at sensitive nuclear sites and observers at military exercises were just around the corner. But Gorbachev was in a hurry, and he was playing by new rules.

NEW PROMISE AFTER THE WALKOUT

The Soviet walkout from the INF and START talks after the deployment of Pershing missiles in West Germany backfired badly. The Kremlin's threats and antinuclear protesters could not stop NATO's new missiles; their rollback could now only be achieved through negotiations. The Soviet Union couldn't afford another ratcheting up of the arms race. Its economy was in dire straits. The Kremlin concluded that "appropriate Soviet-American agreements were the only way out." Gorbachev "exerted pressure on the military and tried to force them to take some practical steps or make concessions."[20] A new plan of action was needed, and Chernenko's death provided this opening.

Gorbachev was intent on changing the enemy image of the Soviet Union in Western capitals. He acted in ways completely unexpected by Reagan administration officials and the U.S. intelligence community. He was a new type of Soviet leader who rejected the "logic of antagonism."[21] Grinevsky recounts how Gromyko trained and promoted Soviet diplomats by their "ability to find fault" with U.S. negotiating positions. The military and the KGB had their own separate reporting channels and could veto new proposals.[22] He cites a Russian proverb, "You can't change what is written." Negotiating positions ossified once stated in a formal document. "Try and back away from such documents. It is nerve wracking and a waste of paper used for correspondence with the capital. The agencies there ask the question: Why concessions now? To whom? And the answer is: to American imperialism."[23]

With the assistance of Shevardnadze and the grudging support of Akhromeyev, Gorbachev shifted gears. He wanted results and he summoned his negotiators to offer ideas that could lead to success. In his first public interview in *Pravda*, he declared, "We regard the improvement of Soviet-American relations not only as extremely necessary, but also as possible."[24] Reagan felt the same way. He strongly wanted to meet face to face with a Soviet leader. He, like Gorbachev, was confident in his powers of persuasion and was eager to dispel wrongful impressions. The summit meeting between Reagan and Gorbachev was set for neutral turf—Geneva—in November 1985. Maneuvering prior to the summit was intense.

OTHERWORLDLY CONSTRUCTS

Reagan's wildly disassociated beliefs—against communism and détente, in favor of deep cuts, nuclear abolition, and an astrodome defense—needed to be stitched together; otherwise they would be completely incoherent in dealings with allies and in negotiations with the Soviet Union. Obstructionists and nuclear dealmakers around Reagan fought pitched battles over the president's priorities. Weinberger, Perle, and their allies appealed at every turn to Reagan's strong attachment to the Strategic Defense Initiative and his deep antipathy toward the Soviet Union. Strobe Talbott, who covered bureaucratic warfare for *Time* magazine, quotes Perle as viewing arms control as a tranquilizer that "puts our society to sleep. It does violence to our ability to maintain adequate defenses."[25] Shultz and his allies countered by appealing to Reagan's antinuclear instincts and his confidence in being able to engage in heroic deal making. Paul Nitze was George Shultz's Svengali.

Nitze's challenge was to figure out a way to pull the antipodal tendencies in Reagan's mind together, and to do so in a way that would leave Weinberger and Perle sputtering. Speaking at the Philadelphia World Affairs Council on February 1985, Nitze unveiled a Reagan-blessed "strategic concept" that could be summarized in a mere four sentences:

> For the next ten years, we should seek a radical reduction in the number and power of existing and planned offensive and defensive nuclear arms, whether land-based, space-based, or otherwise. We should even now be looking forward to a period of transition, beginning possibly ten years from now, to effective non-nuclear defensive forces, including defenses against offensive nuclear arms. This period of transition should lead to the eventual elimination of

nuclear arms, both offensive and defensive. A nuclear-free world is an ultimate objective to which we, the Soviet Union, and all other nations can agree.

Nitze segmented the implementation of this thousand-word strategic concept into three timeframes—a near term, a transition phase, and an ultimate phase. In the near term (a ten-year period), nuclear deterrence would remain very much in place. At the same time, the United States and the Soviet Union would undertake "radical reductions in the number and power of strategic and intermediate-range nuclear arms." Research on the U.S. Strategic Defense Initiative would continue during this time, "as permitted" by the Anti-Ballistic Missile Treaty. During the transition period to follow, the United States would increasingly rely on missile defenses, while also seeking the stabilization of the relationship between offensive and defensive nuclear arms. This transition period, which would be undertaken "as a cooperative endeavor with the Soviets," could lead "to the eventual elimination of all nuclear arms."

Nitze's strategic concept was, at best, simplistic; if he were not in the administration and had anyone else in a position of authority been its author, he would have savaged it. But among the fraternity of deterrence strategists, only Nitze had the standing to offer simplicities. He didn't care about being exposed to criticism by the high priests of nuclear deterrence theory because he outranked them. And besides, Shultz and Nitze weren't interested in getting passing grades from nuclear theologians. Their task was to prioritize and secure deep cuts in nuclear forces. Time phasing was all-important. They knew—as did opponents of treaty making and supporters of the Strategic Defense Initiative—that success in the near term could fundamentally diminish the urgency of more distant pursuits.

A second task before Nitze was to impose criteria that would govern the deployment of U.S. missile defenses. Nitze did this at Philadelphia, as well, announcing three commonsense guidelines. Missile defenses needed to be feasible, survivable, and "cost-effective at the margin"—meaning that an increment of missile defense needed to cost less than an increment of nuclear offense. "If the new technologies cannot meet these standards," said Nitze, "we are not about to deploy them."[26]

In this straightforward and simple way, Nitze managed to shoot down the Strategic Defense Initiative. Reagan's astrodome defense was a fantasy. Even if futuristic technologies could somehow be made to work, were affordable, and then deployed in great numbers, as would be required for continuous protective coverage of missile fields and cities, they could be countered by low-cost, low-technology Soviet space mines that would trail futuristic U.S. deployments. Nonetheless, the Kremlin was habitually anxious about U.S. technological capabilities and short of funds. An astrodome defense might be unachievable, but Moscow would nonetheless be willing to trade deep cuts to prevent the impossible from happening.

Nitze's genius was to frame the terms of domestic debate over the Strategic Defense Initiative by establishing unarguable, commonsense criteria to guide deployments. He explained that the transition period could last decades, during which missile defense deployments meeting his criteria would be pursued and deployed "at a measured pace." Deterrence during the transition would rest on a combination of nuclear arms and missile defenses. As for the ultimate phase, "Given the right technical and political conditions, we would hope to continue the reduction of nuclear weapons down to zero." Nuclear abolition "would be accompanied by widespread deployments of effective non-nuclear defenses" to guard against cheating and breakout. Deterrence would then rest on the ability to deny a successful attack by defensive means: "The strategic relationship could then be characterized as one of mutual assured security."[27] Advocates of SDI were hamstrung; they couldn't dent Nitze's criteria.

Nitze, like Reagan, had antipodal tendencies. Whenever he was on the outside looking in, he was a merciless critic of those who, in his view, failed to appreciate compelling complexities. He was a different man on the inside: clever, remorseless, and energetic in search of constructive outcomes. His strategic concept and criteria for deploying futuristic defenses grounded Reagan's vision and laid the basis for successful negotiations.

Criticism of Nitze was muted. He survived the walk in the woods and was now granted exceptional leeway; pushback was surprisingly slight.[28] Hardliners were stymied by Nitze's hawkish credentials and by commonsense criteria they couldn't oppose. Nitze succeeded in placing the pursuit of astrodome defenses behind the queue of deep cuts. He also succeeded in finding a semblance of coherence in Ronald Reagan's favored pursuits. He described this project as making "a silk purse out of a sow's ear," using SDI to secure deep cuts in nuclear weapons.[29] National Security Advisor McFarlane characterized this gambit as "the greatest sting operation in history."[30]

Nitze's antipodal tendencies were again on display during a heated debate in 1985 over "broad" vs. "narrow" interpretations of the Anti-Ballistic Missile Treaty. When the ABM Treaty was negotiated in 1972, one of its agreed statements clearly stated that in the event that new system components based on "other physical principles" were developed—futuristic defenses like those undergirding Reagan's astrodome defense—they would need to be subject to discussions and agreement to amend the treaty. But what about their development? Did this mean that missile defense interceptors based on "new physical principles" like lasers could move outside of laboratories to be tested? The Heritage Foundation—a bastion of conservatism and staunch Reagan administration ally—issued a report arguing that the treaty provided great leeway in this regard. Then Richard Perle enlisted a Pentagon lawyer to conclude that constraints on development and testing of advanced technologies were loose enough to pursue futuristic concepts for Reagan's astrodome shield.

National Security Advisor McFarlane publicly endorsed this "broad" treaty interpretation on a Sunday morning television show before senior administration officials had discussed its adoption—a radical departure from due process. The Nixon administration sought and received the Senate's consent to ratification based on a "narrow" interpretation of the treaty—that research on advanced concepts could be pursued in laboratories, but not tested and made ready for deployment. The Ford and Carter administrations proceeded accordingly. Suddenly, under the Reagan administration's broad ABM Treaty interpretation, the sky was the limit for developing and testing new concepts for an astrodome defense.

Shultz was furious with McFarlane for preempting a cabinet debate and a presidential decision. Weinberger and Perle were pleased. The fine print mattered, and Shultz characterized Reagan as befuddled "on both sides of the issue."[31] Nitze, who was central in negotiating ABM Treaty constraints, was inclined to agree with the narrow interpretation. Shultz sought advice from Harold Brown, another veteran of the SALT negotiations who concluded that, while the treaty language was unclear, "its spirit was undeniable."[32] Raymond Garthoff, the executive secretary of the U.S. SALT I delegation and drafter of its fine print, also believed that the language and intent of the drafters were clear: Those embracing a broad interpretation were "misreading the negotiating record and distorting the text." Garthoff wrote a detailed refutation of the Reagan administration's "flagrant efforts to distort the historical record," relying on passages in the negotiating record and documents.[33] The lead U.S. negotiator, Gerard Smith, agreed wholeheartedly with Garthoff, as did every other member of the U.S. delegation with one exception.

The exception was Nitze, who was in deal-making mode. He helped kill Carter's SALT II Treaty; now he was aiming for something far better. He knew that his leverage to negotiate deep cuts in Soviet land-based missiles would be enhanced by the broad interpretation. He asked Shultz to task his legal adviser, Judge Abe Sofaer, to reassess the negotiating record. Sofaer concluded that Nitze and his colleagues in the Nixon administration "tried but failed" to persuade Soviet negotiators to accept a restrictive standard of development for advanced technologies. To Nitze's "surprise," after reading Sofaer's assessment he changed his mind, concluding that the broad interpretation was fully justified. "The Soviets had never agreed, in a manner they would consider binding on themselves, that research, development, and testing of systems and components based on other physical principles were prohibited."[34]

Shultz, Weinberger, Nitze, and Perle could all find common ground in arguing that, if the shoe were on the other foot, and if the Soviet Union were pursuing an astrodome defense based on advanced technologies, the Kremlin would not hamstring itself. There was one remaining obstacle to embracing the broad interpretation: it meant trampling on Senate prerogatives. The Senate provided its consent to the ABM Treaty based on the narrow interpretation, and key figures led by Armed Services Committee chairman Sam Nunn were up in arms over the broad interpretation. U.S. allies were, as well. Moscow was outraged.

Shultz and Nitze knew they needed to enhance negotiating leverage, smooth ruffled feathers on Capitol Hill, and reassure allies at one and the same time. This meant embracing and curtailing the broad interpretation at one and the same time. Securing Reagan's endorsement, Shultz delivered a speech in October 1985 saying that the broad interpretation was "fully justified." Then he reeled in the SDI program by announcing that the debate over broad and narrow interpretations was a "moot point" because the program had been structured—and recently affirmed by the president, thanks to Shultz's private intercession—"in accordance with a restrictive interpretation of the Treaty's obligations."[35] Reagan's first meeting with Gorbachev was just five weeks away.

THE GENEVA SUMMIT

The warring bureaucratic camps surrounding Reagan were well represented in Geneva, dubbed the "ship of feuds" by the media. Shultz wanted everyone inside the tent as "a mark of our seriousness of purpose. But there was no room for disagreements."[36] Weinberger's resistance leading up to the summit took the form of delivering a report on Soviet noncompliance with treaties shortly before Reagan was to meet Gorbachev, transmitting it along with an unclassified covering letter. Frank DeSimone, an official working on compliance issues, noted the absence of classification and transmitted Weinberger's letter to this author, who passed it along to a reporter at the *Washington Post*. While Reagan was in route to the summit, the *Post* ran a front-page story headlined "Weinberger Urges Buildup over Soviet Violations." The *New York Times* scooped the *Post* because the *Post*'s editors sat on the story. The *Times* received the letter from another source.[37] Whether or not Weinberger intended his unclassified letter to be leaked, he could hardly have been surprised at the result. His gambit backfired. Reagan and Gorbachev redoubled their commitment to engage successfully, and Shultz subsequently had more running room.

At Geneva, Reagan proposed 50 percent reductions in strategic offensive forces, an interim agreement on Euro-missiles short of the Zero Option, effective verification, and an openness to explore questions related to strategic defenses. Gorbachev had earlier, via Shevardnadze, indicated support for 50 percent reductions to 6,000 warheads each. There were significant differences, however, over what types of missiles would be included and excluded in the 50 percent cuts. As for the Strategic Defense Initiative, Gorbachev insisted that it remain within the strict confines of the Anti-Ballistic Missile Treaty and that offensive cuts be linked to protection of the ABM Treaty. Both leaders sloughed off advice to proceed slowly and invited each other to pay a visit.

The Geneva summit was an unqualified success because both leaders wanted one. Adelman wrote in his reminiscence that it was everything a summit should be. It was "nicely prepared, nicely scheduled in advance, nicely handled and nicely reported."[38] Reagan and Gorbachev took the measure of each other and resolved to keep pressing. Gorbachev readily joined Reagan in declaring that a nuclear war could not be won and must not be fought in the summit communiqué, in which the two leaders also pledged not to seek strategic superiority.

With the benefit of hindsight, the Geneva summit was a turning point. Once these two forces of nature met, naysayers had a harder time and deal makers gained traction. Reagan found "something likeable about Gorbachev. There was warmth in his face and his style." He wrote that "after almost five years I'd finally met a Soviet leader I could talk to."[39] Gorbachev's first reading of Reagan wasn't kind; he found him "not simply a conservative, but a political 'dinosaur,'" whose belief in the Strategic Defense Initiative was "bizarre." And yet, as Gorbachev reflected later, "something important" happened at Geneva. "In spite of everything . . . the human factor had quietly come into action."[40] Shultz was pleased. "The fresh start that the president wanted had become a reality in Geneva, not least because the two leaders had come to like and respect each other."[41]

In Adelman's view, it was the "pivotal summit, one which began the gradual yet momentous transformation of the Reagan administration."[42] Weinberger and Perle made concerted efforts to block serious engagement but failed. To borrow the title of Shultz's memoir, after Geneva, turmoil subsided and the possibility of triumph lay ahead, thanks to the twin sources of leverage provided by NATO's Euro-missiles and the Strategic Defense Initiative.[43] The nearer Reagan moved toward deal making, the more Shultz won his tug-of-war with Weinberger, and the less inclined Weinberger was to follow Perle's advice to seek blocking stratagems. As Garthoff wrote, "The foundation had been laid for later summits, the Intermediate-range Nuclear Forces Treaty, deep cuts in longer-range forces, and a new détente (though not so labeled)."[44]

A BREAKTHROUGH ON INSPECTIONS

Before any agreements could be reached, there had to be a breakthrough on on-site inspections. The Reagan administration needed inspections to override its list of Soviet violations, and Gorbachev needed them to prove that the West was now dealing with a different Soviet Union. He resolved to surmount the opposition of his military and intelligence services.

The breakthrough came in 1986 at the Stockholm negotiations on confidence- and security-building measures. As recounted by Grinevsky, Moscow's Stockholm negotiator, Gorbachev argued that the need of the hour was to deal with "the enormous army and intolerable military-industrial complex that literally crushed the Soviet economy." Gorbachev and Shevardnadze wished to engage in "large-scale politics." To do this, they needed an exemplary achievement, which required breaking the mold cast by Brezhnev and Gromyko, as well as breaking the stranglehold of the Soviet military and intelligence services on creative diplomatic engagement.[45]

Shevardnadze told Grinevsky, "The breakthrough needs to be ensured by concrete deeds. And Stockholm is the most suitable place for this."[46] Opposition to on-site inspections was a mainstay of Gromyko-branded diplomacy since the Acheson-Lilienthal Plan in 1946. President Kennedy was unable to negotiate a comprehensive test ban treaty in 1963 because Nikita Khrushchev wouldn't concede enough on on-site inspections, which the Kremlin viewed as espionage. This Soviet stance remained in place until Gorbachev accepted on-site inspections in the 1986 Stockholm Accord. The failings of a closed society and bureaucratized behavior were painfully on display in the Chernobyl tragedy in April of that year. Gorbachev's patience was wearing thin. With Chernobyl, he had firsthand experience of how institutional resistance magnified nuclear dangers. He was calling for reform and openness, and on-site inspections were the way to underscore his commitment.

As positions narrowed in Stockholm over notifications of military exercises, the last significant issue that could make or break an agreement was the inspection of military exercises. The Politburo had covered this ground before; everyone knew that the Old Guard, the Ministry of Defense and General Staff, were strongly opposed. Consequently, emotions were rubbed raw at the crucial Politburo meeting inside the Kremlin on August 7, 1986, when Gorbachev revisited this issue. Previous battles in making policy had been "acute," and this "was a real war," according to Grinevsky, who Gorbachev and Shevardnadze pitted against Marshal Akhromeyev.[47]

The marshal's last stand wasn't just about protecting state secrets and overturning decades of principled opposition. Nor was it about concealing preparations for surprise attack—the initial reason given to Grinevsky by Marshal Ogarkov for resisting transparency when the talks began three years earlier. There was something else to Akhromeyev's resistance, which he conveyed to Grinevsky before the decisive Politburo meeting: "We have divisions of incomplete strength . . . The shortage of personnel and weapons is appalling. We even have to carry out exercises with dummy rifles . . . You must understand, we cannot let foreigners see all that shame."[48]

At the Politburo meeting, Gorbachev silenced Gromyko, but Akhromeyev boiled over with resentment. He "disagreed violently" with Grinevsky's argument that reciprocal NATO transparency would help Soviet security. Accepting on-site inspections on Soviet territory would, he argued, be "too high a price" to pay, resulting in foreigners "obtaining an opportunity to detect both the strong and weak sides in the system of our combat readiness." This would "facilitate for them selection of directions for their main strikes."[49] Grinevsky countered by arguing that transparency was in line with Gorbachev's reforms and could help reduce the risk of war, allowing necessary reductions in military expenditures.[50]

The outcome of the Politburo meeting was not in doubt, and Akhromeyev knew it. He saw Grinevsky in the anteroom afterward and accused him of treacherous behavior. "The armed forces of the Soviet Union will never, never, never forgive you for this," he seethed. Grinevsky got his revenge by suggesting to Shevardnadze that Akhromeyev be tapped to convey this major change in the Soviet stance before the assembled diplomats in Stockholm, reinforcing how far the Soviet Union had traveled under Gorbachev's new thinking.[51] Akhromeyev conveyed the news everyone was waiting to hear on August 29, 1986.

Less than a month later, negotiations on the Stockholm Accord and its provisions for on-site inspections were completed. Along with other participating states, the Soviet Union agreed to accept up to three inspections per year of military exercises, on the ground, in the air, or both. Sensitive points could be placed off-limits, but inspections could otherwise proceed.

ON TO REYKJAVIK

If the Reagan administration could weave fantasies out of straw, so, too, could the Kremlin. Dobrynin and his colleagues chafed at Reagan's negotiating stance. "Moscow, as well as many in the West," he wrote, regarded Washington's INF and START proposals "as an effort to stake out public positions rather than sincere attempts to reduce nuclear arms."[52] So why not fight fire with fire? Gorbachev planned a major speech in January 1986 on disarmament. The Foreign Ministry worked feverishly to come up with creative ideas, only to be trumped by the General Staff and Ministry of Defense, who advanced a three-stage program for complete nuclear disarmament over a fifteen-year period. Upon hearing this "obvious ploy," Grinevsky relates that the diplomats "exchanged glances and smiled. Kvitzinsky broke into loud demonic laughter . . . The Ministry of Defense had been developing in secret the program for the elimination of nuclear weapons—as if it were a new super secret missile."[53]

If Reagan wanted a world free of nuclear weapons, Moscow wanted one, too. Moscow would join Washington in a game of "arms control chicken"— a throwback to dueling plans for general and complete disarmament in the 1950s. The Kremlin's playbook was obvious: if deep cuts—forget about general and complete disarmament—were achievable, the Strategic Defense Initiative would not be needed. The three-phase plan was "pure propaganda," according to Grinevsky and his fellow negotiators.[54] Two senior Soviet arms control officials later wrote that, although Gorbachev's grand vision was "impractical," it also had "great value as it allowed the Soviet Union to take the political initiative from the United States."[55] The only person who took abolition seriously within the Kremlin was Gorbachev, who wrote in his memoir, "This time we did not use the issue as a means of propaganda as had been done in the past."[56] Gorbachev was as much of a true believer in abolition as Reagan.

Both Gorbachev and his Foreign Ministry were in alignment on the need to make the first phase of nuclear disarmament "concrete and realistic."[57] Included in the first phase would be the elimination of threatening NATO missiles and their Soviet counterparts, as well as 50 percent reductions in longer-range missiles—subjects that Gorbachev and Reagan discussed previously at Geneva. When Reagan was told by Shultz of Gorbachev's proposals, he replied, "Why wait until the end of the century for a world without nuclear weapons?"[58]

The game of disarmament was on. Gorbachev was a man in a hurry and Reagan was also unsatisfied with the diplomatic wrangling in Geneva. Both leaders prided themselves in dispensing with red tape and taking bold decisions. The structure of the revamped negotiations with its three working groups was unwieldy; if anything, it impeded progress. Kampelman wanted to hold all reins in his harness, which hampered movement on Euro-missiles, where prospects of success were most evident. For its part, the Kremlin continued to demand a package deal including Euro-missiles, strategic arms reductions, and space.[59] If this three-ringed circus were to end in a rousing finale, the two ringleaders would have to reengage.

After Reagan's first term, in which nuclear negotiations amounted to playing to the galleries before the Soviet walkout, both Gorbachev and Reagan were ready for something completely different. In a private message, the Kremlin's bold new leader suggested tackling nuclear dangers face to face in a somewhat out-of-the-way place, absent hangers-on and filters. Reykjavik was suitable. Nervousness abounded over the prospective summit. There were only three weeks to prepare after Gorbachev's surprise invite. And prepare for what? Shevardnadze had given notice to expect "serious" proposals, and Reagan wanted to offer serious proposals of his own.

In preparation for Reykjavik, the White House tasked the Office of the Secretary of Defense and the Joint Chiefs to come up with "something big." Their big idea was the elimination of offensive ballistic missiles, or "fast fliers"—oceans spanners as well as missiles of intermediate-range. The remaining U.S. strategic deterrent would be stabilizing, relying on cruise missiles based at sea, in Europe, and on strategic bombers, some of which would also have the ability to penetrate Soviet air defenses.[60] When Gorbachev came bearing detailed, ambitious proposals, the Pentagon would have a counter-proposal ready. It was creative, stabilizing, and very much in Washington's interest if Gorbachev approved. It would also have required a radical restructuring of U.S. strategic forces.

The Reykjavik summit, held on October 11–12, 1986, was the world's highest-stakes poker game. This was the characterization of George Shultz, a man with an excellent poker face.[61] Shultz appeared to be one of only three participants at the summit with no reservations about what transpired. The other two were holding all the chips. Reykjavik wasn't completely unscripted, as there were hurried preparations beforehand. But no one could have anticipated just how Reagan and Gorbachev would deal with substance. Reagan could go into the ether when operating solo and was notoriously dismissive of details. He held only the most elementary grasp of the workings of nuclear strategy and depended heavily on file cards. What he knew for sure was that nuclear deterrence was morally abhorrent. If Gorbachev wanted to tear down the edifice of mutual assured destruction and pursue abolition, Reagan would be all for it—as long as his beloved Strategic Defense Initiative remained in place as an insurance policy.

The story of the Reykjavik summit hinged on the dramatis personae, both supremely confident, impatient, unorthodox risk-takers. The lead actors, the subject matter, and the plot twists were worthy of a Shakespearean play, skipping the exposition. Reagan and Gorbachev both wanted to cut to the chase. The two risk-takers were comfortable meeting at an unscripted summit. Reagan came to Reykjavik expecting exploratory talks and, according to Gorbachev, was wobbly at the outset of their first one-on-one encounter. Reagan had no umbrella in response to the fire hose of bold ideas coming from Gorbachev, so he consulted and read from his note cards. He had difficulty responding to direct questions. As recounted by Gorbachev, "The cards got mixed up and some of them fell on the floor." Sensing Reagan's discomfort, Gorbachev suggested that their foreign ministers join them.[62]

The plot thickened quickly. Gorbachev proposed the elimination of all "strategic offensive arms." The underlying Soviet definition of strategic offensive arms was any platform with sufficient range to reach the Soviet Union. This meant eliminating all strategic forces and "forward-based systems"—aircraft based on land and at sea, intermediate-range missiles, as well as French and British nuclear forces. Challenged by Gorbachev to dispense with stale negotiating proposals, Reagan's team offered the Pentagon's notional proposal to eliminate all ballistic missiles—"fast flyers." Why stop there, asked Gorbachev? How about all bombers, warheads, tactical nuclear weapons, and, for good measure, cruise missiles? Reagan then looked across the table at Gorbachev and reportedly said, "It would be fine with me if we eliminated all nuclear weapons." To which Gorbachev replied, "We can do that. Let's eliminate them. We can eliminate them." All this while Reagan and Gorbachev's military aides carrying the "footballs" with nuclear access codes stood staring blankly past each other in the hallway of the summit venue, Hofdi House.

Neither superpower had previously been led by anyone willing and able to turn hammer, sickle, and eagle's talons against received nuclear wisdom and force structure. At Reykjavik, both leaders were absolutely eager to do so. During their ten and a half hours of negotiations, they entertained the complete abolition of ballistic missiles, nuclear weapons, and offensive nuclear arms, with the terminology shifting and lacking precision. They succeeded in dispensing with most roadblocks to the complete elimination of Euro-missiles with ranges between 500 and 5,500 kilometers and paved the way toward halving strategic nuclear forces. Neither man invited experts at the table to complicate matters; they were accompanied for most of this time only by Shultz and Shevardnadze—who were usually silent—as well as by note-takers and translators. Their retinue of experts led by the 63-year-old Marshal Akhromeyev and the 79-year-old Nitze—two compelling figures in their own right—met for one memorable all-nighter to help pull their leaders' visions closer together.

One consequential outcome of this all-nighter was agreement to count strategic bombers with gravity bombs as "one" in warhead totals for a strategic arms reduction treaty. Another discount was devised for bombers carrying air-launched cruise missiles. These counting rules greatly favored the United States. The logic of doing so was to enhance stability. "Slow fliers" would be treated preferentially because many bombers would have exclusive or primary conventional missions, as they faced heavy air defenses and had far lower alert rates than land-based ballistic missiles. In addition, accurate counts of bomber force loadings would require painfully intrusive inspections. START negotiator Ronald Lehman jokingly argued to his opposite number, Victor Karpov, that counting bomber weapons on alert would require "frisking your mothers."[63] Later, in negotiations on President Barack Obama's New Strategic Arms Reduction Treaty, the Kremlin proposed this discount rule themselves to avoid intrusive inspections at sensitive storage sites.

At Reykjavik Reagan again called for the Zero Option eliminating Euro-missiles. Gorbachev expressed qualifications, wishing to retain some in Asia in deference to his General Staff. As for strategic arms reductions, Reagan wholeheartedly embraced the concept of 50 percent reductions, to which Gorbachev was completely amenable, including cuts in Soviet "heavy" missiles. Gorbachev proposed to accomplish this in five years. When the notion of 50 percent reductions was first advocated by George Kennan in May 1981, this was widely presumed to be beyond the pale.[64] Finalizing this deal would take more time, but it was going to happen. As for Reagan's Strategic Defense Initiative, Gorbachev parried that it would be unnecessary because of deep cuts and abolition. Reagan told Gorbachev that it would remain an essential insurance policy and that he would share its secrets. At this, Gorbachev was incredulous. The impasse over SDI was a deal breaker.

The summit ended abruptly. The experts present but not in the room lacked clarity about what the leaders had discussed, and the leaders lacked precision about what exactly was to be reduced. Shultz reports that Reagan and Gorbachev's commitment to a world without nuclear weapons caused deep discomfort within the State Department and that Perle believed it to be "a disaster, a total delusion."[65] Nitze, in one of his more telling understatements, recounted that at Reykjavik, "There was some confusion on the total elimination of strategic systems as opposed to the total elimination of ballistic missiles."[66] The haste and confusion were two of the reasons why no deals were struck. A third was because Reagan refused Gorbachev's demand to confine the Strategic Defense Initiative to laboratory testing for ten years and proceed thereafter only by mutual consent. Reagan would not sacrifice his beloved astrodome defense, not even for his vision of a world without nuclear weapons.

RECOILING FROM REYKJAVIK

Most commentators and media outlets deemed Reykjavik a failure, taking their cues from the drawn faces of the two leaders hastily leaving Hofdi House. The initial accounts of what transpired were met with a mixture of amazement, sighs of relief, and deep regret. The premier chronicler of U.S.-Soviet relations, Raymond Garthoff, characterized the proceedings as "a historic near miss."[67] Many were grateful for failure. Allies reliant on the U.S. nuclear umbrella were stunned. True believers in nuclear deterrence were appalled. Former secretary of defense James Schlesinger declared Reykjavik "a near disaster from which we were fortunate to escape."[68]

Richard Nixon's judgment was particularly harsh: "No summit since Yalta has threatened Western interests so much as the two days at Reykjavik."[69] Henry Kissinger underlined that the parties where not "anywhere close to a completed agreement, much less a useful one."[70] The INF Treaty was near enough to completion, however, to prompt a flurry of rearguard actions to keep nuclear-armed missiles on NATO soil. Writing in the *Washington Post*, Nixon and Kissinger argued that Moscow's conventional military superiority required nuclear deterrence within the European theater. The treaty would do great damage to "a doctrine—flexible response—which would permit a graduated application of its nuclear power." With the removal of these missiles, efforts to "discourage Soviet nuclear blackmail of Europe" would be badly weakened. Vigilance was required: "Gorbachev has taken the first steps toward reform at home but has not retreated one inch from Moscow's posture abroad. Indeed, his policy can be said to be a subtler implementation of historic Soviet patterns." The architects of the 1972 SALT accords argued: "In retrospect, NATO should not have offered the zero option in the late 1970s. But we have crossed that bridge. The Soviets have accepted our offer."[71]

Another harsh judgment came from Alexander Haig, who expressed the view that U.S. foreign policy was "unhinged" at Reykjavik, and that undaunted support for the Strategic Defense Initiative "provided a welcome pause in the push toward a nuclear-free world."[72] The *Washington Post* editorialized that the summit was an "unfortunate free-wheeling bargaining session."[73] The *New York Times* editorialized, "If the President's purpose . . . was finally to cash in [the Strategic Defense Initiative], and for great arms control gains, he failed."[74] The editorial page of the *Wall Street Journal* characterized the summit as a "big public relations game" and an exercise in "disinformation" that "mercifully" ended in a breakdown.[75]

Unable to figure out Reagan or Gorbachev, Washington's commentariat was even more flummoxed by their interaction. Most observers operated on the twin assumptions that hard-core Republican anticommunists like Reagan were wedded to nuclear weapons, and that any product of the Soviet system, including Gorbachev, couldn't possibly be a real change agent. Nor did America's Kremlinologists grasp what George Shultz intuited—that Gorbachev was impatient because he recognized that the Soviet economy was tanking. At Reykjavik, the curtains parted to reveal Reagan as a man strongly committed to abolition and Gorbachev as a riverboat gambler. Everyone, supporters and skeptics alike, was stunned by reports of what transpired.

Shultz, ever the loyal marine, reflected in his memoir that "the world was not ready for Ronald Reagan's boldness" and that it was "almost too much for people to absorb." [76]

Nixon, Kissinger, and their fellow deterrence strategists seriously misread Gorbachev and the decrepit state of the Soviet Union. The Central Intelligence Agency, continuing a string of misjudgments with the advent of Gorbachev, assumed that Soviet defense spending would ramp up in response to the Reagan's twin challenges of the defense buildup and the Strategic Defense Initiative. Nor did the CIA expect Gorbachev to offer eye-popping proposals at Reykjavik. Instead, as Adelman recounts, Gorbachev came "loaded for bear," intent on breakthrough achievements in part because Soviet defense spending was already three times the U.S. intelligence community's estimate. Shultz and Nitze were right to assume that significant gains could be realized because of Soviet fears that Reagan's astrodome defense could nullify their deterrent. Unlike Nixon and Kissinger, Reagan, Shultz, and Nitze were building up to cut numbers significantly.

As Adelman forthrightly acknowledged, SDI was a "splendidly naïve notion only Reagan could have believed, much less conceived." The U.S. team was unprepared for what transpired at Reykjavik; the much larger Soviet team had a game plan, but neither leader was amenable to handlers. Cautionary advice was not welcome or given. According to Adelman, "Reagan at Reykjavik had been flying solo." Not exactly: Shultz was Reagan's co-pilot, but he was entirely willing to fly by Reagan's instincts.[77]

RECOGNIZING BREAKTHROUGHS

It did not take long for government officials, pundits, and strategic analysts to figure out that Reykjavik was an extraordinary success story for arms control rather than a failure. As Thomas Graham noted, the summit constituted a "sea change . . . nothing thereafter was the same."[78] The principle of 50 percent reductions in strategic forces was agreed upon, and most of the obstacles to a treaty eliminating intermediate- and shorter-range nuclear forces were cleared away at Reykjavik. The INF Treaty was signed in Washington, amidst much pomp and ceremony, fourteen months later. Before leaving office, Gorbachev welcomed Reagan to Moscow, ground central of the "evil empire" that Reagan railed against at the outset of his presidency. When asked by a reporter during a stroll in Red Square whether the opprobrium still applied, he responded, "No. That was another time, another place." The strategic arms reductions that Reagan and Gorbachev envisioned at Reykjavik were finalized in 1991 during George H.W. Bush's term in office. Even deeper cuts followed in 1993.

Reagan and Gorbachev broke the back of the superpower nuclear arms race, giving credence to their mutual pledge that a nuclear war could not be won and must never be fought. If Geneva was the turning point in U.S.-Soviet relations, Reykjavik set the table for world-historic achievements. As Adelman noted, "Reykjavik changed each man, changed the relationship and thus that of the superpowers."[79] The human factor had once again come to the rescue; the world stepped back from Armageddon.

The ambitions of Gorbachev and Reagan were breathtaking. Both deserved the Nobel Peace Prize for their efforts and their crowning achievement, the INF Treaty. One could not have accomplished deep cuts in nuclear forces without the other. But only Gorbachev received the Nobel Peace Prize. Later, in 2009, the Norwegian selectors would award the Peace Prize to Barack Obama, attaching "special importance "to his "vision of and work for a world without nuclear weapons." Obama gave a speech at Prague with brief passages about his vision but was stymied by domestic and international circumstances. In contrast, Reagan aimed high and returned to earth with a clutch of Soviet concessions.

Ironies abounded.[80] Reagan, the unreconstructed Cold Warrior and opponent of détente, succeeded in doing more damage to nuclear orthodoxy than all of his predecessors combined. Any other president who tried to push every last nuclear weapon onto a negotiating table would be subject to impeachment proceedings or worse, like the fictional president played by Frederic March in *Seven Days in May*. Reagan remained untouchable.

Another irony was that Reagan's treasured SDI, the deal-breaker at Hofdi House, became the victim of Reykjavik's successes. Before Reykjavik, Democrats on Capitol Hill had already hamstrung SDI funding. Other restraints were technical in nature: it was too hard to make space-based strategic defenses work and too easy to foil them. The rationale for this pursuit effectively ended with the agreement in principle for 50 percent reductions in strategic forces and the elimination of intermediate-range nuclear forces. The joint communiqué after the Washington summit where the INF Treaty was signed repeated a pledge that neither Washington nor Moscow would seek to achieve military superiority. No formalities were needed for SDI's interment. Instead, the George H.W. Bush administration "grounded" strategic defenses, focusing on land- and sea-based interceptors, as it signed on to deep cuts in strategic offensive forces.

Neither Reagan nor Gorbachev was prophetic enough to foresee these developments in the immediate aftermath of Reykjavik, but the Soviet leader figured this out within the year, persuaded by his academicians. Gorbachev, who knew firsthand that no trade-offs could persuade his negotiating partner to let go of what Adelman called "the pie in the colorful sky of Ronald Reagan's imagination," went about killing SDI with deep cuts.[81] According to Strobe Talbott's near-contemporaneous and often verbatim account based on administration sources, Gorbachev told Reagan at the Washington festivities associated with the INF Treaty signing, "Mr. President, you do what you have to do . . . And if in the end you think you have a system you want to deploy, go ahead and deploy it. Who am I to tell you what to do? I think you are wasting money . . . We are moving in another direction, and we preserve our option to do what we think is necessary . . . And we think we can do it less expensively and with greater effectiveness."[82]

Reagan's instinctive approach to achieve both deep cuts and his Strategic Defense Initiative was sincere but cohered only in his own mind. Reagan had difficulty prioritizing between his competing visions, while his advisers were at loggerheads. Shultz and Nitze sought leverage from Reagan's Strategic Defense Initiative to make deals, while Weinberger and Perle sought the leverage SDI afforded to foreclose deals. Only when Reagan and Gorbachev began to interact could this logjam be broken. In the end, Shultz persevered and won out.

Reagan never abandoned his vision of making nuclear weapons impotent and obsolete, but by choosing to proceed with the INF Treaty and to embrace deep cuts, he effectively grounded his vision of an astrodome defense. In any event, there was no way, using Nitze's criteria, that Reagan's vision could be cost-effective at the margin. Gorbachev figured out that the Soviet Union could defeat SDI with workarounds—primarily deep cuts and cheap countermeasures. The central irony surrounding SDI was that it succeeded despite its impracticality. As Adelman concluded, "SDI never worked as Reagan wished. It worked better."[83]

Ironies abounded in Moscow, as well. By embracing a plan for nuclear abolition to trump Reagan, the Soviet General Staff and Ministry of Defense set in motion a series of events they could not control. As two Kremlin insiders recounted, they "gave (unwittingly, of course) the General Secretary a powerful instrument with which to act."[84] Gorbachev was off and running after Reykjavik. One bold initiative would follow the next. The Foreign Ministry was no longer under Gromyko's lock and key. Positions that were "locked in concrete" were jackhammered.[85] Gorbachev and Shevardnadze pitted the diplomats against the military establishment to whom they were previously subordinate. The Soviet system of decision making was turned on its head. A decision-making process oriented toward saying "yes" to authority now meant endorsing bold proposals. After drawing up plans for abolition, Marshal Akhromeyev was on the defensive. Gorbachev "was so active in implementing the concept [of disarmament] that he achieved substantial success." By endorsing abolition, the Soviet General Staff "became entrapped in their own gambit."[86]

If a deal for abolition had somehow been struck in Reykjavik, it would have unraveled. Reagan and Gorbachev were too far ahead of their governments and publics. Skeptics would have pounced on details and imprecision, just as after the Vladivostok Accord. Vested interests as well as allies would have been up in arms had Reagan and Gorbachev found closure. Their reach far exceeded their grasp. Even so, they changed the paradigm of strategic arms control as they moved to slash force structure and rungs on the escalation ladder. Gorbachev and Reagan both reached for the stars. One came crashing down along with the Union of Soviet Socialist Republics, which was not amenable to his radical ideas. The other now resides in the firmament of America's most successful presidents.

BEHOLD, THE INF TREATY

In December 1987, Gorbachev arrived in Washington to sign the INF Treaty, which eliminated 2,692 missiles in all. It was his and Reagan's finest hour, but the focus was primarily on Gorbachev, who was treated as a rock star by Washington's elite and those lining the streets to wave as his motorcade passed. Defenders of deterrence orthodoxy complained that the United States should never have proposed the Zero Option in the confident belief that it would be rejected by Moscow. Perle and his fellow champions didn't foresee someone who acted like Gorbachev; neither did the Politburo members who elevated him to become general secretary.

Getting to zero was a strange journey. At first, this proposal was offered to facilitate U.S. missile deployments. Then the Reagan administration shifted gears, favoring a militarily significant number of missiles. At Reykjavik, some missiles were permitted for Asia, which caused perturbations in Europe as well as Asia. In reaction, the Zero Option became popular again in Washington. The United States gave up rungs on the escalation ladder, while the Soviet Union gave up decades of diplomatic behavior because Gorbachev was operating on quite different assumptions about the role and value of nuclear weapons—concepts that Reagan shared. None of their predecessors could have struck this deal.

Gorbachev mesmerized the West as much as he worried rearguard remnants of Communist orthodoxy. He was the new Soviet Man intent on transforming his country, embracing Russia's "common European home," and demolishing enemy images. To do this, he needed to confront and change attitudes toward the logic of confrontation. He was willing to pay dearly in a currency he didn't believe in. He understood that the Soviet Union was a Potemkin superpower whose future rested on high-risk reforms that could only work by lessening the grip of centralized control and the military-industrial complex on the Soviet economy. Gorbachev downsized his military's footprint, thereby giving his reforms breathing room.

In the negotiating endgame, Gorbachev dispensed with the need to retain some missiles for Asian contingencies, to the dismay of his diplomats and military officers. As Dobrynin recounted in his memoirs, "In Asia the SS-20s were part of our strategic defenses against China as well as the American bases in Japan and the Indian Ocean, so this certainly represented a major concession."[87] Vladimir Putin would later make amends to his General Staff by deploying missiles that violated the INF Treaty.

Gorbachev and Reagan retained more than enough ocean-spanning missiles and aircraft-delivered weapons to deal with doomsday scenarios—even with the prospective fifty percent reductions that now seemed in the offing. The most salient issue during the Senate's ratification debate on the INF Treaty was whether treaty-prohibited missiles based on futuristic principles would also be covered—an outgrowth of the Reagan administration's belated and expansive reinterpretation of the Anti-Ballistic Missile Treaty. The senator most active in raising doubts about the treaty was Daniel Quayle, whose concerns were mollified by the prospect of becoming George H.W. Bush's running mate. Senators Joseph Biden and Sam Nunn attached language to the resolution of ratification, nailing down the administration's assurances that "futuristics" would be covered.

Reagan and Gorbachev left what remained of the missile defense issue to their successors. In the Joint Communiqué at the conclusion of the Washington summit, Washington and Moscow pledged "to work out an agreement that would commit the sides to observe the ABM Treaty, as signed in 1972, while conducting their research, development, and testing as required, which are permitted by the ABM Treaty, and not to withdraw from the ABM Treaty, for a specified period of time." The focus of U.S. missile defense efforts then shifted to outliers of proliferation concern, like North Korea.

Another major concern was the Soviet record of treaty violations that some in the Reagan administration believed to be quite long. This was the basis of Weinberger's strongly cautionary messages to Reagan before the Geneva summit. Reagan himself, at his first presidential press conference, accused Moscow of lying and cheating in order to achieve its goals.[88] While many citations on the laundry list of Soviet misdeeds were arguable and some were factually incorrect, one was most definitely not: the location of a large radar installation in the interior of the USSR that clearly violated the Anti-Ballistic Missile Treaty. The treaty permitted radars to provide early warning against missile attack as long as they were sited on the periphery of national territory oriented outward. At these locations they were neither defendable nor useful for battle management because they would be destroyed quickly in nuclear exchanges. The Soviet General Staff disregarded this treaty obligation and saved itself considerable expense by building one early warning radar well inland near the city of Krasnoyarsk. To arms control skeptics, the Krasnoyarsk radar was proof positive that the Kremlin had not given up on national missile defenses or the ambition to fight and win a nuclear war. While Gorbachev later proved willing to acknowledge this violation and rectify it, the Krasnoyarsk radar was still standing when Reagan signed the INF Treaty, although construction had stopped.

Reagan was fond of quoting a Russian proverb, "Trust but verify." He and Gorbachev effectively neutralized concerns of Soviet noncompliance with the INF Treaty by pointing to the most expansive and intrusive cooperative inspection provisions ever devised. The Kremlin took its first step to accept on-site inspections at Stockholm the previous year; now under Gorbachev's policies of openness and new thinking, no less that 130 sites would be subject to inspection in the Soviet Union and in Eastern Europe. Five types of inspections were authorized under the treaty: "baseline" inspections to confirm each side's declared holdings; continuous on-site monitoring at a missile production facility; inspections during the elimination of treaty-prohibited items; "close-out" inspections to confirm the status of former missile operating bases, support facilities, and launcher production facilities; and short-notice inspections at any site, active or closed. Each side was allowed a sliding-scale quota of twenty, then fifteen, then ten short notice inspections over the first eighteen years of the treaty's life span. Strict protocols were developed for the conduct of inspections and the equipment allowed. Moscow's only proviso was mutuality: Whatever Washington wished to impose it must also be willing to accept. This guideline curtailed fishing expeditions. A new On-Site Inspection Agency needed to be established.[89]

The Senate voted its consent to the INF Treaty's ratification with only five senators disapproving, in time for President Reagan's visit to Moscow. Moscow's vote on ratification occurred the next day. Gorbachev and Reagan exchanged instruments of ratification on June 1, 1987. On-site inspections began quickly thereafter. The first director of the On-Site Inspection Agency, Roland Lajoie, recruited fellow alumni of the U.S. Military Liaison Mission to help lead inspections. The challenges were daunting, at first—starting up a new organization; dealing with administrative, budgetary, and logistical challenges; developing detailed inspection procedures to supplement treaty text; and negotiating with Russian counterparts on technical details. The work of the military liaison mission in East Germany—the size of Ohio—now expanded across the Soviet Union's twelve time zones as well as across Eastern Europe. Lajoie remembers one inspection in particular, on July 4, 1988: "When I was a military attaché, if I'd gotten close to it, I'd be in great peril. Now I'm being escorted in the front gate and welcomed."[90]

INF negotiator Glitman wrote that Gorbachev succeeded "by warmth" to eliminate threatening missiles—something his predecessors "failed to accomplish by the cold wind of intimidation."[91] Glitman, like most U.S. strategic analysts, presumed that the Soviet deployment of Euro-missiles was a deliberate act to leverage compliant behavior by NATO. Instead, as Soviet insiders reported later, it was a matter of routinized Cold War military behavior. Defense Minister Ustinov proposed to Brezhnev that "obsolete" missiles be replaced, and so it was done. The military got its way and diplomats shrugged. Missile modernization was the purview of generals, not diplomats.[92]

Gorbachev viewed the deployment of new intermediate-range missiles as "an unforgivable adventure, embarked on by the previous Soviet leadership under pressure from the military-industrial complex." The decision to deploy was taken "without the necessary political and strategic analysis of its possible consequences." It was "naïve" to think that the United States and NATO would not respond in disadvantageous ways. "By signing the INF Treaty," Gorbachev wrote, "we had literally removed a pistol held to our head."[93]

This signal accomplishment lasted for three decades, a long time in treaty years between two major powers, considering their shifting geopolitical fortunes. The end came when Putin and the Russian General Staff felt they needed to take back what Gorbachev had given up—the option of targeting both Western Europe and Asia with missiles of intermediate range. While it lasted, the INF Treaty made major contributions. It initiated and then routinized on-site inspections at nuclear-related facilities—inspections that were soon expanded to include bases for strategic forces. While it lasted, the INF Treaty relieved Europe of concerns over a nuclear arms competition. It paved the way for deep cuts in bloated superpower arsenals of longer-range missiles and forged patterns of trust and cooperation that became critical to control nuclear weapons and fissile material when the Soviet Union dissolved.[94]

The symbolism of the treaty was at least as important as its practical effects. Reagan's embrace of abolition and deep cuts enabled a domestic consensus in support of elaborate and ambitious treaty making. This consensus lasted until the George W. Bush administration, which was dismissive of elaborate treaty making, and the advent of Vladimir Putin and a revived Russian Federation, flush with oil revenues and grievances. In Gorbachev's accounting, "The INF Treaty represented the first well-prepared step on our way out of the Cold War, the first harbinger of new times."[95] The "new times" didn't last long, but the decade immediately following the INF Treaty's negotiation was the best of times. The INF Treaty ushered in the golden age of nuclear arms control.

CONSTRUCTIVE FRICTION

Friction fuels nuclear-armed rivals to build up their most fearsome arms. The sources of fuel are abundant and varied. Rivals seek safety from strategic, geopolitical, ideological, religious, and historical competition in deterrence, but they also seek to avoid nuclear war. Since completely unencumbered deterrence is too dangerous, rivals also seek guardrails to their competition, whether tacit or formal. Occasionally, they adopt methods that we call arms control.

Friction between rivals typically generates an excess of arms and a modest amount of arms control. Powerful domestic constituencies support build-ups and resist build-downs. It is easier to place trust in powerful weapons than in diplomacy. Successful arms control requires a fleeting confluence of factors in which the friction that produces arms can be redirected toward diplomatic achievement. These instances are rare. Sometimes they occur after a close encounter with Armageddon. Public insistence for arms control in democratic societies can help leaders place constraints on unfettered competition.

Perceived weakness in closed societies can, as well. All this is necessary but insufficient. Great accomplishments also require leaders willing to take uncommon risks.

These conditions came together in the odd coupling of Ronald Reagan and Mikhail Gorbachev. Their shared beliefs, impatience, and their personal bond enabled extraordinary achievement. Previous conjunctions produced the Limited Test Ban Treaty after John F. Kennedy and Nikita Khrushchev took stock following the Cuban missile crisis. They were prepared to stop the worst aspect of their nuclear competition—testing in the atmosphere—but they could go no further. By way of compensation, the competition ratcheted up with underground testing.

Richard Nixon and Leonid Brezhnev agreed to a treaty banning nationwide defenses but they, too, doubled down on an offensive competition. Gerald Ford and Jimmy Carter were unable to cap the competition they inherited with a SALT II Treaty. Reagan and Gorbachev did far better; they secured a treaty mandating disarmament, without having to take compensating steps. This extraordinary achievement became possible when it seemed most improbable—when the frictions between the nuclear superpowers and between arms control and strategic modernization programs were particularly intense. The conditions for constructive friction are greatest when a Republican administration intent on pursuing strategic modernization programs locks horns with a Democratic-led Congress intent on preventing arms racing, backed up by public opposition to the heightened prospect of nuclear war. These conditions were in effect during the Nixon administration, but were even greater during the Reagan administration.

Nixon and Kissinger stifled opposition to their diplomacy. In contrast, Shultz and Nitze faced intense bureaucratic opposition. They had great diplomatic leverage from strategic modernization programs and from the Strategic Defense Initiative. They engaged in diplomacy against the backdrop of massive public resistance to Euro-missile deployments. Despite the dissonance and noise, conditions for uncommon diplomatic achievement were in place. Republican presidents are usually given wider latitude for treaty making than are Democratic presidents. Republican presidents can also count on the support of the Republican Senate leader, without whom the consent of two-thirds of the Senate is highly problematic.[96]

Reagan was positioned to accomplish feats that were beyond the reach of his predecessors. Success, however, required two uncommon leaders. Reagan and Gorbachev eschewed nuclear orthodoxy. Their respective and mutually

reinforcing beliefs were not evident at the outset, when success seemed unimaginable. At the end of Reagan's first term, Strobe Talbott, the chronicler of
pitched battles within the administration, declared the "Reagan revolution in
arms control" to be "over."[97] Reagan's first term left little room for optimism,
to be sure. Pentagon hardliners drove negotiating positions designed to foreclose agreements. Reagan's extraordinary communication skills could only
go so far; his ideas on nuclear issues didn't cohere, so he badly needed help in
stitching them together in ways that could lead to positive outcomes. Reagan
needed wise counselors—he was only as effective as the people around him.

In actuality, the "revolution" in arms control was just beginning when
Reagan sought reelection. Constructive friction culminated in the INF Treaty
during his second term. Reagan needed help to succeed, and he found it after
the embarrassing Iran-Contra affair when Howard Baker replaced Donald
Regan as White House chief of staff, Frank Carlucci replaced Weinberger,
and Colin Powell succeeded Admiral William Poindexter as national security
advisor. Shultz and Nitze excelled at bureaucratic maneuver. With the advent
of serious negotiations, Shultz was able to wear down the Pentagon's opposition by appealing to Reagan's instinct to become a heroic dealmaker.[98]

One by one, Shultz outlasted the hardliners. Jeane Kirkpatrick resigned
her cabinet-level post as ambassador to the United Nations in April 1985.
She expressed misgivings about the INF Treaty, but supported it in congressional testimony.[99] Perle left government in June 1987. He opposed the INF
Treaty as a private citizen on the grounds that nonnuclear, ground-launched
cruise missiles would be banned, unlike sea- and aircraft-delivered missiles.
He urged the Senate to amend the treaty rather than to "rubber-stamp" it.
This argument was not persuasive since amending the treaty would forego
its benefits and require renegotiation.[100] Weinberger left the Pentagon in November 1987, one month before Gorbachev's arrival in Washington, maintaining a respectful silence on a treaty he strongly resisted. Adelman, another
skeptic of treaty making, dutifully supported the INF Treaty, leaving government two days after the Washington summit.

Too much friction can burn bearings and result in heightened nuclear
danger and even mushroom clouds. These gears could have been stripped
during Reagan's first term, especially during the year of maximum danger
in 1983. Had Andropov remained at the helm in decent health, it is hard
to envision a happy ending to this chapter. Andropov was, however, a very
sick man, and his protégé, Gorbachev, was someone cut from inexplicably
different cloth. Just as important, Reagan realized that a serious crash in

U.S.-Soviet relations was possible toward the end of 1983, after which he changed his course and relied on Shultz to do the steering.

Reagan's vision, Shultz's determination, and Nitze's adeptness were necessary but insufficient for success. Success required a Soviet leader willing to make great concessions to remove NATO's new missiles. Success required a Soviet leader who viewed nuclear weapons and doctrines of deterrence as madness that contributed to bankrupting his country. Gorbachev was as uncharacteristic a leader as Reagan. Reagan was sustained by ingrained beliefs; Gorbachev dispensed with them. Reagan was able to succeed because his instincts about nuclear danger were sound and because he ultimately chose to follow the advice of dealmakers rather than hardliners. He was also able to succeed because the Soviet system was oriented toward following the leader, and that leader was Gorbachev.

Constructive friction thrives on irony. Those who took the hardest line in the negotiations contributed directly to Reagan's success. Weinberger and Perle took stands that fueled massive antinuclear demonstrations; they also took stands that helped produce strong verification provisions. The Zero Option was conceived as a blocking mechanism that became an unforeseen outcome. Reagan's role in this outcome was critical and yet perplexing. At times, especially in small group meetings, including with members of Congress, Reagan could command the stage; at other times, he seemed not altogether present. He had difficulty with details. And yet he succeeded heroically.

Success on a grand scale requires vision, which Reagan possessed in full measure, no less than Gorbachev. Dobrynin was as mystified by Reagan as other observers. He wrote that Reagan's "overriding strength lay in his ability, whether deliberate or instinctive I was never quite sure, to combine the incompatible in the outward simplicity of his approach and in his conviction that his views were correct, even if they were sometimes erroneous or untenable."[101] Ronald Lehman, who worked for Perle and Weinberger, among others, reflected, "There was a lot of Kabuki, soap opera and Sturm und Drang on all sides. But the substantive outcomes were outstanding."[102] Others came to Reagan's rescue, helping him to sort through his grand concepts, offering a realizable path to avoid Armageddon and to leave the stage as a heroic figure.

Reagan was in many ways an innocent, but he wasn't a bystander. He was ill informed but eager for achievements. He had deep-seated beliefs but no geostrategic logic beyond his aphorisms. Among Reagan's close observers, Adelman has written most candidly of his contradictions and mystery: "We know the things Reagan did but do not know how he was able to do them." Adelman asked Kissinger to try to explain this mystery, but Kissinger, too, was at a loss: "'Reagan is different,' he said rather dolefully, 'not like the others. He's sui generis. No, I cannot explain him.'"[103] Mysteries remain. What remains clear is that Reagan was central to reducing nuclear danger because Shultz was a reliable and trusted agent and because Gorbachev was his partner.

As much as fortune smiled on Reagan, fortune deserted Gorbachev. Gorbachev was a heroic figure in the West and a reviled figure at home. His impatience helped produce the INF Treaty, and then during the George H. W. Bush administration, the Open Skies Treaty, the Conventional Forces in Europe Treaty, and the Chemical Weapons Convention. He and Reagan laid the groundwork for subsequent strategic arms reduction treaties. Gorbachev's impatience also led to his downfall. He alienated the Old Guard that tried to remove him but was too damaged to succeed. Their attempted putsch did, however, make Gorbachev's continued leadership untenable. The dissolution of the Soviet Union followed that of the Warsaw Pact.

Gorbachev's accomplishments in arms control were not sustainable. Reverses would follow once Vladimir Putin found his footing. Anatoly Dobrynin's ledger sheet was telling: "Gorbachev increasingly improvised and without consulting our experts would agree to sudden compromises which were often regarded by our military as one-sided concessions to the Americans." These traits became more pronounced over time as "Gorbachev became more active and confident in dealing with disarmament. He wanted to reach his objectives as soon as possible. He was fascinated by the huge challenge of the task and carried away by the cheering international audience. He began to believe in his own exceptional role in history, so he moved forward without seriously contemplating the consequences."[104]

Gorbachev could deconstruct but he couldn't construct. Right until the end of his presidency, he was proposing major structural change, domestic and international. He exhausted the patience of his fellow countrymen and women, who were reeling from economic disruption and the loss of empire. Shevardnadze later wrote that Gorbachev remained a prisoner "of his own nature, his conceptions, and his way of thinking and acting."[105] He never got the hang of democratic politics to support what he was trying to accomplish. How could he? He had no training for the heroic tasks he undertook. The Soviet Union was incapable of fundamental reforms; corruption was too deeply rooted, and habits of mind too incorrigible. After Gorbachev came Boris Yeltsin's erratic behavior and a Great Depression. It was only a matter of time before another strongman would seek to restore order out of chaos, pull the reins of authority tightly into his hands, and revert to familiar choices.

While Gorbachev's stature in Russia plummeted at home, Reagan gained an iconic place in the pantheon of presidents. Garry Wills explained his success this way: "Because he acts himself, we know he is authentic." Reagan was "the great American synecdoche. He was as simple and just as mysterious, as our collective dreams and memories." Reagan was a transmission belt for our collective dreams because "ancient messages traveled through him without friction."[106] For a brief, magical moment in time, Gorbachev shared the stage with Reagan. They were the perfect odd couple. Only they could have broken the back of the nuclear arms race.

APOGEE

Chapter 11

GEORGE H. W. BUSH AT PEAK PERFORMANCE

Key events within a period of ten years always have crucial antecedents, just as their beneficial or punishing effects spill well past a timeframe devised for narrative convenience and explanatory effect. These caveats apply to the ten-year period between 1986 and 1996, the apogee of arms control. The first year of this decade of extraordinary accomplishment was marked by the Reykjavik summit, the Kremlin's acceptance of on-site inspections for military exercises, and work by Pentagon officials to scrub requirements needed for nuclear war-fighting plans, facilitating deep cuts in deployed warheads. The Reykjavik summit opened the door to completing negotiations on the Intermediate Nuclear Forces Treaty that dismantled and destroyed almost 3,000 missiles; other treaties would soon follow.

Reagan set the table for George H. W. Bush, and Bush took complete advantage of his inheritance. No president accomplished more to advance the practice of arms control. In four years, Bush, his national security advisor Brent Scowcroft, and his secretary of state James Baker put the finishing touches on two treaties mandating deep cuts in strategic forces and the warheads they carried, the latter eliminating the most destabilizing land-based missiles; another treaty mandating deep cuts in conventional military capabilities; presidential initiatives to remove the least safe and secure tactical nuclear weapons from forces in the field, resulting in the denuclearization of the U.S. Army and surface ships in the U.S. Navy; a Chemical Weapons Convention establishing norms against the development, possession, and use of these weapons; and a treaty permitting cooperative overflights from Vancouver to Vladivostok.

The decade in which arms control reached its apogee ended with President Bill Clinton's first term. Clinton consolidated and implemented some of the gains negotiated during the Bush administration. He began novel cooperative threat-reduction programs in the former Soviet Union. He brokered agreements confirming the voluntary relinquishment by Ukraine, Kazakhstan, and Belarus of their sudden nuclear inheritance after the Soviet Union's dissolution, paving the way for a permanent extension of the Nonproliferation Treaty. Clinton also led the effort to negotiate a treaty banning nuclear tests, which he characterized as the hardest-fought, longest-sought prize in arms control.

During this ten-year period, the nuclear peace seemed to be well in hand. The sweat equity of diplomats, negotiators, and public advocates, as well as deterrence and arms control strategists, yielded bountiful returns. Many weapons remained in U.S. and Russian stockpiles even after deep cuts, but their deliberate use in warfare seemed inconceivable. Even the testing of these weapons—heretofore considered essential for deterrence and message sending—was prohibited by the 1996 Comprehensive Test Ban Treaty.

The nuclear peace didn't equate to nuclear safety—far from it. New nuclear threats arose from Russia's weakness, proliferation, illicit commerce, and outliers. The possibility of accidents and breakdowns of command and control remained. But the central and most dangerous strategic dilemma of the Cold War—nuclear exchanges between Washington and Moscow that could lead to uncontrolled escalation—appeared to have been put to rest.

At the outset of the Kennedy administration, the founding fathers of nuclear arms control conceptualized what a stabilizing balance of strategic forces might look like. Reagan, Gorbachev, and the demise of the Soviet Union made possible what arms controllers had long sought and what every president before Bush could not possibly hope to accomplish. Bush briefly hesitated and then seized the moment. He turned blueprints into treaties. Had these treaties been ratified and implemented, opposing nuclear forces would have been nonthreatening and ill-suited for surprise attack. But darkness follows dawn, and this was not to be.

THE PERFECTLY PREPARED PRESIDENT AND TEAM

No president came to the Oval Office better trained or equipped to reduce nuclear danger than George Herbert Walker Bush. His father, an investment banker and U.S. senator from Connecticut, began inculcating his son for public service at an early age. At the Phillips Academy, his counselor found Bush to be ambitious and self-confident, reporting that he was athletic, well bred, and well disciplined—the traits of a lifetime. Bush was, in his own words, "a goal kind of guy." His sense of purpose, his accomplishments, and his occasional bowing to political necessity were hallmarks of his career.[1]

Like other young men, whether privileged or not, George Bush answered the distress call of his country after Pearl Harbor. He became the youngest pilot in the navy, flying fifty-eight combat missions in the Pacific. Then came the cloistered environment of Yale. Deciding to build a resumé of his own, Bush left behind the family manse in Greenwich, Connecticut, for Midland, Texas, seeking to make his mark in the oil business. He succeeded, adding wealth and a taste for pork rinds to his career path.

Bush's interests naturally turned to politics. Starting out as chairman of the Harris County (Houston and environs) Republican Party, he aimed high, seeking to become a senator of his adopted home state and, failing that, settling temporarily on being a congressman. President Nixon gave Bush national prominence by appointing him as U.S. ambassador to the United Nations in 1971. He kept his head down during the Watergate scandal when leading the Republican National Committee, and then moved on to become U.S. envoy to China and director of the Central Intelligence Agency.

Bush competed with Ronald Reagan to be the Republican nominee for president in 1980 but couldn't match Reagan's natural ease and likability on the campaign trail. His consolation prize was the vice presidency. For eight years, Bush was the good soldier, traveling extensively and taking on available causes, including the pursuit of a ban on chemical weapons. He was a riddle to Garry Wills, a keen profiler of powerful men: Bush was "both unnecessarily nice and improbably tough," someone who could "rise to genuine nobility of performance and sink to casual ruthlessness."[2] He could be high-minded but obeisant, when necessary, to hard-edged conservatism.[3]

Bush gathered around him the most accomplished and compatible group of foreign policy and national security advisors of any president, before or since. All of them were comfortable with the exercise of power and with each other. James A. Baker III, his secretary of state, was an old friend and campaign manager dating back to Houston, where they were victorious doubles partners at the Houston Country Club. Baker fittingly titled his memoir *The Politics of Diplomacy*; he was a master of domestic and bureaucratic politics, and these skills didn't stop at the water's edge. Bush knew Baker would be competitive, tough, and a strong negotiator.[4]

Baker, like Bush, came from a privileged background. His parents were Houston royalty. His father made his fortune in business and at a law firm bearing his name. James A. Baker III went east to attend The Hill School in Pottstown, Pennsylvania, and then Princeton. Baker attended the University of Texas law school and carved out a successful career working with business clients. Dabbling in government service followed in due course, with Bush as his primary patron. Baker in turn pulled Dick Cheney "out of obscurity" to become deputy secretary of commerce.[5] Baker's career progression had the same stepping-stones as his predecessor as secretary of state. Like George Shultz, Baker served in the marines after Princeton, reached one pinnacle of success as secretary of the treasury before reaching another as secretary of state.

One knowing profile of Baker described him as a mix of genteel, old-money Houstonian, suave citizen of the world, above-it-all statesman, partisan knife-fighter, big-picture visionary, and detail-obsessed consigliere.[6] He was an extremely rare breed—a top-rank political operator as well as an accomplished statesman. Baker succeeded at every assignment, including as chief of staff and secretary of the treasury for Reagan. He had two notable failures as a campaign manager for Gerald Ford and Bush, while winning three others—two for Reagan and one for Bush.

Shultz needed stamina to succeed; what set Baker apart was his political acumen. The last time the State Department was graced with back-to-back secretaries of such accomplishment was when George Marshall passed the baton to Dean Acheson. The timing of both successions could not have been more fortuitous. On both occasions, American power was unparalleled and superior craftsmanship was needed for a world transformed.

After encountering stiff Senate resistance to his choice of John Tower as secretary of defense, Bush turned to Cheney, who gave up a promising career that could have led to the Speakership in the House of Representatives to take on the challenge of running the Pentagon. Bush viewed Cheney as "solid, no-nonsense, and practical."[7] His background had little in common with Baker's except for their mutual love of fly fishing and wide-open spaces. Cheney's father grew up in a small town in Nebraska. He was a cashier in a bank that went belly-up in the Depression. Moving to Wyoming, Cheney's father worked as a public servant for the Soil Conservation Service. His federal service added up to thirty-seven years, including two in the navy during World War II.

Dick Cheney had promise as well as a wild streak. A local Yale alumnus persuaded him to apply, and Cheney headed east for the first time. It was a short stay due to his grades and "various and sundry scrapes with the authorities." He found his footing by marrying his high school sweetheart and attending the University of Wyoming. Cheney began to pursue a doctorate at the University of Wisconsin, but left academics behind when Washington beckoned in the form of a position with an impressive, young Republican congressman, William Steiger. There he met another formidable young congressman, Donald Rumsfeld. Despite rocky first impressions, Rumsfeld hired Cheney to help with congressional relations when appointed by Richard Nixon to run the newly created Office of Economic Opportunity. Frank Carlucci was another recruit, bringing to three the grand total of secretaries of defense incubated in a fledging domestic poverty office.[8]

High-altitude career trajectories in Washington are usually a reflection of drive, innate savvy, serendipity, and mentorship. Cheney worked with Rumsfeld for four years until his boss left to become the U.S. ambassador to NATO, then rejoined him when Ford brought Rumsfeld back to serve as his chief of staff. At the tender age of 33, Cheney found himself as the White House deputy chief of staff, drinking at the fire hose of Ford's presidency. One year later in 1975, he moved up to become chief of staff when Ford shook up his cabinet, firing Secretary of Defense James Schlesinger and replacing him with Rumsfeld. Ford elevated Brent Scowcroft to be his national security advisor and recalled George H.W. Bush from Beijing, making him director of the Central Intelligence Agency—normally a dead end for someone with presidential aspirations. Bush's team of advisers drew from the Ford administration's talent pool, with one notable exception. Rumsfeld didn't have a place in the incoming Bush administration. He was suspected of complicity in moving Bush to the CIA.

The bonds that made Bush's brain trust so tight were forged during the Nixon and Ford administrations. When Bush became president, he surprised no one by appointing Scowcroft for a second tour as national security advisor. They fit together like hand and glove, finishing each other's thoughts. In lieu of autobiographies, they collaborated to reminisce about the momentous developments on their watch. No book like this had been written before, and it is unlikely to be repeated.[9]

Scowcroft's grandfather settled in Utah after migrating west as part of the great "Gathering" of members of the Church of Jesus Christ of Latter-Day

Saints. He was raised in Ogden in idyllic circumstances. Two generations before him had built Scowcroft & Sons, a dry goods, clothes, and hardware business. Brent Scowcroft could have followed in their footsteps but at age 12 he discovered *West Point Today*. The next year he visited West Point and Scowcroft & Sons lost a managing partner. World War II ended before he graduated as a member of the West Point Class of 1947, along with Alexander Haig. Scowcroft was intent on becoming a pilot, but a serious crash took him out of the cockpit and into the classroom.[10]

Scowcroft took courses at Columbia and returned to teach at West Point and later at the Air Force Academy. After a series of Pentagon assignments, his big break, like that of Haig, came from entering Richard Nixon's orbit, first as the president's military assistant, and then as Henry Kissinger's deputy. Scowcroft was utterly reliable and levelheaded—someone that Kissinger could depend on completely. He was a pragmatic implementer and the ultimate team player. Bush wanted an "honest broker" in this position, and there was no chance that, as national security advisor, Scowcroft would seek to play an outsized role, in the Kissinger or Brzezinski mold.[11] Bush allowed his top rank to choose their own deputies. Baker chose Larry Eagleburger; Scowcroft chose Robert Gates, a Soviet expert who would later become the head of the CIA and secretary of defense.[12]

The fourth top-ranked member of the Bush national security team was the chairman of the Joint Chiefs of Staff, Colin Powell. He, too, was introduced to the inner sanctum of national security decision making during the Nixon administration, where he served as a White House Fellow. Powell was born in Harlem and raised in the South Bronx, the son of a shipping clerk and a seamstress, both Jamaican immigrants. He attended public schools and the City College of New York, receiving his degree in Geology. His grades were average, but he found his future by taking the Reserve Officers' Training Course. He graduated as a second lieutenant in 1958 and subsequently served two tours in Vietnam. Political-military affairs suited him. Powell rose through the ranks quickly and, at age 49, became Ronald Reagan's last and best national security advisor. He was only the third army officer to be awarded a fourth star without commanding a division. The other two were Dwight Eisenhower and Alexander Haig.[13]

Cheney has acknowledged a slight hesitancy about plucking Powell from his newly assigned post at Army Forces Command to become chairman of the Joint Chiefs, given the perturbations accompanying Haig's rapid ascent and the baggage that could come with being labeled as a "political" general.

But Cheney quickly shelved his concerns, betting on Powell's executive and personal skills. He won this bet easily.[14]

The director of the Arms Control and Disarmament Agency was Ronald Lehman, who previously held key posts on the staff of the Senate Armed Services Committee, the Office of the Secretary of Defense, and the National Security Council staff. Reagan appointed him as his last negotiator for the Strategic Arms Reduction Talks. The son of a pilot who served in World War II and the Korean War, Lehman was born in the Napa Valley, served in the army for one year in Vietnam, and received a graduate degree and his PhD from Claremont. His dissertation was on Arthur Vandenberg, Robert A. Taft, and Harry Truman. Lehman, deeply immersed in detail as well as substance, rounded out an extraordinary team.

A STRATEGIC PAUSE

Bush was in no hurry to pick up where Reagan left off. He thought Reagan was moving too fast and was too "sentimental" in dealing with Gorbachev. "His natural instinct," as Michael Beschloss and Strobe Talbott wrote, "was to apply the brakes to the Soviet-American relationship, pull over to the side of the road, and study the map for a while."[15] Bush wanted to formulate his own national security policies. "He was," as Linton Brooks recalled, "anxious to prove that he wasn't the third Reagan administration."[16]

Gorbachev, Eduard Shevardnadze, and Shultz wanted to keep pedal to the metal with a strategic arms reduction treaty to follow quickly on the heels of INF Treaty. Gorbachev was especially keen on a signing ceremony for START at the 1988 Moscow summit as "another milestone marking the end of the Cold War."[17] The outlines of a strategic arms reduction treaty were already in hand when Reagan and Gorbachev celebrated the INF Treaty in Moscow. It would allow each superpower 6,000 warheads in the aggregate and, most strikingly, a sublimit of 1,540 warheads atop "heavy" missiles—a long-sought 50 percent reduction in these missiles and in their throw-weight. Throw-weight reductions were a top priority for those opposed to treaty making during the Ford and Carter years, and Gorbachev clarified that they were there for the taking. The top advisers around Reagan at this point—Shultz, Frank Carlucci at the Pentagon, National Security Advisor Colin Powell, and Chief of Staff Howard Baker—were a cohesive unit. The INF Treaty won the Senate's consent with only five naysayers. More progress seemed possible before Reagan would leave office, but it was not to be.

Shultz faced serious resistance in pushing for START, including from George Bush's close associate, Brent Scowcroft. Reagan's penchant for abolition was unnerving. Five days before the INF Treaty signing ceremony, an op-ed by Scowcroft appeared in the *Washington Post,* warning, "The administration seems committed to measures in the fast-moving strategic arms negotiations that could decrease stability and damage our allies' confidence in our deterrent."[18] Shultz assumed that Robert Gates, another likely Bush appointee, also favored a go-slow attitude. Early after becoming secretary of state, Shultz invited Gates and other Soviet experts for a Saturday session on what to make of, and how to deal with, Gorbachev. Richard Burt remembers Gates advising Shultz that Gorbachev was the most dangerous Kremlin leader he had ever observed.[19]

Other powerful voices cautioned restraint before and after the INF Treaty signing. Henry Kissinger published an essay in the *Washington Post* before a trip to Moscow by Shultz to tie down loose ends, arguing that the Zero Option would help Moscow and hurt America's allies.[20] He predicted that the START process would undercut successful deterrence, "stripping away the legitimacy of nuclear weapons" without addressing conventional military imbalances, and argued, "Western military strategy had become progressively separated from rational objectives," leaving the democracies "increasingly suspended between Armageddon and surrender."[21]

Richard Nixon resorted to the unusual device of a letter to the editor in the *New York Times* to offer a warning: "It is very difficult to say anything sane about any proposal to cut the number of nuclear weapons at a time when the euphoria about the signing of the intermediate nuclear forces agreement is understandably dominating the dialogue. People seem to have forgotten that Stalin wanted to ban the bomb in 1945." For Nixon, the issue was "not how much you cut but what you cut and whether strategic stability is improved or jeopardized"—this, despite the deal Gorbachev was ready to sign that would cut greatly into the Soviet Union's nuclear war-fighting posture.[22]

These concerns resonated with Robert Dole, the Senate's Republican minority leader, who argued, "In START, even more than in INF, it is critically important that we move carefully, not quickly." Dole cited differences with Moscow on treaty terms and "uncertainty over our own goals and plans for a post-START world" as reasons for slowing down.[23] The Heritage Foundation also weighed in, cautioning Bush to go slow on START.[24]

Shultz offered a rebuttal to Nixon and Kissinger in *Time* magazine, noting that many nuclear weapons would remain to protect Europe after the

INF Treaty and that, "If the Soviets meet our terms, we should not forgo the benefits of such an agreement, even as we seek the stabilizing reductions in strategic offensive arms that are our highest priority and as we work to redress the conventional imbalance. We are on the right course . . . We should stick with it, collect our winnings, take pride in the success that NATO's steadiness has produced."[25] Shultz knew, however, that he didn't have sufficient backing to proceed quickly.

Momentum on START also stalled because of the inevitable wrangling over fine print. Pavel Palazchenko, the interpreter for Gorbachev and Shevardnadze who was also a Foreign Ministry arms control expert, expressed amazement at "the ability of U.S. and Soviet bureaucracies to entangle any negotiation in a web of abstruse technical details."[26] One of the most vexing issues dealt with cruise missiles, yet another bargaining chip emerging after the 1972 SALT accords that proved to be militarily useful when conventionally armed. Closing the deal quickly on START required top-down impulses, but Vice President George Bush and those whose advice he valued were poised to be at the top. Shultz reluctantly accepted "the naysayers' real pint of blood," which meant placing START in an effective holding pattern.[27]

Gorbachev, as impatient as ever, felt a rapport with the president-elect when he met with him and President Reagan at Governor's Island in New York Harbor in December 1988. The Soviet leader, having received a standing ovation at the United Nations with more bold proposals to transform great power relations, hoped to pick up quickly where he left off with Reagan.[28] As recounted by his interpreter, Gorbachev took pains to explain to Bush, "We have made our choice . . . We want you to know full well how much we have to change. And we want you to understand that the road will be difficult for us." Progress would not happen in a straight line; there would be "some zigzags and maybe even backsliding . . . but the overall direction has been chosen—democracy, freedom and genuine cooperation."[29]

Bush wasn't moved; he still wanted to review the bidding. He was extremely cautious heading into the Governor's Island meeting, even though Colin Powell, who was there as Reagan's national security advisor, sought to put him at ease, advising the president-elect that it was "a courtesy meeting [and] not a summit." In Powell's recollection, Bush responded by saying, "I'm not going to get pinned by this guy. I do not want to be hoodwinked by this guy."[30]

The strategic "pause" was already one year old when Bush took office. All of Bush's advisers supported the strategic pause because it was the "prudent" thing to do—one of Bush's favorite words. Baker recalls that the pause was "very intentional"—on both policy and political grounds. Bush and his advisers wanted "to have our own prism" and "our own imprimatur" on U.S.-Soviet relations."[31] The new president wanted to make his mark and said he was open to "bold and innovative" ideas, but his body language suggested otherwise.[32] Scowcroft believed that a fresh look at the START negotiations was warranted because the Reagan administration had gotten carried away with numbers without an accompanying strategy.[33] Lingering over the specifics was a recoil to Reagan's embrace of abolition.[34] Cheney wanted to go slow at first because he didn't trust Gorbachev. He also thought Gorbachev would fail. It was his job "to make certain we didn't give away the store. There had to be someone voicing the view that, "'Hey, wait a minute. Let's make sure this is for real before we walk down that road.'"[35] Later, Cheney and everyone else recognized the need to be proactive when a nuclear superpower was in the last throes of dissolution.

Robert Gates and the senior staff person dealing with the Soviet Union on the National Security Council, Condoleezza Rice, shared Cheney's views. Gates recalls that he and Rice were both "pretty confident" that Gorbachev would fail. As Gates recalled, at that point, the central question was, "how much business you could get done with Gorbachev, how much you can get out of him that serves our interests before he crashes and burns."[36] When the Soviet Union began to show alarming signs of weakness, Bush and Scowcroft set the pace, either prodding or sometimes circumventing interagency deliberations. In 1989, however, prudence was the watchword; U.S. policy toward the Soviet Union was, at best, sluggish and reactive.

Bush's cautionary approach was reflected in the response of his White House spokesman, Marlin Fitzwater, to yet another Gorbachev initiative—in this instance his May 1989 announcement of a decision to stop arming Nicaragua's Sandinista rebels. Fitzwater characterized Gorbachev as a "drugstore cowboy," a term for which there was no ready Russian translation, but its meaning was unmistakable to the Kremlin. Rather than taking Gorbachev seriously, the Bush White House viewed him as an inauthentic person dressed for a phony part.[37] The month before, Cheney predicted Gorbachev's failure on a television talk show. This caused friction with Baker; it was one thing to harbor doubts privately about successful reform in the Soviet Union but expressing them in public served no useful purpose. Later, Baker had to intercede with Scowcroft to prevent Gates from giving a speech predicting the failure of Soviet reform.[38] These were rare instances of key figures crossing established lanes. For the most part, Bush's national security team was a remarkably cohesive unit. In Cheney's words, "It just all came together, it fit."[39]

PRELIMINARIES

Rather than move directly to complete negotiations on START, the Bush administration initially posed three tests of trust for Gorbachev. The first entailed resurrecting Dwight Eisenhower's proposal for an Open Skies Treaty mandating cooperative aerial flights. This was Robert Blackwill's idea, a strategic analyst on the National Security Council staff. When Eisenhower broached the idea of "open skies" to build confidence and provide early warning of surprise attack, Khrushchev summarily dismissed this proposal as a bald-faced effort to spy on the Soviet Union. Blackwill proposed to resurrect this idea to test Gorbachev's professed commitment to glasnost, or openness.

Gorbachev was amenable to open skies. The advent of reconnaissance satellites had long since opened up the Soviet Union, and he had previously agreed to inspections in the 1986 Stockholm Accord and the 1987 INF Treaty. He was also amenable to expanding the scope of inspections for conventional force reductions. Adding cooperative overflights employing unclassified sensors governed by carefully agreed protocols to this mix would not harm Soviet security and would advance his proposals for a common European home. Open Skies didn't advance U.S. intelligence collection, but it did offer new opportunities to forge ties with states leaving the Soviet orbit, given the treaty's ride- and data-sharing provisions.

The Open Skies Treaty was finalized in 1989, but like the Conventional Forces in Europe Treaty of the following year, it required extensive modifications to accommodate the dissolution of the Warsaw Pact and the Soviet Union. Over time, the Open Skies Treaty's cooperative monitoring arrangements from Vancouver to Vladivostok proved to be eminently adaptable to changing geopolitical conditions, initially reassuring a prostrate Russia of nonhostile NATO intent while forging ties between the United States and former Warsaw Pact countries. After Russia's revival, the treaty's cooperative overflights served to reassure Russia's neighbors of U.S. and NATO support. At the time of its signature, however, the Open Skies Treaty was a check-off item, confirming to the Bush team that Gorbachev meant business, and that more important business could be conducted.

Yet another reason for proceeding slowly on START was hard-crusted doctrine linking conventional and nuclear deterrence in Europe. Orthodoxy held that significantly reduced reliance on nuclear weapons, regardless of their means of delivery, would have the effect of making the conventional force balance in Europe even more critical. The conventional order of battle between NATO and the Warsaw Pact was always imbalanced in Moscow's favor. Bush wanted to secure a treaty mandating deep cuts in tanks and other heavy equipment to stabilize this balance before moving on to START.[40] Deterrence orthodoxy also led Bush and his advisers to push for modernization of nuclear-tipped missiles below the ranges prohibited by the INF Treaty to be based in Europe.

Progress on conventional arms control and reductions typically moved at a glacial pace. Negotiations on "Mutual and Balanced Force Reductions" had groaned on from 1973 without success. A negotiating process to normalize political relations across a divided Europe proved to have greater utility. The 1975 Helsinki "Final Act" included provisions to respect the sovereignty and territorial integrity of the thirty-five signatories, to foster trade, and to protect human rights. Critics roasted Gerald Ford and Henry Kissinger for agreeing to "concessions" that would reinforce Soviet control over the Baltics as well as Eastern and Central Europe. The "Helsinki process" actually loosened these reins. The Final Act's provisions were not fully implemented, but they helped to relax restrictions on emigration from the Soviet Union.

Bush and Gorbachev agreed in 1989 to lend new impetus to a treaty to stabilize the conventional military balance in Europe. These negotiations began as another test of trust for Gorbachev's "new thinking" and intent to curb Soviet military excess. In 1990, they resulted in the Conventional Forces in Europe Treaty that mandated deep cuts in equipment required for large-scale offensive operations. The endgame of these negotiations paralleled momentous change, as Germany was in the process of reunification, the Warsaw Pact was crumbling, and Lithuania was leading an exit of Republics from the Soviet Union. To complicate matters further, the Soviet General Staff sought to protect its holdings by creative accounting measures and early withdrawals, actions that Gorbachev and Shevardnadze seemed hard-pressed to control. The CFE Treaty was no sooner completed than it had to be revised to accommodate the collapse of the Soviet Union. The Bush administration was unwilling to enter a negotiating endgame for START and to ask for the Senate's consent for ratification until Moscow accepted deep cuts in its conventional capabilities.

BUSH CHAMPIONS A CHEMICAL WEAPONS BAN

The third initiative Team Bush pursued before tackling START was reducing stockpiles of chemical weapons. It was widely and correctly presumed that the Soviet Union's stocks of nerve agents exceeded those of the United States. Many strategists extended nuclear deterrence concepts to chemical weapons, presuming that the ability to retaliate in kind was essential to prevent Soviet battlefield use. But U.S. stocks were aging and increasingly unsafe to transport and use. To address these constraints, the Army Chemical Corps proposed to modernize nerve agent munitions, called binaries, so named because their components would reside in separate compartments to facilitate handling. After firing, the components would mix to become lethal nerve agents.

The Army Chemical Corps sought "pre-production" funding for binaries in 1974 and 1975, but these funds were stripped by amendment during debate in the House of Representatives. A "Scoop" Jackson Democrat—Congressman Floyd Hicks from Washington State—achieved these rare successes. He alone among the members of the Armed Services Committee had the standing to pass amendments on the House floor while remaining in the good graces of the committee's leadership, thereby avoiding retribution. This was important because Hicks represented a district laden with defense installations. That he could succeed reflected how widely reviled chemical weapons were and the Army Chemical Corps' lack of clout on Capitol Hill.[41]

The Chemical Corps tried to resurrect the binary program during the Reagan administration, succeeding only with three tie-breaking votes by Vice President Bush in the Senate. Bush didn't want to be known as the man who facilitated a new generation of nerve agents; instead, he wanted leverage to negotiate reduced stockpiles. Once again, Secretary of State Shultz laid the groundwork. On a flight to Stockholm in January 1984 to attend the opening of a European-wide conference on confidence- and security-building measures, Shultz was looking for a bold initiative. Richard Burt, his assistant secretary of state for European affairs, accompanied Shultz and had an idea: Why not announce a prospective draft treaty to eliminate chemical weapons? "We wanted to capture peoples' attention and imagination," Burt recalled, and the chemical weapons' space was available.[42]

Shultz was deeply disturbed by Saddam Hussain's use of chemical weapons against Iranian forces, aided by lax export controls in West Germany and elsewhere. He was intrigued by Burt's suggestion and asked him to call National Security Advisor John Poindexter from the plane to gauge his response. Poindexter gave the green light. Thus, the process of negotiating confidence- and security-building measures in Europe that received little attention in Washington helped not only to midwife Soviet acceptance of on-site inspections but also the Reagan administration's embrace of the Chemical Weapons Convention.[43]

There were no interagency discussions before Shultz announced that the United States would seek the complete and verifiable elimination of chemical weapons. Shultz proposed this initiative while the Reagan administration was holding fast to negotiating positions on the INF and Strategic Arms Reduction treaties that had the Pentagon's blessing and that were widely presumed to be going nowhere. Defense Secretary Weinberger tried and failed to overrule Shultz; his fallback position, conceived by Assistant Secretary of Defense Perle, the man who also conceived the Zero Option, was to insist on "anywhere, anytime" on-site inspections for a chemical weapons ban. Like the Zero Option, this provision was widely viewed as a "treaty killer."

CIA director William Casey opposed the "anywhere, anytime" inspection regime that would open the doors of sensitive facilities from coast to coast. The Pentagon offered a united front, however, with both the Office of the Secretary of Defense and the Joint Chiefs willing to support a treaty with presumably no prospect of the Kremlin's acceptance. There was a collective shrug of shoulders at the State Department and at the Arms Control and Disarmament Agency. Negotiations needed to begin, and presumably over time, the "anywhere, anytime" language would either be revised, or the negotiations would be stymied.[44]

After Reagan backed Shultz, the administration needed to produce a draft treaty text and the proposed Chemical Weapons Convention needed a U.S. champion. Robert Mikulak, ACDA's resident expert on chemical weapons, was the principal drafter of the U.S. proposal. Mikulak took a chemistry course at Hamline University, found a mentor, and was hooked. After earning a doctorate in organic chemistry at MIT, Paul Doty, a Harvard professor with close ties to ACDA, recommended him for a position. Mikulak was hired in 1971. He retired from government service four decades later as the U.S. ambassador to the Chemical Weapons Convention that he helped conceive.

After Shultz's gambit, Mikulak was faced with a political rather than a chemistry problem: Who would be the torchbearer of elimination? Shultz would be focusing on nuclear negotiations. He thought immediately of George Bush, who delivered a U.S. position paper in Geneva on verifying a ban on chemical weapons in 1983. Mikulak sensed that the vice president wanted to be known as someone other than the tie-breaker of votes in the

Senate to resume production of nerve agents. He called someone he knew in the vice president's office to gauge Bush's interest. A positive response came back quickly, and the Chemical Weapons Convention had its champion in Washington.[45]

Bush tabled the hurriedly crafted U.S. draft convention on April 18, 1984. U.S. allies and other states were displeased. Soviet officials were caustic—until Gorbachev replicated his jiujitsu move on the Zero Option by accepting the principle of mandatory challenge inspections in August 1987. By the time Bush became president, the United States and the Soviet Union were already engaged in one-upmanship, with each topping the other's proposals for transparency and chemical weapon destruction.

THE STRATEGIC PAUSE ENDS

With progress underway on Open Skies, the Conventional Forces in Europe Treaty, and the Chemical Weapons Convention, the Bush administration had no compelling reason to delay further the pursuit of strategic arms reductions. The administration's strategic review was, by all accounts, a bust. Scowcroft characterized it as "disappointing." Baker declared the results to be bureaucratic "mush."[46] Powell was impatient, but as chairman of the Joint Chiefs, it wasn't his role to push a policy agenda. His dealings with Soviet leaders and military officers convinced him that Gorbachev and Shevardnadze were in earnest and that they were in a hurry because they were operating from a position of weakness. Shevardnadze unwittingly conceded the point in Vienna during his first meeting with Baker in March 1989, declaring there was "no alternative to success."[47] After Baker's first trip to Moscow in May, he was ready to move into a higher gear.[48]

Bush was also growing impatient. Gorbachev commanded the world stage from the transition period from Reagan to Bush and throughout 1989 with initiatives clarifying his commitment to "new thinking." These proposals were a mixed bag; some were surprising and serious, while others were clearly nonstarters. In September 1988, speaking in western Siberia at Krasnoyarsk, he offered to place a nearby radar that violated the Anti-Ballistic Missile Treaty under international control "for the peaceful exploration of space"—a harbinger of its eventual deactivation. Then at the United Nations in December 1988—just before meeting with Reagan and Bush at Governor's Island—he announced an end to the jamming of foreign radio broadcasts and the unilateral reduction of the Soviet Armed forces and tanks from Eastern Europe, including six tank divisions from East Germany,

Czechoslovakia, and Hungary. He also proposed that all states submit national plans to the United Nations on the conversion of defense enterprises to civilian purposes.

In May 1989, Gorbachev announced that the Soviet Union would no longer supply arms to the Sandinistas in Nicaragua—prompting the "drugstore cowboy" moniker by Fitzwater. He declared himself amenable to the withdrawal of all tactical nuclear weapons from Europe, and privately advised Baker in Moscow of his decision to immediately withdraw 500 of them.

Bush's prudence was no match for Gorbachev's theatricality. Capitol Hill was becoming increasingly restive, with Democrats looking for ways to pare back defense spending. Cheney knew that a proactive approach would be required to help fend off budget cutting beyond what was already in store.[49]

Baker was now ready to make his mark on strategic arms reductions. He had an ally in Powell. Unlike Scowcroft, Cheney, and Gates, Powell had already reached the conclusion that "this game is over." He, too, suspected that Gorbachev would fail, but unlike his colleagues, he believed the most pressing threat would come from Gorbachev's left, not his right.[50]

The pause ended, in Baker's view, because the review didn't "discover any flaws in the prior approach."[51] This wasn't quite true, as Bush and others held serious reservations about Reagan's belief in abolition and in his freelancing. A more convincing reason for the end of the pause was because the administration was taking flak and needed to move on. The pause conveyed a useful message—that Bush & Co. were thoughtful and deliberate—but the passage of time undercut this message. The strategic review didn't carve out a new identity for the president; instead, it reaffirmed that Bush was innately cautious, as was evident by his first tests of Mikhail Gorbachev's bone fides. Gorbachev was passing these tests of trust with flying colors; it was time to pursue strategic arms reductions.

START AND THE COLLAPSE OF EMPIRE

Skeptics of arms control like George Will have argued, "Significant agreements are impossible until they are unimportant, which means until they are not significant." Another variant of this argument is that arms control and reductions have succeeded when least needed and failed when most needed.[52] The Bush administration definitively proved otherwise: arms reduction treaties came when they were most needed, with the Soviet Union collapsing amidst a dangerous surplus of weapons and bomb-making material along with societal implosion. Achieving success required two decades of preliminary work to seize gains quickly when political conditions finally permitted.

The Bush administration's monumental gains were built on a foundation that began in the Eisenhower administration's first efforts to guard against surprise attacks and to seek stabilizing transparency. Nixon contributed the Anti-Ballistic Missile Treaty, without which deep cuts would have been far harder to achieve. Ford and Carter built out the baseline framework from which reductions could occur, and Reagan and Gorbachev had already blessed 50 percent reductions when coming to terms on the Intermediate Nuclear Forces Treaty. The strategic pause became politically inconvenient as public impatience grew alongside Gorbachev's initiatives. There were, however, no penalties for waiting. The administration achieved what it set out to accomplish; it just needed to proceed hurriedly at the end.[53]

New diplomatic initiatives were becoming imperative, first and foremost, because the Soviet Union was falling apart. Gorbachev's interpreter characterized this period as a "tremendous historic whirlwind" in which "the instruments of political management" for stabilization needed to be improvised and seemed woefully insufficient. "History was moving on implacably," he wrote, "and it fell to Mikhail Gorbachev and George Bush to be in the midst of it."[54] Baker verbalized what he had been thinking during the pause in a speech at the Commonwealth Club in San Francisco in October 1989. "Any uncertainty about the fate of reform in the Soviet Union," he said, "was all the more reason, not less for us to seize the present opportunity."[55]

Bush, Scowcroft, and Baker bore the greatest responsibility for managing Soviet decline without explosions, especially ones that could produce mushroom clouds. Arms control and reduction negotiations became essential management tools for Soviet decline. Treaty making was both the manifestation and the instrument of trust building. Bush and Baker, like Reagan and Shultz, became increasingly invested in this work once they connected on a personal level with Gorbachev and Shevardnadze. On Baker's first trip to Moscow in May 1989, Shevardnadze hosted him for a home-cooked Georgian meal with their wives. To Baker, it was the beginning of "a close and warm friendship."[56] Forging a human bond in this way was a shrewd move by Shevardnadze. Baker reciprocated when they met at Jackson Hole, Wyoming, in September 1989 for serious conversation and fishing on the Snake River. Baker and Shevardnadze developed a strong working relationship. "As much as anything else," Baker wrote in his memoir, "the force of friendship based on trust was the reason Shevardnadze and I had been able to accomplish what we did."[57]

At Jackson Hole Baker came to the conclusion that Shevardnadze (and, by extension, Gorbachev) were "for real." One key purpose for this ministerial was to lay the basis for a successful summit at Malta to be held ten weeks later. A long conversation on the plane from Wyoming back to Washington took their personal relationship to a higher level.[58] Shevardnadze let Baker know that the Kremlin was willing to proceed with START even without agreed limits on space-based defenses or an explicit reaffirmation of the original, "narrow" interpretation of the ABM Treaty. This wasn't entirely a surprise, as Gorbachev had previously dropped demands to link constraints on futuristic missile defenses to complete the INF Treaty. It was important, nonetheless, because it clarified Moscow's strong interest in another treaty that enabled cost-cutting.

The concerted Soviet diplomatic and public relations campaign against SDI that began after its surprise unveiling was thus officially interred at Jackson Hole. The Kremlin recognized the futility of taking on SDI frontally and understood that the Bush administration was unencumbered by Reagan's belief system. While pronouncing continued interest in futuristic defenses, Bush, Scowcroft, and Baker had no real desire to move beyond research and development, recognizing the technical and cost challenges of space-based weapons as prohibitive. Cheney knew the lay of this land: "Because it took money away from programs they would rather have, there was never any great enthusiasm on the part of the uniformed military for SDI."[59]

At Jackson Hole, Shevardnadze removed a second major impediment to completing START. He told Baker that the Krasnoyarsk radar, built for convenience and cost-savings in a location prohibited by the Anti-Ballistic Missile Treaty, would be dismantled. The radar's location inland was a concession to the elements. Had it been constructed where it belonged, weather conditions for construction on the periphery of the Soviet northeast would have been brutal, and there was no infrastructure to support a construction project of this magnitude. As one exegesis of the Soviet decision-making process revealed, after much internal study, "The balance was tipped decisively by [Minister of Defense] Dmitri Ustinov and the General Staff . . . The economic rationale proved the determining factor in making this choice. No one, of course, could have imagined at the time that the Krasnoyarsk option would later lead to such serious political complications."[60]

"The serious political complications" came soon enough, as the Krasnoyarsk radar became the unarguable centerpiece of the Reagan administration's long list of Soviet arms control treaty violations. Hardliners pointed to Krasnoyarsk as evidence of the Kremlin's nuclear war-fighting capabilities, while powerful supporters of arms control called out the Kremlin's violation, including Paul Warnke, McGeorge Bundy, George Kennan, Robert McNamara, and Gerard Smith.[61] For all practical purposes, rectifying the violation meant tearing the radar down or leaving it as an unfinished hulk. Shevardnadze took it upon himself "to lance the boil."[62] Once Gorbachev, who wanted and needed START, reconciled himself to this remedy, another important obstacle to a treaty signing ceremony was removed.

A SEASICK SUMMIT IN MALTA

In his memoir, Ronald Reagan wrote that "establishing a personal relationship" with Gorbachev was a precondition to peacemaking.[63] Bush also felt this need for personal contact, as did Gorbachev. Just as in Geneva, when he first met Reagan, Gorbachev expected progress after the human factor kicked in.[64] Once this human connection was made, Bush shed much of his innate caution. Once the Soviet Union started to dissolve, he shed the rest.

One key event in this progression was the Bush-Gorbachev summit in Malta in December 1989. This summit yielded crucial dividends despite the elements that buffeted the dramatis personae in driving winds and uncommonly high seas. The development of a "personal relationship" between Bush and Gorbachev was symbolized most graphically by their collegial joint press conference following their conversations. Scowcroft, who was most hesitant about engaging in summitry with Gorbachev, acknowledged that his concerns were groundless, as there was no "score-keeping" and "one-upmanship."[65]

Bush had waited almost an entire year to have a summit meeting with Gorbachev. He was now primed to clarify his readiness to do business. Malta was where, as his chief of staff, John Sununu, declared, Bush could beat "the timidity rap."[66] His opening remarks were short of major new initiatives but called for fast tracking START, the treaty on conventional force reductions and the destruction of chemical stockpiles. A chemical weapon elimination agreement would make binary nerve gas weapons unnecessary; besides, no U.S. chemical manufacturer wanted to produce them. He also promised Gorbachev something he couldn't deliver—freeing up trade.

In addition, Bush proposed joint monitoring experiments so that the 1974 Threshold Nuclear Test Ban Treaty could finally be ratified and enter into force. This treaty, completed in time for Richard Nixon's last summit in Moscow, permitted tests with yields of 150 kilotons. Elaborate collaborative experiments at U.S. and Soviet test sites could clarify yields that many skeptics of arms control believed exceeded the treaty's allowed threshold. Bush also wanted to propose the elimination of land-based missiles carrying multiple warheads, but he temporarily yielded to the Pentagon's resistance on this issue. Congressional support for new land-based missiles was soft, and Cheney was concerned that it would get softer if the administration offered to bargain them away.

There was a related internal issue that needed to be ironed out. The U.S. position on whether to allow mobile land-based missiles in START had vacillated, dating back to the Johnson administration. Mobile missiles were harder to monitor but also harder to target, and therefore more stabilizing. With advances in on-site inspections and production monitoring in the INF Treaty, Bush dropped U.S. opposition to deploying mobile missiles.

Gorbachev's response to Bush's opening remarks boiled down to "Now I know." He wondered whether Bush was serious about arms control, and he had his answer at Malta.[67] There Gorbachev told Bush that "the Soviet Union was ready not to regard the United States as an enemy."[68] Both leaders heard each other out, exchanged how they thought about current events and their hopes for the future. Powell believes that Malta was where Bush and Gorbachev got their "sea legs. Malta was where they started to realize, '*This guy is for real.*'" Nuclear arms reductions were now high on Bush's agenda. While the key players around Bush worked well together, some were more cautious than others. "From this point on," Powell recalls, "we started to operate on the same harmonic."[69]

CRUISE MISSILES

The major issue standing in the way of completing START was how to deal with cruise missiles, especially those launched from the sea. Gorbachev highlighted this problem at their joint press conference in Malta, declaring that this issue was "impossible to ignore" and a "serious difficulty." Unlike ballistic missiles, cruise missiles never left the earth's atmosphere. They could be programmed to use evasive maneuvers and could have stealthy features to avoid detection and interception.

After their use by Germany in World War II, cruise missiles were eclipsed by the advent of ballistic missiles that could destroy targets in less than thirty minutes, against which there was no effective defense. Cruise missiles received a new lease on life during the Nixon administration as a bargaining chip and as a supplement to the Triad of land- and sea-based ballistic missiles and long-range bombers. Nixon and Kissinger were under fire for the porous

constraints of the 1972 Interim Agreement as well as the parade of new Soviet land-based missiles that their agreement did nothing to stop. Civilians
took the lead in promoting cruise missiles that the military services viewed as
unnecessary and perhaps as a threat to their primary means of delivering deterrence by means of ballistic missiles and bombers. The Nixon White House,
Defense Secretary Laird, and especially his deputy, Bill Clements, overrode
military qualms. When the White House ordered the development of cruise
missiles to begin in 1972, there were no design-to-cost goals, no inventory
requirement estimates, and no operational requirements. The stated reasons
for moving forward were to compensate for giving up nationwide missile
defenses, to hedge against the failure of SALT, and to have a bargaining chip.
None of these rationales were sound. Cruise missiles mattered because they
had great military utility in conventional warfare against ships at sea and
targets on land. For these reasons, and because the navy and the air force
realized they could protect strategic force structure from budget cutters, opposition to cruise missiles melted away within the Pentagon.

Cruise missiles also could be nuclear-armed, which became a serious
source of concern for the Soviet General Staff because they could nullify
their significant investment in air defenses. Once again, they were playing
catch-up. The U.S. technological lead was five years (presumed wrongly by
Clements to be ten), similar to MIRVs. Cruise missiles could be extremely
accurate; effective defenses against them would be costly and probably futile.
The innards of cruise missiles—their guidance, propulsion, and electronics—
were upgradable, and stealthy properties could be added. Even slow-moving
cruise missiles posed a severe threat because of how hard they were to detect,
making them effective instruments of surprise attack. For these reasons, the
Kremlin was intent of eliminating ground-launched cruise missiles as well
as intermediate-range ballistic missiles in the INF Treaty that Reagan and
Gorbachev signed in 1987.[70]

The primary difficulty in negotiating constraints on cruise missiles turned
out to be their military utility in conventional warfare. Another difficulty was
distinguishing between conventional- and nuclear-armed variants. A third
was verifying range limitations. There were no simple or satisfactory answers
to these problems. Unable to reach agreement on cruise missile limitations in
SALT II, the Kremlin and the Carter administration sidestepped this issue in
a protocol of three years' duration. At that time, in 1979, the Pentagon was
contemplating buying new wide-bodied aircraft that could be stuffed with
an average of twenty-eight cruise missiles. Existing bombers could carry as

many as twenty. The range limit of cruise missiles then under consideration was 600 kilometers on ground- and sea-based launchers. Deterrence strategists strongly opposed this provision, presuming that range limits would be carried over in future negotiations.

Later, at Reykjavik, during an all-night negotiating session, Soviet marshal Sergey Akhromeyev conceded to Paul Nitze that each bomber included in a strategic arms reduction treaty would count as one, regardless of the number of cruise missiles they carried. Akhromeyev later offered this same concession to U.S. ambassador Richard Burt when the Bush administration resumed negotiations on START.[71] The Kremlin quickly withdrew Akhromeyev's concession and tried to claw back extremely permissive provisions on air-launched cruise missiles. The Kremlin had scant leverage to do so. As before, the superpower with programs underway was unwilling to constrain them and the disadvantaged side was unwilling to propose meaningful trade-offs. When negotiations on START finally concluded in 1991, its provisions on air-launched cruise missiles seriously undercounted this area of U.S. advantage. Each U.S. heavy bomber would count as ten warheads but could be equipped to carry twice this number. Soviet bombers had less carrying capacity. They could be equipped to carry twelve cruise missiles but would count as having eight.

Limitations on sea-launched cruise missiles also proved to be difficult because they, too, had obvious military utility in conventional warfare. *Janes Fighting Ships* concluded in the Forward to the 1975–76 edition: "The cruise missile has altered the naval equation beyond recognition."[72] The U.S. Navy pursued three variants—an anti-ship, conventional land attack, and nuclear-capable sea-launched cruise missile. All could be launched from torpedo tubes. Conventionally-armed cruise missiles were loaded on battleships reactivated during the Reagan administration, cruisers, and destroyers. In all, cruise missile deployments were planned for almost 150 U.S. surface combatants and submarines. Controls over sea-launched cruise missiles were the longest-sought, hardest-fought provisions in START. They, too, were lax.

NUCLEAR TARGETING

The last bastion of military resistance to civilian control in the Pentagon was the number of weapons required for targeting in the event of a nuclear war. Presidents and secretaries of defense are, of course, briefed on the war plan, known from 1961 to 2003 as the Single Integrated Operational Plan, or SIOP. But presidents habitually resisted knowing the details of these plans and how they were built out. These details are in the hands of the Joint Strategic Targeting Planning Staff, or JSTPS, located in Omaha, Nebraska, the home of the U.S. Strategic Command and its predecessor, the Strategic Air Command.

The military services retained custody of nuclear warheads dating back to the Truman administration. The force structure of the Triad of missiles, submarines, and bombers deemed necessary to execute nuclear war-fighting plans was essentially set during the Eisenhower administration and built out under Presidents Kennedy and Johnson. Warheads were not built to last; they were built to be replaced by more exacting designs, just as old missiles, submarines, and bombers were replaced by newer models. Some delivery vehicles, especially bombers, were modernized but not replaced. Each weapon carried by these delivery vehicles had a deterrent purpose; if deterrence broke down, each was assigned a target. After the basic structure of delivery vehicles congealed, the services sought and received supplementary capabilities, such as MIRVs and cruise missiles, to strengthen deterrence as Soviet nuclear capabilities grew. The duties of building out the war-fighting plan—types of targets and which warheads to be employed against them, the time-phasing of detonations and related nuclear esoterica—fell to the JSTPS.

The SIOP was updated every year in the fall. As warhead totals deriving from MIRVs and cruise missiles increased, targets were added. The process remained highly compartmentalized. Different types of targets could be nearby but would be targeted separately. NATO also possessed nuclear weapons, and NATO targeting was not well coordinated with the JSTPS plan.[73] As Admiral William Crowe wrote in his memoir, "The entire process, of course, was subject to political control. But no political leader would willingly open himself to the charge that he increased America's vulnerability or conceded nuclear superiority to the Soviet Union. That would be tantamount to political suicide."[74] Presidents tended to leave well enough alone, being distinctly incurious about the details of having to fight a nuclear war. The occasional secretary of defense—most notably, Robert McNamara and James Schlesinger—took an interest in targeting options, but even they were hard-pressed to closely follow the implementation of their directives because of the press of other business.

Crowe was the chairman of the Joint Chiefs when the autonomy of the JSTPS was breached. Larry Welch, the air force chief of staff who sat next to him at meetings in the "Tank"—the second-floor conference room in the Pentagon where the service chiefs convened—remembers Crowe fidgeting notably whenever the subject of nuclear weapons came up. Crowe believed in nuclear deterrence and the centrality of ballistic missile-carrying submarines, but he was uncomfortable with nuclear weapons on surface ships and even more uncomfortable about army units with nuclear artillery in the field.[75] Crowe's successor as chairman, General Colin Powell, was strongly inclined to denuclearize the U.S. Army.

Crowe later wrote, "Military people tend to be conservative by nature, and when they are directed to build an arsenal that will bring an adversary to his knees, they will develop a plan to do exactly that." Planning factors congealed as warhead totals and targets grew. The targeting lists, Crowe wrote, "acquired a mystique of their own."[76] The JSTPS worked in near-complete autonomy until Frank Miller began to ask hard questions.

Miller was then a civil servant working in the Office of the Secretary of Defense. He grew up on Horatio Hornblower novels in Manhattan. His father was a physician working for a time in the Philippines for the U.S. Army. His mother, who held a master's degree in genetics from Columbia where she met his father, worked on the Manhattan Project but stayed at home after Miller was born. After graduating from Williams, Miller joined the navy, serving on a destroyer. Three years later, he attended Princeton's Woodrow Wilson School. He tried working at the State Department but it didn't feel right; the Pentagon was a perfect fit.

In 1981, Richard Perle tapped Miller to become an office director working on nuclear issues but not targeting. His portfolio expanded in 1985, when he started investigating the war plan, one aspect at a time. Miller and his small team, including Ed Ohlert, Gil Klinger, and Wayne Lumsden, used creative investigative techniques to gain access to data previously withheld from the Office of the Secretary of Defense on the grounds that civilians did not have a "need to know" these particulars. The more Miller learned, the more he felt compelled to dig deeper.

For starters, the war plan didn't reflect presidential guidance. Ever since McNamara, presidents were supposed to have the option of sparing cities in the event of nuclear exchanges. But given the nature of nuclear weapon effects and the restrictive way urban areas were defined, Soviet cities would have been devastated in nuclear exchanges. Miller went to Perle for backup, and Perle went to Weinberger. They both supported Miller's incursion into the JSTPS's bailiwick. The presidential guidance for "withholds" was clear-cut, reflected in a directive signed by Reagan in October 1981, and yet the methodology employed by the JSTPS clearly negated the concept of sparing cities.

The targeting staff had no effective rebuttal. "It was the first time," Miller recalled, "that civilians had interfered with nuclear targeting."[77] Miller had the bureaucratic savvy to start with an issue where planning clearly violated national policy. "By carefully preparing our analysis, and by ensuring that the Secretary [Weinberger] would back us when we needed it," he wrote, "we demonstrated that henceforth we would be a force to be reckoned with."[778]

Flush with their first victory, Miller and his team next moved on to explore limited nuclear options, a concept of particular interest to James Schlesinger. The Nixon administration's guidance to the targeting staff stipulated the requirement for options that limited "the level, scope and duration of violence . . . in a manner which can be clearly and credibly communicated to the enemy."[79] Every subsequent president signed off on limited nuclear options, but when Miller took a hard look at them, some entailed hundreds of—and in one instance, even a thousand—warheads, delivered by all three legs of the Triad. As there was no way that the Soviet chain of command would view these attacks as limited, such options would invite massive retaliation. After assessing the capabilities of Soviet early warning radars, Miller and his team, again supported by Weinberger, scrubbed these options so that radar operators in the Soviet Union could recognize limited attacks.[80]

Miller's next step was to coordinate U.S. and NATO targeting. A review of both nuclear war-fighting plans revealed NATO pilots would be carrying out missions to destroy targets already obliterated by U.S. ocean-spanning missiles. More coordination followed. Next up, Miller's team took a close look at another aspect of deterrence orthodoxy—the "secure reserve force"—strategic assets that would be withheld, even in large-scale exchanges, to influence post–nuclear exchange outcomes. The targeting staff in Omaha had included land-based missiles in the secure reserve force, which made no sense since they were vulnerable to attack. Other adjustments dealt with capabilities to launch retaliatory strikes while under attack. Capabilities were refined so that, while this option remained, the president did not have to rely on it.[81]

Not one nuclear warhead was reduced by conforming nuclear options to presidential guidance and rationalizing targeting options. These steps were, however, a necessary prelude to a far more consequential review of nuclear targeting authorized by Cheney at the outset of the Bush administration. Few were aware of these changes, and had these scrubs been made public, they would not have been reassuring to domestic audiences deeply uneasy with plans for nuclear warfare. Nor would the Kremlin have found the more efficient and precise allocation of U.S. and NATO nuclear warheads very reassuring.

THE RED-DOT BRIEFING

The service that would be most affected by a fundamental reassessment of the SIOP would be the air force. General Larry Welch, as the air force chief of staff who previously served as commander of the Strategic Air Command, had the standing either to be a change agent or a strong impediment. Welch was born in Guymon, Oklahoma. The first five years of his life were spent in the dustbowl of the Great Plains during the Depression. "Life," he recalled, "was a matter of survival with families moving to where work could be found. While living conditions were harsh, my parent's priority was caring for the family, supporting them in their quests, and instilling the belief in the five children that with perseverance and hard work, there was a better future. I never doubted it." An uncle was a barnstorming pilot who joined the Army Air Force in World War II. He then became a crop-duster, and eventually owned a Cessna dealership. Welsh caught the flying bug from his uncle. He flew combat mission in the Vietnam War and rose through the ranks, becoming the commander of SAC in 1985.[82]

Welch combined an analytical bent with low-key common sense. After his career in the air force, he was enlisted in many blue-ribbon panels while serving as president of the Institute for Defense Analyses. While in uniform, he was too analytical to believe unquestionably in the methodology behind the SIOP. He understood how the war plan would mechanistically apply requirements for damage expectancy against different types of targets. When the estimated kill probabilities fell short—say, 75 percent instead of 95 percent—the JSTPS would assign another weapon to that target. The targeting guidance was being taken so literally that there weren't enough weapons. General Jack Chain, Welsh's successor at the Strategic Air Command, testified on Capitol Hill that, under then-existing guidance, 10,000 weapons were needed—a number that, not coincidentally, equated with warheads carried by the Triad.[83]

Within a month after becoming secretary of defense in March 1989, Cheney received the SIOP briefing in the Tank. He sat between Crowe and Welch; Frank Miller accompanied Cheney, joining with others sitting behind the conference table. General Chain conducted the briefing. Each detonation appeared as a red dot on the expanse of the Soviet Union. As the war plan progressed, more red dots would appear until the "laydown" was complete.

The briefing stunned Cheney. The Soviet Union was awash in red dots. Moscow was completely drowned under a sea of red, as was Kiev. Cheney asked about targeting the Soviet transportation network and was advised that 700 warheads were allocated to this particular set of targets. When Cheney took a close look at the war plan, he recognized its failings. "When you started to peel back the layers and really look carefully . . . and not look at it just in terms of categories of targets, . . . but looking at the number of weapons that were actually going down in a particular geographic area, it didn't make a hell of a lot of sense . . . We were just blanketing stuff."[84]

After the briefing, Welsh recalls Cheney turning to Crowe and asking, "Why are we doing this?" Crowe's response was, "Ask Mr. Nuke"—Welch. Cheney then turned to Welch, and Welch answered, "Because you told us to." Omaha was following the guidance given; the Strategic Air Command and the JSTPS had translated that guidance into 10,000 red dots.[85] Miller, who had advised Cheney in general terms about what to expect, viewed the red-dot briefing as pivotal: "It crystallized the moment."[86] Cheney had gotten to know Miller when, as a member of Congress, they worked together on continuity of government issues in the event of a nuclear war. Cheney was also aware of Miller's prior initiatives to "fix" parts of the SIOP. After the briefing, Cheney tasked Miller to go deeper.

Cheney wanted an answer to a question that no prior secretary of defense had seriously tried to grasp once the Triad of bombers, land-based missiles, and missile-carrying submarines was in place: How many warheads were enough? "His staff," in Colin Powell's retelling, "found the cart now pulling the horse. Every time a new nuclear weapons system came on line, the SIOP targeters went looking for something else to hit, to a point that had become unjustifiable. In the event of war, we were going to aim a warhead at a Soviet bridge *and* the city hall just blocks away." Powell gives Cheney and his civilian analysts full credit for reversing "four decades on encrusted bureaucratic thinking and put nuclear targeting on a rational basis."[87]

Miller and his small team began by investigating a wide range of issues but drilled deepest on three. One involved targeting of the Soviet transportation network. Miller's team determined that targeting key nodes of the transportation network could render it completely dysfunctional without targeting 700 aim points. A second investigation looked at "clustering." For example, the key constituent elements of a Soviet air force base—aircraft shelters, fuel storage, runways, and communication nodes—were individually targeted, even though the entire air base could be destroyed with a single warhead. Miller also looked hard at the targeting around Kiev. The red dot briefing targeted forty warheads against the Ukrainian capital.

Miller went back to Cheney after these preliminary assessments with the conclusion that the Strategic Integrated Operational Plan "was fundamentally broken." It wasn't integrated at all; instead, it was cobbled together and purely additive. The target base and the weapon allocation methodology "were incoherent and riddled with errors." Cheney told Miller to brief his findings to Colin Powell, who had succeeded Crowe as chairman of the Joint Chiefs.

Powell didn't need persuading. Miller recalled that Powell, like Cheney, was ready "to take the whole damn plan down and reconstruct it." Cheney asked Miller what he was going to do about his findings. Miller proposed a zero-based review of the SIOP, but told Cheney that, as a Pentagon civilian, he wasn't authorized to do this. Cheney's response: "You are now." Miller suggested that the Joint Chiefs and Omaha be brought on board and that an "open book" approach was needed. Cheney told Miller to "write the memo" in which he would order a collaborative scrub. Cheney's directive was issued shortly after Thanksgiving, 1989.[88]

The Joint Chiefs knew of Powell's strong endorsement. Omaha was "frosty," but followed orders. The revisions that began in 1985 were concluded in 1991. A systemic approach to targeting was needed. Individual targeting of the entirety of the Soviet electrical power grid, its ground transportation network, and railroad and communication systems was an exercise in overkill; destroying key nodes would suffice.[89] After reducing and rationalizing the SIOP, the number of warheads needed to fulfill presidential guidance dropped precipitously from 10,000 to 5,888. After subtracting targets in newly independent states of the former Soviet Union, warhead requirements for all strategic forces dropped further to between 3,000 and 3,500. The scrub took away grounds for opposition within the Pentagon for steep cuts. The timing was right, as Bush was ready to turn to deep cuts on long-range forces as well as surprising new initiatives to remove tactical nuclear weapons from the field and from naval surface ships as the Soviet Union and Warsaw Pact were dissolving. These treaties and presidential initiatives had the Pentagon's support.[90]

STRATEGIC ARMS REDUCTIONS

After the Malta summit, Baker had running room to finish up negotiations for the Strategic Arms Reduction Treaty, but this was far from easy. Baker's counterpart, Shevardnadze, told him in February 1990 that Gorbachev was receiving strong pushback from Marshal Akhromeyev and others who were "scrutinizing everything that we are doing and they tend to get emotional."[91] The Soviet system was being battered by the difficulties of trying to manage internal and economic reform. External shocks magnified internal ones as it became clear that Gorbachev was not going to intervene in Eastern Europe or even within the Soviet Union against his own principles and values.

While trying to nail down the fine print of START, the Berlin Wall fell, Germany was reunified, Communist governments elsewhere in Eastern Europe toppled, the Lithuanian Parliament declared independence and other Baltic states were preparing their exit from the Soviet Union. It was not a good time for Gorbachev to make concessions on cruise missiles or anything else in START, or to focus on the minutiae of a treaty text that, together with annexes, agreed statements, protocols, memoranda, and related agreements, ran in excess of 700 pages. The Bush administration was undergoing tests of its own with Saddam Hussein's invasion of Kuwait, the defeat of Iraqi forces, and subsequent efforts in Madrid to reinitiate a Middle East peace process.

The basic outlines of the Strategic Arms Reduction Treaty were in place dating back to 1987 when Ronald Lehman was the lead U.S. negotiator. What remained were vexing technical issues and fine print that needed to be written. "Once you get the big stuff done," Lehman noted, "it's hard to get the big guys to care."[92] The START negotiations continued at a plodding pace during the last year of the Reagan administration and during the Bush administration's strategic pause. The Malta summit was an important milepost, but complex issues remained. Among them were prohibiting telemetry encryption during missile flight tests so that data collected could clarify treaty compliance or noncompliance; how to count warheads atop missiles and their downloading; demonstrating the ranges of missiles; verifying mobile missiles; and nailing down parameters of new missile "types"—an issue that caused so much grief during and after the 1972 Interim Agreement.

START was the last Cold War treaty and the first to mandate reductions in strategic forces. To satisfy domestic skeptics, to assuage senatorial concerns, and to reduce the likelihood of compliance issues, the Bush administration was intent to dot every "i" and cross every "t." Baker characterized this work as "going nowhere slowly."[93] A fairer assessment was that the negotiators were going as fast as possible, considering the complexity of the issues they were dealing with. To take but one example, there were a grand total of 136 agreed definitions attached to the treaty text, a gamut running from "accessible" to "weapon-delivery vehicle."

The lead U.S. negotiator responsible for getting the fine print right was a retired navy captain, Linton Brooks. Brooks was the son of a career army officer, growing up with twenty-two different addresses before going to college. He studied physics at Duke while joining the Naval Reserve Officer Training Corps to help defray college expenses. He considered the navy as an adventure, not a career, but discovered that "driving ships" suited him. He started out on destroyers, including one imposing the quarantine during the Cuban missile crisis, and then moved on to nuclear-powered attack and ballistic missile-carrying submarines. Working on nuclear policy issues suited him, first on the National Security Council staff in the Reagan administration, where he was one-third of the "junta" of O-6 (full colonel or captain rank) officers working for Ronald Lehman. The others were Robert Linhart, a brilliant air force officer working on nuclear issues, and Donald Mahley, an army officer who helped shepherd the Chemical Weapons Convention negotiations. From the NSC staff, Brooks then moved to work on START, succeeding Richard Burt as the delegation's head in 1990.

The State Department's representative to START was Edward Ifft, the son of two high school teachers who was drawn toward classes in science and civics. While pursuing a PhD in physics at Ohio State University, he spent a year at Moscow State University, the premier training ground for Soviet diplomats, and moonlighted at the USSR Institute for Physical Problems of the Russian Academy of Sciences. He was hired by ACDA in 1967 and moved over to the State Department five years later, where he specialized in nuclear negotiations.

Shevardnadze provided notice at Jackson Hole in September 1989 of changes in Soviet positions on several major outstanding issues that were delaying the conclusion of START. Reagan's Strategic Defense Initiative and the uncompleted Krasnoyarsk radar would no longer be deal breakers. In addition, Shevardnadze signaled the Kremlin's readiness to move forward with the Threshold Test Ban Treaty and the elimination of chemical weapons. Baker took this as a clear signal that Gorbachev was ready to "close out old issues . . . but also make significant progress."[94] The skids were greased not only for the Malta summit in December but also for a follow-up summit in 1990 when START might be signed. This timetable was too ambitious. By all accounts, wading through the critical minutiae of START was a long, hard slog.[95]

When Gorbachev arrived in Washington in late May 1990 for the follow-up summit after Malta, he had no cards to play. His most pressing concerns were German reunification within NATO and the exit of Lithuania from the Soviet Union. START still wasn't ready for completion. Instead, Bush and Gorbachev signed agreements to destroy 80 percent of their chemical weapon stockpiles, protocols to nuclear testing treaties paving the way for the Senate's consent, and yet another joint pledge to speed up the Conventional Forces in Europe Treaty. The locus of discussion then moved to Camp David, where informality had the same effect between Bush and Gorbachev as the Jackson Hole ministerial did between Baker and Shevardnadze eight months earlier.

Gorbachev told the assembled press, "We spent many hours together and we able to know each other very well. Now we have a good human relationship." Bush wrote later, "We developed a feeling of give and take." There was laughter at Camp David. "The jokes showed the degree of confidence we had reached, and how relaxed we had become." The two leaders wrote personal notes to each other's children. "Gorbachev and I were able to speak heart to heart," recalled Bush, who had earlier resolved not to be hoodwinked by Gorbachev and to avoid Reagan's sentimentalism.[96] Personal ties do not override national interests, but they build trust when agreements are possible. START was certainly possible but would take more time. The new goal was to sign START at the next summit to be held in Moscow in 1991.

More perturbations were unavoidable. Shevardnadze resigned over the use of force to settle nationality issues. (He would return to Gorbachev's side later.) Boris Yeltsin, who reminded Baker of a National Football League tackle, was successfully creating an alternative power center to Gorbachev as chairman of the Russian Supreme Soviet.[97] Baker now made it a habit to visit with Yeltsin as well as with Gorbachev. The Warsaw Pact was crumbling along with the Union of Soviet Socialist Republics. In these death throes the Soviet General Staff was reasserting itself. The end of the Cold War was playing out quickly, and Gorbachev's days were numbered.

In March 1991, Shevardnadze's replacement, Alexander Bessmertnykh, signaled the Kremlin's strong interest in completing the START negotiations. Bessmertnykh, with the chief of the Soviet General Staff, General Mikhail Moiseyev, at his side, resolved the last remaining contentious issues at a meeting in London in July 1991. By then, as Gorbachev's interpreter, Pavel Palazchenko, later wrote, "it had finally dawned on everybody that we were running out of time."[98] But there was still much work to be done: Linton Brooks counted 104 unresolved items in the draft treaty text. Each unresolved issue was bracketed. The solution to bracket removal, as Lynn Rusten, a newcomer at the State Department, recalled, was to move "the entire inter-agency process to Geneva to make real-time decisions."[99]

Those involved in the interagency backstopping process were known as the "Un-Group." The origin of the Un-Group concept traced back to the Reagan administration when Robert Linhard on the National Security Council staff was looking for a way to ease intramural conflicts. Linhard was a well-liked air force colonel from the Bronx who learned that when participants at interagency meetings depended on rank, problems became harder to resolve, so he used his convening powers differently. The basic idea, as Susan Koch, a member of the Un-Group, recalled, was to create a forum where agency representatives, regardless of rank, could "deliver" their building. This meant that they had the confidence of their leadership and could solve problems quickly.[100] Arnold Kanter of the National Security Council staff recreated the Un-Group after early skirmishes between the State and Defense Departments in the Bush administration. Participants varied, but key figures included Reginald Bartholomew at State, ACDA director Ronald Lehman, Stephen Hadley from the pragmatic wing of the Office of the Secretary of Defense, Victor Alessi, a refugee from ACDA, representing the Department of Energy, and Generals John Shalikashvili and Barry McCaffrey representing the Joint Chiefs.[101]

The interagency process never worked better than in the negotiating endgame for START in Geneva. Washington had a willing partner in Moscow. Brooks worked well with his opposite number, Ambassador Yuri Nazarkin, with the Un-Group, and with officials back in Washington. He was easy to work for, engendered trust, was self-effacing, kept everyone in the loop, and had an innate sense of how to manage differences. A few issues needed to be resolved at higher levels, but most of the brackets melted away in long sessions of the Un-Group and their Russian counterparts in Geneva.

Then came the challenge of producing four copies of the finished product so that they could be signed amid pomp and circumstance at a summit meeting in Moscow on July 31, 1991. Special impact printers and special paper were needed for the 700 pages of text. The process was agonizingly slow. James Timbie, another refugee from ACDA now working closely with Baker at the State Department, suggested printing the signature pages first in the event that the entire printing project was not completed in time. It was, but the original documents contained 170 translation and conforming errors.

Marshall Brown, the State Department's legal adviser to START, and a small team subsequently traveled to Moscow in August to correct minor textual errors when the coup against Gorbachev occurred.[102]

When Bush and Baker arrived in Moscow for the START signing ceremony, the event felt anticlimactic to Palazchenko. "It was now clear that the details of arms control had taken altogether too much time," he wrote. "Instead of being an accelerator, arms control was more often a drag."[103] There was no celebratory feel, as with the INF Treaty, because the Soviet Union was in such dire straits. Gorbachev was working on a new Union Treaty, only to have his legs cut out from under him by Yeltsin, who would be the prime beneficiary of the Soviet Union's dissolution.

George Bush wrote about being "emotionally involved" at the START signing ceremony and then moved on to other topics after one short paragraph.[104] Garthoff, the master chronicler of U.S.-Soviet relations, recounts that, by the summer of 1991, strategic arms control had lost its salience, as the Cold War was over, the threat of war had passed, the arms race had lost its rationale." Instead, "the new center of gravity was the economic and political situation."[105]

All this was true but START was no less of an accomplishment. The treaty set limits on 4,900 warheads on missiles. When weapons on bombers were added and heavily discounted, the United States could maintain between 7,000 and 7,500 warheads rather than the 6,000 number advertised. These numbers represented a 25 percent reduction in U.S. strategic forces and a 35 percent reduction for the Soviet Union. Warhead reductions rolled back these arsenals to 1982 levels. The Soviet Union was obliged to dismantle ballistic missiles at a rate of one every 66 hours for seven years. The United States reduced its warheads on land-based missiles by 1,000 and another 1,600 at sea.[106] The Reagan administration's buildup was reversed, and the Kremlin was relieved of spending large sums on missile modernization programs that it could ill afford.

The Soviet Union agreed to 50 percent reductions in its "heavy" missiles, of which 154 missiles carrying 1,540 warheads remained. While U.S. land-based missiles remained vulnerable in their silos (as were stationary Soviet targets), steep cuts in the most threatening Soviet missiles signified how far Gorbachev had moved the Soviet General Staff away from deterrence orthodoxy. In doing so, START went at least halfway to correcting what Paul Nitze, Senator Jackson, and others believed to be the primary shortcoming of SALT. The remaining Soviet throw-weight advantage in land-based missiles wasn't an issue. Deterrence strengtheners cheered for START as loudly as arms control advocates—a rare conjunction. More reductions would follow as the need arose, employing START's fine print. Bush, Scowcroft, and Baker teed them up, with a crucial assist from Cheney, almost as soon as the ink on the treaty's paper was dry.

THE PUTSCH AND THE FIRST PRESIDENTIAL NUCLEAR INITIATIVE

Forty-eight days before the abortive putsch against Gorbachev, this author and other U.S. nongovernmental visitors met with Gennady Yanayev in a well-appointed, roomy office within the Kremlin. Yanayev was Gorbachev's figurehead vice president, apparently with so little to do that he could schedule a meeting with our modest group. He had no visible staff support. Yanayev opened the meeting in typical Soviet style, inviting an exchange of views, and then embarked on the standard twenty-minute ramble in response to the first question asked. In the middle of his exposition, a telephone rang in his outer office. Those sitting around the conference table sat in awkward silence when no one picked up the phone. After about a dozen rings, the caller hung up.

This vignette seemed emblematic after the failed attempt to oust Gorbachev. Gorbachev was, in his own way, as isolated as Yanayev. He was on vacation in his official dacha on the Black Sea coast, disbelieving that a putsch was imminent. In June, Baker had gotten word of a plot to remove Gorbachev and passed along the warning, but his information regarding its timing was wrong and Gorbachev went about his business of drafting and seeking support for a new Union Treaty. For three days in August during the attempted putsch, no one in the United States knew the status of the "football" with the codes authorizing the Soviet use of nuclear weapons. An unsteady and inebriated Yanayev was designated by his fellow plotters as president during the short-lived State of Emergency.

Bush huddled with Scowcroft at the family compound in Kennebunkport, Maine, to discuss these dramatic developments. As Baker recalled, "Just as U.S.-Soviet cooperation was reaching its highest point, Gorbachev's domestic position and the stability of the Soviet state were reaching their lowest levels."[107] Cheney and Baker interrupted fly-fishing vacations to join in crisis management. Before they arrived, Bush seized on Scowcroft's idea of a package of initiatives centering around tactical nuclear weapons. These nuclear warheads were the most difficult to keep safe and secure because they were small and readily transportable.

The questions uppermost in the minds of Bush and Scowcroft were the obvious ones: What would become of thousands of tactical nuclear warheads deployed in Warsaw Pact countries, on surface ships, submarines, depots, Red Army units, and missile bases? And how could the United States best encourage the Kremlin to increase the safety and security of this vast legacy of nuclear excess?

Gorbachev survived the putsch, but his leadership as well as the Soviet Union were on life support. Latvia declared its independence two days after the attempted coup, followed by Ukraine three days after that. Time was of the essence, as was the urgency of signaling steps to remove nuclear weapons from their Cold War footing. Bush wanted ambitious proposals from the military services, and he wanted to announce these initiatives quickly. The original concept was to proceed unilaterally in the hope and expectation that Gorbachev would follow suit. Secretary Cheney and his civilian advisers suggested calling explicitly for reciprocal steps, a recommendation that Bush endorsed.

The chronicler of Bush's Presidential Nuclear Initiatives, Susan Koch, was at this point serving as an assistant director at the Arms Control and Disarmament Agency. She was born in Scranton, Pennsylvania, and grew up in New Bedford, Massachusetts. Her father worked for General Electric; her mother was a grade-school teacher. An excellent student at Mt. Holyoke and then at Harvard, where she took courses from Henry Kissinger, Morton Halperin, and Stanley Hoffmann, Koch joined the Central Intelligence Agency as a Western European analyst. Ronald Lehman, then at the Pentagon, recruited her to help with the INF negotiations, after which she continued to work on nuclear issues for Bush, Bill Clinton, and Barack Obama.

As Scowcroft recalled, after the attempted coup Bush "wanted to stay out in front." He "saw intuitively that there was a new world forming and didn't want to be behind the power curve and be driven either by the Congress and the budget, or by the Pentagon's resistance."[108] Gates recalls that those most cautious about pursuing the kinds of arms control initiatives that Bush wanted were undercut by the Soviet Union's demise. "The irony was," he wrote, "that events played into the President's hand in a way that made their opposition fade away."[109]

Baker was ready to move forward and Powell didn't need prodding. Cheney was also helpful. In Powell's view, Cheney didn't have "a closed mind on nuclear issues. Quite to the contrary, he had demonstrated admirable vision."[110] When Bush directed new initiatives to deal with the possible breakdown of Soviet command and control after the coup, foot dragging wasn't an option.[111] As Cheney recalled, "I believed it was time for bold policy initiatives to cement the downfall of the Soviet Union . . . For me and my colleagues in the Defense Department, the obvious place to begin was with our nuclear arsenal."[112]

The process of coming up with a package of initiatives was irregular. The task went first to the military services before these proposals were vetted by civilians in the Office of the Secretary of Defense. At first, the services proposed proceeding in "a fairly traditional arms control approach," by retaining capabilities and proposing offsetting reductions. Powell, as chairman of the Joint Chiefs, clarified that he wasn't looking for negotiating stratagems. Instead, he wanted "forward leaning" proposals for immediate consideration.[113]

Powell had long "felt we were wasting a lot of money on nuclear weapons." He viewed tactical nuclear weapons as a burden. "Small, artillery-fired nukes . . . were trouble-prone, expensive to modernize, and irrelevant in the present world of highly accurate conventional weapons." Powell had taken a run at denuclearizing the army earlier in the Bush administration but there was too much resistance from Cheney, Pentagon civilians, and the service chiefs. The attempted coup provided the opening Powell needed: "Right after President Bush said we've got to respond to Gorbachev and company, I said, 'I've got an idea.'"[114] The navy was also "agitating to get rid of" tactical nuclear weapons.[115] Powell endorsed every recommendation the Joint Chiefs proposed.

There was one necessary intermediary step: Powell took the Joint Chiefs' recommendations to Cheney. Cheney staffed out these recommendations to a small group of civilians, who amended them slightly. First, while Cheney's staff agreed with removing all ground and naval tactical nuclear weapons from active deployment, they proposed retaining a significant proportion in storage rather than dismantling all of them. The actual language used in President Bush's public announcement was that "many" naval tactical nuclear weapons would be destroyed. Powell subsequently clarified that "many" meant about one-half.

Cheney also added a public challenge for Gorbachev to reciprocate Bush's initiatives. All of this was accomplished in just three weeks' time "with a stack of eight-by-ten slides." As Powell recalled, "There was no paper . . . I don't think you can find a memo. We sat at the President's desk one afternoon and I said, 'Mr. President, I've talked to the Chiefs, and they all agree with this.' . . . In ten minutes, he approved [the recommendations for] tactical nuclear weapons, except for the number we kept in the Air Force for fighter-bomber delivery."[116]

The State Department and the ACDA were engaged only a few days before the Presidential Nuclear Initiative was publicized to help with the roll-out. Bush gave notice to both Gorbachev and Yeltsin shortly before the announcement. Gorbachev said he couldn't respond definitively until reviewing Bush's initiatives but promised a positive response. Yeltsin was also positive and was by nature inclined to top whatever Gorbachev was willing to do. Bush delivered his initiatives in a televised address on a Friday evening, September 27, 1991. The speech came less than five weeks after the attempted coup. It would be the last public presidential address on nuclear weapons.

Never before in the nuclear age have more warheads been taken offline so quickly and without being subject to negotiation. Bush described his initiatives as "the broadest and most comprehensive change in US nuclear strategy since the early 1950s."[117] During his reelection campaign, Bush was critiqued for lacking "the vision thing," but his vision was on clear display after the coup attempt against Gorbachev. He asked his fellow Americans to focus on the need to "provide the inspiration for lasting peace." Given the rapid change in the Soviet Union, he offered reassurance that "we can now take steps to make the world a less dangerous place than ever before in the nuclear age."

Reassurance and reliable lines of communication accomplished what nuclear deterrence could not. Deterrent threats did not reduce a single Soviet warhead or missile when the Soviet Union was failing; diplomacy and arms control accomplished what deterrence could not during this crucial juncture. Prior actions during the Reagan and Bush administrations built sufficient trust so that Gorbachev was in a position to respond favorably to Bush. In conveying messages to Gorbachev and Yeltsin during this trying time, Bush felt that "a real air of cooperation had developed. Perhaps it was how we had stood by Gorbachev and Yeltsin through the coup . . . or the ever-closer relationship and trust that had grown up since Malta and Camp David. In any case, there was a genuine collaborative feeling."[118] Arms control talks forged personal relationships, and personal relationships reinforced perceived national security interests to produce remarkable results.

Bush's initiatives had clear sailing. The *Wall Street Journal*'s editorial page, usually opposed to arms control, declared his initiatives to be "fitting."[119] Bush's national security credentials and those of his team, recently burnished by the expulsion of Saddam Hussein's forces from Kuwait, were impeccable. The Pentagon crafted the initiatives and the diplomats saluted rather than the other way around. The Bush administration had already buried plans to deploy land-based missiles below INF Treaty–prohibited ranges to Europe. This proposal was not popular in West Germany, and with reunification, it made no sense whatsoever. Now Bush announced the removal of all ground-launched tactical nuclear warheads from Europe—about 1,000 artillery rounds and 700 warheads for a ballistic missile with a shorter range than those covered in the INF Treaty. These warheads, and an additional 400 counterparts in U.S. depots, would be destroyed. With respect to the navy, Bush announced that all tactical nuclear weapons would be removed from surface ships, attack submarines, and land-based naval aircraft.

Bush also announced changes in strategic force posture, including an end to the practice of having U.S. strategic bombers on runway alert to foil a surprise attack. An even higher state of readiness was practiced in the 1950s and 1960s, with some bombers in the air at all times, awaiting orders to strike targets in the Soviet Union. These airborne and "strip" alerts resulted in close calls and dangerous accidents. Now they were vestiges of the Cold War. Bush also announced that land-based missiles scheduled for elimination under START would immediately be removed from alert status. He also announced that the Strategic Air Command would be replaced by the U.S. Strategic Command. The name change signified shifting to a joint command and joint development for requirements and targeting. This was a culmination of sorts of the reforms set in motion by Pentagon civilians in the latter years of the Reagan administration, the reaction by Cheney to the red dot briefing in early 1989, and the subsequent scrubbing of the SIOP.

Bush clarified that he was ordering these steps unconditionally, while offering specific ideas on how Gorbachev could take matching action. In addition to relocating tactical nuclear warheads to central storage depots and destroying land- and sea-based tactical nuclear weapons, he focused on Soviet land-based missile programs, suggesting a limit to land-based missile modernization to one new, single-warhead missile, foregoing all programs for MIRVed land-based missiles—an idea Baker had previously raised with Shevardnadze unsuccessfully in March 1990—and confining mobile missiles to garrisons where they would be most safe.

The idea of banning MIRVed land-based missiles was not yet ripe for acceptance, but Bush would return to it immediately after the dissolution of the Soviet Union. The idea of confining mobile missiles in garrisons where they would have been vulnerable to attack required more trust in the Pentagon's change of heart than the Soviet General Staff could summon. Bush went further, suggesting cooperation on safe and secure warhead disposition, command and control, transport, dismantlement and destruction. Much of this work, which was inconceivable during the Cold War, was subsequently carried out after the Bush administration left office.

Bush proposed an additional area of cooperation over missile defenses. Reagan's grand schemes of nullifying ballistic missile attacks and sharing technologies to do so were effectively grounded after the INF Treaty and the sharp upturn in U.S.-Soviet relations. During the war to expel Saddam Hussein's troops from Iraq, Saddam launched missiles against Israel. Bush proposed a conversation with Moscow about adapting the ABM Treaty to address defenses against "theater" ballistic missile threats, as opposed to ocean-spanning missiles.

As for "challenging" Gorbachev to reciprocate, Bush was decidedly diplomatic. He was circumspect about the primary reason for taking the initiative, which was concern over the safety and security of Soviet nuclear weapons. Instead, he stated the obvious: "I do believe more can be done to ensure the safe handling and dismantling of Soviet nuclear weapons." Speaking to his fellow citizens, Bush offered reassurance: "I do not believe that America was at increased risk of nuclear attack during those tense days."

Bush's address was devoid of direct demands, but forward leaning. "If we and the Soviet leaders take the right steps—some on our own, some on their own, some together—we can dramatically shrink the arsenal of the world's nuclear weapons." Other reasons given for his September 1991 Presidential Nuclear Initiative were to "more effectively discourage the spread of nuclear weapons" and to "enhance stability and actually reduce the risk of nuclear war." His pursuit of reciprocity was, however, explicit: "We will closely watch how the new Soviet leadership responds. We expect our bold initiatives to meet with equally bold steps on the Soviet side."[120]

The motivation behind this package was clear in Moscow. The Bush administration, as Palazchenko immediately recognized, "had concluded that the prospect of major upheaval in the Soviet Union was real and decided that the fewer nuclear weapons such a country had in the restive republics, the better."[121] When Gorbachev relayed Bush's proposals to his national security and military advisers, Anatoly Chernaev chaired the meeting. Chernaev, a kindred spirit, asked whether the initiatives were "intended to lead us into some kind of trap, or are they an earnest attempt to start a process of reducing nuclear arms?" A few of the generals present started to quibble. Then Victor Karpov, the acerbic, veteran negotiator from the Foreign Ministry dating back to the Brezhnev years, answered that the proposals were real, and no one gainsaid him. Minister of Defense Marshal Yevgeny Shaposhnikov came late to the meeting, took a quick look at Bush's initiatives, and responded, "Well, it's OK. As for tactical nuclear weapons, it's practically all acceptable. On strategic arms, it's mostly old stuff, but there are some new things—and we must take a fresh look at the whole subject." Shaposhnikov wasn't a nitpicker. His generals fell in line.[122]

Later that day, Palazchenko translated a call from Bush to Gorbachev. The conversation was "warm," but Gorbachev was hesitant to commit to specific responses as he had yet to hear back from Shaposhnikov. In the interim, he welcomed the "spirit" behind Bush's package. Then Bush somewhat sheepishly advised Gorbachev that he intended to reach Yeltsin, as well, and that "I hope you don't mind it."[123] Gorbachev couldn't say no, and both men knew it.

Gorbachev didn't disappoint because Bush was proposing "real" disarmament on a reciprocal basis. His response came a week later on October 5, 1991. In Koch's retelling, it "was faster, wider-ranging, and more positive than even the most optimistic U.S. officials would have predicted."[124] Gorbachev framed his public response with a reference to his campaign for "new thinking," noting that Bush's initiative constituted unmistakable evidence that his philosophy was gaining ground and "widely supported by the world community." He also made reference to "the drive started in Reykjavik," of which Bush's proposals were "a worthy continuation." Gorbachev added, "I know that Boris Yeltsin and leaders of other republics share this opinion."

Gorbachev publicly committed to reductions of tactical nuclear weapon reductions in full measure—the elimination of nuclear artillery, short-range missile warheads, and atomic demolition mines. As Soviet control over the constituent republics and the Warsaw Pact melted, Gorbachev recognized the urgent need to transport warheads back to central storage depots. Like Bush, Gorbachev also announced the removal of tactical nuclear weapons from surface ships, submarines, and land-based naval aircraft. An unspecified number of these warheads would be dismantled, with the rest placed in storage depots.

Gorbachev reciprocated Bush's announcement by stipulating that over 500 land-based missiles, including over 100 MIRVed land-based missiles, would be taken off alert status. He also announced cancelation of a new single-warhead-carrying missile and a short-range nuclear missile for bomb-ers. Then he topped Bush by announcing that he would go below START's 6,000 warhead ceiling, reducing to 5,000 accountable warheads during the treaty's fifteen-year duration. There was more: Gorbachev announced the withdrawal of three ballistic missile-carrying submarines from active duty and proposed a new treaty after START entered into force that would further reduce strategic arms by another 50 percent. For good measure, he announced a 700,000 reduction in Soviet troop levels, upping Bush's announced cut of 500,000 troops.[125]

Gorbachev was amenable to discussions over ballistic missile defense, adding the suggestion of a joint early warning system for ballistic missile launches. Gorbachev also proposed initiatives that he knew would be re-sisted. He challenged Bush to follow his lead and adopt a one-year mora-torium on nuclear testing. After Bush and the Pentagon were reluctant to reciprocate, Democratic majorities on Capitol Hill forced a moratorium, be-ginning in 1992, that continues in place. In addition, Gorbachev called for "a joint declaration" by all nuclear-armed states of a commitment not to use nu-clear weapons first, as well as the complete denuclearization of Europe. Here he was butting his head against the concrete wall of U.S. nuclear doctrine. Warhead requirements could be scaled back, but doctrine was sacrosanct.

THE SECOND PRESIDENTIAL NUCLEAR INITIATIVE

After the coup attempt, Gorbachev returned to Moscow and to a "different country."[126] The competition and abrasiveness between Gorbachev and Yelt-sin were on full display during Bush's START-signing summit in Moscow at the end of July 1991. By the end of the year, Gorbachev's time was up. He had reached, as Strobe Talbott wrote, "the limits of his own vision, effective-ness and mandate."[127] He deserved, as Scowcroft noted, "a less ignominious end," but the times were too turbulent, and it was impossible to orchestrate a fitting departure.[128]

Gorbachev had been outmaneuvered. Yeltsin's Commonwealth of Inde-pendent States reflected emerging realities far more than Gorbachev's pro-posed new Union Treaty. Under Yeltsin's plans, there no longer would be a country called the Soviet Union or a role for Gorbachev. The Russian Fed-eration took control of the institutions of government on October 28. On Christmas Day 1991, the Soviet Union ceased to exist. The red flag with the yellow hammer and sickle came down over the Kremlin, replaced by the tri-color white, blue, and red horizontal bars of the Russian Federation.

Palazchenko recalls much discussion about the transfer of the "football" with the nuclear use codes to Yeltsin, given the latter's "well-known personal character traits." Talbott, President Bill Clinton's point person for Russia, described these traits as "erratic tendencies, boozing, vanity, irascibility, and bouts of depression."[129] As Palazchenko wrote, handing off the football wasn't optional; not to do so "would have created enormous political or technical problems." Relations between the two men were so strained in Gorbachev's final days that plans for a direct handoff were shelved. Instead, Gorbachev made the transfer to Defense Minister Shaposhnikov who, accompanied by two technical assistants, walked the football over to Yeltsin.[130]

Suddenly, the reductions orchestrated with Gorbachev were, as Koch recounts, "astonishing but insufficient."[131] The friction between Gorbachev and Yeltsin worked in Bush's favor when he seized on the need for a second package of initiatives after the Soviet Union's collapse. Yeltsin wasn't about to play second fiddle to Gorbachev; whatever Gorbachev did, Yeltsin could do better. Especially when it came to strategic arms reductions in the midst of economic chaos and when critical production facilities for nuclear forces now resided in newly independent states.

Bush's second package of nuclear initiatives focused on strategic forces. He proposed further downsizing, making a virtue of necessity, since the Congress balked at funding new strategic modernization programs. What the Congress refused to authorize could be added to the mix of other presidential initiatives to give them more heft and to help prompt a forthcoming response from Moscow.[132]

Bush's second batch of unilateral initiatives were announced in his State of the Union Address on January 28, 1992, shortly before Yeltsin's visit to the United States. "With imperial communism gone," Bush announced, the process of reducing nuclear weapons could be accelerated. His "dramatic changes in our strategic nuclear force" included stopping production of B-2 bombers after completing twenty planes; canceling a new single-warhead "Midgetman" land-based missile; stopping production of additional "Peacekeeper" missiles carrying ten warheads each; ceasing production of new warheads for sea-based ballistic missiles; and ceasing additional purchases of advanced air-launched cruise missiles. "These are actions we are taking on our own," Bush declared, "because they are the right thing to do."[133]

Bush notably returned to the idea of eliminating every land-based missile carrying MIRVs, thereby stabilizing the nuclear competition and reversing the opportunity lost by Nixon and Kissinger in the 1972 Interim Agreement.

Defense Secretary Cheney was reluctant earlier to do this, but now he was ready to "put Kissinger's genie back in the bottle."[134] Cheney had overseen the SIOP scrub. With the breakup of the Soviet Union, targeting requirements could be reduced to 3,500 warheads. He was ready to reflect these reductions to eliminate all land-based MIRVed missiles in a second Strategic Arms Reduction Treaty.[135] Yeltsin had already indicated his support for this idea. If MIRVed land-based missiles were eliminated, Bush promised to cancel the Peacekeeper missile, reduce from three to one the number of warheads on Minuteman missiles, reduce the number of warheads on U.S. sea-based missiles by "about one-third," and to convert a "substantial" portion of U.S. strategic bombers to primarily conventional use.

This became the framework for a second Strategic Arms Reduction Treaty. START II would accelerate reductions by approximately 50 percent below those agreed upon just two years earlier. With Cheney and the Joint Chiefs sitting in front of him for the State of the Union address, Bush declared, "The Secretary of Defense recommended these cuts after consultation with the Joint Chiefs of Staff. And I make them with confidence." To members of Congress inclined to cut more, Bush added, "This deep, and no deeper. To do less would be insensible to progress, but to do more would be ignorant of history."[136]

Yeltsin had been notified in advance of the particulars in Bush's speech and responded the following day. He was, in Baker's apt characterization, "a theatrical, wholesale politician, a man prone to larger-than-life gestures." Baker could relate to Yeltsin: for all their differences, he was now dealing with a "street smart" politician.[137] Baker met with a "swaggering" Yeltsin in Moscow ten days before the Soviet Union's official demise with Defense Minister Shaposhnikov notably by his side. Yeltsin offered assurances that he would work collaboratively with the United States on the removal of Soviet nuclear assets left behind in Ukraine, Belarus, and Kazakhstan, dismantling and disabling warheads, providing for safe storage, and undertaking joint planning for nuclear accidents and emergencies. He was also prepared to discuss the de-MIRVing of land-based missiles.

Yeltsin pledged swift ratification of the first Strategic Arms Reduction Treaty and the Conventional Forces in Europe Treaty—pledges that were impossible to keep, given that both were crafted on the assumption that the Soviet Union would remain intact. Russian ratification of START was predicated on strenuous efforts by the Clinton administration to denuclearize newly independent states. The CFE Treaty negotiated in 1990 as well as the Open Skies Treaty negotiated in 1992 required years of readjustment to reflect the demise of the Soviet Union and the Warsaw Pact.[138]

When Bush issued his second set of initiatives on January 29, 1992, Yeltsin couldn't resist another larger-than-life gesture. He believed in nuclear disarmament, as did his foreign minister, Andrei Kozyrev, who was steeped in these matters and who was a practitioner of idealistic internationalism.[139] Yeltsin's speech affirmed that the Russian Federation, as the successor state to the Soviet Union under international law, would be responsible for approving and implementing obligations incurred by Gorbachev. He announced the cessation of production for Backfire and Blackjack bombers as well as air- and sea-launched cruise missiles. He called for speeding up START reductions to 6,000 deployed warheads by four years. Of particular interest was Yeltsin's proposal for a follow-on treaty to reduce accountable strategic warheads to 2,000–2,500 warheads on each side. This was 1,000 warheads deeper than the Pentagon was willing to go.

Yeltsin, like Gorbachev, stated his preference to do more. He wished to negotiate a ban on the production of fissile material for nuclear weapons and to place all remaining air-launched cruise missiles in central storage. He called for the elimination of long-range, sea-launched cruise missiles, ending production of new types of air-launched cruise missiles, ending combat patrols of ballistic missile-carrying submarines, ending anti-satellite weapon tests and eliminating these weapons. The Bush administration had no interest in taking up these proposals.

THE LISBON PROTOCOL

The demise of the Soviet Union threw a "legal monkey wrench" into START's entry into force with the sudden appearance of three newly independent states laden with missiles, bombers, and tactical nuclear weapons.[140] Approximately 1,500 Soviet tactical nuclear weapons were deployed in Belarus, as well as 81 intercontinental ballistic missiles. The newly independent state of Kazakhstan suddenly and temporarily became the fourth largest nuclear-armed state, with over 1,400 warheads carried by strategic forces, including the Soviet Union's most menacing "heavy" missiles, bombers, over 300 nuclear-armed cruise missiles, and hundreds more tactical nuclear weapons. Ukraine's sudden nuclear inheritance was greater, including almost 2,000 warheads on intercontinental ballistic missiles and an even larger number of tactical nuclear weapons, as well as weapons delivered by bombers, temporarily making it the third largest nuclear-armed state. Both the Russian Duma and the

U.S. Congress insisted that all three newly independent states repatriate their nuclear weapons to Russia and join the Nonproliferation Treaty as non-nuclear-weapon states before START could enter into force.

The Bush administration placed a high priority on repatriation. These three states had neither the skills nor the money to maintain warheads and their launchers safely. There were serious concerns about leakage of warheads and fissile material to states of proliferation concern or extremist groups. The well-being of the Nuclear Nonproliferation Treaty depended on Belarus, Kazakhstan, and Ukraine rejecting their nuclear inheritance.

All three states had good reasons to accept warhead repatriation. Belarus was Moscow's most accommodating newly independent neighbor. Its economic fortunes were closely tied to the Russian Federation and ethnic Russians held key positions in its Ministry of Defense and officer corps. Belarus was deeply indebted to Russia and required concessionary prices for imports of natural gas and oil. There was also a popular antinuclear bias, as Belarus was far more adversely affected by the Chernobyl disaster than Ukraine.

Kazakhstan's leader, Nursultan Nazerbayev, had similar reasons to relinquish his nation's sudden nuclear inheritance. More than a million Kazakhs were harmed, some grotesquely, by the 456 nuclear tests the Soviet Union carried out at the test site at Semipalatinsk, including 116 above ground. Like Belarus, Kazakhstan's leadership lacked the ability and funds to assume control over orphaned Soviet warheads, missiles, and bombers. Attempts to do so were unlikely to succeed. They would raise serious hackles in Moscow, Washington, and with Kazakhstan's ethnic Russian minority. These factors also applied to Ukraine's leader, Leonid Kravchuk. All of the newly independent states that inherited nuclear weapons were at a severe diplomatic and economic disadvantage when dealing with Moscow, and all desperately needed Washington's diplomatic, political, and economic support.

Nonetheless, repatriation wasn't easy.[141] Baker worked the phones to line up commitments to denuclearize, using the prospect of presidential meetings at the White House with Presidents Kravchuk and Nazarbayev, as well as economic and political inducements as leverage. It was exasperating work for Baker, who wasn't used to the quick evaporation of commitments he elicited. Nazarbayev and Kravchuk sought security assurances as well as economic assistance and compensation for the fissile material they were relinquishing that could be blended down and used to generate electricity. There were too many loose ends. The finishing touches would have to be provided by the Clinton administration.

Baker was strongly opposed to security assurances placing Kazakhstan and Ukraine on a par with U.S. allies in Europe and Asia, and assumed the Congress would be, as well. James Timbie's creative mind found the solution. Timbie was raised in Marblehead, Massachusetts. His grandfather was a renowned teacher of engineering at MIT, where his dad majored in engineering and then went to work for General Electric. His mom was a homemaker. Timbie went to Princeton and then Stanford to delve into physics. Before receiving his doctorate, Wolfgang Panovsky and Sidney Drell interested him in arms control problems, then helped arrange a position for him at ACDA in 1971. He quickly mastered the technical aspects of negotiating issues and became adept at problem solving, making him indispensable to ACDA directors. With ACDA's star fading, he transferred to the State Department in 1983, where he became indispensable to George Shultz and Baker. As Linton Brooks noted, "Wherever Jim Timbie has been that's where power and influence has been."[142]

Timbie's proposed solution to the security assurance conundrum was to repackage existing assurances embedded in the Organization for Security and Co-operation in Europe's founding document, the 1975 Helsinki Final Act, and the United Nations Charter, as assurances specific to Ukraine, Kazakhstan, and Belarus.[143] Baker finally succeeded in pulling together his counterparts to sign the Lisbon Protocol on May 23, 1992. In this protocol, Belarus, Kazakhstan, and Ukraine promised to join the Nonproliferation Treaty as non-nuclear-weapon states "in the shortest possible time," with all three joining Russia and the United States as parties to the Strategic Arms Reduction Treaty. Baker designed the ceremony at Lisbon to be "austere" and "wordless" because if the foreign ministers spoke, he feared that the event could readily dissolve into a "shouting match."[144] The Lisbon Protocol didn't hold. Neither did other pledges. After making them, the leaders of Kazakhstan and Ukraine again had second thoughts. They wanted more compensation and improved ties to Washington and the West before sending their prized possessions back to the Russian Federation.

Bush asked Baker to leave the State Department in mid-August 1992 to take the reins of his sputtering reelection campaign. With the clock running down on the Bush administration, Baker's successor, Larry Eagleburger, focused on negotiating a second Strategic Arms Reduction Treaty and completing the Chemical Weapons Convention. After receiving a green light from the victorious Clinton campaign to sign the Chemical Weapons Convention and to complete negotiations on a second Strategic Arms Reduction Treaty, the

State Department had little bandwidth left to address backsliding from the Lisbon Protocol.

NUNN-LUGAR

Three days after the August 1991 putsch against Gorbachev failed, Senator Sam Nunn received an urgent call from Moscow. Would he be willing to visit Gorbachev as soon as possible? Nunn happened to be in Budapest and arrived at the Kremlin the following day. Gorbachev meant the visit to be reassuring, but as he tried to answer Nunn's questions about the command and control of Soviet nuclear forces, the Georgia senator was anything but reassured.[145] The air was quickly deflating from Gorbachev's tires, the Soviet Union and its economy seemed to be imploding, and the need of the hour was to lock down grotesquely excess amounts of Soviet bomb-making material and nuclear warheads.

Nunn was born in Macon and grew up in the small town of Perry, Georgia, where his dad was a practicing attorney, farmer, and one-time mayor. He captained his small high school's team to the state basketball championship and moved to Atlanta to attend Georgia Tech before transferring to Emory and staying on to attend Emory Law School. Nunn moved to Washington after graduating in 1962, the first time in his life he had been north of Atlanta. He had a job offer from Carl Vinson, one of the old Southern bulls who looked after the U.S. military's needs on Capitol Hill. Vinson represented a rural district in Georgia for fifty years, rising to become the chairman of the House Naval Affairs Committee in 1931. After World War II, he became chairman of Armed Services Committee after the Naval Affairs and Military Affairs committees merged.

Nunn happened to be Vinson's great-nephew. In his first year of his first job as a committee staffer for Vinson, the 23-year-old Nunn traveled to Europe. As it happened, his trip occurred during the Cuban missile crisis. Thereafter, Nunn was hooked on nuclear issues as well as on Capitol Hill. He began his political career as a state representative and won a highly contested election in 1972 for Senator Richard Russell's Senate seat—another old bull overseeing defense matters. In 1987, Nunn became chairman of the Senate Armed Services Committee. His voice carried on both sides of the aisle, just as Senator Jackson before him. But Nunn, unlike Jackson, could be sympathetic to arms control.[146]

When Nunn returned to Capitol Hill after meeting with Gorbachev, he joined forces with Congressman Les Aspin, the Democratic chairman of the

House Armed Services Committee, to allocate one billion dollars to help Gorbachev from the Defense Authorization Bill then under consideration. There was, however, no consensus to reallocate defense funding to humanitarian aid, and strong resistance to doing so, including from Bush and Cheney. The idea seemed half-baked to many. If the problem was akin to Weimar Germany between the World Wars or a devastated Europe after World War II, something on the scale of the Marshall Plan would be needed, with resources sufficient to stem the downhill slide and lay the groundwork for a lasting friendship. But the failing Soviet Union wasn't Western Europe and members of Congress weren't willing to bail the Soviet Communist Party out; if Cold War peace dividends were to be distributed, they were going to Americans. Nunn tried recrafting this initiative as aiding defense conversion in the Soviet Union, but this, too, fell flat.

Nunn and Aspin withdrew their initiative, but not for long. Circumstances were quickly converging to pave the way for the most successful effort ever initiated by Capitol Hill to reduce nuclear danger. The Carnegie Corporation of New York under the leadership of David Hamburg was already funding programs at Harvard, Stanford, and Brookings to rethink U.S. national security strategy after the demise of the Soviet Union. Hamburg, Ashton Carter, who led the Harvard program at the Center for Security and International Affairs (later to be known as the Belfer Center), and William Perry at Stanford, between Pentagon assignments, had previously traveled with Nunn to the Soviet Union.

Bipartisan support was essential, which was forthcoming after Senator Richard Lugar, the second-ranking Republican on the Senate Foreign Relations Committee, became involved. Lugar's father went to Purdue to study agriculture and to prepare himself for running the family farm in Marion County ten miles southwest of Indianapolis. His mother was a homemaker. Lugar excelled at school, graduating first in his class in high school and at Denison University. He attended Oxford on a Rhodes scholarship, where he was elected president of his class, a unique tribute given to an American that reflected his unassuming but innate political skills. Lugar then volunteered for the U.S. Navy, where he served as an intelligence officer. He was a natural for Indiana politics when internationalism was part of the Republican brand. After two terms as the mayor of Indianapolis, he was elected to the Senate in 1976, where he looked after his two strongest interests—foreign affairs and agriculture—on committees he subsequently chaired.[147]

Lugar invited Carter, Perry, Hamburg, and John Steinbruner of the Brookings Institution to his office to brief him and Senator Nunn on their work. They met on November 19, 1991, just six days after Nunn and Aspin withdrew their amendment. Their discussion revolved around concepts of preventive defense rather than the particulars of what would become the Nunn-Lugar program. Almost as an aside at the end of the meeting, the conversation turned to these particulars. Carter was in the process of completing one collection of essays on how to deal with "Soviet nuclear fission" and was already working on a second.

In the introduction to the first volume, Carter and his colleagues pointed out that the Soviet nuclear command and control was "at root a social and political creation." It could not be insulated "from turmoil throughout the society within which it is embedded." The disposition of the Soviet Union's almost 30,000 nuclear weapons—no one seemed to know the exact number, not even within the Soviet Union—was "a paramount concern of our times. It is one without precedent and therefore without settled guidance. It calls for specific actions to be taken in the near term: there is no option to wait." The authors laid out recommendations to forestall unauthorized use or seizure of Soviet warheads and their means of delivery, their onward proliferation, and "managing the fate of strategic nuclear weapons."[148]

After the November 19 meeting, Nunn and Lugar decided to follow up quickly and to directly engage more of their colleagues. Laura Holgate, a project coordinator on the nuclear fission project, recalls rushing to xerox chapters of the *Nuclear Fission* study for distribution on Capitol Hill. Lugar took it upon himself to round up senators on the Foreign Relations Committee, while Nunn brought colleagues from the Armed Services and other committees. Two days later, over a cholesterol-laden meal of scrambled eggs and bacon, sixteen senators heard Carter's pitch and offered bipartisan support for a funding initiative. Richard Combs, who escorted Senator Nunn as a Foreign Service officer during his trips to the Soviet Union and then went to work for him on the Armed Services Committee staff, attended. Combs recalls that Carter's two key contributions at the breakfast meeting were clarifying specific programs in need of financial support and, more importantly, reframing the initiative toward increasing U.S. national security. Nunn-Lugar would no longer be pegged as a humanitarian initiative. The task of widening the circle of supportive senators then fell to Lugar's staffer, Kenneth Myers, Jr., Combs, and another Nunn staffer, Robert Bell, who was given the difficult assignment of finding language sufficient to bring Senator Jesse Helms, the ranking Republican on the Foreign Relations Committee, on board.[149]

Senators expressed several concerns that took the form of placing conditions on assistance. Helms's primary concern was Soviet compliance with treaty obligations. If this were a condition to Nunn-Lugar funding, no help for safeguarding and dismantling warheads and their means of delivery would have been forthcoming. Helms and his go-between with Nunn's staff, Marshall Billingslea, eventually agreed on language that the Soviet Union needed to be "committed to" complete compliance and to other conditions, including a "substantial" investment by Moscow to dismantle Cold War excess; foregoing military modernization programs exceeding legitimate defense requirements; not using fissile material extracted from dismantled warheads in new ones; facilitating U.S. verification of weapons destruction; and complying with internationally recognized human rights.[150] The most troublesome problem turned out to be a prosaic one—using U.S. contractors and goods and services to deliver Nunn-Lugar assistance whenever possible, which slowed down implementation.[151]

Less than two weeks after Nunn and Aspin failed to attach a Soviet aid provision to the Defense Authorization Bill, an amendment proposed by Nunn and Lugar to the Conventional Forces in Europe Treaty Implementation Act passed by a vote of 86 to 8. Senate Republican minority leader Robert Dole as well as Helms joined Nunn and Lugar in support. The Pentagon was given discretion to shift $400 million dollars in spending for three broad purposes—to destroy nuclear, chemical and other weapons; to transport, store, disable, and safeguard weapons to be destroyed; and to establish verifiable safeguards against the proliferation of these weapons.

Cheney's Defense Department consented to the rechanneling of $400 million in Pentagon funding but wasn't enthusiastic about it. Carter recalls Cheney's deputy, Donald Atwood, reacting this way: "Guys, we just spent fifty years trying to make these people go broke. Why would we ever help them now?"[152] It was unnatural to help, just as the practice of arms control was unnatural, but the Bush administration decided that not helping was unacceptably risky.

The Nunn-Lugar program became public law on December 12, 1991. New funds in the form of direct appropriations for an expanded set of purposes followed at the outset of the Clinton administration. Implementing this initiative enjoyed top-down support from Perry as deputy secretary and later secretary of defense, and with Carter as the assistant secretary of defense with shared jurisdiction over the Nunn-Lugar program. Programming subsequently extended to the Department of Energy and the State Department.[153]

This was the second time that a high-powered group of defense and national security-minded academics in Cambridge, Massachusetts, engaged in perfectly timed studies that influenced the course of arms control. The previous time was in 1960–61, when Donald Brennan, Thomas Schelling, Morton Halperin, and others conceptualized the very practice of arms control. Three decades later, the pressing need was to prevent the fissile material residing in a broken Soviet Union—equivalent to 150,000 Hiroshima bombs—from resulting in mushroom clouds. Arms control had now morphed into what Perry and Carter called "defense by other means," or "preventive defense." Like arms control, Nunn-Lugar programs would be cooperative practices— only now, cooperative threat reduction took previously unimagined forms. The Soviet Union was collapsing, time was of the essence, new thinking was needed, and members of Congress, led by Nunn and Lugar, were up to the task.

THE CHEMICAL WEAPONS CONVENTION

Eliminating chemical weapons was a signature issue for Bush, one that was largely forgotten alongside his other accomplishments. As vice president, Bush tabled draft treaty text banning the production, possession, and use of chemical weapons. As president, Bush pushed Gorbachev for 80 and then 98 percent reductions in existing stockpiles before shedding his cautionary instinct and seizing on abolition. He wanted to finish up negotiations on the Chemical Weapons Convention before leaving office.

Three issues proved vexing during the final negotiating rounds. One was the disposition of old stocks of chemical weapons that Japanese forces left behind in China after World War II. In 1999, both countries signed an agreement in which Japan accepted responsibility for the destruction of these weapons. The second outstanding issue was riot control agents. This issue was settled by prohibiting their use in warfare, but not, as the Senate insisted, for domestic use. The third issue was challenge inspections. After dropping the "anywhere, anytime" language inserted by Perle, the negotiators established the principle of "managed access," allowing host countries to protect sensitive information while taking steps to alleviate compliance concerns. This was an awkward balancing act, but far better than continuing to insist on "anywhere, anytime" inspections at sensitive U.S. locations, a formula that needed to be ditched after Gorbachev called the Reagan administration's bluff.

Bush decided that chemical weapons' proliferation and use by outliers were bigger problems than Soviet cheating and prospective use. For this reason and in deference to protecting industry secrets, he decided on less-than-airtight monitoring procedures. The remaining issues were settled by September 1992, after which the convention was transmitted to the United Nations General Assembly and opened for signature. On January 13, 1993, leaders gathered in Paris to affix their signatures, with Secretary of State Eagleburger among them.[154]

START II

Negotiations on the first Strategic Arms Reduction Treaty took nine years. Negotiations on START II were completed in less than one year—a bullet train compared to a slow freight. Much of the boilerplate that was tediously hammered out in the first agreement could be applied to the second. But the heart of the matter wasn't significant reductions, as important as they were; it was establishing conditions for strategic stability now that the Cold War was over.

The biggest threat to stability resided in silo-based missiles carrying multiple, independently targeted warheads. Each missile could kill many of its opposite number and each was extremely vulnerable. Nixon, Kissinger, and Brezhnev bequeathed this "use or lose" dilemma in the 1972 Interim Agreement. The Bush administration was now seized with the possibility of eliminating land-based missiles carrying MIRVs, and Yeltsin seemed willing. Negotiating this outcome was a rare opportunity—a limited time offer, in Linton Brooks's view. Brooks, whose role as START I's lead negotiator was informally extended to conclude a second treaty, believes that a de-MIRVing agreement would have been impossible to reach six months before and six months after its completion date.[155] Others disagree, but there could be no doubt that a unique window of opportunity became possible only after the coup attempt against Gorbachev. There followed, in quick succession, the dissolution of the Soviet Union and Warsaw Pact, as well as a second scrubbing of the SIOP. START I's limits could be halved.

Earlier, the State Department was inclined toward de-MIRVing silo-based missiles. Baker floated this idea to Bush, who was looking for big ideas prior to the Malta summit. Bush and Scowcroft were favorably disposed and willing to support de-MIRVing all land-based missiles, whether mobile or silo-based. But Cheney then resisted the idea. U.S. land-based missile modernization programs were still in flux and already subject to budget cutting. Bush respected Cheney's preferences.[156] By 1992, Cheney's view had changed. After the coup attempt and after the second SIOP scrub, he had new room to maneuver. He was now ready and willing to pursue warhead reductions and the de-MIRVing of land-based missiles. This was a rare moment: hawks and doves now converged to endorse a radical restructuring of land-based missiles. The long-hoped-for vision of a stable strategic balance—one where Washington and Moscow need not worry about surprise attack—seemed to be at hand.

Cheney felt "especially good about" the two SIOP scrubs because "it badly needed to be done." It also "offered up the opportunity to put stuff on the table" for START II, "because now we had something to trade away."[157] The Pentagon usually resisted measures proposed by arms controllers to downsize deterrence, but there were exceptions. One was when Robert McNamara took the lead in trying to curtail ballistic missile defenses during the Johnson administration. McNamara and his backup team, including Halperin and his boss, Paul Warnke, faced impossible odds. It took time to convince the Kremlin that missile defenses could do more harm than good, and McNamara quickly ran out of time.

Late in the Bush administration the Pentagon was again willing to embrace arms control, but conditions for success were fleeting. The Pentagon insisted on being able to deploy MIRVs in the Nixon administration because they offset the Soviet Union's missile production lines and advantages in throw-weight. Two decades later, the Pentagon was ready to reverse course. The stars were aligned for strategic stability. With Yeltsin and Cheney on board, Bush, Scowcroft, and Baker could accomplish what Nixon and Kissinger could not.

Bush teed up the deal in his last State of the Union Address less than a month after Yeltsin displaced Gorbachev. Bush knew that reducing nuclear danger and weapons was imperative as the Russian Federation was reeling from crisis to crisis. He also knew that Yeltsin couldn't afford to maintain START I force levels, especially with the largest missile-producing plant in the world, with two million square feet of floor space, now residing in a newly independent Ukraine.[158]

It took one year for the details to be worked out. The U.S. and Soviet negotiating teams for START reassembled to work informally together on a second treaty. Most interagency issues could be resolved without going to the Un-Group. Major issues could be handled between Baker and Andrei Kozyrev, Yeltsin's pro–arms control foreign minister. Meeting in London in June 1992, Kozyrev offered Baker two choices: Moscow was willing to agree to Washington's number of launchers but without a MIRV ban on land-based missiles. Alternatively, Moscow could accept the MIRV ban but only with a lower number of launchers. Baker stepped out of the meeting to ask those traveling with him for their preference. Lehman, the director of ACDA, spoke up for de-MIRVing, as did Stephen Hadley, who worked for Cheney. Baker sealed the deal with Kozyrev and de-MIRVing became the centerpiece of START II.

The Bush administration's team of experts worked methodically with their Russian counterparts to complete the treaty text but couldn't finish the job by the time of the U.S. election. When Bush lost, the negotiating team and the team's backstoppers in Washington were advised by Scowcroft to prepare to hand over their unfinished business to the incoming Clinton team. Then came word from Clinton's transition team to proceed full steam ahead. The final text of the START II Treaty reduced permissible warheads per side from 6,000 to 3,000–3,500 on land- and sea-based missiles and intercontinental-range bombers. Yeltsin needed the hyphen because his struggling country couldn't maintain 3,500 warheads on launchers. Unlike START I, the number of warheads on bombers would not be so deeply discounted.

This, alas, is not the end of the story. START II was built on a weak foundation. Yeltsin and Kozyrev seemed unable to keep the Russian General Staff on board. Kozyrev, a severe political liability, resigned in 1996. His successors didn't last very long. The Duma never ratified START II during Yeltsin's turbulent tenure. His hand-picked successor, Vladimir Putin, persuaded the Duma to ratify the treaty seven years after Yeltsin's signature, in 2000, but with conditions. Putin needed leverage against renewed interest on Capitol Hill to deploy national missile defenses during the Clinton administration. The Duma backed up Putin's warning that if "the United States decides to destroy the 1972 ABM Treaty . . . we will withdraw not only from the START II treaty but also the whole system of treaties on limitation and control of strategic and conventional weapons."[159]

And that's just what Putin did, after Clinton's successor, George W. Bush, announced withdrawal from the ABM Treaty three months after the 9/11 attacks on the World Trade Center and Pentagon. Bush and his advisers chafed under the ABM Treaty's constraints, and this time of national vulnerability seemingly clarified the need to take a wide range of protective measures, including missile defenses. The threat of Russian MIRVed land-based missiles had ebbed, given Moscow's dire straits. Besides, both Putin and Bush continued to proclaim that the Cold War was history. So, too, were the ABM Treaty and START II.

BUSH'S LEDGER SHEET

After an initial period of hesitation, George H.W. Bush accomplished in just one term in office far more than any other president in the field of arms control. No administration had a stronger team to seize opportunities before and after the Soviet Union dissolved. Bush took flak for being overly solicitous to Gorbachev, especially when he counseled Ukrainians against breaking away from the Soviet Union, but nothing was lost as a result. Ukraine achieved its independence and Bush helped Gorbachev to accept evolving realities.

The Bush administration's initial tests of trust building with Gorbachev yielded appreciable gains in the form of a treaty mandating deep cuts in conventional capabilities and another establishing cooperative overflights. The origins of both initiatives date back to the Eisenhower administration, and were impossible to imagine until Gorbachev's arrival. The Conventional Forces in Europe Treaty resulted in the dismantlement of 52,000 pieces of military equipment while permitting over 4,000 inspections. The Open Skies Treaty reached the milestone of 1,500 cooperative overflights in 2019, helping to build military cooperation between the United States and former Warsaw Pact and newly independent states. The Chemical Weapons Convention, another signature item for Bush, outlived both of these achievements, establishing a norm against use that only one outlier state, Syria under Bashar al-Assad, and two other national leaders—Kim Jong Un and Vladimir Putin, whose operatives used nerve agents against foes—have disregarded.

Because of the first Strategic Arms Reduction Treaty, the U.S. nuclear arsenal was reduced by 50 percent between December 1990 and December 1994. Further reductions resulted from Bush's Presidential Nuclear Initiatives. This constituted, as Susan Koch has noted, "The most sweeping nuclear arms reductions in history."[160] More was to come. This steep decline in warhead numbers was fostered and enabled by unique circumstances—a president and a team with the national security credentials to take unilateral initiatives, a transformed world leaving the United States as the sole superpower, and a failed adversary that could no longer maintain forces in the field and needed help to reduce them. An unchallenged superpower could afford to take bold steps to reduce the salience of nuclear weapons, and Bush was up to this challenge. Reductions were enabled by the Pentagon's recognition that it needed far fewer warheads for targeting purposes.

Other factors contributed to a recognition at the end of the Cold War that there were limits to the utility of nuclear weapons. U.S. possession of these fearsome weapons did not deter Saddam Hussein from trying to swallow up Kuwait, nor did they help in his defeat. As long-range conventional weaponry gained accuracy, the perceived utility of nuclear weapons narrowed further. As Cheney later reflected, "You give me a few cruise missiles [and] I can shut down any country in the world for a period of time."[161] The bargaining chips that Richard Nixon and Henry Kissinger wanted for SALT II proved their worth—but only when conventionally armed. At the end of the Cold War, nuclear-armed variants were considered excess baggage and subject to recall in the Presidential Nuclear Initiatives.

Bush and Scowcroft were the most seasoned White House team since Nixon and Kissinger, but they made far better decisions under far more favorable circumstances. Baker quickly demonstrated that he was as accomplished in the politics of diplomacy as in domestic politics. In addition, Cheney lent his support to deep reciprocal cuts in strategic offensive forces. The centerpiece of these reductions was the elimination of MIRVed land-based missiles.

It was not to be. George W. Bush was convinced that the ABM Treaty was a relic of the Cold War and that he needed missile defenses against outliers. As forewarned, Putin responded to Bush's withdrawal from the ABM Treaty by withdrawing from START II and beginning to develop a new "heavy" land-based missile that could carry ten or more warheads. The demise of nuclear arms control began to take shape with these two decisions in 2002.

All of this was to come. When George H.W. Bush left office, the state of nuclear arms control could not have been better. No incoming president benefitted more from the nuclear diplomacy of his predecessor than Bill Clinton. With four days to spare before Clinton's inauguration, Bush's national security staff completed the explanatory details on START II and conveyed them to the Senate. The Chemical Weapons Convention was signed during Bush's final week in office, on January 13, 1993.

Bush's achievements and the Soviet Union's collapse freed the electorate to choose a fresh face, someone attuned toward domestic politics and needs. Clinton's winning slogan was "It's the Economy, Stupid!"—but the incoming president didn't have the luxury to dwell exclusively on domestic issues. There were far too many loose ends, including Soviet weapons left behind in newly independent states and a Russian Federation suffering from a Great Depression, unable to assure the safety and security of its bloated arsenal. The global nuclear order needed buttressing in the form of the indefinite extension of the Nonproliferation Treaty and, at long last, a treaty to end nuclear tests. Clinton and his team succeeded in consolidating gains in their first term. Then they stalled out.

Chapter 12

CONSOLIDATING GAINS

The name didn't fit the man: William Jefferson Clinton sounded too formal, with a hint of ancestral lineage. He preferred going by "Bill." He was a preternaturally gifted, instinctual politician, equally adept at connecting with blue-collar workers as with heads of state. His homespun assessments of world leaders and events masked a keen analytical bent. He was, as Leon Panetta described him, "ravenously intelligent," with an undisciplined, perpetually busy, calculating mind.[1]

In stark contrast to his predecessor's pedigree, Bill Clinton had a down-home upbringing. His mother was pregnant when his father, who may have been married three previous times, was thrown from his car in an accident and died by the side of the road. She remarried, choosing an abusive alcoholic. Clinton grew up in a small town named Hope, Arkansas, and derived as much political mileage from this fact as humanly possible. The bright lights of the big city were in Hot Springs. He was living proof that genetics weren't destiny. He was also all too human, temporarily laid low by his biggest character flaw—a lack of discipline—elevated by Republican legislators into an impeachable offense. Then, in characteristic fashion, Clinton rebounded, leaving office with high approval ratings and a strong economy.[2]

Washington, DC, is a magnet for high school class officers from small towns across America. After Clinton's fortuitous selection to attend Boys Nation and a meeting with President John F. Kennedy, Washington was the big city where he wanted to attend college. One of his stated reasons for applying to Georgetown was "to prepare for the life of a practicing politician."[3] He got his first taste of Capitol Hill running errands for Senator William Fulbright, the chairman of the Foreign Relations Committee. The other senator from Arkansas, John McClellan, the chairman of the Appropriations Committee, was more powerful, but Clinton was drawn to foreign policy and a more progressive face of the Old South. Coming from Arkansas had its advantages when competing for a Rhodes scholarship to attend Oxford. From there he traveled widely. Clinton's worldview expanded, but his ambition didn't: he remained fixed on becoming president one day. One roommate at Oxford, Strobe Talbott, whose dream was to become a journalist covering the Soviet Union, easily detected it: "He conveyed a sense not just of direction but of destination."[4]

Clinton had the brains, the energy, and the political skills to realize his ambition. He was a policy omnivore and restless networker. Good fortune favored him. When the time came to run for president, he benefitted greatly from George H.W. Bush's lackluster campaign. Bush seemed out of touch with the concerns of ordinary Americans. It also helped that Bush had put the finishing touches on ending the Cold War. In doing so, the electorate could focus its attention away from the world's trials and tribulations and toward domestic concerns, Clinton's wheelhouse. After three consecutive terms of Republicans in the Oval Office, the electorate voted for change. It was time for a baton pass from the Cold Warriors to the Baby Boomers.

Bill Clinton was the first U.S. president since Richard Nixon who did not need to focus on negotiating strategic arms control. Clinton inherited Bush's successes—the 1991 Strategic Arms Reduction Treaty and START II, hurriedly concluded just before Clinton's inaugural. Talbott became Clinton's principal adviser on Russia. He recounted Clinton's view that strategic arms control was "old business" and "not high on his agenda."[5] His presidential memoir, the memoirs of his two secretaries of state, Warren Cristopher and Madeleine Albright, and even Talbott's firsthand account have little to say about strategic arms control. Instead, when Clinton and his top lieutenants were not preoccupied with domestic issues and fending off Republicans on Capitol Hill, they were focused on other national security priorities, especially managing U.S.-Russian relations and dealing with Balkan wars.

Clinton's talent for improvisation was needed most in managing Boris Yeltsin, Russia's larger-than-life but woefully weak leader of a country living

in chaos. Clinton was intent on keeping U.S.-Russian relations on a hopeful trajectory. He humored Yeltsin, whether he was drinking or sober, and
he tried not to "overwin" by running roughshod over Russian concerns.[6]
Friction was inescapable, however, as Clinton intended to expand NATO,
adapt the Anti-Ballistic Missile Treaty to deal with new missile threats from
outliers, and counter Serbian leader Slobodan Milošević's bloodletting after the breakup of Yugoslavia. No matter how soothingly Clinton explained
these actions to Yeltsin, they resulted in losses of Russian face and a diminished sense of national security—festering sores that would later blow back
against strategic arms control when the Russian economy rebounded under
Vladimir Putin.

Yeltsin was a strong man beset by a weak heart, drinking bouts, depression, and retrograde political factions. During Clinton's first year in office,
Yeltsin survived impeachment when his foes of the Russian Duma fell short
of the two-thirds vote needed. Later that year, Yeltsin directed army units to
fire against the White House, the seat of the Russian legislature, where, during the Soviet Union's death throes, he previously led the defense of Mikhail
Gorbachev against coup plotters. Other political challenges regularly followed. Heading toward the home stretch of his wobbly second presidential
term, Yeltsin appointed five prime ministers in an eighteen-month period.
He was his own worst enemy and yet the best hope for a more democratic
Russia. Clinton acknowledged that, under Yeltsin, Russia was undergoing a
"nonstop nervous breakdown," but that a drunk Yeltsin was "better than
most of the alternatives sober."[7] Yeltsin's legacy as a heroic champion of democracy came to grief, as he managed to hold his failing body together just
long enough to anoint Putin as his successor.

Despite his domestic-first intention, Clinton couldn't afford to ignore
arms control. The unfinished business of the George H.W. Bush administration lay before him. Clinton's foremost task was to consolidate gains. When
the Duma ratified the first Strategic Arms Reduction Treaty in November
1992, it did so with the condition that instruments of ratification would not
be exchanged until Ukraine, Kazakhstan, and Belarus joined the Nonproliferation Treaty as non-nuclear-weapon states. Washington's interests were
aligned with Moscow's. Saddam Hussein's covert nuclear program, discovered after Bush's military campaign, remained indelibly printed on many
minds. No one wanted nuclear warheads and fissile material residing in these
three newly independent states, material that might fall into grasping hands.
Washington, no less than Moscow, wanted to retrieve these weapons from

states that had neither the means nor the expertise to maintain them. Of the three, Ukraine would be, by far, the hardest case.

To help safeguard and reduce the vast remnants of the Soviet Union's nuclear enterprise, the Clinton administration needed to implement a wide range of cooperative measures. Clinton inherited the Nunn-Lugar legislation, but needed to make a success of it. The Pentagon's William Perry willingly took the lead, but other government agencies needed to be enlisted to play key roles. Russian nuclear laboratories and military forces needed help to maintain nuclear safety and security and to prevent bloated stocks of fissile material and warheads from being sold on black markets and used in acts of nuclear terrorism. An entirely novel laboratory-to-laboratory program of collaboration had to be imagined and implemented. The U.S. nuclear laboratories would meet this challenge.

Other Bush agreements awaited implementation. The Chemical Weapons Convention and START II—completed and delivered to Clinton between the time of his election and his inauguration—required the Senate's consent to ratification. The 1970 Nonproliferation Treaty's initial lifespan of twenty-five years would expire on Clinton's watch; the Arms Control and Disarmament Agency would take the lead to extend it indefinitely. Adapting the ABM Treaty to address threats from outliers possessing missiles of increasing range required walking a tightrope between Republicans on Capitol Hill and Russian officials intuitively fearful of any new and better U.S. missile defense programs. On top of this, Clinton aimed to complete negotiations of a treaty ending nuclear weapon testing—the jewel in the crown of arms control, a prize that eluded (or was avoided by) his predecessors.

Consolidating and implementing Bush's gains required adaptation, persistence, and breaking new ground in a practice that Perry and others called cooperative threat reduction. Prospects for extending and building on the achievements of Reagan and Bush seemed bright at the outset of the Clinton administration. Clinton's first term was marked by significant success—the implementation of Nunn-Lugar programs, the denuclearization of Ukraine and Kazakhstan, the indefinite extension of the Nonproliferation Treaty, and completion of the Comprehensive Test Ban Treaty negotiations. And yet the seeds that led to the unraveling of nuclear and conventional arms control were also planted during Clinton's presidency. NATO expansion, the bombing campaigns to stop Serbian war crimes, and Republican pressures to nullify the ABM Treaty occurred on Clinton's watch, harbingers of the downhill slide to come. During his second term, arms control stalled out.

CLINTON'S TEAM

Clinton's choice as secretary of state was Warren Christopher, Cyrus Vance's deputy during the Carter administration. Christopher was, in Talbott's characterization, "courtly and shy to a degree that masked a steeliness that was easy, but unwise, to underestimate."[8] Christopher's father was a small-town banker, broken by the Depression; his mother was the daughter of a Methodist minister. She moved her ailing husband from Scranton, North Dakota, population 300, to the sunny climes of southern California in a futile effort to improve his health. At age 13, Christopher found himself in a foreign land—Hollywood. There he earned income by delivering papers and eventually being paid by the column inch for the *Hollywood Citizen News*.

Christopher received a scholarship to attend Redlands College, where he joined the Naval ROTC. He followed the ROTC program when it shifted to the University of Southern California and, after graduation, was aboard a tanker in the Pacific theater when news of Hiroshima arrived. The juxtaposition of this "awful and wonderful" moment stayed with him. On shore leave, he witnessed Tokyo's devastation by fire bombing, images that lingered for the rest of his life. He attended Stanford Law School where he was chosen for the *Law Review* and was then granted a clerkship for Supreme Court justice William O. Douglas. At the end of his clerkship, Cristopher screwed up his courage to ask Douglas for advice about his future course. Douglas's answer was to "get out into the stream of history and swim as fast as you can."[9]

Christopher then followed a path similar to Caspar Weinberger, joining a law firm and entering California politics. His patron was Governor Pat Brown and his firm, O'Melveny & Myers, offered generous leave for public service. Christopher's first stint in Washington was as deputy attorney general for Ramsay Clark in the Johnson administration. Then came another tour as number two under Vance at the State Department. He was passed over for Senator Edmund Muskie when Vance resigned after the abortive Iranian hostage rescue mission. Christopher was the obvious choice for the top job after Clinton was elected, having run the search that led to Al Gore's appointment as vice president and having served as the incoming president's transition director in Little Rock.

Clinton's first choice as chief of staff, "Mack" McLarty, a childhood friend, didn't work out. The job required, as Christopher wrote, "a Ph.D. in political chemistry" and a wealth of familiarity with Washington—skills that McLarty lacked at that time.[10] McLarty was replaced by Leon Panetta, who possessed these skills in full measure. Clinton's first choice as secretary of defense, Les Aspin, also didn't work out. Aspin demonstrated a formidable intellect on Capitol Hill but had neither the discipline nor the management skills needed for this cabinet-level appointment. He was replaced by his deputy, William Perry, who had both skill sets. Colin Powell's tour as the chairman of the Joint Chiefs of Staff extended through the first ten months of the Clinton administration. He was replaced by General John Shalikashvili, the son of a Polish mother and Georgian émigré father. "Shali" always remembered the CARE packages sent to Europe in 1946 that gave him, a young refugee, "his first taste of peanut butter, his first mouthful of that exotic fruit, raisins, and most importantly, his first glass of powdered milk."[11] He was an inspired choice for the national security problems Clinton faced.

Clinton chose Anthony Lake to be his first national security advisor. Lake was the grandson of a clergyman from Oxford who came to America to teach ecclesiastical history at Harvard. He attended Harvard, studied for two years at Trinity College, Cambridge, and received his PhD from the Woodrow Wilson School at Princeton. Lake joined the Foreign Service and, after two tours in South Vietnam, went to work as a special assistant on the National Security Council staff under Henry Kissinger. He quit the Foreign Service in 1970 after the bombing of Cambodia. Lake then advised Democratic candidates for president, taught at the college level, and wrote at length about hard problems in places like Africa that most Americans preferred not to think about. During the Carter administration, he was Cyrus Vance's director of policy planning at the State Department before Clinton chose him for the corner office in the West Wing. Talbott described Lake as an "experienced, energetic and imaginative thinker."[12]

Talbott was tapped to be the State Department's special ambassador to help with Russia and the newly independent states of the former Soviet Union. His title was long and forgettable, but what mattered more than his title was his long relationship to Clinton, his deep knowledge of the Soviet Union, and his familiarity with nuclear arms control. As a graduate student at Oxford, Talbott was handed the plum assignment of translating Nikita Khrushchev's memoirs that were spirited out of Moscow by *Time*'s bureau chief, Jerry Schecter, with whom he worked previously. Talbott's lasting relationship with Bill Clinton, his housemate, began at Oxford.

Talbott's sense of purpose and sensitivity to world affairs was instilled by his father who, as a navy officer during World War II, worked to prepare the English Channel for the Normandy invasion. He was also a navy diver, retrieving the remains of downed airmen. After surviving World War II, he came home to set up a business in Cleveland as a strong supporter of World Federalism. Talbott's mother was a homemaker. He grew up, first in Dayton and then in Cleveland, with memories of duck-and-cover drills. There was also the unforgettable moment in the chapel at Hotchkiss during the Cuban missile crisis where the head of school told the assembled student body that, whatever God they prayed to—or even if they didn't have a God—it was a good time to get down on their knees.

Cleveland was a city of patchwork ethnicity, including a vibrant Hungarian-American community that reacted strongly when Soviet troops crushed the Hungarian democracy movement in 1956. After the launch of Sputnik in 1957, Talbott was transfixed by the space race. He set his sights on a career in journalism covering the Soviet Union. After Oxford, he began his reporting career in Yugoslavia and was being groomed for Moscow, but after translating Khrushchev's memoirs, Soviet authorities clarified that he was not welcome. He settled comfortably in as a junior diplomatic correspondent in *Time*'s Washington bureau, where sources confided in him like sinners lining up at a confessional. Talbott practiced the journalistic technique of writing first drafts of diplomatic history. He shed light on monumental fights and decisions over nuclear weapons and arms control that were taking placed behind closed doors. Then, like Leslie Gelb and Richard Burt before him, he was offered the chance to practice rather than eavesdrop on nuclear negotiations.[13]

DENUCLEARIZING RUSSIA'S PERIPHERY

The first order of business for the Clinton administration was to secure and then implement the pledges James Baker extracted from Belarus, Kazakhstan, and Ukraine. Clinton needed to have all three join the Nonproliferation Treaty as non-nuclear-weapon states before the NPT's twenty-fifth anniversary review conference to decide the fate of the treaty. The State Department's lawyers stipulated conditions for providing assistance with denuclearization, as did the Congress. These took the form of "umbrella" agreements that specified privileges and immunities for U.S. personnel implementing projects on the ground, including freedom from taxation and liability protections. Negotiations on the fine print of the U.S. umbrella agreement with the Russian Federation took six months and were completed in June 1992. It was signed at the first summit meeting between Bush and Yeltsin.

In October 1992 Belarus, the most pliant of Russia's neighbors, signed its umbrella agreement. As Mitchell Reiss noted, "Belarus did not even pretend to play the nuclear card." It was ready to strike a deal with Moscow, with Washington's help.[14] The Supreme Soviet of Belarus voted overwhelmingly to ratify START I and join the NPT as a non-nuclear-weapon state in February 1993.

Kazakhstan's leader, Nursultan Nazarbayev, had no political opposition and enjoyed a compliant legislature. He could expect popular support for denuclearization, as one million of his citizens suffered from the consequences of Soviet nuclear testing at Semipalatinsk, including 116 tests above ground. Underground tests were also unsafe, often venting deadly radioactive debris over the surrounding farmland.[15] There was no strong nationalist faction in Kazakh politics seeking to stand up to Russia. Decision making was confined to Nazarbayev, a holdover from Soviet rule, and very few men around him. They all believed it was crucial to seek to become a member in good standing of the international community and to have close relations with the United States. In addition, Kazakhstan's leaders exercised no direct control over their sudden nuclear inheritance. Seeking control would have meant a direct confrontation with Moscow.[16]

Kazakhstan's neighbors helped steer Nazarbayev toward denuclearization. Beijing signed a joint statement stating that the two sides would settle any border dispute issues through negotiations in accordance with the established principles of international law. Moscow partially relieved Kazakh security concerns by crafting a Collective Security Treaty with its Central Asian neighbors that was signed in Tashkent in 1992. Baker skillfully used a White House meeting with President Bush to line up Nazarbayev's support for the Lisbon Protocol that was signed the following week. Nazarbayev also signed a Treaty of Friendship, Cooperation and Mutual Aid with Moscow.

To help pave the way for warhead repatriations, the Bush administration sent a large U.S. team led by Reginald Bartholomew of the State Department, Thomas Graham of ACDA, and General Shalikashvili representing the Joint Chiefs. They arrived two weeks after Kazakhstan's independence. The person advancing the team's trip sent word that the Kazakhs had to be paid in cash—$20,000 in small bills—for refueling their aircraft because credit card transactions needed to be cleared at Russian banks that took 10 percent off the top. There were only two people at the newly created Foreign Ministry the U.S. delegation could talk to—the foreign minister and his deputy—so detailed negotiations would have to wait. Nazarbayev told the U.S. delegation that he had received inquiries "from the south" about parting with some of his sudden nuclear inheritance but he wasn't selling. Thereafter, negotiating the details of denuclearization became even more important.[17]

Nazarbayev was a realist. According to Togzhan Kassenova, "He wanted to stall, but he knew he couldn't keep the weapons."[18] With nearly complete freedom of maneuver, Nazarbayev vacillated during the last year of the Bush administration, neither completely confirming nor renouncing his country's nuclear status. He needed Washington's help to carve out an independent space—not just diplomatic recognition but also help with foreign direct investment, access to markets, and loan guarantees. Chevron wanted to invest in the development of Kazakh oil fields, and an umbrella agreement would help. Nazarbayev also needed financial assistance to dismantle Soviet missiles and bombers and to close the Soviet test site—assistance that the Nunn-Lugar program could provide.

By the time Clinton took office, Nazarbayev was clearly pointed in the direction of denuclearization, but he was taking his time, partly because of the rise of Russian nationalism as Yeltsin stumbled. Neither Christopher nor Clinton dwelled on denuclearization efforts in their memoirs; William Perry did, as he was the point person implementing Nunn-Lugar funding. The combined efforts of Baker and Perry succeeded. They were "a winning team," according to U.S. ambassador to Kazakhstan William Courtney.[19] Attention was also paid by Talbott and Christopher, who made an important visit in October 1993, offering $85 million in Nunn-Lugar funds and receiving a pledge from Nazarbayev that he would submit the Nonproliferation Treaty to his parliament, the Mazhilis, by the end of the year. A visit by Vice President Al Gore sealed the deal in December 1993, at which time he signed an umbrella agreement for Nunn-Lugar programs. The Mazhilis then voted overwhelmingly to join the Nonproliferation Treaty without reservations. Nazarbayev presented the instrument of ratification to Clinton at the White House in February 1994.[20]

Heavier diplomatic lifting was needed for Ukraine, whose path to denuclearization was, as William Potter has detailed, long and convoluted.[21] The Bush administration's team of Bartholomew, Graham, and Shalikashvili ran into a brick wall in Kiev in January 1992 when they were advised by the foreign minister and the deputy foreign minister that Ukraine wanted to be the France of the East. Since France had nuclear weapons, Ukraine should have them, too.[22]

The assignment of denuclearizing Ukraine fell to Talbott. Ukraine no longer possessed tactical nuclear weapons, since the Russian military spirited them back home quickly, announcing completion of this task before Ukrainian president Leonid Kravchuk's first visit to the White House in May 1993. Kravchuk was embarrassed. He and his team were rookies when it came to nuclear negotiations, only belatedly understanding the value of the fissile material in warheads that could be modified and used in fuel rods at nuclear power plants to help provide warmth during the Ukrainian winter.

Kiev sought amends when discussing the repatriation of warheads associated with long-range strategic forces orphaned on Ukrainian soil. Ukraine was in terrible economic shape. In 1992 and 1993 alone, Moscow raised oil and gas prices 170 times and threatened to cut off fuel supplies.[23] Paranoia can at times be justified, and the cacophony of loud voices in the Russian Duma calling for overturning Ukrainian sovereignty echoed loudly in Kiev. Ukraine was different from Belarus and Kazakhstan. For Moscow, Belarus was an appendage and Kazakhstan a sideshow. In contrast, the very roots of the Russian state were planted in and around Kiev. Ukraine was an integral part of Tsarist Russia, enjoying independence only briefly after the Tsar was toppled in 1917. This experiment was essentially shut down by Bolshevik fighters by the end of 1921.

There was no change in Ukraine's territorial status until 1954 when Nikita Khrushchev engineered a decree by the Supreme Soviet giving Crimea to Ukraine, perhaps as a byproduct of an internal power struggle. Over three-quarters of Crimea's population was ethnic Russian and many Russians never reconciled themselves to the transfer. This bitter history resurfaced when Vladimir Putin reversed Khrushchev's decree in 2014, annexing Crimea forcibly after Ukrainians took to the streets to send Moscow's favored leader packing.[24]

Kravchuk wanted security assurances and serious compensation for repatriation, as well as leverage over the fate of the orphaned Soviet Black Sea Fleet based at Sevastopol on the southwestern tip of the Crimean Peninsula. He also wanted the steady flow of oil and gas supplies at discounted prices, fuel rods for nuclear power plants, debt relief, and a fair share of Nunn-Lugar funds. The Bush administration's diplomatic strategy of how to deal with the sudden emergence of Ukraine as the world's third-largest nuclear arsenal was to withhold diplomatic recognition until denuclearization. The Clinton administration questioned this approach. Denuclearization required reassurance, and reassurance required broader diplomatic engagement. The more Bush administration officials narrow-casted their approach to denuclearization, the more these weapons appreciated in value and the more concerned Ukrainian officials and legislators became about giving them up.

At their first meeting in May 1993, Talbott recounts that Kravchuk "set an astronomical price" for handing the weapons back—billions of dollars in compensation and a security guarantee to treat an attack on Ukraine as an attack on the United States. Talbott, like Baker before him, was in no position to offer a security guarantee designed for allies. Instead, he offered to help finance warhead repatriation "in exchange for Moscow's assurance, underwritten by the U.S., that Russia would respect Ukrainian independence." Talbott arranged a channel whereby he, his Russian interlocutor Yuri Mamedov, and Ukraine's deputy foreign minister would seek to reach an accord for their bosses to sign off on.[25]

Talbott was told in Moscow that he was on a fool's errand and that ties between Russia and Ukraine were none of his business. Russian ambassador Vladimir Lukin compared them to relations between New York and New Jersey. In Talbott's retelling, the head of the Russian Foreign Intelligence Service (and later foreign minister) Yevgeny Primakov "compared the Ukrainians to children who had gotten their hands on their father's loaded hunting rifle and had the reckless delusion that they could use it to get their own way." Yeltsin could and did override these views, but he needed U.S. help with the repatriation of warheads for strategic forces left behind in Ukraine. Accepting that help required Moscow's recognition that Washington had "no ulterior motive hostile to Russia's interests."[26]

The Clinton administration decided that a broader diplomatic approach would be more persuasive, built upon the three pillars of security assurances, economic assistance, and Nunn-Lugar help with dismantlement. In May 1993, Talbott visited Kiev to lay out this approach. Secretary of Defense Aspin then visited in June to offer Nunn-Lugar assistance, and Secretary Christopher followed up in October to secure an umbrella agreement. Even so, the Ukrainian Parliament, or Rada, added nullifying conditions when it ratified START in November 1993, claiming ownership of all nuclear weapons on national territory. Nor did the Rada endorse the commitments reflected in a side-letter to the Lisbon Protocol from Kravchuk to Bush reaffirming Ukraine's nonnuclear status along with a schedule for transferring all nuclear warheads back to Russia. The Clinton administration recognized that it needed to become more engaged in disputes between Kiev and Moscow over the disposition of the Black Sea Fleet and other contentious issues. Talbott, Steven Pifer on Talbott's staff, and Rose Gottemoeller on the National Security Council staff did so.

They understood that President Clinton's planned trip to Kiev in January 1994 could serve as a forcing function for securing clean Ukrainian assurances on denuclearization and joining both START and the Nonproliferation Treaty as a nuclear-weapon-free state. Perry became the most critical change agent, placing the finishing touches on Ukrainian debt forgiveness, the provision of enriched uranium blended down for fuel rods for nuclear power generation, and Nunn-Lugar funding. Vice President Gore also played a key role with his Russian counterpart, Prime Minister Victor Chernomyrdin.

Still, Kravchuk again got cold feet just as he did before the Lisbon Protocol was signed, prompting a volcanic reaction from Secretary of State Baker that sealed the deal—at least provisionally.[27] Clinton used a brief stopover in Kiev in January 1994 to warn Kravchuk that if he backed out, he invited becoming a persona non grata in Washington and Moscow. The remaining hang-ups in the drafting process then evaporated, including "conforming" the language of a U.S.-Russian-Ukrainian Trilateral Statement signed earlier in Moscow so that it conveyed the same meaning in all three languages. Steven Pifer recounts that the English word "assurance" translates into "guarantee" in both Russian and Ukrainian. This required adding a U.S. statement to the formal negotiating record spelling out Washington's interpretation of the word "assurance," to which the Ukrainian and Russian delegations consented.[28]

The Trilateral Statement was signed by Clinton, Yeltsin, and Kravchuk on January 13, 1994, along with an annex and private letters covering particulars deemed too sensitive for public consumption. The centerpiece of the Trilateral Statement was the security assurances Talbott promised in his first visit to Kiev, with Moscow joining Washington in pledging that relations would be "conducted on the basis of respect for the independence, sovereignty and territorial integrity of each nation." Ukraine promised to transfer all remaining warheads to Russia, with an end date affixed in a private letter. Russia promised debt relief in a private letter, along with a public pledge for down-blended enriched uranium to power Ukrainian reactors.

There was still much work to do. The Rada had to join the Nonproliferation Treaty without disabling conditions. There was no agreed schedule for transferring warheads and dismantling missiles, and agreements in principle for Russia's help to Ukraine needed detailing. To Washington's surprise, the Trilateral Statement helped Moscow and Ukraine iron out implementation. In February 1994, the Rada ratified the first Strategic Arms Reduction Treaty and the Lisbon Protocol without a hitch, but without addressing the Nonproliferation Treaty. Then in March, Clinton hosted Kravchuk at the White House where he announced funding for Nunn-Lugar and economic support. The gears were now meshing. Perry paid personal attention to Nunn-Lugar activities in Ukraine, helped by Ashton Carter, the assistant secretary of defense, and a phalanx of deputies, including Gloria Duffy, Elizabeth Sherwood-Randall, and Susan Koch.

A summit was planned in Budapest in December 1994 to celebrate the achievements of the Organization for Security and Cooperation in Europe. The Clinton administration viewed this summit as a deadline to finally secure Ukraine's accession to the Nonproliferation Treaty as a nuclear-weapon-free state, thereby allowing START's implementation to begin. Once again, Vice President Gore was instrumental in facilitating progress when he visited Ukraine to meet with its newly elected president, Leonid Kuchma.

Kuchma succeeded in securing the Rada's accession to the NPT by an overwhelming vote, but this resolution claimed for Ukraine nuclear weapon–possessing status. Washington, Moscow, and London—the NPT's depository states—resolved this problem by ignoring the Rada's declaration and by a diplomatic note transmitted by Kuchma overriding it. The security assurances that Yeltsin made to Ukraine in Budapest on December 5, 1994, along with Clinton and British prime minister John Major, were to respect the independence, sovereignty, and the existing borders of Ukraine; to refrain from the threat or use of force against the territorial integrity or political independence of Ukraine; to refrain from economic coercion; and to seek immediate United Nations Security Council action if Ukraine should become a victim of an act of aggression. For added effect, the Budapest assurances were transmitted to the UN General Assembly.

For two decades, these security assurances held partly because for long stretches, Ukrainian leaders who ran the country poorly and greedily were beholden to Moscow. When Ukrainians opted to expel Putin's favored proxy, Viktor Yanukovych, and tie their economy more closely to the West in 2014, Putin reacted by carrying out hybrid warfare in eastern Ukraine and by seizing Crimea. The West's security assurances for Ukraine proved to be hollow. Even so, U.S. officials heavily involved in denuclearizing Ukraine believe that they took the right course of action.[29] The global nuclear order would have been shaken had Ukraine not joined the Nonproliferation Treaty as a non-nuclear-weapon state, or had the NPT not been extended indefinitely afterward. Besides, Kiev had no means to maintain an independent nuclear deterrent. Had Kiev tried to do so, it would have forfeited desperately needed Western help to create a viable state.

Nor would the possession and use of nuclear weapons—had Kiev decided to hold onto them—have provided an effective rejoinder against hybrid warfare and the seizure of Crimea. Instead, the use of nuclear weapons in self-defense would have resulted in the utter destruction of Ukraine, with the effects of nuclear detonations wafting well beyond its borders. Would possession alone have sufficed to deter Russian aggression? Those who believe in the deterrent power of offsetting nuclear arsenals do not have history on their side, since there have already been limited border wars between the Soviet Union and China in 1969 and between India and Pakistan in 1999. Whether a nuclear-armed Ukraine would have deterred Putin after the loss of his Ukrainian proxy is unknowable, but far from certain.

Russian aggression was obviously not foreseen at the Budapest summit in 1994; nor was it after Clinton and Yeltsin left office in 2000. Clinton's successor, George W. Bush, met Putin for the first time in Slovenia in 2001, where he "found him very straightforward and trustworthy."[30] Later that year, when Bush announced the U.S. withdrawal from the Anti-Ballistic Missile Treaty, he stated that the world had changed, and that Russia was no longer an enemy. Putin's reaction was muted; he was in no position to react harshly. By the end of the George W. Bush administration, U.S.-Russian relations were on a far different trajectory. At second glance, Bush looked into Putin's soul and found a former KGB officer. Putin, too, was without illusions after NATO expansion included the Baltic states and after Bush's announced intent to include Georgia and Ukraine, as well.

All of this lay in the future. In 1994, the Budapest assurances appeared to be genuine and meaningful. Those who implemented the denuclearization of Ukraine had no second thoughts. General Roland Lajoie, the man responsible for the Pentagon's cooperative threat reduction office, and his team "kept their heads down." He added, "You do the job that's in front of you."[31] It made sense to denuclearize Ukraine and it didn't make sense for Kiev to keep these weapons. "As long as we didn't screw it up," recalled Pifer, who later became the U.S. ambassador to Ukraine, "we were going to get it done."[32] It was a still a hopeful time. The denuclearization of Ukraine, Belarus, and Kazakhstan was a success story for the Clinton administration and for posterity, helping to pave the way for the indefinite extension of the Nonproliferation Treaty.

NEW TOOLS

The Clinton administration developed novel tools to deal with new proliferation dangers associated with Russia's weakened status. A deft approach was required to bring this toolbox to Russia. As Rose Gottemoeller recalled, "We knew they needed help, but they didn't like asking for it."[33] The White House and government agencies, led by the Pentagon and the Department of Energy, seized the moment, eschewing bureaucratic resistance and establishing new ways of doing business to prevent dangerous weapons and materials from falling into new hands. These novel tools—the Nunn-Lugar and "Lab to Lab" initiatives—began in the Bush administration, but both needed to be fully realized during the Clinton administration. Bush and his team saw the need for new mechanisms of cooperative threat reduction but wanted to move slowly since nothing had been done like this before. They were willing to explore, but caution was the watchword.

The initial appropriation of funds for Nunn-Lugar dismantlement programs came out of the Pentagon's budget, which wasn't the way to endear Dick Cheney to the program's objectives. The Nunn-Lugar program needed a steady funding stream, which the Congress enacted under Clinton with strong support from Perry and Carter at the Pentagon. The embrace of Nunn-Lugar would also require contracting and logistics capabilities so that appropriations could be spent in accordance with congressional guidelines. This task was handed to Lajoie. The Defense Nuclear Agency, which supported nuclear testing, became his new fiefdom. Its contracting and logistical capabilities were given a new mission in the newly rebranded Office of Cooperative Threat Reduction.

Lajoie grew up in New Hampshire, the seventh child of a French-Canadian immigrant family. His dad worked in the textile mills. Lajoie was an indifferent student and lacked a sense of purpose until he found himself in an army uniform. He read about the army's foreign area officer program and applied while serving in Vietnam. He learned Russian, and after a second tour in Vietnam, he began a series of assignments, the first at Potsdam with the U.S. Military Liaison Mission, on the front lines of military-diplomatic engagement. Implementing Nunn-Lugar was a dream job. U.S. personnel could now visit sites they had previously "lusted after from afar." The work was "fun," and he made sure that it was implemented without "political baggage." The Pentagon's success encouraged the State Department, the Department of Energy, and other government agencies to become involved.[34]

A second extremely novel program initiated by the Bush administration and taken to a whole new level by the Clinton administration was a "Lab to Lab" program of cooperation among bomb designers and the guardians of nuclear stockpiles. Bush was concerned about the "brain drain" from the old Soviet nuclear weapon complex and asked his secretary of energy, Admiral James D. Watkins, what might be done. Watkins authorized travel by officials from the Los Alamos and Lawrence Livermore Laboratories—including lab directors Siegfried Hecker and John Nuckolls—to meet with their Russian counterparts to explore possibilities. Hecker and Nuckolls came back from their first visit in February 1992 stunned by the openness of their Russian colleagues and by their eagerness to engage. They returned flush with creative ideas for collaboration.

Fortunately, they weren't starting from scratch. During the Reagan administration, Thomas Cochran of the Natural Resources Defense Council and Evgeniy Velikhov of the Soviet Academy of Sciences engaged in collaborative monitoring experiments to detect nuclear weapons at sea—something the U.S. government was disinterested in doing. One consequence of their initiative, as intended, was to prompt Washington and Moscow to take a more active role in verification experiments.[35]

The Joint Verification Experiments conducted during the Reagan years had a specific purpose of better understanding the yields of underground tests. This entailed visiting and instrumenting test sites, which subsequently served as a door opener for Lab to Lab discussions on other subjects. The immediate objective was to clarify yields so that the 1974 Threshold Test Ban Treaty could finally enter into force. Useful ground was broken, and channels of communication opened. Hecker and Nuckolls wanted to expand significantly the scope of Lab to Lab cooperation. Watkins and the White House looked at their "to do" list and scrubbed it. It was too much, too fast. Initial collaborative ventures needed to be limited to basic science.

Hecker and Nuckolls took what the traffic would bear and sought to expand it into a thoroughfare. Siegfried Hecker was born in 1943 and grew up in Austria. Neither parent had more than an eighth-grade education. His father, drafted into the German Army in World War II, never returned from the Russian front. He came to the United States in 1956 and received his PhD from what later became known as Case Western. Hecker fell in love with metallurgy, found a home at Los Alamos, and never looked back. He became the lab's director in 1986, shortly before the Chernobyl accident. Soon thereafter, the Joint Verification Experiments and the Intermediate Nuclear Forces Treaty turned the Cold War nuclear competition on its head.[36]

The incoming Clinton administration was eager to take the initial stirrings of Lab to Lab cooperation to new levels. Clinton and Talbott needed no prompting. The new secretary of energy, Hazel O'Leary, was fully on board, and her deputy, Charles Curtis, was like an offensive lineman in bureaucratic skirmishing, clearing a path for laboratory ball carriers. After Reagan and Bush's achievements, cooperation between the labs no longer seemed completely novel and downside risks seemed manageable. Hecker, Nuckolls, and colleagues at the Sandia National Laboratories found the latitude to head in the directions that were most needed, including, in the jargon of the business, nuclear material accountancy and control. The Russian labs needed help securing fissile material, counting it, and keeping track of it. The long list of creative ideas that Hecker and Nuckolls had drawn up in the winter of 1992 were now in play. Purchasing agreements using Russian overstock of fissile material to help with nuclear power generation in the United States were now possible.[37]

A Presidential Decision Directive issued by Clinton in March 1996 was critical to reaffirming and extending Lab to Lab cooperation. It expressly permitted unclassified collaboration important to a wide range of pursuits, including cooperation on techniques to monitor a zero-yield test ban treaty. These steps were inconceivable during the Bush administration and again became inconceivable later on, when George W. Bush and Vladimir Putin began to spar seriously. Cooperation between the nuclear laboratories depended on U.S.- Russian relations and couldn't be sustained when bilateral conditions deteriorated. Lab to Lab cooperation became a bellwether for the status of arms control. It reached its apogee between 1994 and 1997, became routinized, then began to stall out, and subsequently ended because of opposition on Capitol Hill and in the Kremlin.[38]

NONPROLIFERATION, THE PERMANENT NORM

The Nunn-Lugar and Lab to Lab programs were novel practices that strengthened the norm of nuclear nonproliferation. The timing was right, as the Nonproliferation Treaty text stipulated that, after twenty-five years, state parties would convene "to decide whether the Treaty shall continue in force indefinitely or shall be extended for an additional fixed period or periods." The future of the treaty that President Johnson succeeded in completing and President Nixon succeeded in ratifying was now in Clinton's hands.

The drafters of the NPT stipulated that this decision was to be taken by majority vote.

Holding down the fort at ACDA during the early months of the Clinton administration was its general counsel, Thomas Graham, who became its de facto and temporary director. There were no announcements to fill ACDA leadership positions at the outset of the Clinton administration because of opposition in the State Department led by Under Secretary Lynn Davis, whose portfolio included arms control, and Brian Atwood, who was under secretary for management. They wanted ACDA to be incorporated into the State Department. Graham arranged for Secretary of State Christopher to meet with Muriel Humphrey, the widow of the senator who did more than anyone else on Capitol Hill to create ACDA, where she pleaded the case for reviving the agency. Christopher then overrode Davis and Atwood. John Holum, a veteran of Senator George McGovern's staff and Democratic presidential campaigns, was appointed as the new ACDA director.

The Clinton administration inherited a congressionally mandated moratorium on nuclear testing that was due to lapse in July 1993. Before Holum came on board, Graham participated in deputy secretary and cabinet-level meetings on how best to proceed. Initially, everyone else in the room supported the resumption of testing. Graham's opposition stretched out these deliberations until others came around to his view.

Thomas Graham was born into a political family. Melvin Laird—Nixon's secretary of defense and, before that, a powerful congressman from Wisconsin—was a distant relative. His father was a "mover and a shaker" in Democratic politics in Louisville, Kentucky; his mother was a homemaker. They gave him a "golden childhood" mixed with athletics, Democratic national conventions, and the Kentucky Derby. He attended Princeton and Harvard Law School, interspersed with a two-year stint in the army. At Harvard Law he moonlighted to take courses from Henry Kissinger and Louis Sohn, grandmasters of geopolitics and international law. Perhaps then and there the two major strands of his professional life were interwoven. The practice of law wasn't interesting; instead, he became captivated by the negotiation and legalities associated with treaties, briefly at first in the Pentagon and then at ACDA from 1970 to 1997.[39]

Holum asked Graham what job he wanted; Graham wanted to lead U.S. efforts to indefinitely extend the NPT, the negotiation of which was perhaps ACDA's greatest accomplishment. In deliberating over the U.S. negotiating objective for the crucial 1995 Review Conference, Graham supported indefinite extension with a fallback position of rolling twenty-five-year extensions. The State Department argued strongly for indefinite extension without the fallback position. Robert Einhorn and Ted McNamara of the State Department believed that a strong push from the department's topmost officials on the seventh floor could secure the necessary votes to win by a simple majority, if need be. The Office of the Secretary of Defense backed up State. The United States would seek indefinite extension by consensus if possible, and by majority vote if necessary. There would be no fallback position. McNamara and Einhorn believed that sticks would be more useful than carrots in rounding up votes at the Review Conference.

Christopher followed up with "first person" instructions to U.S. ambassadors directing them to make the case for indefinite extension at foreign ministries. "No government could ignore a personal appeal from the Secretary of State," recalled Einhorn, who was deeply involved in this process. Christopher asked for favorable responses in writing.[40] In the run-up to the 1995 Review Conference, Graham and his closest aide, Susan Burk, a division chief at ACDA, traveled widely. Graham's goal was to prevent the largest voting group—the Non-Aligned Movement—from opposing indefinite extension. Non-nuclear-weapon states wanted leverage on the Permanent Five (or P-5) members on the Security Council to reduce their nuclear forces. Rolling extensions were an obvious leveraging device, but at the risk of having periodic jump-ball treaty tipoffs that could end badly if the P-5 could not or would not reduce their force levels.

Susan Burk grew up in Plainfield, New Jersey. Her father was an oral surgeon and her mother looked after their large brood of seven children. All of them went off to Catholic schools—in Burk's case, Trinity College in Washington, DC—except for a brother who went to the Naval Academy. Committed to working in Washington, she took classes at night and received a graduate degree from Georgetown. Burk got started in the Pentagon and worked for a time on the Intermediate Nuclear Forces Treaty, but the subject matter didn't resonate. With the help of a mentor, she moved to ACDA in 1984, helping Lewis Dunn steer the successful conclusion of the 1985 Review Conference on the Nonproliferation Treaty. She was hooked.

Graham believed indefinite extension by consensus to be a "long shot," but he remained doggedly optimistic.[41] The denuclearization of Ukraine, Kazakhstan, and Belarus helped considerably. Deep cuts in U.S. and Russian nuclear weapons were in train and the perceived value of nuclear weapons was shrinking.

Help in dealing with the Non-Aligned Movement's deliberations came from South Africa, whose last apartheid government, led by President F.W. de Klerk, announced in 1989 that it had secretly possessed and had subsequently destroyed six nuclear warheads. He then handed the reins of power over to Nelson Mandela and the African National Congress. The rationale for South Africa's weapon program—to threaten use so as to prompt help for a beleaguered and isolated white nationalist state threatened by Soviet forces and proxies—melted away with the demise of the Soviet Union. South Africa joined the NPT as a non-nuclear-weapon state in 1991, and under Mandela's leadership became a sterling exemplar of nonproliferation and a leader of the Non-Aligned Movement.[42]

Other factors lent impetus to indefinite extension. The last two holdouts from the P-5, France and China, joined the NPT in 1992. START II, signed in 1993, promised even deeper cuts in U.S. and Russian strategic forces. The Presidential Nuclear Initiatives by Bush, Gorbachev, and Yeltsin promised thousands of reductions in deployed "tactical" nuclear weapons. On July 3, 1993, the Clinton White House issued a press release acknowledging reasons for carrying out additional nuclear tests but concluded that these reasons were outweighed by U.S. "nonproliferation goals." In this statement, Clinton announced that the United States would pursue a Comprehensive Test Ban Treaty in Geneva at the Conference on Disarmament, a reversal of the Bush administration's position. The target date for success was 1996.

In addition, Washington and Moscow worked in concert and coaxed the other permanent members of the Security Council to support a resolution providing "negative security assurances" just before the NPT Review Conference began in April 1995. In these assurances, the P-5 pledged not to use or threaten to use nuclear weapons against NPT members in good standing. ACDA tried to engineer another sweetener—politically, but not legally binding "no first use" pledges. While China's UN ambassador readily accepted a no-first-use formulation, as Graham recalled, "Washington went absolutely berserk over this idea," and it had to be walked back.[43]

The State Department and ACDA worked smoothly together in pursuit of the NPT's indefinite extension. Christopher's "first person" cable produced positive responses. All of the State Department's regional bureaus flooded their respective zones with arguments for indefinite extension. The top two U.S. talking points were that indefinite extension would help establish the basis for further nuclear arms reductions and increase the likelihood of peaceful nuclear cooperation.[44] ACDA's deputy director, Ralph Earle, Larry

Scheinman, and Norman Wulf were heavily involved, as was Einhorn. Burk remembers Dan Poneman of the National Security Council staff, who was overseeing the administration's efforts, saying that he knew securing an indefinite extension wasn't easy, but it also wasn't hard. Easy for him to say, she recalls thinking.[45] But Poneman wasn't wrong: success was in the offing. The question was how smoothly it could be accomplished.

Nongovernmental organizations coalesced in support of indefinite extension under the leadership of Joseph Cirincione at the Stimson Center. Additional high-level impulse was generated by a page-one story in the *New York Times* in January 1995 expressing concerns that indefinite extension was running into difficulties. One sticking point was the lack of enthusiasm by nuclear-armed states to reaffirm their obligation under Article VI of the treaty to seek the abolition of nuclear weapons. An expected flurry of activity and assuring statements by Clinton and other high-level officials followed.[46]

The most important country on Graham's world tour was South Africa. Under Mandela's leadership, South Africa had shifted from a pariah state to a leader of the Non-Aligned Movement. The Review Conference would be his government's "debut" on the world stage. Vice President Gore and Colin Powell, the retired chairman of the Joint Chiefs of Staff, wrote personal notes to Mandela making the case for indefinite extension. If South Africa came on board, opposition from the group of nonaligned nations would be badly undercut.[47]

By the time the NPT Review Conference opened, Einhorn recalled, "We had the votes, and everyone knew this."[48] Gore delivered the opening statement on behalf of Clinton. On the same day, South Africa's representative announced that his country would support indefinite extension, while suggesting proposals that could engender a consensus, or at least a near-consensus decision. These included a statement of principles and objectives for nonproliferation and a "program of action" on disarmament to accompany the resolution on indefinite extension, along with an "enhanced" review process.

This proved to be a winning formula, but there was one missing piece: Egypt and Syria were deeply unhappy with the open secret of Israel's nuclear weapons. In return for looking the other way while Israel was building a nuclear arsenal, President Nixon accepted Golda Meir's artfully vague promise that her country would not be the first "to introduce" nuclear weapons in the region. A consensus or a near-consensus required, in the view of the State Department and ACDA, a nod to concerns in the Arab world.[49]

Graham told conference chairman Jayantha Dhanapala, a distinguished Sri Lankan diplomat, that it would suffice to win indefinite extension by a one-vote margin, but both of them knew that the least divisive way forward was to avoid a floor vote. Dhanapala suggested the device of a "parliamentary consensus" whereby the treaty could be approved without objection. The biggest threat to a consensus vote was the government of Egypt, whose foreign minister, Amr Moussa, told Graham, Burk, and other U.S. officials that Israel needed to take an undefined "concrete step" toward eventual NPT membership. Graham recalls one of Amr Moussa's arguments—that urging indefinite extension was akin to urging a Catholic marriage on a Muslim. Burk's rebuttal: "What's wrong with a Catholic marriage?"[50]

After South Africa, no country received more high-level attention in the run-up to the NPT Review Conference than Egypt. Amr Moussa did not hold a strong hand because Egypt was a substantial recipient of U.S. aid and because the Arab League wouldn't go to the mat with him. Egypt's only card was Washington's evident interest in a consensus vote on indefinite extension. The job of drafting the Middle East Resolution fell mostly to Einhorn and Nabil Fahmy, who later became Egypt's ambassador to the United States and its foreign minister.

Einhorn grew up in Rockville Center on Long Island. His dad was in the export business and his mom was a homemaker. He discovered his calling by "falling into it." He went to Cornell and Princeton, studying diplomatic history with Walter LaFeber and deterrence with Klaus Knorr along the way. His roommate at Princeton was the son of a UN disarmament official, who gave him his first job. James Leonard recruited him to ACDA in 1972, and he moved over to the State Department in 1986, where he was the resident proliferation firefighter when he wasn't doing strategic arms control.

The night before the vote, Madeleine Albright, the U.S. ambassador to the UN, Graham, and Einhorn met with Egyptian and Syrian diplomats and agreed to language on a Middle East Resolution that would accompany the final documents. Initially, they settled on language calling for Middle Eastern states that had not yet joined the NPT to do so. This draft specifically named not only Israel but also Oman and Djibouti, which were not yet members. Both countries opposed being named, as did Israel. Egypt, which had gotten too far in front of the Arab League, then reluctantly agreed to language endorsing a Middle East peace process and "practical steps" toward a zone free of nuclear weapons, "noting with concern" unsafeguarded facilities in the region. The resolution supported "the early realization" of universal adherence to the treaty "as soon as possible." Egypt then refused to co-sponsor this resolution, so the NPT's depository states—the United States, Russia, and the United Kingdom—did so.[51]

On May 8, ACDA director Holum announced that, of the 175 states present and voting, the United States had 105 pledges of support for indefinite extension. That placed the onus on disgruntled capitals. Did they want to play the role of spoilers? None did. Three days later, Dhanapala brought up the resolution affirming the treaty's indefinite extension, asking, "Do I hear objections?" and after waiting a few seconds, he then said, "Hearing none, passed." The other parts of the package deal were similarly affirmed. Egypt was handed a cudgel to use against Israel, but the NPT was now a permanent feature of the global nuclear order. Then by script, as Graham recounts, seventeen nations made speeches denouncing indefinite extension including Egypt, Malaysia and Syria, followed by seventeen nations supporting indefinite extension.[52] The result wasn't perfectly clean, but it was much cleaner than the original transmittal of the NPT to the United Nations, which faced stronger opposition from non-aligned states, two holdouts from the P-5, and some U.S. allies, including West Germany.

Dhanapala subsequently expressed remorse over this result. He wrote in 2017, "The complacency I feared in 1995 is now running rampant—many states view the 1995 indefinite extension as a 'done-deal,' rather than a continuing work-in-progress."[53] His critique of the nuclear-armed states has validity. Complacency was unhelpful enough; it has been replaced by backsliding. The U.S.-Russian arms reduction process has stalled, both have withdrawn from treaty obligations, while Beijing increases its force structure. Three NPT outliers—India, Pakistan, and North Korea—are also building up their nuclear arsenals, while a fourth, Israel, retains its nuclear deterrent. Conditions for deeper cuts and progress toward abolition are absent as relations between nuclear-armed rivals deteriorate.

Contrary to Dhanapala's second thoughts, these conditions point to the wisdom of extending the NPT indefinitely in 1995. Consider, for example, the likely consequences had the NPT been extended for twenty-five years. The treaty would then have been up for a life-extension vote in 2020, hardly an auspicious time, with some possessors backsliding and some abstainers, frustrated by the treaty's lack of impetus toward nuclear disarmament, endorsing a treaty banning nuclear weapons. The NPT process did not—and cannot—propel nuclear-armed states to disarm. Nonproliferation is a necessary condition for a safer global nuclear order, but it is not sufficient to prod arms reductions. These achievements require improved ties between the possessors. Dhanapala did the right thing in 1995, as did the Clinton administration, which fulfilled its promise at the NPT Review Conference to complete negotiations on the Comprehensive Test Ban Treaty the following year.

THE COMPREHENSIVE TEST BAN TREATY

President Jimmy Carter wanted a Comprehensive Test Ban Treaty and appointed two highly capable ambassadors, Paul Warnke and Herbert York, to seek one. At that time, however, the Pentagon and the nuclear laboratories were opposed, and these negotiations came to naught. Bill Clinton was also inclined to pursue a CTBT, under conditions more favorable toward success. The Congress, led by Senators Mark Hatfield, James Exon, and George Mitchell, had imposed a moratorium on testing at the end of the George H.W. Bush administration. This legislation allowed limited testing after nine months, while setting the goal of a comprehensive ban in 1996.

Russia was in no position to resume testing. One of the old Soviet test sites resided in an independent Kazakhstan; the other was above the Arctic Circle, begging for refurbishment. Global public opinion was against the resumption of underground testing and Clinton had already announced in the run-up to the 1995 Nonproliferation Treaty Review Conference that Washington would push hard for a comprehensive ban after the treaty's indefinite extension. For most of 1993, no one was testing.[54]

Another positive development for those who sought a treaty was marked achievement in the science of detecting underground tests. When Presidents Kennedy, Nixon, and Ford sought nuclear testing limitations, the United States depended primarily on "teleseismic" monitoring—trying to decipher the yields of Soviet tests from half a world away. Technical experts presumed that the closer sensors were placed to the test sites, the more accurate their readings might be, especially with a greater understanding of the geology at test sites.

In the 1980s, researchers began to receive encouraging results on the value of monitoring at regional distances—less than 1,500 kilometers from the test sites of countries of interest. Regional seismic data began to be used in earnest in the 1990s. These seismic arrays enabled technical experts to sift through data at higher frequencies, and once seismologists heard tenor rather than baritone notes, detection thresholds fell remarkably lower.[55] Geological data at test sites obtained from Joint Verification Experiments during the

Reagan years provided even greater precision.[56] These experiments also disproved those inclined to see a pattern of Soviet cheating against the Threshold Test Ban Treaty.

When Kennedy first sought a Comprehensive Test Ban Treaty after the Cuban missile crisis, Albert Latter, Edward Teller, and others postulated that a 300-kiloton-yield test with the explosive power of perhaps twenty Hiroshimas could be muffled so as to resemble a one-kiloton yield that presumably would be undetectable.[57] With advances in regional seismic arrays and greater understanding of the geology at test sites, a cheater wishing to carry out a one-kiloton test could have little confidence of going undetected. Those who had long argued that seismic data were being misrepresented to prevent limitations on testing now held the high ground.[58] Finally, a Comprehensive Test Ban Treaty seemed supportable by technical means, reinforced by on-site inspections.

Robert Bell of the National Security Council staff surveyed agency positions at the outset of the Clinton administration and concluded that the Pentagon and the State Department strongly supported the resumption of testing after the congressional moratorium ended. The Congress allowed five tests per year for three years, allocating a few tests for Great Britain to confirm the reliability of existing designs. Bell's canvass also indicated that almost all agencies might support a near-Comprehensive Test Ban Treaty that allowed one-kiloton yields.

ACDA's acting director Thomas Graham took it upon himself to block an interagency consensus on resuming testing in February 1993. He also opposed a test ban allowing one-kiloton yields, arguing that a resumption of testing would be poorly timed in the run-up to the make-or-break twenty-fifth anniversary review conference for the Nonproliferation Treaty. If the United States resumed testing, he argued, others would, as well.

Clinton's cabinet discussed nuclear testing in May. At this point, the one-kiloton threshold idea was dropped in favor of a four-pound threshold—just a whisper of a chain reaction—and there was broad support for a ten-year "escape" clause, where states could opt out of the proposed treaty. Graham again opposed ending the moratorium and found support from John Gibbons, the White House science advisor. The newly confirmed secretary of energy, Hazel O'Leary, said she needed more time to study these issues.

Hazel O'Leary wasn't well versed in nuclear deterrence issues. The daughter of two physicians, she was born and raised in the African American part of Newport News, Virginia, attending segregated classes as a child. She attended Fisk University, got a law degree from Rutgers, and later returned to Fisk as its president. She had worked for a public utility and wasn't a stranger to Washington, but she didn't fit the mold of previous energy secretaries who were supportive of nuclear testing. She was hard working, charming, and after doing her homework, capable of bold decisions.

After getting up to speed, O'Leary came to the conclusion that there was no need to break the moratorium. She brought laboratory officials with her to the next National Security Council meeting later in May to offer supportive technical analysis. After being presented with evidence that the stockpile would not need testing for at least ten years, General Colin Powell, representing the Joint Chiefs, changed his view and supported the continuance of the moratorium. Secretaries Christopher and Aspin held to the view that, since the Congress allowed fifteen tests after the moratorium expired, the United States should carry them out. The meeting ended with another split decision, but opinion was trending toward extending the moratorium. In July, Clinton announced that the United States would extend the moratorium but would reconsider if another nation tested.

The next NSC meeting was in September 1993 amidst intelligence community reports that Beijing was preparing to conduct new tests. This time around, Secretary Aspin spoke first, strongly arguing that "our policy should not be determined by what some people in Beijing do." Secretary Christopher agreed with Aspin. Support for the moratorium at the cabinet level was now firm.[59] The intelligence community's concerns proved warranted as China carried out tests in October 1993, but still the U.S. moratorium held. At this point, Beijing had tested less than forty times; the United States had carried out 1,032 tests. For the first time in memory, the United States supported the annual resolution on the Comprehensive Test Ban Treaty at the United Nations.

Negotiations began in 1994, taking place in Geneva at the Conference on Disarmament, an unwieldy thirty-eight-nation forum that could succeed only with strong U.S. leadership and a united front among the P-5. The U.S. ambassador, Steven Ledogar, was ideally suited for the challenges of multilateral diplomacy. He was shrewd and a good listener, tactically adept, and a force to be reckoned with.

Ledogar was born in Jamaica, Queens, in 1929, the year the stock market collapsed. His father was a lawyer whose practice was devastated by the crash; his mother was a homemaker. Ledogar was a big man—you could lose your hand while shaking his. He grew up attracted to speed and wanted to be a navy fighter pilot. To qualify, he needed to slump his six-foot, five-inch frame to meet the navy's six-foot, four-inch height limit. He went to Fordham before joining the navy and was assigned to the Mediterranean during the Korean War. He then went back to Fordham, taking classes at night for a law degree despite having no intention of litigating. Instead, he took the Foreign Service exam on a lark. Diplomacy and foreign travel suited him. He rose through the ranks of the Foreign Service to be appointed by Ronald Reagan in 1987 as ambassador to conventional force reduction negotiations. He moved from Vienna to Geneva after Bush's election to tackle the Chemical Weapons Convention.

In this, Ledogar succeeded. He now focused on the Test Ban Treaty. One of his colleagues during the CTBT negotiations recalls Ledogar telling the U.S. negotiating team that President Clinton told him he wanted this treaty, and if anyone on his team didn't, they needed to find something else to do.[60] Ledogar was again up to the task. He was, as Robert Bell recalled, "an unsung hero of American diplomacy." No U.S. diplomat accomplished more than Stephen Ledogar in the onerous business of multilateral negotiations.[61]

The P-5 had already promised to finish up the Test Ban Treaty to help with the indefinite extension of the NPT, but Beijing, London, and Paris were deeply ambivalent. To underscore this commitment, the UN General Assembly passed a resolution in January 1996, calling for the treaty to be completed and opened for signature by the fall. Bill Clinton now had another hard deadline. At this time, the "rolling text" of the draft treaty was almost 100 pages long with over 1,200 brackets, reflecting disagreements over language. The conference chair, Jaap Ramaker of the Netherlands, despaired about being able to meet the deadline.[62]

The treaty negotiators borrowed heavily from on-site inspection, challenge inspection, and managed access provisions drawn from the Intermediate Nuclear Forces Treaty and Chemical Weapons Convention. They drew up plans for an International Monitoring System consisting of over 300 monitoring stations and a Technical Secretariat for treaty housekeeping and implementation. The breadth and monitoring capability of this proposed network were impressive, even by the standards of the U.S. intelligence community.

The very low threshold for nuclear testing and the ten-year clause to opt out didn't survive rigorous debate inside the Clinton administration: the P-5 couldn't come up with a common position, and the very low permissible yield threshold invited contentious compliance debates—as did a zero-yield treaty. Supporters of zero argued that anything else would be a sign of bad faith to states without the Bomb that had just agreed to extend the NPT indefinitely. France, which incurred the wrath of many states for resuming tests in the South Pacific during the negotiating endgame, then championed a zero-yield treaty. U.S. experts outside the U.S. laboratory complex, led by Sidney Drell, offered strong rebuttals to those who argued in favor of a low threshold.

As Ledogar, Ramaker, and key leaders among non-nuclear-weapon states drove to meet the deadline for transmitting treaty text to the United Nations, one remaining issue gained prominence: entry into force. The Nonproliferation Treaty required forty states to deposit their instruments of ratification, in addition to the United States, the Soviet Union, and Great Britain, before it could come into effect. Two of the P-5—France and China—were initial holdouts. The NPT consisted of less than sixty members at the outset, growing over time to a global compact of over 190 countries. The Chemical Weapons Convention entered into force upon deposit of the sixty-fifth instrument of ratification. It, too, became a global norm-setter, with over 190 members.

None of these formulas worked for the CTBT. One reason was that the governments of India and Pakistan wanted out. Their nuclear options were shrinking, first with the indefinite extension of the NPT, and now the likely conclusion of a treaty banning all tests. Unlike China, India didn't qualify as a "nuclear-weapon state" under the NPT; only states that tested before 1968 did. New Delhi, however, couldn't accept second-class citizenship in a global nuclear order designed by the P-5, and Pakistan couldn't accept second-class citizenship to India. New Delhi was in a bind. Its founding leader, Jawaharlal Nehru, was one of the earliest and most powerful voices in support of a comprehensive treaty, and India was a consistent champion of nuclear disarmament in the non-aligned world.

And yet India lived in a rough neighborhood where it had fought a border war with China and three with Pakistan. Moreover, there was strong evidence that Beijing was helping Pakistan obtain nuclear weapons. India couldn't feel secure without the Bomb. So, as the negotiations were hurtling toward the fall 1996 deadline, New Delhi did an about-face. Its articulate and forceful negotiator, Arundhati Ghose, argued that the CTBT should be about nuclear disarmament as well as nonproliferation. Unless the P-5 were committed to a certain date when they would dispose of their arsenals, India would not lend its support to a thinly veiled diplomatic effort whose practical effect would hobble its national security options.

India's position was ruinous to the treaty's entry into force. Beijing made it clear that it wouldn't join unless India did, too, and Moscow agreed. Ramaker and the P-5 struggled over formulas; the one they came up with was unwieldy, but seemingly less worse than the other options. The treaty text required forty-four countries with nuclear research or power reactors to deposit instruments of ratification before entry into force. London and Paris were content with this result, as they were unenthusiastic about the CTBT; if they were to take this bitter medicine, others would have to, as well.

This list of forty-four included the P-5, India, Pakistan, North Korea, Iran, Israel, and Egypt. New Delhi would have none of this. Seeing where Ramaker was headed, the government of India effectively withdrew from the negotiations, refused to contribute facilities to the treaty's International Monitoring System, and sought to prevent the transmission of the treaty text to the United Nations, where it could be voted upon. Pakistan was pleased to use India as its heat shield, while supporting the treaty's transmission to the United Nations.[63]

As with the Nonproliferation Treaty in 1968, the Comprehensive Test Ban Treaty needed to be conveyed from Geneva to the UN General Assembly in the absence of a consensus. The governments of Belgium and Australia used creative procedural devices to do so. The vote at the UN in support of the treaty was 158 to 3, with India, Libya, and Bhutan voting nay. Bill Clinton was the first leader to sign the treaty, calling it the longest-sought and hardest-fought prize of nuclear arms control.[64]

NORTH KOREA'S PROLIFERATION CHALLENGE

The North Korean and Iranian nuclear programs have posed the hardest proliferation challenges facing every administration since the toppling of Saddam Hussein. No president has had the bandwidth to tackle both intensively. Clinton focused on North Korea because circumstances gave him little choice, given Pyongyang's ongoing bomb and missile programs. With the help of William Perry, Clinton achieved partial successes, stopping Pyongyang's plutonium pathway to the Bomb while suspending its flight testing of missiles that could carry nuclear weapons. These partial successes would subsequently be nullified after the George W. Bush administration discovered that North Korea was seeking a second pathway to the Bomb using highly enriched uranium.

In 1993, Pyongyang announced its intent to withdraw from the Nonproliferation Treaty and blocked inspections by the International Atomic Energy

Agency. There was ample evidence that North Korea's leader, Kim Jong Il, was pursuing steps necessary to acquire nuclear weapons. In the absence of successful diplomacy, Clinton had two choices—allowing proliferation or taking military action and risking a wider war to prevent it. Perry character- ized this stark choice as between "a disaster and a catastrophe."[65]

Perry issued a public warning that the United States would not permit North Korea to reprocess plutonium and authorized planning for surgical cruise missile strikes at the reprocessing facility at Yongbyon.[66] After an opening provided by a distinguished private citizen prone to freelancing, Jimmy Carter, a U.S. negotiating team led by Robert Gallucci of the State Department succeeded in negotiating an "Agreed Framework" in 1994. The agreement stopped North Korean construction of two nuclear power plants that could have produced plutonium and suspended all reprocessing activ- ity at the sole facility then able to do so. Japan and South Korea agreed to build two proliferation-resistant nuclear power plants to generate electric- ity, and Washington agreed to provide fuel oil to compensate Pyongyang for shutting down the one reactor in operation from which plutonium could be reprocessed.[67]

The Agreed Framework was another first-term success. For a president disinterested in pursuing Cold War–style arms control, Bill Clinton found more than enough to do during his first term on post–Cold War agenda items. He and his team succeeded in consolidating gains, particularly with the implementation of the first Strategic Arms Reduction Treaty after secur- ing the denuclearization of Ukraine and Kazakhstan. Great strides were ac- complished on cooperative threat reduction programs under the leadership of the Pentagon and the Department of Energy. The indefinite extension of the Nonproliferation Treaty provided much needed stability to the global nuclear order. Clinton ended his first term on a high note, completing nego- tiations on the CTBT. He extended the period of arms control's apogee for four more years. The next four would be different.

DEMISE

Chapter 13

STALLING OUT

During Clinton's second term, the most important arms control agenda item inherited from George H.W. Bush was the second Strategic Arms Reduction Treaty, completed just before Clinton's inauguration. START II mandated another 50 percent reduction in deployed forces and, most importantly, prohibited land-based missiles carrying MIRVs. The treaty's ratification and entry into force eluded him. He belatedly sought to improve upon START II's provisions, but to no avail. With revived interest on Capitol Hill in ballistic missile defense programs, and with the Kremlin's habitual impulse to link offensive reductions with constraints on defenses, the START process began to stall out in Clinton's second term. Agreed parameters for regional, or theater, missile defenses against outliers were needed while holding the line against national missile defenses; otherwise, maintaining the Anti-Ballistic Missile treaty and pursuing deeper strategic arms reductions would both be at risk. Clinton's negotiating team succeeded in devising these guidelines, but he lacked partners to implement this agreement. Yeltsin was a spent force during his second term and Republicans in Congress were not inclined to accept limits on defenses of any kind.

NATO EXPANSION

There was another reason for the stalling out of arms control: NATO expansion. No decision by the Clinton administration was more consequential for the future of U.S.-Russian relations, but not at the outset because Russia was in such a weakened state. Clinton's decision to open the doors of NATO to Poland, Hungary, and the Czech Republic was a feel-good exercise, one that made sense both on moral grounds and as a matter of national interest to prevent a vacuum forming in Central and Eastern Europe. Clinton and Perry worked hard to foster cooperative ties between NATO and Russia even while proceeding with NATO expansion. They were even making progress in working with Moscow to stop Serbian bloodletting. One of Talbott's nightmare scenarios—a ground war in the former Yugoslavia—was avoided.[1]

Team Clinton debated the extent of the first tranche of NATO expansion and decided to proceed cautiously. The administration considered economic, diplomatic, and military ties with former Warsaw Pact and newly independent states short of binding alliance memberships, but this "Partnership for Peace" approach was judged to be insufficient and impractical. Aspirants didn't want an alternative to NATO; they wanted a stepping-stone. NATO expansion was a hard "yes" or "no" decision, as Strobe Talbott reflected. "There was no wishy-washy in between."[2] Unless these states were anchored in NATO, Vladimir Putin's disruptive opportunities would be endless. Besides, extending NATO in a limited way didn't present a dilemma for strategic arms control, since Clinton inherited two Strategic Arms Reduction treaties. The Clinton administration's clear intent was to pursue both a freedom agenda and to pocket gains achieved by Bush, Scowcroft, and Baker.

A freedom agenda spoke to America's basic principles; there was nothing about arms control in America's founding documents. Freedom spoke to the heart and facilitated the crossing of political divides. Arms control spoke to the head and was politically contentious. The Bush administration made unprecedented gains in nuclear arms reductions; now the opportunity was at hand to make unprecedented gains in expanding freedom and democracy under the protective umbrella of a military alliance. Talbott believed that NATO expansion "was the right thing to do. The challenge was how to do it right."[3] On this, Perry and Talbott could agree, but Perry wanted to wait. "Timing was all," he argued.[4] He thought NATO expansion in Clinton's second term to be a grave mistake. "We had the opportunity in the 1990s to build a long-lasting cooperative relationship with Russia," he wrote, and "premature" NATO expansion ruined it.[5] Perry made his case and was overruled.

Most leaders in both political parties supported an enlarged NATO, as important domestic constituencies were strongly in favor. For liberal Democrats, NATO expansion was equivalent to expanding and securing freedom eastward; for conservative Republicans, it was all that and more. Washington was securing the gains of geopolitical victory, as well. As Perry characterized this view, "We won the Cold War—get over it."[6] NATO had already expanded once during the George H.W. Bush administration: when Germany became whole, the alliance's eastern border shifted to Poland and the Czech Republic. The issue at hand was whether this was a special circumstance—a fix that would keep a denuclearized, united Germany haltered to the West—or a precedent.

At a February 9, 1990 meeting in Moscow, Secretary of State James Baker assured Mikhail Gorbachev and Eduard Shevardnadze that there would be no extension of NATO's jurisdiction beyond a united Germany for NATO forces "one inch to the east." Baker's handwritten notes of the meeting were as follows: "End result: Unified Ger. Anchored in a *changed (polit.) NATO—whose juris. would not move eastward!" Gorbachev's account of this meeting is similar, with Baker offering two choices: "a united Germany outside of NATO and completely autonomous, without American forces stationed on its territory, or a united Germany that maintains its ties with NATO, but with the guarantee that NATO jurisdiction or troops would not extend east of the current line."[7] Baker's assurance to Gorbachev was short-lived. After he returned to Washington, his colleagues said nothing more about limiting NATO expansion. Moreover, Gorbachev conceded an important point to Bush during their summit in Washington on May 31, 1990—that the Helsinki Accords gave every country the right to choose its own alliances.[8]

Historians, academics, and pundits had long offered cautions about expanding alliances. One Cold War alliance to contain the Soviet Union—the 1954 Southeast Asian Treaty Organization consisting of the United States, France, Great Britain, New Zealand, Australia, the Philippines, Thailand, and Pakistan—had no coherence and no future. Walter Lippmann warned, "An alliance is like a chain. It is not made stronger by adding weak links to it."[9] A.J.P. Taylor, reflecting on the rubble created by warfare between contesting alliances, wrote, "Alliances are worthwhile when they put into words a real community of interests; otherwise they lead only to confusion and disaster."[10] No less a stalwart in the Cold War competition than Henry Kissinger wrote in *Nuclear Weapons and Foreign Policy*, "An alliance is effective . . . only to the extent that it reflects a common purpose and that it represents an accretion of strength to its members."[11] Richard Betts cautioned that "no alliance lasts forever; it can only hope to outlive the threat that inspired it."[12]

These historical references to alliance building had little resonance in 1993, when upbeat appraisals suggested no reason to believe that expansion would pose problems with alliance management, with Russia, or with arms control. NATO was nothing like SEATO. It was a coherent alliance with a strong sense of common purpose containing Soviet power and offsetting the Warsaw Pact. In 1993, the question uppermost in the minds of many strategic thinkers was whether NATO could continue to maintain coherence in a vastly changed European landscape or whether it needed to expand in order to secure tentative democratic gains, thereby giving the alliance a new sense of strategic purpose. Modest expansion followed by due process were the Clinton administration's guidelines. These calculations would be upended by the 2000 election. George W. Bush's election by a one-vote margin of the Supreme Court was accompanied by his decision to push hard and fast to expand NATO membership.

The prophetic voice and most important dissident against NATO expansion was George Kennan. The sage of Princeton, the architect of the policy of containment who predicted the eventual collapse of Soviet power, was now warning that "expanding NATO would be the most fateful error of American policy in the post-cold-war era." It would "inflame the existing nationalistic, anti-western and militaristic tendencies in Russian opinion, restore the atmosphere of the cold war to East-West relations, and impel Russian foreign policy in directions decidedly not to our liking."[13] Kennan was right that containment would eventually lead to the dissolution of the Soviet Union, and he was again prescient about Moscow's reaction to NATO enlargement.

No one in the Clinton administration took Kennan's warnings more seriously than Strobe Talbott. Kennan was to Talbott as Kennedy was to Clinton: an iconic, revered figure.[14] Talbott didn't agree with Kennan, however: "There were new threats to the peace of Europe and dealing with them required military muscle of a kind that only the alliance possessed." The immediate threat was in the Balkans, where Serbian nationalists were engaged in ethnic cleansing. NATO had smoothed out political relations among its member states, and it could continue to function in this way as it expanded. Talbott believed that "Pan-European integration depended both on the Central Europeans joining the major structures of the West, including NATO, and on Russia remaining on a reformist track internally and with its foreign and defense policies."[15] This was a daunting agenda, since the logic of NATO expansion had no obvious end state but almost certainly would provoke a Russian reaction.

Clinton's instincts strongly supported NATO expansion. Secretary of State Christopher wanted to seize the opportunity "to integrate and unify" Europe. Christopher was convinced as early as mid-1993 of an "urgent" need to provide NATO with a new sense of purpose, and that purpose was to help spread democracy and democratic institutions throughout Europe. Expansion would preserve and reinvigorate the alliance.[16] The strongest advocate of NATO expansion in the State Department was Richard Holbrooke, who was the most deeply invested in applying a tourniquet to the bloodshed in the Balkans. Madeleine Albright, the U.S. ambassador to the United Nations during Clinton's first term, whose family left Czechoslovakia behind as the Iron Curtain descended on Eastern Europe, viewed NATO expansion as instrumental "to build a Europe whole and free."[17] When she became secretary of state in Clinton's second term, democracy promotion was her central theme.[18]

The potential consequences for arms control did not figure prominently in arguments over NATO expansion because Bush had accomplished so much with Yeltsin and because Yeltsin had no leverage and no veto power. From Perry's perspective, Clinton and his advisers "put little to no weight at all to the Russian view."[19] It would take many years for Russia to push back strenuously, and if it did, that would only confirm the wisdom of extending alliance ties eastward.

A confident administration with impeccable national security credentials like that of George H.W. Bush might have resisted wholesale NATO expansion. One indicator was that Brent Scowcroft joined with other cautionary voices when the Senate was contemplating the first tranche of NATO expansion.[20] Another indicator was Robert Gates's musings in an oral interview. "At the end of the day," he reflected, the Bush administration would have "kept our focus on our priorities"—Russia and China. At a time of a great humiliation and difficulty for Russia, pressing ahead with expansion of NATO eastward, "when Gorbachev and others were led to believe that wouldn't happen, at least in no time soon . . . probably has not only aggravated the relationship between the United States and Russia but made it much more difficult to do constructive business with them." In lieu of NATO expansion, Gates believed the Bush administration would have tried to find "some kind of bridge, or holding action that wouldn't be satisfactory to the East Europeans, but it would have given them a little something, but not full membership in NATO."[21]

We can only conjecture, since George H.W. Bush, had he been reelected, might well have yielded to political pressures on NATO expansion. The incoming Clinton team started from a very different place. All but one senior official around Clinton was convinced that NATO expansion was a wise and a necessary thing to do. The outlier was Perry. No stranger to bureaucratic maneuver, Perry knew that he couldn't beat something with nothing. His alternative, the Partnership for Peace, would be an "auxiliary" to NATO. The inspiration behind this concept came from Joseph Kruzel, a talented Pentagon official who died tragically when the armored personnel carrier he was riding in crashed in route to Sarajevo. Under the Partnership for Peace, newly independent and former Warsaw Pact states could participate in NATO meetings and committees (without voting rights), attend courses with NATO officers, and conduct joint training with NATO on peacekeeping exercises. This concept showed promise. Its high point was in Bosnia in late 1995, where no less than thirty NATO and "partner" states joined in a peace-keeping mission after gruesome attacks by Serbs against Bosnian Muslims in Sarajevo and Srebrenica. Perry even persuaded Russian defense minister Pavel Grachev to contribute a paratroop brigade under convoluted command and control arrangements.

The Partnership for Peace concept of cooperation without alliance ties was a sound idea but it wasn't politically sustainable at home or abroad. Even its strongest backers, Perry and the chairman of the Joint Chiefs of Staff, John Shalikashvili, argued that membership in good standing in the Partnership for Peace would not be an end in itself, but part of a progression toward eventual NATO membership. They were seeking to buy time, to make members of the Partnership for Peace wait longer for NATO membership, thereby making the concept more digestible to the Kremlin. NATO expansion might be postponed for a decade, in Perry's talking points. This was an untenable position, and he knew it. Newly independent states and those belonging to the defunct Warsaw Pact badly wanted the security that NATO could provide.

Perry persisted and was given the courtesy of a National Security Council meeting on December 21, 1994, to express his reservations. He argued that "a stampede by Eastern European nations to join NATO could remove the opportunity to cooperate with Russia to reduce the threat from nuclear weapons."[22] He was "amazed" at what transpired next. There was no back-and-forth. Neither Christopher nor Lake said a word; Gore was tapped to offer a rebuttal.[23] The fix was in. NATO expansion was never a matter of whether, but when, and how far eastward to push at the outset.

Elite debate over NATO expansion was vigorous. Henry Kissinger called attention to a reality that European allegiances were up for grabs. "Basing European and Atlantic security on a no-man's-land between Germany and Russia runs counter to historical experience." He found Clinton's approach too "ambivalent," and his needle threading with Russia "especially confusing."[24] Zbigniew Brzezinski, like Albright, the beneficiary of a protective parental decision to leave Eastern Europe behind and make a new life across the Atlantic, supported NATO expansion as a creative device for "enlarging democratic Europe" and reinforcing "the practices of peace." Brzezinski and Lake pushed back against Kissinger's concerns of possible Russian meddling via a joint NATO-Russia consultative mechanism. "An expanded alliance," they wrote, "provides a hedge against the unlikely but real possibility that Russia will revert to past behavior. It must also contribute to the goal of preventing that from happening. Integrating Russia into the evolving European security structure advances that goal."[25]

The most prescient and powerful arguments against rushing to expand NATO were offered by former Senate majority leader Howard Baker, newly retired senator Sam Nunn, Scowcroft, and Alton Frye. They worried most about the "contradiction between open-ended NATO expansion and our gravest security priority, mastering the threat of weapons of mass destruction. That task begins with controlling the vast strategic arsenal still present in Russia." They also noted and worried about "early signs of a marriage of convenience between China and Russia," signs that would only grow as NATO headed eastward. The Senate would be wise not to rush to judgment on NATO expansion; otherwise, it "may condemn a vital alliance to the creeping impotence of excessive commitments and clogged decision-making."[26]

Arms Control Association board chairman Stanley Resor gathered fifty prominent individuals to send a bipartisan letter to the White House, arguing that the push for NATO expansion was "a policy error of historic proportions." Co-signers included Raymond Garthoff, Morton Halperin, Fred Iklé, Michael Mandelbaum, Jack Matlock, Robert McNamara, Paul Nitze, Nunn, Richard Pipes, and Paul Warnke.[27] The editorial page writers of *Arms Control Today*, Spurgeon Keeny and Jack Mendelsohn, two former arms control officials, also weighed in against NATO expansion.[28]

Holbrooke wanted the Baltic states to be included in the first tranche, but Perry strongly resisted, and this was beyond what Clinton and Talbott could accept. The first tranche couldn't be too big or too small. Three nations were just right. The Senate voted on May 1, 1998, to approve membership for Hungary, Poland, and the Czech Republic by a vote of 80–19. Republican senator John Warner offered an amendment for a three-year "cooling off" period before considering another tranche. It was defeated by a vote of 59–41. The first tranche of new NATO members was distant from Russia's border. As Clinton promised Yeltsin, this vote was delayed until their second terms. Yeltsin had earlier sought a private commitment from Clinton not to extend membership to republics of the former Soviet Union—a pledge Clinton couldn't possibly make. Clinton and Gore then turned to the business of mollifying Yeltsin and creating a useful mechanism of engagement between NATO and the Russian Federation.

Once NATO was open for new membership and criteria had been established for entry, it was easier to expand than to stop expansion. Clinton's assurance to Yeltsin—that "NATO's governing mission was no longer directed against Russia but against the new threats to peace and stability in Europe"—never gained credibility in the Kremlin or in Russian domestic politics and would soon ring hollow when the floodgates opened in the Bush administration.[29] Deliberations over NATO enlargement were emblematic of the way decisions were made in the Clinton administration. Great care was given to managing consequences and dealing with contending priorities. Smart, experienced officials tried to weave through complex force fields, using rational and empathetic powers of analysis. Clinton welcomed the creation of a new Europe without Cold War divisions—how could he not?

Leon Fuerth, a Foreign Service officer who went to work for congressman and later senator Gore, remaining by his side throughout the Clinton administration, viewed NATO expansion as "a conscious, knowing effort to capitalize on a once in a millennium opportunity." The opportunity came with risks, and Clinton administration officials were aware of them. Would being in an indefensible location for a conventional military defense constitute a barrier to entry? If a state gained entry and reverted to authoritarian tendencies, could alliance members protect democratic norms? These were exceedingly hard questions, but they seemed distant. Fuerth ruefully mused, "It would have been up to the Gore administration to make it work."[30]

ACDA'S DEMISE

Thomas Graham's cunning and persistence managed to extend ACDA's lifespan at the outset of the Clinton administration, but the reprieve was temporary. Senator Jesse Helms, the Republican chairman of the Foreign Relations

Committee, a reliable foe of the agency and its favored pursuits, controlled his committee's calendar. And if the Clinton White House wanted floor votes on the Chemical Weapons Convention, which Helms strenuously opposed, Clinton would have to agree to fold the agency and what was left of its autonomy into the State Department.

Third-tier officials at the State Department had taken a run at absorbing ACDA in 1993 and were told to stand down by Christopher. ACDA was instrumental in putting into practice the novel conceptualization of arms control. It was at the forefront of constraints on nuclear testing and championed the negotiation of the Nonproliferation Treaty over the State Department's misgivings. ACDA was in the trenches of negotiating the 1972 SALT accords and every other accomplishment during the rise of arms control.

ACDA negotiators and employees made many enemies along the way, none more powerful that Richard Nixon and Senator Henry "Scoop" Jackson. Their purge of ACDA's senior ranks after the 1972 SALT accords ran deep. There were premature retirements and odd career postings for civil servants too much in favor of treaty making. Success was always an uphill battle. It was challenging to represent the smallest and least well-endowed government agency in bureaucratic deliberations. There was a constant brain drain from ACDA to more powerful agencies where career opportunities were greater. These losses—including Victor Alessi, Robert Einhorn, Robert Gallucci, James Goodby, Edward Ifft, and James Timbie—were not recouped.

After the halcyon years under Directors William Foster and Gerard Smith, the agency was depleted and hemorrhaging talent. Republican administrations added treaty skeptics to the agency's ranks. Democratic congressional majorities made it easier to hire new talent after Jimmy Carter's election, but the boost was provisional; when Ronald Reagan was elected, another purge followed. ADCA was well led by William F. Burns and Ronald Lehman during the transition from Reagan to Bush, but it wasn't rejuvenated. The agency was at a crossroads by the time Clinton was elected after three successive Republican terms. Confirmations of Democratic nominees were always going to be contentious under Senator Helms's gavel. The choices facing Clinton's transition team for ACDA, led by Rose Gottemoeller with Robert Bell, Dan Caldwell, and Laura Holgate, were obvious: to reinvigorate the agency or, if this proved too onerous, to fold it into the State Department. Clinton never made a command decision; his administration temporized, and eventually folded.

Three studies on the subject were awaiting the Clinton administration. One advisory body, assembled under the auspices of the Carnegie Endowment and the Institute for International Economics, was dominated by State Department officials. This who's who of veteran diplomats was chaired by Richard Holbrooke, and included Madeleine Albright and Peter Tarnoff, who would become Warren Cristopher's third-ranking official. In their "Memorandum to the President-Elect," they recommended abolishing ACDA and folding its residual functions into the State Department. As an indicator of how low ACDA's stature had fallen, one of the signatories was Morton Halperin, who helped launch the arms control movement.[31]

A second study was carried out under the auspices of the State Department's inspector general, and was led by James Goodby, who appears first in these pages at the 1958 Surprise Attack Conference and periodically thereafter. This study endorsed "a specialized, technically competent, and independent arms control institution." It recommended retaining a separate, but reorganized, refocused, and rejuvenated ACDA.[32] The third study was by the Stimson Center. Written by this author, Amy Smithson, and James Schear, it detailed the ways in which ACDA's role and skill sets had been diminished. Benefitting from inputs of previous ACDA directors, the Stimson report proposed fourteen steps to rejuvenate ACDA around the core mission of nonproliferation. If the choice was incorporation instead of rejuvenation, the Stimson report stressed the need for safeguards to protect arms control from being muted in pursuit of the State Department's other, competing priorities.[33]

Clinton's transition team recommended ACDA's rejuvenation, but found no sense of urgency to do this. Months passed without nominees for the directorship and other senior appointments. Clinton's attention was elsewhere. After Christopher heeded Muriel Humphry's advice to keep ACDA alive, the administration nominated John Holum to become the new director in October 1993. Holum was confirmed just before Thanksgiving. A whole year was lost, and the rejuvenation agenda became a dead letter. When Helms demanded that ACDA be folded into the State Department as the price for Senate votes on the Chemical Weapons Convention, Clinton conceded. To lessen the immediate consequences, Holum was appointed as the State Department's under secretary for arms control when the merger took place on April Fools' Day, 1999.

THE CHEMICAL WEAPONS CONVENTION
The Senate's consent to ratify the Chemical Weapons Convention seemed to be a no-brainer. Negotiations began in the Reagan administration, with Vice

President Bush playing a leading role. Negotiations over the convention were completed just before Clinton was elected. The Congress had already mandated the destruction of the U.S. stockpile in 1985; the convention would leverage others to meet this standard and would mark possessors as outliers. It included intrusive verification provisions and challenge inspections.

On top of this, the U.S. chemical industry offered strong support, even with the prospect of foreign inspectors. Industry was already subject to environmental inspections, so dealing with foreigners also seemed manageable, as long as there were provisions to protect trade secrets. The Chemical Manufacturers Association was strongly supportive; its representatives, led by Will Carpenter of Monsanto and Leo Zeftel of Dow Chemical, walked Senate corridors. In a previous dark chapter of the U.S. chemical industry, its leaders opposed the 1925 Geneva Protocol banning the use of poisonous and asphyxiating gasses in warfare; Senate passage took no less than fifty years. This time around, major chemical manufacturers wanted to make amends.

The best time for Clinton to seek the Senate's consent for ratification was soon after taking office, but he had no sense of urgency to do so, and ACDA, the lead prodder for such matters, was in limbo. The longer Clinton waited, the more the convention would belong to him rather than Reagan and Bush. He waited four years. Opponents used the Senate debate as a test bed to develop their tactics. The opposing group of senators and staffers were a minority within the Republican Party when Clinton took office, but their ranks grew as moderate internationalist Republicans retired or lost primary challenges. Their floor leader was Jon Kyl, a tenacious, smart lawyer and lobbyist who rose through the ranks of Arizona politics to become a force in the Senate. Helms, courtly and old-school, was another leading naysayer.[34]

Without the support of the Republican leader, a Democratic president faces long odds in seeking treaty ratification. (The exception was President Barack Obama, who would secure the Senate's consent to ratify New START with four votes to spare without the support of Republican leader Mitch McConnell.) A precondition for success is bringing Republican senators on board early on. As these numbers grow, the calculations of the Republican leader can shift, overriding the inclination to oppose a democratic President in deference to not sharpening the divide within Republican ranks.[35]

Washington politics had not yet become a partisan battleground when the Chemical Weapons Convention was debated. The old-fashioned treaty ratification process—exemplified by the give-and-take between President John F. Kennedy and Republican minority leader Everett McKinley Dirksen on the

1963 Limited Test Ban Treaty—was a gentlemanly game of checkers. (The Senate was very much a male club in Clinton's first term, as there were only seven women in the Senate; there were nine in his second.) Kennedy and his team had to move only a few pieces before the board took shape. Senators could gather afterward to drink bourbon whether they voted "yay" or "nay."

The informal, friendly rules of treaty ratification changed after the Chemical Weapons Convention, as partisan divisions sharpened. The tactics employed by opponents of the CWC were more like a multilevel chess game than a game of checkers. Nongovernmental organizations supported by staunchly conservative funders, led by Frank Gaffney's Center for Security Policy and the Heritage Foundation, flooded Republican offices on Capitol Hill with strained arguments and occasional outright falsehoods against the convention. Administration officials, with Robert Bell at the National Security Council Staff in the lead, supported by Terri Lodge, Lori Esposito Murray, Elisa Harris, and others, were engaged in trench warfare, with wave after wave of concerns and the resurfacing of seemingly settled issues. After finishing negotiations with one small group of Republicans, issues would be relitigated by others.

This work was exhausting, and it was meant to be exhausting. Opponents ran administration officials ragged for a purpose: There was another, higher-stakes ratification debate on the horizon over the Comprehensive Test Ban Treaty. The test bed of the CWC ratification produced the playbook that treaty opponents would then employ against the test ban and against future Democratic presidents. SALT II ratification in the Carter administration was difficult because critics had strong arguments against ratification and because the Kremlin was behaving badly. The CWC was difficult even though the arguments against ratification were weak and the Russian Federation was prostrate.

Ratification wasn't a top priority issue for the State Department, even though it seemed to promise a quick victory. Treaty ratification was ACDA's job, but ACDA was hollowed out. Without top-down insistence, it took the administration's lawyers ten long months to prepare the article-by-article official interpretation of the convention's obligations. The necessary paperwork was finally submitted to the Senate Foreign Relations Committee one day after Holum was confirmed as ACDA director in late November 1993.

Several issues, especially the use of riot control agents, needed to be handled with extreme care, as it was a make or break issue for John McCain—an influential Republican senator on the Armed Services Committee who, as a navy fighter pilot, was shot down and held prisoner in North Vietnam. The convention prohibited the use of riot control agents "as a method of warfare," but McCain and others insisted that their use in hostage rescue operations for downed airmen and others be permitted. Once satisfied on this issue, McCain became a strong supporter.

The long delay in taking up the CWC proved especially costly after Republicans took control of the Senate in the 1994 midterm elections. Senator Helms replaced the mild-mannered, supportive Claiborne Pell as Foreign Relations Committee chairman. Helms was a throwback; the last Republican chairman to hold such strong views against foreign entanglements and treaty making was William Borah of Idaho, who crusaded against U.S. participation in the League of Nations.

After the 1994 midterms, Republican opposition to Clinton hardened. Newt Gingrich was elected Speaker of the House by the new Republican majority. No shrinking violet, Gingrich changed the norms of discourse on Capitol Hill.[36] In the Senate, Republican majority leader Robert Dole, a decorated World War II infantryman, had resigned to run against Clinton in 1996. His place was taken by Trent Lott. Every Republican leader tries to foster a mostly united front during treaty ratification debates, but this proved impossible for Lott with the CWC, as his own caucus was almost evenly divided. The Republican chairmen of the Armed Services (Strom Thurmond) and Intelligence Committees (Richard Shelby), as well as Helms, were all strongly opposed.

The Clinton administration tried to secure the Senate's consent to the CWC in 1996, with Richard Lugar of Indiana and other moderate Republicans joining Democrats to pass a resolution out of the Foreign Relations Committee, circumventing Helms's "poison pill" conditions that would have effectively nullified U.S. obligations. This opening was short-lived, however, as key figures from the Reagan and Bush administrations came out strongly against the convention, including Dick Cheney, Jeane Kirkpatrick, and Caspar Weinberger. They were joined by influential columnists George Will and Charles Krauthammer.

These naysayers succeeded in setting the terms of debate. On top of this, Republican presidential candidate Dole appeared intent not to hand Clinton a legislative victory. He sent a letter to Lott warning against "illusory" arms control agreements and urged Senate delay until U.S. adversaries had ratified the treaty and the U.S. intelligence community could assure its ability to detect even slight violations. Two days before the scheduled vote, the White

House acknowledged it didn't have the two-thirds majority it needed for ratification. Secretary Christopher called Lott and asked that further consideration of the convention be suspended.

Soon after the Clinton administration's climb-down, a hard deadline for the Senate's consent to ratification locked into place. Under the terms of the convention, its entry into force would occur 180 days after the sixty-fifth country deposited its instrument of ratification. On October 31, 1996, Hungary became the sixty-fifth country. Its able diplomat, Tibor Toth, privately approached ACDA deputy director Ralph Earle, asking whether his country should start this clock by finishing up ratification proceedings. Toth was advised to go ahead. Earle knew that if it wasn't Hungary, it would be some other country, and Washington couldn't be making the rounds asking everyone to delay ratification. Under the terms of the convention, if the United States failed to deposit its instrument of ratification by the end of April 1997, it would have been penalized by losing its seat on the convention's implementing body, U.S. nationals would be unable to serve on its Secretariat, and U.S. chemical firms would have been penalized in international commerce. Clinton needed to prepare another assault on Helms's castle.

After Clinton's reelection in November 1996, the CWC was to be his first priority. Clinton was now assisted by Madeleine Albright, who replaced Warren Christopher at the State Department; William Cohen, who took the baton from William Perry at the Pentagon; and Sandy Berger, who moved up as Anthony Lake's deputy to become national security advisor. The most important change of status, however, was that of Robert Dole. Having lost his bid for the presidency, Dole was ready to assume a senior statesman role, as the administration's luck would have it.

After the election, Bell, the National Security Council staffer charged with treaty ratification, resumed hard bargaining with Senator Helms's assistant, Marshall Billingslea. Bell created a binder with forty tabs for the concerns that Billingslea conveyed; after a few months, the binder was almost too unwieldy to lift. But Bell and his colleagues succeeded in coming up with language resolving all but five concerns. These five issues would need to be voted up or down, since their acceptance would effectively kill U.S. involvement. One Helms condition would prevent the United States from becoming a party until China, Iraq, Iran, Libya, North Korea, Syria, and all countries designated by the State Department as state sponsors of international terrorism had ratified the treaty. A second condition would prevent the convention from taking effect until Russia ratified. A third Helms condition called for the renegotiation of two articles of the convention dealing with providing assistance to other state parties so as not to unwittingly abet proliferation. The fourth Helms "killer" amendment barred ratification until the president certified the ability of the intelligence community to detect, with a high degree of confidence, any violation involving as little as one ton of chemical agent. Helms's fifth amendment dealt with rejecting inspectors from countries designated as state sponsors of terrorism—even though the convention allowed member states to reject individual inspectors from approved lists.

Clinton needed a hard deadline and he finally had one. Like the gifted student who waited until the night before to cram for a final exam, he was now pulling levers and working the phones furiously. As much as the deadline focused Clinton, it also empowered opponents of arms control, providing Helms with the leverage he needed to kill ACDA. That was his price of allowing floor votes when negotiating with Joseph Biden, the ranking Democrat on the Foreign Relations Committee. Acting as Clinton's proxy, Biden had no other option but to pay it.

Once again nongovernmental organizations joined the fight over Senate ratification. The Stimson Center served as coordinator for those in support, with John Parachini acting as convener. Stimson's Amy Smithson served as a liaison to the chemical industry, helping with office visits in the Senate. The second time around, the Clinton administration was better at clarifying the convention's lineage to the Reagan and Bush administrations. At a pep rally held on the South Lawn on April 4, Clinton was joined by James Baker and Colin Powell. Baker didn't mince words. "Frankly," he said, "the suggestion that George Bush and Ronald Reagan would negotiate a treaty detrimental to this nation's security is outrageous."[37]

Helms countered the pep rally with hearings. Among those testifying against ratification were three former secretaries of defense—Caspar Weinberger, James Schlesinger, and Donald Rumsfeld. They argued that the treaty would expose U.S. chemical companies to burdensome international inspections, while doing little to affect the actions of pariah states. Clinton expressed "surprise" at this opposition, since active duty and retired military leaders, as well as chemical industry representatives, strongly supported the convention.[38]

The resolution of ratification reflected arduous negotiations between Helms and Biden, Lott and Burger, and Bell and Billingslea. It contained no less than thirty-three conditions and understandings, five of which were Helms's killer amendments. The White House called attention to the twenty-eight conditions on which common ground could be found. Opponents girded for battle over the remaining five. At this point, the White House's "whip count" was still thirteen votes shy of the two-thirds majority needed for ratification.

Then a stroke of luck helped tip the scales. A Republican senator from Utah told Energy Secretary Bill Richardson that he had just met with Dole, who had mentioned that he had been favorably impressed by an appearance by Bell on an April 16 C-SPAN call-in show. Berger, grasping at this news like the proverbial limb overhanging a pit of quicksand, called Dole to offer a private briefing by Bell. Dole agreed, and on Sunday, April 20, Bell walked Dole through the agreed conditions, addressing the concerns Dole had raised in his letter to Senator Lott that resulted in the convention's shelving six months earlier. After the briefing, the former majority leader said, "That sounds convincing to me."[39]

Clinton needed another big event after Helms's hearings. The White House had convened a joint press conference by Madeleine Albright and William Cohen advocating ratification, but Albright and Cohen would not swing any undecided Republican senators. A headliner was needed for the White House's final appeal on April 23. Berger asked Bell to call Dole and try to persuade him to attend. Bell asked, "You mean an hour from now?" Berger replied, "Yes, we really need him." Bell was patched into Dole in his limousine, heading to an appointment. Bell said, "Senator Dole, the President would like very much for you to come to the White House right now and stand with him as he makes a final public appeal for the CWC. If you agree to attend, you will be the headliner. The President will introduce you, and you will speak first." Dole was silent for about fifteen seconds and then said, "Okay."[40]

About thirty minutes later, Dole stood next to President Clinton at the White House podium, urging his former Republican colleagues to vote for the convention. "Is it perfect? No," he said. "But I believe there are now adequate safeguards to protect American interests."[41] With Dole still at the podium, McCain came rushing into the Senate chamber to apprise Helms and Biden, who were engaged in preliminary and soporific sparring over ratification, to give them the news. Majority leader Lott was also taken by surprise.

Lott was now ready to get off the fence. The crucial meeting took place in Lott's office with Berger, Bell, and Lott's, aide, Randy Scheunemann, who previously served in a similar capacity for Dole. In Bell's recollection, "It was surprisingly low key and businesslike. Lott needed a final understanding to clinch the deal, which we viewed as doable and simply a matter of draftsmanship." The last remaining issue had to do with preventing "rogue" states from enhancing their chemical weapon capabilities through CWC-approved trade. Bell and Scheunemann worked up the language and Clinton signed the promissory note.[42]

On April 24, five days before the convention's entry into force, the roll was called. Senator Lott announced that he would support ratification on the grounds that "the United States is marginally better off with it than without it."[43] Taking cues from the former and current Republican leaders, senators who were on the fence got off and voted "aye." All of Helms's five killer amendments were soundly defeated. The final margin was 74 in favor to 26 opposed—seven more than the required two-thirds majority. An exhausted and exhilarated Bell returned to the White House to savor the moment and to receive a heartfelt bear hug from Clinton, who was smoking a victory cigar.

ADAPTING THE ABM TREATY AND SEEKING DEEPER CUTS

The START II Treaty was signed in January 1993; the treaty set such favorable conditions that the Senate consented to its ratification on January 26, 1996, by a vote of 86–4. This was, in effect, Dick Cheney's treaty. He had approved its 50 percent reductions from the preceding agreement after scrubbing targeting requirements and after the Warsaw Pact's dissolution. His trade-off for deeper cuts was the elimination of Russian land-based missiles carrying multiple warheads. An era of strategic stability beckoned.

The problem was that Boris Yeltsin couldn't or wouldn't seek to convince the Duma to ratify START II. And as long as the Duma wouldn't budge, the benefits of START II would remain, in Strobe Talbott's characterization, "in a hiatus." This hiatus lasted the entirety of the Clinton administration.[44] Only in 1997, with the prospect of having no strategic arms reduction treaty to call his own, did Clinton focus on deeper cuts and life-extending measures for the ABM Treaty. Conditions for deeper cuts were reasonably good during Clinton's second term, given the Pentagon's lethargic pursuit of national missile defenses, but Yeltsin either wasn't pressed hard enough on START II ratification, conditions were never ripe for Yeltsin to succeed, or Yeltsin never figured out what came easily to his successor, Vladimir Putin. Faced with an incoming administration bullish on national missile defense and intent on withdrawing from the Anti-Ballistic Missile Treaty, Putin would be able to convince the Duma to ratify START II with the condition that Russia would withdraw from its obligations if George W. Bush walked away from the ABM Treaty.

When Clinton took office, ballistic missile defense activity was mostly in remission. The George H.W. Bush administration had effectively grounded Reagan's Strategic Defense Initiative, choosing to secure instead deep cuts in Soviet and Russian force structure. At the same time, however, the Bush administration's negotiating positions in the Defense and Space Talks would have made the ABM Treaty a dead letter—proposals that there be no restrictions on sensors against missiles attacks, that the United States be permitted additional deployment of fixed, ground-based ABM defenses, and that treaty restrictions on development, testing, and transferring missile defense systems and components be eliminated. The Congress received a commitment in writing from the Clinton administration that it would abide by the "narrow" interpretation of the ABM Treaty, and Clinton dispensed with the Bush administration's negotiating positions.

The missile defense issue seemed like such a backwater in 1993 that the Clinton administration chose not to continue talks on cooperative approaches toward missile defenses begun between James Baker's aide, Dennis Ross, and Soviet deputy foreign minister Yuri Mamedov. This proved unwise, as the Clinton administration decided to address missile defense issues at a technical rather than a political level. The need of the hour was to distinguish between permissible "theater" ballistic missile defenses against outliers like North Korea while preserving the ABM Treaty's prohibition against nationwide defenses. A life extension of the ABM Treaty required demarcation between theater and national missile defenses, but this was no mere technical matter. Demarcation turned out to be the ABM Treaty's last stand.

Critics of the ABM Treaty were on high alert after Clinton and Yeltsin agreed that it remained a "cornerstone of strategic stability"—language that Clinton deemed necessary for Yeltsin's reluctant concession that the United States retained the right to test and deploy effective theater missile defenses. The forum to resolve demarcation issues would be the Standing Consultative Commission created to resolve compliance issues in the SALT I accords. The Clinton administration proposed a two-part agenda for talks. One task was to multi-lateralize the ABM Treaty, since some treaty-related capabilities—in this case, radars—now resided outside the borders of the Russian Federation. James Baker successfully multilateralized the first Strategic Arms Reduction Treaty by adding Ukraine, Kazakhstan, and Belarus because they inherited Soviet missiles; the Clinton administration decided to follow Baker's example.

The second and most important issue dealt with demarcating the performance parameters of acceptable theater missile defense interceptor missiles.

Moscow was open to addressing agreed parameters in stages—first for "low velocity" interceptor missiles suitable for use against outliers, followed by a subsequent agreement for higher-velocity interceptors. Two parameters were paramount: the speed of interceptor missiles and the speed of missiles they used for target practice. A theater missile defense system located close to the Korean Peninsula against rudimentary North Korean missiles did not need ultra-fast interceptor missiles, and these interceptors didn't need to be practiced against targets traveling at ocean-spanning speed. Moscow was unenthusiastic but willing to engage on demarcation, while Republicans on Capitol Hill were unalterably opposed to any constraints on capabilities. The deciding vote, in effect, was cast by North Korea. Once it mastered the technologies of longer-range and ocean-spanning missiles, theater missile defenses would remain necessary but insufficient. National defenses would also be needed.

Talks with Moscow began in 1993. The lead U.S. negotiator was ACDA's Stanley Riveles. Born in Plainfield, New Jersey, his father emigrated from Belarus as a teenager and became a pharmacist. His mother, born in Brooklyn, was a homemaker and a bookkeeper. His grandmother also came over steerage class. Yiddish was spoken at home. Riveles was a classic, overachieving immigrant's son. He went to Yale, played varsity football, and took Russian studies. Then came Cambridge University where he excelled at boxing, followed by a PhD at Columbia on the topic of the Prague spring. He took classes from heavyweight professors—Brzezinski, Seweryn Bialer, and Alexander Dallin. He joined ACDA in the Ford administration and began working on nuclear negotiations in the Reagan administration.

The ABM Treaty backstopped the remarkable achievements of the Reagan and Bush administrations, since the prospect of thick missile defenses would foil deep cuts. The treaty's life extension could therefore facilitate prospects for further reductions, but some in the arms control community viewed the treaty as sacrosanct, opposing demarcation as a slippery slope. Many deterrence strengtheners wanted to kill the ABM Treaty outright. As an expression of Republican opposition to any steps that would extend the ABM Treaty's life, Chairman Helms refused to consider bestowing the rank of ambassador upon Riveles. His delegation was divided about seeking a demarcation agreement, and he enjoyed only spotty high-level support.

The demarcation talks were brutally difficult and tedious. Nevertheless, Riveles and the Russian ambassador to the Standing Consultative Commission General Victor Koltunov made progress on numbers that would give meaning to a demarcation agreement. By early 1994, they reached agreement on the parameters for target missiles. They tuned next to the speed and range of "lower velocity" interceptor missiles. In 1996, they succeeded. The administration maintained that this lower-velocity agreement could be implemented without prejudice to higher-velocity theater missile interceptors then in the works, while stressing that the Pentagon would continue to make compliance judgments on its own programs. Republicans on Capitol Hill strongly disagreed with any negotiated constraints.

Clinton and Yeltsin met at a summit in Helsinki in March 1997 to belatedly tackle the offense-defense equation. Neither man was in great shape: Clinton was hobbled by knee surgery and Yeltsin was reappearing in public after another health scare. The demarcation agreement wasn't their topmost agenda item. This was the summit where Clinton told Yeltsin in no uncertain terms that NATO was expanding eastward, and where he rejected Yeltsin's pleadings that the Baltic states be excluded from future membership.[45]

Then Clinton turned to deal making on demarcation and deep cuts. Clinton used the Helsinki summit to try to break the impasse over the Duma's unwillingness to ratify START II. The administration added two sweeteners: Russia would be given a five-year extension to implement START II, and given the difficulties Moscow faced maintaining START II-sized forces, the United States proposed deeper cuts in a START III Treaty, one that would reduce deployed warheads to 2,000–2,500 from START II's limit of 3,500. The demarcation agreements and the proposal for deeper cuts would not be presented to the Senate for ratification unless and until the Duma consented to ratify START II.

At the presidential palace in Helsinki, Jan Lodal, the Pentagon's technical and policy expert, worked over his calculations and agreed to the terms of a demarcation agreement on faster theater missile defense interceptors with Yuri Mamedov. The two fast velocity interceptor programs then being advanced by the Pentagon could proceed unencumbered. Reaching agreement took less than twelve hours.[46] Clinton left Helsinki on an optimistic note, calling the summit "an unexpected success."[47] Yeltsin had acknowledged the reality on NATO expansion and agreed to a consultative mechanism with NATO; he had, after all, little choice. Agreement on demarcation seemed in hand, and creative ideas were advanced to move the Duma to accept and move beyond START II.

It took a few more months to nail down language for the ABM Treaty multi-lateralization and demarcation accords. On September 27, 1997, Secretary of State Albright and Foreign Minister Primakov were joined by the foreign ministers of Ukraine, Kazakhstan, and Belarus at the Waldorf Astoria Hotel in New York to sign an agreement multilateralizing the ABM Treaty. Riveles and Koltonov attended the ceremony and signed the demarcation accords. It was a sweet moment for Riveles. Despite the bureaucratic hurdles, he accomplished what he set out to do. His work could help maintain the viability of the ABM Treaty while clearing a wide lane for the deployment of theater missile defense.

Clinton and Yeltsin could make progress whenever they met, in part because Clinton was so adept at handling Yeltsin and in part because Yeltsin was a realist. Agreements in principle were all well and good; getting others to agree to them was another matter entirely. After the Helsinki summit, both men returned home to implacable resistance. Clinton found no takers among Republicans on Capitol Hill for his proposed adaptations to the ABM Treaty. The Duma still failed to see the wisdom of approving START II, a treaty that would take away MIRVed land-based missiles, Russia's most effective means of penetrating missile defenses, which Washington appeared intent to deploy. For good measure, Republican majorities on Capitol Hill passed legislation prohibiting deeper U.S. cuts unless and until the Duma ratified START II. To tie this Gordian knot even tighter, the Congress insisted, and the Clinton administration agreed, that the multilateralization and demarcation accords would be presented as ABM Treaty amendments requiring the Senate's consent—after the Duma consented to ratify START II.[48]

Clinton was effectively hemmed in. He had been dealing with brushfires over the ABM Treaty since the start of his presidency. These brushfires turned into firestorms after the 1994 midterm elections, as missile defense deployments figured prominently in the plans and platforms of triumphant Republicans. When North Korea provided the sharper sense of threat by flight testing longer-range missiles, the treaty's days were numbered.

Clinton aptly described national missile defenses as "a giant banana peel."[49] Just when the initial demarcation accords were in hand, they seemed insufficient with the extended range of North Korean missiles. A thin defense of the homeland would be impossible to square with the ABM Treaty. Polarization on Capitol Hill was growing, and the one issue on which there was bipartisan unity—NATO expansion—led to further strains on the treaty because of proposed deployment plans for theater missile defenses in Poland and the Czech Republic.

Republican majorities on Capitol Hill established a blue-ribbon commission led by Donald Rumsfeld to assess missile threats from all azimuths. The commission's composition was unusually broad, including hawkish strategists Paul Wolfowitz, William Graham, and William Schneider, as well as arms control–oriented analysts Barry Blechman and Richard Garwin. Two retired generals, Lee Butler and Larry Welch, provided additional gravitas. The commissioners issued their report in July 1998. Their technical assessment concluded that "the threat to the U.S. posed by these emerging capabilities is broader, more mature and evolving more rapidly than has been reported in estimates and reports by the Intelligence community." Furthermore, "The U.S. might well have little or no warning before operational deployment."[50] Then, placing an exclamation point on these findings, North Korea tried and failed to launch a satellite six weeks later. Thereafter, the ABM Treaty amendments on multilateralization and demarcation became dead letters in the Senate.

At this point, the Clinton administration had effectively lost the terms of public debate over missile defenses. Before leaving the Pentagon, Perry structured an economically and technically defensible ballistic missile defense deployment program. Perry's plan was overly optimistic, as Pentagon procurements moved at a frustratingly slow pace. His intent was, however, sensible. He sought to delay deployments until the threat materialized so as not to rush to deploy immature technology that would quickly need to be replaced at greater cost. Perry was right on the merits: It took North Korea nineteen years to launch an ocean-spanning missile after the failed satellite launch in 1998.

Republicans railed against Perry's plan as lacking urgency. Both the House and the Senate passed legislation by veto-proof majorities in 1999 mandating U.S. policy to "deploy as soon as technologically possible an effective" missile defense system "defending the territory of the United States." The ABM Treaty, as amended, allowed for the defense of a single missile field. To defend the entire territory of the United States against attack would require multiple amendments to the treaty, including radar installations at new locations—in Alaska, for a start—as well as additional interceptor missile bases on U.S. soil, at forward bases, and at sea. Missile defense advocates were also inclined to take another look at space-based defenses. Alternatively, the ABM Treaty could be scrapped entirely so as to design a national missile defense system from the ground up, without constraints.

Clinton was in a bind. At the end of his administration, his choices boiled down to begin construction of the radar installation in Alaska, a location that would require Russian approval and a treaty amendment—both time-consuming and hard to accomplish—or to disregard congressional directives that he had signed into law. He found refuge in how difficult it was for the Pentagon to carry out successful missile defense intercepts. Missile defenses were nowhere near ready for deployment, and contrary to congressional directives, Clinton kicked this can down the road to his successor.

Soon after replacing Yeltsin, Vladimir Putin persuaded the Duma to consent to ratify START II with the proviso that Washington keep the ABM Treaty intact. To up the ante, he announced that U.S. withdrawal would be met not only with Russia's withdrawal from START II but also "from the whole system of treaties on the limitation and control of strategic and conventional weapons."[51] After Bush won the contested 2000 election, he and those around him brushed off these warnings. Putin's maneuvering came too late to rescue the ABM Treaty.

On May 1, 2001—May Day—Riveles, now out of the line of fire as a visiting professor at the National War College, sat in brilliant sunshine on the campus grounds to hear President George W. Bush deliver a major address on the ABM Treaty. "Today's Russia," Bush said, "is not our enemy, but a country in transition with an opportunity to emerge as a great nation, democratic, at peace with itself and its neighbors." This new world, Bush argued, needed "a new framework that allows us to build missile defenses to counter the different threats . . . To do so, we must move beyond the constraints of the 30-year-old ABM Treaty. This treaty does not recognize the present or point us to the future. It enshrines the past."

Bush was cutting the Gordian knot. The offense-defense relationship, codified in the 1972 SALT I accords and recently fretted over in Helsinki by Clinton and Yeltsin, was yesterday's news. Bush would pursue deeper cuts while disposing of the ABM Treaty, playing both ends against the middle and outflanking deterrence strengtheners and arms controllers alike. He told his audience, "We need a new framework that allows us to build missile defenses to counter the different threats of today's world."[52] Riveles felt numb, the way he did the following year when his father died.

THE COMPREHENSIVE TEST BAN TREATY RATIFICATION DEBACLE

Clinton's failure to convince two-thirds of the Senate to provide consent to the CTBT's ratification epitomized the extent to which arms control had stalled out. A prolonged educational campaign was needed to rebut critiques, explain the treaty's monitoring system and its potential benefits—even after India and Pakistan carried out a series of underground tests in May 1998 before announcing moratoria. But treaty supporters favored a fast-track approach, and the Clinton White House agreed. They operated under the false assumption that Republican senators would be loath to vote against a treaty banning nuclear tests before a national election. Instead, Republican senators who were unwilling to support the Chemical Weapons Convention before the 1996 elections were also unwilling to support the CTBT's ratification three years later. Their ranks had, in fact, grown.

Partisan warfare on Capitol Hill was becoming entrenched in Clinton's second term. The CTBT was Clinton's treaty; Reagan and George H.W. Bush opposed it. Even two of the most moderate, internationally minded senators, Richard Lugar and John Warner, thought the vote was premature and voted "nay" along with far more conservative colleagues. Both stressed the need to see whether a novel "stockpile stewardship" program that Clinton proposed could provide high confidence in extending the useful life of U.S. warheads without further testing.[53]

Unbeknownst to the Clinton White House and the treaty's strongest backers on Capitol Hill, Senator Kyl had quietly gained the votes of more than enough Republican senators to kill the treaty outright by September 1999. Once again, Chairman Helms was opposed to ratification and was inclined not to take up the treaty. But he and Lott were goaded by Democratic senators led by Byron Dorgan, a prairie populist with no sense of the vote count, to bring the treaty to the Senate floor. CTBT advocates were counting on public opinion polls indicating that a ban on testing was supported by 70–80 percent of the electorate.

When Lott and Helms did a quick about-face, expressing willingness to take up the treaty under restrictive conditions, Democratic minority leader Tom Daschle and Joseph Biden, the ranking Democrat on the Foreign Relations Committee, were caught in a bind. It would be awkward, at best, to reject Lott's terms after demanding a vote, but they were belatedly aware that they couldn't win. Lott proposed two conditions for a face-saving compromise—that the treaty be withdrawn from the Senate's calendar, and that Clinton promise not to take it up for the duration of his presidency.

The only remaining point of leverage for the White House and Senate Democrats was the prospect of using the CTBT as a cudgel in the upcoming election—hence Lott's second condition. At this juncture, National Security Advisor Sandy Berger seemingly convinced Clinton to stand his ground. "The president believes," Berger told the press corps, "that it is inappropriate for him to say to the world that the United States is out of the non-proliferation business during an election year."[54] Behind the scenes, however, Clinton was willing to compromise, and Daschle and Lott seemed to have a handshake agreement to set the CTBT aside until after the 2000 elections. Due to arcane Senate rules, however, this required unanimous consent among the senators, and for some, as Terry Diebel wrote, "the chance to humiliate Clinton was just too good to pass up."[55] Even though twenty-four Senate Republicans led by Senator Warner and thirty-eight Democrats led by Daniel Patrick Moynihan signed a letter calling for postponement, it was not possible to gain unanimous consent to shelve the treaty.

The debate over the CTBT ratification was short and brutish. The Senate Foreign Relations and Armed Services Committees held a total of four days of hearings. Senate Democrats were unprepared for fast-tracking the CTBT and never issued a report making the case for ratification. The leaders of France, Germany, and Great Britain weighed in with a supportive op-ed. Four former chairmen of the Joint Chiefs of Staff also supported the treaty—Colin Powell, David Jones, William Crowe, and John Shalikashvili.[56]

James Schlesinger was the star witness against the treaty. Five other former secretaries of defense—Dick Cheney, Donald Rumsfeld, Melvin Laird, Frank Carlucci, and Caspar Weinberger—signed a statement opposing ratification. Other notable signers were Bob Dole and Texas governor George W. Bush.[57] Two of the nuclear lab directors—Paul Robinson of Sandia, who was centrally involved in the Reagan administration's Joint Verification Experiments, and Bruce Tartar of Livermore—were notionally in favor but volunteered damaging testimony. Robinson asserted that the ability of Moscow and Beijing to test at low seismic yields would provide "an intolerable advantage."[58] Tartar worried about laboratory personnel recruitment in a no-test environment and that, while the stockpile stewardship program was a good bet, it was not a sure thing. A week before the vote, Henry Kissinger, Brent Scowcroft, and John Deutch entered the fray with an op-ed recommending delay.[59]

On October 13, 1999, the Senate voted 48 in support and 51 in opposition to the CTBT's ratification. Only four moderate Republicans joined with Senate Democrats voting in favor. The Clinton White House's lack of preparedness and situational awareness on Capitol Hill had punishing consequences. After the ragged but successful conclusion of voting on the Chemical Weapons Convention, the shift in the Republican caucus against treaty ratification was notable. Like President Carter, who convinced the Senate with great difficulty to consent to ratify the Panama Canal treaties and then failed on SALT II, Clinton would succeed at treaty ratification once, but not twice.

The main arguments of treaty critics were that the treaty would diminish U.S. deterrence, thus prompting friends and allies to seek the Bomb, that verification wasn't airtight enough, that stockpile stewardship wasn't a sure thing, and that the treaty was "fatally flawed." These arguments have not fared well with the passage of time. Allies did not go their own way because the United States stopped testing, and the treaty's international monitoring system has demonstrated its utility. The labs continued to be exceedingly well funded and the stockpile stewardship program has worked admirably. Two decades after the Senate vote, another critique has gained currency by those opposed to the CTBT—that Russia and China have carried out faint whispers of tests with questionable military utility. These concerns could have been addressed through the treaty's consultation and clarification provisions. If need be, compliance concerns could also have been investigated by the treaty's challenge inspection procedures, but these were voided by the vote against ratification.

Clinton rebounded after the vote on the CTBT. He was, after all, the Comeback Kid. His popularity at the end of his presidency remained high, despite his sexual indiscretion and impeachment. Arms control had difficulty rebounding. Henceforth, as Barack Obama would experience, the price for a Democratic president running the gauntlet of treaty ratification would be like sitting in the dentist's chair for many months at a time. The playbook of naysayers, developed in the CWC ratification debate, was now honed and supported by the swelling ranks of America First senators floating on a rising tide of partisanship.

AN ALTERNATIVE TO WAR ON THE KOREAN PENINSULA

There was one last nonproliferation crisis facing the Clinton administration. In August 1998, North Korea launched a missile over Japanese territory in a failed attempt to launch a satellite. Clinton asked Perry, who had left the Pentagon and returned to Stanford, to lead a review of U.S. policy options. He was assisted by Ash Carter at Harvard and by Wendy Sherman, Robert Einhorn, and James Timbie at the State Department. Perry recruited Japanese and South Korean officials to participate and proceeded to build out an engagement option. In return for normalizing relations with Pyongyang and creating conditions for a peace treaty, Kim Jong Il would need to stop missile flight testing and other hostile acts. If he reacted negatively, Washington and its allies would adopt a more punishing coercive strategy.

In May 1999, Perry and his U.S. team flew to Pyongyang to engage in three days of talks, bringing with them medical supplies for a children's hospital. The talks were a success. The missile flight tests stopped—a moratorium that lasted nearly eight years. North and South Korea initiated a process of rapprochement, symbolized at the 2000 Olympics in Sydney where their teams marched together. In June 2000, Kim Jong Il and South Korean president Kim Dae Jung held a summit meeting in Pyongyang. Then the second-ranking North Korean military official, Vice Marshal Ko Myong Rok, visited Washington with a detailed plan to stop long-range missile testing.[60] He conveyed a request for a presidential visit, but in the competition for Clinton's time before leaving office, he chose to focus on the Middle East peace process. In his stead, Secretary Albright accompanied by Sherman visited Pyongyang in October 2000, receiving brickbats from critics for doing so and for accompanying Kim Jong Il to a massive rally at May Day Stadium ostensibly arranged to help Albright and Sherman "understand North Korean culture and arts."[61]

CLINTON'S LEDGER SHEET

Arms control reached its apogee under George H.W. Bush. Bill Clinton consolidated many of Bush's gains during his first term, adding significant achievements of his own. His greatest achievements were in the area of nonproliferation, including the denuclearization of Ukraine and Kazakhstan, which enabled START I reductions to proceed, the indefinite extension of the Nonproliferation Treaty, the suspension of North Korea's plutonium pathway to the Bomb as well as its most worrisome missile flight tests, and completing negotiations on the Comprehensive Test Ban Treaty. Clinton encouraged the pursuit of cooperative threat reduction with novel programs in the Pentagon and the Department of Energy. The Senate's consent to ratify the Chemical Weapons Convention was a hard slog, but essential. Successful arms control is about norm building, and the Chemical Weapons Convention was fundamental in stigmatizing possession as well as use of these heinous weapons for all but a few outliers. Negotiating the Comprehensive Test Ban Treaty was also crucial for norm building. Despite its rejection by the Senate, all major and regional powers that possess nuclear weapons have not tested for more than two decades.

During Clinton's second term, the process of nuclear arms control stalled out. Clinton needed deadlines, and without them he had the tendency to let matters slide, which proved injurious. His lack of focus and failure to prioritize arms control agenda items while he enjoyed Democratic majorities on Capitol Hill cost him. Yeltsin was accommodating to Clinton's wishes but couldn't or wouldn't secure crucial gains. After NATO enlargement began, Russian backlash against arms control was sure to follow, with crucial assists from George W. Bush and Vladimir Putin.

Clinton and Yeltsin never could untie the knots preventing START II's ratification and implementation. Yeltsin wasn't a reliable partner during Clinton's second term, and Republicans on Capitol Hill tied Clinton in knots over agreements governing nuclear offenses and defenses. When Republicans gained majorities in the House and the Senate, Clinton lost control over the calendar and terms of debate.

After apogee comes a temporary period of weightlessness followed by descent. Clinton and Yeltsin were both adept at patching over impasses; their successors had less interest in doing so. There are no innocent bystanders in the trajectory of arms control, so Clinton and Yeltsin share responsibility for the arc of decline that trailed after them.

Clinton never grasped the imperative to rejuvenate ACDA and failed to pursue ratification of the Chemical Weapons Convention when he enjoyed a Democratic majority in the Senate. The demise of ACDA foreshadowed the coming demise of arms control, and the painful ratification of the convention foreshadowed the Senate's rejection of the Comprehensive Test Ban Treaty.

All of the downside consequences of folding ACDA into the State Department came to pass, just as the agency's supporters predicted. The Clinton administration never did take ACDA off of life support. The State Department didn't champion quick ratification of the Chemical Weapons Convention, and by the time this deadline approached, it was easy for Helms to pull the plug on ACDA. Senator Kyl extracted one more pound of flesh in the voting for the CWC's implementing legislation, authorizing a future president to block "challenge" inspections on U.S. soil on grounds of national security. To date, not one challenge inspection has been carried out under the Chemical Weapons Convention. Nor have they been essential, since the occurrences of chemical weapons' use, as in Syria or when used against political opponents by Putin and against a family member by North Korea's Kim Jong Un, have been grotesquely obvious.

The final vote over the CWC was an eye-opener. A convention negotiated during the Reagan and Bush administrations barely received a majority of support among Republican senators. The final roll call was 29 Republicans in support and 26 against. All of the Senate Republican leadership except Lott voted "nay." This vote should have constituted a flashing red light against trying the ratify the CTBT, but the Clinton White House and Senate Democrats didn't see it. No Republican leader wants to preside over a deeply split caucus to support a Democratic president on treaty ratification. Lott, like Howard Baker before him, would do this once, but not twice.

Attempts to adapt and demarcate the ABM Treaty to expressly permit theater missile defenses were necessary and worthy because without them, the treaty had no future. But these efforts received little top-down interest and reflected what arms control had become—an excruciatingly process of dealing with complex technicalities. Clinton's belated efforts to link demarcation with deeper reductions fizzled out, another casualty of belated timing, domestic politics, and Yeltsin's ineffectuality.

Clinton's interests lay in more compelling international pursuits than arms control. His attention was drawn to stopping Slobodan Milošević's war crimes, avoiding a ground war in the Balkans, and expanding NATO. NATO expansion was a defining move. Clinton opened this door; Bush would rush through it, and arms control suffered as a result.

Descent follows apogee. Clinton administration officials, with rare dissent, thought NATO expansion was a strategic necessity as well as an opportunity to expand democratic governance. They argued that stopping Serbian war crimes over Russian objections was a humanitarian imperative. These arguments were compelling at the time; downside risks and blowback became apparent later when Putin decided that he, too, could employ force and play by his own rules.

There were signs during Clinton's first term that signaled trouble ahead, but they were muffled by real accomplishment. Warning signs became much stronger during Clinton's second term, when progress on arms control stalled. Had Al Gore won the contested Florida vote, the arms control enterprise would likely have fared better, but Gore, too, would likely have had difficulty sustaining achievements and maintaining friendly relations with Putin after the Russian economy revived and after his revanchist tendencies surfaced. Putin reflected Russian political culture far more than Gorbachev and Yeltsin, and Putin rejected much of what he inherited from them.

If Putin was bound and determined to do away with nuclear as well as conventional arms control agreements, then we can largely absolve the occupants of the White House for contributing to this result. The apportionment of blame for the demise of nuclear arms control wasn't one-sided, however. Demise wasn't foreordained; it was the result of conscious choice in both Moscow and Washington. This downturn began during Clinton's second term. The dynamics of arms control changed significantly in the eight years of the Clinton presidency. What began with implementing and negotiating extraordinary achievements ended in a muddle.

As long as Clinton and Yeltsin were on center stage, the structural weaknesses of the arms control enterprise remained masked. Yeltsin needed Clinton's political and economic support, but he couldn't seem beholden to Washington. Clinton needed Yeltsin to say "yes," but in ways that didn't weaken him. Since Yeltsin couldn't afford to say "no," and since Clinton's goals—improving U.S.-Russian and Russian-NATO relations while expanding NATO and seeking relaxation from the ABM Treaty—did not cohere, there were limits to what Clinton and Yeltsin could accomplish. A steep decline in relations between Washington and Moscow followed when leaders who favored masking tape were replaced by leaders who sought separation from treaties.

The business of arms control creaks to a halt when one party overreaches and the other feels disadvantaged by global trends and becomes strong enough to push back. George W. Bush wanted a clean break from inherited constructs. Vladimir Putin was disinterested in shoring up treaties that reflected Russia's loss of empire and constraints on conventional capabilities. He weighed these impulses against his perceived need to maintain working ties with Washington. Putin offered George W. Bush a partnership to combat terrorism after 9/11 and was rebuffed. He remained unruffled when Bush withdrew from the ABM Treaty. Putin was biding his time. He and George W. Bush started off well enough, but by the end of the Bush administration, the demise of arms control was a geopolitical fact of life.

Chapter 14

SHEDDING TREATIES

Bill Clinton and Boris Yeltsin held the enterprise of strategic arms control together with bailing wire and masking tape. They were unable to build on what they inherited, but they managed to keep their inheritance intact. With the changing of the guard from Clinton to George W. Bush and from Yeltsin to Vladimir Putin, the nuclear peace that reached apogee during the decade of 1986–96 began to unravel.

TWO LEADERS BORN OF CRISIS

Bush and Putin were both forged in crucibles of national crisis. Both were easily capable of being underestimated. The highly pedigreed Texas governor knew little of the world before becoming president, but he was smart, clever, intellectually curious, and a quick study. His history of boisterous behavior was long behind him when he raised his hand to take the oath of office. Born again, he chose to live in Texas on parched land—away from the family compounds in Houston and on the Atlantic coast at Kennebunkport. He developed ascetic habits. His three lodestars were his wife, his family, and his Bible. He was deeply centered in facing the storms to come.

Bush entered the White House with a highly sharpened sense of purpose. As Robert Gates observed, "He wanted it to be very clear that he was not in his father's shadow."[1] He intended to govern as if he had won by a landslide instead of a one-vote margin of the Supreme Court. He brought back for encores hardened veterans of his father's administration. They were comfortable with the exercise of power in 1989; now, if anything, they were overconfident in their capabilities. They were also without their level-headed overseers, Bush 41 and Brent Scowcroft.

Putin's outlook was forged in two crises. The first was the loss of Soviet empire, which he witnessed from his post in East Germany. The second came in 2000 when Boris Yeltsin entrusted a Russian Federation in deep economic and political crisis to him—someone barely known beyond the state's security services. Putin was distinguished mostly by what Yeltsin was not. Putin was focused and disciplined, someone with a natural instinct of pulling together the instruments of state control. Once the Russian economy rebounded sufficiently, Putin could exercise significant powers at home but not in distant locales. Bush had ample powers on both fronts, having been granted open-ended authority by the Congress to wage a Global War on Terror after the 9/11 attacks on the World Trade Center and the Pentagon.

GEORGE W. BUSH'S TEAM

Two of the three biggest bulls around Bush—Vice President Dick Cheney and Secretary of State Colin Powell—were in the top tier of his father's administration. The third—Secretary of Defense Donald Rumsfeld—was not. Rumsfeld learned the ropes of bureaucratic maneuver in the Nixon and Ford administrations, where he and Cheney forged strong bonds. Condoleezza Rice and Stephen Hadley received significant upgrades from their service in the George H.W. Bush administration, with Rice serving as Bush's national security advisor and Hadley as her deputy.

Condoleezza Rice was smart, disciplined, and destined for success. She grew up in Birmingham and other cities in Alabama confident in her capabilities, the golden child of a schoolteacher and a pastor who coached basketball on the side. She was a product of the Deep South's African American elite, living in one of the last bastions of segregation. Her loving parents laid out for her classes in piano, ballet, French, typing, and tap dance. No one, however, could be completely insulated from the dire state of race relations in Alabama in the early 1960s. She was attending religious services nearby the 1963 bombing of Birmingham's 16th Street Baptist Church, where one of her friends died.

Rice had the star power, the skills, and the drive to be successful wherever she stopped along the way. In her case, it was the University of Denver, where a Czech émigré, Josef Korbel, introduced her to Soviet studies. Korbel's daughter, Madeleine Albright, had an equally remarkable ascent.

Rice's father moved nearby in Denver, but his career as a school administrator was petering out as his daughter's was beginning to reach exit velocity. A postdoctoral fellowship at Stanford opened up a new world, including introductions to the Republican elite around Ronald Reagan ensconced at the Hoover Institution. Stanford was a comfortable, welcoming place. Academics and administration suited her, when not working in Washington. Rice had a knack for being in the right place at the right time, beginning as a Soviet analyst on the National Security Council staff run by Brent Scowcroft in the George H.W. Bush administration. Her rise was dizzying. Her wealth of talent hid a significant flaw—her failure to offer stiff warnings to George W. Bush that train wrecks were in the offing. Perhaps the reason why she didn't was because Bush wasn't persuadable.[2]

Stephen Hadley possessed all of the qualities of an outstanding national security advisor in the Brent Scowcroft mold. He was quiet, dependable, sound, and discreet. Born in Toledo, Ohio, to an electrical engineer and a homemaker, he traveled the well-worn path of class presidents interested in government who would make their way to Washington. His stops along the way were Cornell during a period of furious campus unrest, and Yale Law School, where he was a "small group-mate" of Hillary Clinton and where he joined the Naval ROTC. Hadley spent his service time in a stint at the U.S. Comptroller's Office. He was hooked on national security. In Republican administrations, he became indispensable wherever he was situated—on the National Security Council staff, where he arrived one month before Richard Nixon's resignation and first worked with Robert Gates; in the Office of the Secretary of Defense under President George H.W. Bush, where he worked on arms control and other issues; and as the deputy national security advisor. When Rice moved from the NSC to become secretary of state during Bush's second term, Hadley took her place. His base of operations during Democratic administrations was the law firm of Shea & Gardner.

Hadley's job as national security advisor was immensely easier than Rice's, who had to deal with Cheney, Rumsfeld, and a disgruntled Colin Powell. In contrast, Hadley, Rice, and Bush "could finish each other's sentences." When Rumsfeld was replaced by Robert Gates in 2007—an old friend and colleague of both Hadley and Rice—the process became smoother still. Cheney's influence on Bush had waned during the second term. As Hadley described, Bush has "had four years of intelligence briefings, four grueling years as President. He knows what he thinks, he knows what he knows . . . He's a different guy. He's confident."[3]

The first term was quite different. Cheney's force field was palpable. He reminded Bush of his "deeply conservative" orientation—perhaps more conservative than the president-elect suspected—when Bush kept returning to him during the vice-presidential search.[4] While Cheney's brand of conservatism wasn't a concern for Bush, surprises were in store. Neither man could reasonably expect the extent to which Cheney's outlook and policy preferences would be affected by the burning cauldron of 9/11.

The thesis that Cheney was the same man during the Bush 41 and Bush 43 administrations doesn't hold up to scrutiny.[5] The clearest evidence to the contrary was the advice Cheney offered on matters of war and peace. He was a cautious, conservative adviser to Bush 41. After 9/11, Cheney became an advocate of extreme measures in extreme cases. He believed that, as long as there was a one percent chance of a nuclear attack against the United States, preemptive action was mandatory. Ron Suskind quotes him as saying, "It's not about our analysis, or finding a preponderance of evidence. It's about our response." Whoever might seek nuclear capabilities for use against the United States—the above quotes were directed against evildoers in Pakistan—needed to be dealt with swiftly and decisively. Prime suspect number one was Saddam Hussein, who had a track record of seeking the Bomb. Cheney viewed every piece of raw intelligence, every report by suspect sources, and every inference through the prism of his "one percent doctrine." Saddam needed to be deposed even if a sound alternative to him couldn't be found.[6]

Cheney, Powell, and Rumsfeld were not in harness, with Powell being the odd man out. Cheney and Powell were often on different wavelengths, and Powell and Rumsfeld sparred routinely. Rice politely noted in her memoir that "there was a good deal of personal respect" and an "equal measure of distrust."[7] Hers was a charitable application of weights and measures. Rumsfeld excelled at bureaucratic maneuver and didn't regard Rice as being in his league. Given all this, Rice had an impossible job. Cheney's force field could be impenetrable, Rumsfeld was elusive and unresponsive, and Powell was quickly becoming an unhappy camper—but one who couldn't leave Rumsfeld to his own devices.[8]

BUSH'S EMPOWERMENT

Bush's extraordinary empowerment was the result of a massive failure by the intelligence community to focus on ample signals amidst the noise of impending, devastating strikes against the U.S. homeland. It was an eerie repeat of Pearl Harbor, where evidence of an attack was abundant but got lost in reams of reporting that failed to connect the dots. In his foreword to Roberta Wohlstetter's account of Pearl Harbor, Thomas Schelling explained this as a "poverty of expectations."[9] During Bush's first year in office, the intelligence community again collected mountains of evidence, but lacked the imagination to predict where and how America would be battered.

Richard Clarke, a frantic aide on the National Security Council staff, and George Tenet, a frazzled Central Intelligence Agency director, conveyed alarming reports of impending terror attacks to the new president and his national security advisor. These reports—including a bell-ringer delivered to Bush and Rice at Bush's ranch in Crawford, Texas, on August 8, 2001, headlined "Bin Laden Determined to Strike in United States"—lacked "actionable" intelligence. No one could say where, when, or how the attacks would happen. Tenet and Clarke were not empowered to convene analysts from the Federal Bureau of Investigation to sit down with the Central Intelligence Agency and other foreign intelligence gatherers to share their most distressing tidbits of information. Only three people—Bush, Cheney, and Rice—could have ordered this to happen and locked the doors until crucial pieces of evidence were connected, especially those of young men, mostly from Saudi Arabia, taking flight training classes who exhibited little interest in landing procedures. None of them did. Rice delegated this to Clarke, but Clarke was too junior and too swamped to connect dots. Cheney went to extra lengths to find plot connections after 9/11, but not before.

The context of decision making after 9/11 helps explain what transpired next. Robert Gates stressed, "Beyond the traumatic effect of the attack itself, I think there was a huge sense among senior members of the administration of having let the country down . . . They had no idea after 9/11 whether further attacks were imminent, though they expected the worst."[10] Bush was saddled by the consequences of this failure and was to be saddled again by the intelligence community's misrepresentation of the evidence used to prosecute another war against Saddam Hussein.

His father's war against Saddam uncovered an advanced nuclear weapon program that the intelligence community failed to detect. Presuming that Saddam was once again seeking the Bomb, Bush, Cheney, Rumsfeld, Rice, and Hadley believed a second war either to be a matter of urgent necessity or a sound, rational choice. It was a time of great anxiety and trauma. To compensate for previously losing signals in noise, the administration removed all filters from intelligence reporting, including the reliability of sources, to receive reports from the field that produced a flood of dire warnings.[11]

Letters containing anthrax were being sent in the mail. A.Q. Khan's network of nuclear commerce—a tangled mix of Pakistani government and military sponsorship and personal profit taking—was publicly revealed after extended scrutiny by the intelligence community. Osama bin Laden and some of his network remained at large. No one knew what they were planning next, and even the most draconian "enhanced interrogation techniques"—the administration's euphemism for torture—on his captured associates could not shed light on these plans. Diplomacy was too passive and slow-moving. The need of the hour was a muscular strategy of compellance. The worst offenders could not be allowed to possess the worst weapons in another attack on the U.S. homeland.

In this mindset, arms control had no role to play against such dire threats. It was too weak a reed. Bush and those around him believed, as George F. Will wrote, "Significant agreements are impossible until they are unimportant, which means until they are not significant."[12] This critique ignored the relationship between halting, hard-won early steps—or even failures—that later contributed to extraordinary outcomes when political conditions subsequently permitted. Bush and his advisers viewed Richard Nixon's Anti-Ballistic Missile Treaty and his father's second Strategic Arms Reduction Treaty as artifacts of the Cold War. Conditions of parity no longer existed. The new world of nuclear dangers was a place where muscle mattered more than diplomatic parchment and where classical strategic arms control would be more of a hindrance than a help.

HARBINGERS OF DEMISE

The demise of arms control was hastened by great hubris and injury. The attacks on 9/11 coincided with a period of unparalleled U.S. power. The trauma of 9/11 also came at a time of Russian weakness, about which Putin could initially do little. The demise of arms control coincided with the revival of Russia's fortunes, but it began with Putin's inclination to disregard treaties that reflected the Soviet Union's weakness and dissolution. At the top of his hit list was the 1990 Conventional Forces in Europe Treaty, one of the signal accomplishments of the George H.W. Bush administration, because it constrained his ability to move troops and equipment on Russian soil. Putin had his own antiterrorism campaigns to fight, centered on Chechnya, and the CFE Treaty constrained his ability to move forces and equipment in Caucasia.

From the very outset, the Russian Army circumvented some numerical limitations of the 1990 Conventional Forces in Europe Treaty and maintained military equipment in excess of agreed provisions for its military campaigns in Chechnya. Russian troops never completely left parts of Georgia and Moldova after they gained independence. In June 2007, after the second large tranche of NATO expansion and after publicly declaring Washington's hostile intent, Putin announced Russia's intention to suspend adherence to the CFE Treaty unless complaints about its restrictive provisions were addressed satisfactorily. In December 2007, Russia formally suspended these obligations.

Bush's animus was focused on the 1972 Anti-Ballistic Missile Treaty, which he believed hampered protection against missile-bearing members of the axis of evil. Bush, like Putin, wanted freedom of action. Both men shed treaties accordingly. START II was one of the crowning achievements of the nuclear peace. If implemented, it would remove the most destabilizing pieces from nuclear war-fighting chessboards. Putin tied its fate to Bush's decision on the ABM Treaty: if the Pentagon sought new missile defense deployments, Moscow would revert to its habitual response, overwhelming them with warhead-laden land-based missiles.

Consequently, the demise of arms control and the nuclear peace began in three different corners of a fabric that took four decades to weave—the ABM Treaty, START II, and the CFE Treaty. The pace of unraveling and the loss of treaties representing the nuclear peace was slow at the outset of Putin's leadership, partly due to the time it would take for the Russian economy to recover sufficiently to rebuild its military and nuclear capabilities, and partly because the nature of a renewed U.S.-Russian competition wasn't yet set. Putin continued to adhere to strategic arms reduction treaties because they placed Russia on a par with the United States, a critical national security interest for Moscow.

Moreover, Bush was ready to find common ground with Putin on deep cuts. Bush had no interest in retaining excess strategic offenses, and cutting back the number of deployable warheads on strategic forces had the additional advantage of reinforcing his messages about withdrawing from the ABM Treaty: The world had changed, Washington and Moscow were no longer enemies, and whether or not Putin withdrew from START II, Bush was ready to cut deeper than his father.

At the outset, Bush delivered mixed messages to Putin. Deep cuts in nuclear offenses would be welcome and reciprocal, given Russia's economic straits. But Putin could only view Bush's withdrawal from the ABM Treaty with unease. Had Bush offered to keep and adapt the ABM Treaty—as Clinton tried to do—in return for START II's ban on land-based missiles carrying multiple warheads, he would have placed Putin in a bind. Bush had leverage over Putin when Russia was reeling in a Great Depression. If Putin moved to deploy MIRVed land-based missiles, Bush could have begun missile defense deployments.

Bush decided not to use this leverage; he and those around him had other priorities. Bush wasn't interested in a trade of keeping the ABM Treaty in place, suitably modified, for Moscow's taking MIRVed land-based missiles off the chessboard. He and his advisers believed that withdrawing from the ABM Treaty was essential to deal with missile threats from outliers and they viewed START II as a dead letter, doubting that Putin would implement it. Putin offered changes to the ABM Treaty to accommodate Bush's perceived missile defense needs, but Bush wanted out. Putin bided his time.

After the Russian economy and military recovered from the chaos of the Yeltsin years, Putin became bolder and the pace of arms control's demise quickened. He made no secret of his grievances when he met with Rice and Ambassador to Russia William Burns in 2006. Putin's message was clear: "Russia was great again," and that Washington had better get used to it.[13] Putin unburdened himself publicly in a talk at the Munich security conference in 2007, bitterly critiquing U.S. policies. Later that year he taught Georgia's rash leader, Mikheil Saakashvili, a harsh lesson, when Saakashvili took the Kremlin's bait and fired on Russian-backed separatists in Georgian enclaves. Putin responded by advancing Russian troops toward Georgia's capital, Tbilisi.

When Putin returned to the Russian presidency in 2008 after a four-year hiatus as prime minister, he was, as Burns observed, "surfing on historically high oil prices and nursing fifteen years of grievances, convinced that the United States had taken advantage of Russia's moment of historical weakness and was bent on keeping it down."[14] Putin felt disrespected by Bush, beginning with when his offer to partner in the fight against terrorism after 9/11 was spurned while his offers of logistical support for U.S. combat troops in Afghanistan were pocketed. In 2008, Putin would begin to flight-test a new ground-launched cruise missile banned by the 1987 Intermediate Nuclear Forces Treaty. Then, after a public revolt in Ukraine that threatened to shift Kiev toward the West in 2014, Putin would launch hybrid warfare in the eastern Donbas region while annexing Crimea. Conditions for arms control would then crater, just as they did after the Soviet invasion of Afghanistan in 1979.

THE UNIPOLAR MOMENT

The trumpeter of muscular unilateralism and what was dubbed as "neocon-servatism" was Charles Krauthammer, who gave a name to the post–Cold War period: it was the "unipolar moment."[15] Krauthammer's rapier-witted columns were reminiscent of Joseph Alsop, who skewered liberals, détentists, and anti–Vietnam War activists in *Washington Post* op-eds during the Cold War. Alsop used his Georgetown salon to extend his influence; Krautham-mer's salon was Fox News.

Brent Scowcroft saw where the unipolar moment was headed after 9/11 and issued a public warning to those who no longer sought his counsel. Writing in the *Wall Street Journal*, he readily acknowledged, "It is beyond dispute that Saddam Hussein is a menace . . . We will all be better off when he is gone." But Scowcroft warned that that "there is scant evidence to tie Saddam to terrorist organizations, and even less to the September 11 at-tacks." Saddam had "little incentive" to make common cause with Osama bin Laden and that there were ways and means short of a preventive war in Iraq to checkmate his regional ambitions.[16] James Baker also weighed in with sobering messages about unilateralism and underestimating force requirements for another war against Saddam. He did not take issue with regime change in Iraq but warned that it could not be achieved "on the cheap." The costs of war, Baker warned, could be great and would no doubt be greater unless supported by a significant international coalition. Diplo-macy wasn't a dirty word—it was "a necessary prerequisite for any success-ful foreign policy."[17]

Krauthammer argued differently—that the time of tepid multilateralism, like that practiced by the Clinton administration, was over. The United States didn't need to ask for anyone's permission; it could intervene decisively "in whatever part of the world it chooses to involve itself." Krauthammer be-littled the multilateral "sheen" that paid obeisance to "the shrine of collec-tive security." The truth of the unipolar moment was that "a dominant great power acts essentially alone," without embarrassment. Krauthammer ac-knowledged that a period of muscular unilateralism could be brief—as little as one decade rather than three or four—if those in power ran the economy "into the ground."[18] In reality, the executive branch and the Congress had no problems with paying for wars by running up the debt; the central problem was the wars themselves, where Gulliver found himself pinned down by the Lilliputians.

WAR MAKING, NOT TREATY MAKING

Bush wasn't ready for 9/11—no newly elected president could possibly be. He knew he had to draw on inner reserves and rise to the occasion. He thought he knew, with strong guidance from Cheney, what he had to do, but he had no feel for what he was getting into. There were no debates over pros and cons of a liberation strategy for Iraq in the National Security Council. This was an extraordinary omission, but dissonance over going to war wasn't perceived as being helpful. Bush was set on this course. The "Vulcans" that Rice gathered to advise Governor Bush during his campaign and who later joined her in the administration were on a similar wavelength. The moniker "Vulcans" was a reference to the civic symbol of Birmingham, Alabama, Rice's hometown, which was once known for its steel production.[19] It accurately described their mindset. Most of the talented group of advisers that helped engineer extraordinary outcomes for President George H.W. Bush lost their bearings after 9/11, just as their principals did.

All of Bush's core advisers during the presidential campaign supported a preventive war, none more so than Paul Wolfowitz, who became Rumsfeld's deputy. Veterans from the Bush 41 administration who returned to the NSC staff also supported deposing Saddam. Robert Blackwill, the idea man behind the Open Skies Treaty and a new NATO formulation characterizing nuclear weapons as "weapons of last resort" when he worked for Scowcroft, was back with big Kissingerian-level ideas about forging a strategic partnership with India and about remaking Iraq. He returned from a stint as U.S. ambassador to India to help briefly with the Iraq project on the National Security Council staff.

Philip Zelikow was trained as a lawyer, succeeded as an academic, and then flourished in the world of national security policy making. He was in on the ground floor of Harvard's Preventive Defense Project with Ash Carter, worked with Blackwill and Rice on German reunification on Scowcroft's National Security Council staff, and served as the staff director of the 9/11 Commission seeking remedies for the intelligence community's failures. He, too, believed that bold policies were needed, and that it was better to be safe than sorry. After sorting out Afghanistan, he and Blackwill joined Wolfowitz in supporting a preventive war against Saddam Hussein and his presumed weapons of mass destruction. By mid-2002, this course was already set. In this view, a preventive war could accomplish what diplomacy could not.[20]

The State Department was skeptical—not just Powell and his deputy, Richard Armitage, but also Richard Haass, the director of policy planning, experts in the Middle East regional bureau led by William Burns, and State's small intelligence shop. These were "Pottery Barn" wars, as Colin Powell described them. U.S. forces could break a country like a piece of pottery. In a store, you pay for the broken item and leave. But when you break a country in a military campaign, you own what you can't fix. Even after spending more than a trillion dollars, as would occur, it was hard to leave without barely concealed failure, if that.[21]

Powell and Armitage could see tragedy ahead, but they couldn't see how to change the sense of purposefulness etched in Bush's face, reinforced with every conversation he had with Cheney. Both Rice and Hadley were clearly on board. Rumsfeld could be obscure but was supportive. Powell was the odd man out, beset with second thoughts. A military man in the striped suit of a diplomat, Powell could resign, making Bush's life even more wrenching in the run-up to war. Or he could remain the good soldier, expressing reservations in private but not laying his body on the train tracks. Powell did, however, let it be known that he advised Bush, "You are going to be the proud owner of 25 million people. You will own all their hopes, aspirations and problems. You'll own it all."[22]

Cheney seethed over Powell's reservations, viewing the Pottery Barn leak as another example of failing to support the president's policies, even being disdainful of them.[23] Powell was the obvious choice to make the case before the United Nations as to why Saddam Hussein needed to be deposed. Cheney and Rumsfeld carried little credibility beyond the precincts of war making, and CIA director George Tenet, who was about to embarrass himself again, could not possibly be the frontperson. So it was that Powell blemished an exemplary career by delivering a slipshod case based on faulty assumptions, bad sourcing, and false information. No matter how deeply Powell tried to scrub his testimony, it wouldn't wash clean. The case that Tenet described as a "slam dunk" to reassure Bush in private, was, in reality, an airball.

The propulsion behind the unipolar moment, fueled by injury and zeal to promote democracy, was too strong. In contrast, multilateralism and diplomacy were tepid instruments of suasion. There was no better reflection of this fusion than the administration's National Security Strategy statement, issued in September 2002. "People everywhere want to be able to speak freely; choose who will govern them; worship as they please; educate their children—male and female; own property; and enjoy the benefits of their labor," it declared. "These values of freedom are right and true for every person, in every society—and the duty of protecting these values against their enemies is the common calling of freedom-loving people across the globe and across the ages."

There would be no more 9/11s: "As a matter of common sense and self-defense, America will act against such emerging threats before they are fully formed . . . History will judge harshly those who saw this coming danger but failed to act. In the new world we have entered, the only path to peace and security is the path of action." Bush's National Security Strategy continued, "To forestall or prevent such hostile acts by our adversaries, the United States will, if necessary, act preemptively." The words "arms control" did not appear in the 2002 National Security Strategy. Zelicow, who bonded with Rice in both Bush administrations, was the primary drafter.[24]

Powell, Rumsfeld, and Cheney all left public service in the Bush administration with impaired reputations. Powell was outmaneuvered by Cheney and Rumsfeld. Bush was clear that the bickering among his most senior advisers needed to stop, and that the appropriate time for Powell to go was after his reelection. Powell expressed a readiness to leave early in 2004 but urged Bush to make a significant shakeup elsewhere, too, especially in the Pentagon. When it became apparent to Powell that he would be the first to go, he tried to overstay.

Rumsfeld finally left the Pentagon in the fall of 2006, after congressional elections returned Democratic majorities to the House and the Senate. Rumsfeld offered his resignation earlier, but Bush was reluctant to change both secretaries of state and defense at the same time. Rumsfeld's tenure at the Pentagon was marked by the prosecution of two punishing wars without the prospect of happy endings, both of which were inappropriately planned, with insufficient troops to stabilize Afghanistan and Iraq—if stabilization were possible. On top of this, Rumsfeld and his administrator in Iraq, Paul Bremmer, demonstrated dreadful judgment in disbanding the Iraqi Army and banning Saddam's Ba'ath Party. No one on Bush's National Security Council sought to stop these decisions—a remarkable dereliction of duty. A surge in U.S. expeditionary forces would temporarily provide a semblance of control but could not compensate for these decisions. The Pottery Barn war in Iraq produced governments more beholden to Tehran than to Washington. Against an endless horizon of sacrifice caused in significant measure by his decisions, Rumsfeld's departing remarks at his mustering-out ceremony were tone-deaf. "Today," he said, "it should be clear that not only is weakness provocative, but the perception of weakness on our part can be provocative, as well."[25]

By the summer of 2006, Cheney was saddled by previous misjudgments, none more so than his predictions that U.S. troops would be met as liberators in Iraq and that the insurgency was "in its last throes" in 2005. He now often disagreed and argued vociferously with Rice in front of Bush, but Rice usually had the support of Gates and Hadley.[26] Bush was a different president in his second term, with a good feel for foreign leaders. He was, however, saddled with the decisions made at the outset of his presidency, leading to outcomes after he left office that belied assertions of victories and missions accomplished. The damaging images that trailed after Bush were emblems of Cheney's intense focus on fighting a global war against terror—the degradations of the Abu Ghraib prison, black sites, and "enhanced interrogation" techniques.

Going to war based on bad intelligence was an embarrassment, but there would be no apologies. The architects of Bush's two unwinnable wars were unrepentant, unlike Robert McNamara, who couldn't keep the pain of Vietnam dammed up inside.[27] Rumsfeld wrote in his memoir that no one lied in the run-up to war. "The far less dramatic truth was that we were wrong."[28] Cheney acknowledged that "much" of what Powell relayed to the United Nations about weapons of mass destruction "was wrong," while holding his aide, Scooter Libby, who compiled this dossier, blameless.[29] Bush acknowledged, "In retrospect, of course, we all should have pushed harder on the intelligence and revisited our assumptions."[30] When it mattered most, however, few questioned the conventional wisdom about Saddam and his ambitions. Iraq was, in Krauthammer's estimation, "the prototype" of a new strategic threat.[31] Saddam was seeking nuclear weapons and he possessed chemical weapons when he was disarmed in the first Gulf War. He presumably had replenished his arsenal and needed to be disarmed again.

AXIS OF EVIL

Iraq was part of the Bush administration's declared axis of evil, an axis that included North Korea and Iran. This phrase, coined by White House speechwriter Michael Gerson, quickly entered the administration's lexicon.[32] "It is a certainty," Krauthammer wrote, "that in the near future there will be a dramatic increase in the number of states armed with biological, chemical and nuclear weapons and the means to deliver them anywhere on earth."[33]

This confident assessment was as erroneous as CIA's estimate of Saddam Hussein's programs. Biological weapons have so far proven to be too dangerous to use, even for dead-enders, while the Chemical Weapons Convention began to establish global norms against production and use. Syria became the worst offender, while nerve agents were used as tools of assassination and punishment by Russian and North Korean agents. These were egregious but still limited cases.

Those interested in nuclear weapons also remained solitary outliers, subject to the Bush administration's threat of preventive war. As Krauthammer wrote in a 2002 retrospective of his essay on the unipolar moment, "The new unilateralism argues explicitly and unashamedly for maintaining unipolarity, for sustaining America's unrivaled dominance for the foreseeable future."[34] Gulliver spent a fortune refurbishing nuclear blunderbusses no leader dared use in the field of battle, while competitors looked elsewhere for comparative advantage. China focused on ways to deny U.S. power projection capabilities. Putin's most significant insight would come later—that hybrid warfare was impervious to the nuclear balance and U.S. conventional might. As for the Lilliputians, their biggest advantage was their staying power.

These new threats could not be addressed by the classical tenets of arms control. Diplomacy had a poor track record with evildoers; Bush would pursue nonproliferation through other means. He would create new and useful coalitions of the willing to isolate suspect states, and he would build on the Clinton administration's "counterproliferation" initiatives to stop proliferation in its tracks. Instruments of counterproliferation included conventional weapons with extended range and great precision. National Security Advisor Rice put this most succinctly in an appearance on one of the talk shows: "We don't want the smoking gun to be a mushroom cloud."[35] President Bush later repeated this formulation in making the case to oust Saddam.

This formulation won the domestic argument hands-down, but it boomeranged on the administration when the intelligence behind this assertion proved to be baseless. The image of mushroom clouds was based on the only physical evidence the intelligence community possessed suggesting Saddam's renewed pursuit of nuclear weapons—his country's purchase of aluminum tubes that might be utilized in making gas centrifuges to produce bomb-making material. For proof in this regard, those inclined to worst-case assessments offered old, never-classified centrifuge plans developed by Gernot Zippe, an Austrian prisoner of war who helped the Soviet Union make these machines. This view was strongly supported by Cheney and embraced by Rice and Bush. Powell's presentation before the United Nations allowed for different interpretations behind the purchase of the aluminum tubes—a shipment of which was intercepted in Jordan—while maintaining a top-line assessment that there could be no doubt that Saddam had resumed work on nuclear weapons.

The U.S. expert who knew the most about Zippe and his centrifuge design was Houston Wood, whose career path involved extended stays at Oak Ridge National Laboratory, working on centrifuge research, and teaching at the University of Virginia, where he received his doctorate. Wood was raised in Baldwyn, Mississippi, where he grew up with chemistry sets. His dad sold insurance and his mom was a homemaker. He discovered his keen interest in and facility for applied mathematics at Mississippi State University. Wood met Zippe at conferences in Europe. The U.S. government invited Zippe to conduct research on centrifuges at the University of Virginia in the late 1950s, after being released as a Soviet prisoner of war. Wood never met Zippe in Charlottesville, but this connection facilitated conversation when they began to meet at European conferences in 1979.

Wood's colleagues at Oak Ridge were skeptical of the thesis that the aluminum tubes Saddam bought were for centrifuges. So, they asked him in 2000 to have a look at the design specifications and drawings of the tubes that Iraq had purchased. The State Department's experts were also skeptical, believing they were far better suited for making missile casings. After fifteen minutes alone with the drawings, Wood emerged to give his Oak Ridge colleagues an unequivocal answer: the tubes were far too thick for centrifuge applications. He was encouraged to doublecheck with Zippe, who confirmed Wood's assessment. The only physical evidence the U.S. intelligence community possessed to support a renewed effort by Saddam to reconstitute his nuclear weapon program actually undermined the public case for going to war being made by Bush, Cheney, and Rice.[36]

THE GREAT UNRAVELING

After 9/11, Washington and Moscow shared a common interest in seeking freedom of action to deal with evildoers. Freedom of action required sloughing off arms control compacts that constrained military options. The unraveling of arms control that began with the ABM Treaty, the Conventional Forces in Europe Treaty, and the START II Treaty met with remarkably little resistance because key building blocks for constructing the edifice of arms control had already begun to crack, some more quickly than others.

One building block was bipartisanship in the United States. Without bipartisanship, diplomatic success was beyond reach. During the Cold War, the Republican Party was instrumental to successful arms control. After the

Cold War ended, the internationalist wing of the Republican Party began to atrophy. America Firsters challenged incumbents; Senator Richard Lugar of Indiana lost his primary challenge in 2012, receiving less that 40 percent of the Republican vote. The new face of the Republican Party was on display during the Senate's ratification of the Chemical Weapons Convention and, even more so, in the defeat of the Comprehensive Test Ban Treaty. During the Cold War, ambitious Democratic politicians jockeyed among themselves as champions of arms control. After the Cold War ended, ambitious Republican politicians positioned themselves as teardown artists, taking aim at negotiated constraints as infringements on U.S. freedom of action.

A second building block for the rise of arms control was the nominal acceptance of "sufficiency" (Nixon and Kissinger), "essential equivalence" (James Schlesinger), or whatever the buzzwords of the day were to reflect the acceptance of a rough balance of strategic offensive forces. Successful strategic arms control and later reductions could only proceed from the public acceptance of rough parity. In reality the twin quests for advantage and the avoidance of disadvantage never went away.[37] After the Cold War ended, equality with Russia was a fiction; the only place it remained was in the numbers associated with strategic arms reduction treaties. Putin needed to be freed of the bonds of START II, but he was content with abiding by equal numbers of strategic forces. The Intermediate Nuclear Forces Treaty was another matter because it zeroed out options his General Staff wished to retrieve. After the dissolution of the Soviet Union and the Warsaw Pact, Moscow measured disadvantage along two axes—missile defense deployments and NATO expansion. As these indicators became more troubling, Putin became less interested in arms control.

A third building block for the rise of arms control was mutual vulnerability. This was the biggest irony of all during the Cold War: That safety was linked to vulnerability and that seeking escape from vulnerability would result in heightened nuclear danger. Even before 9/11, critics found arms control's embrace of vulnerability morally intolerable. After 9/11, most Americans agreed, and the ABM Treaty could be discarded without domestic political consequences. The Bush administration dispensed with the classical tenet of strategic arms control linking strategic offenses with defenses. The world's sole superpower would henceforth decide how to defend itself against missile attacks, and decide, as well, on how much nuclear offense was enough.

A fourth building block for the successful construction of arms control was the decision to accept the inviolability of borders and national sovereignty. Successful conventional arms control and reductions were predicated on the 1975 Helsinki Final Act recognizing a divided Europe. President Gerald Ford was hammered for his decision to accept "captive" European nations; instead the Helsinki Final Act set in motion waves of engagement, including on human rights, that helped loosen Moscow's grip at home and with the Warsaw Pact.

By 2001, all of these conditions for the success of arms control were, at best, tenuous. Bipartisanship in the United States had fallen on hard times. Moderate Republican internationalists were a vanishing breed. As the Washington-based Republican Party gravitated away from internationalism, arms control compacts were increasingly viewed as entanglements or infringements on national sovereignty. Superiority had value; requirements needed to be determined unilaterally, not in concert with a defeated superpower. The acceptance of vulnerability, especially to missile attacks from North Korea and Iran, was beyond the pale.

DEMISE HAPPENS

The pairings of George H.W. Bush with Mikhail Gorbachev and Boris Yeltsin were well suited for apogee; all three wished to seize opportunities. The pairing of Bill Clinton and Yeltsin was well suited for a period of consolidating partial gains followed by stasis, because they could do no more. The pairing of George W. Bush and Vladimir Putin was well suited for a period of decline, as both sought to slough off restraints. There was, however, nothing predetermined about the demise of arms control.

Bush and Putin faced choices that could speed or slow this progression. It was particularly important to Putin to avoid an open rift with Bush. He was the first international leader to call Bush after the 9/11 attacks. He stood down Russian forces after these attacks to help the United States monitor unusually threatening activity, offered to share intelligence on Afghanistan, and used Russian influence to make air bases in former Soviet Republics available to support the war against al Qaeda in Afghanistan. In return, Bush tried to make it easy on Putin while withdrawing from the ABM Treaty and yielded to Putin's desire to turn paper-thin constraints on strategic offenses into a bilateral treaty.

NATO expansion proceeded on a different track, seeming to have a propulsion all its own once Clinton opened this door. Bush took NATO expansion to a different level, making a hash of his and Putin's basic assumptions of U.S.-Russian relations. Yeltsin pleaded with Clinton not to include the Baltic states in NATO expansion. Putin would do no pleading, but he remembered all slights. The rise of arms control required four decades of hard work. The demise of arms control took only two.

The Bush administration waved away Russian security concerns regarding withdrawal from the ABM Treaty and expanding NATO. Europe could now be "whole and free" with the dissolution of the Warsaw Pact and the freedom of former Soviet republics. There were new rules, and these rules reflected imbalance. The process that began with the reunification of Germany within NATO was now well along with the Clinton administration's decision to bring Hungary, Poland, and the Czech Republic into the fold. Bush sped up the process significantly with a second large tranche, including the Baltic states. The strongest argument for doing so was to provide newly independent states protection against a revanchist Russia. This argument reinforced itself as expanding NATO fed Russian revanchism. Putin reached his breaking point when Bush clarified that his democracy agenda didn't end with the second tranche of NATO expansion; he wanted to include Georgia and Ukraine, as well.

Putin's ability to claw back Russian influence along the "near abroad" was limited for the better part of a decade. Under Yeltsin, Russia's economy contracted by almost 40 percent between 1991 and 1998. (By way of comparison, the contraction in the U.S. economy during the Great Depression was 30 percent.) Putin would have to bide his time. His initial pursuit of freedom of action was directed against conventional arms control and eliminating START II's constraint on MIRVing, but little else.

Then, in 2007, after absorbing the insult of a second tranche of NATO expansion, and after Bush expressed his interest in further enlargement, Putin delivered a speech in Munich declaring that U.S. interests had become immutably hostile. The following year Russia began working in the open on a new ground-launched cruise missile in violation of the 1987 Intermediate Nuclear Forces Treaty, retrieving a nuclear option that Mikhail Gorbachev had persuaded his General Staff to give up. And then, shaken by yet another popular revolt against a proxy—the 2014 "Revolution of Dignity" in Ukraine—Putin engaged in a wholesale violation of the post–World War II norm of respecting the territorial integrity and national sovereignty of weaker states.

When Bush took office, he did not expect the downward trajectory with Moscow that his decisions helped propel. He genuinely wished to get off on the right foot with Putin, so much so that, after looking Putin in the eye and into his soul at their first meeting in Slovenia in June 2001, Bush announced his favorable assessment.³⁸ This was a rookie's mistaken phraseology, but it genuinely reflected Bush's desire to put Putin "at ease, win him over [and] establish a good relationship."³⁹ Bush's two terms began with the breezy assertion that Washington and Moscow were no longer enemies and ended with relations in a deep freeze. Completely missing in the memoirs of Bush, Cheney, and Rice was any recognition that cause, especially NATO expansion, might be linked to effect.

TREATY SLAYING AND MAKING

Bush did not do nearly as much damage to arms control as Putin, but he was a significant contributor. Bush issued a National Security Presidential Directive in mid-February 2001 calling for the development of a new "conceptual framework," including a package of deep cuts to accompany withdrawal from the ABM Treaty. This review was overseen by Franklin Miller, who previously found considerable room to reduce warhead requirements while working in the Pentagon. Miller was now a staffer for the National Security Council. Bush made no secret of his intentions, publicly calling for "a new framework that reflects a clear and clean break from the past, and especially from the adversarial legacy of the Cold War." Colin Powell preferred to amend the ABM Treaty rather than giving six months' notice of withdrawal. He was more strongly opposed to the more dramatic option of treaty abrogation, which would have had immediate effect. To at least postpone the inevitable, Powell persuaded Bush to consult with allies that were unenthusiastic about a clean break from the ABM Treaty.⁴⁰

Powell bought time, but not much of it. Republican opposition to the ABM Treaty had become an article of faith by 2000, and Bush's mind was set on withdrawal well before he was elected. He conveyed this view to a meeting with his team of advisers in Crawford in 1999.⁴¹ He also told Putin this at their first meeting in June 2001. In response, Putin and his defense minister, Sergei Ivanov, clarified several times their willingness to adjust the treaty to accommodate U.S. preferences.⁴² At a July 2001 meeting of the Group of Eight industrialized nations in Genoa, Ivanov indicated that he would recommend accepting modifications to the ABM Treaty "if the resulting defenses would not undermine Russia's security."

Then came the 9/11 attacks. Within a week, Georgi Mamedov, deputy minister of foreign affairs, was in Washington to meet with John Bolton, the new under secretary of state for arms control. Mamedov was an old hand working on arms control, first with Dennis Ross in the George H.W.

Bush administration and then with Strobe Talbott under Clinton. Mamedov told Bolton that the attacks "created a new window of opportunity in our relationship." In October, Bush and Putin met at an Asia-Pacific Economic Cooperation forum in Shanghai, where they made progress on coordinating deep cuts but not on the status of the ABM Treaty. Before meeting Bush at his ranch in Crawford the following month, Putin told U.S. journalists that Moscow was ready to compromise on the ABM Treaty and that a deal could be struck, but that Washington was not being forthcoming about the amendments it wanted. "What exactly," Putin asked, did the United States "want changed?"[43]

Bush never had greater leverage on Putin to amend the ABM Treaty. He could have done better than Clinton in this regard, but his mind was made up. Cheney, Rumsfeld, and Bolton were also intent on a clean break, as negotiating amendments could have opened the door to endless haggling. Cheney's priorities had shifted. He was willing to eliminate the Kremlin's land-based missiles carrying multiple warheads in the last lap of the George H.W. Bush administration, but he now wanted to exit the ABM Treaty "the sooner the better," as defending America after 9/11 from missile attacks from the axis of evil took priority. Rumsfeld agreed with Cheney: there should be no limits whatever on testing missile defense interceptors. To highlight this point, Rumsfeld canceled a few planned tests, ostensibly because of treaty constraints.[44]

Bush announced his decision to withdraw from the ABM Treaty on December 13, 2001, after privately advising Putin of this decision in November. As Hadley recalled, Bush tried to be as solicitous as possible to Putin: "He basically said, 'Look, I'm getting out of the ABM Treaty. I have to because I've got to be able to defend the country against countries like Iraq. It's not about you. I don't feel threatened by you. I don't think Russia is going to go to war with the United States.'" Paraphrasing Bush, Hadley continued, "'Quite frankly, I'm not worried about your strategic nuclear weapons. You shouldn't be worried about mine. We should both be worried about the Iranians and we should be cooperating on missile defense to do that. That's what we should be doing.'" In Hadley's retelling, Bush "basically said, 'I want to make this as easy for you as I can. So, you tell me how to do it. I prefer if we both stepped out of the ABM treaty using the right of withdrawal clause. If that doesn't work for you and you prefer that I do it, I'll withdraw. I'd like to do it cooperatively with you, but you tell me what works for you and that's what I'll do.'"[45]

There was no way that Putin could agree to withdraw jointly from the ABM Treaty; it remained valuable to Russia and he wanted to place the onus of withdrawal squarely on the United States. After Bush's unilateral decision to withdraw, Putin's public reaction was muted. He called the decision "mistaken," but added that it "does not pose a threat to the national security of the Russian Federation." Foreign Minister Igor Ivanov acknowledged it was time to move on: "The primary aim now is to minimize the negative consequences of the U.S. withdrawal" and to concentrate on offensive reductions.[46]

By pairing withdrawal with deep cuts—indeed, 40–50 percent deeper than those codified in the 1993 START II Treaty—Bush helped to relieve Moscow's immediate injury and lent credence to his underlying rationale that Washington and Moscow were no longer enemies. At the same time, he disarmed domestic critics seeking arms control. To further ease Putin's concerns, Bush sided with Powell and Rice against Cheney and Rumsfeld by agreeing to codify reductions in a treaty rather than by means of parallel statements of intent.[47]

Bush made this decision on February 12, 2002. His reasoning, according to Bolton, was twofold. First, formality would be consistent with the ten-year duration of an agreement that would extend beyond their terms in office. The second reason for a treaty, in Bolton's recounting, was that Bush was "willing to throw the guy some bones." Bush was solicitous to Putin's domestic optics. Bolton recalls Bush saying, "I want to give him a document he can hold up."[48]

After Miller's internal review, Rumsfeld settled on a range of reductions from 1,700 to 2,200 operationally deployed warheads over a ten-year period. When asked directly by Bush, Miller allowed that even deeper reductions were possible, perhaps down to 1,500 warheads.[49] On November 13, 2001, one month before announcing U.S. withdrawal from the ABM Treaty, Bush publicly announced Rumsfeld's numbers. The steep drop from 3,500 operationally deployed warheads in the second strategic arms reduction treaty negotiated in 1993, but never implemented, reflected how badly Russia had been affected by its Great Depression. In 1993, Yeltsin used his pen to change START II's 3,500 number, adding 3,000 for a range of 3,000–3,500, the lower range reflecting his country's reduced production capacity. Putin's proposed number of strategic warhead reductions was 1,500—too low for Rumsfeld. Putin's number suggested that Russia could field forces half as large as Yeltsin had earlier predicted. Putin continued to press for codification of the reductions in a legally binding treaty that included verification measures.

With Bush's decision in February to accommodate Putin's desire for a treaty, the task of drafting fell to Bolton and Mamedov. Initial sparring didn't last long because Bush and Putin wanted to have an agreement ready for signature at their May 2002 summit in Moscow. The three-page Strategic Offensive Reductions Treaty, or the "Moscow Treaty," was signed by Bush and Putin on May 24. The treaty's preambular language noted the signatories' commitment "to the goal of strengthening their relationship through cooperation and friendship," and the objective of building a "qualitatively new foundation for strategic relations." The treaty's core obligations referenced separate public statements made by Bush and Putin to reduce and limit strategic nuclear warheads "so that by December 31, 2012 the aggregate number of such warheads does not exceed 1,700–2,200."

Bolton characterized the demise of the ABM Treaty and the finalization of the Moscow Treaty as "the end of arms control."[50] His judgment was premature, but he would have a subsequent opportunity to engineer this result in the Trump administration. The Moscow Treaty relied on the voluminous monitoring provisions of the 1991 START Treaty. This treaty would lapse in 2009, while the Moscow Treaty would lapse in 2012. As the Bush administration never got around to negotiating a treaty to extend or supersede START, this meant that there would be no means to monitor warhead limitations for the last three years of the Moscow Treaty, after which all restraints would be null and void. After Barack Obama was elected, filling this gap with a new treaty and monitoring provisions would become his administration's paramount immediate objective.

NONPROLIFERATION POLICY SHIFTS

The period of apogee for nuclear and conventional arms control coincided with the apogee of the Nonproliferation Treaty. The apartheid government of South Africa disassembled its small stockpile before handing the reins over to Nelson Mandela's African National Congress. Ukraine, Kazakhstan, and Belarus gave up their sudden nuclear inheritance and joined the Nonproliferation Treaty as non-nuclear-weapon states. In 1995, the treaty was extended indefinitely. To help engineer this result, possessors pledged to redouble their efforts to complete negotiations on a treaty ending nuclear testing in all environments. The Comprehensive Nuclear Test Ban Treaty was negotiated, as promised, in 1996. One year later, the Vienna-based International Atomic Energy Agency, which pre-dated the Nonproliferation Treaty and which implemented its obligations on abstainers, adopted a "model additional protocol" to expand the ambit of its inspectors. The impetus behind strengthening measures was the discovery of a nuclear weapon–related program in Iraq after the war to expel Saddam Hussein's troops from Kuwait. The IAEA urged widespread adoption of the additional protocol, which was voluntary, not mandatory.

The well-being of the NPT was also reinforced by an ongoing process of strategic arms reductions. The end of the Cold War facilitated deep cuts in U.S. and Russian nuclear forces and warheads. While the second Strategic Arms Reduction Treaty never entered into force, the 2002 Moscow Treaty did, codifying even deeper reductions. These reductions reinforced the NPT's consensual foundations. For non-nuclear-weapon states, this meant accepting inspections to back up their pledges of continued abstinence. For nuclear-weapon-possessing states, this meant working toward nuclear disarmament by reducing the number and salience of their most fearsome weapons. The two states with the largest stockpiles bore the heaviest burdens to reduce. The Moscow Treaty recognized this obligation, explicitly referencing the Non-proliferation Treaty in its preambular language.

Despite these accomplishments, the global system undergirding nonproliferation still had glaring weaknesses. The limits of a consensual approach were clearly evident in the activities of A.Q. Khan's nuclear trafficking network. Constraints on illicit commerce were far too lax. The Bush administration was committed to a more proactive and muscular approach to strengthen the NPT. In May 2003, Bush launched the Proliferation Security Initiative to help stop illegal nuclear trafficking. Interdiction efforts would be undertaken by voluntary coalitions of the willing outside the formal ambit of the NPT. Eleven countries initially joined the Proliferation Security Initiative: Australia, France, Germany, Italy, Japan, the Netherlands, Poland, Portugal, Spain, the United Kingdom, and the United States. Eventually over 100 states signed the initiative's statement of interdiction principles. Russia joined, but China, India, and Pakistan did not.[51]

The best-known Proliferation Security Initiative interdiction was its first. In October 2003, the United States, the United Kingdom, Germany, and Italy worked together to halt and seize a shipment of centrifuge components destined for Muammar Qaddafi's Libya. The point person for this effort on Bush's National Security Council staff was Robert Joseph, a skeptic of arms control with a firm hand in countering proliferation. Qaddafi's many purchases from the A.Q. Khan network remained mostly crated because he lacked a skilled workforce. The Bush administration retrieved Qaddafi's purchases in 2004 in return for lifting sanctions on oil companies and other firms doing business with Libya and embarking on a path to restore diplomatic relations. Within a decade, Qaddafi's ties with the United States had frayed and NATO airstrikes helped to end his rule. His assassination in 2011 became an object lesson to North Korean and Iranian leaders about the potential implications of giving up the nuclear option and thereby inviting regime change.[52]

In 2004, the Bush administration also took the lead in passing a new UN Security Council Resolution 1540, which defined the proliferation of weapons of mass destruction and missiles as threats to international peace and security, thereby actionable for intervention under the UN Charter. Resolution 1540 also levied obligations to deny support to "non-state actors" seeking these weapons or their means of delivery, as well as to implement national legislation and controls to this effect. The Proliferation Security Initiative and Resolution 1540 made meaningful contributions to global nonproliferation efforts.

Other Bush administration initiatives had negative consequences for the NPT. The administration's nuclear posture reinforced and seemingly expanded the role of nuclear weapons for battlefield use. The Pentagon sought new low-yield tactical nuclear weapons and "earth penetrator" warheads to attack deeply buried targets. These plans were blocked on Capitol Hill. Elsewhere, Bush inherited an "Agreed Framework" from the Clinton administration that stopped North Korea's production of plutonium in return for deliveries of fuel oil and the promise of constructing two proliferation-resistant power reactors. The U.S. intelligence community then discovered that, with help from the A.Q. Khan network, Pyongyang was actively pursuing a second route to bomb making by means of gas centrifuges and highly enriched uranium. After this discovery was leaked to the press, Bush withdrew from the Clinton administration's agreement, declaring it to be fatally flawed. The Bush administration was unable to negotiate a better agreement. This pattern—a partial success by a Democratic administration with an outlier state, only to be withdrawn by a Republican administration as being insufficient but not improved upon—would later be repeated with respect to Iran.

Just as key officials in the Reagan administration famously carried out feuds between "dealers" and "squeezers" when negotiating with the Soviet Union, the Bush administration reprised this dynamic over nonproliferation policies. Secretaries of State Powell and Rice were inclined to deal; it was the nature of their job description and they held little expectation that squeezing could result in voluntary or involuntary disarmament. Others, led by Cheney and Bolton, were inclined to squeeze. Rice wrote that Bolton was Powell's "'neocon hire' in deference to the president's desire to have his administration reflect the full range of opinions in the Republican Party." He became "a constant source of trouble" for Powell.[53] His appointment as under secretary of state for arms control—the job that John Holum, the last Arms Control and Disarmament Agency's director, held before him—reflected how far the fortunes of arms control had fallen after ACDA's consolidation into the State Department. Bolton brought with him fellow squeezers, as the exodus of former ACDA officials from the State Department continued.

When Rice became secretary of state in Bush's second term, she fended off suggestions that Bolton become her deputy, writing, "I did not want to repeat Colin Powell's experience. I wasn't sure that I could fully trust John to follow my lead at State, and I didn't want a clash later on should John be—or appear to be—insubordinate."[54] Her creative solution was to remove Bolton as under secretary of state for arms control and to wish him well as the U.S. ambassador to the United Nations. The policy dilemmas of dealing with North Korea and Iran remained. Rice described Bush as "squarely on the hawks' side of the fence," favoring "unrelenting pressure," but harsh sanctions didn't produce regime change, and military strikes against Iran and North Korea seemed more than the traffic could bear with U.S. troops bogged down in Iraq and Afghanistan.[55] The unipolar moment was ending in failed, seemingly endless wars, and yet serious proliferation challenges remained.

A NUCLEAR DEAL FOR INDIA

Just as the Bush administration rejected some of the old tenets of strategic arms control, it also believed that key aspects of long-standing nonproliferation diplomacy needed to be revised. The NPT gained coherence by making the Bomb the essence of the problem, not the Bomb holder. This distinction was necessary during the treaty's formative decades because Washington and Moscow rarely agreed on who to favor and who to punish. Both superpowers could agree, however, that proliferation was unwelcome. Consequently, outliers to the NPT did not enjoy the benefits of nuclear commerce that were available to members in good standing.

The Bush administration held a different view—that not all outliers were alike. Some were evildoers, while others—in particular, India—could become a strategic partner and counterweight to the rise of China. India was a responsible state, deserving the benefits of nuclear commerce. At the same time, rules needed to be tightened for other outliers—including Pakistan—to prevent the most worrisome actors from acquiring the most dangerous weapons. It was okay for reliable states to possess the Bomb; it wasn't okay for outliers.[56]

In a state-centric system, the most powerful state could bend some norms to serve the national interest. Accordingly, Bush set about to persuade the forty-six-member Nuclear Suppliers Group—the only cartel ever designed to prevent profit taking, which operated on the basis of consensus—to make an exception for India to its rules for civil nuclear commerce. The ostensible reason for doing so was to bring India into the "nonproliferation mainstream."

The outlines of this agreement were reached in July 2005 between Bush and Prime Minister Manmohan Singh. In return for the Bush administration's heavy lifting with the Nuclear Suppliers Group, the deal's U.S. backers expected profits, jobs, and a transformed U.S.-India partnership. The U.S.-India Business Council projected a $150 billion commercial opportunity for U.S. firms, producing 27,000 high-quality American jobs.[57] Geopolitics were subtext. The presumed utility of the deal for counterbalancing China's rise was never an explicit part of the administration's argument, in deference to prickly Indian sensibilities about its strategic autonomy. New Delhi viewed itself in exceptional terms, no less than Washington, and would not necessarily do Washington's bidding.

Prior U.S. administrations had worked hard to beef up the Nuclear Suppliers Group by persuading its members to condition nuclear commerce to the acceptance of "full-scope" safeguards that allowed inspectors to confirm that all national activities were for peaceful purposes. Another key requirement was that recipients would foreswear uranium enrichment and plutonium reprocessing activities. India couldn't possibly meet these tests, given its ongoing nuclear weapon programs and how interwoven its commercial and military activities were. The Bush administration judged that the potential benefits of making an exception for India were worth weakening the Nonproliferation Treaty and the Nuclear Suppliers Group.

The India nuclear deal was strongly supported by Rice, Hadley, and Robert Blackwill, who ventured off to India as the U.S. ambassador in June 2001. High policy was Blackwill's forte. He lobbied hard for a "bold and brave nuclear deal," belittling the complaints of nonproliferation advocates as "nagging nannies." Rice's preferred usage was the "high priests" of nonproliferation; in India, the term "nonproliferation ayatollahs" gained currency.[58] Blackwill left his ambassadorial post in July 2003. He worked briefly on Iraq and then, in November 2004, he became the president of Barbour

Griffith & Rogers International, a lobbying firm. In August 2005, the government of India hired Barbour Griffith & Rogers International to promote the nuclear deal.

The Achilles' heel of the NPT was its demonstrable unfairness. Its inequities could only be patched up by consensual agreement between haves and have-nots, where the select few reduced nuclear weapons in return for continued abstinence by the many. The Bush administration's distinction between the Bomb and the Bomb holder challenged the NPT's founding ethos. The India nuclear deal widened divisions between member-states. The NPT's benefits were lopsided, since abstainers that had no interest in acquiring the Bomb had no leverage; nor did they want new nuclear-armed states. Later, the Trump administration opened more distance between abstainers and possessors by arguing that the United States would not seek deeper reductions because of the rise of China. Therefore, if abstainers wanted deeper U.S. reductions, they would be obliged to help create conditions for further disarmament. As a responsible state, the United States could fend off demands from abstainers and make demands of its own. Absent the thin veneer of diplomatic varnish, this message boiled down to the assertion that the national interest of abstainers would best be served by adhering to the NPT even if possessors disregarded the treaty's founding ethos.

The India nuclear deal therefore had far more than symbolic or unique consequence. Those opposed argued that by allowing special dispensation for a treaty outlier, it would become harder to set tougher standards for treaty adherents; that the deal would weaken the Nuclear Suppliers Group practice of consensual decision making; that the proposed deal would heighten Pakistan's sense of insecurity and likely raise its requirements for bomb-making fissile material and weapons; and that the deal would not be consummated, given India's expected demands for indemnification in the event of a nuclear accident. There were long memories in India of a gruesome Union Carbide accident at Bhopal in 1984 where a gas leak resulted in perhaps 3,000 deaths and injuries to over 500,000. Union Carbide's corporate leadership was safely beyond the reach of India's court system. New Delhi demanded provisions for indemnity, while no U.S. nuclear business would build power plants in India without insurance to cover accidents.

The Bush administration easily won debates on Capitol Hill over the India nuclear deal. Most of its asserted benefits proved to be diaphanous, while most of the adverse consequences raised by skeptics were subsequently confirmed. The deal made it harder for possessors to convince abstainers to accept tougher safeguards. The consensus rulemaking of the Nuclear Suppliers Group was weakened. After Washington carved out an exemption for India, China belatedly discovered a "grandfather" clause in an old agreement with Pakistan to construct more power reactors there. Pakistan blocked consensus in the Conference on Disarmament to start negotiations on a treaty to end fissile material production for bomb making and proceeded to ramp up its nuclear arsenal.

The Indian Parliament passed liability legislation for nuclear plant builders and suppliers in August 2010. The two U.S. companies that were to benefit from job creation and nuclear commerce with India—General Electric and Westinghouse—could not accept the financial risk of building power plants in India. Their economic fortunes continued to decline. Heavily subsidized Russian companies were the primary beneficiaries of the Bush administration's nuclear initiative toward India. The Bush administration was right to seek improved ties with India; its instrument to do so was ill chosen.

NATO EXPANSION

The Bush administration proceeded on a fast track to expand NATO. In 2004, Romania, Bulgaria, Slovenia, Slovakia, and the three Baltic states gained membership. A third tranche involving Albania, Croatia, and Macedonia (when a dispute with Greece over its name could be sorted out) would be next in line. Bush didn't want to stop there—he was strongly in favor of including Georgia and Ukraine, as well. Rice noted the obvious in her memoir: "As the Alliance moved steadily east, Moscow's tolerance was being tested." She was warned in no uncertain terms by her ambassador to Moscow, William Burns, that the process of expanding NATO eastward, particularly with regard to Ukraine, would cross a red line for Putin.[59] Rice didn't heed this advice. Moscow needed to know, as she wrote in her memoirs, that "the Cold War is over and Russia lost."[60]

Bush's memoir barely addresses the possible contribution of NATO expansion to the deterioration of relations with Russia. He wrote, "I viewed NATO expansion as a powerful tool to advance the freedom agenda. Because NATO requires nations to meet high standards for economic and political openness, the possibility for membership acts as an incentive for reform."[61] Bush was right about states being on their best behavior in order to join; neither he nor other advocates of expansion foresaw how some members would revert to antidemocratic habits once inside NATO's protective umbrella. Cheney's memoir is silent on this subject.

Secretary of Defense Robert Gates picked his battles carefully. He wrote in his memoir that including the Baltic states into NATO "was the right thing to do," after which the process should have slowed down. Moving too quickly was a "mistake." In his view, U.S. ties to Russia were badly mishandled after George H.W. Bush left office. Rotating troops through bases in Bulgaria and Romania was a "needless provocation." Washington "ignored" Russia's long historical ties to Serbia and opposition to Kosovo's independence. Trying to bring Georgia and Ukraine into NATO "was truly overreaching." Asking parents to send their sons and daughters to war to defend them made no sense. In his view, "NATO expansion was a political act, not a carefully considered military commitment, thus undermining the purpose of the alliance and recklessly ignoring what the Russians considered their own vital national interests." He noted that "the president had strong convictions about certain issues . . . and trying to persuade him otherwise was a fool's errand." NATO expansion was one such subject, and Gates "dutifully" supported Bush's decisions.[62]

Putin's slow burn reached a boil after the second tranche of NATO expansion, particularly with the inclusion of the Baltic states. At an annual security conference held in Munich on February 12, 2007, Putin dispensed with pleasantries "to say what I really think about international security problems." He took direct issue with the unipolar moment, as it was premised on "one center of authority, one center of force, one center of decision-making. It is world in which there is one master, one sovereign. And at the end of the day this is pernicious not only for all those within this system, but also for the sovereign itself because it destroys itself from within." For Putin, the unipolar model was "not only unacceptable but also impossible in today's world." Unilateral action didn't solve problems. Instead, "an almost uncontained hyper use of force—military force—in international relations" was "plunging the world into an abyss of permanent conflicts."[63]

In 2008, Bush upped the ante. After popular discontent with misrule in Georgia and Ukraine brought to power leaders inclined to distance their countries from Moscow, Bush strongly favored placing both in the queue for NATO membership. Rice views this as the breaking point for Russian tolerance, but Putin's speech at the Munich security conference the year before suggests otherwise.[64] During cabinet deliberations Rice, whose area of specialization was Russia, offered Bush pros and cons about the wisdom of lining up Georgia and Ukraine for NATO membership, knowing all the while that Bush "was a strong supporter of their applications." Secretary of Defense Gates withheld cautionary judgment, knowing Bush would not heed it.

Thus, on the most consequential decision President Bush made in his second term affecting relations between Washington and Moscow—to invite Georgia and Ukraine to join NATO—his secretary of state offered mild reservations and his secretary of defense stayed silent. Bush was all in. In his view, Moscow's potential threat to the independence of Georgia and Ukraine only strengthened their case for membership into NATO. Rice recalls Bush saying near the end of the cabinet meeting, "If these two democratic states want [to apply for NATO membership], I can't say no." She "admired his principled stand."[65]

German chancellor Angela Merkel and French president Nicolas Sarkozy were deeply skeptical about inviting Georgia and Ukraine into NATO. The issue would have to be hashed out at an April 2008 NATO summit in Bucharest. Germany's foreign minister, Frank-Walter Steinmeier, made the case against including Georgia and Ukraine, given their weak and mercurial governments, lingering governance and corruption issues, and tense relations with Russia. Poland led the rebuttal, with other eastern European states concurring. Moscow's concerns should not, in their view, be a determining factor, arguing that a unified Germany would not have entered NATO on these grounds. This argument effectively quieted German opposition.

The newest NATO members viewed the further expansion of the alliance eastward as a matter of national security. The final communique of the Bucharest summit welcomed "Ukraine's and Georgia's Euro-Atlantic aspirations for membership in NATO. We agreed today that these countries will become members of NATO."[66] Germany and France didn't fall on their swords, resolving to take subsequent blocking action. This was, as William Burns noted, the worst of all possible outcomes: "indulging the Ukrainians and Georgians in hopes of NATO membership on which we were unlikely to deliver, while reinforcing Putin's sense that we were determined to pursue a course he saw as an existential threat."[67]

The die was now cast for active Russian measures against both countries, foreclosing their NATO membership. Reading the tea leaves after an acrimonious meeting between Putin and Georgia's Saakashvili in June 2006, Burns, then the U.S. ambassador to Russia, forewarned Washington that Georgia's rash young leader could have Georgia's territorial integrity or NATO membership, but not both.[68] In the end, Saakashvili got neither. He played into Putin's hands by responding to the shelling of villages from the Russian-backed autonomous enclave with a Georgian military offensive. Russian troops and armor then pushed easily into Georgian territory, threating the capital, Tbilisi. In Robert Gates's retelling, "The Russians set a trap and a headstrong, impetuous Saakashvili walked right into it."[69]

The Russian Army had regained its coherence and capabilities. The march toward Tbilisi was an object lesson to unruly neighbors. Russian forces never completely returned to their barracks, and for good measure, Moscow conferred independence on the autonomous zones it created on Georgian soil. Rice's memoir offers an odd coda to this overt, albeit small-scale exercise of Russian power. "Moscow could still invade a small neighbor and defeat its Army as in the old days," she wrote. "But it could no longer march to the capital and overthrow the government."[70] There was, however, no need for Putin to occupy the Georgian capital. His goals were achieved without extreme and politically costly measures. Russia's neighbors would take note, and Georgia was not going to be a member of NATO.

In 2014, Putin would take more extreme measures in response to another popular movement, this time in Ukraine, to send a corrupt, Russian-backed leader packing. Ukrainian membership in NATO was, as Burns knew, "the reddest of red lines for Putin." Putin warned Burns in March 2008 that Russia "would do all in our power" to prevent Ukraine's membership in NATO, to which Burns added his own strong cautionary messages to Rice.[71] In response to the loss of a reliable crony in Kiev, Putin engaged in "hybrid" warfare, backing local leaders in resource-rich areas in eastern Ukraine with a mix of regular troops and freelancers. Putin also arranged for the annexation of Crimea, taking back the gift that Nikita Khrushchev gave to Ukraine in 1954. The rise of arms control was built atop the norm of respecting national sovereignty and territorial integrity, codified in the 1975 Helsinki Final Act. After Moscow's assault on Ukraine, arms control would go into temporary cold storage, just as it did after Soviet troops entered Afghanistan.

New borders and states were created in Balkan wars after Yugoslavia imploded; Putin's assaults on Georgia and Ukraine were different. They were premeditated acts of a strong state to carve up weak neighbors. Moscow viewed its predatory actions through a completely different lens than Washington. In the Kremlin's view, the United States had demonstrated in Serbia, in Kosovo, and with NATO expansion that might made right, and that Washington lived in a state-centric rather than a rules-based system. Putin could play by these rules, too, and he now had the military capabilities and economy to throw Russia's weight around. When Germany argued unsuccessfully against putting Georgia and Ukraine in the queue for NATO expansion, Berlin warned against getting involved in "frozen" conflicts around Russia's periphery.[72] Moscow's conflict with Ukraine was now frozen, as were plans to include both countries into NATO.

BUSH'S LEDGER SHEET

The practice of arms control had already stalled out when George W. Bush and Vladimir Putin replaced Bill Clinton and Boris Yeltsin. When Bush left office, the demise of arms control was well along. Bilateral relations, which began with Bush's affirmations that the Cold War and adversarial relations were over, ended with Washington and Moscow at loggerheads and Putin declaring publicly that Washington was a danger to others—and to itself. Bush overreached badly and Putin pushed back hard once the Russian economy revived.

When U.S.-Russian relations deteriorate, arms control deteriorates. Three treaties representing important aspects of the nuclear peace—the Anti-Ballistic Missile Treaty, the second Strategic Arms Reduction Treaty, and the Conventional Forces in Europe Treaty—were cast aside. The twin deaths of the ABM Treaty and START II were decisive. Vice President Cheney offered no rebuttal when Bush cast aside his crowning achievement—the abolition of MIRVed land-based missiles—in order to defend against missile threats from the axis of evil. Putin authorized a cruise missile program that constituted a material breach of the Intermediate Nuclear Forces Treaty. This and other treaties would be jettisoned when Donald Trump was paired with Putin. During Bush's second term, tensions increased, and reassurance receded as NATO expanded. Communication channels remained open, but not for constructive business.

The progressive demise of treaties did not mean reverting to the worst conditions of the Cold War. Nuclear arsenals were a small fraction of Cold War levels, nuclear testing moratoria remained in place, as did the fundamentals of nuclear deterrence. The death of treaties representing the nuclear peace didn't make a nuclear war inevitable; it did mean increased friction and dangerous military practices. Strategic arms reductions were unaffected at the outset of the unraveling process because Moscow valued equal force levels with the United States. Conventional arms control was a different matter, as Putin had no interest in constraining freedom of action to move military equipment and troops within and just beyond Russian borders.

There would be a respite from the death of treaties during the Obama administration, in part because Obama couldn't bring himself to exit the Intermediate Nuclear Forces Treaty that Russia was clearly violating. Obama would take advantage of Dmitri Medvedev's one term as president, securing the New Strategic Arms Reduction Treaty in 2010, extending verification arrangements for ten years, superseding the flimsy Moscow Treaty. New START was a major accomplishment, given the trajectory of U.S.-Russian relations, but it would be a placeholder and little more. Despite appearances, it wouldn't mandate deeper cuts than the Moscow Treaty because of generous warhead counting rules.

The demise of arms control began in earnest with treaty withdrawals by Bush and Putin. Bush was confident in U.S. power and Putin never doubted and systematically nurtured the return of Russian nationalism. Both men knew exactly what they were doing when they discarded treaties, but they didn't foresee where this would lead. Bush could have amended the ABM Treaty to his liking, but he chose an alternative path even before taking office. He and those around him believed strongly that the treaty's shackles needed to be removed, even though effective interceptors for national defense against sophisticated countermeasures would remain beyond technical reach for decades into the future and perhaps indefinitely. Putin was thus relieved of START II's ban on land-based missiles carrying multiple warheads, and in 2020 began to deploy the worst possible variants of this kind—liquid-fueled behemoths based in silos. These missiles were the easiest for his military-industrial complex to produce and pay for. They took longer to prepare for launch than the time required to destroy them. The problem of reciprocal fears of surprise attack that START II would have shelved would return front and center when Putin began deploying his new "use or lose" missiles.

Bush's record on nonproliferation was mixed. On the positive side of the ledger, the Bush administration pursued deep cuts in strategic forces. It could claim notable achievements in the Proliferation Security Initiative and UN Security Council Resolution 1540. Saddam Hussein and his sons would no longer plague Iraq. Reconstruction of an Iraqi nuclear program that Saddam was unable to restart seems remote. Libya's ineffectual program was shut down and Israeli aircraft destroyed a nascent Syrian nuclear program built with help from North Korea. In addition, the Bush administration carried out two effective crisis management interventions on the subcontinent. After militant groups based in Pakistan and linked to Pakistan's military and intelligence services carried out an attack against the Indian Parliament building in 1999, Powell and Richard Armitage adroitly intervened to avoid a war between these two newly nuclear-armed states. In 2008, Rice and Hadley provided an Indian government that wished to avoid war with an exit strategy after luxury hotels, the main train station, and a Jewish Center in Mumbai were attacked by militants based in Pakistan.

On the negative side of the nonproliferation ledger, the two hardest proliferation cases became more intractable. Eight years passed without effective constraints on Iran's nuclear and missile programs. Bush and his advisers deemed constraints on North Korea's nuclear and missile programs inherited from the Clinton administration to be insufficient. These constraints were rejected without replacement or improvement. North Korea withdrew from the Nonproliferation Treaty in 2002 and tested its first nuclear device in 2006 along with fourteen missile flight tests during Bush's presidency. Rice overcame Bush's skepticism about diplomacy with North Korea and strong internal resistance, primarily from Cheney, to engage Kim Jong Il with regional stakeholders and major powers for "six party" talks. These talks produced a notional agreement on nuclear disarmament as well as implementation plans. Pyongyang agreed to partial measures, including blowing up the cooling tower at its reactor producing plutonium, but its declared holdings of nuclear capabilities was incomplete, and Pyongyang was unwilling to agree to verification arrangements in writing. The six-party talks broke down in December 2008.

Elsewhere, the India nuclear deal accelerated warhead and missile production on the subcontinent. Pakistan blocked negotiations on a fissile material "cutoff" treaty and began constructing new plutonium production reactors. New Delhi ramped up its own programs. The Bush administration's preventive wars and new framework for assessing proliferation, with friendly states receiving "passes" and suspect states being subject to pressure campaigns, had corrosive effects on the Nonproliferation Treaty's consensual foundations. Subsequently, abstainers felt less obliged to adopt strengthened safeguards on their civil nuclear programs, while possessors felt less obliged to take steps to reduce the number and salience of their nuclear weapons. Five-year treaty review conferences became more contentious. Abstainers began to look elsewhere to hold possessors accountable, with some focusing their efforts on drafting and promoting a treaty banning nuclear weapons. On balance, the NPT was weakened during the Bush years.

From Eisenhower to Bush, the superstructure of arms control was constructed with two building permits: one was U.S. international standing and the other was a sound basis for cooperation between Washington and Moscow. The Bush administration's wars in Afghanistan and Iraq imposed heavy costs on U.S. international standing, as well as on those prosecuting them, on foreign combatants and noncombatants. These wars did not gravely damage U.S.-Russian relations because Moscow (and Beijing) benefitted from U.S. misfortunes. Nor did these wars damage prospects for arms control. The decline of bilateral relations, and thus the misfortunes of arms control, came instead from NATO expansion, especially plans to include Georgia and Ukraine within the alliance. Secondary causes related to U.S. plans for missile defense deployments and grievances over Balkan wars and Kosovo's independence.

Bush and his advisers walked in full stride through the door of NATO expansion that the Clinton administration opened. The hubris of the Bush administration's freedom agenda came back to haunt. There is hardly a nod in the memoirs of Bush and Rice that Putin's behavior was influenced by NATO's headlong expansion. Rice is completely dismissive of any link in this regard. The essence of the problem, in her view, was not Washington's over-reaching, but "Russia's ability to come to terms with the post–Cold War order."[73] Bush attributes Putin's aggressiveness to "Russia's newfound wealth," defensiveness about his domestic record, and his intent to expand Russia's sphere of influence.[74] There is truth to these explanations, but they don't acknowledge a feedback loop from the Bush administration's decisions.

The demise of arms control that began with Bush and Putin was both a tragedy and a case of murderous intent. The tragedy was that the basis for long-standing strategic stability was in place with both the ABM Treaty and START II, and that once the interwoven fabric of arms control began to unravel, it was hard to stop until all of the treaties that Washington or Moscow found bothersome were discarded. By jettisoning treaties, Bush and Putin also jettisoned the reassurance treaties provided. Both men did what they felt they needed to do and didn't dwell on long-term consequences.

Some of the unraveling was bound to happen because Moscow and Washington were intent on loosening these bonds. But the fundamental unease of the relationship—and thus the extent of unraveling to come—was rooted in the Bush administration's freedom agenda that placed Washington and Moscow on a collision course. Putin's splenetic speech before the 2007 Munich Security Conference included a pointed reference to NATO enlargement: "The process of NATO expansion has nothing to do with modernization of the alliance. We have the right to ask, 'Against whom is this expansion directed?'"[75] Placing Georgia and Ukraine in the queue of NATO expansion was intolerable to the Kremlin. Putin had the means to block their membership, and his blocking actions hastened the demise of arms control.

Expanding NATO also raised significant problems for the alliance's political cohesion and military effectiveness. The extent of NATO expansion to the Baltic states led to defense requirements that couldn't be met by conventional forces alone. Western strategic analysts convinced themselves that Moscow was intent to "escalate to de-escalate" by using tactical nuclear weapons in campaigns against the Baltic states. This scenario led to the pursuit of new low-yield nuclear strike options to be delivered by U.S. missile-carrying submarines. These calculations harkened back to the Cold War. Putin had something different in mind. His model of hybrid and cyber warfare made Russian resort to the early use of nuclear weapons unnecessary.

NATO was much larger as a result of the Bush administration, but it wasn't stronger, either politically or militarily. Given the limited military means of new NATO member states, an expanded alliance would necessarily take on more of a political coloration, but political cohesion suffered as Hungary and Poland reverted to authoritarian tendencies under NATO's protective umbrella.

Arms control treaties were not the only or the most important aspect of a rules-based international order that began to fray badly as a result of actions taken by Bush and Putin. Bush's rationale for invading Iraq on the basis of anticipatory proliferation required agile interpretations of international law. Vice President Cheney dispensed with them. "The only legitimacy we really need," he argued, "comes on the back of an M1A1 tank."[76] This argument also suited Putin, who took a backseat to no one in his disregard for international law, dismissing the territorial integrity and national sovereignty of his neighbors.

Putin also dispensed with treaty obligations without bothering to announce his prospective intent to withdraw from compacts constraining his freedom of action. During the Bush administration, Russian missile flight testing continued that was prohibited by the INF Treaty signed by Gorbachev and Reagan. Russia also violated the Open Skies Treaty by restricting flights over "independent" enclaves in Georgia and over Kaliningrad, a Russian outpost on the Baltic Sea. The more Putin violated treaty obligations the more Republicans on Capitol Hill demanded U.S. treaty withdrawals.

The actions of Bush and Putin resulted in the undoing of arms control. Both leaders bent norms to their liking. Bush considered himself, as Robert Gates observed, "tougher and more idealistic than his father."[77] He also lacked his father's geopolitical instincts and prudence. Bush 41 was surrounded by wise counsel; Bush 43's advisers reinforced bad decisions far more than they questioned them. Bush sent U.S. expeditionary forces into two unwinnable wars without exit strategies. In Afghanistan, it was essential to disrupt and defeat al-Qaeda. Dealing with the Taliban was another matter entirely, and once in, there was never a good time to leave valued partners behind. The situation in Iraq was equally murky after toppling Saddam. "One of the principal outcomes," as Gates acknowledged, "had been to empower Iran, so it upset the balance in the region."[78]

As for NATO expansion, Bush bequeathed to his successors a much larger alliance that would inevitably become less politically coherent and less militarily purposeful over time. One consequence of Bush's overreaching on NATO expansion was the transition, in less than a decade's time, of U.S.-Russian relations from mutual positivism to mutual recrimination. The most punishing national security decisions of the Bush presidency—his responses to 9/11 in the first term and his pursuit of NATO expansion to include Georgia and Ukraine in the second—saddled his successors with limited room to maneuver and recover. Bush faced hard choices with humility and confidence, but without his father's cautionary instincts and wise counselor, Brent Scowcroft. His bold choices proved to be his undoing and contributed greatly to the undoing of arms control.

Chapter 15

REALITY OVERTAKES HOPE

The state of the nuclear peace depends on the state of relations between nuclear-armed rivals. Trend lines in U.S.-Russian relations were deteriorating when the candidate of hope and change, Barack Obama, replaced George W. Bush in the White House. Obama's nemesis was Vladimir Putin, with whom he met in July 2009 to hear a litany of grievance. The essence of Putin's complaint was that Bush pursued a post–Cold War order at Russia's expense, particularly with NATO expansion.[1] Putin was intent to push back against U.S. overreaching, and his agenda included dismantling arms control arrangements that Mikhail Gorbachev and Boris Yeltsin endorsed during times of grave weakness.

Obama had breathing room, however. His timing was typically fortunate, as his first term coincided with Putin's decision to temporarily cede the Russian presidency in 2008 to Dmitri Medvedev. Obama seized on this opening, offering Medvedev a "reset" and partially mend the fabric of arms control. Medvedev seemed willing to reset relations with Washington, but Putin was waiting in the wings and negative trendlines were already deeply grooved. Even more troubling developments were in the offing, when Putin returned to the presidency in 2012 to disregard treaty constraints during Obama's second term.

With the Russian economy on the mend, prospects for deeper cuts were daunting, as these forces constituted the Kremlin's strong suit. From

Moscow's perspective, deeper reductions would require constraints on U.S. missile defenses—constraints that weren't politically feasible for Obama given advances in North Korea's missile programs and opposition on Capitol Hill. Whether he could achieve deep cuts or not, Obama needed a new treaty governing strategic offenses quickly because the Bush-Putin Moscow Treaty signed in 2002 depended on verification provisions embedded in the first Strategic Arms Reduction Treaty, and START I was set to expire during Obama's first year in office. Without a new treaty, the practice of strategic arms control dating back to Richard Nixon's 1972 Interim Agreement would be lost.

Putin wasn't the only roadblock. Obama sought to reduce the salience and number of nuclear weapons when they were becoming more valuable to the leaders of China, India, Pakistan, and North Korea as well as Russia.[2] Stabilization measures were becoming more pressing but harder to accomplish as jockeying increased between nuclear-armed rivals. Obama aimed high, but quickly adjusted to ground realities. The book written by Obama's speechwriter and close adviser, Ben Rhodes, was aptly titled *The World as It Is*, in contrast to the one Obama hoped to change in lasting ways. Obama reprised Rhodes's book title for a section of his memoir, *The Promised Land*, in which he wrote, "You learn to measure progress in smaller steps."[3] Much of his ambitious arms control agenda fell by the wayside.

Obama demonstrated that U.S. leadership could still make a difference in strategic arms control and nonproliferation, but presidential leadership wasn't enough. Major successes come during upswings in cooperation between major powers. Obama's presidency was marked by growing friction between Washington and both Moscow and Beijing. Achievements were still possible, but they were also reversible because of hyper-partisanship in Washington. While Obama achieved a verifiable treaty to extend strategic arms control, which the administration called New START, the Kremlin resisted deeper cuts. He made strides locking down dangerous fissile material in a series of Nuclear Security Summits, and most surprising of all, he orchestrated a verifiable agreement that significantly limited Iran's bomb-making capacity. Then came a black swan event—the election of Donald Trump. The mutually convenient and toxic partnership of Trump and Putin—one a serial treaty withdrawer, the other a serial violator—would leave arms control in a battered state. Before the denouement of arms control, however, there was an interlude of hope.

THE EMBODIMENT OF HOPE

Barack Hussein Obama owed his election to the hope he engendered and to public perceptions of his predecessor's failings. John McCain, his Republican opponent, stumbled during the campaign, reinforcing Obama's case for younger leadership. He personified, as his campaign slogan advertised, "hope you can believe in." He also inherited harsh realities. Bush bequeathed to him a national economic crisis and two unwinnable wars from which exits would be excruciatingly difficult. The election result—with Obama winning 53 percent of the popular vote—reflected the electorate's strong desire to turn the page. Voters seemed to be looking for a different kind of boldness than Bush offered. Bill Clinton and Bush trumpeted the United States as the indispensable nation; the country that Obama led felt like the overextended nation.

Obama's mantra about avoiding "stupid stuff" applied, above all, to avoiding another war without an exit strategy. On the campaign trail, Obama distinguished between the war in Afghanistan, which he viewed as necessary, with the war in Iraq, which he viewed as a tragic error. His victory in the primaries against Hillary Clinton and subsequent election were partly the result of his early opposition to the war to topple Saddam Hussein and remake Iraq. He wasn't a pacifist, however. Obama authorized Navy SEALs to kill Osama bin Laden and airpower to stop Muammar Qaddafi from slaughtering his domestic opposition, hastening his demise. Chaos ensued, but there would be no U.S. boots on the ground to stabilize or remake Libya. Targeted killings by drone strikes rose markedly under Obama, who downsized Bush's Global War on Terror to disrupting, dismantling, and defeating Islamic terror networks. Drone strikes didn't win hearts and minds in the Islamic world. They were, however, an effective substitute to committing more ground forces in seemingly intractable conflicts. Obama increased U.S. expeditionary forces in Afghanistan, but success, no matter how narrowly defined, remained elusive. He soon learned the same lesson in Afghanistan as the Bush administration learned in Iraq: changing the course of events in the Islamic world by force of Western arms was at best a draining proposition.

When the Bush administration misused hard power, America's soft power became collateral damage. Joseph Nye described soft power as "the ability of a country to structure a situation so that other countries develop preferences or define their interests in ways consistent with its own." Nye's short-form definition—"getting others to want what you want"—seems too narrow.[4] A broader, nontransactional definition of soft power measures a country's attractiveness. Likability matters in international relations, even if it doesn't matter as much as hard power and a strong economy.

Likability extends to political leaders and their policies. The Bush administration's reliance on hard power reflected the topmost priority of preventing another 9/11. For this, it was better to be feared than liked. Vice President Dick Cheney became the personification of America's hard power. Obama was the personification of American soft power. The son of a wayward Kenyan father and an adventurous mother from Kansas was the living embodiment of the promise of America to achieve a more perfect union. His name, his skin color, and his background were different. His demeanor wasn't stiff; it was serenely graceful. He could mimic Al Green crooning love ballads and could shoot hoops. He didn't kill animals for sport or for food. Constituencies could relate to him that previously felt far removed from the White House. Obama struck chords that hadn't been played by any of his predecessors.[5]

Obama was a vessel that people at home and abroad could fill with their aspirations or their fears. For some, aspirations were so great that they were bound to be disappointed. Others couldn't relate to Obama or were unalterably opposed to what they presumed he stood for. For all his oratorical skills, Obama couldn't change minds, and for all the coverage he received, he remained a mysterious figure. He came across as both an idealist and a pragmatist. He had a magnetic personality and yet he also came across as detached and aloof. He possessed intellectual depth, but he could connect with crowds. He mostly kept his cool and could flash a magnificent smile. He was a gifted leader, but he disliked retail politics. The Senate taught him important lessons about Washington, but it didn't teach him management skills.

Obama added strong aspirations atop those of his supporters. His interest in reducing nuclear danger dated back to college and was sharpened under the tutelage of Senator Richard Lugar when both served on the Foreign Relations Committee. Obama was intent to reduce the numbers and salience of nuclear weapons in the United States and elsewhere. His election gave new hope to those who believed that it was possible to abolish nuclear weapons after the Cold War ended. The urtext in this regard was penned by four elder statesmen—George Shultz, William Perry, Henry Kissinger, and Sam Nunn—who wrote an op-ed in 2007 supporting the vision of a world without nuclear weapons.

The "four horsemen" wrote that "U.S. leadership will be required to take the world to the next stage—to a solid consensus for reversing reliance on nuclear weapons globally as a vital contribution to preventing their proliferation into potentially dangerous hands, and ultimately ending them as a threat to the world." Cold War constructs of nuclear deterrence needed to be rethought. New threats, especially Iran's and North Korea's nuclear programs, as well as the threat of nuclear terrorism, demanded new approaches. "Reliance on nuclear weapons" to counter these threats, they argued, "is becoming increasingly hazardous and decreasingly effective." The alternative to "a new nuclear era that will be more precarious, psychologically disorienting, and economically even more costly than was Cold War deterrence" was to take seriously the goal of abolition. The need of the hour was to "rekindle the vision shared by Reagan and Mr. Gorbachev." They called for changing hair-trigger readiness to use nuclear weapons and for substantial reductions.[6]

These were heady times. The agenda of the four horsemen (Kissinger subsequently had second thoughts and dropped out) heightened expectations about abolition. Just three months after taking office, Obama addressed the abolition agenda briefly in a highly anticipated speech delivered before a crowd of perhaps 30,000 enthusiasts in Prague. Obama reworked many of the speeches Rhodes prepared for him, but his agenda was too packed to edit this one.[7] Obama began with a commonplace observation—that nuclear weapons were the most dangerous legacy of the Cold War. Then he echoed the Bush administration: "In a strange turn of history, the threat of global nuclear war has gone down, but the risk of a nuclear attack has gone up." His reference points were North Korea, which tested a missile the day of his speech, Iran, and nuclear terrorism. Obama rejected a fatalistic approach to proliferation, equating it to fatalism about the eventual appearance of mushroom clouds. He reaffirmed the Nonproliferation Treaty's basic bargain of abstinence in return for steps toward disarmament.

Then Obama offered the message that many came to hear: "Today I state clearly and with conviction America's commitment to seek the peace and security of a world without nuclear weapons." He added, by way of qualification, "I'm not naive. This goal will not be reached quickly, perhaps not in my lifetime. It will take patience and persistence." Then he took another swipe at fatalism, echoing his campaign's theme: "We must ignore the voices who tell us that the world cannot change. We have to insist, 'Yes we can.'"

The Prague speech tried to revive and reclaim the vision of Ronald Reagan and Mikhail Gorbachev. Obama promised to take "concrete steps towards a world without nuclear weapons," to "reduce the role of nuclear weapons in our national security strategy and urge others to do the same," and to negotiate a new "legally binding and sufficiently bold" strategic arms reduction treaty, pointing the way to further cuts. There was more: Obama sought "to include all nuclear weapons states in this endeavor," promised to "immediately and aggressively" pursue ratification of the Comprehensive Test Ban Treaty and start negotiations on a compact to end global production of bomb-making fissile material."[8]

Obama the pragmatist didn't edit Obama the idealist before delivering the Prague speech. It cost him. The "Prague agenda" became a yardstick for the administration's unfulfilled ambitions. It was too bold and too overt, lending a sense of greater urgency to those seeking to clip his wings. He would be hard-pressed to change U.S. nuclear doctrine, even with the world's most capable conventional forces, let alone persuade others to reduce the salience of nuclear weapons. The Prague agenda was, however, sweet music to the ears of arms controllers in the United States and Europe, as well as to the committee awarding the Nobel Peace Prize. Obama's response upon hearing that he had received this high honor was expletive-laden. He immediately realized that he would need to deal with even more unrealistic expectations. As a partial corrective, Obama's speech after accepting the Peace Prize was about when the use of force was necessary.

Obama wasn't a true believer in nuclear weapons, but he couldn't move others to modify contrary beliefs. He had no strong attachment to the particulars of nuclear deterrence or to targeting requirements in the event deterrence failed. He vocalized in private what all his predecessors dating back to Eisenhower no doubt felt when being briefed about nuclear war-fighting plans. He reportedly said, "Let's stipulate that all of this is insane," before bowing to the reality that plans and doctrine were needed.[9]

At the outset, Obama's topmost arms control challenge was to rehabilitate strategic arms control, given that existing limits and inspections would lapse at the end of his first year in office. New multilateral accords dealing with fissile material, the pursuit of Senate ratification of the Comprehensive Test Ban Treaty, and a code of conduct for responsible space-faring nations— another campaign promise—would have to wait. The Nuclear Security Summits, New START, and a nuclear deal with Iran would constitute Obama's legacy in this domain. All were notable achievements, all mended a fraying fabric of arms control, and all would be hard to sustain after he left office.

TEAM OBAMA

The two heavyweights in Obama's cabinet were Secretary of State Hillary Clinton and Secretary of Defense Robert Gates. Clinton, bested by Obama in a long and sometimes testy primary campaign, was a surprise choice. Picking her helped Obama to mend fences and helped Clinton showcase her talents and develop her expertise on foreign policy—all of which were expected to provide propulsion for another run for the White House. Obama persuaded Gates, whose sense of duty to troops in war zones was palpable and deep, that they were on a close enough wavelength for him to stay at the Pentagon for two more years. Gates knew that he was providing "cover" for Obama as a Bush holdover, but he was at peace with this as long as he could help shape Obama's approach to the issues that mattered most to him—attending to the two wars Obama inherited and avoiding a third with Iran. Clinton and Gates lent a pragmatic bent to Obama's foreign and national security policies, much to the discomfort of his progressive backers. Gates wrote that he and Clinton formed a "very strong partnership, in part because it turned out we agreed on almost every important issue." He was surprised to find Clinton "smart, idealistic but pragmatic, tough-minded, indefatigable [and] funny."[10]

Leon Panetta, a former congressman, head of the Office of Management and Budget, and chief of staff under Bill Clinton, was another surprise pick to lead the Central Intelligence Agency. Panetta was the son of Italian immigrants who settled in Monterey, California, and succeeded from scratch in the restaurant business. They sold the business to buy land and plant walnut trees in the Carmel Valley. Their son could always be counted on to answer "yes" when called to serve a country where immigrants and their children were welcomed and could realize their dreams. He was a likable politician who could absorb new portfolios and manage large organizations—a rare skill set. Gates identified Panetta as a worthy successor to care for the troops and run the Pentagon, and Obama readily concurred. Obama's choice as national security advisor was the retired commandant of the Marine Corps, James Jones. Jones was chosen in part to counter images of Obama as an untethered peacenik. He was by all accounts a poor fit, becoming the odd man out to Obama's White House confidants Tom Donilon and Denis McDonough.

The memoirs of Obama, Clinton, Gates, and Panetta have little or nothing to say about traditional arms control and the Prague agenda. Likewise, John Kerry and former senator Chuck Hagel followed by Ashton Carter at the Pentagon—the successors to Clinton and Gates—paid little attention to strategic arms control. As always, the urgent displaced other issues that were merely important. Carter was the best equipped secretary of defense since William Perry and Harold Brown to work on arms control, by virtue of his brainpower and previous Pentagon assignments working on policy, acquisition, and management. Earlier in his career, he was instrumental in preventing "loose nukes" in the former Soviet Union, but as secretary of defense, he was disinterested in strategic arms control, focusing instead on arrows rather than olive branches. Proliferation was a different matter entirely. Kerry, along with Energy Secretary Ernest Moniz, Under Secretary of State Wendy Sherman, technical expert James Timbie, and many others, focused hard on negotiating with Iran.[11]

NEW START

No president since Jimmy Carter was as committed to nuclear arms control and as conversant with its details as Barack Obama. The White House's coordinator for arms control issues, Gary Samore, was struck by Obama's absorptive capacity for substance and detail, as well as his commitment to "making a mark."[12] But Obama, for all his talents, lacked the ability to rewrite the script in which he played a starring role or to change his Russian co-star, Vladimir Putin. Obama entered the stage when arms control was already in a period of decline for reasons that were beyond his ability to reverse. Putin, the embodiment of revived Russian fortunes, was, as William Burns described, "cocky, cranky, aggrieved and insecure"—not the traits one would wish for in a negotiating partner.[13]

In Jimmy Carter's day, negotiating strategic arms control was the province of the director of the Arms Control and Disarmament Agency and the secretary of state. Strategic arms reductions no longer merited this degree of attention. During the Obama administration, it was the bailiwick of an assistant secretary or under secretary of state. The administration's negotiator was Rose Gottemoeller. She was, as Mike McFaul described her, "knowledgeable about the issues, calm in demeanor, persistently optimistic, and a team player." Negotiating strategic arms control was "an assignment of a lifetime for her." McFaul handled the Russia portfolio on the National Security Council staff and was then assigned his dream job as U.S. ambassador to Russia.[14]

Gottemoeller grew up in Columbus, Ohio, and Dearborn, Michigan. Her father was an insurance executive and her mother a housewife. Like other baby boomers, she held lasting memories of duck-and-cover drills. After the Soviet Union launched Sputnik, her dad took her outside to watch as the satellite passed overhead. She attended Georgetown University, studied Russian, and then went to George Washington University. Her first job was as a research assistant to Thomas Wolfe at RAND who was writing a book on the Strategic Arms Limitation Talks. As a Council on Foreign Relations Fellow during the George H.W. Bush administration she was placed at the State Department, where she got her first taste of strategic arms reduction negotiations. She wanted more. During her stint in the Clinton administration, one of Gottemoeller's assignments was to negotiate a space cooperation agreement with Moscow that bore fruition with the International Space Station, another object that could be readily seen in the night sky. Gottemoeller spent the three years prior to joining Obama as director of the Carnegie Endowment's Moscow Center, where she met periodically with Anatoly Antonov, who would become her counterpart negotiator.

Brad Roberts, who worked on nuclear issues at the Pentagon during the Obama administration, wryly noted that the 2002 Moscow Treaty stapled together the proposed U.S. and Russian force structures and called the result arms control.[15] Previous treaties also reflected force levels deemed to be essential. The three-page Moscow Treaty did not obligate reductions in "operationally deployed" warheads until the last minute of the last day of the treaty's ten-year duration, after which all obligations would be null and void. Without START's monitoring provisions, the Moscow Treaty had no weight-bearing capacity. But START was due to expire three years before the Moscow Treaty—ten months into the new administration. The White House wanted Gottemoeller to negotiate a new treaty in six months so that the Senate's consent to ratification could be completed before START's expiration date of December 5, 2009.

Negotiations began in April 2009, with both sides needing to plumb and refresh institutional memory, since the START negotiations ended eighteen years earlier. The pressure to complete the negotiations quickly intensified when Moscow was unwilling to extend START's verification provisions after its expiration because, as Gottemoeller recalled, "they said it contravened their national law on security—they needed a legally binding treaty to override domestic legislation (as do we). Second, because they were concerned that we would leave the negotiating table or slow-roll completion of the new treaty, just leaving START verification measure in place."[16] The negotiations proceeded with unnatural speed, but not fast enough for the Obama White House, which believed that faster progress could be achieved by micromanagement and by elevating Gottemoeller's blood pressure.[17] The Russian delegation was caught between Medvedev's desire for a treaty and Putin's qualms, but Medvedev managed to keep the negotiations on track. There were still issues to haggle over, trade-offs to accept, and repeated efforts by Moscow to limit U.S. missile defense programs.

Medvedev welcomed Washington's "reset" policy and was a willing partner in the talks. Putin remained a hovering presence, however, and in December 2009 he gave a talk in Vladivostok in which he worried aloud that U.S. missile defenses could disrupt the strategic balance and facilitate aggressive acts.[18] Gottemoeller went to bed that night wondering if the negotiations would be stymied, but Medvedev managed to stay the course. The Russian negotiating team, led by Antonov, proceeded in workmanlike fashion. Drawing heavily from the fine print from START I's provisions, U.S. and Russian negotiators were able to complete the 180,000-word treaty text and annexes in record time. On March 24, 2010, just one year after the start of negotiations, New START was ready for signature. Obama and Medvedev did so in Prague on April 8. New START reduced nuclear forces to 1,550 accountable deployed nuclear weapons on a total of 700 intercontinental ballistic missiles, ballistic missile-carrying submarines, and heavy bombers. These limits were to be met by February 2018, three years before the treaty's expiration date. Washington and Moscow could structure their strategic forces any way they wished and could keep 100 additional launchers in reserve, limiting capabilities to "break out" from treaty constraints.

The deployed warhead total was nominally down from the Moscow Treaty's 1,700–2,200 warhead limits, but there was a catch: New START adopted an old "counting rule" where bombers counted as one regardless of how many nuclear weapons they carried. The negotiating history of this bomber counting rule was tortuous, with Washington and Moscow switching positions at various times. This time around, the Obama administration was willing to assign bombers with a larger count of attributable warheads, backed up by inspections of storage bunkers at bomber bases, but Moscow vetoed this idea, not willing to allow this degree of transparency. By counting bombers as carrying one warhead only, New START undercounted deployed warheads by upward of 1,000 weapons.

New START extended verifiable strategic arms control for another crucial decade. Each party had the right to conduct eighteen inspections per year; by 2020, the number of these inspections exceeded 300. The numbers and types of inspections were streamlined from START because there were far fewer facilities to inspect and because both Washington and Moscow sought relief from the expense and delays associated with preparing for and hosting so many inspections. Provisions for the exchange of telemetry from missile flight tests—data that could, for example, determine the number of warheads released by a missile—were also streamlined because confirmation could be provided by radiation detection devices during on-site inspections at missile bases.

New START didn't qualify, in Obama's estimation, as a "world-changing" accomplishment.[19] That standard was reserved for the Cold War–ending compacts negotiated in the Reagan and George H.W. Bush administrations. Instead, New START was, to borrow the lexicon of the Joint Chiefs of Staff after SALT II was negotiated in the Carter administration, modest but useful. It was critically important to extend verifiable strategic arms control, but deterrence strengtheners were unimpressed, criticizing New START's verification standards and claiming that the treaty's ostensibly equal limitations actually favored Moscow. Arms controllers expressed disappointment that New START did not produce deeper cuts. Obama was willing to reduce further—his administration's internal reviews indicated that reductions to 1,000 deployed warheads would not be detrimental to U.S. national security—but he did not have a willing partner in Putin, and he would proceed only in parallel with Russian reductions.

Putin's return to the presidency in 2012 effectively ended the reset in U.S.-Russian ties. He reminded Obama of a ward boss from Chicago, "except with nukes and a UN Security Council veto."[20] Nonetheless, Obama sought once more to reduce deployed warheads by another third when he met with Putin in 2013. Putin responded that the initiative was premature, as New START's mandated reductions would take five more years to implement. After this meeting in Berlin, relations plummeted with Putin's annexation of Crimea and hybrid warfare against Ukraine.

There would be no improvement on New START's terms on Obama's watch, nor would there be another summit meeting with Putin. Another complicating factor was China's rise, evident not just in terms of economic growth but also in its pursuit of a navy that could project power within and beyond territorial waters, as well as more assertive steps to extend its writ over contested islands in the South China Sea. Beijing historically placed a much lower priority on expanding its strategic nuclear forces but clearly had the means to do so—a mutual concern of Moscow and Washington. This was one of the arguments levied against New START during the Senate's ratification debate and would later be highlighted by the Trump administration as a reason not to extend New START for five years beyond its 2021 expiration date.

Obama courted heavyweights to help with ratification. At a gathering in the Roosevelt Room in the White House, he listened to helpful ideas from

Henry Kissinger, James Baker, Brent Scowcroft, Sam Nunn, and others. Ratification seemed eminently manageable. New START did no harm and gave the process of verifiable strategic arms control a crucial ten-year life extension. "If we can't do this," he told his august visitors, "we can't do anything."[21] Six former Republican secretaries of state—Kissinger, George Shultz, Baker, Lawrence Eagleburger, Colin Powell, and Condoleezza Rice—endorsed New START.[22] President George H.W. Bush supported ratification. U.S. allies in Europe and Asia were relieved to see a verifiable extension of strategic arms control. The Pentagon was fully supportive. The chairman of the Joint Chiefs of Staff, Mike Mullen, was instrumental in breaking negotiating impasses, and the Pentagon's negotiators, Ted Warner and Mike Elliot, were stanchions during the negotiations and the ratification debate.

New START skirted the neuralgic issue of missile defenses. The only nod given to Moscow's concerns within the treaty text was preambular language noting the "interrelationship between strategic offensive arms and strategic defensive arms." The treaty itself imposed only one limitation on U.S. missile defense programs—that interceptor missiles would not replace nuclear-armed intercontinental ballistic missiles in their silos—an option the Pentagon had no interest in pursuing.[23]

Critics were not mollified. In twenty-one days of hearings (twelve less than devoted to the tragic events at Benghazi where the U.S. ambassador to Libya and others lost their lives), they expressed concerns that future U.S. missile defense efforts would be subject to Russian vetoes and that silo-based intercontinental-range conventional strike capabilities would be hampered. Presidential candidate Mitt Romney set the tenor for opponents by asserting that the treaty "gives far more to the Russians than to the United States" and that "New START is a major victory for Russia." Opponents offered no prospect for success in negotiating a better alternative to New START, nor any substitute for the on-site inspections and other cooperative monitoring practices embedded in the treaty.[24] John Bolton opined that the treaty was "profoundly misguided" and could "cripple America's long-range conventional warhead delivery capabilities."[25]

None of the arguments against New START have withstood the passage of time. Missile defenses remained hampered by technical challenges and U.S. conventional global strike capabilities proceeded apace. Instead, the primary underlying rationales behind the campaign against New START were to make the Obama administration pay as high a price as possible in terms of support for strategic modernization programs and to deter the administration from coming back to the Senate with another treaty mandating deeper cuts. Both objectives were served by making the New START ratification process prolonged and painful. The leader of this effort in the Senate was again Jon Kyl, who reprised tactics developed during the fights over the Chemical Weapons Convention and Comprehensive Test Ban Treaty. The person Obama deputized to work with senators to secure the necessary two-thirds majority was Vice President Joe Biden. And the person Biden deputized to help him was his deputy national security advisor, Brian McKeon.

Biden worked the phones, helped immensely by the support of the Foreign Relations Committee chairman and ranking member John Kerry and Lugar. McKeon and Gottemoeller moved their base of operations to the Capitol building and Senate corridors during the final push for ratification. State Department officials Alex Bell, Lynn Rusten, and others dutifully answered over a thousand "questions for the record" asked by senators. The administration extinguished countless brushfires in the run-up to the ratification vote.

Obama and Biden were skeptical that Kyl would vote for New START, but they were intent not to provide him with ammunition to use with undecided Republican senators. The administration committed itself to strategic modernization of all three legs of the Triad as well as to upgrade the Department of Energy's nuclear weapon–related facilities. It topped off its previous budget plans, adding five billion dollars to partially address Kyl's demands, upping the amount pledged for modernization to $210 billion over ten years, including $85 billion for warhead-related work. These pledges, which necessarily could not commit a new administration after Obama left office, sufficed for ratification purposes. They constituted a significant down payment for the projected cost of well over one trillion dollars to fully fund strategic modernization programs for the Triad over a three-decade span.

Kyl lost the ratification vote but succeeded in wearing down administration officials over a seven-month-long process. Senate Republicans dashed the administration's hope for a quick and easy New START ratification and Putin dashed their hopes for deeper reductions in a follow-on accord. The roll call vote on New START was close, with the administration prevailing by four votes, 71–26. Kyl pocketed the administration's commitment for strategic modernization programs and voted "nay." John McCain, who was instrumental in the ratification vote in favor of the Chemical Weapons Convention, was aggrieved by the Obama administration's "Don't Ask, Don't Tell" policy with regard to the sexual orientation of members of the armed forces. McCain voted "nay." New START became the only nuclear arms control

treaty ever ratified without the support of the Republican leader. Mitch Mc-
Connell voted "nay," but at the urging of Lugar, he indicated that he would
not seek to impose party discipline and that this would be a "conscience"
vote. Thirteen Republican senators voted for ratification. McKeon, Biden's
point person for ratification, watched from the Senate gallery. The vote tally
was exactly as Biden predicted. McKeon then returned to the White House
to drink a glass of champagne in the Oval Office.

Gottemoeller served on the front lines in both the Clinton and Obama
administrations. The burden of "an accumulation of tactical decisions" and
week after week of fighting fires on Capitol Hill took its toll. Rounding up
two-thirds of the Senate was exhausting work. After succeeding, she noted,
the natural response was to say, "We're done," and not to repeat the process.
She was, however, game to try again—this time on the Comprehensive Test
Ban Treaty—but there was little enthusiasm in the White House or elsewhere
in the executive branch to charge up this hill.[26] Obama barely discusses the
struggle for New START's ratification in his memoir. After so much effort
and so much resistance, the realist in him was ready to move on. "We didn't
get a second bite of the apple," said Rusten.[27] Neither did President Carter
after the Panama Canal treaties nor Clinton after the Chemical Weapons
Convention.

The "one bite of the apple" standard for Democratic presidents was underscored when the Senate voted on the United Nations Convention on the
Rights of Persons with Disabilities in December 2012. The convention was
modeled on U.S. legislation—the Americans with Disabilities Act—which became public law in 1990. Proponents argued that the United States would
not incur new obligations and that by voting for ratification, Senators would
be urging other nations to follow Washington's example. Opponents argued
that the United States would be ceding sovereignty to the United Nations.
The White House's ratification effort took too much for granted, thinking
ratification assured. Despite the dramatic entrance in a wheelchair of former
Republican Senate leader Robert Dole—89 years old and recently released
from the Walter Reed National Military Medical Center—to signal his support, a majority of Senate Republicans were unmoved. They voted "nay,"
blocking ratification.

NUCLEAR SECURITY SUMMITS

There are no shortcuts to diplomatic success in the hardest proliferation cases,
but there are shortcuts to acquiring bomb-making capabilities. The collapse

of the Soviet Union raised the specter of fissile material, bomb-making parts, and entire devices falling into the hands of outliers. Obama, like his predecessors, accorded a very high priority to implementing new safety and security measures against illicit commerce.

Obama's signature initiative was a series of Nuclear Security Summits where world leaders would focus on the challenge of securing bomb-making materials. President Eisenhower's "Atoms for Peace" initiative inadvertently opened this door by providing research reactors fueled with highly enriched uranium to U.S. friends and allies. Obama inherited a situation where more than fifty countries possessed poorly safeguarded weapon-usable fissile material. In addition, 150 countries possessed radioactive sources such as cobalt and cesium that have medical, industrial, and agricultural uses. These radioactive sources cannot produce a mushroom cloud, but when combined with conventional explosives can be used as "dirty" bombs that spread radiation and fear. Nuclear weapons are weapons of mass destruction; dirty bombs have been called "weapons of mass disruption."[28]

In 1997, at the Clinton administration's urging, a summit meeting in Moscow of the Group of Seven—states with the world's largest economies—plus Russia was devoted to post–Cold War proliferation dilemmas. The Bush administration expanded the scope of these efforts by creating in 2002 the Global Partnership Against the Spread of Weapons and Materials of Mass Destruction, which had a broader scope, encompassing nuclear, chemical, and biological weapon–related terrorism. In 2005, Bush championed more expansive provisions for the Convention on Physical Protection of Nuclear Materials negotiated in the Carter administration. Bush successfully broadened the scope of the original convention, making it obligatory for states to protect nuclear facilities and source materials in storage and transport.

There were four summits in all, held in Washington (2010), Seoul (2012), The Hague (2014), and again in Washington (2016). The administration's goals for the summits were to create a process to help leaders familiarize themselves and embrace the issue, to prompt concrete steps to reduce proliferation danger, and to strengthen institutions with responsibilities to promote responsible nuclear stewardship and to prevent acts of nuclear terrorism.

Summit meetings require significant staff preparation. They serve as a forcing function to prompt "deliverables"—commitments that accompany a summit communique and reflect progress on agenda items. The deliverables at the first Nuclear Security Summit came to be known as "house gifts." Just as guests bring gifts when coming to dinner, Obama administration officials clarified that national leaders would be expected to announce concrete steps to improve nuclear security when visiting Washington. Beginning at the second summit in Seoul, the practice of bundling comparable commitments began; these were called "gift baskets."

The Nuclear Security Summit process was a White House initiative staffed primarily by National Security Council staffers. Those working on the Nuclear Security Summits used terminology for other summits to describe the hierarchy of staff support. The leaders who attended the summit were assisted by "sherpas" who worked together in advance of the summit. Sherpas were assisted by "sous-sherpas" who, in turn, were assisted by "yaks." President Obama's sherpa for the first two summits was Samore, who previously worked on the hardest proliferation cases during the Clinton administration. In all, Samore served seventeen years in government, beginning with the Lawrence Livermore National Laboratory. He helped Robert Gallucci negotiate the 1994 Agreed Framework designed to block North Korea's plutonium pathway to nuclear weapons. The sherpa for the third summit was Elizabeth Sherwood-Randle, who also served in the Clinton administration, working at the Pentagon to reduce nuclear danger after the collapse of the Soviet Union. After working on the National Security Council staff during the Obama administration, Sherwood-Randle served as deputy secretary at the Department of Energy. Laura Holgate, the sous-sherpa for the first three summits, served as the sherpa for the 2016 summit.

One key responsibility at the outset of the summit process was "building the guest list." If too many leaders came, the process would be unwieldy. Obama wanted an interactive summit and a seminar-like atmosphere for the first summit, not a long and deadening series of official statements. The guest list reflected states with key facilities required to make nuclear weapons, geographical representation, and diverse opinions about the Nonproliferation Treaty regime. Samore and Holgate came up with forty-two countries—notably similar to the Comprehensive Test Ban Treaty's list of states whose ratifications were required for entry into force. Representatives from the European Union and the International Atomic Energy Agency were also invited. Two presumed spoilers—Iran and North Korea—were purposefully excluded to maintain focus on the topic at hand. Subsequently, others were invited to participate. The dates for the first summit needed to be changed because the organizers didn't check with the First Lady's calendar: the initial dates conflicted with the spring break of the Obama daughters.

The first Nuclear Security Summit took place on April 12–13, 2010. It was the largest gathering of world leaders ever to be in Washington at one time. Obama consumed a three-inch briefing book to make informed interventions; other national leaders did, as well. By one accounting, participants brought a total of 935 "house gifts" and 39 "gift baskets" to the four summits.[29] Seventeen countries consented to remove, dispose of, or minimize the use of highly enriched uranium. The number of countries with mushroom cloud–making material on their territory was more than halved. [30]

One important outgrowth of the Nuclear Security Summits was the proliferation of "Centers of Excellence"—national institutions created to focus on subjects of greatest interest and perceived need, such as nuclear forensics in the Netherlands and border security in Lithuania. The summit process became a spur for China, India, Pakistan, Japan, and South Korea to upgrade existing training programs and invest in institutions dedicated to nuclear security.

The Nuclear Security Summit process depended on U.S. leadership to maintain momentum. Russia attended the first three summits, but chose not to attend the fourth in the aftermath of its annexation of Crimea. "Summit fatigue" became a factor, and after four summits, the locus of attention shifted to "action plans" for multilateral organizations. The burden of maintaining progress on nuclear security issues fell to the International Atomic Energy Agency, which convenes international conferences where countries could exchange lessons learned. Absent strong impulses from key nuclear possessors and abstainers, the propulsion for improvements in nuclear security declined after Obama left office.

THE PROLIFERATION CALCULUS

Nuclear proliferation has proceeded more slowly than has often been projected. One reason is the establishment of a global norm of nonproliferation embodied in the Nonproliferation Treaty. Most state parties to the NPT have come to view the Bomb as being immoral, unnecessary, or too expensive to seek. Another reason is that American presidents reinforced the nonproliferation norm by providing a protective umbrella over allies. Over time, other reasons for restraint became apparent. Some national leaders came to the conclusion that possessing the Bomb would actually diminish national security by damaging relations with benefactors, by the imposition of sanctions, or by prompting rivals to seek the Bomb. Yet another reason for restraint was the prospect of being on the receiving end of punishing and embarrassing air strikes.

The apartheid government of South Africa voluntarily dismantled its nuclear weapons prior to peaceful regime change. Ukraine, Kazakhstan, and Belarus gave up their sudden nuclear inheritance, convinced that their security would be diminished by retaining Soviet weapons. Nuclear ambitions have also been dashed by incompetence (Libya), air strikes (Israel, directed against Iraq and Syria), and warfare (the 1991 U.S. war in Iraq). Nonetheless, when national leaders are absolutely intent to acquire the Bomb and the means to deliver it, they usually succeed. Since the NPT was negotiated in 1968 only four states—Israel, India, Pakistan, and North Korea—have done so. The last of this lot, North Korea, did so during the George W. Bush administration's watch.

At any given time, there will be outliers to global nonproliferation norms. The hardest cases do not lend themselves to permanent successes. Partial successes are still possible, however, when an outlier is in no hurry or not fully committed to acquiring the Bomb, or when the outlier has other options to meet its national security objectives. Partial successes are also possible when a state wishes to shed its outlier status to engage in international commerce, delaying nuclear and missile programs and buying time for more diplomacy. If and when political, regional, and geopolitical conditions become more conducive to nonproliferation, partial successes can lead to bigger successes.

Skeptics of nonproliferation diplomacy argue that partial successes are a mirage, as outliers intend to disregard or circumvent concessions at their convenience. Some skeptics clearly state their preference for military measures to nullify an outlier's nuclear capabilities. Military strikes might also result in partial or temporary successes—at the risk of wider warfare—because nuclear capabilities can be reconstituted.

There have been three instances of partial diplomatic successes in extremely hard cases: The Agreed Framework and later the moratorium on missile testing with North Korea negotiated during the Clinton administration, and the nuclear deal with Iran during the Obama administration. The length of delay associated with partial diplomatic successes depends on the most impatient party to the agreements reached. In the North Korean and Iranian cases, the most impatient party was Washington. Republican administrations, not Pyongyang and Tehran, walked away from partial successes, but couldn't improve upon them.

THE IRAN NUCLEAR AGREEMENT

Administrations committed to nonproliferation diplomacy have limited bandwidth. The Clinton administration chose to engage with North Korea; the Obama administration engaged with Iran. When Obama took office, North Korea already possessed rudimentary atomic weapons and was ramping up its capacity to produce more powerful thermonuclear weapons. Partial diplomatic accomplishments could not reverse North Korea's possession of the Bomb. Military strikes risked hellish consequences, making reliance on deterrence and diplomatic containment the soundest options. There was, as Jon Wolfsthal concluded, "no pathway to success" to eliminate North Korea's nuclear arsenal.[31] In contrast, Tehran hadn't yet acquired nuclear weapons and was taking its time to do so. There was still a chance, as the U.S. negotiator Wendy Sherman surmised, that Iran's leaders could be extricated from "the jam" they were in—if they were not fully committed to acquiring the Bomb.[32]

Negotiating with Iranian officials, like negotiating with North Koreans in the 1990s and with Soviet diplomats during the Eisenhower and Nixon administrations, constituted a perilous voyage into the unknown. Iranians that negotiated with the United States risked much if they were perceived to be weakening national security. Sherman, who negotiated with North Korea as well as Iran over nuclear issues, noted that "the stakes were very different" for the negotiators. "Our reputations might be challenged, but we could move forward. They could face labor camps, imprisonment, or worse."[33]

Iran was a complicated country with evident domestic unrest. Iran's elected officials needed to heed powerful constituencies deeply resentful of Washington that were determined not to make concessions. U.S. negotiators also faced daunting political and diplomatic challenges. Space for negotiations could nonetheless be found because Iran had clear societal needs that its theocratic leaders and Revolutionary Guard Corps could not ignore. U.S.-led sanctions were squeezing Iran hard and they could be harder still. If Iran's leaders wished to engage in commerce and had enough backing, a nuclear deal could enable Tehran to break through its international isolation.

The U.S. intelligence community assessed with high confidence that Tehran "halted its nuclear weapons program" in the fall of 2003, after the second U.S. war against Saddam Hussein removed the primary threat Iran faced and provided an object lesson to Iranian rulers.[34] In 2003, Iran also began talks with the United Kingdom, France, and Germany over its nuclear program.

As long as Washington remained on the sidelines, these talks weren't going anywhere, even with the addition of Russian and Chinese negotiators.

While Iran had ceased working on weaponization in 2003, its scientists continued working on uranium enrichment, efforts that began to produce results in February 2006.[35] An electricity-generating nuclear reactor at Bushehr came online in 2011 after Russia provided the enriched uranium to begin its operation under the International Atomic Energy Agency's inspections. It was far from clear, however, whether Tehran could count on foreign supplies for reactor fuel in the future. Iranian enrichment facilities could provide fuel for Bushehr and other power reactors Iran expected to build with Russian support, as well as for a small research reactor in Tehran whose lineage dated back to Eisenhower's "Atoms for Peace" initiative.

Nuclear reactors generating electricity typically use uranium enriched to 4 percent; research reactors can use uranium enriched to 20 percent; the standard for nuclear weapons is 90 percent. The responsibility to monitor whether enrichment programs conform to peaceful uses under the Nonproliferation Treaty rests with the International Atomic Energy Agency. In 2007, Iranian officials began operating an enrichment facility outside of the IAEA's purview, in contravention of UN resolutions. Another enrichment facility was being secretly constructed underground. As these facilities were not under inspection by the IAEA, it was reasonable to assume that they would serve military purposes. The U.S. intelligence community identified other facilities consistent with a program to produce nuclear weapons, including a reactor from which plutonium could be reprocessed to make bombs. At Secretary Condoleezza Rice's urging, President Bush agreed to have William Burns and other U.S. diplomats join Great Britain, France, Germany, Russia, and China as well as the European Union to sit at the table with Iran. This July 2008 meeting elicited no interest by Iranian negotiators in a temporary freeze of both enrichment and sanctions.

Harsh critics of any negotiated settlement, led by Israeli prime minister Benjamin Netanyahu, demanded the complete elimination of Iran's nuclear infrastructure. In this view, partial constraints, regardless of duration, amounted to an acceptance of Iran's nuclear ambitions. Obama knew that Netanyahu's absolutism was a recipe for failed diplomacy, followed by military strikes. He was determined to give deal-making a chance as long as a diplomatic settlement verifiably blocked all pathways to an Iranian bomb. But diplomacy hadn't been tried with Iran for thirty-five years. Burns, who took his Foreign Service entrance exam in 1979, shortly after U.S. diplomats were held hostage at the U.S. Embassy in Tehran, framed the challenge aptly: "Iran seemed a menacing and impenetrable presence, too big and dangerous to ignore, but too intransigent to engage. It was a minefield for diplomats, and nobody had a good map."[36] Obama and Hillary Clinton handed this challenge to Burns.

Burns inherited an interest in public service and nuclear diplomacy from his father, William F. Burns, whose interest in the field was imprinted when, as a colonel, he commanded a base in West Germany with poorly secured tactical nuclear weapons that was attacked by the Baader-Meinhof gang. He went on to represent the Joint Chiefs of Staff at the Intermediate Nuclear Forces Treaty negotiations and worked at the State Department before becoming the director of the Arms Control and Disarmament Agency in the last year of the Reagan administration.

The younger Burns attended college at La Salle and then received his master's degree and doctorate from Oxford under the tutelage of Hedley Bull, who wrote books about anarchy and arms control. Burns's doctoral thesis was on economic aid to Egypt. The disruptions caused by his father's military postings was good training for his thirty-three-year diplomatic career, where he acquired deep expertise from multiple assignments in the Middle East and dealing with the Kremlin.

Obama was willing to concede an Iranian enrichment program because the Iranians already had one that was a source of national pride and that they insisted was a basic right. Only a bombing campaign with broader, dangerous ramifications could nullify it—for a time. As Burns put it, "There was no way you could bomb, sanction or wish" Iranian enrichment away.[37] If Iran's leaders were willing to verifiably curtail its uranium enrichment to levels consistent with peaceful uses, as well as forego a plutonium pathway to the Bomb, a deal could be struck. In return, there would be sanctions relief and the release of Iranian assets frozen in Western banks. Progress could only be realized in stages, first with an interim agreement, followed by a comprehensive one.

Obama wasn't seeking regime change. Neither was he willing to accept an Iran in possession of nuclear weapons. He was committed to take actions short of air strikes, including cyber warfare, to create difficulties for Iranian centrifuge operations. One cyber operation, known as Stuxnet, subsequently became widely publicized.[38] In the event that diplomacy failed, Obama retained military options to temporarily disable Iran's nuclear activities, including those buried deep underground.

During Obama's first term, prospects for successful negotiations with an Iran led by Supreme Leader Ali Khamenei and President Mahmoud Ahmadinejad appeared exceedingly remote. In a disputed election result, the guardians of Iran's revolution awarded Ahmadinejad a second term in 2009. Thousands were arrested in the protests that followed, and Washington imposed additional sanctions. Ahmadinejad increased to 19,000 the number of centrifuges enriching uranium at low levels.

The Obama administration looked for openings to engage with Ahmadinejad and found one when, in June 2009, Tehran contacted Mohamed ElBaradei, the Egyptian director general of the IAEA, requesting assistance because its supply of enriched uranium fuel for the Tehran Research Reactor was about to be exhausted. Tehran's request for assistance was genuine, but it came with an inference: if ElBaradei wasn't responsive, Iran could enrich to 20 percent to provide for its research reactor needs. From 20 percent enrichment, it would be a short step-jump to bomb-grade material.

ElBaradei notified Washington, where Robert Einhorn at the State Department and Samore on the National Security Council staff seized on the idea of a fuel swap. They devised a complicated, creative proposal to provide an external source of assured and safeguarded enrichment services, either from Russia or France. For payment in return, Iran would send its very low enriched uranium outside its borders, diminishing stocks that could be further enriched and used for making bombs. Russian authorities and ElBaradei were enthusiastic about the plan, which Burns presented to Iran's nuclear negotiator and secretary to the Supreme National Security Council, Saeed Jalili, in October 2009.

Jalili saw value in changing the narrative about Iran's nuclear activities. The month before meeting with Burns, the U.S. intelligence community confirmed the existence of the secret underground enrichment facility at Fordow, which Obama revealed publicly alongside the British prime minister and the French president. When Burns proposed the fuel swap and opening up the secret facility to ElBaradei's inspectors, Jalili was receptive. The facility at Fordow was subsequently opened to ElBaradei's inspectors, but Jalili encountered stiff opposition to the fuel swap, which fell apart over Iranian counterproposals, backtracking, and technical complications. After Supreme Leader Khamenei pronounced the swap "naïve and perverted," tougher sanctions followed.[39]

In June 2013, a very different type of Iranian leader, Hassan Rouhani, was elected president on the coattails of a young electorate desiring a better future than that offered by their theocratic leaders, the Revolutionary Guard Corps, and Ahmadinejad. The authorities honored the election result and Obama had more of an opening. After Rouhani's election and the appointment of Javad Zarif as foreign minister, it was time to try once more for a breakthrough. Effective sanctions were in place, but they were viewed by Washington's negotiating partners as a means to a diplomatic end. "When our leverage had reached a kind of critical mass," Burns recounted, "we had to use it or risk losing it." With Rouhani's election, "it was time to put diplomacy to a rigorous test."[40]

Even before Rouhani's election, Obama sent Burns and Jake Sullivan to Oman to see whether Tehran might usefully engage with Washington. Burns had by then risen to the second-ranking position at the State Department after previously serving as the U.S. ambassador to Jordan and Russia. Sullivan grew up in Minneapolis in a middle-class family. His father worked on the business side of the *Minneapolis Star-Tribune* and later at the University of Minnesota's journalism school; his mother worked as a public-school teacher. He excelled at Yale and Oxford, then returned to Yale for a law degree. The practice of law couldn't compete with his interest in public policy. Sullivan worked on Capitol Hill for Senator Amy Klobuchar and served as Hillary Clinton's director of policy planning at the State Department before moving over to work for Vice President Joe Biden.

Burns and Sullivan provided their Iranian counterparts the outline of this deal during a secret trip to Oman in February 2013. The United States had considerable leverage in these talks. International sanctions were biting, and the new government in Iran badly needed sanctions relief and hard currency. It was wise to have begun talks with Ahmadinejad, in Burns's view, providing continuity for Rouhani and buy-in from Khamenei.[41] Another round of secret talks with Rouhani's emissaries in Oman, held in September 2013, was more encouraging. The outlines of an interim agreement built around a six-month cessation of nuclear-related activities in return for the release of some of Iran's money frozen by Western banks was agreed upon, with details to be haggled over later. The talks resumed in New York alongside the UN General Assembly session later in September, where Secretary of State John Kerry, with a draft agreement in hand, had his first direct engagement with Iranian foreign minister Zarif. Rouhani and Obama had a polite phone call before Rouhani left New York, another encouraging sign.

Secret talks resumed in October 2013 in Oman. Burns and Sullivan were now joined by Wendy Sherman, the State Department official who would lead the U.S. delegation to the multilateral negotiations that would resume in November. It was time to advise Washington's negotiating partners—the European Union, France, Germany, Great Britain, Russia, and China—and other interested parties of what had transpired without their knowledge. By this time, bracketed or contested issues in the draft interim agreement had been whittled down to only five or six items. Burns was "genuinely surprised we had come such a long way in such a short time."[42]

The remaining differences in the first-phase interim agreement, called the Joint Plan of Action, were hammered out in Geneva and announced on November 24. Iran agreed to freeze its nuclear program for six months, a rollback of the enrichment level of its uranium stocks down from 20 percent, along with intrusive monitoring. In return it gained modest relief from sanctions along with a commitment of no new sanctions for the next six months. Netanyahu called this outcome "the deal of a century" for Iran.[43] The reception on Capitol Hill was divided, and not just along partisan lines. Republicans lined up against any agreement allowing nuclear infrastructure in Iran that could be used for bomb making. Some Democrats were inclined to agree, most notably Senator Chuck Schumer and other Jewish members of Congress.

A comprehensive agreement took eighteen more months to negotiate in what Sherman characterized as a "staggeringly laborious process" involving seven teams with a combined 100 negotiators.[44] Kerry and Zarif served as prime movers.[45] Kerry had previously promoted a nuclear deal with Iran publicly and privately as chairman of the Senate Foreign Relations Committee. In Burns's characterization, Secretary of State Kerry aimed high, "was unintimidated by long odds," and was ready "to take big risks and even bigger falls."[46] He received help from Energy Secretary Moniz when high-level reinforcement was needed on technical detail. Moniz's grandparents came to America from the Azores. He grew up in the blue-collar precincts of Fall River, Massachusetts. His father was a factory worker at the Firestone plant and his mother was a homemaker. Moniz excelled at math and physics at Boston College, Stanford, and MIT. He had the look, if suitably attired by an imaginative portrait painter, of an adventurous Portuguese sea captain. Moniz's opposite number was Ali Salehi, the head of Iran's Atomic Energy Organization, another MIT alumnus.

The hard slog of negotiating the agreement fell to Sherman. She was raised by socially progressive parents. Her father was wounded at Guadalcanal, settled in Baltimore, and found success in the real estate brokerage business. Her mother was a homemaker who went to community college and then into real estate. Her father's commitment to civil rights and opposition to redlin-ing—discriminatory lending practices that blocked African Americans from obtaining home mortgages and that devalued their properties—dramatically affected her father's income.

Sherman was trained as a social worker but her commitment to pub-lic policy shifted her focus from retail to wholesale. She was drawn to and worked for a local politician, Barbara Mikulski. Sherman became her chief of staff when Mikulski was a congresswoman and then a senator. Her aperture opened further when Warren Christopher recruited her to become his assis-tant secretary of state for legislative affairs in the Clinton administration. She returned to the State Department working for Hillary Clinton and Kerry as the department's third-ranking official.

As negotiations with Iran progressed from the first-phase Joint Plan of Action to the comprehensive agreement, opposition on Capitol Hill and from Netanyahu intensified in ways that were previously considered to be beyond the pale. The Republican Speaker, John Boehner, surprised the administra-tion by extending an invitation to Netanyahu to speak to a joint session of Congress, knowing full well that he would excoriate the deal. Kerry, who met with the Israeli ambassador the day before this announcement, was blind-sided by this "total departure from protocol and tradition." The Congress, Kerry later wrote, was no longer being run "as an institution belonging to the country and history, but on behalf of a party and the moment."[47]

Netanyahu's address on March 3, 2015, reminded his audience that Iran remained a revolutionary state that sought the annihilation of Israel, was unalterably committed to acts of terror, and was "gobbling up nations" in the Middle East. "Don't be fooled," Netanyahu warned. Turning to the nu-clear agreement, he asserted that it would "not prevent Iran from developing nuclear weapons. It would all but guarantee that Iran gets those weapons, lots of them." Obama's first "major concession," Netanyahu declared, was to "leave Iran with a vast nuclear infrastructure" and a breakout time of perhaps a year to produce the Bomb. International inspections would be of little help, since inspectors could only document violations, not stop them. Obama's second major concession was that "virtually all the restrictions on Iran's nuclear program will automatically expire in about a decade," after which Tehran planned to retain 190,000 centrifuges. "That's why this deal is so bad," he argued. "It doesn't block Iran's path to the bomb; it paves Iran's path to the bomb."

Netanyahu ended with flourishes. "This deal won't change Iran for the better; it will only change the Middle East for the worse." He added, "This deal won't be a farewell to arms. It would be a farewell to arms control." He argued that Iran needed to change its behavior and ambitions; otherwise a deal would be folly. Then Netanyahu hinted broadly about what he really wanted: "Nuclear know-how without nuclear infrastructure doesn't get you very much. A racecar driver without a car can't drive. A pilot without a plane can't fly. Without thousands of centrifuges, tons of enriched uranium or heavy water facilities, Iran can't make nuclear weapons."[48]

Never has an ally so abused the hospitality of its host and principal benefactor. Netanyahu could do so because he correctly presumed that Israel would have immunity from retaliation on Capitol Hill. He had previously made the same arguments in private to the Bush administration and found an ally in Vice President Cheney, but Defense Secretary Gates convinced Bush against military strikes that could initiate a third war in the region.[49] Netanyahu knew he would again lose the argument with Obama, but he had a better chance of winning it on Capitol Hill.

Netanyahu's concerns about Iran's larger regional ambitions were fully warranted as Tehran remained active in Yemen, Iraq, and Lebanon, while continuing to support proxies against Israel. Netanyahu's presumption about Iranian cheating was not accurate, at least for the agreement's truncated duration. His characterization of the expiration dates of various provisions and the allowances Iran were granted were also inaccurate. Obama's rejoinder to Netanyahu's grave breach of alliance protocol was to point to the obvious— that he "didn't offer any viable alternatives." He was, in effect, proposing no deal with no negotiable constraints and a military solution.[50]

Less than one week after Netanyahu savaged the Obama administration's diplomatic effort, Senator Tom Cotton issued an "open letter" to Iranian leaders signed by 47 of his 54 Republican colleagues. The ostensible purpose of the open letter, released on March 9, 2015, was to "enrich" Tehran's understanding of the U.S. Constitution and executive-congressional relations. The co-signers urged Iran's leaders to "seriously consider" that, while Obama was soon to leave office, many of them would still be in the Senate and that the election results could produce a president with a similarly jaundiced view of any agreement signed by the outgoing administration. Obama's deal could be nullified "with the stroke of a pen." Moreover, "Congress could modify the terms of the agreement at any time."[51]

The Obama administration was incensed by Cotton's public letter but didn't have strong, detailed rebuttals, as the Joint Comprehensive Plan of Action had not yet been finalized. Obama's public reaction was restrained: "It's somewhat ironic to see some members of Congress wanting to make common cause with hard-liners in Iran."[52] His mild irony was no match for the heavy guns aimed at him. Norms were being battered. It was unprecedented, as Kerry later wrote, "to intervene directly with foreign leaders and to try to undermine a sitting president in the middle of a negotiation, let alone one where the stakes were so high. It was irresponsible and reckless."[53]

The framework for the Joint Comprehensive Plan of Action was completed the next month, in April 2015. The last details of the 159-page text, including annexes, were finalized in July. In the text of the agreement, Tehran "reaffirmed" that "under no circumstances will Iran ever seek, develop or acquire any nuclear weapons" and that it would accept constraints to "ensure that Iran's nuclear program will be exclusively peaceful." Tehran accepted surprisingly long delays in key pathways to acquire nuclear weapons. The agreement banned reprocessing for fifteen years. Uranium enrichment would be capped at less than 4 percent for fifteen years. Iran's stocks of low enriched uranium would also be capped, requiring the removal of 98 percent of its stockpile. The International Atomic Energy Agency's inspectors would carry out continuous monitoring of Iranian uranium mines and mining activities for twenty-five years as well as continuous monitoring of centrifuge production facilities for twenty years, after which Iran's facilities would be subject to periodic inspections in perpetuity. The agreement placed limits on the number and type of centrifuges, requiring the dismantling or mothballing of 13,000 centrifuges. The core of Iran's lone plutonium production reactor would be removed, and the reactor disabled. In return for these steps, sanctions would be removed in stages.[54]

The number and type of centrifuges permitted under the agreement were predicated on the Obama administration's baseline requirement that the agreement leave Iran approximately one year away from acquiring its first nuclear weapon if Tehran decided to break out from its obligations.[55] Adjusting one number—for example, the number of centrifuges of a certain type—meant adjusting others in what Sherman described as "the world's most complex and consequential Rubik's cube."[56] The conduct or interference with inspections would provide warning of cheating, along with U.S. intelligence gathering. With early indications of a material breach, sanctions could be snapped back, and U.S. air strikes could be carried out.

Why did Iran's leaders accept these comprehensive constraints? Perhaps, as skeptics argued, because they could wait them out, or perhaps this was an elaborate charade as Tehran had no intent to abide by them. The alternative supposition—that Iran's leaders were not hell-bent to actually possess nuclear weapons—was barely articulated. The comprehensive agreement's details couldn't make a dent in Republican opposition on Capitol Hill. The terms of debate were predicated on Iranian malevolence for which there was ample evidence, and majorities in the House and the Senate were opposed to partial victories. At the same time, congressional leaders were not inclined to accept responsibility for killing the deal and its useful limitations.

Consequently, the White House and congressional leaders agreed to package the deal as a politically binding agreement rather than as a treaty. The ostensible and valid reasons for doing so were because seven parties were involved and because unilateral changes to the agreement's numbers and interactive sequencing mechanisms would defeat it. There was a more prosaic reason, as well: it was clear after Netanyahu's speech and Cotton's letter that strong Republican opposition would doom a treaty. A politically binding agreement under Obama's executive authority would typically require simple majorities in both the House and Senate. Even this wasn't possible, as the fate of the Iran nuclear deal would be decided during a presidential campaign in which none of the Republican contenders supported it and one, Donald Trump, characterized it as "the worst deal in history."[57]

To implement the deal, the administration sought and received the support of congressional leaders for arcane procedures whereby the agreement would be rejected only if a resolution of disapproval passed both the House of Representatives and the Senate. The resolution of disapproval passed in the House by a very wide margin—269 to 162—with all Republicans and 25 Democrats voting to disapprove. The administration's focus was on the Senate. According to Senate rules, a resolution of disapproval could be stalled or filibustered by supporters of the deal. A total of 60 senators were needed to invoke cloture, thereby defeating a filibuster. This meant that the Obama administration needed 41 senators to support the agreement or, failing that, 34 senators to sustain Obama's veto. The vote in the Senate was 58 calling for an end to the filibuster against 42 supporters of the deal—one more vote than necessary. The much-maligned Senate filibuster saved the Iran nuclear agreement.

By structuring the vote in this convoluted manner, Senate leaders gave diplomacy a chance. At the same time, opponents were given, in effect, a free pass: they could go on record against a deal that wasn't good enough without having to assume the burden of killing it. There were no penalties for demanding a tougher agreement. There were also no assurances that a deal opposed by majorities in both the House and the Senate could survive for very long.

Obama's agreement with Iran was a significant success, but it marked a new low in terms of support on Capitol Hill for nonproliferation diplomacy. Partisanship had become a severely limiting condition, another manifestation of the demise of arms control. Not one Republican voted to support an agreement whose terms verifiably blocked all pathways to an Iranian bomb for at least fifteen years. The votes on Capitol Hill, as Wendy Sherman noted, "reflected the life of politics in our time."[58] Obama's only option to begin implementing the nuclear deal was a politically binding agreement that could readily be cast aside by his successor. Trump announced his withdrawal in May 2018.

James Timbie worked on the technical aspects of the agreement, avoiding the spotlight, as usual. He was described by Burns as "a quiet national treasure" for his more than four decades of involvement in arms control. Timbie viewed his work on the Iran nuclear agreement as the most satisfying contribution of his career. The negotiators were starting from scratch, trying to accomplish something that had never been done before. The stakes were extremely high and "the alternative to success was war."[59] In reflecting on Trump's decision to kill the agreement, National Security Advisor Susan Rice wrote that "it's hard to imagine how we will ever again verifiably dismantle Iran's nuclear program short of war—and even then only temporarily."[60] Congressional majorities didn't support it, but neither did they seek military strikes against Iran's nuclear facilities. The nuclear agreement with Iran was left in the Bardo, a suspended state after death and before potential resurrection.

THE INF TREATY VIOLATION

The 1987 Intermediate Nuclear Forces Treaty was unique. It didn't control or reduce nuclear force structure; instead, it banned entire categories of missiles of less than intercontinental range. The Soviet General Staff wasn't happy with this treaty, preferring to retain perhaps 100 or more missiles for military contingences related to Asia as well as Europe. Gorbachev persuaded his military advisers to do without these missiles and to accept the Zero Option to eliminate highly threatening U.S. missiles then being deployed in Europe.

Some deterrence strengtheners in the United States, including Richard Nixon, Henry Kissinger, and James Schlesinger, were also uneasy about the Zero Option. Eliminating all ground-based, nuclear-armed missiles from Europe would, they argued, remove rungs on escalation ladders. Moreover, forward-based missiles exemplified Washington's commitment to the defense of its NATO allies.[61]

Putin and the Russian General Staff were intent on retrieving a military option that Gorbachev was willing to give up. In his scathing talk in 2007 at the Munich security conference, Putin publicly complained about the INF Treaty's lack of "universal character." Others were "working on these systems and plan to incorporate them as part of their weapons arsenals." (One notable omission in Putin's list of missile-holders was China.) "Only the United States and Russia," he said, "bear the responsibility to not create such weapons systems."[62]

Two former Soviet experts who played key roles in Cold War arms control negotiations have shed light on the Kremlin's decision making. They write that "no one could have foreseen that the [INF negotiating] process would end with the Zero Option." The Soviet General Staff approved of but was deeply unhappy with this result, as well as with Gorbachev's negotiating style. As time passed, "as expected, the after-the-fact criticisms of the INF Treaty in the Soviet Union were very sharp, especially on the part of retired Soviet military," that the USSR "made great concessions without any reasons." In these accounts, the INF Treaty "was presented as an act of unilateral disarmament."[63]

The Soviet ambassador to the United States during this period, Anatoly Dobrynin, added further context, writing in his memoirs, "Gorbachev increasingly improvised and without consulting our experts would agree to sudden compromises which were often regarded by our military as one-sided concessions to the Americans." Giving up INF-range missiles for Asian contingencies added salt to these wounds: "In Asia the SS-20s were part of our strategic defenses against China as well as the American bases in Japan and the Indian Ocean, so this certainly represented a major concession."[64]

Two decades after the INF Treaty was negotiated, Putin could begin to put these pieces back on the chessboard, confident that the United States and NATO would have great difficulty matching ground-based deployments. After obliquely hinting at doing so in his Munich speech, the first flight test of ground-based missiles prohibited by the INF Treaty began in 2008. This was a deeply inauspicious time for U.S.-Russian relations. President Bush publicly announced his strong support for Georgia and Ukraine to become NATO members in April 2008. In August of that year, Russian troops threatened Georgia's capital, Tbilisi. When the flight testing of Russia's new cruise missile began, prospects for improved U.S.-Russian relations were dim, just as prospects of improved U.S.-Soviet relations were dim when a core group of the Soviet Politburo decided to invade Afghanistan three decades earlier.

Early on, it wasn't clear that the cruise missile being flight-tested violated INF Treaty provisions; had the missile been sea-based or launched from aircraft, it would not have been a violation. In 2011, preliminary U.S. intelligence assessments pointed toward land basing and thus a violation of the treaty's core provision not to deploy ground-based missiles of ranges between 500 and 5,500 kilometers. Key legislators were notified of the problem. By 2013 further analytical assessment left no room for doubt. Gottemoeller raised U.S. concerns with Russia's ambassador to the United States, Sergey Kislyak, and then with the Russian deputy foreign minister, Sergei Ryabkov, in May.[65] In all, Gottemoeller raised this issue with Russian colleagues over twenty times.[66] The Obama administration held off on publicly announcing a violation in the State Department's annual report on treaty compliance in 2013, recognizing that the chances of rectification would likely vanish after a public guilty verdict.[67] Initially, Russian officials denied that the missile in question existed. Russian representatives at international conferences minimized the issue as being "technical" and solvable. It was neither.

Arms control compliance concerns can be successfully resolved when the actions taken do not constitute material breaches that gut central treaty provisions, when relations between the parties are on an upswing, and when they wish to reaffirm their treaty obligations. None of these conditions were applicable in this case. Putin may well have concluded there was nothing of value to be lost and something to be gained by violating the INF Treaty. Bilateral relations plummeted further when Russia's forces and proxies began military operations in eastern Ukraine and Crimea in February 2014. In July, the State Department issued its compliance report declaring Russia in violation of the INF Treaty.[68]

In 2019 the Russian government acknowledged the existence of the ground-launched cruise missile, even putting it on display, while claiming that it did not have range capabilities prohibited by the INF Treaty, despite flight testing and dimensions to the contrary.[69] Russian officials also raised compliance concerns over U.S. activities, including the possibility that ground-based, theater missile defense interceptors could be changed out and replaced by treaty-prohibited land-attack cruise missiles.[70] While this blame game played out, Moscow deployed six battalions of the treaty-prohibited cruise missile, totaling perhaps 100 launch-ready missiles and spares.[71]

The cover story offered for the INF Treaty violation was as flimsy as for the Krasnoyarsk radar. The radar violation could be rectified because Gorbachev was in charge and because he wanted to reduce military expenditures and to sign a strategic arms reduction treaty. The INF Treaty violation was not rectifiable because Putin was in charge, the missile in question reflected a military requirement, technical "fixes" to reduce its range could be easily reversed, and Putin wished to be relieved of a treaty constraint that didn't apply to China.

The violation could not be rectified for another reason, as well: Washington couldn't respond to Moscow's missile deployments in the same way as Jimmy Carter and Ronald Reagan did—in a highly threatening manner that could induce negotiating trade-offs. Reagan inherited Carter's Euro-missile programs and succeeded in deploying them on NATO soil, prompting Gorbachev to accept Reagan's Zero Option. A repeat of this scenario wasn't attractive or available to the Obama administration. As Putin likely figured, no NATO country was willing to host nuclear-armed ground-based missiles during Obama's watch—even if Obama had been willing to do so, which he was not. During the apogee of arms control, as Ben Rhodes reflected, "We could count on Russia being on its back foot as we enlarged NATO."[72] Deploying INF Treaty–prohibited missiles was a form of retaliation; it was one way for Putin to put NATO on the back foot.

The Obama administration was in a quandary. Staying in the treaty made less sense with every new missile battalion that Moscow deployed, but Obama wasn't ready to leave. He passed this violation over to Donald Trump, who casually announced the U.S. exit at a political rally in Nevada. Putin got what he wanted—freedom of action, while Trump received brickbats from those who wanted to repair the Russian breach rather than withdraw from the treaty. The Pentagon also welcomed freedom of action to deploy intermediate-range missiles for contingencies against China as well as Russia. Given allied sensitivities in Asia and Europe, U.S. cruise missiles would be deployed offshore or delivered by aircraft, at least initially.

The death of the INF Treaty had outsized consequences. The treaty was a cornerstone of the nuclear peace. It mandated true disarmament, backed up by intrusive inspections, paving the way for deep cuts in bloated Cold War strategic forces. By signing the INF Treaty, Reagan and Gorbachev ended the

Cold War nuclear competition. The treaty's death was as freighted with symbolism as its negotiation. Other treaty deaths would follow.

ENDGAME

Obama could mend and extend verifiable strategic arms control, but deeper reductions eluded him. He didn't have a willing partner in Putin, not only with respect to deeper cuts but also for extending New START for an additional five years, as the treaty permitted, contingent on joint U.S.-Russian agreement. The timing and the conditions during Obama's second term weren't right to do business with Putin. Moscow said that discussions on an extension could not begin until 2018, when New START's ceilings were to be met. The Kremlin was then also insisting that its concerns about missile defenses and "prompt, conventional global strike" forces be addressed in any conversation about extension. There were other matters to contend with, including Russia's annexation of Crimea, its military presence in eastern Ukraine, and its flight testing of a missile prohibited by the INF Treaty.

Obama was also strongly disinclined to intrude upon the prerogatives of his successor, whom he assumed would be Hillary Clinton. Gottemoeller believed that New START's extension in her administration would be "an early and easy win for arms control."[73] Another consideration was Defense Secretary Carter's disinclination to reward Putin's misbehavior by means of arms control.[74] Extending New START would have required the expenditure of political capital. Obama had no reason to hoard it once he knew that Trump would be his successor, but he never revisited the issue. Extending New START would be Trump's decision to make or not make.

There was not much left of the Prague agenda as the Obama administration drew to a close. One outstanding issue was steering U.S. nuclear doctrine away from using nuclear weapons first. U.S. allies that felt reassured by the U.S. nuclear umbrella were uneasy with this change in U.S. declaratory policy. At the peak of U.S. power when the Soviet Union was imploding in 1990, President George H.W. Bush and Secretary of State James Baker persuaded NATO to accept a "weapons of last resort" formulation. An alternative—that the "sole purpose" of nuclear weapons is to deter their use by others—would also serve to reduce the salience of nuclear weapons in U.S. national security policy.

The point person to revisit changes in doctrine was Jon Wolfsthal, who served on Vice President Joe Biden's staff at the outset of the administration and returned to the National Security Council staff in 2014 to reenergize the

Prague agenda. Wolfsthal grew up in New York City, the son of a jeweler who worked on the diamond exchange and a schoolteacher. He went to college at Emory, found a mentor, was politically active, and joined the freeze movement. He learned the ropes of bureaucratic maneuver but was stymied by the Pentagon's indifference or resistance to the Prague agenda.

Vice President Biden delivered the Obama administration's last word on the Prague agenda nine days before Trump was sworn in to become president. Biden delivered remarks that were originally prepared for Obama to an audience at the Carnegie Endowment for International Peace. "Given our non-nuclear capabilities and the nature of today's threats," he said, "it's hard to envision a plausible scenario in which the first use of nuclear weapons by the United States would be necessary. Or make sense. President Obama and I are confident we can deter and defend ourselves and our Allies against non-nuclear threats through other means."[75] This was not a pledge of no first use, but it was the closest the Obama administration could come to it as a time when other states possessing nuclear weapons seemed to be relying more on them. Biden would have a chance to revisit this issue later.

OBAMA'S LEDGER SHEET

One definition of successful diplomacy, offered by Henry Kissinger, is "the patient accumulation of partial successes."[76] Patience is, however, a rare commodity in the United States when the subject is nuclear arms control. The accumulation of partial successes requires more continuity that hyper-partisanship allows. Wendy Sherman, whose patience was tested in negotiating the fine print with North Korean and Iranian diplomats, wrote, "Each solution is only sufficient to its time and place and the ripeness of a solution."[77] Time and place yielded only partial but important successes in the Obama administration.

Extending the process of verifiable strategic arms control for ten more years was a major accomplishment. New START helped mend the unraveling process, providing breathing space until something better could be negotiated, but the reset with Moscow ended when Putin reclaimed the Russian presidency in 2012. Putin's military campaign in eastern Ukraine, the annexation of Crimea, and the ongoing violations of the INF Treaty mocked attempts at ambitious strategic arms reductions.

After decades of slow-motion modernization of its nuclear forces, China accelerated the pace of warhead production while adding numbers to its intermediate-range missiles and strategic forces. India and Pakistan resumed border clashes, marked by cross-border air strikes, while increasing fissile material stocks and warhead numbers. North Korea walked away from Obama's attempt to revive multilateral talks in 2009 and carried out its second test of a nuclear device. Its sixth test in 2017 demonstrated a higher-yield thermonuclear capability.[78] Nuclear danger was outpacing diplomacy on several fronts as Obama left the White House.

Obama's Nuclear Security Summits were notable successes. Continued progress in this domain depends on whether a national leader has the standing and influence to provide the necessary impetus. The Nuclear Security Summits were new, but not headline news. The nuclear deal with Iran was, in contrast, major news. Negotiations with Iran accomplished something unexpected—fifteen or more years' worth of verifiable constraints on Tehran's bomb-making capabilities. Those who opposed the agreement believed it was bound to fail and that partial solutions in the hardest proliferation cases were insufficient. Partial successes are, however, all that is usually on offer in the hardest cases.

The Obama administration negotiated an agreement that seemed impossible at the outset of the secret talks in Oman. A nation hell-bent to acquire nuclear weapons—a nation that rejects deterrence and that seeks to annihilate its enemies—does not accept a fifteen-year hiatus in this pursuit. Either Iran's leaders were content with keeping the nuclear option open but not acquiring the Bomb, or they never intended to abide by their obligations. We will never know because Donald Trump walked away from the agreement reached. Just as George W. Bush walked away from nuclear and missile constraints on North Korea, Trump withdrew from the Iran nuclear agreement with nothing better to replace it.

Arms control can, when successful, limit and reduce the most dangerous weapons devised by human ingenuity. Over time, arms control can also reinforce norms against the battlefield use and testing of these weapons. At the outset of the strategic arms control talks in 1969, Richard Nixon and Henry Kissinger believed that arms control could also stop unwanted actions by a negotiating partner. Their attempt to impose linkage failed, as would others. Indeed, Nixon and Kissinger flaunted linkage by bombing Hanoi, Haiphong Harbor, and other targets in North Vietnam, resulting in Soviet casualties, as they were preparing for a summit in Moscow to sign the 1972 Interim Agreement and Anti-Ballistic Missile Treaty. The Kremlin fully returned the favor, seeking geopolitical advantage in distant locales during strategic arms control negotiations.

The linkage question also haunts nonproliferation diplomacy. For those who believe in the utility of arms control and nonproliferation agreements, reducing weapon capabilities in verifiable ways suffices. For critics, reducing weapon capabilities without stopping bad behavior in other domains is insufficient. When the behavior of an outlier is particularly unsettling, advocates of linkage win this debate. Iran's leaders provided fodder for opponents of the 2015 Joint Comprehensive Plan of Action when they didn't curtail their attempts to extend Iranian influence at the expense of U.S. friends in the region.

It was probably hard enough for Iran's leaders to agree to meaningful limits to prevent bomb making; imposing constraints on other fiefdoms controlled by the Revolutionary Guard Corps may well have been beyond the pale. The history of nuclear arms control is replete with instances of concessions in one sphere being accompanied by compensatory actions in another. The Obama administration had hoped to prevent Tehran from acquiring nuclear weapons and, in doing so, to gain a foothold for improved U.S.-Iranian relations. Obama succeeded on the nonproliferation front for the short period of time that the agreement lasted, but changing the character of the Iranian regime, like mollifying domestic critics and altering the trajectory of the demise of arms control, was beyond his powers to achieve. The Iran nuclear agreement was an extraordinary accomplishment, but it had too many powerful opponents in too many places to survive for very long.

The nuclear peace was unraveling. Major power competition was sharpening. Friction between nuclear-armed states in Asia was growing. The Nonproliferation Treaty's connective tissue between nuclear possessors and abstainers was dissolving. Trendlines were moving away from the Prague agenda. Barack Obama entered the White House with big plans, far bigger than what the traffic would bear. Major successes in arms control require partnership and bipartisanship, and Obama didn't have willing partners in Moscow and among Republicans on Capitol Hill. He did as well as he could with what he had to work with. A black swan election would jeopardize or reverse his hard-won gains, hastening the demise of arms control.

DENOUEMENT

Chapter 16

DONALD TRUMP AND VLADIMIR PUTIN

Black swan events are like top-of-the-Richter-scale earthquakes that occur in major metropolitan areas: they aren't unprecedented or completely unexpected, but we take refuge in thinking of them as once-in-a-century occurrences, like the 1906 earthquake that demolished San Francisco. Pandemics on the scale of the Spanish flu in 1918–20 were beyond living memory until the COVID-19 pandemic appeared a century later. Unlike localized devastation from earthquakes or floods, black swan events have global consequences. To experience one is unnerving. We now live at a time when hundred-year floods occur every few years. So, too, do black swan events. The United States has experienced no less than four in a span of only twenty years and is reeling from their consequences. The 2016 election that elevated Donald J. Trump to the White House was a black swan event, facilitated by previous ones.

The unipolar moment of the United States lasted barely a decade, from the fall of the Berlin Wall in 1991 to the fall of the Twin Towers in 2001, truncated by black swan events and by domestic divisions. First came the 9/11 attacks following on the heels of a disputed presidential election. Two debilitating wars without victory, each costing well in excess of one trillion dollars, followed. The second black swan event was the collapse of the subprime mortgage market in 2007–8, along with investment banks holding worthless paper, sparking a global recession that lasted eighteen months in the United States. Gross Domestic Product fell by over 4 percent, and unemployment peaked at 10 percent.[79] Global trade contracted by almost 10 percent, investment declined by 9 percent, and global unemployment quadrupled.[80]

Trump's election was the third black swan event in this progression, causing more global aftershocks. Elevated by the Electoral College to command the nuclear "football" despite garnering nearly three million fewer votes than Hillary Clinton, he was a president like no other. The fourth black swan event, a novel coronavirus, arrived during the fourth year of Trump's presidency. The global pandemic resulted in unemployment levels of 40 million U.S. citizens. Manufacturing outputs largely stopped for a quarter of the calendar, and global supply chains were broken. The World Bank projected a contraction of the global economy by 5 percent in 2020, contraction of the U.S. economy by 6 percent, and contraction of the collective economies of advanced countries by 7 percent.[81]

The aftershocks of these black swan events in the United States were magnified by social and economic inequality and by troubled race relations. Conditions for domestic alienation and unrest grew because of extreme income inequality exacerbated by the two great recessions in 2007 and 2020, the second of which raised U.S. jobless rates to Depression-era levels. During an earlier time of great turmoil, President Richard Nixon found comfort in his silent majority. Trump relied on his vocal minority. He could have cultivated bipartisan support because he had no deep, prior party affiliation, but this wasn't his nature. He postured in office the way he campaigned—to rouse his base. Trump took pride in generating commotion, and he succeeded well beyond his imaginings. The phenomenon of Barry Goldwater's presidential campaign in 1964 to pare back government prompted the historian Richard Hofstadter to ask, "When, in our history, has anyone with ideas so bizarre, so archaic, so self-confounding, so remote from the basis American consensus, ever got so far?"[82] Goldwater lost in a landslide; Trump, to whom Hofstadter's characterization amply applied, won in a squeaker.

Just as the election of Barack Obama was inconceivable without George W. Bush's presidency, so, too, was the election of Trump inconceivable without Obama preceding him. Obama was a visual affront to much of the Republican Party's base. He represented the advent, not too far in the future, of a minority-majority electorate. In response, Republican office holders in Washington hunkered down to secure White minority rule. Support was provided and grievances nurtured by right-wing radio and television programming. Unlike Bill Clinton who also faced a gauntlet of ceaseless negative commentary, Obama's personal life gave his critics no grounds for complaint. He exuded graciousness, empathy, and compassion. His family and inner circle were free of scandal and self-dealing. He remained, however, an immutable Rorschach test. Whatever he did or said was admired by some and hated by others. George W. Bush could relate.

Obama took brickbats for expanding health care while avoiding new unwinnable wars. Critics of his administration's national security policy homed in on vacuums created in Iraq and Libya—the former from U.S. troop withdrawals, the latter from the use of air power—that he was loath to fill with boots on the ground. His administration left Libya in a state of chaos after helping to topple Muammar Qaddafi. The U.S. ambassador to Libya was one of the casualties, attacked and killed by Islamist extremists in the U.S. consulate at Benghazi during the ensuing chaos. Obama's secretary of state and presumed successor, Hillary Clinton, took the brunt of a subsequent political attack. There were eight separate Republican-led congressional investigations into this tragic incident, lasting over two years—longer than the commissions investigating Pearl Harbor, the assassination of President John F. Kennedy, and the 9/11 attacks.[83]

The streams of invective directed against Obama and Hillary Clinton partially explained Trump's election. She, like Al Gore, was well prepared to become president but was a wooden candidate on the hustings, someone who hid her most appealing personal traits behind layers of protective covering. Enough voters had second thoughts about bringing Bill Clinton back for a "best man" encore and who much preferred the populism of her Democratic rival, Bernie Sanders, to provide Trump with an opening. Clinton's gender was a factor, as was Vladimir Putin's pro-Trump campaign that added new eddies in social media channels already overflowing with poison and disinformation. In an evenly divided electorate, the outcome hung on many contributing factors. Trump's victory surprised himself, his domestic opposition, and a world puzzled by what had become of the United States of America.

A DIFFERENT REPUBLICAN PRESIDENT

Republican presidents were central to the rise of arms control; they were also central to its demise. Richard Nixon began the process of controlling nuclear arms, Ronald Reagan broke the momentum of the arms race, George H.W. Bush presided over the apogee of arms control, and George W. Bush cut deeply into deployed warheads. Democrats in the White House worked the problem with competence and commitment but had less room to maneuver because of domestic opposition. Great accomplishments were within reach only when circumstances permitted—and only then with a combination of sound presidential judgment, instinct, and situational awareness. Mastery of detail helped but was less important than political dexterity. When geopolitics and domestic politics were unforgiving, mastery of detail was of little help.

Great achievements eventually became possible after Nixon and Kissinger negotiated the 1972 SALT accords. The linkage between limits on defenses and controls and then reductions on offenses was set in these accords. The Anti-Ballistic Missile Treaty was necessary but insufficient to subsequent success because its accompanying Interim Agreement was so porous that it would take time to first cap and then reduce arsenals. The big payoffs came when the Soviet Union was mortally wounded, when nuclear excess could be greatly reduced, and when channels of cooperation established through arms control negotiations could be applied to improving the safety and security of warheads and fissile material in a broken country and truncated empire.

When the Cold War ended, the tenets of strategic arms control changed. George W. Bush dispensed with the ABM Treaty; henceforth, the United States would defend itself against missile threats and size its nuclear forces as it saw fit. If Moscow was willing to accept the results, then deals could be struck. Bush's withdrawal from the ABM Treaty had similar downstream consequences as Nixon's Interim Agreement. Both decisions made it harder for their successors to negotiate deeper cuts in strategic offenses. With Vladimir Putin as a willing partner, Bush set a course that would lead to the unraveling of arms control. When Trump was paired with Putin, the unraveling of arms control accelerated greatly.

Bush's decisions were not impulsive; they reflected calculated choice. The world had changed, and the rules-based system of strategic arms control—a system that accorded a defeated superpower equal status—no longer applied. Trump wasn't inclined toward geopolitical calculation; his attention span was too limited and his mind too scattered. He was disinterested in substance and lacked the talent for political dexterity. Trump operated in a wholly different way—by impulse and by demeaning others. Nixon had a controlling, disturbed personality, but Nixon's insecurities and toxicity paled in comparison to Trump's.[84]

China was one of the two major beneficiaries of Trump's cavalier and disrespectful approach toward allies. The extent of the damage was hard to calculate, since allies rarely walk through exits. They do, however, make accommodations and take compensatory measures, subtle and sometimes pointed. Beijing cast a longer shadow as Trump diminished U.S. standing in Asia and elsewhere, especially in response to the novel coronavirus pandemic that radiated from Wuhan to the rest of the world on the wings of air travel.

The second major beneficiary was Russia. Putin's investment in the 2016 U.S. election paid handsome dividends. Trump never gainsaid Putin, as if repaying a debt or advancing a prospective commercial interest. Putin sought freedom of action and the recoupment of losses. The two men and the moment were perversely aligned. Trump saw little value in the agreements he inherited. Putin, too, wanted freedom of action and had proven himself to be a serial treaty violator. The unraveling of arms control would have been difficult to mend no matter who had won the 2016 U.S. election. With Trump's election and his pairing with Putin, the denouement of post–Cold War arms control was at hand.

TEAM TRUMP AND AMERICA FIRST

The slogan "America First" thrives on public alienation born of income disparity, job losses, and declining family fortunes. When these conditions are reinforced by unpopular wars, the Republican Party hears the siren call of isolationism.[85] Wars in Iraq and Afghanistan generated a reaction similar to the isolationist sentiment of the 1920s and 1930s—after a world war that didn't end all wars, as advertised. The new chairman of the Senate Foreign Relations Committee was Jim Risch, a staunch defender of American sovereignty. Risch's America First credo harkened back to the previous isolationist era when another Idahoan, William Borah, chaired the committee. Cold War era Republican presidents pursued international engagement and negotiated arms control treaties. The Cold War was long over when Trump raised the banner of America First, disrupted alliance ties, withdrew from international compacts, and left strategic arms control barely alive on a ventilator.

The advent of 24/7 news cycles on cable television provided those with the loudest voices to campaign for airtime and positions in new administrations. The ceaseless grilling of Clinton over Benghazi was a case in point. A congressman representing Wichita, Kansas, Mike Pompeo, was a Trump skeptic during the presidential primary campaign but found favor by interrogating Clinton mercilessly. Trump appointed him as the head of the Central Intelligence Agency, discovered a soulmate, and then moved him over to the State Department.

Pompeo's predecessor at the State Department, Rex Tillerson, was a captain of industry at Exxon Mobil. Presidents had tapped corporate leaders to become secretary of defense, with decidedly mixed results. George Shultz, who was president of the Bechtel Corporation, was the only captain of industry chosen to run the State Department before Tillerson. Shultz was wise in the ways of Washington, having previously run the Treasury and Labor Departments in the Nixon administration. Tillerson had no prior experience in the corridors of government. He never navigated this transition and his corporate leadership practices did not work well at the State Department. He soon lost the support of his workforce. It was beneath Tillerson's dignity to curry favor with Trump, which ensured a short tenure.

Trump chose James Mattis to be his secretary of defense. Mattis was a four-star marine general with a storied resumé. Another retired general with an intellectual bent, H.R. McMaster, was Trump's initial choice as national security advisor. Still another general, John F. Kelly, was picked to head the Department of Homeland Security and then became Trump's chief of staff. Trump grew tired of their advice. McMaster lasted fourteen months in the job; Mattis left the Pentagon in December 2018, the final straw being Trump's intention to remove U.S. troops from the Syrian-Turkish border, placing at grave risk friendly Kurdish troops and civilians. Kelly's tenure as chief of staff lasted seventeen months.

Every secretary of defense since William Perry viewed arms control as a peripheral interest, at best. Mattis was no different. There was no evident pushback to Trump's negative views about Obama's New START. Mattis focused instead, with support from Tillerson, on preventing Trump from withdrawing from the Iran nuclear agreement. They succeeded during Trump's first year in office but lost this battle in 2018. Mattis also understood the utility of the Open Skies Treaty—a legacy item of President George H.W. Bush—as an alliance-strengthening tool, even with Russian violations at the margins of the agreement. Mattis directed Pentagon officials to stop resisting the procurement of replacement aircraft and upgraded sensors to carry out ride-sharing flights over Russia. This, too, was a losing battle; Trump withdrew from the Open Skies Treaty in May 2020.

In the four years of the Trump administration, the churn was so great that no fewer than fifteen persons were either confirmed or acting secretaries of state, defense, and national security advisor. The Trump administration set the record for the longest period of time in U.S. history without a Senate-confirmed secretary of defense—202 days.[86] In all, there were six acting and confirmed secretaries of defense. The State Department was a ghost ship drifting under Tillerson and listing to starboard under Pompeo. In the first two years of the Trump administration, one-fifth of the highest-ranking officials—career ministers, minister counselors, and counselors—retired. More fled during Trump's last two years.[87]

The intelligence community was also poorly led. Trump's last appointee to be the director of national intelligence was John Ratcliffe, who represented the congressional district in Texas that once sent Sam Rayburn to Washington. Ratcliffe auditioned for the job by staunchly defending Trump during his impeachment hearings. Nixon, who prided himself on his knowledge of international affairs, chose a renowned geopolitical strategist, Henry Kissinger, as his national security advisor. Trump cycled through four national security advisors in four years. The one that mattered most was the third, John Bolton.

THE TREATY SLAYER

Bolton, like Trump, fashioned himself as a hyper-realist, taking pride in disregarding diplomatic nuance. Never one to look for shades of gray, the title of Bolton's first memoir was *Surrender Is Not an Option*. His second memoir, *The Room Where It Happened*, was scathing in its criticism of Trump, depicting a chaotic administration in which every presidential engagement with a foreign leader became an exercise in damage control. Bolton believed that Trump was poorly served by those around him. He gives Trump high marks, however, for shedding arms control agreements, which Bolton considered to be long overdue.[88]

Bolton was born and raised in a working-class neighborhood in Baltimore. Neither of his parents finished high school. His father was a firefighter who needed a second job to help pay the bills; his mother was a homemaker. Bolton's pugnacity seems to have come from his father. He was fueled by resentment rather than gratitude. Bolton directed his ire against those with liberal belief systems, especially those with an unearned sense of entitlement. He worked hard and was exceptionally smart. He escaped his environs by winning a scholarship to attend a boarding school. Scholarships also helped pay for an education at Yale, where he graduated summa cum laude. He joined the National Guard in 1970 to avoid serving in Vietnam because he wasn't going "to waste time on a futile struggle."[89] Next came Yale Law School and a position at the law firm of Covington & Burling.

Like Paul Warnke, who also worked at Covington & Burling, Bolton's attachment to the law was entirely situational, depending on who won the presidency. He was an oppositionist by nature, and he could be more effective in opposition from the inside than on the sidelines. When Ronald Reagan won, Bolton left his law firm to pay his dues working at the Agency for International Development. In Reagan's second term, he returned to the executive branch to work for Attorney General Ed Meese at the Justice Department. When George H.W. Bush won, James Baker tabbed him to be the assistant secretary of state working on the United Nations and international organizations. After helping Baker during the contested vote count in Florida in 2000, Bolton wanted to become the second- or third-highest-ranking official at the State Department. Colin Powell, who was directed to find a place for Bolton by Bush's political operation, offered him the position of under secretary of state for arms control instead.

Bolton's mission in life belied his job title. In his view, arms control agreements were appendages of the liberal international order that constrained Washington's freedom of maneuver and that needed to be ditched. His memoir of government service for George H.W. Bush included a chapter titled "Cutting Gulliver Loose." He undercut Powell by opposing diplomacy to deal with North Korea's nuclear program and sought to dispose of the Anti-Ballistic Missile Treaty as quickly as possible. Scrapping the treaty was anathema to arms controllers, which made it all the more satisfying. Bolton likened treaty killing to "a desecration of their sacred scrolls." If treaties were unavoidable, they should take the form of the three-page Treaty of Moscow he helped negotiate in 2002; phone book–sized treaties were passé. Bolton made enemies along the way within the executive branch, on Capitol Hill, and especially among treaty supporters, but he relished doing so, considering being "scorned and derided" as a badge of honor.[90]

In the maneuvering for positions in George W. Bush's second term, Bolton sought to become a deputy to either Condoleezza Rice at the State Department or National Security Advisor Stephen Hadley. Both steered him away from their domains and toward New York as the U.S. ambassador to the United Nations. There were many dragons to be slain there. Bolton had made too many enemies in the Senate to be confirmed as ambassador, so Bush gave him a sixteen-month recess appointment to circumvent the Senate's confirmation process. Bolton left government with a much higher profile and a sharpened sense of grievance. He settled into a new position at the American Enterprise Institute, becoming a prominent critic of Barack Obama on Fox television, thereby coming to the notice of Donald Trump.

Bolton's tenure as national security advisor was only seventeen months long. He was at odds with Trump's overtures toward Kim Jong Un in North

Korea, his soft approach toward Putin, his withdrawal of U.S. troops from Syria at the expense of America's Kurdish allies, and Trump's attempt to dangle aid in return for help from Ukraine's newly elected president in his bid for reelection. Despite these differences, working for Trump was an uncommon opportunity for Bolton—the chance of a lifetime. Trump was susceptible to the advice of the last person he spoke to—as long as it accorded with his instincts—and Bolton's corner office in the West Wing was only a few steps away from the Oval Office. His first memoir, *Surrender Is Not an Option*, included a section on "So Many Bad Deals to Kill, So Little Time." Bolton would make good use of his time working for Trump.

THE OPPOSITIONIST IMPULSE

Bolton viewed arms control as a hopeless and naïve endeavor. This belief system has deep roots among some deterrence strengtheners, dating back to the writings of Robert Strausz-Hupé, Robert Kintner, Edward Teller, and others who were greatly unsettled by the Eisenhower administration's first tentative interactions with Soviet negotiators. This belief system led some, including Teller, to oppose President John F. Kennedy's treaty stopping atmospheric nuclear tests. Senator Henry Jackson, Richard Perle, Richard Pipes, William van Cleave, and others were greatly dismayed by the forays of Presidents Nixon, Ford, and Carter into strategic arms control. No one was more adept and articulate in expressing this belief system than Perle, who characterized arms control as a soporific that would dull the electorate and prevent deterrence-strengthening measures.[91] These views gained prominence in President Reagan's first term before he hitched his wagon to dealmakers led by George Shultz and Paul Nitze.

In Republican administrations, opponents of agreements reached or sought were sidelined, co-opted, temporarily appeased, or overruled. Nixon sent Strausz-Hupé off to be ambassador to Sri Lanka. He quieted critiques of the SALT I accords by sacking the leadership of the Arms Control and Disarmament Agency and all but two members of his negotiating team. Reagan smothered critics in soothing bromides, but discontent resurfaced after the INF Treaty. Skeptics of arms control were as stunned as everyone else by the demise of the Soviet Union and fully supported George H.W. Bush's remarkable achievements.

Muffled criticism in Republican administrations became full-throated when Democrats won the White House. Carter, Clinton, and Obama faced a torrent of criticism that curtailed their ambitions. Generational change in the

Republican Party sharpened this criticism. Party elders like Kissinger, Shultz, Brent Scowcroft, and Baker were dealmakers. Far below them in organizational charts, skeptics of arms control were being credentialed. With the passage of time, dealmakers left the stage, and those who opposed agreements that curtailed freedom of action rose through the ranks. In their view, the demise of the Soviet Union made deal making optional, if not unnecessary. Trump's victory was a victory for opponents of arms control who had paid their dues and risen through the ranks; they were empowered as never before. Bolton was their titular head, who suppressed his disdain for Trump in order to serve in his administration to limit damage. His definition of damage limitation included killing arms control agreements. After Tillerson and Mattis left, even stays of execution were hard to come by.

Bolton's counterpart at the State Department was Christopher Ford, who served as an assistant secretary of state. Ford received his bachelor's degree, summa cum laude, from Harvard, studied at Oxford as a Rhodes scholar, and received a law degree from Yale. Instead of practicing law in between stints in the executive branch, he worked on Capitol Hill and for the Hudson Institute. Bolton was a bulldozer; Ford was articulate, thoughtful, and in his polite way, cutting. In Ford's view, thinking about arms control had devolved into a "distinctive subculture" that had lost its way. Arms controllers had stopped focusing on "managing competitive dynamics of the security environment and clashing security interests." They had lost sight of pathological Russian behavior, particularly evident in Ukraine and in Moscow's noncompliance with treaties. In doing so, arms controllers were captured by their own pathologies—the "identity politics of virtue signaling and consciousness raising." They remained focused on the goal of disarmament, believing the problem was a lack of political will rather than the unforgiving competitive dynamics of major power competition.[92]

Ford's critique of the insularity of arms controllers was accompanied by an unwillingness to acknowledge, let alone critique, the insularity of deterrence strengtheners. He opposed the "virtue signaling" of arms controllers while finding virtue in new applications for tactical nuclear weapons and the full panoply of strategic modernization programs. Ford endorsed all of this on moral grounds—as instruments of war prevention—without addressing how his moral code would fare in the event that deterrence failed, nuclear weapons were used, and uncontrolled escalation ensued. In Ford's pantheon of virtues, deterrence could provide what arms control could not—even though the humanitarian laws of warfare that he championed could be obliterated after the first appearance of a mushroom cloud, which he dutifully supported if circumstances demanded. This was, after all, a core belief of deterrence strategists. Ford didn't dwell on the consequences of deterrence failure; few deterrence strengtheners did. And yet, if deterrence failed, escalation control was unlikely to succeed because deterrence was predicated on upping the ante. How, then, could deterrence and the likelihood of uncontrolled escalation be squared with the humanitarian laws of warfare? The worst aspects of deterrence needed to be defanged by arms control, but Ford was notably reticent on the virtues of arms control—at least as practiced by others.

After Trump's first year in office, opponents of arms control were clearly in the ascendancy. They had the ear of cabinet members who either didn't need convincing or didn't try to hold back the tide. As for new negotiating positions, administration officials typically sought outcomes that diplomacy couldn't deliver. What others considered invitations to fail, they considered righteous pathways to success. In this view, it was essential to set the bar high, otherwise outcomes would fall short. Then, if diplomacy failed, the United States would become stronger by being unencumbered.

These arguments were not new; they were reprised from the first Reagan administration, where skeptics proposed agreements that they presumed the Kremlin's Old Guard would never accept. This approach backfired, producing unexpected successes when negotiations took a wholly unexpected turn as Reagan revealed himself to be an abolitionist and was paired with Mikhail Gorbachev, who matched Reagan in his disdain for nuclear orthodoxy. What worked for Reagan couldn't possibly work for Trump, because Reagan turned to pragmatic dealmakers in his second term and because Putin wasn't Gorbachev. Besides, Trump and those around him had no interest in negotiating a new arms reduction treaty. Instead, they sought a pause as new U.S. missiles, submarines, and bombers were being readied for deployment. In this view, further reductions would only invite Beijing to accelerate the growth of its strategic forces.

The Trump administration's posture of resistance to strategic arms reductions was clear. In contrast, its nonproliferation diplomacy was muddled. North Korea was treated much differently than Iran. Trump engaged in invective and then flirtation with Kim Jong Un, without effect. In the case of Iran, the Trump administration demanded denuclearization without offering or being willing to accept trade-offs to achieve it. Instead, the administration's demands for denuclearization were accompanied by tougher sanctions and a maximum pressure campaign. A sanctions-oriented approach and a refusal to negotiate conveyed steadfastness and resolve while avoiding the perceived pitfalls of a negotiating process. Unlike complete denuclearization in the hardest proliferation cases, sanctions were achievable. And if sanctions did not succeed in prompting concessions or regime change, then more sanctions would follow. If squeezing harder failed and prompted greater nuclear danger, military action would become more warranted.

DEALING WITH THE HARDEST CASES

Toward the end of the Clinton administration, Clinton tapped William Perry to devise a strategy to stop Pyongyang before it acquired nuclear weapons and the missiles that could reliably loft them across the Pacific. Perry engaged North Korea's neighbors and U.S. allies to help craft a diplomatic strategy. The result was a bold offer—normal ties and economic benefits to Pyongyang in return for denuclearization.[93] Time was short, however, and success was only partial. The George W. Bush administration discovered that North Korea's leader Kim Jong Il was working on a second pathway to acquire nuclear weapons after mothballing the first. Bush then chose to back away from Perry's approach. His administration also found complete denuclearization an elusive goal. By the end of the Bush administration, North Korea possessed nuclear weapons and the means to deliver them against U.S. allies, making military options to destroy these weapons even more risky.

Iran lagged behind North Korea in producing the Bomb and the missiles to carry them long distances. The Obama administration took up the challenge of stopping Iran from making nuclear weapons through diplomacy, defining success in partial terms. Critics of the agreement assessed this deal to be an abject failure because it did not meet the denuclearization standard and because they assumed that Tehran would not abide by its commitments, which were deemed to be too short in length in any event. Tehran's troubling behavior in the Middle East provided critics with more grounds for disaffection and opposition.

Trump inherited this situation and Bolton sought to affect it. Their pairing was predictably fractious. On most matters, at least in Bolton's retelling, they disagreed. Mutual disenchantment was inevitable. Bolton viewed himself as being a serious practitioner of geopolitics. Trump's interest here, as elsewhere, was skin-deep. During their time together, Bolton concluded that Trump was ruled by self-regard; all else was secondary, including the national interest. It did not take long for Bolton to find Trump's dealings with foreign leaders and lack of knowledge about the world appalling. He characterized

Trump as erratic, impulsive, and stunningly uninformed, while overtly seeking help from China's Xi Jinping as well as Ukraine's Volodymyr Zelensky for his reelection campaign.[94]

Trump's approach to North Korean leader Kim Jong Un, who succeeded Kim Jong Il in 2011, was particularly egregious, in Bolton's view, because it lacked consistency and flirted with vainglorious deal making. Trump opening gambit reflected Nixon's "mad man" theory of deterrence—a belief that wild threats coming from someone who might just be capable of following through with them could instill caution or prompt favorable outcomes.[95] One of Trump's cardinal principles was unpredictability to keep others off guard. Provocations served this purpose, as well.[96] Borrowing from Pyongyang's idiom, Trump warned, "North Korea best not make any more threats to the United States. They will be met with fire and fury like the world has never seen."[97] Next came personal slights, including a reference to North Korea's leader as "little rocket man."[98] Kim Jong Un volleyed back with "I will surely and definitely tame the mentally deranged U.S. dotard with fire."[99]

Then, abruptly, Trump switched gears and engaged in a campaign of flattery toward Kim Jong Un. He rejected diplomatic preliminaries and decided to engage in summitry, meeting the North Korean leader in Singapore in 2018 and in Hanoi in 2019, in addition to a brief visit to the Demilitarized Zone. After his first summit with Kim, Trump declared, "There is no longer a nuclear threat from North Korea."[100] Before their second encounter, Trump told supporters attending a political rally that Kim "wrote me beautiful letters" and "we fell in love."[101] Trump's employment of flattery in service to deal making with Kim Jong Un was, in Bolton's view, "strikingly naïve and dangerous."[102] It was also ineffectual.

Sustained diplomatic engagement was not a hallmark of the Trump administration. Trump's first national security advisor, H.R. McMaster, with a nod to the international relations theorist Hans J. Morganthau, characterized Trump-like behavior as "strategic narcissism."[103] Trump wasn't just a narcissist; he was a fabulist, as well. His varied approaches to North Korea had no lasting, positive effect. After the atmospherics dissipated, Kim Jong Un realized that nothing would come from these photo opportunities, and signaled steps to strengthen deterrence.

ALL FALL DOWN

The marriage of convenience between Trump and Bolton lasted long enough to kill some of the agreements that Bolton believed were contrary to the national interest. His influence on Trump's thinking predated his arrival and lasted after his departure, despite their bitter estrangement. For example, the provenance of Trump's proposal for trilateral count-every-warhead talks with Russia and China can be traced to Bolton's tenure at the White House, where Bolton publicly telegraphed a move that would play out after he left. Bolton's purpose was to derail a long extension of Obama's New START. His first order of business, however, was extrication from Obama's nuclear deal with Iran. Trump was inclined to withdraw during his first year in office but was temporarily dissuaded from doing so by Tillerson, Mattis, and McMaster.

On his first day at the office, Bolton directed the National Security Council staff to prepare for withdrawal from Obama's politically binding compact with Iran.[104] The same month that Bolton replaced McMaster, Pompeo replaced Tillerson, leaving Mattis, who had already lost Trump's confidence, alone in opposition to withdrawing from the Iran nuclear deal. One month after Bolton and Pompeo joined the administration, Trump announced the U.S. withdrawal, declaring, "This was a horrible, one-sided deal that should have never, ever been made. It didn't bring calm, it didn't bring peace, and it never will."[105] Trump then sparred with Europe, Russia, and China over the reimposition of sanctions as Tehran reacted with countermoves to increase enrichment levels. Trump had no inclination or interest to improve on Obama's terms. He also had no enthusiasm for another war in the Middle East.

Next up was the Intermediate Nuclear Forces Treaty. In August 2018, Bolton told his Russian counterpart, Nikolai Patrushev, that U.S. withdrawal from the treaty was "a real possibility, even though there was no official U.S. position." This degree of frankness, in Bolton's view, "must have astounded" his Russian interlocutors.[106] Bolton was confident about Trump's predilections, which he astutely reinforced. Six months later, Trump announced the U.S. withdrawal from the INF Treaty. He was fully justified in doing so. Putin had authorized a material breach of the treaty and the Russian General Staff subsequently deployed battalions of missiles expressly prohibited under its terms. Corrective action wasn't possible as long as these missiles were deemed essential to Russian national security. In announcing the U.S. withdrawal, Trump said, "We cannot be the only country in the world unilaterally bound by this treaty, or any other."[107]

Two months later, in April 2019, Trump announced U.S. withdrawal from the Arms Trade Treaty during remarks at the annual meeting of the National Rifle Association. The object and purpose of the Arms Trade Treaty are to prevent the illicit international trade in conventional arms, including tanks, armored personnel carriers and small arms, as well as to bolster international humanitarian law. Negotiations on the treaty at the United Nations concluded in 2013, after which Obama sent the treaty to the Senate for its advice and consent, but no action was subsequently taken. Trump's "unsigning" of the treaty had no practical effect since prospects for U.S. ratification were remote. His reasoning, as he told conference-goers: "We will never allow foreign bureaucrats to trample on your Second Amendment freedom."[108] This wasn't the first instance of domestic politics upending arms control, but it was the least substantive.

Before leaving the White House, Bolton signaled the impending U.S. withdrawal from the Open Skies Treaty. He left funeral arrangements to his acolyte on the National Security Council staff, Tim Morrison, who worked previously for Senator Kyl. After calling on U.S. friends and allies to try to improve Russian compliance and finding progress to be inadequate, the administration announced its withdrawal from the Open Skies Treaty in May 2020, disregarding a provision of public law requiring prior notice to Capitol Hill.[109]

The treaty was first broached by President Eisenhower in 1955 as a device to allay concerns about surprise attacks and rejected by the Kremlin as giving license to espionage. President George H.W. Bush resurrected the idea to test Gorbachev's sincerity about *glasnost*, or openness, and Gorbachev was amenable. Since 2002, when cooperative overflights by aircraft carrying unclassified sensors began, over 1,500 Open Skies flights were carried out. A novel feature of the treaty was its ride-sharing provisions, whereby the United States could bring along treaty partners, including former members of Warsaw Pact and the newly independent states of Georgia and Ukraine, sharing unclassified data with them.

Putin wasn't complying fully with the Open Skies Treaty, but unlike the INF Treaty, his violations were marginal, easily circumvented and nullified. Putin rejected overflights of the enclaves he carved out of Georgian soil. He also limited them over Kaliningrad, a Russian outpost between Poland and the Baltic states, after an extended Polish overflight completely shut down the enclave in 2014. Russian violations prompted U.S. countermoves restricting air space over Hawaii and Alaska in greater measure than Moscow's limits. Putin softened his opposition to overflying Kaliningrad, but added a new insult, designating an airfield in Crimea as a refueling spot for U.S. Open Skies aircraft.

As justification for withdrawal, Trump administration officials stressed Russian violations and data gathering from Russian overflights of the United States that could be useful for cyber warfare. Whether true or not, this vulnerability was widely shared. Canceling Russian overflights served no protective purpose against cyber warfare, as subsequent Russian hacks of the State Department, the Department of Homeland Security, and other governmental agencies confirmed. The most glaring vulnerabilities to cyber warfare entered through the back door, not overhead. In announcing the U.S. withdrawal, Pompeo warned Moscow that it had six months to rectify its noncompliance—as if Putin would have second thoughts about ending U.S. ride sharing with former Soviet Republics and Warsaw Pact members. Walking away from the Open Skies Treaty was a gift from Trump to Putin and another point of divergence between Washington and its friends and allies in Europe.

THE WITHDRAWAL DOCTRINE

Donald Trump's National Security Strategy, issued in December 2017, had no lasting import. Its promises were ephemeral, reflections of a moment in time and a temporary supporting cast. This document promised "a strategy of principled realism that is guided by outcomes, not ideology." It also promised to "lead in multilateral organizations so that American interests and principles are protected." Noting the threat of naturally occurring outbreaks of viruses, Trump's National Security Strategy pledged to "strengthen our emergency response and unified coordination systems to rapidly characterize outbreaks, implement public health containment measures to limit the spread of disease, and provide surge medical care—including life-saving treatments." It affirmed that "diplomacy is indispensable to identify and implement solutions to conflicts in unstable regions of the world short of military involvement" and resolved to "upgrade our diplomatic capabilities to compete in the current environment." There was also a promise to "champion American values and offer encouragement to those struggling for human dignity in their societies." And this: "The United States will deepen collaboration with our European allies and partners to confront forces threatening to undermine our common values, security interests, and shared vision. The United States and Europe will work together to counter Russian subversion and aggression."[110]

Despite Trump's erratic behavior and statements, patterns emerged from his decisions. He proudly advertised his National Security Strategy as an "America First foreign policy in action"—and that it was.[111] Richard Haass, who worked in both Bush administrations, suggested the name of a doctrine to accompany Trump's actions. He called it the Withdrawal Doctrine.[112] Every withdrawal from an agreement or institution subtracted Washington's international standing and ability to influence outcomes. And almost every withdrawal contributed directly or indirectly to increasing the shadows cast by China and Russia around their peripheries. The scope of the Trump administration's retreat extended well beyond arms control compacts, to include withdrawal from the Trans-Pacific Partnership trade agreement and the Paris Climate Agreement, both finalized in the Obama administration where they faced strenuous opposition from Republicans on Capitol Hill. The Trump administration dealt with trade issues bilaterally. There was no pretense of diplomatic activity to address climate change.

Each withdrawal was trumpeted as a victory for Trump's America First strategy. The United Nations remained a reliable punching bag. Bolton had successfully distanced the United States from the International Criminal Court during the George W. Bush administration by withdrawing from its founding Rome Statute. The United Nations Education, Scientific and Cultural Organization, dominated by Third World nations, was a frequent target for its cultural programming with anti-Israel overtones. The Reagan administration withdrew from UNESCO in 1984. The George W. Bush administration rejoined in 2003, but after a vote making Palestine a member of UNESCO in 2011, the United States stopped paying its dues and lost its voting rights. The Trump administration announced a second withdrawal from UNESCO in December 2018.

The Trump administration withdrew from the U.N. Human Rights Council in June 2018 because of its focus on Israeli activities toward Palestinians and the poor human rights record of some of the states represented. China was elected to the Human Rights Council after the Trump administration's departure. The United States fell badly in arrears paying its dues for peacekeeping operations. Trump announced U.S. defunding of the World Health Organization during the coronavirus pandemic in April 2020, ostensibly for its pro-China bias. In May, Trump announced intent to withdraw.

Other withdrawals pointed to dire consequences for U.S. allies recruited to help wage the George W. Bush administration's global war against terror. In October 2019, Trump withdrew military support for the Kurds in Syria, ceding this ground to Turkish forces who were the sworn enemy of Kurdish fighters. Trump repeatedly called for ending the U.S. troop presence in Afghanistan and initiated negotiations with the Taliban for a peace agreement, during which the Taliban trained their fire on a battered Afghan

National Army. The Taliban generally respected a cease-fire with U.S. forces to facilitate their departure, with the notable exception of reports of bounties on U.S. troops paid to Taliban fighters by Russian agents.[113] The government of Afghanistan, rent by division and utterly dependent on foreign aid, mostly from the United States, had good reason to wonder about the duration of its existence.

Prime Minister Winston Churchill cautioned President Franklin Delano Roosevelt in 1940 before U.S. "Lend-Lease" support was forthcoming by cabling that "the voice and force of the United States may count for nothing if they are withheld too long."[114] The voice and force the United States counted for far less as a result of the Trump administration's America First strategy and its serial withdrawals from international compacts. Not all of Trump's withdrawals were baseless: unilateral compliance with the INF Treaty in the face of ongoing Russian material breaches was neither wise nor warranted, and the indefinite participation of U.S. ground forces in Afghanistan was unsustainable. The sum total of U.S. withdrawals, however, suggested a broader disengagement, one keenly felt by U.S. allies and friends in Europe and Asia.

Allies received the brunt of Trump's plainspokenness. Early in his presidency Trump called NATO "obsolete" and openly wondered why the United States would fight a war for its newest members, Montenegro and North Macedonia.[115] He cast public scorn-by-tweet on German chancellor Angela Merkle, French president Emmanuel Macron, British prime minister Theresa May, and Canadian prime minister Justin Trudeau.

Russian president Vladimir Putin was notably unscathed by Trump's penchant for denigrating foreign leaders. When asked at a press conference after their July 16, 2018 summit meeting in Helsinki about Putin's denial of interfering in the U.S. presidential election, Trump said, "I don't see any reason" why Putin wouldn't be telling the truth. Senator John McCain reacted by calling Trump's remarks "one of the most disgraceful performances by an American president in memory." John Brennan, Central Intelligence Agency director under Barack Obama, found Trump's remarks to be a treasonable offense.[116] Trump was similarly supportive of China's leader, Xi Jinping, until he pivoted against him during the coronavirus pandemic.

NUCLEAR SCATTERSHOTS

On U.S. nuclear posture, Trump's public comments touched all bases. At various times he called for winning a nuclear arms race, capping the nuclear competition, suggesting abolition, threatening first use and massive nuclear destruction, and calling for deep cuts.[117] He asked aides whether nuclear detonations might be employed to counter hurricanes and mused about increasing the U.S. arsenal tenfold, then denigrated leaks of these conversations as "fake news."[118] Because Trump's views on nuclear weapons were so scattershot, they were widely discounted except by those most worried about his behavior. A more reliable indicator of the administration's underlying approach to nuclear weapons was the unclassified version of the Office of the Secretary of Defense's Nuclear Posture Review, released in February 2018.

The Pentagon's Nuclear Posture Review concluded that global threat conditions had "worsened markedly" since 2010. The hopeful period following the end of the Cold War was over, replaced by an era of major power competition. China and Russia were increasing the role that nuclear weapons played in their security calculations. As a consequence, the Pentagon advised that "the current environment makes further progress toward nuclear arms reductions in the near term extremely challenging." The United States needed "a flexible, tailored nuclear deterrent strategy" to deter potential adversaries. "For any President, the use of nuclear weapons is contemplated only in the most extreme circumstances to protect our vital interests and those of our allies." The goal of the U.S. nuclear posture "is to convince adversaries that they have nothing to gain and everything to lose from the use of nuclear weapons."[119]

The Posture Review's language regarding nuclear deterrence reflected continuity with previous defense reviews and a sharp discontinuity about the utility of pursuing further reductions in nuclear arms. The Trump administration's strategic modernization programs, like those of the Obama administration, reflected an across-the-board commitment to replace the old with the new. Whereas a Hillary Clinton administration might have trimmed these purchases, the Trump administration fully supported them. The Pentagon added a new wrinkle—deploying low-yield warheads atop some ballistic missiles on submarines. The purpose of this program was for contingencies where the Kremlin might seek to "escalate to de-escalate," a growing concern of deterrence strengtheners. These programs, plus the costs of nuclear warhead production and infrastructure upgrades, if fully funded, were projected to far exceed a trillion dollars over the course of the next three decades.[120]

ENFORCEMENT

If expenditures for nuclear weapon–related programs were a reliable indicator of security, the United States would be the safest country in the world by a considerable margin. And yet the world was becoming, as the Pentagon and intelligence community rightly assessed, a more dangerous place. Rivalries among nuclear-armed states were heating up, aggressive acts were on the rise, and international institutions were badly weakened. Insecurities were also rising on the domestic front as a result of the pandemic, joblessness, and racial strife. On top of this, Trump added the denigration of arms control, a withdrawal doctrine, and a dismissive approach to diplomacy. Arms control compacts were being shed without something better to replace them, alliances were fraying, nuclear capabilities in North Korea and Iran were growing, competition with China was becoming more worrisome, as was Putin's behavior. Chinese and Russian space warfare capabilities were becoming more pointed, as was cyber warfare. This panoply of security concerns would have challenged any U.S. president; they were accentuated further as the U.S. government was being hollowed out by weak appointments, nonappointments, and the departure of skilled, experienced personnel, including those versed in arms control.

The 2018 Trump Nuclear Posture Review added a new condition for acceptable arms control—that agreements be "enforceable." While the administration remained "receptive to future arms control negotiations if conditions permit and the potential outcome improves the security of the United States, its allies, and partners," it did not entertain much hope for success. "Further progress is difficult to envision," the report added, "in an environment that is characterized by nuclear-armed states seeking to change borders and overturn existing norms, and by significant, continuing non-compliance with existing arms control obligations and commitments."[121]

Enforcing arms reduction and treaty compliance aren't entirely new concepts; they have a failed past. After World War I, the victorious European powers tried to enforce onerous provisions of the Treaty of Versailles on a prostrate Germany. Germany was forced to pay reparations, the Rhineland was demilitarized and occupied by foreign inspectors, the size of the German Army and the tonnage of its capital ships were strictly limited, submarine construction was prohibited, as was the creation of a German Air Force. These enforcement provisions were unsustainable as the Weimar Republic failed and as German grievances grew. Reparations dried up, the occupiers went home, and German armament factories resumed production. Enforcement provisions were no match for Germany's sense of victimization.

Later on, enforcement came to the fore with the Acheson-Lilienthal Plan. Enforcement provisions were plainly needed for abolition, as Bernard Baruch argued before a fledgling United Nations in 1946. The UN was then a new institution in which many invested great hope. Baruch proposed that it have enforcement powers to control dangerous uses of atomic energy. The United States proposed that permanent members of the UN Security Council give up their veto power and help stand up a vast inspection corps. Baruch's concept of enforcement was quickly rejected by the Soviet Union. This fading chapter in disarmament diplomacy presents a Catch-22 dilemma that pertains to this day: when political and geopolitical conditions are not amenable to abolition, enforcement is required but not feasible.

Enforceable arms control and reduction in compacts between nuclear-armed states or by means of a supranational authority remain beyond reach. States possessing the Bomb have persuasive means to reject enforcement and, besides, the UN is in a period of decline. What, then, did the Trump administration's Nuclear Posture Review have in mind when stating enforcement as a requirement for new arms control compacts? No explanation was forthcoming, nor could one be reasonably expected. Every arms control agreement since the Bomb's appearance has been based on mutual interest. The parties found sufficient common ground to reach agreement, they possessed national means to monitor compliance, and eventually they supplemented technical observation with cooperative inspections. No force majeure could be exercised against a nuclear-armed competitor, nor was it required. When compliance questions arose, concerns were discussed and clarified. Sometimes corrective actions were taken. Other compliance concerns were not correctable because they reflected the deliberate exploitation of loopholes that negotiators were instructed to carve out. On rare occasions, Moscow deliberately disregarded treaty constraints and on even rarer occasions, such as the INF Treaty, its noncompliance constituted a material breach.

All of the nuclear agreements reached during and after the Cold War had consultative provisions. None had enforcement provisions. If compliance concerns could not be met, there was always the option of taking matters to the United Nations, but when major powers with veto rights disagree, this will be a symbolic or hollow exercise. When faced with noncompliance, states that possess nuclear weapons sought their own remedies. If noncompliance were slight, remedies were, as well; if noncompliance were serious, serious remedial action was available, including treaty withdrawal. Only two American presidents concluded that treaties no longer served U.S. national security interests—George W. Bush and Trump.

Diplomacy to address compliance concerns was messy, but not as messy as enforcement by means of war and occupation. Military means of enforcement against small states possessing nuclear weapons posed exceptional risks, which is why North Korean leaders have strived to possess a nuclear deterrent. In such cases, sanctions are the standard remedy, but sanctions are unlikely to roll back nuclear programs for leaders who are convinced they need to possess nuclear weapons.

Enforcement is not a remedy associated with deterrence and diplomacy; it's a concept that appeals to those with little faith in deterrence and diplomacy. The word "enforcement" did not appear in any of the agreements that constituted the nuclear safety net during and after the Cold War. When the Trump administration declared that enforcement was a requirement for new arms control compacts, it was, in effect, foreclosing the possibility of new agreements that could meet its standards. Trump withdrew from the one agreement where enforcement was most applicable—the Iran nuclear agreement with "snap back" provisions for the reimposition of sanctions. The logic of Trump's withdrawal from the Iran nuclear agreement, followed by Tehran's countermoves to increase its holdings of enriched uranium, pointed toward remedial strikes against Iran's nuclear weapon–related facilities. This form of enforcement is more likely without negotiated agreements than with them.

LAST TREATY STANDING

The last remaining caps and inspections on U.S. and Russian strategic forces resided in New START, the treaty that Obama and Dmitri Medvedev signed in 2010. New START's ten-year duration began the following year, meaning its expiration date would arrive within two weeks after the inauguration of the winner of the 2020 election. Its provisions could be extended for up to five years by mutual agreement, it could be superseded by a new agreement, or it could lapse. Obama chose not to act on extending New START, as Putin was then imposing conditions for doing so. Besides, during the latter years of the Obama administration, U.S.-Russian relations had deteriorated badly over Ukraine and Russia's material breach of the INF Treaty. Obama decided to leave this decision to his successor, presumably Hillary Clinton.

When Trump won enough Electoral College votes to become president, opposition to New START among deterrence strengtheners gained official sanction. One argument against extending New START for five years was that its focus on numbers and reductions had become misguided; what mattered more, in the view of critics, were behavior patterns, a focus on warheads rather than their means of delivery, and changing China's status from a free rider to a constrained party. Critics argued that New START's reductions had not improved the behavior of either Russia or China. Nor did New START address "nonstrategic nuclear weapons"—short-range tactical nuclear weapons that Russia was presumed to be increasingly relying upon, and intermediate- and medium-range missiles that both Russia and China were upgrading and deploying. In sum, New START was too limited in scope. It focused on the wrong units of account and didn't address emerging security concerns.

These arguments didn't address how U.S. security would be advanced in the absence of strategic arms control or by increasing force structure and deployed warheads—options that were also available to Russia and China. Nor did they acknowledge the wide gap between U.S. and Chinese deployed warheads. Beijing was doubling the size of its deployed warheads over the next decade—to perhaps 400—while the Pentagon was allowed upward of 2,500 deployed warheads under New START when lax counting rules for warheads on bombers were included, with perhaps another 1,300 warheads in reserve or awaiting disassembly.[122]

When Secretary of Defense Robert McNamara marked out the baseline for the U.S. strategic deterrent in the Kennedy and Johnson administrations, U.S. forces were to consist of 41 missile-carrying submarines, 1,000 silo-based missiles, and 250 bombers. As a result of the post–Cold War treaties negotiated by George H.W. Bush, George W. Bush, and Barack Obama, U.S. deployed forces had shrunk to 18 submarines (each with 24 tubes to deliver missiles carrying multiple warheads), 66 bombers dedicated to nuclear missions, and 400 single-warhead-carrying missiles in vulnerable silos. Because of the high cost of modernizing the Triad, additional shrinkage was already conceded for the number of missile-carrying submarines, and further cuts for budgetary reasons could occur in the number of replacement bombers and land-based missiles. Critics of New START's extension argued that either it should be short or that it was time for a pause in further reductions, as they would encourage Beijing to seek parity or at least to close the distance between U.S. and Chinese strategic forces.

John Bolton's was the loudest voice in the room against New START. During the Obama administration, he opposed the treaty as unilateral disarmament and questioned the "rush" toward deeper reductions.[123] A year before being tapped to become the national security advisor, Bolton publicly applauded Trump's view that New START was another bad Obama agreement. The treaty was, he wrote, "an execrable deal, a product of Cold War nostrums about reducing nuclear tensions. Arms-control treaties, properly conceived and drafted, should look like George W. Bush's 2002 Treaty of Moscow: short (three pages), with broad exit ramps and sunset provisions."[124]

In his first phone call to Trump, Putin inquired about extending New START, and after a halting initial reaction and hurried consultation with those around him in the Oval Office, Trump reportedly characterized it as another one of the Obama administration's bad deals.[125] In one fleeting exchange, the opportunity for a quick treaty extension was lost. There was an upside, however: Putin dropped his conditions to New START's extension. Extending New START for the permissible five-year period would not have been a heavy lift for Trump. One reason to do so was that it would likely take the better part of five years to successfully engage China and devise a broader formula for arms reductions. Another was that it would take that long and far longer for new U.S. submarines, bombers, and ocean-spanning missiles to be fielded. Moreover, Putin's conditions would likely be reintroduced in any new negotiating format. On the other side of the equation, New START was Obama's treaty, and Trump was predisposed to oppose rather than extend it.

For over three years, Trump administration officials didn't hint publicly at what they had in mind as a replacement for New START. In private, Bolton conveyed the message in August 2018 to his Russian counterpart that "it was unlikely we could agree to a five-year extension." Bolton took delight in doing so, as "Moscow and most US liberals were praying for" a five-year extension.[126] On June 18, 2020, Bolton revealed his advice to Trump in an interview to the *Washington Beacon*, saying, "Cold War–style, bilateral strategic arms negotiations don't make sense when you're in a multipolar nuclear world." China needed to be brought into the talks.[127] A month later Bolton delivered a speech before the National Conservative Student Conference, where he announced that New START was "flawed from the beginning" and "unlikely" to be renewed. "Why extend a flawed system just to say you have a treaty?" The flaw Bolton identified was the noninclusion of tactical nuclear weapons. "We need to focus on something better, and we will."[128]

Bolton left the White House the following month, having succeeded in shaping Trump's views toward New START and precipitating Trump's withdrawal from the Open Skies Treaty. Morrison stayed behind to attend to these matters until Trump's impeachment inquiry. After leaving, he wrote an opinion piece applauding the president's fondness for upsetting apple carts. "The President should not shy away from this disruption," Morrison opined, "but he should also be wary of the unelected bureaucracy in his midst that may not support his bold call for the modernization of arms control."[129] It takes a whole of government effort, along with dedicated leadership, to negotiate agreements that reduce nuclear danger and nuclear weapons. It takes only a small number of well-placed, dedicated individuals to tear these agreements down.

There was no formal public rollout of Trump's replacement for New START, and no briefing for reporters by the president or the secretary of state. The first public suggestion of an ambitious alternative came in April 2019 when an unidentified senior White House official—most probably Morrison—said, "The president has made clear that he thinks that arms control should include Russia and China and should include all the weapons, all the warheads, all the missiles." He went on to liken this out-of-the-box, innovative, and bold initiative to Trump's ambitious outreach to North Korean leader Kim Jong Un.[130] Senator Cotton worked closely with Bolton and Morrison, serving the dual roles of trial-balloon launcher and downfield blocker. A case in point was his proposed Senate resolution in calling for withdrawing from the Open Skies Treaty—seven months before Trump acted.[131]

The State and Defense Departments signed off on the plan championed by Bolton, Cotton, and Morrison to improve upon New START. Trump proposed counting every Russian and Chinese warhead. Further reductions would be placed on hold. The administration announced the appointment of Marshall Billingslea to spearhead the new nuclear talks on April 10, 2020. Billingslea was a Treasury Department official working on sanctions and a former staff member for Senator Jesse Helms on the Foreign Relations Committee, where he fully shared Helms's skepticism of arms control compacts, especially those produced by Democratic administrations.

The administration announced plans for Billingslea to meet with the Russian deputy foreign minister, Sergei Ryabkov, on the same day as announcing that it was formally withdrawing from the Open Skies Treaty. Billingslea and Morrison appeared at a Hudson Institution event on May 21, 2020, to provide the bare outline of a grand trilateral compact to count warheads.[132] Seeking to engage a dubious Moscow and a rejectionist Beijing, Billingslea warned of the possibility of an arms race: "We know how to win these races, and we know how to spend the adversary into oblivion."[133] Beijing nonetheless quickly opted out, and Moscow waived off Trump's suggestion that it help change Beijing's mind.[134]

Every president since Gerald Ford and Jimmy Carter sought limitations on warheads linked to their means of delivery. The Trump administration's proposal sought neither. Instead, Trump endorsed an ambitious transparency measure at a time when U.S.-Russian relations were toxic and U.S.-Chinese relations were at a low point over the novel coronavirus. Trump's goals of counting every warhead and engaging Beijing were unobjectionable. They were also a diversion. Further reductions would presumably have to await a full accounting of existing warheads, if then. The administration never publicly indicated a willingness to extend New START for more than one year. This short duration was initially pegged to Beijing's failure to engage in negotiations, and later on Moscow's unwillingness to partake of bold and innovative diplomacy. Whatever the reason, the administration was consistent about seeking an early exit from New START.

The Trump administration also endorsed a companion initiative formulated by Christopher Ford to fend off calls from the Nonproliferation Treaty's abstainers who were clamoring for deeper cuts. The need of the hour, Ford argued, was creating conditions for nuclear disarmament. He argued that a rote process of reductions, regardless of international conditions, was otherworldly. Instead, reductions could only proceed when conditions were conducive to disarmament. There was clear merit to this argument, just as there was merit to counting every warhead. Both initiatives were, however, predicated on the nonrecognition of nuclear excess. The Trump administration's initiatives to create conditions for nuclear disarmament and to count every warhead had another common feature: they shifted the burden to others before further reductions could occur.[135]

NEW START ON A VENTILATOR

The great edifice of strategic arms control and reductions was built over four decades of hard diplomatic labor. The process began in November 1969 with Leonid Brezhnev asking his chief SALT negotiator to choose which prison he wanted to be interned at if he revealed state secrets. Initially, the Kremlin refused to provide data on Soviet strategic forces. Success came slowly at first, and then with a rush: During the apogee of arms control, there were hundreds of on-site inspections at production facilities and missile bases.

Republican administrations did much of this heavy lifting. As the Soviet Union dissolved, President George H.W. Bush seized the moment to dramatically reduce Cold War arsenals. A peace dividend was at hand. Accepting deep cuts was also a way to help Moscow reduce launchers it could not afford and to place warheads in secure storage, awaiting their dismantlement. The arsenals that remained were still excessive; another Republican president, George W. Bush, would attend to that. Obama's New START was built upon this foundation. Trump was dismissive of this construction project. His National Security Strategy and the Pentagon's Nuclear Posture Review cast doubt on the value of strategic arms control, let along the possibility of new agreements in an era of intensified competition among major powers. And yet Trump was persuaded by Bolton to propose a radical departure from anything negotiated by his predecessors. It wasn't a hard sell: proposing something bold and different appealed to Trump's instincts. It suited his nature to do things differently, to disrupt, and to leave his critics sputtering.

None of the treaties negotiated by Trump's predecessors counted and inspected every single Russian warhead for strategic forces. Counting rules were applied, and they applied only to deployed forces. Strategic bombers could clearly carry a great many warheads but were assigned charitable counting rules. No arms control and reduction agreement between Washington and Moscow covered, let alone counted and inspected, nondeployed warheads and "nonstrategic" or tactical nuclear weapons. And no previous agreement covered or counted Chinese strategic forces, let alone warheads.

Visionary goals like counting every warhead and creating conditions for nuclear disarmament have utility. They can help point to a safer future. There is also utility in challenging conventional thinking. The Trump administration was right to challenge Beijing to engage in arms control and to accept transparency and constraints on its nuclear forces. As long as Beijing remains an outlier and a free rider, bilateral U.S.-Russian reductions that reinforced the Nonproliferation Treaty's fundamental bargain between possessors and abstainers would be modest, at best.

A balanced assessment of aspirational goals also requires an assessment of the motives behind their advancement. The Trump administration had little standing to make the case for creative, visionary proposals. Its track record was one of general hostility to inherited agreements, serial withdrawals from agreements, and deep skepticism about the utility of new compacts. It was foursquare against deeper reductions. Another test of aspirational goals is the lengths to which an administration will go to seek their accomplishment. Those who advanced the Trump administration's initiatives might reasonably have called for a five-year extension of New START, as Putin announced his readiness to accept, in order to make headway on visionary initiatives. A long New START extension could provide time and stabilization needed to gain traction for better outcomes, but the Trump administration wasn't interested in extending New START beyond one year. Nor were prospects of success improved when lead negotiator Billingslea resorted to tweets to either embarrass or prompt Beijing to participate in these discussions. Billingslea brought miniature Chinese flags to the first engagement with his Russian counterpart in June 2020 to underscore Beijing's failure to attend. His props improperly replicated the Chinese flag.

Diplomacy was not the administration's strong suit; but this wasn't diplomacy, it was showmanship. Trump, as was his habit, paid little attention to the diplomatic labor of working on a more ambitious and expansive negotiating agenda. Preparations were hurried and haphazard. The initiative to count every warhead was offered just four months before a presidential election. There was no evidence of laying the groundwork to facilitate progress in Moscow or Beijing. The principal backers of Trump's negotiating concept fully expected their wildly ambitious proposal to be rejected by Beijing. If they expected to receive anything more than a polite hearing by Moscow, they were unpleasantly surprised as Putin awaited the election results.

Beijing absented itself from the proceedings and the Trump administration dropped its condition for Chinese engagement in order to extend New START for a brief period. Its final pre-election offer was to condition a short, one-year extension of New START to progress with Moscow on its count-every-warhead agenda. Since New START could only be extended by joint agreement, the administration's leverage to engineer this result was only as strong as Trump's prospects against the Democratic Party's standard bearer, Joe Biden. Putin clearly preferred Trump over Biden, but not to the extent of accepting the Trump administration's offer. Moscow nominally engaged, while awaiting the possibility that a new U.S. administration would offer new terms of engagement.

Trump had another option, but he forfeited it by pursuing his count-every-warhead proposal. He could have unilaterally withdrawn from New START, an option he had previously exercised on four other agreements. Doing so before the November election, however, would have diminished his prospects for winning. Doing so after losing the election to Biden would be ineffectual, since withdrawal would not come into effect until ninety days after its announcement, during which time the newly inaugurated president would reverse it. Had Trump won a second term, he might well have let the agreement lapse, or for emphasis, exercised the U.S. right of withdrawal. There was another option—treaty abrogation that would dispense with the waiting period necessary for withdrawal. Treaty abrogation, however, could only be invoked if "supreme" national interests were at immediate risk. This was too far a reach, even for Trump's advisers.

With Biden's victory, the decision was out of Trump's hands. The length of an extension was Biden's decision to make jointly with Putin, soon after the inauguration. Backers of the count-every-warhead proposal could still take some solace. They had changed the subject away from further arms reduction, at least temporarily. They also established their own baseline for complaint at whatever a Biden administration could engineer in this domain; whatever their successors could accomplish would come up short by their standards.

The incoming Biden administration would face the same dilemmas of how to deal with Putin's grievances and treaty violations and how best to counter the growth of Chinese nuclear and power projection capabilities. It wouldn't be easy. Modernization cycles were again out of phase. While Russian and Chinese production lines were warm, U.S. production lines were not. Russia was producing both strategic and intermediate-range missiles once banned by the INF Treaty. China was never constrained by the INF Treaty; more than 90 percent of its missile production lines was stamping out INF-type missiles.[136] The Pentagon, by contrast, was just beginning to deploy INF-range cruise missiles while waiting for the next generation of ocean-spanning ballistic missiles, submarines, and bombers.[137]

Biden and his team faced hard choices on how best to proceed. Whatever they decided, they could expect Republicans on Capitol Hill to give them little slack.

TRUMP'S LEDGER SHEET

Hillary Clinton likened her role as secretary of state to promote U.S. leadership abroad as a relay race.[138] She traced this form of rarified baton-passing back to Dean Acheson and the other stewards of American leadership from the origins of the Cold War onward. While it was true that presidential campaigns accentuated differences and that new presidents embarked on new initiatives, there was usually more continuity than change from one administration to the next. The norm of baton-passing, along with many others, was battered by the Electoral College victory of Donald Trump. Trump personified discontinuity rather than continuity. He dropped the baton, not by accident or inadvertence, but by personal habit.

Trump pursued, in William Burns's characterization, a "shock and awe campaign against professional diplomacy . . . born of equal parts ideological contempt and stubborn incompetence."[139] He denigrated allied leaders and corroded relationships built on decades of common purpose and sacrifice. His words stung but didn't wound because few took his words seriously. He cast off agreements that allies valued like old advertising campaigns that no longer suited his brand. The major benefactors of his penchant for disparaging allies and withdrawing from international agreements and institutions were Beijing and Moscow.

Putin had his own reasons to discard arms control agreements that no longer suited, foremost among them the Conventional Forces in Europe Treaty and the Intermediate Nuclear Forces Treaty. There was no way to fix Russian violations of the INF Treaty; U.S. withdrawal was warranted by Putin's blatant disregard for its central prohibition. Trump's withdrawal from the Open Skies Treaty over nonsubstantive but irritating constraints imposed by Putin was a gift to the Kremlin and to hardened arms control oppositionists on Capitol Hill, and an affront to friends and allies. Other withdrawals placated his core base of support, as was the case with the Arms Trade Treaty, which was announced with flair at a National Rifle Association gathering.

Trump inherited a verifiable agreement with Iran that blocked pathways to the Bomb and provided early warning of noncompliance for at least fifteen years. This accord was negotiated with, and had the support of, Russia, China, and Europe. Trump joined with those who did not believe in the utility of deterrence and diplomacy in boxing in Iran's leaders. Trump's withdrawal, followed by enrichment activities by Tehran that the agreement was designed to prohibit, left Washington and Tehran back on a collision course. As for North Korea, Trump's quixotic personal diplomacy with Kim Jong Un came to naught, as was widely predicted.

Trump left rubble in his wake. True to his word, he disrupted. After four years in the White House, he had no arms control achievement to point to. He doubled George W. Bush's total of withdrawals from arms control agreements. He defined achievement as tearing down the accomplishments of his predecessors. No lessening of any preexisting nuclear condition occurred on Trump's watch. Together with Vladimir Putin, a serial treaty violator, Trump dismantled much of the great inheritance accomplished by their predecessors. They left strategic arms control, as central as deterrence in keeping the nuclear peace, in limbo.

REVIVAL

Chapter 17

REAFFIRMING NORMS, REDUCING NUMBERS

There have been no mushroom clouds in warfare for the past three-quarters of a century despite tens of thousands of detonations-in-waiting with doctrines spring-loaded for use. The nuclear peace has held even as pairings of nuclear-armed rivals have increased fourfold. Tribute for this great accomplishment is usually paid to deterrence, but this answer is, at best, only half right. Deterrence has dangerous ritual behaviors. It is designed to succeed by the threat of harsh punishment. When deterrence is strengthened, threats become more pronounced. A nuclear rival usually reciprocates with strengthening measures of its own. The resulting nuclear competition is deeply unsettling, and those under the Bomb's protection do not feel safer as a result. Their discomfort cannot be alleviated with threats of even greater destructive effect.

Deterrence between adversaries without some form of reassurance is unsafe. Reassurance, like deterrence, has its own rituals, the most formal of which entail negotiating, signing, and implementing treaties. Those who seek safety by means of strengthening deterrence typically argue that arms control agreements are unreliable and that treaties fail. There is truth to these arguments: Reassurance, like deterrence, is not a permanently safe condition. Many treaties do not last for more than three decades, if that. It is also true that deterrence fails. The nuclear peace cannot count only on deterrence or on instruments of reassurance, including arms control; to be extended, the nuclear peace requires embracing both.

Rivals that possess nuclear weapons compete seriously. Because they compete, they occasionally find themselves in harrowing crises. Competition requires guardrails, norms, and stabilization measures to avoid mushroom clouds. Arms control can provide these essential needs. Deterrence, left to its own devices, cannot. Deterrence needs stabilization and mechanisms to reduce nuclear danger. Deterrence without the reassurance provided by arms control will not end well.

Nuclear deterrence is inherently unstable because it is based on the prospect of inflicting greater punishment. Because deterrence fails and because arms control treaties can be impermanent, norms are central. When deterrence breaks down and when treaties are cast aside, norms can still remain in place. The most crucial norm is not crossing the nuclear threshold in warfare to gain advantage or to avoid disadvantage. Once there is first use in a war between nuclear-armed rivals, there almost assuredly will be second use. Uncommon efforts by national leaders under extreme duress would be required to prevent uncontrolled escalation. Escalation control is an intellectual construct conceived in great hubris that has never been tested to withstand circumstances that are completely unique and incomprehensibly dangerous. The way to avoid nuclear escalation control is to not use these weapons in the first place. Nuclear use kills both deterrence and the remnants of arms control.

The norm of nonbattlefield use is reinforced by the norm of not testing nuclear weapons. Together these norms set nuclear weapons apart from other instruments of warfare. They are central to the nuclear peace. A third, related norm that sets nuclear weapons apart is that of nonproliferation: states that do not possess the Bomb agree not to seek it. If we are to extend the nuclear peace and revive arms control, we are obliged to reaffirm these core norms, and to nurture others, as well.

While norms are fundamental, the purposes of arms control are broader: Arms control seeks to stabilize the competition between rivals and to reduce nuclear danger. Treaties were designed for these purposes, but there is more to arms control than treaties. The nuclear peace was also nurtured by codes of conduct, tacit or explicit. Arms control opened new lines of communication. Some were technical in nature, such as "hotlines." Other lines of communication were opened between leaders, military establishments, and experts. This practice was utterly novel at first but became routinized. Arms control succeeded so well that, when conditions permitted, the deployed warheads and the means to deliver them long distances possessed by Washington and Moscow were reduced by 85 percent. Deterrence helped produce conditions for these reductions; the reductions themselves flowed from obligations embedded in treaties.

The end of the Cold War was accompanied by disinterest in arms control. Other concerns became paramount, especially climate change. Russia under Vladimir Putin was intent to change the post–Cold War order. He violated treaties that codified Moscow's loss of empire and reversed other decisions made by his predecessors. The Republican Party became hostile to arms control. Presidents George W. Bush and Donald Trump jettisoned treaties in favor of freedom of action. Other nuclear-armed rivals weren't ready for arms control. One consequence was to rely more heavily on deterrence. As relations between rivals deteriorated and as channels of communication atrophied or never opened, crises became more frequent and more hair-raising.

Diplomacy isn't optional if the United States and other nuclear rivals wish to navigate through harrowing crises without warfare and dampen nuclear arms competitions. Reassurance can take many forms. Treaties are the hardest to negotiate and, in the United States, the hardest to enter into force. Other instruments can take the form of strengthened norms, guardrails, and stabilization measures. Not everyone will be reassured by the revival of arms control. Opposition will come, as before, from those who believe that deterrence will be weakened and that deals struck will be unfair. And yet national leaders will turn, sooner or later, to the varied practices of arms control because relying on deterrence alone is far too dangerous.

The most precious jewels in the crown of arms control have been extraordinary treaties that have prevented nuclear proliferation, greatly reduced nuclear forces, and banned nuclear testing. Other treaties banned chemical and biological weapons. The negotiation of ambitious treaties seems beyond reach in the near future for several reasons, beginning with the partisan divide in the United States. A Republican Party that champions national sovereignty is likely to oppose ambitious treaties advanced by Democratic presidents. We also customarily define success in arms control by numbers: the lower the numbers, the better the treaty. Deep reductions are also beyond reach as long as Washington is divided about their advisability, Moscow refuses to accept them, and Beijing refuses to engage in trilateral numbers-based treaty making unless its numbers are equal to those granted to the United States and Russia.

Audacious treaty making is beyond reach because it requires more than figuring out how to stabilize triangular interactions between the United States, Russia, and China. The global geometry of nuclear competition is now reflected in two interlocking triangles (the second involving China, India, and Pakistan) and no less than four paired rivalries—the United States and Russia, the United States and China, China and India, and India and Pakistan. This complex geometry suggests that the revival of arms control will entail new as well as familiar arrangements.

Political fashions and national security calculations change over time. The diplomacy of reconciliation that has been out of fashion might someday return. If this appears remote, what are we to do in the interim? I propose a shift in our thinking about arms control, which has long been focused on treaties and numbers. I propose that instead of ambitious treaties, we now seek audacious goals by means of the daily accretion of small victories. This can be accomplished by extending norms against the battlefield use of nuclear weapons and nuclear testing. I suggest that the numbers that matter most are zero mushroom clouds and zero nuclear tests. I propose that we seek to extend these zeroes to the 100th anniversary of the atomic bombing of Hiroshima and Nagasaki.

The norm of nonuse in warfare is already three-quarters of the way toward this goal. While all states that possesses nuclear weapons conduct nuclear experiments, all but one have refrained from testing them for over twenty years. The outlier—North Korea—reinforces this norm because testing reaffirms its outlier status. The two crucial norms of not using nuclear weapons in warfare and not testing them have been extended for many reasons—foremost among them is that these norms are the hardest to break. We can succeed in extending the non-battlefield-use norm because, in deep crises, national leaders and their hawkish advisers considering first use have no good answer to the question "And then what?" The no-testing norm can be extended because the political and geopolitical costs of being the first to resume and to prompt a cascade of further testing are extremely high. These norms become harder to break every day, every month, and every year they are extended.

If we succeed in extending these two norms on a daily basis until the 100th anniversary of the atomic bombings of Hiroshima and Nagasaki, nuclear weapons will be perceived as having very little military utility, despite the enduring calculations of deterrence strategists. As a consequence, their numbers will be reduced as rival leaders reallocate resources to far more useful instruments of national power. If this seems wildly unrealistic, consider how far we have traveled in fencing off what were once considered "war winning" weapons from actual battlefield use. Consider, too, the efforts recounted in these pages to stop nuclear testing, which seemed like another Herculean task. Achieving the goal of extending these two norms to 2045 is not nearly as hard as establishing and maintaining them up until now. We can succeed in the future in the same way that others have succeeded before us—one day at a time and one crisis at a time—by rousing and asserting ourselves whenever the battlefield use and testing of nuclear weapons are contemplated and appear imminent.

The companion norm of nonproliferation also remains crucial. The last state to cross this threshold—North Korea—did so in 2006. The immediate predecessors, India and Pakistan, tested nuclear devices in 1998. There are many reasons for this elongated timeline, including the efforts described in these pages to negotiate the Nonproliferation Treaty, to reaffirm its founding ethos of abstention linked to the pursuit of disarmament, to build out the ranks of state parties, and to improve safeguards against dangerous practices. New challenges to the viability of the Nonproliferation Treaty are clearly within view; success in extending this norm until the 100th anniversary of the atomic bombing of Hiroshima and Nagasaki, as with the norms on non-battlefield use and no testing, will be hard but achievable.

To reinforce these three fundamental norms, I advocate reaffirmations of the canonical pledge by Ronald Reagan and Mikhail Gorbachev that a nuclear war must not be fought and cannot be won. I also seek advancement of another norm—the norm of not threatening to use nuclear weapons. The respect for the national sovereignty and territorial integrity of states, and the peaceful settlement of disputes, are crucial norms. When these norms are broken, we are obliged to impose costs on the norm breaker. Arms control then takes a hiatus, but we return to its practices to reduce nuclear danger. We revive arms control out of need, not sentimentalism.

Existing treaties still matter greatly. The revival of bilateral strategic arms control between Washington and Moscow rests on the foundation of extending New START and updating it. Besides the Nonproliferation Treaty, three other surviving treaties are in need of reinforcement: the Comprehensive Test Ban Treaty, the Chemical Weapons Convention, and the Biological Weapons Convention. One of these treaties, the Comprehensive Test Ban, has not entered into force but remains a bulwark against the resumption of nuclear testing.

The history of nuclear arms control described in these pages is one of reducing excess. Nuclear excess continues to exist, as the United States still possesses nearly 6,000 warheads; Russia's stockpile could be greater. The

United States and Russia, with by far the two largest arsenals, are obliged to pursue further reductions and to reduce nuclear danger on a bilateral track. Reductions could be undertaken unilaterally to reallocate funds for usable instruments of national defense or for other purposes. Alternatively, further reductions could be pursued in parallel by means of a politically binding agreement. If enough Republican senators could be persuaded to lend their support, and if the effort and expense of ratification are not too high, another round of reductions could take treaty form.

Bilateral strategic arms control, while essential, is too narrow a pursuit. There are other important vectors of nuclear danger. India and Pakistan as well as China and India clash over disputed borders. The next limited war between states possessing nuclear weapons, like the last, could well be between India and Pakistan. China has engaged in power projection, increasing the likelihood of crises with the United States. Vladimir Putin has elevated cyber-intrusion campaigns to new heights. The militarization of space is well advanced, with China, the United States, and Russia leading the way. Codes of conduct to prevent dangerous military-related activities on the ground, at sea, in the air, and in space, as well as in the cyber domain, need to be clarified and implemented properly. The United States, Russia, China, Great Britain, and France—the Permanent Five members of the UN Security Council, all of whom possess nuclear weapons—have convened periodic meetings on nuclear-related issues, limiting themselves to lowest common denominator initiatives. Its membership reflects the Cold War nuclear order, not the post–Cold War challenges to it. Even if P-5 deliberations on nuclear issues could somehow become more purposeful, their deliberations are unlikely to have a direct bearing on the actions of India and Pakistan, each of which possesses growing, three-digit-sized nuclear arsenals.

The Trump administration proposed a novel trilateral agreement to count every U.S., Russian, and Chinese warhead. This formula was bound to fail. Beijing refused Trump's proposal and the Kremlin responded by reviving long-standing calls for France and Great Britain to engage in strategic arms control. Because guardrails, norms, and stabilization measures are needed for all crisis-prone regions and because all nuclear dilemmas are connected, I suggest creating a broader forum of engagement that includes India and Pakistan as well as the United States, Russia, China, Great Britain, and France. I acknowledge great complications with this approach, and yet expanding the scope of dialogue might paradoxically increase prospects for success—if the focus of conversation is on norms rather than numbers. I also suggest a multilateral build-down approach where these seven states reduce the size of their arsenals as they modernize them. This approach is admittedly prone to derailment, but I lay out the logic for it, a logic that serves arms control's fundamental objectives of stabilization and reduction of nuclear danger. These ideas are explained in further detail below.

ADDING REASSURANCE TO DETERRENCE

So far, the first two detonations in warfare over Hiroshima and Nagasaki have been the last, much to the surprise of those who revealed the Bomb and those who were stunned to learn about it in August 1945. The subsequent record of nonbattlefield use constitutes an extraordinary success story—the most unacknowledged diplomatic success of the Cold War. There was no master plan to accomplish this success. Instead, success happened by accretion, by uncommon restraint, by chance, by luck, by respect for our common humanity, and by a sense of dread about retaliation.

Most people during the early, virulent Cold War competition expected further use of nuclear weapons in warfare. The Bomb, after all, had lived up to the expectation that drove its designers: it was a "war-winning" weapon. Because it was a war-winning weapon, the Soviet Union needed to have its own nuclear arsenal. And once both superpowers possessed the atomic bomb, followed by far more destructive hydrogen bombs, the nuclear peace depended initially and only on the mutual threat of horrific destruction.

Deterrence was never more dangerous than in its formative decades. New technologies to deliver the Bomb were being perfected, including technologies associated with ocean-spanning ballistic missiles that seemed ideally suited to surprise attack. Production lines for missiles, submarines, and strategic bombers reflected wartime urgency. New weapon designs were developed and needed to be tested. Every test was a demonstration of resolve and declaration of readiness to use nuclear weapons. Initially, weapon designs were tested in the atmosphere. The mushroom cloud became the indelible image of nuclear danger. Nuclear weapons and their means of delivery were kept in a high state of readiness for use, even though safety mechanisms to prevent accidental and unauthorized detonations were initially woefully inadequate.

The Bomb and all of its accoutrements of deterrence didn't make Americans feel safer. President Eisenhower recognized that deterrence was too narrow and too toxic a base to keep the nuclear peace. He therefore authorized the first awkward engagements with Soviet negotiators on measures short of abolition. Eisenhower's insight—that deterrence needed reassurance to succeed—was acknowledged by all his successors during the Cold War. The obvious common ground was mutual survival. The essence of mutual survival was the nonuse of nuclear weapons in warfare. No treaty ever enshrined this norm. In fact, Washington and Moscow adhered to military doctrines incorporating the first use of nuclear weapons if the need arose. Eisenhower almost talked himself into considering nuclear weapons as just another instrument of warfare, but he always had second thoughts when pressed to push the proverbial red button. No U.S. or Soviet leader crossed the nuclear threshold. The reasons for their restraint went far beyond the precepts of nuclear deterrence, which were too coldly analytical to account for how human beings act in deep crisis.

The norm of nonuse evolved, as one crisis after the next passed without a decision to seek temporary tactical advantage by using nuclear weapons first. In virulent passages of the Cold War, deterrence strengtheners obsessed over a massive "bolt out of the blue" attack. This worst-case scenario rested on the improbable assumption that a leader would risk the end of days to somehow achieve a victory at a price far, far greater than those who lost previous wars. President Kennedy rejected advice to undertake a preventive war and preemptive strikes during the 1962 Cuban missile crisis, as have other presidents in lesser crises with nuclear-armed states. These crises clarified that deterrence could fail. With this recognition came treaties and other instruments of arms control to stabilize nuclear rivalry and to reduce nuclear danger.

The diplomacy of arms control has gone out of fashion. Multilateral treaty negotiations are moribund. As treaties have been discarded, what forms will reassurance now take? How can we extend the nuclear peace in a world of growing competition between rivals that possess nuclear weapons and deep partisan division in the United States? The decade of extraordinary treaty making between 1986 and 1996 is long behind us. Reassurance is unlikely to be found in ambitious treaty making and deep cuts will elude us for the foreseeable future. And yet we cannot be indifferent to the numbers of nuclear weapons because increased numbers usually equate to increased nuclear danger, while reductions reflect reduced threat levels. Limitations and inspections on U.S. and Russian strategic forces remain necessary. They are also insufficient to reduce nuclear danger when friction between other nuclear-armed rivals is growing. These complex conditions suggest that the revival of arms control requires broader scope. A broader scope that includes all nuclear-armed rivals is unlikely to be found by formalizing numerical limitations. A more promising approach lies in extending key norms.

NO USE

The norm against battlefield use has survived despite great errors in judgment, faulty intelligence, and poor situational awareness in crises. This norm gained strength after each and every crisis and close call. "Something quite unanticipated happened," wrote Thomas Schelling, a founding father of arms control. "Rather, something widely expected didn't happen."[1] The chronicler of the norm of nonuse, Nina Tannenwald, rightly characterizes it as "the most important phenomenon of the nuclear age."[2] Without this norm, we are truly lost. Reaffirming and maintaining the norm of nonuse in warfare is the fundamental basis for any strategy to revive nuclear arms control. A norm that has survived for seventy-five years can be broken tomorrow, or the day after. The nuclear future will turn on how well we defend this norm in future crises involving nuclear-armed rivals.

The norm of nonuse is typically tested most severely during the first fifteen years of a nuclear rivalry when arsenals rise precipitously, when technological advances are embraced, and when there are few, if any, guardrails to the competition. This period is usually marked by harrowing crises and clashes over sensitive locales and contested borders. For the United States and the Soviet Union, the severest tests were over Berlin and Cuba. The flashpoints for the Soviet Union and China, as well as for India and Pakistan, were over contested borders. Deterrence in these cases was not yet fully formed, and reassurance was nonexistent.

It took fifteen years after the Bomb's appearance for the practice of arms control to be conceptualized in the United States. The initial conceptualization focused on behavioral practices and stabilization measures rather than numbers. The key concern back then, as explained in a primer written by Thomas Schelling and Morton Halperin, was to ease reciprocal fears of a surprise attack.[3] Schelling and Halperin proposed a broader conception of national security in which deterrence and arms control could be synthesized, but opposing camps formed quickly. Staunch believers in deterrence instinctively opposed steps for reassurance because they weakened credible threats, while arms controllers took strong exception to proposals for more credible threats. This endless tug-of-war in the United States remains hard-wired between arms controllers who believe that deterrence strengtheners go too far, and deterrence strengtheners who believe that arms controllers go too far.

The first, most obvious and essential arms control step—the cessation of atmospheric testing because of its clear public health hazards—was opposed by deterrence strengtheners like Edward Teller on the grounds that health hazards were overblown or were justified in moral terms to check Soviet Communism. Every subsequent step that arms controllers sought was subject to criticism on the grounds of weakening credible threats. No arms control measure struck at the very essence of deterrence strategy more than the 1996 Comprehensive Test Ban Treaty, the culmination of four decades of effort since Eisenhower was first lobbied by his scientific advisers to entertain this radical notion. President Clinton characterized this treaty as the longest-sought, hardest-fought accomplishment in the canon of arms control. It was a bitter pill to swallow for deterrence strengtheners, since limits on nuclear testing constituted surrogate constraints on the credible threat of battlefield use.

The norm of not testing nuclear weapons has great symbolic and political value because it buttresses the norm against mushroom clouds on battlefields. The absence of testing for over two decades by the United States, Russia, China, Great Britain, France, India, Pakistan, and Israel did not constrain replacement programs for missiles, submarines, and bombers, as well as other means to deliver reliable warhead designs. The norm of not testing did, however, reinforce the essential distinction that nuclear weapons were a breed apart. When the Bomb first appeared, Bernard Brodie edited a book that introduced the term "the absolute weapon."[4] Abolition wasn't possible, but by categorizing the Bomb in this way, Brodie began to build the scaffolding to set it apart from other instruments of warfare.

In truth, the absolute weapon wasn't really absolute, since it lent itself to the quest for relative advantage, or at least the avoidance of relative disadvantage. Arms control initially became a public imperative because of atmospheric testing and then because there seemed no end to the number of warheads both superpowers were building. Nuclear "overkill" became a household word. Then came greater accuracies for warheads launched half a world away, enabling "counterforce" strikes against missiles in their silos and other hardened targets. The nuclear arms race wasn't self-regulating, as some early critics of negotiating with the Kremlin like Robert Strausz-Hupé projected it would become.[5] Instead, it was growing more dangerous. Arms control was needed to stabilize the nuclear competition. The absolute weapon absolutely required forms of reassurance to accompany deterrence in order to create conditions for the nuclear peace.

Arms control didn't explicitly prevent the first use of nuclear weapons in warfare by treaty. This norm relied mostly on moral and prudential restraints. Some nuclear doctrines expressly allowed first use, while others were suspect for promising no first use. These nuclear use doctrines didn't take sufficient account of the human factor. The seventy-five-year-long record of nonbattlefield use can only be partially explained by deterrence theory, threats of mutual retaliation, diplomacy, reassurance, and arms control. Missing in this standard list, besides luck, is the factor of human connectedness. Some close calls have been averted by human beings far down as well as at the top of the chain of command who chose not to open the Gates of Hell.

These individuals appear fleetingly in this and other texts. They are not household names, but we owe much to their allegiance to our common humanity. Vasili Alexandrovich Arkhipov was the captain aboard a Soviet Foxtrot diesel submarine during the Cuban missile crisis that was being depth-charged to the surface to enforce President Kennedy's quarantine of Cuba. No U.S. official suspected at that time that Foxtrot submarines carried nuclear-armed torpedoes. No one knew at that time that the captain, second captain, and deputy political officer on board this particular submarine had made a private compact that if they were unable to reach authorized channels, they would make their own decision about firing a nuclear weapon. If all three voted in favor, they would do so. If the vote was not unanimous, they would hold their fire. On October 27, 1962, two of the three officers voted to fire their torpedo. Arkhipov voted nyet.

Stanislav Petrov was the commanding officer of a post dedicated to providing early warning of missile attacks. During the night shift on September 26, 1983, he saw indications of what looked like the opening salvo of a U.S. surprise attack on his screen. It was a year of great nuclear danger, when new counterforce NATO missiles were being deployed in Europe and nuclear negotiations had broken down. Petrov was faced with the choice of notifying superiors during a period of heightened alert, superiors who would then notify key members of the Politburo, including a general secretary with paranoid tendencies, Yuri Andropov. Andropov, like his minister of defense and another Politburo member, the head of Soviet intelligence, was convinced that the Reagan administration intended to fight and sought to win a nuclear war. Petrov chose not to send his warning up the chain of command, assuming a technical malfunction. He did not follow regular procedures, thereby helping to extend the post-Nagasaki record of nonbattlefield use.

The norm of nonbattlefield use—the norm upon which every other element of keeping the nuclear peace rests—has been sustained because during periods of great crisis, individuals under intense pressure held due regard for the survival of their fellow human beings. So far, national leaders in sufficient and sometimes barely sufficient control of events, regardless of nationality, religion, authoritarian tendencies, and grotesque treatment of their fellow citizens, have not wished to be the person responsible for opening the Gates of Hell by authorizing the first use of nuclear weapons. The individual who crosses the nuclear threshold for the first time since Nagasaki will live in infamy thereafter—if there is recorded history after the use of nuclear weapons. This pillar of the nuclear peace remains in place in the absence of treaties. It is in perpetual need of strengthening.

National leaders who have resolved in the privacy of their own consciousness to do their utmost not to use nuclear weapons have nonetheless been entirely willing to preside over plans for battlefield use. Some may even have taken comfort in these plans. For most leaders, nuclear doctrines for use are tolerable as long as they remain in locked safes.[6] The appearance of a single mushroom cloud, for whatever reason, makes escalation control deeply problematic in a crisis. How does a national leader who authorizes the use of a mushroom cloud in warfare signal stoppage? How does an opponent armed with nuclear weapons not react in kind, or up the ante? The possibility of uncommon restraint exists, particularly for a stronger adversary, but so, too, does the possibility of retaliating in greater strength.

The precepts of nuclear escalation control, like the precepts of arms control, are the provenance of gifted analytical minds—in this case, Herman Kahn, Henry Kissinger, Paul Nitze, and James Schlesinger, among others. Nuclear escalation control, unlike arms control, has never been tested in the real world. After first use, the theorems of escalation control would be tested by human beings under unimaginable strain. Computer and human simulations suggest abject failure. Individuals with a profound sense of consequence might produce better results; the future of human, animal, and plant life depends on it if the nuclear threshold is crossed.

The superstructure of deterrence theory fails with first use and collapses without escalation control. This edifice has a weak point at its core, like the death star in *Star Wars*. The weak point is humanitarian laws of warfare, to which advocates of nuclear deterrence must and nominally do accept fealty. Without escalation control, there is no way to square the first use of nuclear weapons with the precepts of international humanitarian law. The strongest safeguard against disproportionate and possibly incalculable damage is to not cross the nuclear threshold first. The value of first use is unalterably diminished by the prospect of subsequent use. The norm of nonbattlefield use has been extended as a result of these calculations, which remain in place even as treaties have been discarded.

The U.S. first-use policy was firmly rooted in the context of the Cold War when NATO's conventional forces in Europe were weaker than those of the Warsaw Pact. The military context is starkly different today. Now, first-use contingencies are postulated for a NATO alliance that has expanded to outposts such as the Baltic states that are hard to defend by conventional means, as well as for allies in Asia facing North Korea and China. Deterrence strengtheners have sought new ways to be able to employ low-yield warheads to control escalation in such contingencies, mirroring what they view as Russian nuclear-use doctrine. Why Vladimir Putin would see value in crossing the nuclear threshold first remains puzzling, when he has demonstrated success in hybrid, information, and cyber warfare without having to come anywhere near to it. Nonetheless, mirror imaging—emulating what you presume your adversary is able to do—remains an enduring and troubling aspect of the nuclear competition, with or without treaties.

The weakest link of extended deterrence has never been the absence of nuclear weapons with low yields available for use. Instead, the weakest link of extended deterrence is the very notion of first use. First use prompts retaliatory use because that is the very essence of deterrence. When deterrence fails, the use of nuclear weapons in warfare compounds failure. Prospects for escalation control are never better than before the nuclear threshold is crossed, and never worse than after its crossing. Actual, as opposed to hypothetical, first use kills nuclear deterrence. It is likely to kill what remains of arms control, as well.

Nuclear first use by the United States is not the answer to localized military contingencies in the Baltics, against China, or on the Korean Peninsula, where U.S. conventional military advantages cannot quickly be brought to bear. Far better answers lie in acquiring conventional capabilities, as usable military instruments matter far more than weapons a president will do his or her utmost to avoid using. Thinking about deterrence and war-fighting as combining nuclear and conventional arms is fundamentally unsound. The nuclear peace rests on setting nuclear weapons apart.

After decades of nonuse, first-use doctrines have credibility problems. There is no compelling evidence that the threat of first use—as opposed to the possession of nuclear weapons—has helped to deter war or lesser forms of aggression. First-use postures have not prevented limited wars between nuclear-armed rivals. Two have already occurred—the Soviet Union against China in 1969 and Pakistan against India in 1999. First-use postures have not changed the outcome of these wars; nor have they prevented dangerous crises. "No First Use" doctrines also have credibility problems. China and India have both adopted No First Use postures, but deterrence strengtheners do not place great credence in China's doctrine, just as Pakistan's strategic enclave does not believe India's declarations. Crises will occur whether nuclear-armed states adopt first use or No First Use postures. The outcome of future crises will not depend on nuclear doctrine; they will depend on the disposition of usable weapons and forces near the crisis, the stakes in dispute, and the risk-taking disposition of national leaders.

Why, then, not drop the pretense and fully embrace No First Use? Because Donald Trump has made a hash of alliance relationships in an era of major power competition and because adopting a No First Use posture would unsettle allies even more. So far, there are no instances of a state that has relied upon the threat of first use that has subsequently thought better of it and embraced No First Use. (For a time, the Kremlin advertised this change, but subsequent revelations after the Cold War ended proved these declarations to be false.) An additional reason is that seeking to change U.S. first-use doctrine is a battle whose effort is greater than the reward. Rebuttals are easy, beginning with the obvious one that Russia doesn't accept No First Use. Pakistan won't accept No First Use either and India is hedging its bets. Embracing No First Use would not make the United States demonstrably safer, nor is it likely to change the calculations of other states possessing nuclear weapons. Doctrinal debates don't expand public support, and besides, nuclear orthodoxy usually wins doctrinal debates, as Obama administration officials can attest.

The George H.W. Bush administration temporarily succeeded where the Obama administration later came up short. Bush, Scowcroft, and Baker attached great importance to signaling Gorbachev that the Soviet retreat from East Germany would not be met with a reaffirmation of U.S. nuclear orthodoxy. During the apogee of arms control, Bush and Baker convinced Margaret Thatcher, a deeply skeptical British prime minister, and more willing NATO allies to drop the formulation of first use. Baker skillfully maneuvered consensus support for the alternative formulation of "weapons of last resort," as Thatcher was not willing to risk an Anglo-American clash on this issue. The resulting NATO communique also dropped the terminology of "flexible response" and "forward defense."[7]

Despite massive reductions in Cold War-sized arsenals, we still live in a world of over 13,000 nuclear weapons. The use of one of these weapons in warfare can result in a slow motion or speedy chain reaction of detonations. The United States is highly unlikely to be the first user of nuclear weapons, despite the Pentagon's nuclear doctrine. Since nothing is ever assured when it comes to nuclear weapons except the dangers inherent in first use, public opposition to first use in democratic societies remains essential. Official doctrine speaks to the calculations of deterrence strategists; popular campaigns under the banner of No First Use speak to our common humanity. Extending the record of nonbattlefield use requires assuring allies as well as respecting public opinion. Nuclear doctrine is too important to remain solely in the hands of deterrence strategists. It is conceived behind closed doors; when unleavened by public consent, it becomes otherworldly, lending itself to excess. By speaking to different audiences, the defenders and opponents of nuclear orthodoxy can in this instance serve a complementary purpose in extending the norm of not using nuclear weapons in warfare.

If the doctrinal adoption of No First Use remains out of reach and ill-timed, what phraseology best supports the most important norm backstopping the nuclear peace? Public defenders will continue to champion No First Use. I prefer a variation on this theme that lends itself to broader public support and that makes rebuttals harder. I suggest the phrase "No Use" because these words resonate and move beyond doctrinal debate into the domains of common sense and public safety. The phraseology of No Use is readily understandable and simple. Deterrence strengtheners have occasionally used simple, reasonably sounding formulations to their advantage because they require multiple paragraphs of rebuttal. The phraseology of No Use reverses this dynamic. The formulation that the George H.W. Bush administration endorsed—"weapons of last resort"—is pointed but less succinct. An alternate approach is to declare that the "sole purpose" of nuclear weapons is deterrence. Both constructions are better than reaffirming first use and both would prompt fewer perturbations for extended deterrence than No First Use.

There are no shortcuts to extending the historical record of nonbattlefield use when the global nuclear order—which encompasses two triangular competitions and four pairings of nuclear-armed rivals—raises many possibilities of use. Whatever the formulation one prefers—No Use, sole purpose, weapons of last resort, or No First Use—success is achieved one day at a time and one crisis at a time, despite nuclear doctrines poised toward use. Political campaigns supportive of arms control have helped to stigmatize the use of nuclear weapons in the past; they remain essential in the future. American presidents have been well served by public opposition to doctrinal orthodoxy, even when they have found it particularly unwelcome.

One of the great early struggles in arms control was countering the expectation that the use of nuclear weapons would be inevitable. The inevitable hasn't happened in the past three-quarters of a century and need not happen in the future. Setting the goal of a century without the battlefield use of nuclear weapons seems daunting. Political campaigns for noble end-states typically peter out. Campaigns to abolish nuclear weapons, for example, lose steam because domestic and geopolitical conditions become roadblocks. The sooner the proposed end state for abolition, the more politically unrealistic it seems; the more distant the end state, the easier it becomes to discount its probability and to lose focus. Success in a norm-building approach is far easier, as the seventy-five-year record of nonbattlefield use attests. Success happens every day, every month, and every year without battlefield use. We succeeded yesterday, we can succeed today, and the day after that by rising to the defense of No Use during the next crisis. My proposal of setting the goal of nonbattlefield use to the 100th anniversary of the detonations over Hiroshima and Nagasaki isn't original; it has been passed on to me from Lewis Dunn.[8] If enough of us focus on this goal, the likelihood of success will increase.

We can achieve this goal even when domestic U.S. politics are riddled with partisanship, when the Republican Party has lost its moorings, and when competition between major powers and nuclear-armed rivals is sharpening. No treaty ratification is needed to extend the norm of No Use, which can continue on the same moral and prudential grounds that have produced success for seventy-five years. Heightened competition between the United States and China does not make crossing the nuclear threshold any more likely; it makes extending the norm of nonbattlefield use and the revival of public activism in support of arms control more imperative. The norm of No Use was fragile during Cold War crises in the 1940s, 1950s, and 1960s. It is much stronger now but is in serious need of reinforcement.

The challenges posed by Moscow do not require nuclear use. Putin's irredentism pales by comparison to the extent of NATO expansion after the Cold War ended. The loss of Soviet dominion cannot be reversed. Moscow does not have the resources, the lure, or the military muscle to regain its former holdings. Putin's pushback was directed at the farthest reaches of the George W. Bush administration's hubris in seeking to extend NATO to include Georgia and Ukraine. Putin's annexation of Crimea, as with the Soviet annexation of the Baltic states, will go unrecognized, and the occupation of eastern Ukraine by his proxies can be made more costly, as have prior instances of Moscow's overreaching.

Nuclear weapons remain Moscow's strong suit, but the use of these weapons risks all, and Putin is not a great risk taker. He has found other means to seek to undermine democracies, such as the use of hybrid, information, and cyber warfare. The use of nuclear weapons is a self-defeating substitute for them. Putin's gains have been abetted by Washington's mistakes. They can be nullified by better U.S. decisions, not by the battlefield use of nuclear weapons. A strategy that extends the norm of nonbattlefield use has no downsides because first use risks far more than whatever might be gained.

NO TESTING

Conventional weapons and missiles are regularly tested. Nuclear weapons have been stigmatized to the extent that they are not. National leaders acknowledge that nuclear weapons are a breed apart by not breaking moratoria to resume testing. These constraints were partial at first, allowing underground tests, followed by limitations on their yield. After four decades of episodic diplomatic ambition, test constraints became comprehensive—or nearly so—in 1996. That was when, at Clinton's urging, negotiations on a Comprehensive Test Ban Treaty were completed, as promised, one year after the Nonproliferation Treaty was indefinitely extended.

Clinton tried and failed to secure the Senate's consent to ratification in 1999. Senate Republicans found the risks of permanently ending testing and their antipathy toward Clinton stronger than the arguments in favor of ratification. Clinton authorized an expensive and open-ended "stockpile stewardship" program so that U.S. nuclear laboratories could provide assurance of the efficacy of existing warhead designs without further testing, but this initiative was unproven in 1999. Internationally minded Republican stalwarts in the Senate, including John Warner and Richard Lugar, believed ratification to be premature until the stockpile stewardship program had demonstrated its efficacy.

Even when the Senate consents to ratify the CTBT, other hurdles to the treaty's entry into force will remain. No less than forty-four states possessing the Bomb or the infrastructure to produce one need to consent to ratification. This was the price that reluctant leaders in Great Britain, France, Russia, and

China extracted before agreeing to terms. Eight holdouts remain—the United States, China, India, Pakistan, Israel, Egypt, Iran and North Korea. And yet the treaty has still performed its declared function, fostering moratoria that are now over two decades old. The Soviet Union stopped testing in 1990, the United States in 1992, and China in 1996. India and Pakistan started and stopped in 1998. Testing moratoria have served as a surrogate for entry into force.

The norm of not demonstrating prowess through nuclear testing, like the norm of no battlefield use, has taken hold in the absence of a treaty in force codifying its terms. Both norms require and have received daily affirmation. Every day without a nuclear test is a success story, and every subsequent day increases the degree of political difficulty associated with being the first national leader that resumes testing. The only state that has tested since 1998 has been North Korea. No other nuclear-armed state has wished to follow its example. If, however, the United States, Russia, or China were to decide to resume testing, a cascade of tests is likely to follow. Continued moratoria reflect these calculations. The passage of time without testing doesn't foreclose a future cascade, but the longer moratoria continue, the harder it will be for a national leader to become the norm breaker.

The central object and purpose of the Comprehensive Test Ban Treaty is that signatories pledge "not to carry out any nuclear weapon test explosion or any other nuclear explosion." The Clinton administration deemed further precision regarding this definition both as unwarranted and as an invitation to workarounds. The CTBT does not prohibit nuclear experiments. Every state that possesses nuclear weapons conducts them. The Clinton administration advocated a "zero yield" standard for the treaty, meaning that experiments involving nuclear material not produce "a self-sustaining, supercritical chain reaction." The Clinton administration stated its understanding that Russia and China understood and accepted this standard.[9]

In 2020, the Trump administration publicly questioned whether Russia and China are adhering to the Clinton administration's standard. The State Department's 2020 report on this matter does not charge Moscow and Beijing with a material breach because the Comprehensive Test Ban Treaty has not entered into force. Nor does it assert that nuclear experiments like those described have military utility. Rather, the Trump administration asserted that Russia has not adhered to the zero-yield standard and that China's actions "raise concerns," suggesting a weaker evidentiary base for China's citation.[10]

Treaty opponents will argue that any experiment above zero yield defeats the object and purpose of the CTBT. Supporters will argue otherwise, as miniscule yields do not facilitate the advanced development and certification of new warhead designs. Before a serious effort is made to again seek the Senate's consent to ratification, a formal, common understanding among the United States, Russia, and China of the zero-yield standard will likely be needed, along with new monitoring devices at the locations where experiments are conducted.

These whispers are all that remain from a legacy of almost 2,000 nuclear tests. Existing warhead designs and variations do not require new testing. The certification of entirely new warhead designs would. Extending the two-decade-long norm against testing depends primarily on decisions made in Washington, Moscow, and Beijing. An important constraint against the resumption of testing is a common understanding that whatever gains might be pocketed in pursuing an exacting new warhead design would be outweighed by the collective advances of others that resume testing. Old technologies and designs suffice to underscore deterrence. As long as existing designs remain durable and duplicable—and their plutonium cores might well last a century or more—there is no need to resume underground tests.[11]

Moratoria on testing are an important stabilization measure for the complex geometry of global nuclear competition. Any doubts on this score can be dispelled by imagining the impact of a cascade of testing by the United States, Russia, and China in one triangle, and by China, India, and Pakistan in the other. The treaty of greatest help to stabilize both triangles has already been negotiated but has not entered into force. The Senate's consent to ratify the CTBT could set in motion positive cascade effects, as China has repeatedly declared a readiness to ratify, but only after the U.S. Senate provides its consent. To affirm this sequencing, the Senate could insist that the United States not deposit its instrument of ratification until China, India, and Pakistan ratify. India will not sign and ratify until China ratifies, and Pakistan will not sign and ratify until India does. Both competitive triangles could benefit from this cascade of ratifications. And yet those who argue that it is necessary to engage Beijing and to change China's status from a free rider to an active participant in strategic arms control oppose the Senate's consent to ratify the CTBT. No single step by Washington would provide greater reinforcement in extending the twin norms against nonbattlefield use and nuclear testing.

Ratification seems a distant prospect during a time of rampant partisanship on Capitol Hill. It will happen eventually, either because of losses in the ranks of America First Republican senators or a Republican president who is ready to take this step. This possibility is not completely far-fetched, given the variation of post–Cold War Republican presidents. In the meantime, the extension of the nuclear peace and the revival of prospects for nuclear arms control depend on extending testing moratoria.

Patience as well as insistence can be a virtue. In the case of the CTBT, patience is a necessity. It took fifty years for two-thirds of the Senate to support ratification of the 1925 Geneva Protocol that banned the use of poisonous and asphyxiating gases, like those used indiscriminately during World War I. The Senate is now halfway toward this lamentable historical marker, as the CTBT was negotiated a quarter-century ago. As long as moratoria on testing are extended, we can continue to wait. It should not take fifty years for enough Republican senators to regain their international moorings and to recognize the immense obstacles that must be overcome before resuming tests. The Nevada Test Site will remain open for nuclear experiments but not for tests that shake the casinos in Las Vegas. The Stockpile Stewardship program is a major success story. The U.S. nuclear laboratories have done their part and continued bipartisan support for stockpile stewardship is assured.

The passage of time without nuclear testing makes ratifications more likely. No state possessing nuclear weapons wants to use them on battlefields. Every state's nuclear enclave would welcome resumed testing, but with every passing day, it becomes harder to do so. Thanks to the work of previous generations, it is harder to cross the nuclear use and testing thresholds than to maintain them. Continued success in protecting these two essential norms can compensate for shortcomings on other fronts, such as the absence of ambitious treaty making. The longer these norms are honored, the more nuclear weapon stockpiles will be reduced, with or without treaties.

NONPROLIFERATION

The third crucial norm undergirding the nuclear peace is nonproliferation. Given the attention paid to North Korea and Iran—the two hardest proliferation cases—it is easy to overlook how deeply rooted the norm of nonproliferation has become and the degree to which the pace of proliferation has been slowed. This is a remarkable success story that began when the Arms Control and Disarmament Agency overcame the State Department's reservations to negotiate the Nonproliferation Treaty. This treaty was ACDA's greatest legacy, a reminder of why having a dedicated cadre of leaders and experts within the executive branch focused on arms control matters. Since ACDA's demise, the State Department's expertise on arms control and the priority accorded to this pursuit have not fared well.

The North Korean proliferation problem lends itself to diplomatic management but not solutions. Kim Jong Un has succeeded in producing nuclear weapons and the means to deliver them against U.S. allies and against the U.S. homeland. In doing so, he has gained some measure of protection against suffering the fate of Saddam Hussein and Muammar Qaddafi. Air strikes, like those Israel carried out against nuclear facilities in Iraq and Syria, seem unlikely against North Korea, as no presidential adviser or occupant of the Oval Office could be confident of their complete success to enforce denuclearization, let alone neutralize North Korea's other capabilities to punish Seoul and other cities. Under these circumstances, U.S. and allied security, as well as the avoidance of war on the Korean Peninsula, rests on the twin pillars of containment and deterrence.

North Korea is producing more, and more powerful, nuclear weapons. Diplomacy could yet succeed in limiting North Korean nuclear capabilities, while abolition seems unrealizable. Whether Pyongyang's stockpile growth prompts further proliferation depends on its behavior and on the strength of U.S. alliance ties to South Korea and Japan. While these relationships have corroded during the Trump administration, they remain capable of repair. The elements of containment and deterrence that matter most in both cases are mending diplomatic ties, maintaining forward-deployed forces and missile defense capabilities, and enhancing conventional military capabilities in the region.

Kim Jong Un will continue to act out in search of leverage and rewards. Sanctions will remain in place until this pattern of behavior changes. There is no evidence that he wishes to place at risk that which he holds dear. Consequently, there is no need to overreact to provocations that leave his regime more isolated. There will be a need, however, to react to provocations that harm U.S. allies. Diplomacy with Kim Jong Un can be resumed without Donald Trump's bluster, erratic behavior, and delusions. Partial diplomatic gains may once again be achievable, but only after Kim Jong Un realizes that better offers are illusionary. Nuclear threats do not help in this regard. A long game is called for—as long as it takes for North Korea's leader to change course to help his economy grow.

Iran, unlike North Korea, has yet to cross the nuclear threshold, but the timeline for doing so has shortened considerably since Trump walked away from the agreement struck by Obama and by other leaders in Europe, China, and Russia. In the case of Iran, as with North Korea, the most likely candidates to seek the Bomb if Washington's diplomatic exertions fail are states that have historically depended on the United States for their sense of security. Washington's standing and influence to prevent these states—principally Saudi Arabia, Egypt, and Turkey—from acquiring nuclear weapons has been greatly diminished and is only partially recoverable.

If Iran's leaders move resolutely toward possession of nuclear weapons, they invite U.S., if not Israeli, air strikes that will set back Tehran's nuclear ambitions, further impair Iran's ability to sell oil, and wreak even more damage to the Iranian economy. Consequently, while a concerted Iranian push for nuclear weapons remains a possibility, further incremental steps appear more likely, as Tehran seeks leverage in return for sanctions relief. Distinguishing between leverage in the form of reversible actions and the pursuit of bomb making will lie in the eyes of the beholder. Renewed diplomatic efforts to curtail Tehran's nuclear capabilities face formidable challenges, not the least of which is hardened opposition among congressional majorities, as was the case during the Obama administration.

It is a testament to those who have been dedicated to nonproliferation norm-building and to the centrality of the NPT that both remain in decent shape despite North Korea's nuclear stockpile and Iran's posturing near to, but below, possession. Decades of purposeful diplomatic effort have paid off. Sanctions have become far more effective tools to deal with outliers, cyber warfare, and other forms of sabotage have been added to the nonproliferation toolkit, and military options remain available in rare cases. Even so, new proliferation challenges lie ahead, depending on how the North Korean and Iranian cases play out. What makes new challenges different is that the most likely aspirants to acquire the Bomb in the future have all been friends of the United States in the past.

Since the Cold War ended, Democratic presidents have attempted to revive nonproliferation diplomacy and Republican presidents have viewed these efforts with skepticism. Despite cyclical diplomatic successes and setbacks, the third key norm of nonproliferation abides. With more appreciation for its consensual foundations, the norm of nonproliferation can become stronger still. If this sounds Pollyannaish, consider the surprisingly slow track record of nonproliferation, and how many times predictions of cascading proliferation danger have proven to be false.

NO THREATS TO USE NUCLEAR WEAPONS

The three central norms of no battlefield use, no testing, and nonproliferation remain in place despite the demise of arms control treaties and increased friction between the Bomb's possessors and abstainers. Related norms are in need of reinforcement, including the norm to improve safety and security for fissile material. Another important norm is in need of affirmation—the norm of not threatening to use nuclear weapons. Like the norm of no testing, a norm of not threatening to use nuclear weapons impinges on the prerogatives of possessors. I propose that we seek to stigmatize brandishing and threatening to use nuclear weapons, just as we have stigmatized the testing of nuclear weapons.

Nuclear threats can be explicit or thinly veiled. They can be rhetorical or inferential, such as when forces that are integral to planning for nuclear weapons' use are deployed to forward areas or their alert rates are increased to place an adversary on notice. Those who have studied nuclear threat making have found no shortage of examples, with Washington leading all other states by a considerable margin, and with Moscow coming in second.[12]

Nuclear threat making dropped precipitously after the Cold War ended. Moscow was in no position to make them, and Washington relied instead on conventional military instruments of suasion along with diplomatic and economic levers.[13] The United States did not threaten the use of nuclear weapons when Russian troops threatened the Georgian capital of Tbilisi in 2008, when Putin carried out hybrid warfare in eastern Ukraine and annexed Crimea in 2014, and when he authorized wholesale cyber intrusions in 2020.

When the Cold War ended, the greatest incidence of nuclear threat making shifted to the subcontinent, as India and Pakistan experienced a series of harrowing crises before and after they tested nuclear devices in 1998. The first fifteen years of the U.S.-Soviet rivalry were the most nuclear threat-laden. The peak period of threat making between India and Pakistan has lasted longer.[14] Measures of reassurance haven't begun to catch up to increases in nuclear capabilities on the subcontinent. Pakistan's conventional capabilities lag behind India, so Pakistan has resorted to threat making in crises, believing that they would prompt both caution by New Delhi and U.S. crisis management. Pakistani threats typically prompt Indian rejoinders.

Threats and counterthreats have so far reinforced rather than altered the territorial status quo in the disputed region of Kashmir.

Beijing has issued far fewer threats with nuclear overtones than Washington and Moscow, as is consistent with China's declared No First Use posture. Beijing has, however, occasionally threatened nuclear use, beginning with its 1969 border clash with the Soviet Union. The most instances of Chinese threat making with nuclear overtones have occurred over the status of Taiwan.[15] As tensions with the United States over Taiwan's status increase, veiled or explicit nuclear threat making might, as well.

Threats during crises between nuclear-armed rivals has not changed outcomes since they could be countered in kind. The possession of nuclear weapons has so far deterred worst cases—nuclear exchanges and full-scale conventional wars—but they haven't compelled wanted behavior, even when a nuclear-armed adversary clearly lags behind in the competition. Nor do nuclear weapons help in warfare against abstainers. The outcomes in these wars have favored the abstainers, as has been evident in the military misadventures of the United States and the Soviet Union in Afghanistan. The determining factors in the outcome of crises and wars are usually the coercer's ability to impose its will by conventional military means, the competing stakes in dispute, and the presumed costs of military conflict.[16]

The presumption that more nuclear firepower equals greater coercive power is more intuitive than real. This presumption helped fuel the superpower nuclear competition during the Cold War, just as it fuels the two interlocking triangular nuclear competitions and the four bilateral rivalries at present. Nuclear weapons have instilled caution in crises and border clashes, thereby helping the weaker state to defend, without helping the stronger state to impose its will. The most credible threats of nuclear use occur when a state lacks conventional military capabilities or finds itself in a desperate situation with its back to the wall.

These arguments and the case studies to back them up fall on deaf ears to those who find safety in nuclear advantage in crises and in the event the nuclear threshold is crossed. Taking this view to its logical conclusion, the greatest advantages in crises and limited warfare derive from enjoying nuclear superiority. The purpose of nuclear superiority, in this view, is not to fight and win, but to avoid having to fight. It follows that, if outright superiority cannot be achieved, nuclear advantage is still worth gaining because it provides coercive bargaining leverage.[17]

Real crises and real warfare have defeated these arguments, and with it, the utility of nuclear threat making. Just as absolute nuclear advantage has not prevented defeat in wars against highly motivated abstainers, an advantageous nuclear order of battle has not provided leverage against a state able to retaliate in kind. Nuclear threat making, whether against an unarmed or similarly armed opponent, lacks credibility after a seventy-five-year-long record of nonbattlefield use. These threats reflect poorly on the threat maker, who broadcasts being unsettled at least as much as being resolved. Even so, trend lines of nuclear threat making could well increase, as dangerous military practices are on the upswing in all four pairings of nuclear-armed rivals.

The stigmatization of nuclear threat making is gaining ground among abstainers, as reflected in the Treaty on the Prohibition of Nuclear Weapons that includes a provision banning this practice. Nuclear-armed states will steer clear of the Prohibition Treaty, but leaders care about their public image and the practice of arms control has helped to constrain behavior. Possessors do not use nuclear weapons in war, and they do not test them. Just as the practice of arms control can affect what leaders do, it can affect what they say. I propose that we try to relegate nuclear threat making to outliers; when they threaten use, they reinforce their outlier status. Leaders of states that wish to be regarded as responsible stewards of nuclear weapons do not threaten mushroom clouds. The incidence of nuclear threats can be reduced by stigmatizing the threat maker.

THE CANONICAL PLEDGE

Late in 1983, Ronald Reagan began to appreciate how disturbed key Politburo members were by his rhetoric, his policies, and his administration's actions. His first corrective step was to announce before the Japanese Diet that "a nuclear war can never be won and must never be fought" on November 11, 1983. Even as he was speaking in Tokyo, U.S. and NATO authorities were engaged in an exercise, Able Archer 83, that greatly worried key members of the Politburo. Reagan's formulation before the Diet didn't change any material aspect of the strategic competition, but it was a start. All good affirmations require repetition. Reagan repeated his during his 1984 State of the Union address. Speaking at one and the same time to the U.S. Congress and the Kremlin, he said, "There is only one sane policy, for your country and mine, to preserve our civilization in this modern age: A nuclear war cannot be won and must never be fought. The only value in our two nations possessing nuclear weapons is to make sure they will never be used."[18] Reagan's canonical statement was, in effect, an approximate declaration of No Use. Repeating it a second time still wasn't convincing because very few people were then aware that Reagan was dead set against Armageddon happening on his watch and that he harbored abolitionist views. When Reagan and Gorbachev jointly repeated this formulation at their Geneva summit in 1985, skeptics began to take notice.

The hard edges of nuclear doctrines can be softened by leadership declarations of responsible nuclear stewardship. Reagan's formulation was a sharp and necessary contrast to the Pentagon's nuclear posture and his secretary of defense's public commitment to prevail in the event of a nuclear war of extended duration. Straightforward declarations of No Use raise questions about extended deterrence; Reagan's unerring talent for strategic communication found the right public approximation. Temperatures during a period of heightened competition between nuclear-armed states could be lowered if leaders include the canonical affirmation that a nuclear war cannot be won and must never be fought in the summit communiques after every bilateral or larger group meeting. The canonical pledge might then serve as the basis for action plans to affirm public declarations.

RESPECTING NATIONAL SOVEREIGNTY

If the norms of responsible behavior among major powers and nuclear-armed rivals are weak, prospects for arms control cannot be strong. Strategic arms control has always been predicated on the principles of respecting the territorial integrity and national sovereignty of states and of the peaceful settlement of disputes. Arms control comes to a temporary halt when nuclear-armed states disregard these norms. Prospects for the Senate's consent to ratify SALT II were troubled before the Soviet invasion of Afghanistan and ended after it. Similarly, prospects for arms control ground to a temporary halt in 2014 when Putin annexed Crimea and conducted hybrid warfare in eastern Ukraine. When these norms are trashed, arms control efforts go into cold storage as the reflexive response of leaders is to spend more for national defense. When circumstances dictate, arms control is taken out of cold storage. Reagan initiated negotiations on intermediate-range nuclear forces within two years of the Soviet invasion of Afghanistan while making the Kremlin pay dearly for its decision.

Norms that are broken are in need of repair. While refusing to recognize the violation of the territorial integrity and national sovereignty of states by a nuclear-armed rival, American presidents have pursued the imperatives of stabilizing nuclear competitions and reducing nuclear danger. At the same time, they have increased costs to the norm breaker through varied means. The United States negotiated with the Soviet Union over the limitation and reduction of nuclear arsenals while refusing to recognize the Kremlin's engorgement of the Baltic states and its control over unwilling Eastern European populations. Likewise, the United States can negotiate with Moscow to reduce nuclear danger while refusing to recognize Russia's annexation of Crimea and while making the Russian presence in eastern Ukraine more painful and costly. This template has succeeded in the past, and it can succeed again.

CHALLENGES FROM RUSSIA AND CHINA

Russia and China are serious competitors, but they are not pre–World War II Germany and Japan. They want to increase their spheres of influence at the expense of the United States, not engage in aggressive wars to occupy their neighbors. The Russian annexation of Crimea is not the functional equivalent of the German occupation of the Sudetenland in 1938. Russia is not on the march; it spends heavily on nuclear weapons to cover manifold weaknesses. It seeks toeholds abroad in failed states like Syria, Venezuela, and Libya. It has carved out autonomous zones in Georgia that only Nauru, Nicaragua, Syria, and Venezuela recognize. Moscow's sole natural ally, Belarus, is restive. Putin's Russia has managed to contain itself by poor governance, economic malpractice, and systemic corruption. As a consequence, a strategy of containment by the United States is not a heavy lift. It requires less sums that are now devoted to nuclear weapon programs and more attention to what William J. Burns calls "America's tool of first resort"—diplomacy. Russia's weaknesses will remain exploitable, while U.S. weaknesses can be mended.[19]

Threats posed by China are more challenging than those posed by Russia because China's capacity for growth is greater despite its demographic challenges, because Beijing has invested strategically in usable military and economic instruments of power, and because Beijing seeks to achieve around its periphery what the United States has enjoyed close to home—a security environment conducive to its interests, unencumbered by external challenges. Xi Jinping engages in muscle flexing toward China's neighbors while effectively challenging the U.S. Navy's freedom of action in the South and East China Seas. Beijing's pattern of behavior there, along the contested border with India, and in its dealings with Hong Kong, makes all its neighbors uncomfortable, including friends and allies of the United States. China has invested smartly in technologies that exploit the Pentagon's reliance on too few and too vulnerable high-end naval combatants. Beijing, like Moscow, has practiced its belief that silicon can wreak havoc over steel through cyber warfare. Some are alarmed by China's strategic modernization programs, as well. The number of Chinese nuclear warheads could double in size over the next decade, although it will continue to lag far behind U.S. and Russian totals. Its force levels will grow as the number of U.S. missile defense interceptors and Indian missiles grow. Like the United States, Russia, and India, China will replace old means to deliver nuclear weapons with better ones.

The status of Taiwan is an obvious flashpoint between Washington and Beijing. China does not accept that a national border exists across the Taiwan Strait and Washington has conceded this point since the Carter administration declared a "one China" policy in 1979. A military move by Beijing against Taiwan would nonetheless be momentous in many ways, one of which would be its dramatic impact on prospects for including China in a multilateral process of arms control. Future crises over Taiwan's status will be marked by asymmetrical conventional power equations favoring the mainland. Coercive maneuvering is likely to grow, just as coercive maneuvering between the United States and Russia is likely to grow after Donald Trump's electoral defeat. Friction is most likely to involve naval capabilities operating in close quarters, while the Bomb remains ever present in the background. The United States has work to do to counter China's military advances and to repair diplomatic and economic instruments of national power. These will be required whatever Beijing's approach to Taiwan might be. The battlefield use of nuclear weapons is not among them.

REASSESSING ARMS CONTROL OBJECTIVES IN NEW CIRCUMSTANCES

As Thomas Schelling and Morton Halperin wrote, arms control was conceptualized to open useful channels of communication. It was pursued "to avoid false alarms and misunderstandings." Channels developed through arms control could provide insight and utility for crisis management. Arms control could help signal reassurance. Strategic competitors needed to know that "restraint on the part of potential enemies will be matched by restraint on our own." They conceived of arms control as pursuing a "mutual interest in the avoidance of a war that neither side wants, in minimizing the costs and risks of the arms competition, and in curtailing the scope and violence of war in the event it occurs."[20]

The original precepts of arms control still apply, as do the difficulties in achieving them. The objective of arms control to lessen risk taking was initially achieved by means of the Anti-Ballistic Missile Treaty that recognized national vulnerability. It then took decades of work to reduce dangers associated with offensive capabilities because diplomacy lagged behind technological advances that neither superpower was willing to forego. As for significantly reducing or at least controlling costs, arms control failed until the demise of the Soviet Union. Before then, cost controls were weak because presidents endorsed strategic modernization programs to accompany agreements reached, the competition was unflagging, and the price extracted for treaty ratification by deterrence strengtheners was high. Later on, when the size of deployed forces was greatly reduced, budgetary outlays remained high because replacement costs were exorbitant.

As for the objective of curtailing the scope and violence of war in the event it occurs, arms control succeeded primarily by setting nuclear weapons apart from other instruments of warfare. Even deep arms reductions could not ensure the curtailment and scope of violence if the nuclear threshold were crossed, followed by uncontrolled escalation. Arms control can continue to help with mutual reductions of weapons that national leaders are deeply reluctant to use, and to provide cost savings that can be applied to other needs. This was accomplished in the past by focusing on numbers. Numbers can be reduced by treaties, executive agreements, or tacit understandings. Numbers can also be reduced significantly over time by extending the three key norms of nonuse, not testing, and nonproliferation.

These three norms have survived even as treaties have been discarded. Continued adherence to these norms will be absolutely essential if even modest new arms reduction agreements are beyond reach. In the near term, it will be hard to negotiate much deeper reductions when deterrence strengtheners in the United States and Russia dig in their heels, when China, India, and Pakistan increase the size of their arsenals, and when competition between states that possess nuclear weapons is becoming sharper. The problem of reducing nuclear danger has become enlarged. If arms control is to be revived, its scope must be enlarged, as well.

NUMBERS

When nuclear arms control was conceived at the outset of the Kennedy administration, its central design feature was stabilization, not numbers. Schelling and Halperin treated reductions as an "open question." In their view, reductions might make sense in some areas and increases in others. To advance stabilization, they focused on qualitative aspects of the competition and the way nuclear weapons were deployed. The "essential feature" of arms control was "the recognition of common interest," not numbers.[21]

A numbers-based approach to stabilization was challenging but feasible in a bipolar competition. With China's ascent, a numbers-based approach to strategic arms control becomes far more complicated. Beijing has long-standing reasons to remain aloof from numbers-based strategic arms control since its forces and warhead totals pale by comparison to those of the United States and Russia. Neither Moscow nor Washington is willing to accept Beijing in a trilateral compact except as a second-tier state, a status that Beijing is unlikely to accept. Seeking China's inclusion would thus incentivize Beijing to compete harder than before. While China has increased the pace of its strategic modernization programs as U.S. offensive and defensive capabilities evolve, its priorities appear to lie in platforms, techniques, and weapons that have demonstrable military utility. In contrast, Moscow relies on high numbers of warheads atop missiles. Its nuclear forces are the last vestiges of Moscow's Cold War status. The Kremlin's high-cost insurance policies reflect perpetually wariness of U.S. missile defense plans, while keeping an eye out for China's growing arsenal. The Kremlin also believes it gains geopolitical leverage from its nuclear forces, despite plentiful evidence to the contrary. Deterrence strengtheners in Washington are also extremely wary of deeper reductions, however modest.

Numbers provide a snapshot of progress, stagnation, or backsliding to reduce nuclear danger. The Biden administration took office in a period of backsliding, with across-the-board strategic modernization programs in Russia and the United States, and growing strategic forces in China, India, and Pakistan. The geometry of nuclear competition, featuring two triangular and four bilateral rivalries, presents significant barriers to success in numerical arms reduction. Bilateral U.S.-Russian reductions remain difficult but possible; multilateral numerical limits are another matter.

Prior multilateral attempts to limit the most fearsome weapon systems did not fare well. During the years between the two World Wars, naval powers engaged in arms control. "Capital ships" were the strategic forces of this era. Heavy tonnage warships with sixteen-inch guns could traverse long distances and appear offshore to deliver threatening messages or heavy firepower. At the instigation of Secretary of State Charles Evans Hughes, a three-tiered ratio system was devised in the 1922 Washington Naval Treaty.

Great Britain and the United States were evenly situated in the top tier, Japan was in the second tier, and France and Italy were in the third tier. These ratios were adjusted at the 1930 London Treaty, where Secretary of State Henry L. Stimson led the U.S. delegation. These treaties did not take into adequate account dramatic changes in the technology of naval warfare represented by the advent of the submarine and the aircraft carrier. They were bedeviled by workarounds, violations, exclusions, and most of all, by the clear intent of two states—Japan and Germany—to radically alter the status quo in the Pacific and in Europe. Japan was a signatory to naval limitations; Germany was not.[22]

This troubling history would intrude on any effort to devise ratios among states that possess nuclear weapons at a time of advancing technologies and sharpened competition. Thorny issues of definition and scope would bedevil a ratio-based system of arms limitation. What would the range limitations be for the missiles to be counted? Would they include intermediate- and medium-range missiles like those formerly banned under the 1987 INF Treaty, as well as ocean-spanning missiles? Would missiles designed for ballistic missile defense count along with missiles used for offensive purposes? How would missiles designed to carry either conventional or nuclear warheads be counted? All of this, and more, would need to be sorted out if a ratio-based approach for Russia, the United States, and China could be agreed upon. China is unlikely to accept constraints if India doesn't, and India wouldn't accept limits if Pakistan remains an outlier. Devising numerical ratios among China, India, and Pakistan would be a very tall order.

A numerical approach to multilateral strategic arms control is just too hard. And yet numbers matter because they reflect the state of competition between possessors and because additions tend to be more destabilizing than stabilizing. Numbers also matter because the more they rise, the more they undermine the norm of nonproliferation. If bilateral strategic arms control is necessary but insufficient, if it is important for China to engage in nuclear restraint, and if a hierarchical, multilateral ratio-based system is impractical, where does this leave us?

Sometimes, when the nature of a problem seems intractable, the wisest course might just be to expand the scope of the problem. Because numbers matter greatly and because numerically based, multilateral strategic arms control is beyond our grasp, I propose that we pursue multilateral norm extension among the United States, Russia, China, France, Great Britain, India, and Pakistan. The key norms of No Use, no testing, and nonproliferation can be strengthened and extended even when multilateral numerical limitations and reductions are beyond reach. Over time, success in extending these three norms can lead naturally to reduced numbers—with or without treaties.

SEVEN-NATION NORM BUILDING

U.S. and Russian negotiations began very late in the Trump administration, with neither expressing an interest in further arms reductions because of China's trajectory. Moscow responded to the Trump administration's call for Beijing's participation in trilateral talks by reviving calls for France and Great Britain to be included—a negotiating position that dates back to the first strategic arms limitation talks. Paris and London would bring expertise to any negotiation but expressed no enthusiasm to engage—stances that also date back to the Nixon administration. Their nuclear arsenals and force structures are not threatening. They have no pressing disputes that could lead to the use of nuclear weapons. Nor are they increasing the size of their force structure.

In contrast, the force structures of China, India, and Pakistan are growing. They have disputed borders and border clashes. China and India, like India and Pakistan, have no substantive security dialogue over nuclear weapons and nuclear risk-reduction measures. There are no bilateral measures in place that place limits on interactive nuclear competitions in Asia. Convening a triangular nuclear forum with China, India, and Pakistan is unlikely because New Delhi would be outnumbered. This triangular competition is as resistant to hierarchical ratios as the triangular competition among the United States, Russia, and China.

Dangerous military practices are rising in both triangular competitions and in all four bilateral rivalries. Every pairing of nuclear-armed rivals could benefit from the establishment of guardrails, the reinforcement of norms, and the acceptance of stabilization measures. Codes of conduct governing dangerous military practices exist but are in need of reaffirmation between Washington and Moscow. They barely exist for China, India, and Pakistan. Just as it is worthwhile to change China's role from a free rider to a participant, it is also worthwhile to seek ways to change the status of India and Pakistan from free riders to participants. Common restraint measures are applicable to all four pairings of nuclear-armed rivals. Progress in this daunting agenda might have a greater chance of success if everyone has a seat at the table, as well as France and Great Britain.

Engaging seven states in multilateral discussions on nuclear restraint, norm building, and risk reduction would be complicated and difficult, but not as difficult as seeking these results in bilateral or trilateral discussions. For all of the manifold difficulties seven-nation discussions would face, there is sufficient connective tissue to try. All seven have significant concerns about the intentions and capabilities of states with dynamic nuclear modernization programs. Each state has its own reasons to participate, as well as to be wary. None of the states with dynamic modernization programs are willing to relax requirements unless others do.

All seven states have respected the norm of nonbattlefield use, but further reinforcement is needed for the crises that lie ahead. All seven have adhered to nuclear test moratoria for more than twenty years. Discussions on how to strengthen this norm among the seven could produce tangible results. Bilateral lines of communication could become more meaningful as a consequence of discussions initiated in a seven-nation forum. India and Pakistan might see value in having seats at the high table of nuclear possessor states. Their participation could also complicate matters even more as Pakistan would seek to bring bilateral disputes to the table. Ground rules would be necessary at the outset to clarify that bilateral issues are off-limits. If India and Pakistan are ready to participate, it would be harder for Beijing to remain an outlier. Each of the five states with dynamic nuclear modernization programs has good reason to engage—as long as everyone engages.

A MULTILATERAL BUILD-DOWN

Seven-nation discussions centered around norm building might yield dividends. But what about numbers? Numbers cannot be completely divorced from norms, and yet a direct approach to discuss numbers is bound to fail. Washington and Moscow have a long history of negotiating numbers, but no one else does. It would be senseless to try to set ratios and hierarchy for all seven states. China, India, and Pakistan do not even advertise or acknowledge numbers—a situation comparable to the beginning of U.S.-Soviet strategic arms limitation talks when Washington provided the data for both superpowers. Setting a hierarchical order for the Asian competition would be particularly problematic, as China rarely acknowledges challenges by India, and Pakistan would be unlikely to accept an inferior position to India. All three would be as unwilling to accept intrusive inspections at sensitive sites as the Soviet Union was until 1986.

I propose an indirect approach: that the seven consider a norm of building down numbers as new nuclear armament is deployed. This isn't a new idea. During the Reagan administration, Alton Frye conceived the concept of a strategic build-down.[23] Frye was writing at a time of intense debate in the United States over Soviet intentions, the Reagan administration's negotiating stance, and the Pentagon's strategic modernization programs. One severe crisis followed another during 1983, and negotiations over arms reductions were deadlocked. Frye's build-down concept was an attempt to break domestic and negotiating impasses. Under his proposal, both superpowers would be obliged to reduce as they modernized. Frye's concept of a superpower strategic build-down was overtaken by events. The elevation of Gorbachev and his pairing with Reagan opened up extraordinary negotiating outcomes and led to deep cuts in opposing arsenals.

The build-down concept still has great utility, however, and might be considered and adapted for use in seven-nation discussions. This approach would avoid some of the problems inherent in trying to devise a ratio-based system, but not all of them. Under a build-down regime, states do not have to agree to a hierarchy or a ratio-based system. Instead, they would proceed from where they already are. States would, however, be obliged to acknowledge numbers that other states have already discovered for themselves by observation from space and by other means, just as the Soviet Union did at the onset of the strategic arms limitation talks. Nations would also be obliged to confirm what other states will eventually discover with respect to their plans to modernize nuclear forces. Nothing would prevent them from proceeding with modernization plans, but they would be obliged to reduce in agreed fashion as they replace old systems with new ones.

There are many potential advantages in attempting to apply a build-down concept to seven states. Among the advantages are making a virtue of budgetary necessity. It will be difficult for Washington and Moscow to afford replacing existing missiles, submarines, and bombers on a one-for-one basis, given the exorbitant costs of doing so, and other calls on national resources. China is the country most able to afford a nuclear buildup and is engaged in doing so. And yet China's claims for the value of nuclear weapons are far more modest than those of the United States and Russia. India has strong domestic constraints on defense spending. Pakistan doesn't, but can least afford it.

China's long-held position is that the United States and Russia must build down to its level. It would be harder to maintain this position if the United States, Russia, India, Pakistan, France, and Great Britain are inclined to consider a multilateral build-down scheme. Depending on the particulars, a multilateral build-down could alleviate security concerns for both triangular nuclear competitions and all four pairings of nuclear rivals. Drawing down multilaterally might well be less difficult than drawing down bilaterally or trilaterally. Strategic modernization would continue, but at a lesser scale under a build-down regime.

There are many difficulties that would have to be surmounted if a multilateral build-down concept were to be agreed upon, beginning with agreed baselines for a multilateral build-down. States would need to be willing to accept transparency beyond their comfort levels. They would need to release verifiable information on their holdings and their plans. Under a build-down, states might hold on to older systems longer than would otherwise be the case so that they can be traded off later, as modernization proceeds. This is a minor problem. Others are more significant.

Difficult questions regarding the scope of a multilateral build-down would need to be addressed. Would missile defense interceptors be included in national counts, and if so, what threshold capabilities would make a missile defense interceptor accountable? If defenses are included in national totals, states would presumably insist on being free to choose between offense and defense and to have freedom to mix, depending on their perceived national security interests. Another difficult issue relates to the unit of account for a multilateral build-down. Would the unit of account be warheads, delivery vehicles, or both? Would intermediate- and medium-range missiles be counted along with ocean-spanning missiles and strategic bombers? If so, what would be the range threshold for inclusion? How would missiles above the range threshold be considered if they are deployed with conventional and not nuclear warheads? And how would states distinguish between nuclear and conventionally armed missiles? How would advancing technologies, such as hypervelocity glide missiles, be treated?

These and other questions could well lead to different answers about inclusion and exclusion, based on each nation's security perspectives. The pursuit of preferred outcomes could provide incentives to participate in seven-nation talks. Perhaps trade-offs could be agreed upon, or perhaps these divisions would be so great as to foreclose agreements. Discussions about a multilateral build-down are likely to be prolonged because of differing U.S. and Russian perspectives, and because China, India, and Pakistan have had no prior basis for such discussions. Great Britain and France might not wish to engage in a build-down, arguing that they already adhere to minimum deterrence postures. Or they might see value in doing so, given budgetary constraints. Given all this and more, multilateral discussions about establishing a build-down norm might not make headway. Even so, there are good reasons for exploratory talks, even if positive outcomes remain distant.

The reaffirmation of norms need not await exploratory discussions about a build-down. Seven-nation talks might proceed in phases. Norm building and the construction of guardrails and stabilization measures would come first. Successful results could facilitate multilateral talks over a build-down. Even if agreements are not reachable or fully inclusive, preliminary discussions with free riders could still have utility. Negotiating a multilateral build-down would be a difficult and time-consuming task. Nonetheless, it might be useful to begin thinking through this approach and assessing different parameters on how best to proceed.

CONCLUSION

Deterrence isn't self-regulating; it's self-generating. Nuclear deterrence without reassurance is dangerous and prone to catastrophic failure. The basis for reviving arms control rests on this recognition. Arms control was conceived to advance public safety in ways that deterrence alone could not possibly provide. Paul Warnke often said that if arms control was torn down, it would have to be rebuilt. The burden of reconstruction falls on us.

We will revive arms control because our lives depend on it. We will revive arms control because deterrence without reassurance is too dangerous and crisis prone. Guardrails, norms, and stabilization measures can take many forms; reinvention depends on our creativity and wisdom. It also depends on the state of relations between nuclear-armed rivals. If their competition sharpens, and if national leaders are content to intensify that competition, then no proposals to reverse course will succeed. If and when leaders decide to pursue course corrections, or if and when leaders change, opportunities will arise. When they do, it is essential to have plans in mind on how best to proceed.

A standard critique of arms control riffs off of what Samuel Johnson is believed to have said about second marriages: The pursuit of arms control, in this jaundiced view, constitutes the triumph of hope over experience. Not true. Many who remarry live happily ever after. More to the point, arms control didn't fail. Arms control cut deeply into nuclear excess; it created a nonproliferation norm for nuclear weapons and disarmament norms for chemical and biological weapons. Most importantly, arms control set nuclear weapons apart from other instruments of warfare. Without arms control, it is highly unlikely that we would have survived three-quarters of a century without the battlefield use of nuclear weapons.

Accomplishments in this field are never unblemished. Outliers can be easily identified because they do not abide by the foundational norms of arms control. Most treaties are not everlasting. Some never enter into force or do so after extended waits. Others, like the Anti-Ballistic Missile Treaty and Intermediate Nuclear Forces Treaty, served useful purposes for three decades but not longer. These treaties accomplished what they set out to do until one of the parties wanted to be relieved of constraints.

Foundational norms are advanced by and can outlast treaties. Three of them—no use of nuclear weapons in warfare, no testing, and nonproliferation—are stanchions of the nuclear peace. These norms have taken hold; it is our responsibility to extend them. Despite many setbacks, norms-based arms control endures. Norms can be extended even in a period of intense polarization on Capitol Hill and sharpened competition between states possessing nuclear weapons. Treaties, by comparison, fare less well when domestic and geopolitical circumstances change. There will be a next phase of arms control because the need to stabilize competition between nuclear-armed rivals is everlasting. The future of arms control will build on successes, require re-invention, and explore new possibilities.

My approach accepts ground realities and does not place upon arms control the impossible burden of transcending them. For this reason, these pages do not dwell on abolition. While I endorse visionary end states and salute those who seek them, I also recognize political and geopolitical conditions that militate against these agendas. Political will cannot be manufactured when ground realities do not permit success. I steer clear of grand treaty making in deference to deep partisan divides and the complications posed by the complex geometry of nuclear-tinged competitions. We are obliged to be agile; if new treaties remain beyond reach, there are other ways to proceed, including by executive agreement, politically binding accords, tacit agreements in the form of parallel steps, or by unilateral measures.

While I do not seek ambitious treaties, I do seek visionary outcomes by other means. I advocate a synthesis of pragmatism and idealism. Seeking the nonuse of nuclear weapons in warfare for a full century after Hiroshima and Nagasaki is extraordinarily ambitious, as is seeking to extend testing moratoria until 2045. And yet these goals are achievable because the norms of No Use and no testing are the hardest for any national leader to break. Unlike a treaty calling for abolition, extending the norms of No Use and no testing lend themselves to a sense of daily accomplishment. Every day that passes without use or testing is a victory. Setbacks can happen tomorrow, which is why these norms demand our protection, as well as game plans in the event they are broken.

Convening a seven-nation forum to reaffirm norms might well be a bridge too far. Implementing a build-down norm for all seven nations lies even farther afield. These ideas are nonetheless worth exploring. Every major accomplishment in arms control seemed inconceivable when first advocated, including the permanent cessation of nuclear testing. I was a teenager when the United States and the Soviet Union stopped testing in the atmosphere. When I graduated high school, there were over 60,000 nuclear weapons on this planet. At present, there are 13,000. Our parents and grandparents never expected to reach, let alone pass, the seventy-five-year mark for the absence of mushroom clouds on battlefields, or the twenty-year mark on testing moratoria, and yet here we are. Those who practiced arms control accomplished great things; they have left more work for us to do. It is now up to us to extend the nuclear peace. When we get knocked down, we pick ourselves up and press forward.

We live at a time of great lamentation, when profound success stories go unrecognized. The absence of mushroom clouds on battlefields, the cessation of testing, deep nuclear arms reductions, and a near-universal membership in the Nonproliferation Treaty are profound successes. We are, however, capable of backsliding as well as accomplishment. We make bad decisions as well as good ones. Much of the edifice of nuclear arms control has been torn down. It's up to us to rebuild it. Success is again possible because failure would be too costly.

ACKNOWLEDGMENTS

I have been granted the gift of meaningful work, and for this I am grateful to funders who have supported the Stimson Center's mission to pursue pragmatic steps toward ideal objectives. Stimson is now in the strong hands of Brian Finlay, who was gracious in his support for this book project. The MacArthur Foundation provided grant support for this book and decades of assistance to the Stimson Center. My sincere thanks go to Emma Belcher, Theo Kalionzes, Angela Schlater, Julia Stasch, Robert Gallucci, and Jonathan Fanton. The Carnegie Corporation of New York has also steadfastly supported the Stimson Center and my work. Carnegie's continued supply of oxygen has nurtured the living, breathing, purposeful organism that is Stimson, now over seventy talented people strong. I am deeply indebted to Vartan Gregorian, Deana Arsenian, Carl Robichaud, Patricia Nicholas, and Stephen Del Rosso. I am also grateful to Penny Willgerodt, John Redick, and the Board of the Prospect Hill Foundation for helping with research assistance during the last furlong of writing this book.

Chapter reviewers have improved my analysis and saved me from myself many times. Len Ackland and Lewis Dunn read and commented on my chapters, pointing out weaknesses in plot lines and passages where I had gotten out over my skis. I am also grateful to chapter readers Kenneth Adelman, Barry Blechman, Dan Caldwell, Toby Dalton, Kelly Eplee, Alton Frye, James Goodby, Rose Gottemoeller, Ronald Lehman, Edward Levine, Franklin Miller, Stanley Riveles, and Spencer Weart. I am also indebted to two anonymous reviewers. Alan Harvey and Caroline McKusick at Stanford University Press provided invaluable editorial advice. Susan Karani, Stephanie Adams, and Bridget Kinsella helped shepherd this book to market. Paul Tyler did an extraordinary job of copyediting. Errors that remain are on me. I am grateful to Tobiah Waldron for preparing the index and to Rob Ehle for the cover art.

Participants at Stimson Center brainstorming sessions helped me to organize my thoughts. My thanks go to Justin Anderson, Linton Brooks, Susan Burk, Anita Friedt, Matthew Fuhrmann, Rebecca Gibbons, Morton Halperin, Matthew Kroenig, Sara Kutchesfahani, Brad Roberts, Joan Rohlfing, Lynn Rusten, Scott Sagan, Todd Sechser, Nina Tannenwald, Heather Williams, and Jon Wolfsthal.

This book has been enriched by interviews with, among others, Kenneth Adelman, Robert Barry, Alex Bell, Robert Bell, Barry Blechman, Linton Brooks, Matthew Bunn, Susan Burk, Richard Burt, Richard Combs, Pierce Corden, William Courtney, Nancy Dorfman, Robert Einhorn, Marcie and William S. Foster III, Alton Frye, Leon Fuerth, Leslie Gelb, James Goodby, Rose Gottemoeller, Gregory Govan, Thomas Graham, Jr., Michael Guhin, Morton Halperin, John Harvey, Siegfried Hecker, Laura Holgate, Edward Ifft, Togzhan Kassenova, Susan Koch, David Koplow, Roland Lajoie, Ronald Lehman, Jan Lodal, Kenneth Luongo, Jenifer Mackby, Monte Mallin, Brian McKeon, Ted McNamara, Robert Mikulak, Franklin Miller, William Perry, Steven Pifer, Alan Platt, John Redick, Dan Reicher, Paul Richards, Stanley Riveles, Brad Roberts, Frank Rose, James Rubin, Gary Samore, Adam Scheinman, Alice Schelling, Thomas Scoville, Wendy Sherman, George Shultz, Walter Slocombe, James Steinberg, Strobe Talbott, James Timbie, Frank von Hippel, Paul Sommer Warnke, Stephen Warnke, Lawrence Weiler, Larry Welsh, Jon Wolfsthal, Houston Wood, John Woodworth, Norman Wulf, Rachel York, and Sybil York. I have respected the wishes of others who requested anonymity.

For help with sources and data gathering, special thanks go to three persons who are stanchions for those of us who work on nuclear issues: Daryl Kimball at the Arms Control Association, Hans Kristensen at the Federation of American Scientists, and Amy Woolf at the Congressional Research Service. I also received research assistance from Shannon Bugos, Dan Caldwell, Kelsey Davenport, James Goodby, Carol Krepon Ingall, Rhianna Kreger, Polly Nayak, Robert S. Norris, Joshua Pollack, Leon Ratz, John Redick, Kingston Reif, Dean Rust, Todd Sechser, James Siebens, Melanie Sisson, Rachel Stohl, and Margaret Warnke. Sean Maguire has doggedly tracked down details and drank from my fire hose of requests with good cheer. My thanks also go to Katie Holmes, Heather Byrne, and Kirk Lancaster.

William Burr walked this novice through archival research procedures. For archival investigations, my thanks go to Valoise Armstrong at the Dwight D. Eisenhower Presidential Library and Museum, Hailey Philbin at the John F. Kennedy Library, and Lara Hall at the Lyndon Baines Johnson Presidential Library. For access to the Herbert York papers, I am thankful to the special collections staff at the Geisel Library at the University of California at San Diego. With travel curtailed by the COVID-19 virus, I received help from those who sifted through archives before me, including James Goodby, who shared papers from the Kennedy Library, and Judith Reppy, who dug through the Cornell University archives. Dan Caldwell provided me with shortcuts to the Henry M. Jackson papers at the University of Washington. For delving into the papers of Herbert Scoville, my thanks go to Thomas Scoville. For help with Stephen Ledogar's papers, I am indebted to Lucy (Ledogar) van Beever. For inspiration, my thanks go to Lovely Umayam, a rare find, whose work combines artistic sensibility with serious policy chops.

Most of all, my thanks go to my beloveds and their beloveds, who support me and excuse my preoccupations. The wisest member of our family, by far, is Sandra Savine, also known as Alessandra, Mom, Nonna, and the Queen of the Slipstream. I have been fortunate in many things, but never more so than in our partnership for over four decades, through thick and thin, in sickness and in health. Josh and Misha, and their partners, Sarah and Kenny, are extraordinary human beings. Their kids, Quinn, Clara, Zander, and Leland Michael, light me up.

The revival of nuclear arms control will rest on the talent and energy of those already committed to this task and those who will join them. The future will be in good hands. Perseverance has accomplished extraordinary feats in the past and can do so again. Those who helped me write this book believe, as I do, in an obligation to transmit what we have experienced and learned, as well as to avoid repeating painful chapters of our nuclear history. If readers take away from these pages a renewed appreciation for arms control and a deeper commitment to prevent mushroom clouds, this book will have served its purpose.

ANNEXES

Dwight Eisenhower

Antarctica Treaty 1959

John F. Kennedy

Hot Line Agreement 1963

Limited Nuclear Test Ban Treaty 1963

Lyndon Baines Johnson

Outer Space Treaty 1967

Latin American Nuclear Free Zone Treaty 1967

Nonproliferation Treaty 1968

Richard M. Nixon

Seabed Treaty 1971

Agreement on the Prevention of Nuclear War 1971

Hot Line Modernization Agreement 1971

Biological Weapons Treaty 1971

Anti-Ballistic Missile Treaty 1972

Interim Agreement on Offensive Forces 1972

Threshold Nuclear Ban Treaty 1974

Gerald R. Ford
Helsinki Final Act 1975
Treaty Banning Peaceful Nuclear Explosions 1976

Jimmy Carter
Treaty Banning Environmental Modification 1977
International Atomic Energy Agency Safeguards Agreement 1977
Strategic Arms Limitation Treaty II 1979
Convention on Physical Protection of Nuclear Material 1980

Ronald Reagan
Hot Line Modernization Agreement 1984
Nuclear Risk Reduction Centers 1985
Intermediate Nuclear Forces Treaty 1987

George H.W. Bush
Conventional Forces in Europe Treaty 1990
Strategic Arms Reduction Treaty I 1991
Open Skies Treaty 1992
Strategic Arms Reduction Treaty II 1993

Bill Clinton
Agreed Framework (North Korea) 1994
Comprehensive Test Ban Treaty 1996

George W. Bush
Withdrew from ABM Treaty 2001
Moscow Treaty 2002
Proliferation Security Initiative 2003
Withdrew from North Korean Agreed Framework 2003

Barack Obama
New Strategic Arms Reduction Treaty 2010
Arms Trade Treaty 2013
Iran Nuclear Agreement 2015

Donald Trump
Withdrew from Iran Nuclear Agreement 2018
Withdrew from Intermediate Nuclear Forces Treaty 2019

Withdrew from Arms Trade Treaty 2019
Withdrew from Open Skies Treaty 2020

Source: Dan Caldwell

ANNEX 2
NORMS ESTABLISHED BY ARMS CONTROL
AND DISARMAMENT AGREEMENTS

*When the United States is a party to the agreement.

Types of Agreement, Date Signed, and Date Entered into Force

1. NORM: *Regional Nuclear Weapon–Free Zones*
    1.1 Antarctica Treaty* 1959, 1961
    1.2 Outer Space Treaty* 1967, 1967
    1.3 Treaty of Tlatelolco (Latin America)* 1967, 1968
    1.4 Seabed Treaty* 1971, 1982
    1.5 Treaty of Rarotonga (South Pacific) 1985, 1986
    1.6 Treaty of Bangkok (Southeast Asia) 1995, 1997
    1.7 Treaty of Pelindaba (Africa) 1996, 2009
    1.8 Central Asia Treaty 2006, 2009

2. NORM: *Nuclear Test Constraints*
    2.1 Limited Test Ban Treaty* 1963, 1963
    2.2 Threshold Test Ban Treaty* 1974, 1990
    2.3 Peaceful Nuclear Explosives Treaty* 1976, 1990
    2.4 Comprehensive Test Ban Treaty 1996, Not ratified

3. NORM: *Communicate for Crisis Management and Prevention*
    3.1 Hot Line Agreement* 1963, 1963
    3.2 Accidents Measures Agreement* 1971, 1971
    3.3 Hot Line Modernization Agreement* 1971, 1971
    3.4 Basic Principles of Relations (US & USSR)* 1972, 1972
    3.5 Incidents at Sea Agreement* 1972, 1972
    3.6 Agreement on the Prevention of Nuclear War* 1973, 1973
    3.7 Prevention of Dangerous Military Practices* 1989, 1989

4. NORM: *Nuclear Nonproliferation*
    4.1 International Atomic Energy Agency founded* 1956
    4.2 Nonproliferation Treaty * 1968, 1970

4.3 Nonproliferation Treaty Exporters Committee (Zangger Committee)* 1974

4.4 Nuclear Suppliers Group* 1975

4.5 US-IAEA Safeguards Agreement* 1977, 1980

4.6 Convention on Physical Protection of Nuclear Material 1980, 1987

4.7 Missile Technology Control Regime* 1987

4.8 Cooperative Threat Reduction Program* 1991

4.9 Agreed Framework with North Korea* 1994, 1994

4.10 Proliferation Security Initiative* 2003

4.11 UN Resolution 1540* 2004

4.12 Iran Nuclear Agreement* 2015, 2015

5. NORM: Disarmament

5.1 Geneva Protocol 1925, 1928

5.2 Biological Weapons Convention* 1972, 1975

5.3 INF Treaty* 1987, 1988

5.4 Convention on Certain Conventional Weapons* 1982

5.5 Treaty on the Prohibition of Nuclear Weapons 2020

6. NORM: Environmental Protection

6.1 Antarctica Treaty* 1959, 1961

6.2 Limited Test Ban Treaty* 1963, 1963

6.3 Environmental Modification Agreement* 1977, 1978

7. NORM: Control and Reduce Strategic Arms Limitations

7.1 Anti-Ballistic Missile Treaty* 1972, 1972

7.2 Interim Agreement on Offensive Forces* 1972, 1972

7.3 ABM Protocol* 1974, 1974

7.4 SALT II Treaty* 1979, Not ratified

7.5 START I Treaty* 1991, 1994

7.6 START II Treaty* 1993, Not implemented

7.7 SORT/Moscow Treaty* 2002, 2003

7.8 New START* 2010, 2011

8. NORM: No Production, Possession, and Use of Chemical and Biological Weapons

8.1 Geneva Protocol on Chemical Weapons* 1925, 1928

8.2 Biological Weapons Convention* 1972, 1975

8.3 Australia Group 1985

8.4 Chemical Weapons Convention* 1993, 1997

9. NORM: *Reduce or Do Not Use Certain Conventional Weapons*

9.1 Convention on Certain Conventional Weapons 1982, 1983

9.2 Conventional Forces in Europe Treaty 1990, 2003

9.3 UN Register of Conventional Arms* 1992

9.4 Land Mine Treaty 1997, 1999

9.5 Cluster Munitions Convention 2008, 2010

9.6 Arms Trade Treaty* 2013, 2014

Source: Dan Caldwell

NOTES

All interviews are by author and all email communications are to author unless otherwise noted.

CHAPTER 1

1. See Robert Jay Lifton, *The Broken Connection* (New York: Simon and Schuster, 1979), 284.

2. Spencer R. Weart, *The Rise of Nuclear Fear* (Cambridge, MA: Harvard University Press, 2012), 57. Also see Weart, *Nuclear Fear: A History of Images* (Cambridge, MA: Harvard University Press, 1988).

3. See Paul Boyer, *By the Bomb's Early Light: American Thought and Culture at the Dawn of the Atomic Age* (New York: Pantheon Books, 1985), 3.

4. See Campbell Craig and Sergey Radchenko, *The Atomic Bomb and the Origins of the Cold War* (New Haven, CT: Yale University Press, 2008).

5. Henry Lewis Stimson, "The Decision to Use the Atomic Bomb," *Harper's Magazine* 194 (February 1947): 100.

6. See Lynn Eden, *Whole World on Fire: Organizations, Knowledge & Nuclear Weapons Devastation* (Ithaca, NY: Cornell University Press, 2003).

7. Norman Cousins, "Modern Man Is Obsolete," *Saturday Review of Literature*, August 18, 1945, 5.

8. U.S. House of Representatives, Committee on Military Affairs, *Atomic Energy Hearings on H.R. 4280*, 79th Cong., 1st Sess. (October 9 and 18, 1945); Vannevar Bush, *Modern Arms and Free Men: A Discussion of the Role of Science in Preserving Democracy* (New York: Simon and Schuster, 1949); Leslie R. Groves, *Now It Can Be Told: The Story of the Manhattan Project* (New York: Harper, 1962); and Robert S. Norris, *Racing for the Bomb: General Leslie R. Groves, The Manhattan Project's Indispensable Man* (South Royalton, VT: Steerforth Press, 2002).

9. Wayne A.R. Leys, "Human Values in the Atomic Age," in *The Impact of Atomic Energy, ed. Robert A. Dahl (Philadelphia: Annals of the American Academy of Political and Social Science, 1953)*, 127.

10. Weart, *The Rise of Nuclear Fear*, 62.

11. See Garrett M. Graff, *Raven Rock: The Story of the US. Government's Secret Plan to Save Itself—While the Rest of Us Die* (New York: Simon & Schuster, 2017); and Edward M. Geist, *Armageddon Insurance: Civil Defenses in the United States and Soviet Union, 1945–1991* (Chapel Hill: University of North Carolina Press, 2019).

12. Herman Kahn, *On Thermonuclear War* (Princeton, NJ: Princeton University Press, 1961), 34.

13. J. Robert Oppenheimer, "Physics in the Contemporary World," Arthur D. Little Memorial Lecture at MIT, Cambridge, MA, November 25, 1947.

14. See Kai Bird and Martin J. Sherwin, *American Prometheus: The Triumph and Tragedy of J. Robert Oppenheimer* (New York: Vintage Books, 2007); and Alice Kimball Smith, *A Peril and a Hope: The Scientists Movement in America, 1945–47* (Chicago: University of Chicago Press, 1965).

15. See Kati Marton, *The Great Escape: Nine Jews Who Fled Hitler and Changed the World* (New York: Simon & Schuster, 2006).

16. James Franck, Donald J. Hughes, J.J. Nickson, Eugene Rabinowitch, Glenn T. Seaborg, J.C. Stearns, and Leo Szilard, *"Report of the Committee on Political and Social Problems," Manhattan Project, Metallurgic Laboratory, University of Chicago, June 11, 1945 (the Franck Report)*, US National Archives, Record Group 77, Records of the Chief of Engineers, Manhattan Engineer District, Harrison-Bundy File, Folder 76, 7–10.

17. Stimson, "Decision to Use the Atomic Bomb," 97–107. Also see Henry L. Stimson and McGeorge Bundy, *On Active Service in Peace and War* (New York: Harper and Brothers, 1948); Sean L. Malloy, *Atomic Tragedy: Henry L. Stimson and the Decision to Use the Bomb against Japan* (Ithaca, NY: Cornell University Press, 2008); and Barton J. Bernstein, "The Quest for Security: American Foreign Policy and International Control of Atomic Energy, 1942–1946," *Journal of American History* 60, no. 4 (March 1974).

18. See Alex Wellerstein, "A 'Purely Military' Target? Truman's Changing Language about Hiroshima," *Restricted Data: The Nuclear Secrecy Blog,* January 19, 2018. The Stimson Center re-gifted the folios from the briefing Groves gave to Harvey Bundy to the Hiroshima Peace Memorial Museum in July 2016.

19. Bird and Sherwin, *American Prometheus,* 332.

20. See Nina Tannenwald, *The Nuclear Taboo: The United States and the Non-Use of Nuclear Weapons Since 1945* (Cambridge: Cambridge University Press, 2007), 133.

21. Sidney Shallet, "First Atomic Bomb Dropped on Japan; Missile Is Equal to 20,000 Tons of TNT; Truman Warns Foes of a 'Rain of Ruin'," *New York Times,* August 7, 1945, 1–2.

22. Michael J. Yavenditti, "The American People and the Use of Atomic Bombs on Japan: The 1940s," *The Historian* 36, no. 2 (February 1974): 224–47.

23. See Lawrence Cottrell and Sylvia Eberhardt, *American Opinion on World Affairs in the Atomic Age* (Princeton, NJ: Princeton University Press, 1948).

24. Henry DeWolf Smyth, *Atomic Energy for Military Purposes: The Official Report on the Development of the Atomic Bomb under the Auspices of the United States Government* (Washington, DC: Superintendent of Documents, 1945), 223.

25. Robert A. Dahl, "Atomic Energy and the Democratic Process," in Dahl, ed., *The Impact of Atomic Energy,* 1–7.

26. Paul R. Baker, ed., *The Atomic Bomb: The Great Decision,* 2nd ed. (Hinsdale, IL: Dryden Press, 1976), 143–44.

27. Robert M. Hutchins, *The Atomic Bomb versus Civilization,* Human Events pamphlet for December 1945 (Washington, DC: Human Events, Inc.), 5–13.

28. Paul F. Boller, "Hiroshima and the American Left: August 1945," *International Social Science Review* 57, no. 1 (1982): 25.

29. "Horror and Shame," editorial, *Commonweal Magazine,* August 24, 1945.

30. Reinhold Niebuhr, "Our Relations to Japan," *Christianity and Crisis* 5 (September 17, 1945): 5–6.

31. "Hiroshima—and After: America's Atomic Atrocity," editorial, *Christian Century,* August 29, 1945. Reproduced in *The Christian Century Reader* (New York: Association Press, 1962), 263.

32. See Boyer, *By the Bomb's Early Light,* 179–239.

33. See Richard Rhodes, *The Making of the Atomic Bomb* (New York: Simon & Schuster, 1986); Jennet Conant, *109 East Palace: Robert Oppenheimer and the Secret City of Los Alamos* (New York: Simon & Schuster, 2005); Jon Hunner, *Los Alamos: The Growth of an Atomic Community* (Norman: University of Oklahoma Press, 2004); and Kai and Sherwin, *American Prometheus.*

34. Niels Bohr, "Memorandum to President Roosevelt, July 3, 1944," in *Niels Bohr—Collected Works, vol. 11, The Political Arena (1934–1961),* ed. Finn Aaserud (Amsterdam: Elsevier, 2005), 106.

35. United States Department of State, "A Report on the International Control of Atomic Energy," Washington, DC, March 16, 1946.

36. Bird and Sherwin, *American Prometheus,* 424.

37. See Margaret L. Colt, *Mr. Baruch* (Boston: Houghton Mifflin, 1957).

38. Barton J. Bernstein, "The Quest for Security: American Foreign Policy and International Control of Atomic Energy, 1942–1946," *Journal of American History* 60, no. 4 (March 1974): 1004.

39. President Harry Truman, Radio and Television Report to the American People on the Situation in Korea, September 1, 1950, www.presidency.ucsb.edu/documents/radio-and-television-report-the-american-people-the-situation-korea.

40. See Kevin Ruane, *Churchill and the Bomb in War and Cold War* (London: Bloomsbury Academic, 2016).

41. John Hersey, *Hiroshima* (New York: Alfred A. Knopf, 1946).

42. J. Robert Oppenheimer, "Atomic Weapons," *Proceedings of the American Philosophical Society* 90 (January 1946): 9.

43. Robert Wilson, book review of *Brighter Than a Thousand Suns,* in *Scientific American,* December 1958, in *Arms Control: Readings from Scientific American* (San Francisco: W.H. Freeman, 1973), 17.

44. "Atomic Education Urged by Einstein," *New York Times,* May 25, 1946, 11.

45. Frederick Seitz and Hans Bethe, "How Close Is the Danger?" in *One World or None,* ed. Dexter Masters and Katherine Way, 3rd ed. (New York: New Press, 2007), 117.

46. Arthur H. Compton, "Introduction," in *One World or None, ed.* Dexter Masters and Katherine Way, 1st ed. (New York: McGraw-Hill, 1946), v.

47. H.H. Arnold, "Air Force in the Atomic Age," in Masters and Way, *One World or None,* 1st ed., 26.

48. Norman Cousins and Thomas K. Finletter, "A Beginning of Sanity" (a review of the Acheson-Lilienthal Plan), *Saturday Review of Literature* 29 (June 15, 1946): 9.

49. Albert Einstein, "The Way Out," in Masters and Way, *One World or None,* 3rd ed., 211.

50. J.R. Oppenheimer, "The New Weapon: The Turn of the Screw," in Masters and Way, *One World or None,* 1st ed., 22, 25.

51. Arnold, "Air Force in the Atomic Age," in Masters and Way, eds., *One World or None,* 3rd ed., 84.

52. Walter Lippmann, "International Control of Atomic Energy," in Masters and Way, eds., *One World or None,* 3rd ed., 184.

53. Bernard Brodie, "War in the Atomic Age," in *The Absolute Weapon: Atomic Power and World Order, ed. Bernard Brodie* (New York: Harcourt Brace, 1946), 21–69. Also see Barry H. Steiner, *Bernard Brodie and the Foundations of American Nuclear Strategy* (Lawrence: University of Kansas Press, 1991).

54. See Fred Kaplan, *The Wizards of Armageddon* (New York: Simon & Schuster, 1983).

55. Herbert F. York, *The Advisors: Oppenheimer, Teller, and the Superbomb* (San Francisco: W.H. Freeman, 1976), ix.

56. Joseph L. Lyon, Melville Klauber, John W. Gardner, and King S. Udall, "Childhood Leukemias Associated with Fallout from Nuclear Testing," *New England Journal of Medicine* 300, no. 8 (February 22, 1979): 397–402.

57. Bird and Sherwin, *American Prometheus,* 417–18. Also see York, *The Advisors.*

58. York, *The Advisors,* 52–53.

59. James R. Killian, *Sputnik, Scientists, and Eisenhower: A Memoir of the First Special Assistant to the President for Science and Technology* (Cambridge, MA: MIT Press, 1977), 8. Also see Istvan Hargittai, *Judging Edward Teller: A Closer Look at One of the Most Influential Scientists of the Twentieth Century* (Amherst, NY: Prometheus Books, 2010); and Edward Teller with Judith Shoolery, *Memoirs: A Twentieth-Century Journey in Science and Politics* (Cambridge: Perseus, 2001).

60. Rachel York, interview, La Jolla, CA, March 8, 2019.

61. York, *The Advisors,* 5.

62. Harold C. Urey, "Should America Build the H-Bomb?" *Bulletin of the American Scientists* 6, no. 3 (March 1950).

63. See Ken Young and Warner R. Schilling, *Super Bomb: Organizational Conflict and the Development of the Hydrogen Bomb* (Ithaca, NY: Cornell University Press, 2020); Richard Pollenberg, ed., *In the Matter of J. Robert Oppenheimer: The Security Clearance Hearing* (Ithaca, NY: Cornell University Press, 2002); Priscilla McMillan, *The Ruin of J. Robert Oppenheimer and the Birth of the Modern Arms Race* (New York: Viking, 2005); Bird and Sherwin, *American Prometheus,* 455–550; and York, *The Advisors,* 52.

64. Hans A. Bethe, "The Hydrogen Bomb," *Bulletin of the American Scientists* 6, no. 4 (1950): 102.

65. Herbert York, "Preface," in *Arms Control: Readings from Scientific American* (San Francisco: W.H. Freeman, 1973), v.

66. National Security Council Report, NSC 68, "United States Objectives and Programs for National Security," April 14, 1950, History and Public Policy Program Digital Archive, US National Archives, http://digitalarchive.wilsoncenter.org/document/116191.

67. Letter provided by Thomas Scoville.

68. Gerard C. Smith, *Disarming Diplomat: The Memoirs of Ambassador Gerard C. Smith, Arms Control Negotiator* (Lanham, MD: Madison Books, 1996), 15–16.

69. See Robert S. Norris, "Known Nuclear Tests Worldwide, 1945–1998," *Bulletin of the Atomic Scientists* 54, no. 6 (November–December 1998): 65–67;

Defense Nuclear Agency, *Comprehensive History of Cold War Nuclear Weapon Development and Testing, 1947–1997* (Washington, DC: Defense Threat Reduction Agency, 2002); Terrence R. Gosling, *Atmospheric Nuclear Testing, 1951–1963* (Washington, DC: U.S. Department of Energy, 2006); Richard L. Miller, *Under the Cloud: The Decades of Nuclear Testing* (New York: Free Press, 1986); Elizabeth Tynan, *Atomic Thunder: British Nuclear Testing in Australia* (Yorkshire: Pen & Sword, 2018); Kim Holmes, *Moruroa, French Polynesia, French Nuclear Test Zone* (Roulaix: La Provence, 2017); and John Lewis Wilson and Xue Litai, *China Builds the Bomb* (Stanford: Stanford University Press, 1988).

CHAPTER 2

1. Robert S. Norris and Hans M. Kristensen, "Global Nuclear Weapons Inventories, 1945–2010," *Bulletin of the Atomic Scientists* 66, no. 4 (2010): 77–83.

2. National Cancer Institute, "Get the Facts about Exposure to I-131 Radiation," updated August 3, 2013.

3. See Laurence S. Kaplan, *Harold Stassen: Eisenhower, the Cold War, and the Pursuit of Nuclear Disarmament* (Lexington: University of Kentucky Press, 2018).

4. See W.W. Rostow, *Open Skies: Eisenhower's Proposal of July 21, 1955* (Austin: University of Texas Press, 1982).

5. Ian Neil Gibson, *Six Futile Weeks?: The 1958 Surprise Attack Conference* (Oxford: Oxford University Press, 1994), 66.

6. George B. Kistiakowsky, *A Scientist at the White House: The Private Diary of President Eisenhower's Special Assistant for Science and Technology* (Cambridge, MA: Harvard University Press, 1976), xlvi.

7. James R. Killian, *Sputnik, Scientists, and Eisenhower: A Memoir of the First Special Assistant to the President for Science and Technology* (Cambridge, MA: MIT Press, 1977), 175–76.

8. James Goodby, interview, Washington, DC, January 31, 2019.

9. See RAND and Albert Wohlstetter, "The Delicate Balance of Terror," Report P-1472, 1958; and Albert Wohlstetter, "The Delicate Balance of Terror," *Foreign Affairs* 37, no. 2 (1959): 211–34.

10. "Testimony by Ambassador William C. Foster before the Senate Subcommittee on Disarmament, January 30, 1959," *Documents on Disarmament, 1945–1959, Volume II: 1957–1959* (Washington, DC: U.S. Department of State, 1960), 1,358.

11. See Milton Katz, *Ban the Bomb: A History of SANE, the Committee for a Sane Nuclear Policy, 1957–1985* (Westport, CT: Frederick A. Praeger, 1987).

12. See Lawrence S. Wittner, *Confronting the Bomb: A Short History of the World Nuclear Disarmament Movement* (Stanford: Stanford University Press, 2009).

13. Herman Kahn, "The Arms Race and Some of Its Hazards," *Daedalus 89*, no. 4 (Fall 1960): 765.

14. Robert Straus-Hupé, William R. Kintner, and Steffan T. Possony, *A Forward Strategy for America* (New York: Harper & Brothers, 1961), ix, 210, 323–24. Also see Robert Straus-Hupé, William R. Kintner, James E. Daugherty, and Alvin J. Cottrell, *Protracted Conflict: A Challenging Study of Communist Strategy* (New York: Harper & Brothers, 1959).

15. Herbert F. York, *Making Weapons, Talking Peace: A Physicist's Odyssey from Hiroshima to Geneva* (New York: Basic Books, 1987), 82. Also see Stephen B. Libby and Karl A. Van Bibber, eds., *Edward Teller Centennial Symposium: Modern Physics and the Scientific Legacy of Edward Teller* (Hackensack, NJ:

World Scientific, 2010); and William J. Broad, *Teller's War: The Top-Secret Story behind the Star Wars Deception* (New York: Simon & Schuster, 1992).

16. See, for example, William R. Van Cleave and S.T. Cohen, *Tactical Nuclear Weapons: An Examination of the Issues* (New York: Crane, Russak, 1978); and Van Cleave and Cohen, *Nuclear Weapons, Policies, and the Test Ban Issue* (New York: Frederick A. Praeger, 1987).

17. Edward Teller and Albert L. Latter, *Our Nuclear Future: Facts, Dangers and Opportunities* (New York: Criterion Books, 1958), 124. The *Life* magazine issue appeared in February 10, 1958.

18. Linus Pauling, *No More War* (New York: Dodd Mead, 1958), 115.

19. Pauling, *No More War*; and Linus Pauling, "Pauling vs. Teller [Letter to the Editor]," *Life* 44, no. 11 (1972): 21.

20. "Fallout and Disarmament: A Televised Debate between Linus Pauling and Edward Teller," televised by KQED, San Francisco and other public television channels, February 20, 1958, http://scarc.library.oregonstate.edu/coll/pauling/peace/video/1958v.3-greatandterrible.html.

21. See Keith Myers, "In the Shadow of the Mushroom Cloud: Nuclear Testing, Radioactive Fallout, and Damage to US Agriculture, 1945 to 1970," *Journal of Economic History* 79, no. 1 (2019): 244–74.

22. Sidney Hook, "General and Complete Disarmament as a Policy Goal," in Herman Kahn, Thomas C. Schelling, Sidney Hook, et al., *The Prospects for Arms Control* (Philadelphia: MacFadden Books, 1965), 157.

23. York, *Making Weapons, Talking Peace*, 83.

24. See Fred Charles Iklé, Hans Spier, Bernard Brodie, Alexander L. George, Alice Langley Hsieh, and Arnold Kramish, "The Diffusion of Nuclear Weapons to Additional Countries: The 'Nth Country' Problem," RAND, RM-2484-RC, February 15, 1960.

25. See Harold Karan Jacobson and Eric Stein, *Diplomats, Scientists and Politicians: The United States and Nuclear Test Ban Negotiations* (Ann Arbor: University of Michigan Press, 1966); Bernard G. Bechhoefer, *Postwar Negotiations for Arms Control* (Washington, DC: Brookings Institution, 1961); Robert A. Divine, *Blowing on the Wind: The Nuclear Test Ban Debate, 1954–1960* (New York: Oxford University Press, 1978); James J. Wadsworth, *The Price of Peace* (New York: Frederick A. Praeger, 1962); and James W. Spanier and Joseph L. Nogee, *The Politics of Disarmament: A Case Study in Soviet-American Gamesmanship* (New York: Frederick A. Praeger, 1962).

26. Henry A. Kissinger, "Nuclear Testing and the Problem of Peace," *Foreign Affairs* 37, no. 1 (October 1958): 1–18.

27. Hanson Baldwin and William Sullivan, "U.S. Atom Bomb Blasts 300 Miles Up Mar Radar, Snag Missile Plan: Called 'Greatest Experiment'," *New York Times*, March 19, 1959; and Jack Raymond, "Quarles Says Atom Shots Aided Weapons Research in Attack and in Defense," *New York Times*, March 20, 1959. Also see Mark Wolverton, *Burning the Sky: Operation Argus and the Untold Story of the Cold War Nuclear Tests in Outer Space* (New York: Overlook Press, 2018).

28. Wadsworth, *The Price of Peace*, 24.

29. See Defense Nuclear Agency, *Comprehensive History of Cold War Nuclear Weapon Development and Testing: Atomic and Hydrogen Bomb Development, Post-War Treaties* (Washington, DC: Defense Nuclear Agency, 2002), 110–27.

CHAPTER 3

1. Morton Halperin, interview, Washington, DC, February 6, 2019.

2. *Daedalus* 89, no. 4 (Fall 1960); Donald G. Brennan, ed., *Arms Control, Disarmament, and National Security* (New York: George Braziller, 1961); and

Thomas C. Schelling and Morton H. Halperin, *Strategy and Arms Control* (New York: Twentieth Century Fund, 1961).

3. Donald G. Brennan, editor's preface, in Brennan, *Arms Control, Disarmament, and National Security*, 12.

4. Jerome B. Wiesner, foreword, in Brennan, *Arms Control, Disarmament, and National Security*, 14.

5. Donald G. Brennan, "Setting and Goals of Arms Control," in Brennan, *Arms Control, Disarmament, and National Security*, 37.

6. Robert B. Bowie, "Basic Requirements of Arms Control," in Brennan, *Arms Control, Disarmament, and National Security*, 43, 46.

7. Thomas C. Schelling, "Reciprocal Measures for Arms Stabilization," in Brennan, *Arms Control, Disarmament, and National Security*, 170, 172.

8. Nancy Dorfman, telephone interview, July 27, 2019.

9. Dorfman, telephone interview, July 27, 2019. Also see Robert Dodge, *The Strategist: The Life and Times of Thomas Schelling—How a Game Theorist Understood the Cold War and Won the Nobel Prize* (Singapore: Marshall Cavendish, 2006); and Andrew Schelling, *Towards Acturus* (Albuquerque: La Alameda Press, 2007)

10. Morton Halperin, telephone interview, July 23, 2019; and Morton H. Halperin, *If Only You Do Not Want the Credit: A Memoir of Life in Washington*, forthcoming.

11. Morton Halperin, interview, Washington, DC, February 6, 2019

12. Schelling and Halperin, *Strategy and Arms Control*, 1–2.

13. Schelling and Halperin, *Strategy and Arms Control*, 142.

14. Edward A. Gullion, Acting Deputy Director of the United States Arms Control Administration, to the Kennedy Administration, undated, Papers of John F. Kennedy, Presidential Papers, President's Office Files, Box 69a, "Arms Control and Disarmament Agency (ACDA)," John F. Kennedy Library, Boston, MA.

15. See Lawrence S. Kaplan, *Harold Stassen: Eisenhower, the Cold War, and the Pursuit of Nuclear Disarmament* (Lexington: University Press of Kentucky, 2018).

16. Secretary of Defense Robert Lovett, "Congressional Concerns and Dissenting Views," 138 Cong. Rec., Part 17 (September 15, 1992), 25,138.

17. Herbert F. York, *Arms and the Physicist* (Woodbury, NY: American Institute of Physics Press, 1995), xii. Also see York, *Making Weapons, Talking Peace: A Physicist's Odyssey from Hiroshima to Geneva* (New York: Basic Books, 1987).

18. "Disarmament Agency," Hearings Before the Committee on Foreign Relations, U.S. Senate, 87th Cong., 1st Sess., on S.2180 (1961), 162.

19. "Disarmament Agency," Hearings Before the Committee on Foreign Relations, U.S. Senate, 87th Cong., 1st Sess. (1961), 177–78. Also see Arnold A. Offner, *Hubert Humphrey: The Conscience of the Country* (New Haven, CT: Yale University Press, 2018); and Carl Solberg, *Hubert Humphrey: A Biography* (New York: W.W. Norton, 1984).

20. See "Arms Control and Disarmament," *Hearings Before the Preparedness Investigating Committee of the Committee on Armed Services*, U.S. Senate, 87th Cong., 2d Sess. (1962).

21. See John W. Spanier and Joseph L. Nogee, *The Politics of Disarmament: A Study in Soviet-American Gamesmanship* (New York: Frederick A. Praeger, 1962); and Bernhard G. Bechhoefer, *Postwar Negotiations for Arms Control* (Washington, DC: Brookings Institution, 1961).

22. Marcie Foster and William C. Foster III, telephone interviews, February 19, 2019 and March 1, 2019.

23. See David L. Snead, *The Gaither Committee, Eisenhower, and the Cold War* (Columbus: Ohio State University Press, 1999); and Morton H. Halperin, "The Gaither Committee and the Policy Process," *World Politics* 13, no. 3 (April 1961): 360–84.

24. William C. Foster, recorded interview by Charles T. Morrisey, August 5, 1964, 1, John F. Kennedy Library Oral History Program.

25. Adrian S. Fisher, interview, October 31, 1968, 17, Lyndon Baines Johnson Oral History Collection.

26. Lawrence Weiler, telephone interview, February 9, 2019.

27. Matthew Bunn, telephone interview, March 28, 2019.

28. Judith Reppy, telephone interview, July 16, 2019; and Cornell University Faculty Biographical files, #47-10-3394, Division of Rare and Manuscript Collections, Cornell University Library, Ithaca, NY.

29. Thomas Scoville, telephone interview, June 20, 2019.

30. Edward Teller and Allen Brown, *The Legacy of Hiroshima* (New York: Doubleday, 1962), 180.

31. Letter to the Editor, *Washington Post,* February 10, 1962.

32. James Goodby, electronic message, February 21, 2019.

33. William C. Foster, recorded interview by Charles T. Morrissey, August 5, 1964, John F. Kennedy Library Oral History Program, 31.

34. "Commencement Address at American University, Washington, D.C., June 10, 1963," John F. Kennedy Presidential Library and Museum, Boston, MA.

35. See Rudy Abramson, *Spanning the Century: The Life of W. Averell Harriman, 1891–1986* (New York: William Morrow, 1992); Walter Isaacson and Evan Thomas, *The Wise Men: Six Friends and the World They Made* (New York: Simon & Schuster, 1986); and W. Averell Harriman, *America and Russia in a Changing World: A Half Century of Personal Observation* (Garden City, NY: Doubleday, 1971).

36. See Glenn T. Seaborg with Benjamin S. Loeb, *Kennedy, Khrushchev and the Test Ban* (Berkeley: University of California Press, 1981).

37. Seaborg with Loeb, *Kennedy, Khrushchev and the Test Ban,* 242.

38. George Bunn, *Arms Control by Committee: Managing Negotiations with the Russians* (Stanford: Stanford University Press, 1992), 33.

39. William C. Foster, recorded interview by Charles T. Morrissey, August 5, 1964, John F. Kennedy Library Oral History Program, 27.

40. President John F. Kennedy and Prime Minister Macmillan to Chairman Khrushchev, April 15, 1963, Papers of John F. Kennedy, Presidential Papers, National Security Files, Box 184, "Union of Soviet Socialist Republics: Subjects, Khrushchev Correspondence, 4/15/63–5/8/63."

41. See Harold Karan Jacobson and Eric Stein, *Diplomats, Scientists, and Politicians: The United States and the Nuclear Test Ban Negotiations* (Ann Arbor: University of Michigan Press, 1966); and Seaborg with Loeb, *Kennedy, Khrushchev and the Test Ban.*

42. Adrian S. Fisher, recorded interview, May 13, 1964, John F. Kennedy Library Oral History Program, 78. Also see Foster, recorded interview, August 5, 1964, 31.

43. U.S. Congress, Senate, Committee on Armed Services, Preparedness Investigating Subcommittee, *Interim Report on the Military Implications of the Proposed Limited Nuclear Test Ban* (1963). Also see Benjamin S. Loeb, "The Limited Test Ban," in *The Politics of Arms Control Treaty Ratification,* ed. Michael Krepon and Dan Caldwell (New York: St. Martin's Press, 1991), 167–228; and Bunn, *Arms Control by Committee,* 18–49.

44. See Raymond L. Garthoff, *A Journey through the Cold War: A Memoir of Containment and Coexistence* (Washington, DC: Brookings Institution Press, 2001), 154–64; Raymond L. Garthoff, "Banning the Bomb in Outer Space," *International Security* 5, no. 3 (Winter 1980/1981): 25–40; and Ram S. Jakhu, "Evolution of the Outer Space Treaty," in *50 Years of the Outer Space Treaty: Tracing the Journey*, ed. Ajey Lele (New Delhi: Pentagon Press, 2017).

45. Jonathan Reid Hunt, "Into the Bargain: The Triumph and Tragedy of Nuclear Internationalism during the Mid-Cold War, 1958–1970," PhD diss., University of Texas at Austin, December 2013, 40.

46. Bunn, *Arms Control by Committee*, 64–75.

47. See "A Report to the President by the Committee on Nuclear Proliferation," January 21, 1965, https://nsarchive2.gwu.edu//NSAEBB/NSAEBB1/nhch7_1.htm; and Hal Brands, "Rethinking Nonproliferation: LBJ, the Gilpatric Committee, and U.S. National Security Policy," *Journal of Cold War Studies* 8, no. 2 (2006): 83–113.

48. Transcript, Adrian S. Fisher Oral History Interview II, November 7, 1968, electronic copy, LBJ Library, 24.

49. Foster, recorded interview, August 5, 1964, 38.

50. See Reid Hunt, "Into the Bargain."

51. See William C. Potter, "The Origins of US-Soviet Non-proliferation Competition," in William C. Potter and Sarah Bidgood, *Once and Future Partners: The United States, Russia and Nuclear Non-proliferation* (London: Routledge, 2018); Bunn, *Arms Control by Committee*, 59–106; Roland Popp, Liviu Horovitz, and Andreas Wenger, *Negotiating the Nuclear Non-Proliferation Treaty: Origins of the Nuclear Order* (London: Routledge, 2017); Ian Bellamy and Coit D. Blacker, eds., *The Nuclear Non-proliferation Treaty* (London: Frank Cass, 1985); Mohamed Ibrahim Shaker, *Nuclear Non-Proliferation Treaty: Origin and Implementation, 1959 to 1979* (New York: Oceana, 1980); and George Bunn and Roland M. Timerbaev, "Security Assurances to Non-Nuclear-Weapon States," *Nonproliferation Review* 1, no. 1 (Fall 1993): 11–21.

52. See John Robert Redick, "The Politics of Denuclearization: A Study of the Treaty for the Prohibition of Nuclear Weapons in Latin America," unpublished PhD diss., submitted to the University of Virginia, 1970. Also see Thomas Graham, Jr., *The Alternate Route: Nuclear-Weapon-Free Zones* (Corvallis: Oregon State University Press, 2017); and Ramesh Thakur, ed., *Nuclear Weapons-Free Zones*, (Basingstoke: Palgrave MacMillan, 1998).

CHAPTER 4

1. Aleksandr G. Savel'yev and Nicolai N. Detinov, *The Big Five, Arms Control Decision-Making in the Soviet Union* (Westport, CT: Praeger, 1995), 3–13.

2. See James Cameron, "From the Grass Roots to the Summit: The Impact of US Suburban Protest on US Missile-Defence Policy, 1968–72," *International History Review* 36, no. 2 (2014): 342–62.

3. "Text of McNamara Speech on Anti-China Missile Defense and U.S. Nuclear Strategy," *New York Times*, September 19, 1967, 18.

4. Jack Ruina, interview, "War and Peace in the Nuclear Age: At the Brink," March 4, 1986, WGBH Media Library & Archives, http://openvault.wgbh.org/catalog/V_269A8450EA2841C7B46A4132ED833FFD.

5. "Legends of the Law: A Conversation with Paul C. Warnke," District of Columbia *Bar Report,* June/July 1968, www.dcbar.org/bar-resources/publications/washington-lawyer/articles/legend-warnke.cfm.

6. "Text of McNamara Speech on Anti-China Missile Defense," 18.

7. Herbert York, *Race to Oblivion: A Participant's View of the Arms Race* (New York: Simon and Schuster, 1970), 195.

8. See Michael Charlton, *The Star Wars History—From Deterrence to Defence: The American Strategic Debate* (London: BBC, 1986).

9. McGeorge Bundy, *Danger and Survival: Choices about the Bomb in the First Fifty Years* (New York: Random House, 1988), 549.

10. Memcon of Luncheon, 23 June 1967, 13:30, Glassboro, LBJ Library, Austin, TX; and Rostow interview by John M. Clearwater, March 11, 1993, in John M. Clearwater, *Johnson, McNamara, and the Birth of SALT and the ABM Treaty, 1963–1967* (Dissertation.com, 1999).

11. Raymond L. Garthoff, *A Journey through the Cold War: A Memoir of Containment and Coexistence* (Washington, DC: Brookings Institution, 2001), 209.

12. Morton Halperin, interview, Washington, DC, February 6, 2019; and Morton H. Halperin, "The Decision to Deploy the ABM: Bureaucratic and Domestic Politics in the Johnson Administration," *World Politics* 24, no. 2 (October 1972): 62–95.

13. Robert S. McNamara, "The Dynamics of Nuclear Strategy," *Department of State Bulletin*, October 9, 1967, 443–51.

14. Richard B. Stolley, "Defense Fantasy Come True: Secretary McNamara Explains the Logic behind the New ABM System," *LIFE Magazine*, September 29, 1967, 28a–28c.

15. See Ted Greenwood, *Making the MIRV: A Study of Defense Decision Making* (Cambridge: Ballinger, 1975); and Ronald L. Tammen, *MIRV and the Arms Race: An Interpretation of Defense Strategy* (New York: Praeger, 1993).

16. See Clearwater, *Johnson, McNamara*; and Jerome H. Kahan, *Security in the Nuclear Age* (Washington, DC: Brookings Institution, 1975).

17. See James Cameron, *The Double Game: The Demise of America's First Missile Defense System and the Rise of Strategic Arms Control* (New York: Oxford University Press, 2018), 80–105; Glenn T. Seaborg with Benjamin S. Loeb, *Stemming the Tide: Arms Control in the Johnson Years* (Lexington: D.C. Heath, 1987); Clearwater, *Johnson, McNamara*; and Garthoff, *A Journey through the Cold War*, 188–220.

CHAPTER 5

1. Michael Guhin, telephone interview, February 17, 2020. Also see Jonathan B. Tucker and Erin R. Mahan, "President Nixon's Decision to Renounce the U.S. Offensive Biological Weapons Program," Center for the Study of Weapons of Mass Destruction, National Defense University, Case Study 1 (Washington, DC: National Defense University Press, October 2009); Gregory Koblentz, *Living Weapons: Biological Weapons and International Security* (Ithaca, NY: Cornell University Press, 2009); and Jonathan B. Tucker, "A Farewell to Germs: The U.S. Renunciation of Biological and Toxin Warfare, 1969–1970," *International Security* 27, no. 1 (2002): 107–48.

2. See Gerard C. Smith, *Disarming Diplomat: The Memoirs of Ambassador Gerard C. Smith, Arms Control Negotiator* (Lanham, MD: Madison Books, 1996).

3. Raymond L. Garthoff, *A Journey through the Cold War: A Memoir of Containment and Coexistence* (Washington, DC: Brookings Institution, 2001), 243; and Philip Farley, interview, "War and Peace in the Nuclear Age," WGBH Media Library & Archives, November 10, 1986, http://openvault.wgbh.org/catalog/V_B1AF905A6FC5403C81A5AD8B9085B1B1.

4. Thomas Graham Jr., *Disarmament Sketches: Three Decades of Arms Control and International Law* (Seattle: University of Washington Press, 2002), 17; and Gerard C. Smith, *Doubletalk: The Story of the First Strategic Arms Limitations Talks* (Garden City, NY: Doubleday, 1980), 370–78, 109–10.

5. See Jenny Thompson and Sherry Thompson, *The Kremlinologist: Llewellyn E. Thompson, America's Man in Cold War Moscow* (Baltimore: Johns Hopkins University Press, 2018).

6. Howard Stoertz was a board member of the Stimson Center. When the author spied a vintage copy of *The Absolute Weapon* nestled in a perfect dust jacket on his bookshelf in Herndon, Virginia, and asked to borrow it, it felt like asking for temporary possession of one of his children.

7. Aleksandr G. Savel'yev and Nicolai N. Detinov, *The Big Five, Arms Control Decision-Making in the Soviet Union* (Westport, CT: Praeger, 1995), 2, 3, 9.

8. Jonathan Haslam, *Russia's Cold War: From the October Revolution to the Fall of the Wall* (New Haven, CT: Yale University Press, 2011), 261–62.

9. Ambassador Thomas Graham Jr., Foreign Affairs Oral History Collection, Association for Diplomatic Studies and Training, October 12, 2001, 55.

10. *Documents on Disarmament—1970* (Washington, DC: United States Arms Control and Disarmament Agency, 1971), 20–33.

11. See James Cameron, *The Double Game: The Demise of America's First Missile Defense System and the Rise of Strategic Arms Control* (New York: Oxford University Press, 2018).

12. "Minutes of National Security Meeting, Document 36," June 18, 1969, *Foreign Relations of the United States*, 1969–76, vol. 34, National Security Policy, 1969–72, 139.

13. Smith, *Doubletalk*, 119.

14. Alton Frye, *A Responsible Congress: The Politics of National Security* (New York: McGraw-Hill, 1975), 47–95; and Frye, interview, Washington, DC, May 2, 2019.

15. See Anne Cahn, *Eggheads and Warheads: Scientists and the ABM* (Cambridge, MA: MIT Press, 1971); and "Strategic and Foreign Policy Implications of ABM Systems," Hearings Before the Subcommittee on International Organizations and Disarmament Affairs of the Committee on Foreign Relations, 91st Cong., 1st Sess., Part I (March 1969).

16. "ABM, MIRV, SALT and the Nuclear Arms Race," Hearings Before the Subcommittee on International Organization and Disarmament Affairs, Committee on Foreign Relations, 92nd Cong., 2d Sess. (March 1969), 344–45.

17. Graham, *Disarmament Sketches*, 3. Also see Dale Van Atta, *With Honor: Melvin Laird in War, Peace and Politics* (Madison: University of Wisconsin Press, 2008).

18. "Strategic and Foreign Policy Implications of ABM Systems," 205, 171, 262, 263.

19. "Arms Control Implications of Current Defense Budget," Hearings Before the Committee on Foreign Relations, Subcommittee on Arms Control, International Law and Organization, 92nd Cong., 1st Sess. (1971), 177.

20. "Strategic and Foreign Policy Implications of ABM Systems," 3–21.

21. Richard L. Miller, *Under the Cloud: The Decades of Nuclear Testing* (New York: Free Press, 1986), 387. Also see Ernest J. Sternglass, "The Death of All Children," *Esquire*, September 1969, 1a–1d; and Sternglass, "Infant Mortality and Nuclear Tests," *Bulletin of the Atomic Scientists* 25, no. 4 (April 1969): 18–20.

22. Richard Perle, "Commentary: Arms Race Myths vs. Strategic Competition's Reality," in *Nuclear Heuristics: Selected Writings of Albert and Roberta*

Wohlstetter, ed. Robert Zarate and Henry Sokolski (Carlisle, PA: Strategic Studies Institute, 2009), 382.

23. See Johan J. Holst and William Schneider, Jr., eds., *Why ABM? Policy Issues in the Missile Defense Controversy* (Elmsford, NY: Pergamon Press, 1969); William R. Kintner, ed., *Safeguard: Why the ABM Makes Sense* (New York: Hawthorn Books, 1969); and Abram Chayes and Jerome B. Wiesner, eds., *ABM: An Evaluation of the Decision to Deploy an Antiballistic Missile System* (New York: Harper & Row, 1969).

24. Richard L. Garwin and Hans A. Bethe, "Anti-Ballistic-Missile Systems," *Scientific American* 218, no. 3 (March 1968): 21–31; George W. Rathjens, "The Dynamics of the Arms Race," *Scientific American* 220, no. 4 (April 1969): 15–25; Herbert F. York, "Military Technology and the National Security," *Scientific American* 221, no. 2 (August 1969): 17–29; G.W. Rathjens and G.B. Kistiakowsky, "The Limitation of Strategic Arms," *Scientific American* 222, no. 1 (January 1970): 19–29; and Herbert Scoville, Jr., "The Limitation of Offensive Weapons," *Scientific American* 224, no. 1 (January 1971): 15–25.

25. D.G. Brennan, "The Case for Missile Defense," *Foreign Affairs* 47, no. 3 (April 1969): 433–48; and McGeorge Bundy, "To Cap the Volcano," *Foreign Affairs* 48, no. 1 (October 1969): 1–20.

26. Paul C. Warnke, "National Security: Are We Asking the Right Questions?" *Washington Monthly* 1, no. 9 (October 1969): 27.

27. Edward Teller, "Nearing the Moment of Truth," *National Review* 21, no. 25 (July 1, 1969): 630.

28. "Hearings Before the Committee on Armed Services," U.S. Senate, *Authorization for Military Procurement, Research and Development, Fiscal Year 1970, and Reserve Strength,* Part 2 (April 1969), 1109–456.

29. William Beecher, "Missile to Carry Warhead Cluster," *New York Times,* January 20, 1967, 1.

30. Hanson Baldwin, "Soviet Antimissile System Spurs New U.S. Weapons," *New York Times,* February 5, 1967, 1.

31. "Strategic and Foreign Policy Implications of ABM Systems," 199; and "Agreement on Limitation of Strategic Offensive Weapons," Hearings Before the Committee on Foreign Affairs, House of Representatives, 92nd Cong., 2d Sess. (1972), 80.

32. "ABM, MIRV, SALT, and the Nuclear Arms Race," Hearings Before the Subcommittee on Arms Control, International Law and Organization of the Committee on Foreign Affairs, United States Senate, 91st Cong., 2d Sess. (March–June 1970), 53.

33. "ABM, MIRV, SALT, and the Nuclear Arms Race," 91.

34. *Congressional Record,* September 24, 1971, S-33314.

35. Murrey Marder, "Israel Seen Getting Aid, No New Jets," *Washington Post,* March 22, 1970, A-1.

36. Frye, *A Responsible Congress,* 70, 82.

37. "Arms Control Implications of Current Defense Budget," Hearings Before the Subcommittee on Arms Control, International Law and Organization of the Committee on Foreign Relations, United States Senate, 92nd Cong., 1st Sess. (1971), 2, 210.

38. "ABM, MIRV, SALT, and the Nuclear Arms Race," 61.

39. "ABM, MIRV, SALT, and the Nuclear Arms Race," 9.

40. See Cameron, *The Double Game,* 107–35.

41. Graham, *Disarmament Sketches,* 42.

42. Savel'yev and Detinov, *The Big Five,* 25.

43. William G. Hyland, *Mortal Rivals: Superpower Relations from Nixon to Reagan* (New York: Random House, 1987), 43.

44. Smith, *Doubletalk*, 154.

45. "Transcript of Secretary Henry Kissinger's Background Press Briefing," December 3, 1974, in *Survival* 17, no. 4 (July 1, 1975): 191–98.

46. Richard Nixon, *RN: The Memoirs of Richard Nixon* (New York: Simon & Schuster, 1978), 524. Also see Henry Kissinger, *White House Years* (Boston: Little, Brown, 1979), especially 542–44; Smith, *Doubletalk,* 154–78; and Hyland, *Mortal Rivals*, 43.

47. Henry Kissinger, "A New Approach to Arms Control," *Time,* March 21, 1983.

48. Anatoly Dobrynin, *In Confidence: Moscow's Ambassador to America's Six Cold War Presidents* (New York: Random House, 1995), 212.

49. Raymond L. Garthoff, *Détente and Confrontation: American-Soviet Relations from Nixon to Reagan* (Washington, DC: Brookings Institution, 1985), 137–41, 139n34.

50. Smith, *Doubletalk,* 173–74.

51. Savel'yev and Detinov, *The Big Five,* 8.

52. Richard M. Nixon, *The Real War* (New York: Warner Books, 1980), 253–55.

53. See Thomas C. Schelling, *The Strategy of Conflict* (New York: Oxford University Press, 1963), 188.

54. See William Burr and Jeffrey P. Kimball, *Nixon's Nuclear Specter: The Secret Alert of 1969, Madman Diplomacy, and the Vietnam War* (Lawrence: University Press of Kansas, 2015).

55. See Strobe Talbott, *The Master of the Game: Paul Nitze and the Nuclear Peace* (New York: Alfred A. Knopf, 1988); and Paul H. Nitze, *From Hiroshima to Glasnost: At the Center of Decision* (New York: Grove Weidenfeld, 1989).

56. "Address by President Nixon to the Congress, June 1, 1972," *Documents on Disarmament—1972* (Washington, DC: United States Arms Control and Disarmament Agency, 1974), 254; and Bernard Gwertzman, "Nixon Flies Home and Tells Nation of Summit Gains," *New York Times,* June 2, 1972, 1.

57. Dr. Henry Kissinger, "Congressional Briefing on the Strategic Arms Limitation Treaty and Agreement," June 15, 1972, *Weekly Compilation of Presidential Documents*, vols. 1–8 (January–June 1972), 1049.

58. "Strategic Arms Limitation Agreements," Hearings Before the Committee on Foreign Relations, United States Senate, 92nd Cong., 2d Sess. (1972), 5, 27.

59. "Congressional Briefing on SALT I in the State Dining Room, June 15, 1972," *Documents on Disarmament—1972* (Washington, DC: United States Arms Control and Disarmament Agency, 1974), 304.

60. William R. Van Cleave, "Implications of Success or Failure of SALT," in *SALT: Implications for Arms Control in the 1970s,* ed. William R. Kintner and Robert L. Pfaltzgraff, Jr. (Pittsburg: University of Pittsburgh Press, 1973), 322.

61. "Agreement on Limitation of Strategic Offensive Weapons," Hearings Before the Committee on Foreign Affairs, House of Representatives, 92nd Cong., 2d Sess. (1972), 93.

62. Smith, *Doubletalk,* 332; and Garthoff, *Détente and Confrontation,* 168.

63. Smith, *Doubletalk,* 99.

64. See testimony of Secretary of Defense Melvin Laird, "Military Implications of the Treaty on the Limitation of Anti-Ballistic Missile Systems and the Interim Agreement on Limitation of Strategic Offensive Arms," Hearings Before the Committee on Armed Services, U.S. Senate, 92nd Cong., 2d Sess. (1972), 165;

and testimony of SALT Ambassador Gerard Smith, "Military Implications of the Treaty on the Limitation of Anti-Ballistic Missile Systems and the Interim Agreement on Limitation of Strategic Offensive Arms," Hearings Before the Committee on Armed Services, U.S. Senate, 92nd Cong., 2d Sess. (1972), 364.

65. Graham, *Disarmament Sketches,* 47.

66. Nitze, *From Hiroshima to Glasnost,* 249; and Smith, *Doubletalk,* 156.

67. Richard M. Nixon, *RN: The Memoirs of Richard Nixon* (New York: Grosset & Dunlap, 1978), 388.

68. Smith, *Doubletalk,* 225; and Nitze, *From Hiroshima to Glasnost,* 304.

69. Smith, *Disarming Diplomat,* 177.

70. Glenn T. Seaborg with Benjamin S. Loeb, *The Atomic Energy Commission under Nixon: Adjusting to Troubled Times* (New York: St. Martin's Press, 1993), 83.

71. "Military Implications of the Treaty on the Limitation of Anti-Ballistic Missile Systems and the Interim Agreement on Limitation of Strategic Offensive Arms," Hearings Before the Committee on Armed Services, U.S. Senate, 92nd Cong., 2d Sess. (1972), 3.

72. "Strategic Arms Limitation Agreements," Hearings Before the Committee on Foreign Relations (1972), 60, 1.

73. William J. Perry, *My Journey at the Nuclear Brink* (Stanford: Stanford University Press, 2015), 54.

74. Paul H. Nitze, "Limited Wars or Massive Retaliation?," review of *Nuclear Weapons and Foreign Policy* by Henry A. Kissinger, *The Reporter,* September 5, 1957, 40–41.

75. Foreign Relations of the United States, 1969–1976, "SALT I, 1969–1972," vol. 32 (Washington, DC: U.S. Government Printing Office, 2010).

76. Foreign Relations of the United States, 1969–1976, "SALT I, 1969–1972," vol. 32 (Washington, DC: U.S. Government Printing Office, 2010), 453.

77. Dobrynin, *In Confidence,* 200.

78. Nitze, *From Hiroshima to Glasnost,* 340.

79. *Strategic Arms Limitation Agreements,* Hearings Before the Committee on Foreign Relations, U.S. Senate, 92nd Cong., 2d Sess. (1972), 66.

80. "American-Soviet Agreement of the Prevention of Nuclear War, June 22, 1973," *Weekly Compilation of Presidential Documents* 9, no. 25 (June 25, 1973): 822, and "Agreement Between the United States of America and the Union of Soviet Socialist Republics on Measures to Improve USA-USSR Direct Communications Link, September 30, 1971," *Documents on Disarmament—1971* (Washington, DC: U.S. Government Printing Office, 1972), 635–39.

81. Hyland, *Mortal Rivals,* 53–54.

82. Smith, *Doubletalk,* 454–55.

83. Henry Kissinger, *Years of Upheaval* (Boston: Little, Brown, 1982), 256.

84. John Newhouse, *Cold Dawn: The Story of SALT* (New York: Holt, Rinehart and Winston, 1973), 269.

CHAPTER 6

1. Gerard C. Smith, *Doubletalk: The Story of the First Strategic Arms Limitations Talks* (Garden City, NY: Doubleday, 1980), 444.

2. Smith, *Doubletalk,* 441–46.

3. U. Alexis Johnson: *The Right Hand of Power: The Memoirs of an American Diplomat* (Englewood Cliffs, NJ: Prentice-Hall, 1984), 603–4.

4. See National Security Decision Memorandum 197, November 18, 1972, in "SALT II, 1972–1980," *Foreign Relations of the United States, 1969–1976,* vol. 33 (Washington, DC: U.S. Government Printing Office, 2013), 30–33.

5. See National Security Decision Memorandum 213, May 3, 1973, in "SALT II, 1972–1980," *Foreign Relations of the United States, 1969–1976*, 78–80.

6. See National Security Decision Memorandum 213, May 3, 1973, in "SALT II, 1972–1980," *Foreign Relations of the United States, 1969–1976*, 78–80.

7. Raymond L. Garthoff, *Détente and Confrontation: American-Soviet Relations from Nixon to Reagan* (Washington, DC: Brookings Institution, 1985), 328–29.

8. "SALT II, 1972–1980," *Foreign Relations of the United States, 1969–1976*, 83; and Johnson, *The Right Hand of Power*, 591, 582–91. Also see Garthoff, *Détente and Confrontation*, 327–28; and Paul H. Nitze, *From Hiroshima to Glasnost: At the Center of Decision* (New York: Grove Weidenfeld, 1989), 335–36.

9. Arkady N. Shevchenko, *Breaking with Moscow* (New York: Alfred A. Knopf, 1985), 303.

10. See Alexander L. George, "The Basic Principles Agreement on 1972: Origins and Expectations," in Alexander L. George, *Managing U.S.-Soviet Rivalry: Problems of Crisis Prevention* (Boulder, CO: Westview Press, 1983), 107–18.

11. "American-Soviet Agreement on the Prevention of Nuclear War, June 22, 1973," *Documents on Disarmament—1973* (Washington, DC: U.S. Arms Control and Disarmament Agency, 1975), 283.

12. Garthoff, *Détente and Confrontation*, 338.

13. "SALT II, 1972–1980," *Foreign Relations of the United States, 1969–1976*, 118.

14. "SALT II, 1972–1980," *Foreign Relations of the United States, 1969–1976*, 175.

15. Edward Ifft, telephone interview, February 17, 2020.

16. See Edward Ifft, "The Threshold Test Ban Treaty," *Arms Control Today* 39, no. 2 (March 2009): 55–59; and Jan Lodal, interview, McLean, VA, February 12, 2020.

17. Ambassador Thomas Graham Jr., recorded interview, Foreign Affairs Oral History Collection, Association for Diplomatic Studies and Training, Arlington, Virginia (October 12, 2001), 54.

18. "News Conference in Moscow, July 3, *Department of State Bulletin* (July 29, 1974), 215.

CHAPTER 7

1. See James Cannon, *Gerald R. Ford: An Honorable Life* (Ann Arbor: University of Michigan Press, 2013).

2. "Memorandum from the President's Assistant for National Security Affairs (Kissinger) to President Ford," October 18, 1974, "SALT II, 1972–1980," *Foreign Relations of the United States, 1969–1976*, 342–48.

3. U. Alexis Johnson: *The Right Hand of Power: The Memoirs of an American Diplomat* (Englewood Cliffs, NJ: Prentice-Hall, 1984), 605.

4. "Minutes of a Meeting of the National Security Council," December 2, 1974, October 18, 1974, "SALT II, 1972–1980," *Foreign Relations of the United States, 1969–1976*, 393.

5. Johnson, *The Right Hand of Power*, 606.

6. Johnson, *The Right Hand of Power*, 614.

7. "Minutes of a Meeting of the National Security Council," October 18, 1974, "SALT II, 1972–1980," *Foreign Relations of the United States, 1969–1976*, 349–67.

8. See Robert J. Pranger and Roger P. Labrie, eds., *Nuclear Strategy and National Security: Points of View* (Washington, DC: American Enterprise Institute Press, 1977), 396–415.

9. Henry Kissinger, *Years of Upheaval* (Boston: Little, Brown, 1982), 1173.

10. See "Jackson Offers Plan for Nuclear Arms Cut," *Washington Post*, March 27, 1975; and "Nonproliferation Issues," Hearings Before the Subcommittee on Arms Control, International Organizations and Security Agreements, Committee on Foreign Relations (1975), 14–15, 78.

11. Paul H. Nitze, "Assuring Strategic Stability in an Era of Détente," *Foreign Affairs* 54, no. 2 (January 1976): 187, 201.

12. Raymond L. Garthoff, *Détente and Confrontation: American-Soviet Relations from Nixon to Reagan* (Washington, DC: Brookings Institution, 1985), 446.

13. Gerard C. Smith, "SALT after Vladivostok," *Journal of International Affairs* 29, no. 1 (Spring 1975): 7–18.

14. Minutes of a Meeting of the National Security Council, September 17, 1975, "SALT II, 1972–1980," *Foreign Relations of the United States, 1969–1976*, 468.

15. Nitze, "Assuring Strategic Stability," 211, 216–17.

16. Testimony of Richard Perle, "The Role of Arms Control in U.S. Defense Policy," Hearings Before the Committee on Foreign Affairs, U.S. House of Representatives, 98th Cong., 2d Sess. (1984), 48.

17. Remarks of James Schlesinger to the Overseas Writers Club, January 10, 1974, reprinted in *Survival* 16, no. 2 (1974): 86–90. Also see *Report of Secretary of Defense James R. Schlesinger to the Congress on the FY 1975 Budget and FY 1975–1979 Defense Program, March 4, 1974* (Washington, DC: U.S. Government Printing Office, 1974), 4.

18. Testimony on March 4, 1974 in "U.S.-USSR Strategic Policies," Hearings Before the Subcommittee on Arms Control, International Law and Organization, Committee on Foreign Relations, U.S. Senate, 93rd Cong., 2d Sess. (1974), 10.

19. "Hearing on U.S.-U.S.S.R. Strategic Policies," 7.

20. "Interview with General George Brown," *U.S. News and World Report*, February 25, 1974, 63.

21. Alan Platt, interview, Washington, DC, June 11, 2019; and Alan Platt, *The U.S. Senate and Strategic Arms Policy, 1969–1977* (Boulder, CO: Westview Press, 1978), 84–85.

22. *Congressional Record*, June 4, 1975, S9623.

23. *Congressional Record*, June 10, 1974, S18486.

24. See Donald Mackenzie, *Inventing Accuracy: A Historical Sociology of Missile Guidance* (Cambridge, MA: MIT Press, 1990); Alton Frye, *A Responsible Congress*, 91–95; Wolfe, *The SALT Experience*, 136–53; and Platt, *The U.S. Senate and Strategic Arms Policy*, 71–97.

25. "Memorandum of Conversation," September 19, 1975, "SALT II, 1972–1980," *Foreign Relations of the United States, 1969–1976*, 482–87.

26. Henry Kissinger, *Years of Renewal* (New York: Simon and Schuster, 1999), 301.

27. Kissinger, *Years of Renewal*, 302.

28. "U.S. Intelligence Agencies and Activities: Risks and Control of Foreign Intelligence," Hearings Before the Select Committee on Intelligence, U.S. House of Representatives, 94th Cong., 1st Sess., Part 5 (1975), 1622. Also see Elmo R. Zumwalt, Jr., *On Watch: A Memoir* (New York: Quadrangle Books, 1976).

29. Johnson, *The Right Hand of Power*, 536–37.

30. Melvin Laird, "Is This Détente?" *Readers Digest*, July 1975, 54–57.

CHAPTER 8

1. See Jonathan Alter, *His Very Best: Jimmy Carter, A Life* (New York: Simon & Schuster, 2020); and Stuart E. Eizenstat, *Jimmy Carter: The White House Years* (New York: Thomas Dunne Books, 2018).

2. See Justin Vaisse, *Zbigniew Brzezinski: America's Grand Strategist* (Cambridge, MA: Harvard University Press, 2018).

3. Walter Slocombe, telephone interview, July 10, 2019.

4. William Perry, interview, Palo Alto, CA, May 29, 2019. Also see William J. Perry, *My Journey at the Nuclear Brink* (Stanford: Stanford University Press, 2015).

5. See David S. McLellan, *Cyrus Vance* (Totowa, NJ: Rowman & Allanheld, 1985).

6. Strobe Talbott, *Endgame: The Inside Story of SALT II* (New York: Harper & Row, 1980), 39.

7. See Paul H. Nitze, "Atoms, Strategy and Policy," *Foreign Affairs* 35, no. 2 (January 1956): 187–98.

8. See *An Evolving US Nuclear Posture*, Steering Committee of the Project on Eliminating Weapons of Mass Destruction, Report no. 19 (Washington, DC: Henry L. Stimson Center, 1995); and Paul H. Nitze, "A Threat Mostly to Ourselves," *New York Times*, October 28, 1999.

9. See Albert Wohlstetter, "Is There a Strategic Arms Race?" *Foreign Policy, no.* 15 (Summer 1974): 3–20.

10. Paul Warnke, "Apes on a Treadmill, *Foreign Policy,* no. 18 (Spring 1975): 12–29. Also see Paul Sommer Warnke, "Conflicting Views of the U.S.-Strategic Competition: Tracing the Warnke-Wohlstetter Debate across the Pages of *Foreign Policy,*" master's thesis, Middlebury Institute of International Studies, December 14, 2018.

11. Nicholas Thompson, *The Hawk and the Dove: Paul Nitze, George Kennan, and the History of the Cold War* (New York: Henry Holt, 2009), 265.

12. Barry Blechman, interview, Washington, DC, May 15, 2019.

13. Paul H. Nitze, *From Hiroshima to Glasnost: At the Center of Decision* (New York: Grove Weidenfeld, 1989), 345.

14. Blechman, interview, May 15, 2019.

15. Alton Frye, interview, Washington, DC, May 2, 2019.

16. United States Senate, Committee on Armed Services, "Consideration of Mr. Paul C. Warnke to be Director of the U.S. Arms Control and Disarmament Agency and Ambassador," Hearings, February 22–28, 1977, 95th Cong., 1st Sess. (Washington, DC: U.S. Government Printing Office, 1977), 206, 186, 183.

17. Thompson, *The Hawk and the Dove,* 265–66; Stephen Warnke, interview, Washington, DC, April 15, 2019.

18. Interview with Paul C. Warnke, Oral History Project, United States Courts, Historical Society of the District of Columbia Circuit, 63.

19. Nitze, *From Hiroshima to Glasnost,* 355.

20. See Oral History Project, United States Courts, Historical Society of the District of Columbia Circuit; Interview with Paul C. Warnke, "Legends in the Law: A Conversation with Paul C. Warnke," *District of Columbia Bar Report*, June/July 1998; Oral History interview with Paul Warnke, Lyndon Baines Johnson Presidential Library; Stephen Warnke, interview, Washington, DC, April 15, 2019.

21. Raymond L. Garthoff, *Détente and Confrontation: American-Soviet Relations from Nixon to Reagan* (Washington, DC: Brookings Institution, 1985), 563.

22. See Cyrus Vance, *Hard Choices: Critical Years in America's Foreign Policy* (New York: Simon and Schuster, 1983), 48; and Garthoff, *Détente and Confrontation*, 801–7.

23. Leslie Gelb, telephone interview, July 1, 2019; Jimmy Carter, *Keeping Faith: Memoirs of a President* (New York: Bantam Books, 1982), 216–19; and Garthoff, *Détente and Confrontation*, 801–7.

24. See Albert Wohlstetter, "Is There a Strategic Arms Race?" *Foreign Policy*, no. 15 (Summer 1974): 3–20. Also see Ann Hessing Cahn, *Killing Détente: The Right Attacks the CIA* (University Park: Pennsylvania State University, 1988).

25. Richard Pipes, "Why the Soviet Union Thinks It Could Fight and Win a Nuclear War," *Commentary* 74, no. 1 (July 1977): 21; Nitze, "Atoms, Strategy and Policy," 189–90; and Paul H. Nitze, "Assuring Strategic Stability in an Era of Détente," *Foreign Affairs* 54, no. 2 (January 1976): 211–12.

26. Pipes, "Why the Soviet Union Thinks It Could Fight," 26–30.

27. University of Washington Manuscript Collection, Henry M. Jackson, Accession #3560–6, Box 12, Folder 113.

28. "Memorandum from the President's Assistant for National Security Affairs (Brzezinski) to President Cater," March 18, 1977, "SALT II, 1972–1980," *Foreign Relations of the United States, 1969–1976*, 665–72.

29. "Presidential Directive/NSC-7," March 23, 1977, "SALT II, 1972–1980," *Foreign Relations of the United States, 1969–1976*, 684–86. Also see Zbigniew Brzezinski, *Power and Principle: Memoirs of the National Security Adviser, 1977–1981* (New York: Farrar, Straus, Giroux, 1983), 156–64.

30. Talbott, *Endgame*, 61.

31. Ambassador Thomas Graham Jr., recorded interview by Charles Stuart Kennedy, Foreign Affairs Oral History Collection, Association for Diplomatic Studies and Training, Arlington, VA, April 24, 2002, 70.

32. "Presidential Directive/NSC-7," March 23, 1977, "*SALT II, 1972–1980,*" *Foreign Relations of the United States, 1969–1976*, 684–86.

33. Carter, *Keeping Faith*, 218–19.

34. Transcript, "Legends in the Law: Paul C. Warnke," District of Columbia Bar Report, June/July 1998, www.dcbar.org/bar-resources/publications/washington-lawyer/articles/legend-warnke.cfm.

35. "Memorandum From Secretary of State Vance and the Director of the Arms Control and Disarmament Agency (Warnke) to President Carter," August 30, 1977, "SALT II, 1972–1980," *Foreign Relations of the United States, 1969–1976*, 742.

36. Vance, *Hard Choices*, 57–58.

37. See Richard Burt, "Neutron Bomb Controversy Strained Alliance and Caused Splits in the Administration," *New York Times*, April 9, 1978, 18; "The Heated Debate over the Neutron Bomb," *Washington Post*, March 31, 1978, A19; and Sherri L. Wasserman, *The Neutron Bomb Controversy: A Study in Alliance Politics* (New York: Praeger Books, 1983).

38. "Telegram from Secretary of State Vance to the Department of State," April 20, 1978, "SALT II, 1972–1980," *Foreign Relations of the United States, 1969–1976*, 826.

39. "Memorandum from the President's Assistant for National Security Affairs (Brzezinski) to President Carter," November 16, 1977, "SALT II, 1972–1980," *Foreign Relations of the United States, 1969–1976*, 795–96.

40. "Memorandum from Secretary of Defense Brown to President Carter," January 6, 1978, "SALT II, 1972–1980," *Foreign Relations of the United States, 1969–1976*, 798–805.

41. Vance, *Hard Choices,* 37.

42. See Paul C. Warnke, "The Domestic Politics of Arms Control," Center for International and Strategic Affairs, University of California at Los Angeles, CISA Working Paper no. 60, undated, unpublished paper, 9–10. Also see George D. Moffett, *The Limits of Victory: The Ratification of the Panama Canal Treaties* (Ithaca, NY: Cornell University Press, 1985); and Michael Krepon and Dan Caldwell, eds., *The Politics of Arms Control Treaty Ratification* (New York: St. Martin's Press, 1991).

43. Bill Prochnau, "Mormon Church Joins Opposition To MX Program," *Washington Post,* May 6, 1981, A1. Also see *MX Missile Basing* (Washington, DC: U.S. Office of Technology Assessment, September 1981); Herbert Scoville, Jr., *MX: Prescription for Disaster* (Cambridge, MA: MIT Press, 1981); and J.G. Barlow, *Insuring Survivability: Basing the MX Missile* (Washington, DC: Heritage Foundation, 1980).

44. Walter Slocombe, telephone interview, July 10, 2019.

45. Perry, *My Journey at the Nuclear Brink,* 50.

46. "Memorandum from Secretary of Defense Brown to President Carter," August 3, 1978, "SALT II, 1972–1980," *Foreign Relations of the United States, 1969–1976,* 862.

47. Brent Scowcroft et al., "Report of the President's Commission on Strategic Forces," April 6, 1983 (Washington, DC: U.S. Government Printing Office, 1983), www.cia.gov/library/readingroom/docs/CIA-RDP85M00364R001101620009-5 .pdf.

48. "Memorandum of Conversation, Document 210," September 12, 1978, *Foreign Relations of the United States, 1969–1976,* vol. 33, SALT II, 1972–1980, 869.

49. "Hearings on the Military Implications of the Treaty on the Limitation of Strategic Offensive Arms and Protocol Thereto (SALT II Treaty)," Part 1, U.S. Senate, Committee on Armed Services, 96th Cong., 1st Sess. (1979), 155.

50. "Memorandum of Conversation," September 2, 1978, "SALT II, 1972–1980," *Foreign Relations of the United States, 1969–1976,* 869, 870.

51. Zbigniew Brzezinski, *Power and Principle: Memoirs of the National Security Adviser, 1977–1981* (New York: Farrar, Straus, Giroux, 1983), 337–38.

52. Leslie Gelb, telephone interview, July 1, 2019.

53. Thomas Graham Jr., interview, Association for Diplomatic Studies and Training Foreign Affairs Oral History Project, March 25, 2013, 91–92.

54. Johnson, *The Right Hand of Power,* 622.

55. Paul H. Nitze, "Is SALT II a Fair Deal for the United States?," May 16, 1979, reproduced in part in *SALT Handbook: Key Documents and Issues, 1972–1979, ed. Roger P. Labrie* (Washington, DC: American Enterprise Institute for Public Policy Research, 1979), 667–74.

56. "Documentation," *International Security* 1, no. 1 (Summer 1976): 183.

57. American Security Council, *An Analysis of SALT II* (Boston: Coalition for Peace through Strength, 1979), reprinted in *SALT Handbook: Key Documents and Issues, 1972–1979,* 674–85.

58. "Statement of the Board of Directors on the SALT II Agreements," June 18, 1979, in *SALT Handbook: Key Documents and Issues, 1972–1979,* 685–95.

59. See Dan Caldwell, *The Dynamics of Domestic Politics and Arms Control: The SALT II Treaty Ratification Debate* (Columbia: University of South Carolina Press, 1991).

60. "The SALT II Treaty," Hearings Before the Committee on Foreign Relations, U.S. Senate, 96th Cong., 1st Sess., Part 2 (1979), 20, 31.

61. Gelb, telephone interview, July 1, 2019.

62. "The SALT II Treaty," Hearings Before the Committee on Foreign Relations, U.S. Senate, 96th Cong., 1st Sess., Part 1 (1979), 88, 93, 302, 373–74, 436, 438.

63. "The SALT II Treaty," Hearings Before the Committee on Foreign Relations, U.S. Senate, 96th Cong., 1st Sess., Part 4 (1979), 2, 233, 346–47.

64. "The SALT II Treaty," Hearings Before the Committee on Foreign Relations, U.S. Senate, 96th Cong., 1st session, Part 3 (1979), 152, 153, 156.

65. "Military Implications of the Treaty on the Limitation of Strategic Offensive Arms and Protocol Thereto," Hearings Before the Committee on Armed Services, U.S. Senate, 96th Cong., 1st Sess., Part 3 (1979), 1116, 1086, 1259.

66. "The SALT II Treaty," Report of the Committee on Foreign Relations, U.S. Senate, Together with Supplemental and Minority Views (November 19, 1979), 455.

67. "The Military Implications of the SALT II Treaty," Report of the Armed Services Committee, U.S. Senate, 96th Cong., 1st Sess. (December 20, 1979), 19.

68. Robert G. Kaiser, "Senate Committee Says SALT Not in America's Best Interest," *Washington Post,* December 21, 1979, A3.

69. Ralph Earle II, interview, Association for Diplomatic Studies and Training Foreign Affairs Oral History Project, February 1, 1991, 38.

70. Talbott, *Endgame,* 279.

71. "Hearings on the Military Implications of the Treaty on the Limitation of Strategic Offensive Arms and Protocol Thereto (SALT II Treaty)," Part 1, U.S. Senate, Committee on Armed Services, 96th Cong., 1st Sess. (1979), 155.

72. See Thomas W. Wolfe, *The SALT Experience* (Cambridge, MA: Ballinger, 1979), 244.

73. Garthoff, *Détente and Confrontation,* 824.

74. Brzezinski, *Power and Principle,* 3.

75. Slocombe, telephone interview, July 10, 2019.

76. Carter, *Keeping Faith,* 265.

77. Wolfe, *The SALT Experience,* 243.

CHAPTER 9

1. Edmund Morris, *Dutch: A Memoir of Ronald Reagan* (New York: Random House, 1999).

2. George Shultz, interview, Stanford, CA, May 28, 2019.

3. Arthur M. Schlesinger, Jr., "Foreign Policy and the American Character," *Foreign Affairs* 61, no. 1 (Fall 1983): 5–6.

4. Pat Buchanan, "Has Conservative Hour Passed?" *Human Events* 44, no. 1 (January 2, 1988).

5. Kenneth Adelman, *The Great Universal Embrace: A Skeptic's Guide to the Politics of Disarmament* (New York: Simon and Schuster, 1989), 295.

6. Kenneth Adelman, *Reagan at Reykjavik: Forty-Eight Hours That Ended the Cold War* (New York: Harper Collins, 2014).

7. Strobe Talbott, *The Master of the Game: Paul Nitze and the Nuclear Peace* (New York: Alfred A. Knopf, 1988), 18.

8. Raymond Garthoff, *The Great Transition: American Soviet Relations and the End of the Cold War* (Washington, DC: Brookings Institution Press, 1994), 759.

9. See Paul Lettow, *Ronald Reagan and His Quest to Abolish Nuclear Weapons* (New York: Random House, 2006); and Martin and Annelise Anderson, *Reagan's Secret War: The Untold Story of His Fight to Save the World from Nuclear Disaster* (New York: Crown Books, 2009)

10. See Jack F. Matlock, Jr., *Reagan and Gorbachev: How the Cold War Ended* (New York: Random House, 2005). Also see Don Oberdorfer, *The Turn: From the Cold War to a New Era—The United States and the Soviet Union, 1983–1990* (New York: Poseidon Press, 1991).

11. Kenneth Adelman, interview, Rosslyn, VA, November 7, 2019.

12. Quoted in Morris, *Dutch*, 616.

13. Alexander Haig, *Caveat: Realism, Reagan and Foreign Policy* (New York: Macmillan, 1984), 85; Adelman, *The Great Universal Embrace*, 27; David Stockman, *The Triumph of Politics: Why the Reagan Revolution Failed* (New York: Harper & Row, 1986), 435; and Peggy Noonan, *What I Saw at the Revolution: A Political Life in the Reagan Era* (New York: Ballantine Books, 1991), 277.

14. Lewis Dunn, electronic communication, September 2, 2019.

15. Mikhail Gorbachev, *Memoirs* (New York: Doubleday, 1996), 568.

16. See Matlock, *Reagan and Gorbachev*, 319.

17. Shultz, interview, May 28, 2019.

18. Gorbachev, *Memoirs*, 524, 526.

19. Matlock, *Reagan and Gorbachev*, 106–8.

20. Pavel Palazchenko, *My Years with Gorbachev and Shevardnadze: The Memoir of a Soviet Interpreter* (University Park: Pennsylvania State University Press, 1997), 28.

21. See Richard M. Nixon and Henry A. Kissinger, "An Arms Agreement—on Two Conditions; The Former President and the Former Secretary of State Offer Their Advice," *Washington Post*, April 26, 1987, D7.

22. James A. Baker, III, *The Politics of Diplomacy: Revolution, War and Peace, 1989–1992* (New York: G.P. Putnam's Sons, 1995), 26.

23. Paul H. Nitze, *From Hiroshima to Glasnost: At the Center of Decision— A Memoir* (New York: Grove Weidenfeld, 1989), ix.

24. Caspar Weinberger, *Fighting for Peace: Seven Critical Years in the Pentagon* (New York: Warner Books, 1990), 29.

25. Shultz, interview, May 28, 2019.

26. Richard Burt, interview, Washington, DC, September 5, 2019.

27. Hedrick Smith, "Reagan Putting His Stamp on U.S. Policies: At Home and Abroad, a Change of Course," *New York Times*, January 30, 1981, A11.

28. Adelman, interview, November 7, 2019; and Kenneth Adelman, "Sell Hard, Take Risks," *The Washingtonian*, September 1986, 129.

29. Kenneth Adelman, electronic communication, November 11, 2019; and Thomas Graham, Jr., *Disarmament Sketches: Three Decades of Arms Control and International Law* (Seattle: University of Washington Press, 2002), 102–3.

30. Anatoly Dobrynin, *In Confidence: Moscow's Ambassador to America's Six Cold War Presidents* (New York: Random House, 1995), 432.

31. Cyrus Vance, *Hard Choices: Critical Years in America's Foreign Policy* (New York: Simon and Schuster, 1983), 18–19.

32. "Minutes of a National Security Council Meeting," *Foreign Relations of the United States, 1981–1988*, vol. 3, Soviet Union, January 1981–January 1983 (Washington, DC: U.S. Government Printing Office, 2016), February 6, 1981, 39.

33. Jack Mendelsohn, Association for Diplomatic Studies and Training Foreign Affairs Oral History Project, February 12, 1997, 108.

34. Talbott, *The Master of the Game*, 164.

35. U. Alexis Johnson: *The Right Hand of Power: The Memoirs of an American Diplomat* (Englewood Cliffs, NJ: Prentice-Hall, 1984), 609.

36. Richard Halloran, "Pentagon Draws Up First Strategy for Fighting a Long Nuclear War," *New York Times*, May 30, 1982, 1, 12; and George C. Wilson,

"Preparing for Long War Is Waste of Funds, Gen. Jones Says," *Washington Post,* June 19, 1982, A3.

37. Richard Halloran, "Weinberger Defends His Plan on a Protracted Nuclear War," *New York Times,* August 10, 1982, A8.

38. Robert Scheer, "U.S. Could Survive War in Administration's View," *Los Angeles Times,* January 16, 1982, A1.

39. Linda Charlton, "Groups Favoring Strong Defense Making Gains in Public Acceptance," *New York Times,* April 4, 1977, 50.

40. John Woodworth, interview, Batesville, VA, June 6, 2019; Richard Burt, interview, Washington, DC, September 5, 2019. Also see Thomas Graham Jr., *Disarmament Sketches: Three Decades of Arms Control and International Law* (Seattle: University of Washington Press, 2002), 106–11; Maynard W. Glitman, *The Last Battle of the Cold War: An Inside Account of Negotiating the Intermediate-Range Nuclear Forces Treaty* (New York: Palgrave Macmillan, 2006), 54–56; Nitze, *From Hiroshima to Glasnost,* 366–70; and Strobe Talbott, *Deadly Gambits: The Reagan Administration and the Stalemate in Nuclear Arms Control* (New York: Alfred A. Knopf, 1984), 43–70.

41. "Memorandum of Conversation," *Foreign Relations of the United States, 1981–1988,* vol. 3, Soviet Union, January 1981–January 1983, 276.

42. Paul C. Warnke, "'Zero' May Mean Nothing," *New York Times,* January 26, 1983, A23.

43. Herbert Scoville, Jr., "Poor Record on Arms," *New York Times,* February 12, 1984, D19.

44. "A Cop-Out Solution?" *Wall Street Journal,* March 28, 1983, 22.

45. "Missiles, Resisting the Pressure," *Los Angeles Times,* March 15, 1981, Part IV, 4.

46. Nitze, *From Hiroshima to Glasnost,* 374.

47. John Woodworth, interview, Batesville, VA, June 14, 2019.

48. Maynard W. Glitman, *The Last Battle of the Cold War: An Inside Account of Negotiating the Intermediate-Range Nuclear Forces Treaty* (New York: Palgrave Macmillan, 2006), 13.

49. Glitman, *Last Battle of the Cold War,* 65.

50. Garthoff, *The Great Transition,* 513. Also see Talbott, *Deadly Gambits,* 231–76.

51. Dobrynin, *In Confidence,* 486.

52. Judith Reppy, telephone interview, July 16, 2019; and Lynn Eden, "Randy Forsberg in Our Time," paper presented at a conference at Cornell University, September 14, 2018. Also see Randall Caroline Watson Forsberg, *Towards a Theory of Peace: The Role of Moral Beliefs* (Ithaca, NY: Cornell University Press, 2019).

53. Reppy, telephone interview, July 16, 2019.

54. "Calling for a Mutual and Verifiable Freeze on and Reductions in Nuclear Weapons," Hearings and Markup before the Committee on Foreign Affairs, U.S. House of Representatives, 98th Cong., 1st Sess. (1982), 20.

55. "Nuclear Arms Reduction Proposals," Hearings Before the Committee on Foreign Relations, U.S. Senate, 97th Cong., 2d Sess. (1982), 294.

56. "Nuclear Arms Reduction Proposals," 106.

57. Margot Hornblower, "Alternate A-Freeze Plan Passes: House Approves Reagan-Backed Bill, 204 to 202; House Passes Reagan Plan for A-Freeze," *Washington Post,* August 6, 1982, A1. Also see Randall Forsberg, Alton Frye, and Federation of American Scientists, *Seeds of Promise: The First Real Hearings on the Nuclear Arms Freeze* (Andover, MA: Brick House, 1983); and Douglas C. Waller,

Congress and the Nuclear Freeze: An Inside Look at the Politics of a Mass Movement (Amherst, MA: University of Massachusetts Press, 1987).

58. Nitze, *From Hiroshima to Glasnost,* 375–86; Glitman, *Last Battle of the Cold War,* 73–79; Woodworth, interview, June 14, 2019.

59. Nitze, *From Hiroshima to Glasnost,* 375.

60. Glitman, *Last Battle of the Cold War,* 76.

61. Burt, interview, September 5, 2019.

62. Talbott, *Deadly Gambits,* 54.

63. Weinberger, *Fighting for Peace,* 344.

64. Talbott, *Deadly Gambits,* 136.

65. Nitze, *From Hiroshima to Glasnost,* 387–88; and Talbott, *Deadly Gambits,* 116–61.

66. George P. Shultz, *Turmoil and Triumph: My Years as Secretary of State* (New York: Charles Scribner's Sons, 1993), 271.

67. Shultz, interview, May 28, 2019.

68. Presentation at the World Affairs Council at the Cosmos, Club, Washington, DC, March 1, 1983.

69. See McGeorge Bundy, "Maintaining Stable Deterrence," *International Security* 3, no. 3 (Winter 1978–79), 6.

70. Henry Kissinger, "The Future of NATO," in *NATO, The Next Thirty Years: The Changing Political, Economic, and Military Setting, ed.* Kenneth Myers (Boulder, CO: Westview Press, 1980), 4.

71. Ben Fischer, *A Cold War Conundrum: The 1983 Soviet War Scare* (Washington, DC: Central Intelligence Agency, 1997), 3.

72. See, for example, International Institute for Strategic Studies (IISS), *The Military Balance, 1983–84* (IISS: London, 1983); Robert S. Norris and Thomas B. Cochran, *U.S.-U.S.S.R. Strategic Offensive Forces, 1946–1989* (Washington, DC: Natural Resources Defense Council, 1990); and Central Intelligence Agency, Office of Soviet Analysis, USSR: Economic Trends and Policy Developments, Joint Economic Committee Briefing Paper (September 14, 1983).

73. Dobrynin, *In Confidence,* 611.

74. Robert M. Gates, *From the Shadows: The Ultimate Insider's Story of Five Presidents and How the West Won the Cold War* (New York: Simon & Schuster, 2006), 258.

75. Gorbachev, *Memoirs,* 196–97.

76. Oberdorfer, *From the Cold War to a New Era,* 66.

77. See Alan Dobson, "Ronald Reagan's Strategies and Policies: Of Ideology, Pragmatism, Loyalties, and Management Style," *Diplomacy & Statecraft* 27, no. 4 (2016): 746–65.

78. Fischer, *A Cold War Conundrum,* 17.

79. Cathleen Fisher, "Controlling High Risk Naval Operations," in *Naval Arms Control: A Strategic Assessment, ed.* Barry M. Blechman and William J. Durch (New York: St. Martin's Press, 1991), 29–92. Also see Fischer, *A Cold War Conundrum,* 7–10.

80. Francis X. Clines, "Reagan Denounces Ideology of Soviet as 'Focus of Evil'," *New York Times,* March 9, 1983, 1.

81. See "Soviet Capabilities for Strategic Nuclear Conflict, 1982–1992," National Intelligence Estimate NIE 11–3/8–83, February 15, 1983," in *Intentions and Capabilities: Estimates On Soviet Strategic Forces, 1950–1983,* ed. Donald P. Steury (Washington, DC: U.S. Government Printing Office, 1996), 491–500.

82. "NIE 11-4-82: The Soviet Challenge to US Security Interests," in Steury, *Intentions and Capabilities,* 475.

83. Shultz, *Turmoil and Triumph*, 507.

84. Dobrynin, *In Confidence*, 502, 513, 540; Garthoff, *The Great Transition*, 137–38. Also see John W. Parker, *Kremlin in Transition*, vol. I (Boston: Unwin Hyman, 1991).

85. Shultz, *Turmoil and Triumph*, 252.

86. Shultz, *Turmoil and Triumph*, 701, and Talbott, *Deadly Gambits*, 231. Also see Hedrick Smith, *The Power Game: How Washington Works* (New York: Ballantine Books, 1988), 603–16.

87. Caspar W. Weinberger, *Fighting for Peace: Seven Critical Years in the Pentagon* (New York: Warner Books, 1990), 307.

88. Shultz, *Turmoil and Triumph*, 250.

89. Talbott, *The Master of the Game*, 193.

90. Robert McFarlane, *Special Trust* (New York: Cadell and Davies, 1994), 228. Also see Martin and Annalise Anderson, *Reagan's Secret War: The Untold Story of His Fight to Save the World from Nuclear Disaster* (New York: Random House, 2009), 352.

91. See, for example, McGeorge Bundy, George F. Kennan, Robert S. McNamara, and Gerard Smith, "The President's Choice: Star Wars or Arms Control," *Foreign Affairs* 63, no. 2 (1984), 275–76; Harold Brown, "Is SDI Technically Feasible?" *Foreign Affairs* 64, no. 3 (1985), 435–54; and Ashton B. Carter and David N. Schwartz, eds., *Ballistic Missile Defense* (Washington, DC: Brookings Institution, 1984).

92. John F. Burns, "Andropov Says U.S. Is Spurring a Race for Nuclear Arms," *New York Times*, March 27, 1983, 1.

93. Christopher Andrew and Oleg Gordievsky, *Instructions from the Centre: Top Secret Files on KGB Foreign Operations, 1975–1985* (London: Hodder and Stoughton, 1991), 112.

94. Hugo Young, *One of Us: A Biography of Mrs. Thatcher* (London: Macmillan, 1989), 17.

95. Talbott, *The Master of the Game*, 232–33; and Shultz, *Turmoil and Triumph*, 264.

96. Patrick Buchanan, "The Act of a Criminal Regime," *Washington Times*, September 2, 1983, 3A.

97. See Don Oberdorfer, *The Turn* (New York: Simon and Schuster, 1991), 49–57. Also see Garthoff, *The Great Transition*, 118–41; David E. Hoffman, *The Dead Hand: The Untold Story of the Cold War Arms Race and Its Dangerous Legacy* (New York: Doubleday, 2009), 72–89; Alexander Dallin, *Black Box, KAL 007 and the Superpowers* (Berkeley: University of California Press, 1985); and Seymour M. Hersh, *The Target Is Destroyed* (New York: Random House, 1986).

98. Dobrynin, *In Confidence*, 537, 539.

99. Oleg Grinevsky and Lynn M. Hansen, *Making Peace: Confidence and Security in a New Europe* (New York: Eloquent Books, 2009), 117–19.

100. D.F. Ustinov, "To Struggle for Peace, to Strengthen Defense Capability," *Pravda*, November 19, 1983; and Colonel L.V. Levadov, "Results of the Operational Training of NATO Joint Armed Forces in 1983," *Military Thought*, no. 2 (February 1984): 67, cited in Garthoff, *The Great Transition*, 140.

101. See Nate Jones, ed., *Able Archer 83: The Secret History of the NATO Exercise That Almost Triggered Nuclear War* (New York: New Press, 2016); Oberdorfer, *The Turn*, 65–68; Hoffman, *The Dead Hand*, 89–95; and Garthoff, *The Great Transition*, 138–42.

102. Director of Central Intelligence, *Implications of Recent Soviet Military Political Activities*, Special National Intelligence Estimate 11-10-84, May 18, 1984 (Langley, VA: Central Intelligence Agency, 1984), 5.

103. President's Foreign Intelligence Advisory Board, "The Soviet 'War Scare'," Declassified Report, February 15, 1990, in *The 1983 War Scare Declassified and For Real*, ed. Nate Jones, Tom Blanton, and Lauren Harper (Washington, DC: National Security Archive, 2015), National Security Archive Electronic Briefing Book no. 533. Also see Ben McIntyre, *The Spy and the Traitor: The Greatest Espionage Story of the Cold War* (New York: Random House, 2018); Gordon Brooke-Shepherd, *The Storm Birds* (New York: Weidenfeld & Nicholson, 1989); and Christopher Andrew and Oleg Gordievsky, *KGB: The Inside Story of Its Foreign Operations from Lenin to Gorbachev* (New York: Harper Collins, 1990).

CHAPTER 10

1. Don Oberdorfer, *The Turn: From the Cold War to a New Era—The United States and the Soviet Union, 1983–1990* (New York: Poseidon Press, 1991), 65.

2. George Shultz, interview, Stanford, CA, May 28, 2019.

3. See Simon Miles, *Engaging the Evil Empire: Washington, Moscow, and the Beginning of the End of the Cold War* (Ithaca, NY: Cornell University Press, 2020); Hedrick Smith, "Reagan's Address: Trying a New Tactic," *New York Times*, January 17, 1984, A9; and Anatoly Dobrynin, *In Confidence: Moscow's Ambassador to America's Six Cold War Presidents* (New York: Random House, 1995), 545.

4. William Beecher, "Reagan's Secret Arms Letter," *Boston Globe*, February 12, 1984, 1.

5. Kiron K. Skinner, Annelise Anderson, and Martin Anderson, eds., *Reagan: A Life in Letters* (New York: Free Press, 2003), 743.

6. Shultz, interview, May 28, 2019.

7. Grinevsky and Hansen, *Making Peace,* 203, 213.

8. George P. Shultz, *Turmoil and Triumph: My Years as Secretary of State* (New York: Charles Scribner's Sons, 1993), 521.

9. See Maynard W. Glitman, *The Last Battle of the Cold War: An Inside Account of Negotiating the Intermediate-Range Nuclear Forces Treaty* (New York: Palgrave Macmillan, 2006), 204.

10. See Thomas Graham Jr., *Disarmament Sketches: Three Decades of Arms Control and International Law* (Seattle: University of Washington Press, 2002), 118.

11. Aleksandr G. Savel'yev and Nikolay N. Detinov, *The Big Five: Arms Control Decision-Making in the Soviet Union* (Westport, CT: Prager, 1995), 68.

12. Glitman, *Last Battle of the Cold War,* 125.

13. Savel'yev and Detinov, *The Big Five,* 124.

14. Savel'yev and Detinov, *The Big Five,* 124.

15. See Glitman, *Last Battle of the Cold War,* 151–72.

16. Gregory Govan, interview, Charlottesville, VA, August 5, 2017; Roland Lajoie, telephone interview, September 4, 2019; and Gregory Govan, "War Stories and Sober History," keynote presentation at Military Liaison Mission Conference and Reunion, Potsdam, Germany, June 21, 2019. Also see Thomas S. Lough, *The Origins of the Military Liaison Missions in Germany,* Research Report 65–1 (Washington, DC: U.S. Arms Control and Disarmament Agency, 1965).

17. Govan, "War Stories and Sober History."

18. Roland Lajoie, telephone interview, September 4, 2019.

19. Govan, interview, August 5, 2019.

20. Sagel'yev and Detinov, *The Big Five,* 92.

21. Mikhail Gorbachev, *Memoirs* (New York: Doubleday, 1996), 415.

22. Grinevsky and Hansen, *Making Peace,* 354, 142.

23. Grinevsky and Hansen, *Making Peace,* 176.

24. "Interview of M.S. Gorbachev with an Editor of the Newspaper *Pravda*," *Pravda*, April 8, 1985. From Garthoff, *The Great Transition*, 213n46.

25. Strobe Talbott, *Deadly Gambits: The Reagan Administration and the Stalemate in Nuclear Arms Control* (New York: Alfred A. Knopf, 1984), 348.

26. "Document 23: SDI and a Three-Phase Plan for the Global Elimination of Nuclear Weapons: Address by the President's and Secretary of State's Special Adviser on Arms Control Matters (Nitze) before the World Affairs Council, Philadelphia, February 20, 1985," *American Foreign Policy Current Documents—1985* (Washington, DC: U.S. Department of State, 1986), 78.

27. "Document 23: SDI and a Three-Phase Plan," 76–80.

28. Nitze, *From Hiroshima to Glasnost*, 405.

29. Talbott, *The Master of the Game*, 18.

30. Talbott, *The Master of the Game*, 204.

31. Shultz, *Turmoil and Triumph*, 581.

32. Shultz, *Turmoil and Triumph*, 579.

33. Raymond L. Garthoff, *A Journey through the Cold War: A Memoir of Containment and Coexistence* (Washington, DC: Brookings Institution Press, 2001), 357–58. Also see Raymond L. Garthoff, *Policy vs. the Law: The Reinterpretation of the ABM Treaty* (Washington, DC: Brookings Institution Press, 1987).

34. Nitze, *From Hiroshima to Glasnost*, 415.

35. Shultz, *Turmoil and Triumph*, 582.

36. Shultz, *Turmoil and Triumph*, 512.

37. See Walter Pincus, "Weinberger Urges Buildup over Soviet Violations," November 18, 1985, A1; and "Text of Weinberger Letter," *Washington Post*, November 17, 1985, A30. Also see Michael R. Gordon, "Weinberger Urges U.S. to Avoid Vow on 1979 Arms Pact," *New York Times*, November 16, 1985, 1, 6.

38. Kenneth L. Adelman, *The Great Universal Embrace: Arms Summitry—A Skeptic's Account* (New York: Simon and Schuster, 1989), 22.

39. Ronald W. Reagan, *Ronald Reagan: An American Life* (New York: Simon & Schuster, 1990), 635, 641.

40. Gorbachev, *Memoirs*, 524, 526.

41. Shultz, *Turmoil and Triumph*, 606.

42. Adelman, *The Great Universal Embrace*, 125.

43. Shultz, *Turmoil and Triumph*, 535–38.

44. Garthoff, *The Great Transition*, 239.

45. Grinevsky and Hansen, *Making Peace*, 475, 447.

46. Grinevsky and Hansen, *Making Peace*, 530.

47. Grinevsky and Hansen, *Making Peace*, 570.

48. Grinevsky and Hansen, *Making Peace*, 572.

49. Grinevsky and Hansen, *Making Peace*, 576.

50. Grinevsky and Hansen, *Making Peace*, 576–78.

51. Grinevsky and Hansen, *Making Peace*, 576–81.

52. Dobrynin, *In Confidence*, 487.

53. Grinevsky and Hansen, *Making Peace*, 436–37.

54. Grinevsky and Hansen, *Making Peace*, 438.

55. Savel'yev and Detinov, *The Big Five*, 93.

56. Gorbachev, *Memoirs*, 530.

57. Grinevsky and Hansen, *Making Peace*, 438.

58. Shultz, *Turmoil and Triumph*, 700.

59. Glitman, *Last Battle of the Cold War*, 110–17; Savel'yev and Detinov, *The Big Five*, 123–26.

60. Ronald Lehman, telephone interview, December 4, 2019; and Ronald Lehman, electronic communication, July 21, 2020.

61. David Hoffman, "Iceland Talks: One Word Chills Hope," *Washington Post*, October 19, 1986, A1, A37.

62. Gorbachev, *Memoirs,* 537. Also see Pavel Palazchenko, *My Years with Gorbachev and Shevardnadze: The Memoir of a Soviet Interpreter* (University Park: Pennsylvania State University Press, 1997), 55.

63. Lehman, telephone interview, December 4, 2019.

64. Milt Freudenheim, "Kennan: Are We Nuclear Lemmings?" *New York Times,* May 24, 1981, sec. 4, 2.

65. Shultz, *Turmoil and Triumph,* 701.

66. Nitze, *From Hiroshima to Glasnost,* 436.

67. Garthoff, *The Great Transition,* 286.

68. James Schlesinger, "Reykjavik and Revelations: A Turn of the Tide?" *Foreign Affairs* 65, no. 3 (1987): 429.

69. Richard M. Nixon, *1999: Victory without War* (New York: Simon & Schuster, 1988), 191.

70. Henry Kissinger, "Fundamental Agreements Do Not Happen Overnight," *Washington Post*, October 19, 1986, H8.

71. Richard M. Nixon and Henry A. Kissinger, "An Arms Agreement—On Two Conditions; The Former President and the Former Secretary of State Offer Their Advice," *Washington Post*, April 26, 1987, D7.

72. Alexander M. Haig, Jr., "Arms Reduction for Its Own Sake," *St. Louis Post Dispatch,* October 26, 1986, 31.

73. "Cold in Iceland," *Washington Post*, October 13, 1986, A24.

74. "Derailment at Reykjavik," *New York Times*, October 13, 1986, A18.

75. "Reykjavik Saga," *Wall Street Journal*, October 14, 1986, 32.

76. Shultz, *Turmoil and Triumph,* 777.

77. Kenneth L. Adelman, *Reagan at Reykjavik: Forty-Eight Hours That Ended the Cold War* (New York: Broadside Books, 2014), 93, 188.

78. Graham, Jr., *Disarmament Sketches*, 125.

79. Adelman, *Reagan at Reykjavik,* 2.

80. See Michael Krepon, *Better Safe Than Sorry: The Ironies of Living with the Bomb* (Stanford: Stanford University Press, 2009).

81. Adelman, *Reagan at Reykjavik,* 77.

82. Talbott, *The Master of the Game,* 363–64.

83. Adelman, *Reagan at Reykjavik,* 314.

84. Sagel'yev and Detinov, *The Big Five*, 93.

85. Gorbachev, *Memoirs*, 213.

86. Sagel'yev and Detinov, *The Big Five*, 93.

87. Dobrynin, *In Confidence*, 630.

88. Lee Lescaze, "Reagan Denounces Soviets But Speaks Gently of Iran," *Washington Post,* January 30, 1981, A1.

89. See Joseph P. Harahan, *On-Site Inspections under the INF Treaty: A History of the On-Site Inspection Agency and INF* (Washington, DC: U.S. Government Printing Office, 1993).

90. Lajoie, telephone interview, September 4, 2019.

91. Glitman, *Last Battle of the Cold War,* 235.

92. Dobrynin, *In Confidence,* 432.

93. Gorbachev, *Memoirs,* 572.

94. See Avis Bohlen, William Burns, Steven Pifer, and John Woodworth, "The Treaty on Intermediate-Range Nuclear Forces: History and Lessons Learned,"

Brookings Arms Control Series, Paper 9, December 2012, www.brookings.edu/wp-content/uploads/2016/06/30-arms-control-pifer-paper.pdf.

95. Gorbachev, *Memoirs,* 443.

96. See Michael Krepon, "Conclusions," in *The Politics of Arms Control Treaty Making,* ed. Michael Krepon and Dan Caldwell (New York: St. Martin's Press, 1991), 399–471.

97. Talbott, *Deadly Gambits,* 352.

98. Shultz, interview, May 28, 2019.

99. "NATO Defense and the INF Treaty," Hearings, Senate Committee on Armed Services, Part 1, 100th Cong., 2d Sess. (1988), 68.

100. Richard Perle, "What's Wrong with the INF Treaty," *U.S. News & World Report* 101, no. 12 (1988): 46.

101. Dobrynin, *In Confidence,* 607.

102. Lehman, telephone interview, December 2, 2019.

103. Adelman, *Reagan at Reykjavik,* 324, 322.

104. Dobrynin, *In Confidence,* 629, 632.

105. Eduard Shevardnadze, *The Future Belongs to Freedom* (New York: Free Press, 1991), 220.

106. Garry Wills, *Reagan's America: Innocents at Home* (Garden City, NY: Doubleday, 1987), 1, 4.

CHAPTER 11

1. Jon Meacham, *Destiny and Power: The American Odyssey of George Herbert Walker Bush* (New York: Random House, 2015), xix, 33–38.

2. Garry Wills, "The Ultimate Loyalist," *Time,* August 22, 1988, 23.

3. See Mimi Swartz, "The Texanhood of George H.W. Bush," *Texas Monthly,* January 2, 2019; and Meacham, *Destiny and Power.*

4. George Bush and Brent Scowcroft, *A World Transformed* (New York: Random House, 1998), 18.

5. James A. Baker III, interview, March 17, 2011, George H.W. Bush Oral History Project, Miller Center, University of Virginia, 11. Also see Peter Baker and Susan Glasser, *The Man Who Ran Washington: The Life and Times of James A. Baker III* (New York: Doubleday, 2020).

6. S.C. Gwynne, "James Baker Forever," *Texas Monthly,* January 20, 2013.

7. Bush and Scowcroft, *A World Transformed,* 23.

8. See Richard B. Cheney, interview, March 16–17, George H.W. Bush Oral History Project, Miller Center, University of Virginia; and Dick Cheney, *In My Time: A Personal and Political Memoir* (New York: Simon & Schuster, 2011), 11–109.

9. See Bush and Scowcroft, *A World Transformed.*

10. See Bartholomew Sparrow, *Brent Scowcroft and the Call of National Security* (New York: Public Affairs, 2015).

11. Bush and Scowcroft, *A World Transformed,* 18.

12. See Robert M. Gates, *From the Shadows: The Ultimate Insider's Story of Five Presidents and How They Won the Cold War* (New York: Simon & Schuster, 1996).

13. See Colin Powell, *My American Journey* (New York: Random House, 1995).

14. Cheney, interview, March 16, 2000, Miller Center, 38–39.

15. Michael R. Beschloss and Strobe Talbott, *At the Highest Levels: The Inside Story of the End of the Cold War* (Boston: Little Brown, 1993), 9, 11.

16. Linton Brooks, telephone interview, November 12, 2019. Also see Bush and Scowcroft, *A World Transformed,* 7.

17. Mikhail Gorbachev, *Memoirs* (New York: Doubleday, 1996), 581.

18. Brent Scowcroft, John Deutch, and R. James Woolsey, "The Survivability Problem," *Washington Post,* December 3, 1987, A23.

19. Richard Burt, interview, Washington, DC, September 5, 2019; and George P. Shultz, *Turmoil and Triumph: My Years as Secretary of State* (New York: Charles Scribner's Sons, 1993), 121–22, 780.

20. Henry Kissinger, "Forget the 'Zero Option,'" *Washington Post,* April 5, 1987, C2.

21. Henry Kissinger, "A Dangerous Rush for Agreement," *Washington Post,* April 24, 1988, D-8.

22. Richard M. Nixon, "It's What You Cut," *New York Times,* December 20, 1987, E18.

23. "Statement of Senator Bob Dole: The President Departs for the Moscow Summit with Gorbachev, May 25, 1988," Robert J. Dole Press Releases, Box 1, Folder 38, Robert and Elizabeth Dole Archive and Special Collections, University of Kansas.

24. Kim Holmes, "In the Nuclear Arms Talks, Go Slow on START," Heritage Foundation Backgrounder, January 11, 1989.

25. George P. Shultz, "A Reply to Nixon and Kissinger," *Time* 129, no. 20 (1987): 40.

26. Pavel Palazchenko, *My Years with Gorbachev and Shevardnadze: The Memoir of a Soviet Interpreter* (University Park: Pennsylvania State University Press, 1997), 54.

27. Shultz, *Turmoil and Triumph,* 1,085.

28. Gorbachev, *Memoirs,* 640.

29. Palazchenko, *My Years with Gorbachev and Shevardnadze,* 106.

30. Powell, interview, December 16, 2011, Miller Center, 10.

31. Baker III, interview, March 17, 2011, Miller Center, 3.

32. Bush and Scowcroft, *A World Transformed,* 8.

33. Bush and Scowcroft, *A World Transformed,* 7–13.

34. Powell, interview, December 16, 2011, Miller Center, 9.

35. Cheney, interview, March 17, 2000, Miller Center, 107.

36. Robert M. Gates, interview, July 23, 2000, George H.W. Bush Oral History Project, Miller Center, University of Virginia, 8.

37. David Hoffman, "Gorbachev 'Gambit' Challenged," *Washington Post,* May 17, 1989, A1.

38. Molly Moore, "Cheney Predicts Gorbachev Will Fail, Be Replaced," *Washington Post,* April 29, 2019, A17; Baker, *The Politics of Diplomacy,* 70–71, 156–58.

39. Cheney, interview, March 17, 2000, Miller Center, 97. Also see Jeffrey A. Engel, *When the World Seemed New: George H.W. Bush and the End of the Cold War* (Boston: Houghton Mifflin Harcourt, 2018).

40. Bush and Scowcroft, *A World Transformed,* 43, 59, 73.

41. The author served as Congressman Hicks's legislative assistant.

42. Richard Burt, telephone interview, October 29, 2019.

43. See John Borawski, *From the Atlantic to the Urals: Negotiating Arms Control at the Stockholm Conference* (Washington, DC: Pergamon-Brassey's, 1988); Oleg Grinevsky and Lynn M. Hansen, *Making Peace: Confidence and Security in a New Europe* (New York: Eloquent Books, 2009); Johnathan B.

Tucker, *War of Nerves: Chemical Warfare from World War I to Al-Qaeda* (New York: Anchor Books, 2006), 103–58; and Nicholas Badalassi and Sarah B. Snyder, eds., *The CSCE and the End of the Cold War: Diplomacy, Societies and Human Rights, 1972–1990* (New York: Berghahn Books, 2019).

44. Shultz, *Turmoil and Triumph*, 238–39; Tucker, *War of Nerves*, 160–61; Robert Mikulak, telephone interview, October 15, 2019.

45. Mikulak, telephone interview, October 15, 2019.

46. Bush and Scowcroft, *A World Transformed*, 53; Baker, *The Politics of Diplomacy*, 68.

47. Baker, *The Politics of Diplomacy*, 67.

48. Baker, *The Politics of Diplomacy*, 39.

49. Cheney, interview, March 16, 2000, Miller Center, 89, 109–10.

50. Powell, interview, December 16, 2011, Miller Center, 10–11.

51. Baker III, interview, March 17, 2011, Miller Center, 3–4.

52. George F. Will, "Is Iranian Containment the Only Option?" *Washington Post*, May 13, 2018, A21.

53. Baker III, interview, March 17, 2011, Miller Center, 4.

54. Palazchenko, *My Years with Gorbachev and Shevardnadze*, 106–7.

55. See Baker, *The Politics of Diplomacy*, 155–56.

56. Baker, *The Politics of Diplomacy*, 65, 77–78. Also see Don Oberdorfer, *The Turn: From Cold War to a New Era* (New York: Simon & Schuster, 1991), 370; Palazchenko, *My Years with Gorbachev and Shevardnadze*, 133–34; and Raymond L. Garthoff, *The Great Transition: American-Soviet Relations and the End of the Cold War* (Washington, DC: Brookings Institution, 1994), 379; Beschloss and Talbott, *At the Highest Levels*, 121.

57. Baker, *The Politics of Diplomacy*, 577.

58. Oberdorfer, *The Turn*, 371–72.

59. Cheney, interview, March 17, 2000, Miller Center, 117.

60. Aleksandr' G. Savel'yev and Nikolay N. Detinov, *The Big Five: Arms Control Decision-Making in the Soviet Union* (Westport, CT: Praeger, 1995), 99.

61. Hearings, "The Treaty between the United States of America and the Union of Soviet Socialist Republics on the Elimination of Their Intermediate-Range and Shorter-Range Missiles," Senate Committee on Foreign Relations, 100th Cong., 2d Sess. (1988), 181; and McGeorge Bundy, George F. Kennan, Robert S. McNamara, and Gerard Smith, "The President's Choice: Star Wars or Arms Control," *Foreign Affairs* 63, no. 2 (1984), 275.

62. Beschloss and Talbott, *At the Highest Levels*, 118.

63. Ronald Reagan, *An American Life* (New York: Simon & Schuster, 1990), 12.

64. Gorbachev, *Memoirs*, 524, 526. Also see Garthoff, *The Great Transition*, 405.

65. Bush and Scowcroft, *A World Transformed*, 173. Also see Gates, *From the Shadows*, 475–76.

66. Beschloss and Talbott, *At the Highest Levels*, 149.

67. Oberdorfer, *The Turn*, 379.

68. Palazchenko, *My Years with Gorbachev and Shevardnadze*, 156.

69. Powell, interview, December 16, 2011, Miller Center, 16. Italics in the original.

70. See Robert L. Pfaltzgraff, Jr., and Jacquelyn K. Davis, *The Cruise Missile: Bargaining Chip or Defense Bargain* (Cambridge: Institute for Foreign Policy Analysis, 1976); Richard K. Betts, *Cruise Missile: Technology, Strategy, and Politics* (Washington, DC: Brookings Institution, 1981); Dennis M. Gormley, *Missile*

Contagion: Cruise Missile Proliferation and the Threat to International Security (New York: Praeger, 2008); and Janne Nolan, *Trappings of Power: Ballistic Missiles in the Third World* (Washington, DC: Brookings Institution, 1991).

71. Burt, interview, September 5, 2019.

72. John E. Moore, ed., *Janes Fighting Ships, 1975–1976* (New York: Franklin Watts, 1975), 91.

73. See, for example, U.S. Air Force, *Targeting—Covering Target Characteristics, Weaponeering, Mensuration, Collateral Damage, Tasking Cycle, Campaign Assessment, and Effects-Based Operations*, Air Force Doctrine Document 3–60 (Maxwell Air Force Base, Alabama: U.S. Air Force Doctrine Center, 2018); Government Accountability Office, *Strategic Weapons: Nuclear Weapons Targeting Process*, NSIAD-91-319FS (Washington, DC: Government Accountability Office, 2013); Fred Kaplan, *The Bomb* (New York: Simon & Schuster, 2020); and Desmond Ball and Jeffrey Richelson, eds., *Strategic Nuclear Targeting* (Ithaca, NY: Cornell University Press, 1988).

74. William J. Crowe, *The Line of Fire: From Washington to the Gulf, the Politics and Battles of the New Military* (New York: Simon & Schuster, 1993), 258.

75. Larry Welch, telephone interview, October 23, 2019.

76. Crowe, *The Line of Fire*, 257.

77. Franklin Miller, interview, Washington, DC, October 11, 2019.

78. Franklin Miller in Lee Butler, *Uncommon Cause: A Life at Odds with Convention*, Part II (Denver: Outskirts Press, 2016), 9.

79. "National Security Decision Memorandum 242, Document 31," January 17, 1974, *Foreign Relations of the United States, 1969–1976, vol. 35, National Security Policy, 1973–1976* (Washington, DC: U.S. Government Publishing Office, 2014), 142–46.

80. Miller, interview, October 11, 2019.

81. Miller, interview, October 11, 2019; Miller in Butler, *Uncommon Cause*, 6–13; and Janne Nolan, *The Guardians of the Arsenal: The Politics of Nuclear Strategy* (New York: Basic Books, 1989), 248–64.

82. Larry Welch, electronic communication, November 7, 2019.

83. Welch, telephone interview, October 23, 2019; and Miller in Butler, *Uncommon Cause*, 13.

84. Cheney, interview, March 17, 2000, Miller Center, 109.

85. Welch, telephone interview, October 23, 2019.

86. Miller, interview, November 7, 2019.

87. Colin Powell, *My American Journey* (New York: Ballantine Books, 1995), 540–41.

88. Miller in Butler, *Uncommon Cause*, 14; Franklin Miller, interview, Washington, DC, November 7, 2019.

89. Crowe, *The Line of Fire*, 259.

90. Miller, interviews, Washington, DC, October 11, 2019, November 7, 2019, and November 8, 2019; Miller in Butler, *Uncommon Cause*, 13–17.

91. Baker, *The Politics of Diplomacy*, 237.

92. Lehman, telephone interview, December 12, 2019.

93. Baker, *The Politics of Diplomacy*, 247.

94. Baker, *The Politics of Diplomacy*, 151.

95. Edward Ifft, interview, Washington, DC, December 2, 2019; Lehman, telephone interview, December 4, 2019; and Brooks, telephone interview, December 16, 2019.

96. "News Conference of President Bush and President Mikhail Gorbachev of the Soviet Union," June 3, 1990, *Weekly Compilation of Presidential Documents*

26, no. 13 (April 2, 1990) (Washington, DC: Government Publishing Office, 1990), 875; Bush and Scowcroft, *A World Transformed,* 287–89; and Beschloss and Talbott, *At the Highest Levels,* 9.

97. Baker, *The Politics of Diplomacy,* 142.

98. Palazchenko, *My Years with Gorbachev and Shevardnadze,* 286.

99. Lynn Rusten, telephone interview, April 27, 2020.

100. Susan Koch, interview, Washington, DC, February 13, 2020.

101. See Baker, *The Politics of Diplomacy,* 660.

102. Ambassador Thomas Graham Jr., recorded interview, Foreign Affairs Oral History Collection, Association for Diplomatic Studies and Training, Arlington, VA, May 10, 2013, 131.

103. Palazchenko, *My Years with Gorbachev and Shevardnadze,* 299.

104. Bush and Scowcroft, *A World Transformed,* 514.

105. Garthoff, *The Great Transition,* 466.

106. Beschloss and Talbott, *At the Highest Levels,* 370.

107. Baker, *The Politics of Diplomacy,* 472.

108. Brent Scowcroft, interview, November 12, 1999, George H.W. Bush Oral History Project, Miller Center, University of Virginia, 77–78.

109. Gates, interview, July 23, 2000, Miller Center, 13. Also see Gates, *From the Shadows,* 530.

110. Powell, *My American Journey,* 540.

111. Susan Koch, interview, Washington, DC, October 11, 2019.

112. Cheney, *In My Time,* 232.

113. Susan J. Koch, *The Presidential Nuclear Initiatives, 1991–1992,* Center for the Study of Weapons of Mass Destruction, Case Study 5 (Washington, DC: National Defense University Press, 2012), 7–8.

114. Powell, interview, December 16, 2011, Miller Center, 8–9; Powell, *My American Journey,* 540.

115. Susan Koch, interview, Washington, DC, October 11, 2019.

116. Powell, interview, December 16, 2011, Miller Center, 9.

117. Bush and Scowcroft, *A World Transformed,* 546.

118. Bush and Scowcroft, *A World Transformed,* 546.

119. "Who Needs Arms Control?" *Wall Street Journal,* September 30, 1991, A12.

120. Koch, *Presidential Nuclear Initiatives,* 7–10; "Address to the Nation on United States Nuclear Weapons Reductions, September 27, 1991," *Public Papers of the Presidents of the United States: George Bush, 1991, Book II—July 1 to December 31, 1991* (Washington, DC: U.S. Government Printing Office, 1992), 1220–24.

121. Palazchenko, *My Years With Gorbachev and Shevardnadze,* 328.

122. Palazchenko, *My Years With Gorbachev and Shevardnadze,* 328–29.

123. Palazchenko, *My Years With Gorbachev and Shevardnadze,* 329–30.

124. Koch, *Presidential Nuclear Initiatives,* 14.

125. "Gorbachev's Remarks on Arms Cuts," *New York Times,* October 6, 1991, A12.

126. Palazchenko, *My Years with Gorbachev and Shevardnadze,* 315–16.

127. Strobe Talbott, *The Russia Hand: A Memoir of Presidential Diplomacy* (New York: Random House, 2002), 19.

128. Bush and Scowcroft, *A World Transformed,* 556.

129. Talbott, *The Russia Hand,* 10.

130. Palazchenko, *My Years with Gorbachev and Shevardnadze,* 360–61.

131. Koch, interview, October 11, 2019.

132. Koch, *Presidential Nuclear Initiatives*, 2.

133. "Address before a Joint Session of the Congress on the State of the Union, January 28, 1992," *Public Papers of the Presidents of the United States: George Bush, 1992–93, Book I—January 1 to July 31, 1992* (Washington, DC: U.S. Government Printing Office, 1993), 158.

134. Miller, telephone interview, November 26, 2019.

135. Miller in Butler, *Uncommon Cause*, 16; Miller, interview, November 7, 2019.

136. "Address before a Joint Session of the Congress on the State of the Union, January 28, 1992," *Public Papers of the Presidents of the United States*, 158.

137. Baker, *The Politics of Diplomacy*, 475.

138. Baker, *The Politics of Diplomacy*, 569–73.

139. Garthoff, *The Great Transition*, 782.

140. Mitchell Reiss, *Bridled Ambition: Why Countries Constrain Their Nuclear Capabilities* (Baltimore: Johns Hopkins University Press, 1995), 97.

141. See William Walker, "Nuclear Weapons and the Former Soviet Republics," *International Affairs* 68, no. 2 (April 1992): 255–77; Reiss, *Bridled Ambition*; Steven Pifer, *The Eagle and the Trident: U.S.-Ukraine Relations in Turbulent Times* (Washington, DC: Brookings Institution Press, 2017); and William C. Potter, "The Politics of Nuclear Renunciation: The Cases of Belarus, Kazakhstan, and Ukraine," Stimson Center Occasional Paper no. 22, April 13, 1995.

142. Brooks, telephone interview, December 16, 2019.

143. Steven Pifer, telephone interview, January 29, 2020.

144. Baker, *The Politics of Diplomacy*, 663.

145. Robert Bell, telephone interview, January 30, 2020.

146. See Roland McElroy, *The Best President the Nation Never Had: A Memoir of Working with Sam Nunn* (Macon, GA: Mercer University Press, 2017).

147. See John T. Shaw, *Richard G. Lugar, Statesman of the Senate: Crafting Foreign Policy from Capitol Hill* (Bloomington: Indiana University Press, 2012); and "Senator Richard Lugar Oral History Interviews," September 13, 2016, Randall L. Tobias Center for Leadership Excellence at Indiana University / Purdue University Indianapolis.

148. Kurt M. Campbell, Ashton B. Carter, Steven E. Miller, and Charles A. Zraket, *Soviet Nuclear Fission: Control of the Nuclear Arsenal in a Disintegrating Soviet Union*, CSIA Studies in International Security, no. 1 (Cambridge, MA: Center for Science and International Affairs, Harvard University, November 1991), i–v. Also see Graham Allison, Ashton B. Carter, Steven E. Miller, and Philip Zelikow, eds., *Cooperative Denuclearization: From Pledges to Deeds*, CSIA Studies in International Security, no. 2 (Cambridge, MA: Center for Science and International Affairs, Harvard University, 1993).

149. Laura Holgate, interview, Washington, DC, January 6, 2020; Richard Combs, telephone interview, January 27, 2020; Robert Bell, telephone interview, February 5, 2020.

150. Bell, telephone interview, January 30, 2020.

151. Combs, telephone interview, January 27, 2020. Also see the Soviet Nuclear Threat Reduction Act of 1991, H.R. 3807, 102nd Cong., 1st Sess. (December 21, 1991).

152. Ash Carter, *Inside the Five-Sided Box: Lessons from a Lifetime of Leadership in the Pentagon* (New York: Random House, 2019), 80.

153. See Carter, *Inside the Five-Sided Box*, 80–81; Richard Combs, "U.S. Domestic Politics and the Nunn-Lugar Program," in *Dismantling the Cold War: U.S. and N.I.S. Perspectives on the Nunn-Lugar Cooperative Threat Reduction*

Program, ed. John M. Shields and William C. Potter (Cambridge, MA: MIT Press, 1997), 41–60; and Paul I. Bernstein and Jason D. Wood, "The Origins of Nunn-Lugar and Cooperative Threat Reduction," Center for the Study of Weapons of Mass Destruction Case Study 3 (Washington, DC: National Defense University, April 2010).

154. Beschloss and Talbott, *At the Highest Levels,* 120. For more on chemical weapons and the Chemical Weapons Convention, see Jonathan Tucker, *War of Nerves: Chemical Warfare from World War I to Al-Qaeda* (New York: Random House, 2006).

155. Brooks, telephone interview, December 16, 2019.

156. Beschloss and Talbott, *At the Highest Levels,* 144–46.

157. Cheney, interview, March 17, 2000, Miller Center, 110.

158. Thomas B. Cochran, William M. Arkin, Robert S. Norris, and Jeffrey I. Sands, *Nuclear Weapons Databook, vol. 4, Soviet Nuclear Weapons* (Cambridge, MA: Ballinger, 1989), 77.

159. Michael R. Gordon, "Putin Wins Vote in Parliament on Treaty to Cut Nuclear Arms," *New York Times*, April 15, 2000, A1. Also see Talbott, *The Russia Hand,* 389.

160. Koch, *Presidential Nuclear Initiatives*, 21.

161. Cheney, interview, March 17, 2000, Miller Center, 110–11.

CHAPTER 12

1. Leon Panetta, *Worthy Fights* (New York: Penguin Press, 2014), 96.

2. See George Stephanopoulos, *All Too Human: A Political Education* (Boston: Little, Brown, 1999); John F. Harris, *The Survivor: Bill Clinton in the White House* (New York: Random House, 2006); and David Maraniss, *First in His Class: A Biography of Bill Clinton* (New York: Simon & Schuster, 1995).

3. Bill Clinton, *My Life* (New York: Alfred A. Knopf, 2004), 115.

4. Strobe Talbott, *The Russia Hand: A Memoir of Presidential Diplomacy* (New York: Random House, 2002), 11.

5. Talbott, *The Russia Hand,* 43.

6. Talbott, *The Russia Hand,* 245.

7. Talbott, *The Russia Hand,* 409, 185.

8. Talbott, *The Russia Hand,* 38.

9. Warren Christopher, *Chances of a Lifetime* (New York: Scribner, 2001), 9–22.

10. Christopher, *Chances of a Lifetime,* 162.

11. "Remarks by General John Shalikashvili, Chairman of the Joint Chiefs of Staff, CARE 50th Anniversary Symposium," Washington, DC, May 10, 1996, in Dan Caldwell, *World Politics and You* (Englewood Cliffs, NJ: Prentice Hall, 2000), 227

12. Talbott, *The Russia Hand,* 37.

13. Strobe Talbott, Association for Diplomatic Studies and Training Foreign Affairs Oral History Project, July 26, 2016; Strobe Talbott, telephone interview, March 13, 2020.

14. Mitchell Reiss, *Bridled Ambition: Why Countries Constrain Their Nuclear Capabilities* (Baltimore: Johns Hopkins University Press, 1995), 137.

15. See Michael Krepon, Peter D. Zimmerman, Leonard S. Spector, and Mary Umberger, eds., *Commercial Observation Satellites and International Security* (New York: St. Martin's Press, 1990), 108–9. Also see Alexandra Genova and Phil Hatcher-Moore, "This Is What Nuclear Tests Leave in Their Wake," *National*

Geographic Magazine, October 13, 2017, www.nationalgeographic.com/photo graphy/proof/2017/10/nuclear-ghosts-kazakhstan/.

16. See Togzhan Kassenova, "Kazakhstan and the Global Nuclear Order," *Central Asian Affairs* 1 (2014): 273–86; and Anuar Ayazbekov, "Kazakhstan's Nuclear Decision Making, 1991–92," *Nonproliferation Review* 21, no. 2 (2014): 149–68.

17. Ambassador Thomas Graham Jr., recorded interview, Foreign Affairs Oral History Collection, Association for Diplomatic Studies and Training, Arlington, VA, June 12, 2013, 134.

18. Togzhan Kassenova, telephone interview, February 3, 2020.

19. William Courtney, telephone interview, March 8, 2020.

20. See William C. Potter, "The Politics of Nuclear Renunciation: The Cases of Belarus, Kazakhstan, and Ukraine," Stimson Center Occasional Paper no. 22, April 13, 1995, 16–19; and Reiss, *Bridled Ambition*, 138–50.

21. Potter, "The Politics of Nuclear Renunciation," 19–26. Also see Reiss, *Bridled Ambition*, 90–150; and Steven Pifer, "The Trilateral Process: The United States, Ukraine, Russia and Nuclear Weapons," Brookings Arms Control Series, Paper no. 6 (Washington, DC: Brookings Institution, May 2011).

22. Graham, recorded interview, Association for Diplomatic Studies and Training, 134–35.

23. Reiss, *Bridled Ambition*, p. 101.

24. See Serhil Plokhy, *The Gates of Europe: A History of Ukraine* (New York: Basic Books, 2015); and Rajan Menon and Eugene B. Rumer, *Conflict in Ukraine: The Unwinding of the Post-Cold War Order* (Cambridge, MA: MIT Press, 2015).

25. Talbott, *The Russia Hand,* 79–80.

26. Talbott, *The Russia Hand,* 80–81.

27. Graham, recorded interview, Association of Diplomatic Studies and Training, 136; and Thomas Graham Jr., *Disarmament Sketches: Three Decades of Arms Control and International Law* (Seattle: University of Washington Press, 2002), 135–36.

28. Steven Pifer, "The Trilateral Process," 23–24.

29. Steven Pifer, telephone interview, January 19, 2020; Rose Gottemoeller, telephone interview, February 14, 2020

30. "The President's News Conference with President Vladimir Putin of Russia in Kranj, June 16, 2001," *Public Papers of the Presidents of the United States: Administration of George W. Bush, 2001, Book I—January 20 to June 30, 2001* (Washington, DC: U.S. Government Printing Office, 2002), 689.

31. Roland Lajoie, telephone interview, January 9, 2020.

32. Pifer, telephone interview, January 29, 2020.

33. Gottemoeller, telephone interview, February 14, 2020.

34. Lajoie, telephone interviews, January 9, 2020 and March 19, 2020.

35. See Thomas B. Cochran, "The Black Sea Experiment," presentation at "From Reykjavik to New START: Science Diplomacy for Nuclear Security in the 21st Century," sponsored by the National Academy of Sciences and the U.S. Institute of Peace, January 19, 2011, www.nrdc.org/sites/default/files/nuc_11024apdf.

36. Siegfried Hecker, interview, Stanford, CA, May 28, 2019.

37. See Siegfried Hecker, ed., *Doomed to Cooperate: How American and Russian Scientists Joined Forces to Avert Some of the Greatest Post–Cold War Nuclear Dangers* (Los Alamos, NM: Bathtub Row Press, 2016), vols. 1 and 2.

38. Hecker, telephone interview, March 17, 2020; National Security Council and National Security Council Records Management Office, "PDD-47—Nuclear

Scientific and Technical Cooperation with Russia Related to Stockpile Safety and Security and Comprehensive Test Ban Treaty, CTBT Monitoring and Verification, 3/4/1996."

39. Graham, *Disarmament Sketches*, 3–19; Graham, interview, Washington, DC, March 19, 2019.

40. Robert Einhorn, telephone interview, February 27, 2020.

41. Graham, *Disarmament Sketches,* 260; Graham, telephone interview, April 21, 2020; Susan Burk, telephone interview, February 26, 2020.

42. See David Albright and Andrea Stricker, *Revisiting South Africa's Nuclear Weapons Program: Its History, Dismantlement, and Lessons for Today* (Washington, DC: Institute for Science and International Security, 2016); Nic Von Wielligh and Lydia Von Wielligh-Steyn, *The Bomb: South Africa's Nuclear Weapons Programme* (Pretoria: Litera, 2015); and Uri Friedman, "Why One President Gave Up His Country's Nukes," *The Atlantic,* September 9, 2017.

43. Graham, recorded interview, Association for Diplomatic Studies and Training, 179.

44. Graham, *Disarmament Sketches,* 266.

45. Burk, telephone interview, February 26, 2020.

46. Barbara Crossette, "Atom Arms Pact Runs into a Snag," *New York Times,* January 26, 1995, A1.

47. Burk, telephone interview, February 26, 2020.

48. Einhorn, telephone interview, February 27, 2020.

49. See Avner Cohen, *Israel and the Bomb* (New York: Columbia University Press, 1998); and Avner Cohen, *The Worst Kept Secret: Israel's Bargain with the Bomb* (New York: Columbia University Press, 2010).

50. Graham, *Disarmament Sketches,* 268.

51. The Conference of the Parties to the Treaty on the Non-Proliferation of Nuclear Weapons, *Resolution on the Middle East,* NPT/CONF.1995/32 (Part I), Annex (May 12, 1995), https://unoda-web.s3-accelerate.amazonaws .com/wp-content/uploads/assets/WMD/Nuclear/1995-NPT/pdf/Resolution _MiddleEast.pdf.

52. Graham, recorded interview, Association for Diplomatic Studies and Training, 179.

53. Jayantha Dhanapala and Tariq Rauf, *Reflections on the Treaty of the Non-Proliferation of Nuclear Weapons: Review Conferences and the Future of the NPT* (Stockholm: Stockholm International Peace Research Institute, 2017), 101.

54. See Maurice A. Mallin, "The Comprehensive Nuclear Test Ban Treaty: A Case Study," Washington, DC: National Defense University, Center for the Study of Weapons of Mass Destruction, Case Study 7, February, 2017; Keith A. Hansen, *The Comprehensive Test Ban Treaty: An Insider's Perspective* (Stanford: Stanford University Press, 2006); and Steve Fetter, *Toward a Comprehensive Test Ban Treaty* (Cambridge, MA: Ballinger, 1988). Also see Graham, *Disarmament Sketches,* 237–56.

55. Paul Richards, telephone interview, March 16, 2020.

56. See C. Paul Robinson, "The Joint Verification Experiment and the Nuclear Testing Talks," in *Doomed to Cooperate: How American and Russian Scientists Joined Forces to Avert Some of the Greatest Post-Cold War Nuclear Dangers,* ed. Siegfried S. Hecker (Los Alamos, NM: Bathtub Row Press, 2016), vol. 1, 85–98.

57. See, for example, A.L. Latter, R.E. LeLevier, E.A. Martinelli, and W.G. McMillan, "A Method of Concealing Underground Nuclear Explosions," *Journal of Geophysical Research* 66, no. 3 (1961): 943–46.

58. See Lynn R. Sykes, *Silencing the Bomb: One Man's Quest to Halt Nuclear Testing* (New York: Columbia University Press, 2017).

59. Graham, *Disarmament Sketches,* 243.

60. Edward Ifft, interview, Washington, DC, December 2, 2019.

61. Robert Bell, telephone interview, February 5, 2020; Robert Mikulak, telephone interview, February 5, 2020; and Lucy (Ledogar) van Beever, telephone interview, February 6, 2020.

62. Mallin, "Comprehensive Nuclear Test Ban Treaty," 6.

63. See Rebecca Johnson, *Unfinished Business: The Negotiation of the CTBT and the End of Nuclear Testing* (Geneva: United Nations, 2009); and Jaap Ramaker, Peter D. Marshall, Robert Geil, and Jenifer Mackby, *The Final Test: A History of the Comprehensive Nuclear-Test-Ban Treaty Negotiations* (Vienna: Provisional Technical Secretariat of the Preparatory Commission for the Comprehensive Nuclear-Test-Ban Treaty Organization, 2003).

64. Alison Mitchell, "Clinton, at U.N., Signs Treaty Banning All Nuclear Testing," *New York Times*, September 25, 1996, A1.

65. William J. Perry, *My Journey at the Nuclear Brink* (Stanford: Stanford University Press, 2015), 103.

66. Perry, *My Journey at the Nuclear Brink,* 106.

67. See Jonathan D. Pollack, *No Exit: North Korea, Nuclear Weapons and International Security* (London: Routledge, 2011).

CHAPTER 13

1. Strobe Talbott, telephone interview, March 13, 2020.

2. Talbott, telephone interview, March 13, 2020.

3. Strobe Talbott, *The Russia Hand: A Memoir of Presidential Diplomacy* (New York: Random House, 2002), 92–93.

4. William J. Perry, *My Journey at the Nuclear Brink* (Stanford: Stanford University Press, 2015), 126.

5. Perry, *My Journey at the Nuclear Brink,* 152.

6. William Perry, interview, Palo Alto, CA, May 28, 2019.

7. Mary Elise Sarotte, "A Broken Promise? What the West Really Told Moscow about NATO Expansion," *Foreign Affairs* 93, no. 5 (2014): 92–97; Mikhail Gorbachev, *Memoirs* (New York: Doubleday, 1996), 682–83; and Talbott, *The Russia Hand,* 441n1. Also see Joshua R. Itzkowitz Shifrinson, "Deal or No Deal? The End of the Cold War and the U.S. Offer to Limit NATO Expansion," *International Security* 40, no. 4 (April 2016): 7–44; and Svetlana Savranskaya and Thomas Blanton, eds., *NATO Expansion: What Gorbachev Heard*, National Security Archive Electronic Briefing Book no. 613 (Washington, DC: National Security Archive, 2017).

8. George Bush and Brent Scowcroft, *A World Transformed* (New York: Alfred A. Knopf, 1998), 282.

9. Walter Lippmann column, *Today and Tomorrow*, August 5, 1952.

10. A.J.P. Taylor, *Origins of the Second World War* (New York: Antheneum, 1985), 246.

11. Henry Kissinger, *Nuclear Weapons and Foreign Policy* (New York: Harpers & Brothers, 1957), 237.

12. *Richard K. Betts, "NATO's Mid-Life Crisis," Foreign Affairs 68, no. 2 (1989):* 39.

13. George F. Kennan, "A Fateful Error," *New York Times,* February 5, 1997, A23.

14. Talbott, *The Russia Hand,* 14.

15. Talbott, *The Russia Hand*, 92–93.

16. Warren Christopher, *Chances of a Lifetime* (New York: Scribner, 2001), 272–73, 276.

17. Madeleine Albright, *Madam Secretary: A Memoir* (New York: Harper-Collins, 2003), 254, 266.

18. Albright, *Madam Secretary,* 504.

19. Perry, interview, May 28, 2019.

20. Howard Baker Jr., Sam Nunn, Brent Scowcroft, and Alton Frye, "Will Expansion Undercut the Military?" *Los Angeles Times*, March 26, 1998, B9.

21. Robert M. Gates, recorded interview by Miller Center Staff, July 24, 2000, George H.W. Bush Oral History Project, Miller Center, University of Virginia, 101.

22. Perry, *My Journey at the Nuclear Brink,* 116.

23. Perry, *My Journey at the Nuclear Brink,* 128–29.

24. Henry A. Kissinger, "U.S. Must Embrace the Expansion of NATO," *Los Angeles Times*, January 12, 1997, M2.

25. Zbigniew Brzezinski and Anthony Lake, "For a New World, a New NATO," *New York Times*, June 30, 1997, A11.

26. Baker et al., "Will Expansion Undercut the Military?"

27. "Opposition to NATO Expansion," *Arms Control Today* 27, no. 4 (1997): 25.

28. See Jack Mendelsohn, "NATO Expansion: A Decision to Regret," *Arms Control Today* 27, no. 4 (1997): 2; Spurgeon M. Keeny Jr., "NATO Expansion: Time for Damage Control," *Arms Control Today* 28, no. 2 (1998): 2.; and Jack Mendelsohn, "Tranche Fever," *Arms Control Today* 28, no. 3 (1998): 2.

29. Bill Clinton, *My Life* (New York: Alfred A. Knopf, 2004), 750.

30. Leon Fuerth, interview, Washington, DC, February 12, 2020.

31. "Harnessing Process to Purpose," Memorandum to the President-Elect (Washington, DC: Carnegie Endowment for International Peace and Institute for International Economics, 1992), 16.

32. "New Purposes and Priorities for Arms Control," a report to Sherman M. Funk, Inspector General of ACDA (Washington, DC: ACDA, December 14, 1992).

33. Michael Krepon, Amy Smithson, and James A. Schear, "Restructuring for the Post-Cold War Era," Occasional Paper no. 13, December 1992 (Washington, DC: Stimson Center). Also see "Does the Arms Control and Disarmament Agency Have a Future?" Occasional Paper no. 8, March 1992 (Washington, DC: Stimson Center).

34. See Jonathan B. Tucker, "U.S. Ratification of the Chemical Weapons Convention," Center for the Study of Weapons of Mass Destruction, Case Study 4, December 2011 (Washington, DC: National Defense University Press); and Michael Krepon, Amy E. Smithson, and John Parachini, "The Battle to Obtain U.S. Ratification of the Chemical Weapons Convention," Occasional Paper no. 35, July 1997 (Washington, DC: Stimson Center).

35. Michael Krepon and Dan Caldwell, eds., *The Politics of Arms Control Treaty Ratification* (New York: St. Martin's Press, 1991).

36. See Julian E. Zelizer, *Burning Down the House: Newt Gingrich, the Fall of a Speaker, and the Rise of the New Republican Party* (New York: Penguin Press, 2020).

37. Steven Lee Myers, "Clinton Mobilizes Bipartisan Effort on Chemical Arms," *New York Times*, April 5, 1997, A1.

38. Clinton, *My Life*, 753.

39. Robert Bell, telephone interview, February 5, 2020.

40. Bell, telephone interview, February 5, 2020; and Tucker, "U.S. Ratification of the Chemical Weapons Convention," 19–20.

41. Adam Clymer, "Some in the G.O.P. Move to Back Ban on Chemical Arms," *New York Times*, April 24, 1997, A1; Peter Baker and Helen Dewar, "Dole Raises Hopes of Chemical Treaty Backers," *Washington Post*, April 24, 1997, A1; and Francis X. Clines, "Dole No Senator, but Might as Well Be," *New York Times*, April 24, 1997, A6.

42. Tucker, "U.S. Ratification of the Chemical Weapons Convention," 21; and Robert Bell, electronic communication, March 7, 2020.

43. "In Their Own Words: Three Senators, For and Against" *New York Times*, April 25, 1997, A10.

44. Talbott, *The Russia Hand,* 376.

45. Clinton, *My Life*, 750; Talbott, *The Russia Hand,* 238–41.

46. Jan Lodal, telephone interview, March 13, 2020.

47. Clinton, *My Life,* 752. Also see Thomas W. Lippman, "Clinton, Yeltsin Agree on Arms Cuts and NATO," *Washington Post*, March 22, 1997.

48. Steven Lee Myers, "U.S. and Russia Agree to Put Off Deadline for Arms," *New York Times,* September 27, 1997, A1; and John M. Goshko, "U.S., Russia Reaffirm Nuclear Pact," *Washington Post*, September 27, 1997, A16.

49. Talbott, *The Russia Hand*, 390.

50. Donald H. Rumsfeld et al., "The Report of the Commission to Assess the Ballistic Missile Threat to the United States," July 15, 1998 (Washington, DC: U.S. Government Publishing Office, 1998), 5–6.

51. Michael R. Gordon, "Putin Wins Vote in Parliament on Treaty to Cut Nuclear Arms," *New York Times*, April 15, 2000, A1.

52. "Remarks at the National Defense University, May 1, 2001," *Public Papers of the Presidents of the United States: Administration of George W. Bush, 2001, Book I—January 20 to June 30, 2001* (Washington, DC: U.S. Government Printing Office, 2002), 471, 472.

53. See Terry L. Diebel, "Inside the Water's Edge: The Senate Votes on the Comprehensive Test Ban Treaty," Pew Case Studies in International Affairs, Case 263, Institute for the Study of Diplomacy, Georgetown University, 2003; and Diebel, "The Death of a Treaty," *Foreign Affairs* 81, no. 5 (September–October 2002): 142–61.

54. Eric Schmitt, "A Plan Is in Works to Put Off a Vote on Test Ban Pact," *New York Times*, October 12, 1999, A12.

55. Diebel, "The Death of a Treaty," 149.

56. Jacques Chirac, Tony Blair, and Gerhard Schroder, "A Treaty We All Need," *New York Times,* October 8, 1999, A27; and United States Congress, Senate Committee on Foreign Relations, *Final Review of the Comprehensive Test Ban Treaty, October 7, 1999*, 106ᵗʰ Cong., 1st Sess. (2000), 3.

57. United States Congress, Senate Committee on Armed Services, *Comprehensive Test Ban Treaty, October 6 and 7, 1999*, 106th Cong., 1st Sess. (2000), 33.

58. United States Congress, Senate Committee on Armed Services, *Comprehensive Test Ban Treaty, October 7, 1999*, 106th Cong., 1st Sess. (Washington, DC: U.S. Government Publishing Office, 2000), 135.

59. John Deutch, Henry Kissinger, and Brent Scowcroft, "Test-Ban Treaty: Let's Wait Awhile," *Washington Post*, October 6, 1999, A33.

60. Wendy R. Sherman, *Not for the Faint of Heart: Lessons in Courage, Rower & Persistence* (New York: Pubic Affairs, 2018), 106.

61. Albright, *Madame Secretary*, 467.

CHAPTER 14

1. Robert Gates, interview, July 9, 2013, George W. Bush Oral History Project, Miller Center, University of Virginia, 76.

2. See Condoleezza Rice, *No Higher Honor: A Memoir of My Years in Washington* (New York: Crown, 2011); Marcus Mabry, *Twice as Good: Condoleezza Rice and Her Path to Power* (New York: Rodale, 2007); and Elizabeth Bumiller, *Condoleezza Rice: An American Life* (New York: Random House, 2007).

3. Stephen J. Hadley, interview, October 31, 2011, George W. Bush Oral History Project, Miller Center, University of Virginia, 17, 19.

4. Dick Cheney, *In My Time: A Personal and Political Memoir* (New York: Simon & Schuster, 2011), 264.

5. James Mann, *The Great Rift: Dick Cheney, Colin Powell, and the Broken Friendship That Defined an Era* (New York: Henry Holt and Company, 2020), 222.

6. Ron Suskind, *The One Percent Doctrine: Deep inside America's Pursuit of Its Enemies since 9/11* (New York: Simon & Schuster, 2006), 62; and Peter Baker, *Days of Fire: Bush and Cheney in the White House* (New York: Doubleday, 2013).

7. Rice, *No Higher Honor,* 16.

8. See Rice, *No Higher Honor,* 13–22; James Mann, *The Great Rift;* and Bumiller, *Condoleezza Rice.*

9. Roberta Wohlstetter, *Pearl Harbor: Warning and Decision* (Stanford: Stanford University Press, 1962), viii. Also see Donald Rumsfeld, *Known Unknowns: A Memoir* (New York: Penguin, 2011), xiv–xv.

10. Robert Gates, *Duty: Memoirs of a Secretary at War* (New York: Alfred A. Knopf, 2014), 93.

11. Gates, *Duty,* 93.

12. George F. Will, "Is Iranian Containment the Only Option?" *Washington Post,* May 13, 2018, A21.

13. William J. Burns, *The Back Channel: A Memoir of American Diplomacy and the Case for Its Renewal* (New York: Random House, 2019), 202.

14. Burns, *The Back Channel,* 202.

15. Charles Krauthammer, "The Unipolar Moment," *Foreign Affairs* 70, no. 1 (1990/1991): 23–33.

16. Brent Scowcroft, "Don't Attack Saddam," *Wall Street Journal,* August 15, 2002, A12.

17. James A. Baker III, "The Right Way to Change a Regime," *New York Times,* August 25, 2002, C9.

18. Krauthammer, "The Unipolar Moment," 24, 25, 26.

19. Rice, *No Higher Honor,* 3–5.

20. See James Mann, *The Rise of the Vulcans: The History of Bush's War Cabinet* (New York: Penguin Books, 2004).

21. See Thomas E. Ricks, *Fiasco: The American Military Adventure in Iraq* (New York: Penguin Group, 2006); and Michael R. Gordon and General Bernard E. Trainor, *Cobra II: The Inside Story of the Invasion and Occupation of Iraq* (New York: Random House, 2006).

22. Bob Woodward, *Plan of Attack* (New York: Simon and Schuster, 2004), 150. Also see Robert Draper, *To Start a War* (New York: Penguin Press, 2020).

23. Cheney, *In My Time,* 381.

24. President George W. Bush, *The National Security Strategy of the United States of America* (Washington, DC: The White House, 2002), introduction, 15.

25. Rumsfeld, *Known Unknowns,* 710.

26. Rice, *No Higher Honor*, 17; Gates, *Duty*, 584; and Peter Baker, *Days of Fire: Bush and Cheney in the White House* (New York: Doubleday, 2013), 3–11.

27. See Robert S. McNamara, *In Retrospect: The Tragedy and Lessons of Vietnam* (New York: Vintage, 1995).

28. Rumsfeld, *Known Unknowns*, 449.

29. Cheney, *In My Time*, 396.

30. George W. Bush, *Decision Points (New York: Random House, 2010)*, 242.

31. Krauthammer, "The Unipolar Moment," 30.

32. Bumiller, *Condoleezza Rice*, 173–75.

33. Krauthammer, "The Unipolar Moment," 30.

34. Charles Krauthammer, "The Unipolar Moment Revisited," *National Interest* 70 (2002): 17.

35. CNN's *Late Edition with Wolf Blitzer*, September 8, 2002.

36. Houston Wood, telephone interview, April 1, 2020. Also see David Barstow, William J. Broad, and Jeff Gerth, "The Nuclear Card: The Aluminum Tube Story, How White House Embraced Suspect Iraq Arms Intelligence," *New York Times*, October 3, 2004, A1.

37. See James Cameron, *The Double Game: The Demise of America's First Missile Defense System and the Rise of Strategic Arms Limitation* (New York: Oxford University Press, 2018).

38. Patrick E. Tyler, "Bush and Putin Look Each Other in the Eye," *New York Times*, June 17, 2001, 10.

39. Hadley, interview, October 31, 2011, Miller Center, 40.

40. See James Cameron, *Double Game;* and Lynn F. Rusten, "U.S. Withdrawal from the Antiballistic Missile Treaty," Center for the Study of Weapons of Mass Destruction Case Study 2 (Washington, DC: National Defense University Press, January 2010).

41. Hadley, interview, November 1, 2011, Miller Center, 83.

42. John Bolton, *Surrender Is Not an Option: Defending America at the United Nations and Abroad* (New York: Simon & Schuster, 2007), 72.

43. Rusten, "U.S. Withdrawal from the Antiballistic Missile Treaty," 4–9.

44. Bolton, *Surrender Is Not an Option*, 61.

45. Hadley, interview, October 31, 2011, Miller Center, 36.

46. "FM Ivanov Says Russia Regrets U.S. Withdrawal from the ABM Treaty," *Interfax*, June 13, 2002, translated in Foreign Broadcast Information Service CEP20020613000005.

47. Bolton, *Surrender Is Not an Option*, 69–70.

48. Bolton, *Surrender Is Not an Option*, 77.

49. Franklin Miller, telephone interview, April 2, 2020.

50. Bolton, *Surrender Is Not an Option*, 82.

51. See Robert G. Joseph and Susan Koch, *The Proliferation Security Initiative: A Model for Future International Collaboration* (Fairfax, VA: National Institute for Public Policy, August 2009).

52. See Robert G. Joseph, *Countering WMD: The Libyan Experience* (Fairfax, VA: National Institute Press, 2009); and David E. Sanger, "U.S. Lifts Bans on Libyan Trade, but Limits on Diplomacy Remain," *New York Times*, April 24, 2004, A1.

53. Rice, *No Higher Honor*, 158.

54. Rice, *No Higher Honor*, 306.

55. Rice, *No Higher Honor*, 159.

56. See George Perkovich, "Global Implications of the U.S.-India Deal," *Daedalus* 139, no. 1 (2010): 20–31.

57. See Sridhar Krishnaswami, "Indo-US N-Deal a Historic Opportunity," *India Abroad*, March 22, 2006; and J. Sri Raman, "The U.S.-India Nuclear Deal—One Year Later," *Bulletin of the Atomic Scientists*, October 1, 2019.

58. Robert D. Blackwill, "The India Imperative," *National Interest* 90 (2005): 10; Rice, *No Higher Honor*, 129, 437; and Gopalan Balachandran, "It's Not about Pakistan's Reactor but US Reaction," *Indian Express*, July 27, 2006.

59. See Burns, *The Back Channel*, 457–59.

60. Rice, *No Higher Honor*, 674.

61. Bush, *Decision Points*, 430.

62. Gates, *Duty*, 157–58, 94.

63. Vladimir Putin, "Putin's Prepared Remarks at 43rd Munich Conference on Security Policy," *Washington Post*, February 12, 2007, www.washington post .com/wp-dyn/content/article/2007/02/12/AR2007021200555.html; and Thom Shanker and Mark Landler, "Putin Says U.S. Is Undermining Global Stability," *New York Times*, February 11, 2007, A1.

64. Rice, *No Higher Honor*, 670.

65. Bush, *Decision Points*, 430–31; and Rice, *No Higher Honor*, 671–72.

66. "Bucharest Summit Declaration," NATO, Bucharest, April 3, 2008, www .nato.int/cps/en/natolive/official_texts_8443.htm.

67. Burns, *The Back Channel*, 239.

68. Burns, *The Back Channel*, 221.

69. Gates, interview, July 8, 2013, Miller Center, 49.

70. Rice: *No Higher Honor*, 692.

71. Burns, *The Back Channel*, 222, 238.

72. Rice, *No Higher Honor*, 673.

73. Rice, *No Higher Honor*, 693.

74. Bush, *Decision Points*, 432–33.

75. Thom Shanker and Mark Landler, "Putin Says U.S. Is Undermining Global Stability," *New York Times*, February 11, 2007, 1.

76. Burns, *The Back Channel*, 172.

77. Gates, interview, July 8, 2013, Miller Center, 14.

78. Gates, interview, July 9, 2013, Miller Center, 88.

CHAPTER 15

1. William J. Burns, *The Back Channel: A Memoir of American Diplomacy and the Case for Its Renewal* (New York: Random House, 2019), 277–78; and Mike McFaul, *From Cold War to Hot Peace: An American Ambassador in Putin's Russia* (Boston: Houghton Mifflin Harcourt, 2018), 130–34.

2. See Brad Roberts, "On Creating the Conditions for Nuclear Disarmament: Past Lessons, Future Prospects," *Washington Quarterly* 42, no. 2 (Summer 2019): 7–30.

3. Barack Obama, *The Promised Land* (New York: Crown, 2020), 483.

4. Joseph S. Nye Jr., "Soft Power," *Foreign Policy* 80 (1990): 168; and Joseph S. Nye Jr., *Bound to Lead: The Changing Nature of American Power* (New York: Basic Books, 1990), 31.

5. See Obama, *The Promised Land*.

6. George P. Shultz, William J. Perry, Henry A. Kissinger, and Sam Nunn, "A World Free of Nuclear Weapons," *Wall Street Journal*, January 4, 2007, A15.

7. Ben Rhodes, *The World as It Is: A Memoir of the Obama White House* (New York: Random House, 2018), 41–42.

8. "Remarks in Prague, April 5, 2009," *Public Papers of the Presidents of the United States: Barack Obama, 2009, Book I—January 20 to June 30, 2009* (Washington, DC: U.S. Government Printing Office, 2010), 439–44. Also see Helene

Cooper and David E. Sanger, "Citing Rising Risk, Obama Seeks Nuclear Arms Cuts: Warns of Spread of Bomb Technology in Black Market," *New York Times*, April 6, 2009, A1.

9. Fred Kaplan, *The Bomb: Presidents, Generals, and the Secret History of Nuclear War* (New York: Simon & Schuster, 2020), 243–44.

10. Robert Gates, *Duty: Memoirs of a Secretary at War* (New York: Alfred A. Knopf, 2014), 283, 290.

11. See Ash Carter, *Inside the Five-Sided Box: Lessons from a Lifetime of Leadership in the Pentagon* (New York: Random House, 2019). Also see Leon Panetta, *Worthy Fights* (New York: Penguin Press, 2014); Hillary Rodham Clinton, *Hard Choices* (New York: Simon & Schuster, 2014); John Kerry, *Every Day Is Extra* (New York: Simon and Schuster, 2018); Rhodes, *The World as It Is*; Wendy Sherman, *Not for the Faint of Heart: Lessons in Courage, Power & Persistence* (New York: Public Affairs, 2018); Susan Rice, *Tough Love: My Story of the Things Worth Fighting For* (New York: Simon & Schuster, 2019); and James Mann, *The Obamians: The Struggle inside the White House to Redefine American Power* (New York: Penguin Books, 2013).

12. Gary Samore, telephone interview, May 11, 2020.

13. Burns, *The Back Channel*, 206.

14. McFaul, *From Cold War to Hot Peace*, 139.

15. Brad Roberts, telephone interview, April 20, 2020.

16. Rose Gottemoeller, electronic communication, April 24, 2020.

17. See Rose Gottemoeller, *A Personal Memoir of the New START Treaty Negotiations*, forthcoming.

18. Ellen Barry, "Putin Says U.S. Antimissile Plan Stands in Way of New Arms Treaty," *New York Times*, December 30, 2009, A6.

19. Obama, *The Promised Land*, 484.

20. Obama, *The Promised Land*, 466.

21. Jon Wolfsthal, telephone interview, April 28, 2020.

22. Henry A. Kissinger, George P. Shultz, James A. Baker III, Lawrence S. Eagleburger, and Colin L. Powell, "Why New START Deserves GOP Support," *Washington Post*, December 2, 2010, A25; and Condoleezza Rice, "New START: Ratify with Caveats," *Wall Street Journal*, December 7, 2010, A19.

23. Craig Whitlock, "For Deterrent, U.S. Looks to Conventional Warheads," *Washington Post*, April 8, 2010, A1.

24. Mitt Romney, "Obama's Worst Foreign Mistake," *Washington Post*, July 6, 2010, A13; and Mitt Romney, "Eight Problems with the New START," *National Review Online*, July 26, 2010.

25. John Bolton, "New Start Is Unilateral Disarmament," *Wall Street Journal*, September 8, 2010, A19.

26. Rose Gottemoeller, telephone interview, February 14, 2020.

27. Lynn Rusten, telephone interview, April 27, 2020.

28. See Charles D. Ferguson and William C. Potter, *The Four Faces of Nuclear Terrorism* (New York: Routledge, 2005).

29. Michelle Cann, Kelsey Davenport, and Jenna Parker, "The Nuclear Security Summit: Accomplishments of the Process" (Washington, DC: Arms Control Association and Partnership for Global Security, March 2016).

30. See Amandeep S. Gill, *Nuclear Security Summits: A History* (New York: Palgrave Macmillan, 2020).

31. Tomoko Kurokawa, "Determinants of the Nuclear Policy Options in the Obama Administration: An Interview with Jon Wolfsthal," *Journal for Peace and Nuclear Disarmament* 1, no. 2 (2018): 521.

32. Sherman, *Not for the Faint of Heart*, 29.

33. Wendy Sherman, telephone interview, May 18, 2020.

34. National Intelligence Council, *Iran: Nuclear Intentions and Capabilities*, National Intelligence Estimate, November 2007, 5.

35. Sharon Squassoni, *Iran's Nuclear Program: Recent Developments* (RS21592), Congressional Research Service, Library of Congress, August 3, 2006, 3.

36. Burns, *The Back Channel*, 338.

37. Burns, *The Back Channel*, 362.

38. See Kim Zetter, *Countdown to Zero Day: Stuxnet and the World's First Digital Weapon* (New York: Broadway Books, 2014); and David E. Sanger, *Confront and Conceal: Obama's Secret Wars and Surprising Use of American Power* (New York: Crown, 2012), 188–225.

39. Thomas Erdbrink and William Branigan, "Iran's Khamenei Rejects U.S. Outreach," *Washington Post*, November 4, 2009, A12.

40. Burns, *The Back Channel,* 384.

41. Burns, *The Back Channel*, 368.

42. Burns, *The Back Channel*, 376.

43. Michael R. Gordon, "West and Iran Seen as Nearing a Nuclear Deal," *New York Times*, November 8, 2013, A1.

44. Sherman, *Not For the Faint of Heart,* 130.

45. Burns, *The Back Channel*, 382.

46. Burns, *The Back Channel,* 248. Also see Sherman, *Not for the Faint of Heart,* 32.

47. John Kerry, *Every Day Is Extra* (New York: Simon & Schuster, 2018), 504.

48. "Joint Meeting to Hear an Address by His Excellency Binyamin Netanyahu, Prime Minister of Israel," *Congressional Record* 161, no. 36, House of Representatives, 114th Cong., 1st Sess. (March 3, 2015), H1528–1531.

49. Gates, *Duty*, 388–89; Robert M. Gates, interview, July 8–9, 2013, George W. Bush Oral History Project, Miller Center, University of Virginia, 88–89.

50. Peter Baker, "In Congress, Netanyahu Faults 'Bad Deal' on Iran," *New York Times*, March 4, 2015, A1.

51. Senator Tom Cotton et al., *An Open Letter to the Leaders of the Islamic Republic of Iran*, March 9, 2015, www.cotton.senate.gov/?p=press_release&id=120.

52. Peter Baker, "G.O.P Senators Write to Tehran on Nuclear Pact," *New York Times*, March 10, 2015, A1.

53. Kerry, *Every Day Is Extra*, 505.

54. United States Department of State, "Joint Comprehensive Plan of Action," July 14, 2015, 2, https://2009–2017.state.gov/documents/organization/245317.pdf.

55. Kerry, *Every Day Is Extra,* 505–6.

56. Sherman, *Not for the Faint of Heart*, x.

57. Mark Landler and Maggie Haberman, "Clinton and Trump, in Speeches, Vow to Protect Israel but Differ on the Means," *New York Times*, March 22, 2016, A18; and Abby Phillip and Jenna Johnson, "Presidential Candidates Promise They Will Stand by Israel," *Washington Post*, March 22, 2016, A4.

58. Wendy Sherman, telephone interview, May 18, 2020.

59. Burns, *The Back Channel*, 359; and James Timbie, interview, Livermore, CA, February 20, 2020. Also see Kerry, *Every Day Is Extra,* 523.

60. Rice, *Tough Love*, 418.

61. Richard M. Nixon, "It's What You Cut," *New York Times,* December 20, 1987, E18; Henry Kissinger, "Forget the 'Zero Option'," *Washington Post,* April 5, 1987, C2; and James Schlesinger, "Nuclear Deterrence, the Ultimate Reality," *Washington Post,* October 21, 1986, A17.

62. Vladimir Putin, "Putin's Prepared Remarks at 43rd Munich Conference on Security Policy," *Washington Post,* February 12, 2007, www.washingtonpost .com/wp-dyn/content/article/2007/02/12/AR2007021200555.html.

63. Aleksandr' G. Savel'yev and Nikolay N. Detinov, *The Big Five: Arms Control Decision-Making in the Soviet Union* (Westport, CT: Praeger, 1995), p. 138.

64. Anatoly Dobrynin, *In Confidence: Moscow's Ambassador to Six Cold War Presidents* (New York: Random House, 1995), 629, 630.

65. Michael R. Gordon, "Russians' Test Called Breach of Missile Pact," *New York Times*, July 29, 2014, A1.

66. Rose Gottemoeller, "US-Russian Nuclear Arms Control Negotiations—A Short History," *Foreign Service Journal* 97, no. 4 (2020): 30.

67. See U.S. Department of State, *Adherence to and Compliance with Arms Control and Nonproliferation Agreements and Commitments, 2013* (Washington, DC: U.S. Department of State, 2013), 8.

68. U.S. Department of State, *Adherence to and Compliance with Arms Control and Nonproliferation Agreements and Commitments, 2014* (Washington, DC: U.S. Department of State, 2014), 8.

69. Neil MacFarquhar, "Russia Shows Off New Cruise Missile and Says It Abides by Landmark Treaty," *New York Times,* January 23, 2019, A7.

70. See Hearings, United States House of Representatives, Committee on Armed Services, Subcommittee on Strategic Forces, *INF Withdrawal and the Future of Arms Control: Implications for the Security of the United States and Its Allies,* 116th Cong., 1st Sess. (February 26, 2019), 3–6, 36–56.

71. See Hans M. Kristensen and Matt Korda, "Russian Nuclear Forces," *Bulletin of the Atomic Scientists* 76, no. 2 (March 9, 2020): 113; and Amy F. Woolf, *U.S. Russian Compliance with the Intermediate Range Nuclear Forces (INF) Treaty: Background and Issues for Congress* (R43832), Congressional Research Service, Library of Congress, August 2, 2019.

72. Michael Crowley, "What Worries Ben Rhodes about Trump," *Politico,* January/February 2017, www.politico.com/magazine/story/2017/01/obama -foreign-policy-legacy-ben-rhodes-donald-trump-china-iran-214642.

73. Rose Gottemoeller, telephone interview, May 28, 2020.

74. Frank Rose, telephone interview, May 25, 2020.

75. The White House, "Remarks by the Vice President on Nuclear Security," January 11, 2017, https://obamawhitehouse.archives.gov/the-press-office/2017/ 01/12/remarks-vice-president-nuclear-security.

76. Henry Kissinger, *Diplomacy* (New York: Simon & Schuster, 1994), 836.

77. Sherman, *Not for the Faint of Heart,* 166.

78. David E. Sanger and Choe Sang-Hun, "North Korea Nuclear Test Draws U.S. Warning of 'Massive Military Response,'" *New York Times,* September 2, 2017, A1.

CHAPTER 16

1. *The 2007–2009 Recession: Similarities to and Differences from the Past* (R40198), Congressional Research Service, Library of Congress, October 6, 2010, 1, 2.

2. M. Ayhan Kose, Naotaka Sugawara, and Marco E. Terrones, "What Happens during Global Recessions?" in *A Decade after the Global Recession: Lessons*

and Challenges for Emerging and Developing Economies, ed. M. Ayhan Kose and Franziska Ohnsorge (Washington, DC: World Bank Group, 2019), 92.

3. World Bank, *Global Economic Prospects, June 2020* (Washington, DC: World Bank, 2020), 4.

4. Richard Hofstadter, "A Long View: Goldwater in History," *New York Review of Books* 11, no. 15 (1964): 20.

5. David M. Herszenhorn, "Benghazi Panel Finds No Misdeeds by Clinton," *Washington Post,* June 29, 2016, A1; and Mark Landler and Amy Chozick, "Clinton Unscathed by Benghazi Report: No Significant News in 800-Page Document on Her Role in 2012 Attack," *New York Times,* June 30, 2016, 6.

6. See Mary L. Trump, *Too Much and Never Enough: How My Family Created the World's Most Dangerous Man* (New York: Simon & Schuster, 2020).

7. See Charles A. Kupchan, *Isolationism: A History of America's Efforts to Shield Itself from the World* (New York: Oxford University Press, 2020).

8. Helene Cooper, "Senate Confirms Esper as Defense Secretary, Filling a Long-Vacant Job," *New York Times,* July 24, 2019, A16.

9. See Uzra S. Zeya and Jon Finer, "Revitalizing the State Department and U.S. Diplomacy," Council on Foreign Relations, November 2020, https://cdn.cfr.org/sites/default/files/report_pdf/csr89_final.pdf.

10. John Bolton, *The Room Where It Happened: A White House Memoir* (New York: Simon & Schuster, 2020), 459–479.

11. John Bolton, *Surrender Is Not an Option: Defending America at the United Nations and Abroad* (New York: Simon & Schuster, 2007), 11.

12. Bolton, *Surrender Is Not an Option,* 55, 19, 83.

13. Strobe Talbott, *Deadly Gambits: The Reagan Administration and the Stalemate in Nuclear Arms Control* (New York: Alfred A. Knopf, 1984), 348.

14. See "The Politics of Arms Control: A Discussion with Assistant Secretary Christopher Ford," *International Institute for Strategic Studies,* February 11, 2020, www.iiss.org/events/2020/02/the-politics-of-arms-control.

15. William J. Perry, *My Journey at the Nuclear Brink* (Stanford: Stanford University Press, 2005), 103–9.

16. John Bolton, *The Room Where It Happened,* 223–45, 287–318, 445–82.

17. See William Burr and Jeffrey P. Kimball, *Nixon's Nuclear Specter: The Secret Alert of 1969, Madman Diplomacy and the Vietnam War* (Lawrence: University Press of Kansas, 2015), 52. Also see Fred Kaplan, *The Bomb: Presidents, Generals and the Secret History of Nuclear War* (New York: Simon & Schuster, 2020), 100–120; and Jeffrey P. Kimball, *Nixon's Vietnam War* (Lawrence: University of Kansas Press, 1998), 63–86.

18. Stuart Jefferies, "The 'Nuclear Football'—The Deadly Briefcase That Never Leaves the President's Side," *The Guardian,* August 22, 2016, 9. Also see William J. Broad and David E. Sanger, "Issue in Race: Can President Be Kept from Hitting Button?" *New York Times,* August 5, 2016, A1.

19. Peter Baker and Choe Sang-hun, "In Chilling Nuclear Terms, Trump Warns North Korea," *New York Times,* August 9, 2019, A1.

20. Julie Hirschfeld Davis, "In Risky Game, Trump Taunts a Touchy Dictator," *New York Times,* September 25, 2017, A1.

21. Peter Baker and Somini Sengupta, "Trump Moves to Widen U.S. Trade Sanctions against North Korea," *New York Times,* September 22, 2017, A11.

22. Peter Baker and Choe Sang-hun, "President Claims His Talks Ended Nuclear Threat," *New York Times,* June 14, 2018, A1.

23. Anne Gearan and Aaron Blake, "In W. Va., Trump Turns Kavanaugh Nomination Fight into GOP Rallying Cry," *Washington Post,* September 30, 2018, A10.

24. See Bolton, *The Room Where It Happened,* 77–126.

25. H.R. McMaster, *Battlegrounds: The Fight to Defend the Free World* (New York: Harper Collins, 2020), 130–31, 255.

26. Bolton, *The Room Where It Happened,* 48–49.

27. Mark Landler, "Trump Abandons Iran Nuclear Deal He Long Scorned," May 8, 2018, A1.

28. Bolton, *The Room Where It Happened,* 161.

29. Anne Gearan, Paul Sonne, and Carol Morello, "U.S. to Withdraw from Nuclear Pact with Russia," *Washington Post,* February 2, 2019, A1.

30. Missy Ryan and John Hudson, "In NRA Speech, Trump Pulls U.S. Support for Global Arms Pact," *Washington Post,* April 28, 2019, A2.

31. David E. Sanger, "Trump to Pull Out of Open Skies Treaty in Latest Arms Accord Retreat," *New York Times,* May 22, 2020, A20.

32. President Donald J. Trump, *The National Security Strategy of the United States of America* (Washington, DC: The White House, 2017), 1, 4, 9, 33, 28, 38, 48.

33. Trump, *National Security Strategy of the United States of America,* 1.

34. Richard Haass, "Trump's Foreign Policy Doctrine? The Withdrawal Doctrine," *Washington Post,* May 27, 2020, A21.

35. Charlie Savage, Eric Schmitt, and Michael Schwirtz, "Russia Offered Afghans Bounty to Kill U.S. Troops, Officials Say," *New York Times,* June 27, 2020, A1.

36. Winston S. Churchill, *Their Finest Hour* (Boston: Houghton Mifflin, 1949), 24.

37. Audrey Carlsen and Jugal K. Patel, "Trump's Policy Reversals, in His Own Words," *New York Times,* April 15, 2017, A10; "Trump to Montenegro: Drop Dead," *New York Times,* July 23, 2018, A18.

38. Katie Reilly, "John McCain Calls Trump's Press Conference with Putin 'One of the Most Disgraceful Performances by an American President'," July 16, 2018, https://time.com/5339932/john-mccain-statement-trump-putin-meeting/; and Jason Le Miere, "Ex-CIA Head Says Donald Trump Committed 'Treasonous,' Impeachable Offense during Putin Press Conference," *Newsweek,* July 16, 2018, www.newsweek.com/donald-trump-putin-treasonous-brennan-cia-1026468.

39. See Ben Kesling and Paul Sonne, "Trump Supports Strengthening of Nuclear Arsenal," *Wall Street Journal,* December 23, 2016, A5; Jake Sherman and Anna Palmer, "POLITICO Playbook: The World According to Trump," *Politico,* October 22, 2019, www.politico.com/newsletters/playbook/2019/10/22/the-world-according-to-trump-487485; Rebecca Morin, "Trump: U.S. Will Cease Building Nuclear Arsenal If Other Countries Stop First," *Politico,* February 12, 2018, www.politico.com/story/2018/02/12/trump-nuclear-arsenal-404491; "Remarks by President Trump and Prime Minister Trudeau of Canada before Bilateral Meeting," *White House Press Releases, Fact Sheets and Briefings,* October 11, 2017; and "How Trump Has Exposed Our Warped Priorities," *Topeka Capital Journal,* October 23, 2016, A4.

40. Jonathan Swan and Margaret Talev, "Scoop: Trump Suggested Nuking Hurricanes to Stop Them from Hitting U.S.," *Axios,* August 25, 2019, www.axios.com/trump-nuclear-bombs-hurricanes-97231f38-2394-4120-a3fa-8c9cfoe3f51c.html; Antonia Noori Farzan, "Trump Denies That He Suggested Nuking Hurricanes; But the Government Once Studied the Idea," *Washington Post,* August 26, 2019, www.washingtonpost.com/nation/2019/08/26/trump-nuclear-weapons-hurricane/; Courtney Kube, Kristen Welker, Carol E. Lee, and Savannah Guthrie, "Trump Wanted Tenfold Increase in Nuclear Arsenal, Surprising Military," *NBC News,* October 11, 2017, www.nbcnews.com/news/all/trump-wanted-dramatic

-increase-nuclear-arsenal-meeting-military-leaders-n809701; and Peter Baker and Cecilia Kang, "NBC Nuclear Arsenal Story Prompts a Threat by Trump," *New York Times*, October 12, 2017, A14.

41. United States Department of Defense, *Nuclear Posture Review, February 2018* (Washington, DC: U.S. Department of Defense, 2018), Secretary's Preface, ii, iii, v.

42. Congressional Budget Office, *Approaches for Managing the Costs of U.S. Nuclear Forces, 2017 to 2046, October 2017* (Washington, DC: Congressional Budget Office, 2017), 1.

43. United States Department of Defense, *Nuclear Posture Review*, xvi, xvii, 73.

44. See W.J. Hennigan and John Walcott, "The U.S. Expects China Will Quickly Double Its Nuclear Stockpile," *Time*, May 29, 2019, https://time.com/5597955/china-nuclear-weapons-intelligence/; and Hans M. Kristensen and Matt Korda, "United States Nuclear Forces, 2020," *Bulletin of the Atomic Scientists* 76, no. 1 (January 2020): 46–60.

45. John Bolton, "New Start Is Unilateral Disarmament," *Wall Street Journal*, September 8, 2010, A19; and John Bolton and John Yoo, "Why Rush to Cut Nukes?" *New York Times*, November 10, 2010, A35.

46. John Bolton, "Trump's New Start with Russia May Prove Better Than Obama's," *Wall Street Journal*, February 13, 2017, A17.

47. Johnathan Landay and David Rhode, "Exclusive—In Call with Putin, Trump Denounced Obama-era Nuclear Arms Treaty—Sources," Reuters, February 9, 2017, https://news.trust.org/item/20170209171124–868gh.

48. Bolton, *The Room Where It Happened*, 161.

49. Bill Gertz, "Bolton: China Continuing Cyberattacks on Government, Private Networks," *Washington Free Beacon*, June 18, 2019, https://freebeacon.com/national-security/bolton-china-continuing-cyberattacks-on-government-private-networks/.

50. "A Nuclear Treaty's Final Word," *Washington Post*, August 1, 2019, A20; Shervin Taheran and Daryl G. Kimball, "Bolton Declares New START Extension 'Unlikely'," *Arms Control Today* 49, no. 6 (2019): 22; and Kingston Reif, "Bolton Renews New START Criticism," *Arms Control Today* 49, no. 7 (2019): 28.

51. Tim Morrison, "Trump Should Continue to Follow His Instincts on Arms Treaty," *CNN*, December 5, 2019, www.cnn.com/2019/12/05/opinions/trump-china-russia-arms-treaty-morrison/index.html

52. Kylie Atwood and Nicole Gaouette, "Trump Admin Aiming for Major Nuclear Deal with Russia and China," *CNN*, April 26, 2019, www.cnn.com/2019/04/25/politics/trump-nuclear-deal-russia-china/index.html. The following month, Senator Tom Cotton co-sponsored a Senate resolution, "The New START Treaty Improvement Act," that would withhold funds to extend the treaty unless it included China and covered Russia's entire inventory of nuclear warheads. "Senators Cotton, Cornyn, and Rep. Cheney Introduce New START Treaty Improvement Act," *Federal Information & News Dispatch*, May 13, 2019.

53. Tom Cotton, "The Open Skies Treaty Is Giving Russia Spying Capabilities. End It," *Washington Post*, December 10, 2019, www.washingtonpost.com/opinions/2019/12/10/open-skies-treaty-is-giving-russia-spying-capabilities-end-it/.

54. Michael R. Gordon, "U.S. Seeks to Include Beijing in Arms Pact," *Wall Street Journal*, May 22, 2020, A1.

55. David Sanger, Eric Schmitt, and Edward Wong, "As Virus Toll Preoccupies U.S., Rivals Test Limits of American Power," *New York Times*, June 1, 2020, A5.

56. David Wainer and Nick Wadhams, "Russia Signals It Won't Lean on China to Join Arms Control Talks," *Bloomberg News,* June 9, 2020, hwww .bloomberg.com/news/articles/2020-06-09/russia-signals-it-won-t-lean-on-china -to-join-arms-control-talks?utm.

57. Christopher Ford, "Our Vision for a Constructive, Collaborative Disarmament Discourse," Remarks at the Conference on Disarmament March 26, 2019, www.state.gov/t/isn/rls/rm/2019/290676.htm; and "The Politics of Arms Control: A Discussion with Assistant Secretary Christopher Ford," International Institute for Strategic Studies, February 11, 2020, www.iiss.org/events/2020/02/ the-politics-of-arms-control.

58. Missile Defense Project, "Missiles of China," *Missile Threat*, Center for Strategic and International Studies, June 14, 2018, January 13, 2020, https:// missile threat.csis.org/country/china/.

59. See Vince Manzo, *Nuclear Arms Control without a Treaty? Risks and Options after New START* (Arlington, VA: CNA, 2019), www.cna.org/CNA_files/ PDF/IRM-2019-U-019494.pdf.

60. Hillary Rodham Clinton, *Hard Choices* (New York: Simon & Schuster, 2014), 21.

61. William J. Burns, *The Back Channel: A Memoir of American Diplomacy and the Case for Its Renewal* (New York: Random House, 2019), 390.

CHAPTER 17

1. Thomas C. Schelling, "Foreword," in *Arms Control and a Changing Environment, ed. Jeffrey A. Larsen* (Boulder, CO: Lynne Rienner, 2002), iii.

2. Nina Tannenwald, *The Nuclear Taboo: The United States and the Non-Use of Nuclear Weapons since 1945* (Cambridge: Cambridge University Press, 2007), 1. Also see T.V. Paul, *The Tradition of Non-Use of Nuclear Weapons* (Stanford: Stanford University Press, 2009).

3. Thomas C. Schelling and Morton H. Halperin, *Strategy and Arms Control* (New York: Twentieth Century Fund, 1961), 121.

4. Bernard Brodie, ed., *The Absolute Weapon: Atomic Power and World Order* (New York: Harcourt, Brace, 1946).

5. Robert Strausz-Hupé, William R. Kintner, and Stefan T. Possony, *A Forward Strategy for America (*New York: Harper & Brothers, 1961).

6. See Fred Kaplan, *The Bomb: Presidents, Generals, and the Secret History of Nuclear War* (New York: Simon & Schuster, 2020).

7. See Philip Zelikow and Condoleezza Rice, *Germany Unified and Europe Transformed: A Study in Statecraft* (Cambridge, MA: Harvard University Press, 1995), 300–324.

8. Lewis A. Dunn, "The Strategic Elimination of Nuclear Weapons: An Alternative Global Agenda for Nuclear Disarmament," *Nonproliferation Review* 24, nos. 5–6 (2017): 401–35.

9. "Scope of the Comprehensive Nuclear Test-Ban Treaty," U.S. Department of State Fact Sheet, Bureau of Arms Control Verification and Compliance, https:// 2009–2017.state.gov/t/avc/rls/212166.htm.

10. United States Department of State, *Adherence to and Compliance with Arms Control and Nonproliferation Agreements and Commitments,* 2020 (Washington, DC: U.S. Department of State, 2020), 7–8.

11. See R.J. Hemley et al., *Pit Lifetime* (JSR-06–335), JASON, MITE Corporation, January 11, 2007; and U.S. Department of Energy and U.S. Department of Defense, *National Security and Nuclear Weapons in the 21st Century* (Washington, DC: U.S. Departments of Energy and Defense, 2008).

12. See Barry M. Blechman and Stephen S. Kaplan, *Force without War: U.S. Armed Forces as a Political Instrument* (Washington, DC: Brookings Institution, 1978).

13. See Melanie W. Sisson, James A. Siebens, and Barry M. Blechman, eds., *Military Coercion and US Foreign Policy: The Use of Force Short of War* (New York: Routledge, 2020).

14. Samuel Black, *The Changing Political Utility of Nuclear Weapons: Nuclear Threats from 1970 to 2010,* (Washington, DC: Stimson Center, 2010), www.stimson.org/wp-content/files/file-attachments/Nuclear_Final_1.pdf.

15. John W. Lewis and Xue Litai, *Imagined Enemies: China Prepares for Uncertain War* (Stanford: Stanford University Press, 2006), 65; and Black, *Changing Political Utility of Nuclear Weapons,* 15–23.

16. See Todd D. Sechser and Matthew W. Fuhrmann, *Nuclear Weapons and Coercive Diplomacy* (New York: Cambridge University Press, 2017).

17. See Matthew Kroenig, *The Logic of American Nuclear Strategy: Why Strategic Superiority Matters* (New York: Oxford University Press, 2018).

18. "Address before a Joint Session of the Congress on the State of the Union, January 25, 1984," *Public Papers of the President of the United States: Ronald Reagan, Book I: January 1 to June 29, 1984* (Washington, DC: U.S. Government Publishing Office, 1986), p. 93.

19. See William J. Burns, *The Back Channel: A Memoir of American Diplomacy and the Case for Its Renewal* (New York: Random House, 2019), 388–423.

20. Schelling and Halperin, *Strategy and Arms Control,* 1.

21. Schelling and Halperin, *Strategy and Arms Control,* 2.

22. See Emily Goldman, *Sunken Treaties: Naval Arms Control between the Wars* (University Park: Pennsylvania State University Press, 1994); Robert Gordon Kaufman, *Arms Control during the Pre-Nuclear Era: The United States and Naval Limitation between the Two World Wars* (New York: Columbia University Press, 1990); Richard Fanning, *Peace and Disarmament: Naval Rivalry and Arms Control, 1922–1933* (Lexington: University Press of Kentucky, 1995); and Thomas H. Buckley, "The Washington Naval Treaties," in *The Politics of Arms Control Treaty Ratification, ed.* Michael Krepon and Dan Caldwell (New York: St. Martin's Press, 1991), 65–124.

23. Alton Frye, "Strategic Build-down: A Context for Restraint," *Foreign Affairs* 62, no. 2 (Winter 1983): 293–317.

INDEX

Aaron, David, 174
Abel, I. W., 110
Able Archer, 225–30, 517
ABM Protocol, 538
ABM Treaty: 9/11 attacks and, 318, 399–400, 404; adapting, 371–77; Belarus and, 375; Bolton and, 404, 406, 468; Brezhnev and, 6, 127, 130, 148, 188; Carter and, 129, 239; Clinton and, 324–25, 371–77, 383–84; George H. W. Bush and, 136, 303, 320, 372–73, 404; George W. Bush and, 318–20, 335, 371–72, 377, 384, 391–92, 400–405, 416–17, 419, 464, 536; Interim Agreement and, 123–24, 127, 129, 132–37, 464, 538; Kazakhstan and, 375; Kissinger and, 456; limited use of, 529; McNamara and, 101, 122; moral issues and, 134, 400; Multiple Independently Targetable Reentry Vehicles (MIRVs) and, 122, 127, 130, 132, 319, 375, 392, 416; Nixon and, 122, 127, 129–30, 132, 135–37, 148, 281, 390, 456, 464, 535; norms and, 529, 538; North Korea and, 372, 375–76; Nunn and, 240, 254; Putin and, 318–20, 371, 377, 384, 391–92, 401, 403–5, 416–17, 419, 464; Reagan and, 136, 238–41, 254–55, 303,

372–73; reassessing arms control objectives and, 521; Shevardnadze and, 282; Smith and, 155; Ukraine and, 375; Warnke and, 97, 132
Absolute Weapon, The (Brodie, et al), 36, 110
Accidents Measures Agreement, 537
Acheson, Alice, 69
Acheson, Dean, 69, 118, 135, 169, 268, 489
Acheson-Lilienthal Plan: abolition of bomb and, 20, 27–31, 35, 41, 47, 71, 242, 480; moral issues and, 20, 27–31, 35, 41, 47, 71, 242, 480; Moscow veto of, 47; Oppenheimer and, 20, 28–31; Stimson and, 27
Adams, Ruth, 213
Adelman, Kenneth, 194–96, 202, 204, 241–42, 250–52, 259–61
Advanced Research Projects Agency, 96
Afghanistan: Carter and, 182, 187, 189; George W. Bush and, 17, 392, 394, 396, 401, 409, 415, 418, 421; norms and, 517–18; Obama and, 424, 452; Reagan and, 218, 229; Soviets and, 187, 218, 229, 392, 401, 415, 452, 516, 518; Trump and, 465, 477–78
AFL-CIO, 70
African National Congress, 341
Agent Orange, 106

country problem and, 55; Strategic Arms Limitation Talks (SALT) and, 132; surprise attacks and, 50; Talbott and, 327–28; Ukraine and, 331, 415; unilateral moratorium of, 51–52
Killian, James, 50, 52, 65, 98, 110, 117
Kim Dae Jung, 381
Kim Jong Il, 351, 380–81, 418, 472–73
Kim Jong Un, 319, 382, 468, 471, 473, 485, 490, 513
Kintner, Robert, 52, 469
Kirkpatrick, Jeane, 202, 259, 367
Kislyak, Sergey, 452
Kissinger, Henry, 56; analytical mind of, 504; anti-ballistic missiles (ABMs) and, 114–15, 127–37, 155, 456; Arms Control and Disarmament Agency (ACDA) and, 106–15, 123, 131, 136; balance sheet of, 127–34; Brezhnev and, 146, 148–49, 153, 156, 161, 316; Brzezinski and, 163, 270, 361; Carter and, 162–65, 168–69, 172, 174, 176–77, 180–85, 188–89; Charles River Gang and, 59, 62; Clinton and, 327, 339, 357, 361, 379; Comprehensive Test Ban Treaty (CTBT) and, 379; constructive friction and, 258; as dealmaker, 109, 115, 122–23, 153, 159, 470; détente and, 162; diplomacy and, 128, 320, 455; Dobrynin and, 124, 126, 130–31, 133, 172; Ford and, 152–56, 159–61; four horsemen and, 425–26; George H. W. Bush and, 270, 272, 276, 284, 299, 306–7, 316–17, 320, 433; Gromyko and, 148; Halperin and, 62, 165, 299; Helsinki Final Act and, 276; INF Treaty and, 272; New START and, 433; Nixon and, 105–15, 122–38, 142–51, 400, 451, 456, 464, 467; North Atlantic Treaty Organization (NATO) expansion and, 361; Nuclear Weapons and Foreign Policy and, 133, 357; Obama and, 425–26, 455; Reagan and, 197–98, 201, 217–18, 249–50,

258, 261; Reykjavik summit and, 249–50; Scowcroft and, 149, 152, 159, 270, 320, 379, 394, 433, 470; Strategic Arms Limitation Talks (SALT) and, 176, 464; Vladivostok Accord and, 126, 153–56, 159, 161, 172, 182, 198; Warnke and, 151; Years of Upheaval and, 155; Zero Option and, 272, 451
Kistiakowsky, George, 48–49, 52, 65, 78, 84, 98, 117, 120
Klerk, F. W. de, 341
Klinger, Gil, 288
Klosson, Boris, 143
Knorr, Klaus, 343
Koch, Susan, 213, 296, 299, 304, 306, 319, 334
Kohler, Foy, 76, 172
Koltunov, Victor, 373–75
Ko Myong Rok, 381
Korbel, Josef, 386
Korean Armistice Agreement, 73
Korean War, 31, 42, 68, 142–43, 182, 271, 348
Korniyenko, Georgii, 111–12, 175, 187, 225
Kosygin, Alexei, 86, 98–99
Kozyrev, Andrei, 308, 318
Krauthammer, Charles, 367, 393, 397–98
Kravchuk, Leonid, 309, 331–34
Kremlinology, 47, 81, 99, 110, 227, 249
Kruzel, Joseph, 360
Kuchma, Leonid, 334
Kupperman, Charles, 182
Kurds, 466, 469, 477
Kuwait, 88, 293, 302, 320, 407
Kvitsinsky, Yuli, 214–16, 232, 244
Kyl, Jon, 365, 378, 382, 434, 475

Lab to Lab initiative, 336–38
LaFeber, Walter, 343
Laird, Melvin: Carter and, 180; Comprehensive Test Ban Treaty (CTBT) and, 379; Ford and, 160; Nixon and, 106–7, 114, 117, 120–22, 129, 131–32, 144, 285, 339; Strategic Arms Limitation Talks (SALT) and, 106–7, 114, 117, 120–22, 129, 131–32, 144, 180, 285

Printed in the USA
CPSIA information can be obtained
at www.ICGtesting.com
JSHW020833071123
51599JS00002B/3